DATE DUE

BRODART, CO.   Cat. No. 23-221

Accountability for Killing

Accountability for Killing

Moral Responsibility for Collateral Damage in America's Post-9/11 Wars

NETA C. CRAWFORD

OXFORD
UNIVERSITY PRESS

OXFORD
UNIVERSITY PRESS

Oxford University Press is a department of the University of Oxford.
It furthers the University's objective of excellence in research, scholarship,
and education by publishing worldwide.

Oxford   New York

Auckland   Cape Town   Dar es Salaam   Hong Kong   Karachi
Kuala Lumpur   Madrid   Melbourne   Mexico City   Nairobi
New Delhi   Shanghai   Taipei   Toronto

With offices in

Argentina   Austria   Brazil   Chile   Czech Republic   France   Greece
Guatemala   Hungary   Italy   Japan   Poland   Portugal   Singapore
South Korea   Switzerland   Thailand   Turkey   Ukraine   Vietnam

Oxford is a registered trademark of Oxford University Press
in the UK and certain other countries.

Published in the United States of America by
Oxford University Press
198 Madison Avenue, New York, NY 10016

Library of Congress Cataloging-in-Publication Data
Crawford, Neta C.
Accountability for killing : moral responsibility for collateral damage in America's post-9/11 wars /
Neta C. Crawford.
pages cm
Includes bibliographical references and index.
ISBN 978–0–19–998172–4 (hardback : alk. paper)   1. Military ethics—United States.
2. Civilian war casualties.   3. War victims.   4. Guilt and culture—United States.   5. War—Moral and
ethical aspects—United States.   I. Title.   II. Title: Moral responsibility for collateral damage in America's
post-9/11 wars.
U22.C73 2013
172'.42—dc23
2013011951

1 3 5 7 9 8 6 4 2
Printed in the United States of America
on acid-free paper

For Rose Jordan Crawford, a bright, beautiful, earnest, and generous life.
I write with the hope and determination that you may live in a less violent world.

CONTENTS

LIST OF FIGURES

LIST OF TABLES

PREFACE

Paradigm shifts in a nation's foreign and military policy are relatively rare. On 23 May 2013, United States President Barack Obama reoriented counterterrorism policy in a speech at the National Defense University. For the first time, Obama addressed the use of drone aircraft strikes against leaders of terrorist organizations in some detail. Obama argued that the drone strikes were militarily effective and legal, but also said: "To say a military tactic is legal, or even effective, is not to say it is wise or moral in every instance." The President admitted that concern for civilian casualties and accountability had prompted the development of the drone policy guidance:

> Much of the criticism about drone strikes—both here at home and abroad—understandably centers on reports of civilian casualties. There's a wide gap between U.S. assessments of such casualties and nongovernmental reports. Nevertheless, it is a hard fact that U.S. strikes have resulted in civilian casualties, a risk that exists in every war. And for the families of those civilians, no words or legal construct can justify their loss. For me, and those in my chain of command, those deaths will haunt us as long as we live, just as we are haunted by the civilian casualties that have occurred throughout conventional fighting in Afghanistan and Iraq.[1]

President Obama acknowledged that the questions raised by US drone strikes were hardly unique. "As was true in previous armed conflicts, this new technology raises profound questions—about who is targeted, and why; about civilian casualties, and the risk of creating new enemies; about the legality of such strikes under

---

[1] Barack Obama, "Remarks by the President at the National Defense University," 23 May 2013, http://www.whitehouse.gov/the-press-office/2013/05/23/remarks-president-national-defense-university.

U.S. and international law; about accountability and morality."[2] Obama then outlined the new guidance for drone strikes against terrorists, including the requirement that "before any strike is taken, there must be near-certainty that no civilian
can be killed or injured—the highest standard we can set."[3]

These issues—the causes, consequences, legality, accountability, and morality of
civilians killed and injured by US military operations in Afghanistan, Pakistan, Iraq,
and Yemen—are at the center of this book. The criticisms of US caused civilian
casualties in drone strikes are the manifestation of growing distress over civilian
casualties by all causes, and the concern among US officials that harming civilians is
counterproductive because it makes new enemies for the US.

When the President asserted that drone strikes were legal and effective, he was
alluding to long-standing debates over the law of war, civilian immunity and military
necessity. When Obama said that accounts of civilian casualties by drone strikes
were disputed, he might well also have been talking about the arguments about the
counts of civilian casualties more generally in these wars. I explore the questions of
military necessity, proportionality, risk, and the disputed estimates of US-caused
civilian casualties in part I.

When the president set a standard of near certainty that no civilian would be killed
in drone strikes outside war zones, the policy was the culmination of years of evolution of US policy and practice. I trace that evolution—starting with the Bush administration's acceptance of the inevitability of civilian casualties early in these wars, to the
gradual development of policy and procedures to minimize those civilian casualties at
the level of military organizations. By publicly addressing and institutionalizing measures to reduce civilian casualties caused by drone strikes with a new policy guidance,
the Obama administration exemplifies the assumption of moral responsibility and the

---

[2] *Ibid.*

[3] The president also stated:

> Beyond the Afghan theater, we only target al Qaeda and its associated forces. And even then,
> the use of drones is heavily constrained. America does not take strikes when we have the abil-
> ity to capture individual terrorists; our preference is always to detain, interrogate, and prose-
> cute. America cannot take strikes wherever we choose; our actions are bound by consultations
> with partners, and respect for state sovereignty.
>
> America does not take strikes to punish individuals; we act against terrorists who pose a
> continuing and imminent threat to the American people, and when there are no other govern-
> ments capable of effectively addressing the threat.

Ibid. Also see the 23 May 2013 White House, "Fact Sheet: U.S. Policy Standards and Procedures
for the Use of Force in Counterterrorism Operations Outside the United States and Areas of Active
Hostilities," http://www.whitehouse.gov/the-press-office/2013/05/23/fact-sheet-us-policy-standar
ds-and-procedures-use-force-counterterrorism and the "Background Briefing by Senior Administration
Officials on the President's Speech on Counterterrorism." 23 May 2013, http://www.whitehouse.gov/
the-press-office/2013/05/23/background-briefing-senior-administration-officials-presidents-speech-co.

exercise of moral agency. The US Air Force and Army also institutionalized measures for civilian casualty mitigation in their air and ground operations. Later, I discuss additional measures the military could take to reduce the likelihood of causing civilian casualties.

President Obama also implicitly acknowledged that oversight for the drone strike program had been lacking when he said, "I've asked my administration to review proposals to extend oversight of lethal actions outside of warzones that go beyond our reporting to Congress." Obama mentioned several potential mechanisms for oversight.

> Each option has virtues in theory, but poses difficulties in practice. For example, the establishment of a special court to evaluate and authorize lethal action has the benefit of bringing a third branch of government into the process, but raises serious constitutional issues about presidential and judicial authority. Another idea that's been suggested—the establishment of an independent oversight board in the executive branch—avoids those problems, but may introduce a layer of bureaucracy into national security decision-making, without inspiring additional public confidence in the process. But despite these challenges, I look forward to actively engaging Congress to explore these and other options for increased oversight.[4]

The Obama administration became much more transparent about the drone strike program after the President's reelection in 2012.[5] Yet, oversight of U.S. wars has not only been inadequate in the area of drone strikes, but across the entire spectrum of military operations that leads to civilian casualties, as I describe in the chapter on political responsibility. Although no solution is perfect, there are several steps that could improve accountability and decrease risk to civilians, as I discuss in the chapters on political and public moral responsibility and the conclusion.

The Obama administration's redirection of the war on terror and the institutionalization of drone strike policies and procedures suggest that while the United States may have entered a new phase in its counterterrorism wars, the questions of moral responsibility and accountability for killing civilians will not go away.

Nor will the question of trade-offs and risks assumed or transferred to others disappear. One of the most difficult trade-offs I discuss is the relationship between civilian protection and protection of one's own soldiers—force protection. President Obama also acknowledged trade-offs and risks to US forces and civilians when he said, "It is also not possible for America simply to deploy a team of Special Forces to capture every terrorist. Even when such an approach may be possible, there are places where it would pose profound risks to our troops and local civilians."[6]

---

[4] Obama, "Remarks by the President at the National Defense University."

[5] The May 2013 speech was preceded in late 2012 by the release of an unclassified Department of Justice White Paper, "Lawfulness of a Lethal Operation Directed Against a U.S. Citizen Who Is a Senior Operational Leader of Al-Qa'ida or An Associated Force," Draft 8 November 2012.

[6] Obama, "Remarks by the President at the National Defense University."

It is my hope that this book provides the necessary background—histori-cal, legal, and moral—for grappling with these challenging questions. In the end, *Accountability for Killing* is about moral reasoning in war at all levels, from individual soldiers, to commanders, to organizations, within political institutions, and among the public, and how moral agency and accountability can be improved. There is probably no better path to the improvement of our capacities for moral reason and the exercise of moral agency than engaging in the concrete and complex realities of an important and difficult case.[7]

---

[7] This book would have been much more difficult to research without the internet. However, web pages occasionally move to new addresses, or disappear, and data is sometimes updated by sources without explanation or notice. Some sources, such as the Congressional Research Service or the United Nations Assistance Mission in Afghanistan, may update figures for prior years in their most recent reports. My larger arguments should still hold even if these sorts of changes occur. Nevertheless, I have done my best to insure the accuracy of the citations and data.

Introduction

A pattern seems to have developed of periodic embarrassments provok-
ing momentary outrage: Marines urinating on dead insurgents, NATO
helicopters killing children collecting firewood, the burning of Korans at
a U.S. base, the murder of 17 civilians in their homes. The reality on the
other hand, is that between these intermittent headlines, Afghans die less
sensational deaths, suffer less dramatic travails, and survive less repug-
nant but equally traumatic violence on a regular basis.[1]

Viewed as a liberator by many here in the early days of the war, the
American military has fallen steadily in Afghan's eyes as civilian casualties have mounted amid a steady trickle of episodes of brutality against
and outright murder of Afghans.[2]

In all types of operations, failure to mitigate CIVCASs [civilian casual-
ties] can jeopardize success.[3]

In late May 2013, President Obama announced limits on its secret drone strike program in Pakistan and Yemen in part to address concerns that too many civilians
were harmed or killed in the strikes. Policy makers apparently feared the backlash
against the U.S. when civilians are harmed in the strikes undermined the larger goals
of the drone strike program. The fact of civilian killing in war, its cause, its consequences, and the responsibility for it, are the subject of this book.

"Collateral damage," an anodyne phrase—invented by lawyers and perhaps
first used in a military context by Thomas Schelling in 1961 to describe something
very concrete, the unintended deaths and injury of civilians in a US-Soviet nuclear
war—reduces the experience of killing to abstraction.[4] As America's post-9/11 wars

---

[1] Luke Mogelson, "Pacifists in the Crossfire," *New York Times Magazine*, 20 May 2012, p. 44.

[2] Elisabeth Bumiller and Matthew Rosenberg, "4 Marines in Video with Dead Taliban are
Identified," *New York Times*, 14 January 2012, p. A5.

[3] Department of the Army, *Civilian Casualty Mitigation*, Army Tactics, Techniques, and Procedures,
No. 3-37.31 (Washington, DC: Department of the Army, 18 July 2012), p. 1-8.

[4] Thomas C. Schelling, "Dispersal, Deterrence, and Damage," *Operations Research*, vol. 9, no. 3
(May/June 1961): 363–370.

wind down, and the soldiers return, it may become increasingly difficult to recall the incidents of civilian killing that happened far away to those strangers "over there." Rachel Manley, poet, memoirist, and novelist wrote that: "Time shrinks time. Old time becomes simply a number of things we know, a set of images that are one horizon, like the entire world reduced to a map and the years to one day."[5] The length of the wars, our physical distance, and, soon, our chronological remove from the fighting may contribute to a further blurring of the reality. Most of us hardly understand what happened to American soldiers and their allies. But the trace of each bullet, bomb, burn, and brain injury is written on the bodies of survivors and their families. New incidents of collateral damage will occur as long as the United States continues to wage war. Now and again it will pay to recall some of those incidents in detail.

Ishaqi Iraq, north of Baghdad, 15 March 2006: At about 2:30 A.M., US troops approached a house and attempted to capture and kill what they believed were number of insurgents in a home US intelligence indicated was being used as a safe house. According to US Major General William Caldwell, "As the enemy fire persisted, the ground force commander appropriately reacted by incrementally escalating the use of force from small arms fire to rotary wing aviation, and then to close air support, ultimately eliminating the threat."[6] The United States used at least one AC-130 gunship and ground fire in their assault on the house. Although the numbers were disputed, at least eleven, and as many as thirteen, noncombatants were killed by US forces in Ishaqi that day. One of those deaths was of the suspected terrorist Ahmad Abdallah Muhammad Nais al-Utai, or Hamza. Uday Faris al-Tawafi, suspected of making roadside bombs, was also killed. The civilians killed were the family of Faez Khalaf, who was killed in the attack. Khalaf's brother said: "[The] killed family was not part of the resistance; they were women and children. The Americans have promised us a better life, but we get only death."[7]

The noncombatant deaths—of six adults and five children ranging in ages from about 6 months to 75 years old—were explained as collateral damage.[8] US military investigators found US actions in Ishaqi to be appropriate. "The investigating officer concluded that possibly up to nine collateral deaths resulted from this engagement, but could not determine the precise number due to collapsed walls and

---

[5] Rachel Manley, *Slipstream: A Daughter Remembers* (Toronto: Random House, 2000), p. 68.

[6] Caldwell, quoted in John D. Banusiewicz, "Probe Clears Coalition Forces of Wrongdoing in March 15 Raid," American Forces Press Services, News, US Department of Defense, 3 June 2006. http://www.defense.gov/News/NewsArticle.aspx?ID=16139. Banusiewicz also said, "Caldwell noted that Arab and Western media have focused a great deal of attention recently on allegations of coalition troops killing innocent civilians in Iraq."

[7] Quoted in John Ward Anderson, "Up to 13 Killed in U.S. Assault," *Washington Post*, 16 March 2006, http://www.washingtonpost.com/wp-dyn/content/article/2006/03/15/AR2006031501709.html.

[8] Richard A. Oppel Jr., "Commander Cleared in Deadly Raid in Iraq; Calls Troop's Response Appropriate," *International Herald Tribune*, 5 June 2006, p. 3.

heavy debris."[9] US forces were accused by local Iraqi police of deliberately shooting the eleven people before blowing up the building.[10] The police report said, "The American forces gathered the family members in one room and executed 11 people, including 5 children, 4 women and two men, then they bombed the house, burned three vehicles and killed their animals."[11]

US Major General William Caldwell, who reported on the results of an official US investigation of the incident, disputed allegations that US troops executed the family that was living in the house. Rather, Caldwell said, "The investigation revealed the ground force commander, while capturing and killing terrorists, operated in accordance with the rules of engagement governing our combat forces in Iraq."[12] During his remarks about Ishaqi, Caldwell acknowledged that there was considerable concern about how the US military was behaving in Iraq. "Temptation exists to lump all these incidents together," he said, "however, each case needs to be examined individually."[13] If the initial US investigation is correct, this is an incident of inadvertent killing of civilians—collateral damage. But what if we do not simply examine each case individually? What if we add them up?

The unintentional killing of civilians in war is at the root of perhaps the most difficult moral dilemmas that soldiers and their commanders' face. Civilians can be located near military targets. Schelling was writing in 1961 about dispersing US nuclear bombers away from US cities so that there was the possibility of lower collateral damage in case of a nuclear war. On the other hand, unscrupulous belligerents may even play on their adversary's restraint by deliberately placing civilians in harm's way, to act as human shields, or to score propaganda points when those civilians are killed or injured. Or, the disruption of an enemy's command and control apparatus or its ability to make weapons may be understood to require the destruction of power facilities or other infrastructure that also serves civilian

[9] Caldwell, quoted in Banusiewicz, "Probe Clears Coalition Forces of Wrongdoing in March 15 Raid."

[10] BBC News, "New 'Iraq Massacre' Tape Emerges," 2 June 2006, http://news.bbc.co.uk/2/hi/middle_east/5039420.stm.

[11] Matthew Schofield, "Iraqi Police Report Details Civilians' Deaths in Ishaqi at Hands of U.S. Troops," *McClatchy*, 19 March 2006, http://www.mcclatchydc.com/2006/03/19/122733/iraqi-police-report-details-civilians.html.

[12] Caldwell, quoted in Banusiewicz, "Probe Clears Coalition Forces of Wrongdoing in March 15 Raid."

[13] Caldwell, quoted in Banusiewicz, "Probe Clears Coalition Forces of Wrongdoing in March 15 Raid." On 27 March 2006, the UN Special Rapporteur on Extrajudicial, Summary or Arbitrary Executions Philip Alston raised questions about the attack in a cable to the US Secretary of State, noting that autopsies "revealed that all corpses were shot in the head and handcuffed." http://wikileaks.org/cable/2006/04/06GENEVA763.html. After the cable surfaced in late 2011, Iraqi officials said they would reopen their investigation. Annie Gowen, "Iraq to Reopen Probe of Deadly 2006 Raid," *Washington Post*, 2 September 2011, http://www.washingtonpost.com/world/middle-east/iraq-to-reopen-probe-of-deadly-ishaqi-raid/2011/09/02/gIQAT0hSwJ_story.html.

needs—so-called "dual-use" facilities. Should the United States or any great power back off in those cases or continue with their mission, even if it means noncombatants will die or be injured? The attempt to avoid harming civilians, if it for instance means a soldier or pilot must come closer to a potential target in order to determine whether civilians are present, may put one's soldiers at greater risk.

Under international law, civilians—defined as those who are not combatants—are not to be deliberately attacked. Most US soldiers do not deliberately kill or injure civilians. More often the killing of noncombatants is inadvertent; no one intended to kill or injure civilians. Rather, the noncombatants were caught in the crossfire between combatants, or killed at checkpoints when they were mistaken for attackers, or they were bombed in homes or in wedding parties that the US military thought or knew were being used by insurgents as cover. The civilians unintentionally harmed in war are called "collateral damage," or in new Pentagon jargon, "civcas."

Such noncombatant injury and death at the hands of troops following the "rules of engagement" has been relatively commonplace in Iraq, Afghanistan, and Pakistan. Some civilians have been deliberately massacred. Others have been abused by soldiers. But, though those incidents make may sicken our hearts and justly command a great deal of media attention, deliberate massacre is relatively uncommon. A much more common way for noncombatants to die is as collateral damage. These thousands of deaths and injuries were considered ordinary and inevitable. And so, in some ways, this book underscores how a significant problem can persist with little notice, and even grow, if it is seen by at least some as natural and inevitable.

Civilians have died in accidents and in ways that are foreseen and even authorized. Civilian deaths and injuries outrage the populations where the United States is engaged in military operations. A July 2011 headline on the front page of the *New York Times* read, "Night Raids Curbing Taliban, But Afghans Cite Civilian Toll."[14] Similarly, a front page article in October 2010 in the *New York Times*, "A Grim Portrait of Civilian Deaths in Iraq," reported previously unknown killings of Iraqi civilians by US forces and stated, "The pace of civilian deaths served as a kind of pulse, whose steady beat told of the success, or failure, of America's war effort."[15] During these wars, the US military came to believe that civilian casualties vitiate military progress, and thus preventing collateral damage became an urgent military priority. An article in the US coalition's International Security Assistance Force (ISAF) newsletter to its troops in Afghanistan stressed the importance of reducing civilian casualties for the success of its counterinsurgency (COIN) operations in the strongest terms: "No matter how hard we try to reduce CIVCAS, unless we bring

[14] Carlotta Gall, "Night Raids Curbing Taliban, But Afghans Cite Civilian Toll," *New York Times*, 9 July 2011, p. A1.

[15] Sabrina Tavernise and Andrew Lehren, "A Grim Portrait of Civilian Deaths in Iraq," *New York Times*, 22 October 2010, http://www.nytimes.com/2010/10/23/world/middleeast/23casualties.html.

them down to zero, we risk mission accomplishment."[16] Yet despite their efforts, Afghanistan's leader Hamid Karzai repeatedly protested the killing of civilians by ISAF forces. For example, after four airstrikes reportedly killed dozens of civilians in May 2012, Karzai said that the incidents were "unacceptable." Karzai's spokesperson stated, "President Karzai said if the lives of Afghans are not safe then strategic coopera- tion between the two countries will lose its meaning and concept."[17]

Collateral damage, the unintended harm to civilians in the course of a military operation, is legal and generally considered inevitable, an ordinary aspect of war. As US General Michael Ryan, who was in charge of NATO air operations during 1999 in Kosovo said: "Our politicians need to understand that we will do our best to make airpower [as] clean and painless as they want us to, but it is not going to work out that way. People die in airpower conflicts. There is collateral damage. There is unintended loss of life. When they choose to employ us, to take us to war, when they choose to use military force to solve a problem that politicians could not, then they need to grit their teeth and stay with us."[18] The Pentagon's manual for collat- eral damage mitigation says: "Military forces conduct operations among civilian populations; CIVCASs [civilian casualties] have always been a tragic consequence of armed conflict."[19] In other words, "collateral damage" deaths are to be expected.

In the view of many soldiers, because collateral damage is considered inevitable, con- cern for collateral damage should not get in the way of force protection or accomplish- ing the mission. Lieutenant Colonel Nathan Sassaman lost respect for a commander who refused to use all artillery power available to him because the Colonel "feared the collateral damage that might result from such an action." Sassaman reasoned: "Well, collateral damage is one of the costs of war. You try to minimize it, of course, but it's going to happen. War is imprecise and unpredictable. It is, in a word, terrible. If you aren't willing to accept collateral damage as a cost of doing battle, then you shouldn't engage the military in the first place."[20]

American soldiers and officials often say that civilian deaths in war are both tragic and regrettable. For example, in July 2002 when the United States mistakenly killed thirty people in a wedding party in Afghanistan, President Bush apologized for the "tragedy" and Colonel Roger King, a US officer in Afghanistan, said: "The US govern- ment extends its deepest sympathies to those who may have lost loved ones or who

---

[16] Isaac Larson, "Afghan Perceptions of Civilian Casualties," *COIN Common Sense*, vol. 1, no. 1 (February 2010): 3.

[17] CNN Wire Staff, "Karzai Calls Civilian Casualties Unacceptable," *CNN*, 7 May 2012, http:// articles.cnn.com/2012-05-07/asia/world_asia_afghanistan-casualties_1_dozens-of-afghan-civilians- airstrike-sangin?_s=PM:ASIA.

[18] General Michael C. Short, Commander, Allied Air Forces, Southern Europe, Air Force Association, Air Warfare Symposium 2000, 25 February 2000. http://www.afa.org/aef/pub/short200.asp.

[19] Army, *Civilian Casualty Mitigation*, p. 1-1.

[20] Nathan Sassaman, with Joe Layden, *Warrior King: The Triumph and Betrayal of an American Commander in Iraq* (New York: St. Martin's Press, 2008), p. 159.

may have suffered any injuries. Coalition military forces take extraordinary measures to protect against civilian casualties."[21] Frank Wuterich, who was charged in relation to the deaths of twenty-four Iraqi civilians in Haditha apologized after pleading guilty to dereliction of duty, saying, "But even with the best intentions, sometimes combat actions can cause tragic results."[22] In commenting on a 2012 UN report on civilian casualties in Afghanistan, the NATO ISAF spokesperson said: "The priority of ISAF has been and will be on limiting civilian casualties. This past year, ISAF-caused civilian casualties have generally declined since a peak in July 2011, representing the lowest number of ISAF-caused civilian casualties since 2009. However, we realize that there is much work to be done yet in reducing these tragic cases of loss of civilian lives.... Again, every civilian casualty is tragic and detrimental to ISAF. We will continue to do everything possible to prevent civilian casualties throughout 2012."[23] A top Obama administration official, John Brennan, described the deaths of civilians in US drones strikes in similar terms:

> As the president and others have acknowledged, there have indeed been instances when, despite the extraordinary precautions we take, civilians have been accidently killed or worse—have been accidentally injured, or worse, killed in these strikes [sic]. It is exceedingly rare, but it has happened. When it does, it pains us, and we regret it deeply, as we do any time innocents are killed in war. And when it happens we take it very, very seriously. We go back and we review our actions. We examine our practices. And we constantly work to improve and refine our efforts so that we are doing everything in our power to prevent the loss of innocent life. This too is a reflection of our values as Americans.[24]

The dominant paradigm of legal and moral responsibility in war stresses both intention and individual accountability. Deliberate killing of civilians is outlawed, and international law blames individual soldiers and commanders for such killing because, as I argue in chapter 4, the dominant view of agency is a theory of

---

[21] George W. Bush, quoted in Leela Jacinto, "The Hidden Costs of War in Afghanistan," ABC News, 9 July 2002. http://abcnews.go.com/International/story?id=79913&page=1#.T5lVcM0dfyw. Col. King, quoted in Luke Harding, "No US Apology over Wedding Bombing," *The Guardian*, 2 July 2002, http://www.guardian.co.uk/world/2002/jul/03/afghanistan.lukeharding.

[22] Quoted in Mary Slosson, "Marine Spared from Jail Time in Iraq Killings," *Reuters*, 25 January 2012, http://www.reuters.com/article/2012/01/25/us-marine-haditha-idUSTRE80M1U620120125. Six of the seven soldiers originally charged in the Haditha killings had their charges dismissed.

[23] ISAF Spokesman, "Operational Update 6 February 2012," NATO, International Security Assistance Force, Headquarters, Kabul, Afghanistan, 2012.

[24] John Brennan, "The Efficacy and Ethics of U.S. Counterterrorism Strategy," 30 April 2012, Woodrow Wilson International Center for Scholars, http://www.wilsoncenter.org/event/the-efficacy-and-ethics-us-counterterrorism-strategy.

individual autonomous moral agency. Killing civilians is legal and may be forgiven if it was unintended, incidental, and considered proportional to a militarily necessary operation. As the noted Israeli legal scholar Yoram Dinstein argues: "There is no way to avert altogether harmful consequences to civilians flowing from attacks against military objectives. Accidents are beyond control by human beings. So are weapon malfunctions."[25] While the deliberate massacre of civilians is condemned, the "unintended" killing of civilians is too often dismissed as unavoidable, inevitable, and accidental. In sum, the very law that protects noncombatants from deliberate killing allows unintended killing. An individual soldier may be sentenced to life in prison, or death, for deliberately killing even a small number of civilians, but the large-scale killing of dozens or even hundreds of civilians may be forgiven if it was unintentional—incidental to a military operation.

What are the causes of foreseeable collateral damage and who has moral responsibility for these deaths? Is "collateral damage" simply an unavoidable consequence of all wars? Why, when the US military tries so hard to limit collateral damage, does so much of it seem to occur? Or, are the numbers of deaths actually quite low by historical standards? These episodes were both foreseeable and often foreseen. Indeed, over the years that I observed the wars and read of many of these incidents, it became clear that the military had some control over what it described as tragic accidents. Collateral damage is not only or always an unforeseen "accident."

"Collateral damage" is defined in US military documents as: "Unintentional or incidental injury or damage to persons or objects that would not be lawful military targets in the circumstances ruling at the time. Such damage is not unlawful so long as it is not excessive in light of the overall military advantage anticipated from the attack."[26] This definition focuses on the intentions of the attacker (military advantage) and the (unintended) outcome to civilians or civilian objects. What is missing here and, I argue, in much of the analysis of collateral damage incidents is a sense of the different ways collateral damage occurs—the causal path to civilian deaths and the ways that those deaths may be foreseeable and foreseen. Thinking of collateral damage as "tragedy" is the wrong frame—it implies inevitability and fate when experienced observers and soldiers know that accidents are only one kind of collateral damage. Thus, I suggest that it is important to consider three types of collateral damage, all legal under international law: genuine unforeseen and perhaps unforeseeable accidents, foreseeable systemic incidents, and foreseen double effect.

Type 1: Genuine Accident Collateral Damage.　Sometimes military planners and soldiers do not anticipate that civilians will be at risk in a particular operation, but civilians are nevertheless harmed. We think of these as accidents. But there are

---

[25] Yoram Dinstein, "Collateral Damage and the Principle of Proportionality," in David Wippman and Mathew Evangelista, eds., *New Wars, New Laws? Applying the Laws of War in the 21st Century* (Ardsley, NY: Transnational Publishers, 2005), pp. 211–224, 212.

[26] US Air Force, *Targeting*, Air Force Doctrine Document 2-1.9 (U.S. Air Force, 8 June 2006), p. 113.

really, as others have observed, at least two kinds of "accidents." There are those accidents that arise in situations that are unusual and quite unlikely. No one wanted the outcome and no one could have reasonably foreseen it. I call those, "genuine accidents." There may be a lot of genuine accidents in war because the violence, displacement, and general high level of fear in war create unsafe conditions. Then there are foreseeable and preventable "accidents."

Type 2: Systemic Collateral Damage. Yoram Dinstein argues that the category of lawful collateral damage includes those incidents that "emanate from human error or mechanical malfunction and when that occurs there is no stigma."[27] I argue that the category of accident can be too large and conceal too much. Human error is sometimes (although not always) caused by putting people in situations where such errors are more likely. For example, as Dinstein suggests, "It is typical during the Afghanistan War—where the equipment used by the US has been the most advanced—collateral damage to civilians has repeatedly occurred, with bombing mistakes reported almost as a matter of routine (including mistakenly bombing a Red Cross complex in Kabul, in 2001, on two separate occasions)."[28] Similarly, a weapons malfunction can be unforeseen, but some weapons malfunction more often than others and in ways that are foreseeable. The fuzzy line between systemic collateral damage and accidents is illustrated by cases where individual soldiers are undisciplined in their use of force or are too ready to use force.[29] One such incident of indiscipline may be an anomaly—many indicative of systemic features of training or small unit norms.

Charles Perrow calls some events "normal accidents" in the sense that although they are undesired and uncommon, they should be expected (even if they are not actually expected). These incidents are in fact likely to occur, Perrow suggests, when organizations that perform highly risky activities are complex and tightly coupled, so that errors can cascade.[30] In a normal accident we can anticipate a failure or undesired outcome in the routine conduct of operations even though no one wants that result. For example, a normal accident in war occurs when soldiers drive fast through narrow streets because they are likely to harm those who cannot move out of the way. Or we know that when soldiers combine night operations, such as raids, with certain weapons or tactics, some number of civilians will likely die because it is difficult to distinguish between combatants and noncombatants. Or we know that when tens of thousands of weapons, such as cluster munitions, with a known

[27] Yoram Dinstein, *The Conduct of Hostilities under the Law of International Armed Conflict*, 2d ed. (Cambridge: Cambridge University Press, 2010), p. 125.

[28] Ibid., p. 135.

[29] Mark Martins, "Rules of Engagement for Land Forces: A Matter of Training, Not Lawyering," *Military Law Review*, vol. 143, no. 1 (Winter 1994): 1–160.

[30] Charles Perrow, *Normal Accidents: Living with High Risk Technologies* (Princeton: Princeton University Press, 1999).

failure or "dud" rate, of say 5 percent, are used in an urban area, many civilians are at risk. We do not know when or who, but these are operations with risks that can calculated. Indeed, I argue, many times the incidental deaths were, if not foreseen, they were foreseeable. C. A. J. Coady argues, "The plea of 'accident' or 'mistake' does not necessarily avoid blame, since much accidental damage in war should have been foreseen and been avoided." Coady then goes on to argue that "a good deal of accidental killing of enemy civilians in war exhibits a culpable lack of concern for their lives and safety."[31]

In other words, these systemic "normal accident" type collateral damage incidents are often not true accidents in the sense of being unforeseen and unpreventable, even as the deaths or injury were not intended. On the other hand, systemic collateral damage killing is not the product of simple recklessness or gross negligence. The fact is that many of these incidents are foreseeable, often foreseen, and the probability of causing death is sometimes calculated using computerized algorithms.[32] The incidence of civilian death fluctuates depending on changes in rules of engagement or choice of weapons; it can be ratcheted up or down. For example, as I describe later, in 2006 when US military leaders decided that they must reduce the US killing of Iraqi civilians in "escalation of force" incidents at checkpoints and changed procedures, the number of civilians killed at checkpoints fell from about six per week to an average of one per week.

Failures of foresight and corrective action are often not simply the failure of a single bureaucrat; the failure may be systemic if the organization's practices and beliefs are structured so that normal accidents predictably recur, if it is extremely difficult to notice patterns of pernicious outcomes, or when there is little incentive to "add things up." The structural context is one where collateral damage becomes a normal accident.

In some or arguably many of these instances, we can speak of organizational responsibility in the sense that such an outcome should have been foreseen because such operations frequently lead to civilian harm—due to the rules of engagement, the choice of weapons, or conditions under which such operations are approved to take place. The rules of engagement and weapons choices are, respectively, cognitive and structural biases that lead to predictable outcomes—normal accidents. "In bureaucracies, certain patterns of fault are common enough that we should expect any competent official to anticipate them and to take reasonable precautions to

---

[31] C. A. J. Coady, "Bombing and the Morality of War," in Yuki Tanaka and Marilyn B. Young, eds., *Bombing Civilians: A Twentieth Century History* (New York: The New Press, 2009), pp. 191–214, 206. Mistakes may lead to accidents. See John Austin, "A Plea for Excuses," *Proceedings of the Aristotelian Society*, 1956–1957. http://www.ditext.com/austin/plea.html.

[32] C. A. J. Coady has argued that there are two kinds of collateral damage. He called one type of "foreseen but unintended damage 'incidental damage,'" which he contrasts with "accidental damage." C. A. J. Coady, "Collateral Immunity in War and Terrorism," in Igor Primoratz, ed., *Civilian Immunity in War* (Oxford: Oxford University Press, 2007), pp. 136–157, 142.

avoid them or at least to minimize their harmful consequences."[33] For many years, the US military failed to fully understand the problem of systemic collateral damage in Afghanistan and Iraq. By mid-2012, it is fair to say that the US military had grasped the essential details of the problem and had moved to correct it.

Type 3: Foreseen Proportionality/Double Effect Killing.   In some cases, the civilian deaths were foreseeable, foreseen, and judged to be worth the military advantage that would result from an operation. Under the doctrine of double effect, which comes from the Just War tradition, it is acknowledged that noncombatants may die in the course of military operations. These deaths may be excused if they were an unintended consequence of a necessary military operation and if some effort was made to "minimize" civilian casualties. Killing civilians is accepted on some level. It is planned, and it is excused when it is thought to be militarily necessary and not excessive. Further, the operation must be proportionate; the good of the military operation must outweigh the negative consequences of the operation. On the other hand, if dozens of civilians are killed, albeit inadvertently, so that only one soldier may be killed, the proportionality principle may be violated.

In this scenario of foreseen, but unintentional, civilian killing, the military has set a certain level of acceptable risk for collateral damage death or injury. Attempts to reduce the number of civilians harmed will be made. But the operation may be allowed to proceed on the judgment that the civilian losses are justified in light of the value of the military objective (proportionality) and that there was no other way to be effective (necessity). This is a consequentialist acceptance of civilian killing where the death was anticipated and considered justified.

This type of collateral damage—which I also call proportionality/double effect killing—describes the rule of the early days of Operation Iraqi Freedom when a ceiling of an anticipated thirty or more civilian deaths was the trigger for seeking the approval of the president or Secretary of Defense. An operation with fewer civilian deaths anticipated could proceed without such approval. Thus, during the early days of the war in Iraq, a Pentagon official said, "If it is a high enough value target, you accept a higher risk of casualties."[34] The law excuses and becomes an excuse. The US unmanned drone strikes which target militant leaders often involve such calculations, where the potential for a successful targeted killing is weighed against the risk to civilians. According to the chief of the Obama administration's counterterrorism effort, John Brennan, after US officials ensure that they are acting against a legitimate military target, "we only authorize a strike if we have a high degree of confidence that innocent civilians will not be injured or killed, except in the rarest of circumstances."[35]

---

[33] Dennis F. Thompson, "Moral Responsibility of Public Officials: The Problem of Many Hands," *American Political Science Review*, vol. 74, no. 4 (December 1980): 905–916, 913.

[34] Eric Schmitt, "Rumsfeld Says Dozens of Important Targets Have Been Avoided," *New York Times*, 24 March 2003, p. 12.

[35] Brennan, "The Efficacy and Ethics of U.S. Counterterrorism Strategy."

Military necessity acts as permission or, from some perspectives, could be seen as a loophole that permits operations that knowingly endanger civilians. Or, as I heard a Marine Corps Lieutenant Colonel say, necessity is a "moral allowance."[36] Similarly, Senator John McCain said after the United States killed Afghan civilians in October 2001 that the United States should not be too concerned with noncombatant casualties in Afghanistan: "Issues such as Ramadan or civilian casualties, however regrettable and however tragic…have to be secondary to the primary goal of eliminating the enemy."[37]

My research on US-caused collateral damage deaths in Afghanistan, Iraq, and Pakistan, as well as drone strikes in Yemen, yielded several findings. First, collateral damage of all types is not a rare outcome. Further, after many years of hearing these killings declared tragic accidents, I found that there are more collateral damage killings of the second and third type—systemic normal accidents and proportional foreseen double effect killing—than we might think. The focus here is on the moral responsibility for both systemic and proportionality/double effect collateral damage. It is particularly important that the systemic collateral damage incidents be recognized as distinct from genuine accidents: many civilians are harmed in ways that were foreseeable and either were, or should have been, foreseen.

These were sobering findings. Yet there are pieces of good news here. First, although soldiers still "snap" and massacre civilians or desecrate the bodies of those they kill, they do so relatively infrequently. Indeed, while the aggregate numbers are uncertain, unintended deaths caused by the US and allied military force operations far outnumber those more widely publicized incidents where US soldiers "snap" and intentionally kill Iraqi and Afghan noncombatants. And, unlike the Taliban in Afghanistan, militants in Pakistan, and insurgents in Iraq, who have deliberately targeted civilians, the US military works quite hard to protect civilians. Second, although there is sometimes a relatively low level of concern for civilian harm when military necessity is understood to be high, as an institution, the US military has often taken great care to avoid harm to civilians in Afghanistan, Iraq, and Pakistan. Indeed, collateral damage estimation and mitigation are institutionalized within the US military. The increased US effort to reduce inadvertent killing of civilians, which includes new training, routines and procedures, using the advice of military lawyers, and the development of computerized algorithms to predict, estimate, and minimize collateral damage, have at times been quite successful. These are admirable measures, and there can be little doubt that both the organizational capacity and effort to assess potential harm to civilians and to ameliorate it has improved. For instance, in Afghanistan in the period between 2008 and 2011, even as the United States and its allies increased their overall forces and the intensity of military

---

[36] Lt. Col. Ian Houck, at the conference on "Civilian Devastation" at George Mason University, Fairfax, VA, March 2009.

[37] Russ Buettner, "Stray U.S. Bombs Kill 13: Friends and Foes Angered," *Daily News*, 29 October 2001, p. 14.

operations against insurgents, pro-government forces cut the total number of civilians killed in collateral damage incidents in half according to the United Nations.[38] This book thus also is a case study of organizational learning—how an organization began to see a problem differently and adapted itself to address the problem.

The incident of civilian killing in Afghanistan described below, well known at the time, is illustrative of the tactical, strategic, and moral issues that are explored here. It suggests the distinctions, and the thin lines, between genuine accident, systemic collateral damage, and double effect killing. It also illustrates how the US military learned from the incident.

Garani and Ganjabad, Afghanistan, 4 May 2009

On the night of 4 May 2009, an estimated 300 Taliban used both light and heavy weapons to attack Afghan police checkpoints along a highway in the Bala Baluk district of Farah Province. The objective of the Taliban assault was apparently to obtain control of the highway and the neighboring villages of Garani and Ganjabad. The Taliban would then be able to use their control to gain the revenue from the local opium harvest. In response to a request by the Afghan police, US Marines and Afghan National Army forces entered the area and engaged with the Taliban for several hours in what was described as heavy fighting. The villagers took shelter from the fighting in several homes.

Here is where accounts begin to differ, yielding significant variations and revisions in both the reports of what happened that night, in the tally of civilian death and injury, and in the causal and moral responsibility for the civilian deaths. The villagers said the fighting ended by 6 P.M. and that the Taliban had withdrawn. Jamil Ahmad told the New York Times, "The battle finished and the Taliban retreated. They did not stay in the villages."[39] Men went out for evening prayers and had returned. All agree that US Special Operations Forces called in close air support, which arrived and began bombardment about 8 P.M. The aircraft dropped several bombs that struck houses in the villages. Villagers said that when the aerial bombing began, they again sought shelter in several larger homes. "I heard a loud explosion and the compound was burning and the roof fell in."[40] At the end of the raid at least six houses were completely destroyed, although later reports said twelve houses were destroyed. The surviving villagers took days to pull surviving victims and body parts

---

[38] United Nations Assistance Mission to Afghanistan, *Annual Report on Protection of Civilians in Armed Conflict* (Kabul, Afghanistan, 2011), pp. 1-2. Pro-government forces include the Afghan National Security Forces and the international military forces operating in Afghanistan.

[39] Elizabeth Bumiller and Carlotta Gall, "Officials Say U.S. Raids Killed Some Afghan Civilians," *New York Times*, 8 May 2009, p. A4.

[40] A surviving victim, Nazo, quoted in Carlotta Gall and Taimor Shah, "Afghans Recall Airstrike Horror, and Fault U.S.," *New York Times*, 15 May 2009, p. A1.

out of the rubble. An Afghan legislator, Mohammad Naim Farahi, said that "the governor [of Farah Province] said that the villagers have brought two tractor trailers full of pieces of human bodies to his office to prove the casualties that had occurred."[41]

The initial report of the incident in the *New York Times* ran under the headline "Afghans Say U.S. Raid Killed 30 Civilians," but the article also indicated that the United Nations had found evidence that ninety civilians had been killed.[42] A report in the *New York Times* the next day indicated that the United States was investigating and following up on what it said were reports that the Taliban had actually killed the civilians themselves by using grenades. A Pentagon spokesperson told the press, "We cannot confirm the report that the Taliban executed these people."[43]

The *New York Times* reported that the Governor of Farah Province said that perhaps as many as 130 civilians died in the incident. Speaking in Afghanistan, US Secretary of Defense Robert M. Gates said that the United States and the coalition "do everything we possibly can to avoid civilian casualties" and that the incident would be investigated.[44] The United States continued to insist that if there were any civilian deaths, uncertainty remained about both the numbers harmed and the cause of the killing. Secretary Gates said: "We all know that the Taliban use civilian casualties, and sometimes create them, to create problems for the United States and our coalition partners. We have to wait and see what happened in this—in this particular case."[45] Secretary Gates promised to make amends for any—"even one"—civilian casualty. But he reiterated the Pentagon's position that the United States should not necessarily be blamed for the killing.

> First of all, I believe, in many instances, the Taliban used civilians as shields. They mingle with civilians and then attack ISAF partners. And so while there have been civilian casualties caused by American and our coalition partners' troops, the reality is that in virtually every case, they have been accidental. Whereas when the Taliban creates civilian casualties, it has been deliberate, as part of their strategy for trying to build an adversarial relationship, between the Afghan people and those who are trying to help the Afghan government.
>
> Our technical capabilities provide certain assets, but the reality is this is, at the end of the day, a war on the ground, in rural areas, village by village,

---

[41] Carlotta Gall and Taimor Shah, "Civilian Deaths Imperil Support for Afghan War," *New York Times*, 7 May 2009, p. A1.

[42] Taimoor Shah and Carlotta Gall, "Afghans Say U.S. Raid Killed 30 Civilians," *New York Times*, 6 May 2009, p. A10.

[43] Quoted in Gall and Shah, "Civilian Deaths Imperil Support for Afghan War."

[44] Ibid.

[45] "Press Conference with Secretary Gates from Kabul, Afghanistan," US Department of Defense, News Transcript, 7 May 2009. http://www.defense.gov/transcripts/transcript.aspx?transcriptid=4416.

block by block. And very often, modern techniques are very limited in what they can contribute to this fight. It's one of the reasons why at home I have been seeking additional capabilities for our troops who are here in the fight.

As I said, we deeply regret any civilian casualty. But fundamentally, people need to recognize that exploiting civilian casualties and often causing civilian casualties are a fundamental part of the Taliban strategy. And it is a measure of the ruthlessness with which they fight.[46]

More than a week after the attack, the *New York Times* published an article that contained several conflicting reports of the number of people killed in the bombing of Garani. Surviving villagers gave Afghan government officials a list of 147 dead; the Afghan government said 140 civilians had died and 25 were wounded; an Afghan human rights organization, Afghanistan Rights Monitor reported at 117 dead including 61 children; and the United States believed, according to the reporters, that "even 100 [killed] is an exaggeration."[47]

The controversy over the numbers killed and their identities continued for several more weeks even as the newly appointed US ambassador to Afghanistan, Lt. General Karl W. Eikenberry went to Farah, near Garani, on the 19th of May and apologized for the incident. Eikenberry promised that the coalition would change its tactics to diminish the threat to civilians.[48] Yet, as the debate over Garani unfolded, NATO announced that its forces killed eight civilians in an airstrike in Helmand Province on the 19th of May.[49] The following day, a US military spokesperson asserted that not all the victims in Garani were civilians; the list of Afghans killed "included more than civilians."[50] The United States released an estimate that "60-65 Taliban extremists" were killed, "while at least 20-30 civilians may have been killed during the fighting."[51] As Secretary of Defense Gates said during his visit to Afghanistan, "I think the key for us is, on those rare occasions when we do make a mistake, when there is an error, to apologize quickly, to compensate the victims quickly, and then carry out the investigation."[52]

Although the Pentagon promised to release a video of the attack, the video was never released. The US Central Command (CENTCOM) made a summary of the

[46] Ibid.

[47] Gall and Shah, "Afghans Recall Airstrike Horror and Fault U.S."

[48] Carlotta Gall, "U.S. Envoy Vows to Help Cut Afghan Civilian Deaths," *New York Times*, 20 May 2009, p. A10.

[49] Sabrina Tavernise, "U.S. Counts Civilian Toll at Far Below Afghan Tally," *New York Times*, p. A10.

[50] Ibid.

[51] Radio Free Europe, Radio Liberty, "NATO Says New Airstrike Likely Killed Afghan Civilians," 20 May 2009, http://www.rferl.org/articleprintview/1735658.html.

[52] Dexter Filkins, "U.S. Toughens Airstrike Policy in Afghanistan," *New York Times*, 22 June 2009, p. A1.

results of its investigation public on 18 June 2009, revealing that four F/A-18F and a B-1B bomber were involved in the attack on Garani. The F/A-18Fs were used to drop flares, strafe the area with machine gun fire, and drop bombs. The first B-1B strike released three 500-pound bombs, set for an air burst. This strike destroyed a mosque and an adjacent building. A second B-1B strike released two 500-pound and two 2,000-pound bombs. One building was destroyed and another three were "heavily damaged." The third B-1B strike, less than 30 minutes later dropped a single 2,000-pound bomb on a building where the "B-1B Commander and the ground force commander," seeing "similarly sized adults moving rapidly in the dark…away from friendly forces" believed the Taliban had taken shelter.[53]

All told, the B-1B dropped a total of five 500-pound bombs and two 2,000-pound bombs—all of which were equipped with GPS guidance systems—in three strikes after sunset. The CENTCOM report suggested that it was the munitions from the last two strikes of the B-1B bomber that "likely" did the damage to the civilians and "may have resulted in civilian casualties."[54] US investigators concluded that it was only the last two B-1B strikes which violated the procedures the United States had previously instituted to avoid civilian casualties.[55] The image in figure I.1 is from the unclassified report of the incident.

CENTCOM reported the Afghan Independent Human Rights Commission estimate that there were as many as 86 civilians killed in the assault. Indeed, the Afghan Independent Human Rights Commission report said that there were some witness accounts "and other sources" that suggested "the 11 other adult males reported killed in these three compounds were also civilians."[56] The CENTCOM reported killing "at least 78 Taliban" and "approximately 26 civilians."[57]

The 2,000- and 500-pound bombs which caused the destruction in Garani carried by the B-1B were regularly deployed in Afghanistan and also Iraq. A typical 2,000 pound bomb (and there are several versions, both guided and unguided) contains nearly 1,000 pounds of tritonal explosive. The lethal radius of a 2,000-pound bomb—the distance from the center of the blast within which nearly everything will be destroyed—is approximately 115 feet (35 meters). Thus, the lethal area of a 2,000-pound bomb is more than 41,400 square feet. The lethal radius of a 500-pound bomb

---

[53] USCENTCOM's Unclassified Executive Summary, "U.S. Central Command Investigation into Civilian Casualties in Farah Province, Afghanistan on 4 May 2009," Central Command, 18 June 2009, p. 9.

[54] Ibid.

[55] Ibid., pp. 2 and 9.

[56] Afghanistan Independent Human Rights Commission, "Balabook Incident" Press Release, Kabul, 26 May 2009, p. 2.

[57] USCENTCOM's Unclassified Executive Summary, "U.S. Central Command Investigation into Civilian Casualties in Farah Province, Afghanistan on 4 May 2009," Central Command, 18 June 2009, p. 11.

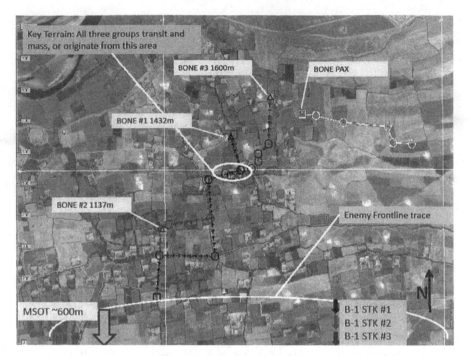

Figure I.1 US image of Garani, Afghanistan.
Source: USCENTCOM, Unclassified Executive Summary, "U.S. Central Command Investigation into Civilian Casualties in Farah Province, Afghanistan on 4 May 2009."

is about 65 feet (20 meters), and its lethal area is thus about 13,270 square feet. By comparison, the area of an American football field is 57,600 square feet.[58]

The image in figure I.2 of the blast from a 2,000-pound bomb dropped by a US B-1B bomber on the town of Yatimchay, in Helmand Province during Operation Mar Lew in Afghanistan in June 2009 illustrates the range of destruction of such a weapon.[59]

When large bombs are used in close air support of ground operations, US troops need to be some distance away to reduce the risk of injury or to avoid being injured altogether by the blast or flying debris. For instance, when a 2,000-pound bomb is dropped, soldiers should be at least 3,000 feet away, and for a 500-pound bomb, soldiers should be at least 1,600 feet away, to avoid being harmed by the shrapnel. Thus, although the GPS guided 2,000-pound bombs (JDAMs) are accurate to an

---

[58] The area of a US football field is 120 yards by 53.3 yards.

[59] Chris Hughes, "We Witness the Dangers Our Troops Face in Afghanistan Minefield," 1 June 2009, http://www.mirror.co.uk/news/top-stories/2009/06/01/a-walk-into-the-valley-of-death-115875-21405430/. For NATO video of the assault, see "NATO Ministers Meet on Afghanistan in Dutch Town," http://www.youtube.com/watch?v=hPrUFoCXzSc, viewed on 13 July 2009.

Figure I.2 Effects of a 2,000-pound bomb on an Afghan Village.
Source: NATO video, "NATO Ministers Meet on Afghanistan in Dutch Town." http://www.youtube.com/watch?v=hPrUFoCXzSc.

average of about 30 feet, the damage caused by the bombs could not be described as pinpoint.

Risk estimate distances for combat, estimating the "percent of friendly casualties that may result from an air strike against an enemy threat" for a 2,000-pound bomb are between 738 and 1,640 feet.[60] For example, on 4 December 2001, US Special Forces in Afghanistan under fire from the Taliban called in a close air support airstrike. A B-52 responded and dropped a 2,000-pound satellite guided JDAM bomb in what turned out to be too close to the Special Forces position—the US troop coordinates had been mistakenly programmed as the target. The bomb fell approximately 100 meters (328 feet) away from the troops and killed three US soldiers, five Afghan soldiers fighting with the United States, and seriously wounded nineteen other Special Forces troops. A few hours after the incident a reporter asked Admiral John Stufflebeem to explain how troops 100 meters away from the strike could have been hurt: "That's a long way away. Is somebody in danger a football field away?" Stufflebeem replied, "A 2,000-pound weapon is a devastating weapon....As a pilot, when I would drop a 2,000-pound weapon, I wanted at least 4,000 feet of separation from that weapon when it went off."[61] But in combat, the

[60] These distances are, respectively, for 10 percent and a 1 percent probability of incapacitation. U.S. Army, Marine Corps, Navy, and Air Force, *J-Fire: Multiservice Procedures for the Joint Application of Firepower* (FM 90-20) (Langley, AFB: Air Land Sea Application Center, November 1997), pp. 58–59.

[61] Stufflebeem, "DoD News Briefing—ASD PA Clarke and Rear Adm. Stufflebeem," http://www.defense.gov/transcripts/transcript.aspx?transcriptid=2600, 5 December 2001. In this case, the bomb landed where it was supposed to. Also see Carl Conetta, "Disappearing the Dead: Iraq, Afghanistan, and the Idea of 'New Warfare,'" Project on Defense Alternatives Research Monograph 9, 18 February 2004 (Cambridge, MA: Commonwealth Institute, 2004), p. 25.

use of air power entails risks for one's own troops when they are in contact with the enemy. Admiral Stufflebeem was describing what might be called best-case scenario—minimizing risks to one's own soldiers by maximizing their distance from the target. But, as Stufflebeem also said, "As a pilot, I can do everything perfectly with a perfect weapons system and still cannot account for every weapon going exactly where it's supposed to go. And that's just a fact of unfortunate life here in this case."[62]

Civilians are also clearly in danger when large weapons are used. The CENTCOM report on Garani clearly notes what Afghan's had reported: that several structures in the area were destroyed either directly or were damaged or destroyed by the blast effects of the 2,000-pound bombs. The Afghans report pulling both dead bodies and survivors out of buildings that had been reduced to rubble in Garani. The American ambassador to Afghanistan, Karl Eikenberry questioned the use of 2,000-pound bombs on houses.[63] When US General Dan McNeill was asked in a television interview in May 2009 about the Garani incident, and questioned more specifically about the possibility of reducing the use of heavy bombs by the interviewer, Ray Suarez, General McNeill said that the United States did not only use 2,000-pound bombs.

RAY SUAREZ: Well, General McNeill, you heard Marc Garlasco. American military leaders keep assuring the Afghans they're trying to minimize civilian casualties. How do you do that? What can you change?

GEN DAN MCNEILL: I agree with Marc that we have to work all the time and steadily at our activities to review them, to assess them, and make sure we're applying our resources in the best way we can, because, as Admiral Mullen said, any time a noncombatant is harmed or killed, we do harm to our own cause.

RAY SUAREZ: Well, Marc Garlasco just suggested using lower collateral damage bombs. Would that help? Using instead of 2,000-pound bombs on civilian targets—on human targets, using, perhaps, less lethal ones or with lethality spread over a less widespread area?

GEN. DAN MCNEILL: Let me address that question, Ray. By your question, you're suggesting that every aerial munition drop is a 2,000-pound bomb, and nothing could be further from the truth.

As a NATO commander, I cannot recall the number of times that I sat with a lawyer on one side to make judgments on the law of armed conflict and the likelihood of harm to things that were clearly considered noncombatants and a weaponeer who was advising me on what was available and what could be applied.

[62] Stufflebeem, "DoD News Briefing—ASD Clarke and Rear Adm. Stufflebeem."
[63] Gall, "U.S. Envoy Vows to Help Cut Afghan Civilian Deaths."

So NATO imposes some really strict steps and concepts to execute aerial munition attacks. And, frankly, I think they're good. Are they always perfect? I'm not advertising that; certainly, they are not.

But I think there are far more episodes that go relatively uneventful than this tragic episode that we're discussing right now and the others that have gone before it.

But I do not disagree with Marc. We have to work everyday to make it better. We have to work harder. We have to reduce the harm and deaths to noncombatants.[64]

On the other hand, a spokesperson for NATO ISAF forces in Afghanistan, Lt. Commander Christine Sidenstricker, told a reporter that: "The fact remains that civilians were killed because the Taliban deliberately caused it to happen.... There is nothing—in the story, or that we've seen or heard elsewhere— that says our actions led to additional collateral damage or civilian casualties. And regardless, the fact remains that civilians were killed because the Taliban deliberately caused it to happen. They forced civilians to remain in places they were attacking from."[65]

On 2 July 2009, the new American commander in Afghanistan, Stanley McChrystal issued a new "tactical directive" to the NATO ISAF and US forces which, according to officials, was in part a response to the incident at Garani: "We don't want another Granai [*sic*]. The tactical gains simply don't outweigh the costs."[66] Under the new tactical directive, the United States would restrict the use of airstrikes to cases where coalition troops were in danger of being overrun. "When we shoot into a compound, that should only be for the protection of our forces." General McChrystal emphasized that: "Air power contains the seeds of our own destruction if we do not use it responsibly. We can lose this fight."[67]

In a declassified portion of the tactical directive, McChrystal stated that:

I expect leaders at all levels to scrutinize and limit the use of force like close air support (CAS) against residential compounds and other locations likely to produce civilian casualties in accordance with the guidance. Commanders must weigh the gain of using CAS against the cost of civilian casualties, which in the long run make mission success more difficult and

[64] "U.S. Considers Ways to Prevent Civilian Deaths While Battling Afghan Insurgency," PBS Newshour, 21 May 2009, http://www.pbs.org/newshour/bb/asia/jan-june09/afghan2_05-21.html.

[65] Noah Schachtman, "Despite Damning Report, U.S. Blames Taliban for Air Strike Deaths," Danger Room, 3 June 2009, *Wired*, http://www.wired.com/dangerroom/2009/06/deadly-us-airstrikes-broke-rules-report-says-military-continues-to-blame-taliban/.

[66] A "senior military official," quoted in Yochi J. Dreazen, "U.S. Revisits Afghan Battle Rules," *Wall Street Journal*, 24 June 2009, http://online.wsj.com/article/SB124571281804038963.html.

[67] Quoted in Filkins, "U.S. Toughens Airstrike Policy in Afghanistan."

turn the Afghan people against us.... The use of air-to-ground munitions and indirect fires against residential compounds is only authorized under very limited and prescribed conditions.[68]

General McChrystal's directive acknowledged the increased risk to troops in his tactical directive. "I recognize that the carefully controlled and disciplined employment of force entails risks to our troops—and we must work to mitigate that risk wherever possible. But excessive use of force resulting in an alienated population will produce far greater risks. We must understand this reality at every level in our force." On 17 July 2009, two weeks after the publication of McChrystal's directive, thirteen civilians were wounded and at least five were killed in a US close air support strike in Kandahar, Afghanistan.[69]

What happened at Garani was far from unique: from the use of large bombs in a populated area, the proximate cause of the killing; to confusion about how many and the identities of those killed; to the questions of moral responsibility for the deaths. Garani did add an incentive for the well-known US tactical directive. But, as I describe in chapter 2, changes in rules of engagement following similar incidents had been made before, notably twice in the previous year, and civilians were still being killed in what many felt was a persistent and frustrating regularity. Thus, Garani is an example of systemic collateral damage, the kind that is foreseeable, and perhaps should have been foreseen. The fact that the rules of engagement were changed after Garani suggests that the systemic nature of this kind of collateral damage—that it was predictable given the rules of engagement and other features of the situation—was recognized by commanders and organizational responsibility was taken to reduce the likelihood of similar future incidents.

I began to think about the causes and moral responsibility for US caused civilian casualties after the US invasion of Afghanistan in October 2001. Al Qaeda had deliberately targeted civilians in New York and Washington in September on the view that they were not innocent. By contrast, the United States said it would avoid harm to civilians and instead would liberate Afghans from the Taliban. Yet, I wondered why there were seemingly many instances "collateral damage" killing of Afghan civilians in 2001 and 2002. Was the United States, as the Pentagon argued, conducting a war with relatively few civilian casualties? Were those deaths unavoidable? More important, who was morally responsible for the injury and death of noncombatant Afghans—the US military or the Taliban and Al Qaeda, as then Secretary of Defense Rumsfeld argued? The same questions arose in Iraq when many civilians died, and later, as the US escalated its "drone" strikes against the Taliban and Al

---

[68] Declassified excerpt from NATO Tactical Directive, 2 July 2009, released by NATO ISAF Headquarters, 6 July 2009.

[69] Taimoor Shah and Carlotta Gall, "U.S. Strike Kills Civilians, Afghans Say," *New York Times*, 17 July 2009, p. A8.

Qaeda into Pakistan, killing noncombatants. In Yemen, of those killed by US drone strikes meant to target Al Qaeda leaders, as of late 2012, 21 percent were counted as civilians by the conservative *Long War Journal*.[70]

It seemed that in many instances the United States had adhered to the letter of international law in attempting to minimize civilian casualties, but the conduct of operations suggested fatalism about civilian casualties that bordered on indifference. Reflecting this fatalism, when the United States inadvertently killed civilians very early in the war in Afghanistan, Secretary of Defense Donald Rumsfeld said: "Now in a war, that happens. There is nothing you can do about it."[71] Yet, inadvertent killing was often foreseen and indeed its likelihood the subject of calculations. Moreover, I was struck by the great attention given to incidents of deliberate killing of civilians by US soldiers, though it seemed that far more civilians were injured and killed unintentionally in these wars. Because the military said it was trying to avoid harming civilians, there seemed to be both a political and public tolerance for inadvertent harm to noncombatants; any inadvertent killing was the fault of the enemies of the United States for either starting the wars or resisting US occupation. Collateral damage is certainly legal under certain conditions—when it is unintentional and proportionate to the military advantage gained. How does legal responsibility for deliberate killing differ from moral responsibility for inadvertent killing? Who was morally responsible for those deaths?

As I raised these questions at conferences attended by members of the US military and civilian analysts, I heard a strong defense of US efforts to avoid civilian harm. I heard arguments that US conduct in these wars was characterized by the greatest care, compared to past wars, to avoid harming civilians and that concern for civilian life was, historically, the "American way of war." I heard a defense of military necessity and the desire to protect US forces in combat areas. But I also heard concern from members of the military, expressed by Majors, Lt. Colonels, and Colonels that the United States was not doing enough to protect civilians in Afghanistan and Iraq. These concerns were eventually echoed publicly by higher ranking officers such as this US Brigadier General speaking from Afghanistan: "I mean, we are so focused on the population and we are very attuned to civilian casualties. And I mean, they were very important in Iraq, but here they have taken on a whole new level of importance it seems."[72] By mid-2009, it seemed that the US command had learned that not enough was being done to protect civilians in Afghanistan and that

---

[70] http://www.longwarjournal.org/multimedia/Yemen/code/Yemen-strike.php.

[71] Donald H. Rumsfeld, U.S. Secretary of Defense Donald H. Rumsfeld, DoD News Briefing—Secretary Rumsfeld and Gen. Myers, Monday, October 29, 2001. http://www.defense.gov/transcripts/transcript.aspx?transcriptid=2226.

[72] DoD News Briefing with Brig. Gen. Lawrence Nicholson from Afghanistan, 8 July 2009 http://www.defense.gov/transcripts/transcript.aspx?transcriptid=4442.

minimizing "collateral damage" would be a priority. Yet, it is not always so easy to admit civilian killing and to take responsibility for it.

Outline of the Argument

One incident of unintended civilian killing is a singular tragedy. Frameworks of mistake, accident, or tragedy direct our attention to the event, and to individuals, but they foreshorten our analysis. Thousands of episodes of civilian killing, over months and years and in different war zones, that follow a similar pattern of cause and effect, suggest a different sort of understanding is necessary, one that helps us distinguish genuine accidents from "normal accidents" and the unintended deaths that are the result of a strategic choice about proportionality and military necessity. The chain of moral responsibility for systemic collateral damage and double effect/proportionality killing begins much further back in time and includes more factors than can be found on the battlefield. Specifically, beliefs about war and the law of war, choices made by individual actors, and the constraining and enabling effects of institutions and organizational procedures may produce collateral damage and make it difficult for us to recognize how individual tragedies "add up."

In Part I, I explain the terms used here and describe the scope and scale of collateral damage in recent US wars. Chapter 1, "Moral Grammar and Military Vocabulary," clarifies the concepts of collateral damage and moral responsibility, as well as terms such as combatant, noncombatant, and civilian as they are used in international law and ethics. Other terms, such as force protection and risk transfer are also key concepts. Sustained attention to the terms is necessary because the fact of repeated incidents of unintended harm or killing of civilians is not simple. Collateral damage is legal and regrettable at the same time. Moral responsibility includes the primary responsibility to reduce the likelihood of collateral damage and the secondary responsibility to act to reduce collateral damage in case those with primary responsibility fail to do so. The underlying moral grammar—the structure of moral reasoning—is partially revealed by attention to the vocabulary.[73]

The first section of chapter 2, "How They Die," describes how the US military became concerned with the problem of collateral damage in Afghanistan and Iraq. The second part of the chapter, after briefly describing the difficulty of counting the dead in these wars, gives estimates of aggregate collateral damage and provides some of the details of how Afghan, Pakistani, Iraqi, and Yemeni civilians have been injured or killed in these wars despite the US military's best efforts. We know much more about US casualties and maiming. We know much less about the suffering caused by the United States and each month brings different accounts and disputes of the numbers and the causes of those deaths.

---

[73] On the other hand, although the analysis of philosophy, international law, and political science were essential, I limit the use of the specialist terms associated with those disciplines.

The focus on the aggregate numbers and details is important to provide a sense of the scale and the causes of unintended civilian killing. First, while newspaper accounts and some analysis tend to describe the incidents of civilian killing as isolated incidents, adding them up suggests that the repetitious nature and the scale of unintended civilian death have perhaps been underestimated. While there were certainly fewer civilians killed by the United States and its allies than there would have been if the policy was either to deliberately target civilians, or one of gross indifference to protecting the lives of civilians, collateral damage killing has nevertheless been a frequent and costly occurrence. By my estimate, there were about 22,000 collateral damage deaths in the major US war zones in Afghanistan and Iraq over the years between late 2001, when the war in Afghanistan began, and late 2012, after eleven years of war. But, as I discuss, there are formidable obstacles to an accurate accounting of civilian casualties. The first difficulty is defining the scope of the US wars, which have arguably also extended to Pakistan and Yemen, with US drone strikes, and support and training for US allies in those countries. Yet the difficulties in counting the dead and injured are greatest in Pakistan and Yemen, where few media have penetrated the areas where the United States conducts its drone strikes. The idea that drone strikes are an antidote to conventional war that will produce far fewer civilian casualties than conventional air strikes is questionable when one examines the data. Between 500 and 2,000 civilians may have been killed in Pakistan and dozens of civilians have also been killed in Yemen by US drone strikes between 2002 and 2012. Further, the United States is fighting militants in Pakistan with the help of the Pakistani military, which has itself killed more than 13,200 civilians since 2008. In sum, depending on how one counts, the United States and its allies are likely responsible about 22,000 collateral damage deaths in Afghanistan and Iraq. If the collateral damage deaths caused by U.S. allies in Pakistan and Yemen are included, then the United States and its allies are responsible for an additional 16,000 collateral damage deaths and thousands of injuries in those war zones.

Second, the causal chain that produces repeated incidents of collateral damage can only be illuminated and understood by examining how the incidents occur. We need an understanding of the facts on the ground in order to get at the moral responsibility for collateral damage. One of those facts is that when the United States emphasizes the protection of civilians, it has succeeded; but at the same time it may increase risk to its own soldiers.

Part I introduces the idea that collateral damage is not necessarily an unforeseeable tragic accident and that collateral damage is a significant moral and political problem. It concludes with an analysis of the place of civilian casualties in international ethics and international law. It then addresses the primary causal and moral responsibility for repeated episodes of collateral damage. Actors and institutions with primary responsibility are causally proximate to the harm. Specifically, the causal and moral chain that leads to collateral damage begins with actors' beliefs about war, specifically the tensions between the normative value placed on preventing civilian deaths with the values of military necessity and proportionality. The ways that these values are balanced can increase the vulnerability of civilians. The causal and moral chain of responsibility then includes the institutionalization and operationalization of beliefs within the military organization.

Chapter 3, "Norms in Tension" explores the system of normative beliefs and international law that is concerned with civilian immunity, military necessity, and force protection. I describe the moral reasoning that creates and excuses the category of collateral damage and ask whether foreseeable deaths ought to be excused. In the cases of Afghanistan, Iraq, and Pakistan, the United States has taken important measures to reduce the effect of war on civilians. The current US wars illustrate the uneven balance or what may be better described as a deep tension between protecting noncombatant civilians, force protection, and military necessity. The notion of "necessary" military operations can be understood too broadly and that because deaths may often be foreseeable, we should not allow the doctrine of double effect to excuse unintended civilian deaths. Thus, while "collateral damage" might well be legal, there is still a moral problem that points to a legal lacuna.

The second cause of systemic collateral damage is the way beliefs structure practices at the levels of those primarily responsible for making war and protecting civilians, namely individual soldiers, commanders, and the military organization itself. International law since the Nuremberg and Tokyo War Crimes Tribunals has tended to see military atrocity as deliberate acts undertaken by individuals or ordered by commanders. When individuals violate orders and kill noncombatants, they are or should be prosecuted. It would be much neater if there were a bright line, or even better, a huge chasm separating the moral responsibility of individuals and institutions for intentional and unintentional harm. There is no such bright line. It is probably wrong to put the sole blame for either deliberate killing or systemic collateral damage on soldiers, the second most vulnerable class of individuals, after noncombatants, in any war.

I argue that moral responsibility should be understood broadly in the case of collateral damage and in some cases the deliberate killing of civilians. War is necessarily a collective or corporate act; individual agency is constrained in war and war could not be undertaken and prosecuted without the work of large, organized groups. Individual commanders and organizations must bear moral responsibility in cases of systemic collateral damage. Readers expecting that I will ascribe moral responsibility for collateral damage killing only one set of actors will thus be disappointed; moral responsibility for collateral damage is shared among individual and collective agents. As Dennis Thompson rightly notes, "there is no fixed pool of responsibility such that when one person's share goes up another's must go down."[74]

---

[74] Dennis Thompson, "Ascribing Responsibility to Advisors in Government," *Ethics*, vol. 93, no. 3 (April 1983): 546–560, 554. Thompson may or may not, however, subscribe to my particular way of understanding moral responsibility as being shared among individuals in their roles and within institutions such as military organizations or Congress.

Part II focuses on understanding moral responsibility for collateral damage at the level of those with primary responsibility for war—soldiers, commanders, and military organizations. Because the paradigm understanding of moral responsibility focuses on individuals and intentions, I had to first untangle individual from collective moral responsibility for systemic collateral damage. Thus, I begin the analysis of individual moral responsibility by reviewing cases where the moral responsibility for killing noncombatants is ostensibly clear—the deliberate killing of civilians by US soldiers in the era when protecting noncombatants became a priority.

Chapter 4, "When Soldiers 'Snap': Bad Apples and Mad Apples," examines cases where the members of the US military have gone against their orders and deliberately killed civilians. These are atrocities and war crimes on the assumption that the individuals are autonomous moral agents who could have done otherwise. Perhaps the most famous incident in US history is the March 1968 My Lai massacre where as many as five hundred Vietnamese civilians were slaughtered by US soldiers. My Lai led to reforms intended to decrease the likelihood of such killing. Despite these reforms, there have been a number of high-profile incidents where soldiers and some civilian contractors "snapped" and deliberately killed Iraqi and Afghan civilians. What are the causes of these incidents? Are they isolated events, attributable to a few "bad apples" or combat stress? Does US military training and the counterinsurgency mission tend to produce these atrocities? The psychiatrist Robert Lifton argues that counterinsurgency war itself is an "atrocity producing situation." I show that the theory of individual moral responsibility for atrocity and war crimes should, at a minimum, be questioned in light of the fact that individual moral agency is constrained in war. Or, as Dick Couch, a former Navy SEAL and instructor at the US Naval Academy, argues: "We must consider the system as well as individuals. It may not be just a few bad apples in the barrel; it may be that we have a barrel that allows for both good and bad apples."[75] I show how training, the culture of obedience, and the fear that is omnipresent in war diminish individual moral agency. I also suggest how individual soldiers can and sometimes do nevertheless act to increase their moral agency.

Chapter 5, "Command Responsibility," outlines the legal doctrine of command responsibility and continues to explore the overlapping terrain of individual and group responsibility. By focusing on the role of military and top civilian commanders in preventing deliberate and collateral damage, I begin to explore the frameworks of role and shared moral responsibility. Commanders are morally and legally responsible, but like individual soldiers, commanders operate within a military organization, and we can only understand their moral responsibility by attending to how individual agency is constrained by the organization. I then describe the way command responsibility is understood in the United States with regard to collateral

[75] Dick Couch, *A Tactical Ethic: Moral Conduct in the Insurgent Battlespace* (Annapolis: Naval Institute Press, 2010), p. 5.

damage. Specifically, commanders are responsible for establishing the rules of engagement and ensuring that training and operations lead to victory and the observance of the laws of war. I use two cases to explore how commanders' oversight and attitudes can promote or fail to promote respect for noncombatants—US air operations in Bosnia in 1995 and the siege of Fallujah in 2004. In the first instance, civilian protection was a priority and operations were designed and redesigned to avoid collateral damage. In Fallujah, there was less concern about collateral damage and even a loss of distinction. I conclude the chapter with discussions of ways that commanders can exercise greater moral responsibility in war.

But to put the onus of moral responsibility on individual soldiers and commanders is to foreshorten the time horizon and narrow the institutional and normative context—important elements in the causal chain that makes civilian death in war more or less likely. The understanding of moral agency in war that I develop here considers a wider temporal and social domain than the usual focus on what happens on a battlefield, at "the tip of the spear," between soldiers and those they kill. In other words, the preparation for and waging of war is a social system entailing structural requirements and effects, as well as having implications for individual agency.

Chapter 6, "Organizational Responsibility," moves back along the causal chain and is a turning point in my analysis where I move from individual responsibility to collective responsibility and where I show how organizations are what I call "imperfect" and how the US military has evolved in its understanding of collateral damage. Organizations are both the embodiment of physical resources and the institutionalization of beliefs, organizational knowledge, and routines. To be able to argue that the military is organizationally responsible for collateral damage, I make a short detour to philosophy and organization theory to show that organizations can be and are imperfect moral agents and that the US military is a moral agent. Because most scholarly work on moral agency focuses on individuals, the chapter necessarily breaks new ground by integrating organization theory with a theory of imperfect moral agency.[76] In fact, the methodological individualism that has dominated the social sciences and philosophy—specifically, the assignment of all agency and moral responsibility to individuals—has gotten in the way of recognizing systemic collateral damage.

While some measures for minimizing civilian harm were in place at the start of these wars, it arguably took the military a long time and many civilians killed to see

---

[76] There is a rich and growing literature on collective moral responsibility. Overviews include Peter A. French and Howard K. Wettstein, *Midwest Studies in Philosophy*, Volume 30: *Shared Intentions and Collective Responsibility* (Boston: Blackwell, 2006); Larry May and Stacy Hoffman, eds., *Collective Responsibility: Five Decades of Debate in Theoretical and Applied Ethics* (New York: Rowman and Littlefield, 1991); Tracy Isaacs, *Moral Responsibility in Collective Contexts* (New York: Oxford University Press, 2011); Christian List and Philip Pettit, *Group Agency: The Possibility, Design, and Status of Corporate Agents* (Oxford: Oxford University Press, 2011).

the enormous political and strategic costs of collateral damage and to recognize that its procedures could be and should be changed. Once recognized, however, commanders and the services focused on developing and improving means to minimize collateral damage. Rules of engagement were modified, and algorithms, weapons, operations, and ethics training were improved to meet the requirement for civilian protection. Examples illustrate how, on the one hand, institutional beliefs and practices can sometimes set the stage for systemic collateral damage and excuse them. Other examples show how the military acted to reduce collateral damage.

Throughout the wars, the US military has acted as an imperfect moral agent, and its gradual recognition of the problem of collateral damage, its initial ad hoc responses to the problem, and the gradual institutionalization of a program of civilian casualty mitigation illustrates a cycle of moral agency and a process of organizational learning. I argue that this process has been, with exceptions, mostly positive. But I also show where and how the US military could further act to reduce systemic and proportionality/double effect collateral damage.

Part III focuses on secondary moral responsibility for civilian casualties—the responsibility of political actors, namely those within states and the public who do not have primary responsibility for collateral damage, but in their respective roles, are or ought to be monitoring the conduct of war and, when commanders and the military fail to adequately do so, act to force those with primary responsibility to address the problem. I argue that these actors have indirect causal responsibility for war and are responsible moral agents.

Chapter 7, "Political Responsibility," focuses on the role of civilian political institutions' oversight of the military with respect to protecting noncombatants. Prior to the twentieth century, to the extent that there was a concern about noncombatants, the US military was largely responsible for policing its own conduct. In the middle of the twentieth century, US civilian political leadership began to exercise more control and attempted to safeguard noncombatants. This concern was understood by some to have reached an extreme when the White House vetted targets during the Vietnam War partially on the basis of the risk to noncombatants. In part as a reaction to what was perceived as undue interference by civilian authorities and exaggerated concern for noncombatants, the military took control for targeting back and institutionalized it. Yet today the responsibility for the conduct of war is still an area of contention between civilian institutions and the military. I argue that although civilian leaders in the executive branch can and often do exercise oversight, the other branches, namely Congress and the Judiciary have taken much less interest in civilian protection. I propose guidelines for the civilian oversight of the military's preparation for war and its conduct in war.

Chapter 8, "Public Conscience and Responsibility for War," recalls the perennial disputes about the role and public responsibility for war. At least in democracies, militaries only fight the wars "we" tell them to fight and in broad outlines, only use the weapons we buy for them and, in theory, only follow the strategies that we approve. But that is only in theory. When it is argued that the public has some moral responsibility for undertaking war (*jus ad bellum*), most observers stop there, leaving the oversight of military conduct in war (*jus in bello*) to the military and civilian political leadership.

But, although the public often exercises little interest in or oversight of war, I argue that their causal and moral responsibility extends to the conduct of war. When the military fails to adequately protect noncombatants, the political public has moral responsibilities to monitor civilian casualties and to constrain the military. Because it is difficult for the general public to take responsibility for war—to move beyond moral bystander-ship—it is essential to lower the barriers to participation in this most crucial of public policy areas. I offer some suggestions for how the public can increase its capacities for moral agency. I also discuss the public's duties to US soldiers: principals (civilian leaders and the public) have the duty to ensure that their agents (soldiers and private security contractors) are not put at undue risk.

While I am arguing that Americans should hold themselves morally responsible and politically accountable for the conduct of war, that does not make the citizens of the United States legitimate military targets for Al Qaeda or any other terrorist organization or army. Terrorists want to argue that as citizens of a democracy we are responsible for US foreign policy and are thus legitimate targets. Thus, there is a paradox. Citizens in a democracy can share responsibility for their government's foreign policy but not be legitimate military targets because there is an important distinction between a direct combat role and a political role. The moral responsibility of the public is a political charge to action of a democratic citizenry to hold all other actors (including individual soldiers, private military contractors, commanders, the military organization, and civilian officials and institutions) who are constitutive of the social organization of war, to account.

The final chapter, "Collateral Damage and Frameworks of Moral Responsibility," ties the arguments together. It also offers concrete steps that could be taken immediately to reduce the occurrence of incidents of collateral damage.

Four Reasons Noncombatant Killing Should Concern Us

The first reason to be concerned about harm to noncombatants is the sense of moral wrongness of killing civilians. Although international law and a concern for what happens to others living far away from us in countries that are at war with us may not be uppermost in our minds during a time of war, a concern for humanity and human rights is an important part of an emerging international society and what may ultimately be the foundation for sustainable peace. Intentionally killing or harming noncombatants is deeply offensive to most of humanity because those noncombatants did nothing to deserve their ill-treatment. They do not control their leaders, and they may not even agree with the aims of the war they are caught up in.

It is thus considered a grave moral breach and a grave breach of international law to intentionally kill noncombatants.

Killing civilians is not only wrong when it is deliberate, it also sometimes wrong when it is unintended yet foreseeable. The idea that most incidents of "collateral damage" are unforeseen and unpreventable accidents may be mistaken. As I show in the next chapters, some of the individual incidents of "collateral damage" are not genuine accidents at all, but rather, part of a morally troubling pattern of failing to correct procedures that lead to foreseeable and foreseen death or valuing military necessity and force protection, in calculated trade-offs (the proportionality/double effect type of collateral damage), over civilian life. In the case of proportionality/double effect trade-offs, I cannot say what the "right" trade-off between civilian protection and military necessity is, but I can say that given how military necessity is a notoriously elastic concept we ought to weight civilian protection more heavily than the United States has at times done in these wars.

To say we care about the lives of the "enemy" state's civilians is not to say how much we care about them. And how much we care will determine the amount of risk citizens ask soldiers to take in war to see that they are protected. Do we care about them as much as we care about our own civilians? Usually not. But should we care about them as much? The presumption here is that those civilians in distant countries where the United States is fighting who are not directly participating in combat are just as presumptively innocent as civilians in the United States. They deserve as much care as we would want to be taken with our own lives.

The second reason we should care about noncombatant death is the pragmatic reason identified by the US military: winning increasingly depends on not killing civilians. While some might argue that the military should not be so concerned with noncombatants that it constrains their military operations and the capacities of individual soldiers to achieve their missions, the pragmatic argument is that there is such strong moral disapprobation associated with harming and killing "innocents" that survivors tend to rehearse and mourn those deaths, and the pain becomes a cause for grievance and anger. Indeed, outrage at civilian deaths can be more charged than sorrow of the deaths of one's own soldiers, who after all, expected that they might be killed and at least had the training and the weapons to defend themselves. Moreover, even accidentally harming civilians, in ways that are thought to be the result of callousness, indifference, or recklessness, is often equated by the victims, as essentially the same as deliberate harm. After all, the family member is just as dead, whether the death was intentional or unintended.

The US wars in Afghanistan, Pakistan, and Iraq, though undertaken for different purposes—respectively to root out, arrest, or destroy Al Qaeda and to eliminate the regime of Saddam Hussein and turn Iraq into a democracy—turned into counter-insurgency wars. The theory of victory in such wars is that one must both destroy or capture insurgents and win the "hearts and minds" of the population. Clearly, winning hearts and minds means, commanders argue, that the United States must

stop killing civilians. The US military and political leadership in both the Bush and
Obama administrations were gradually convinced that the steady killing and maiming of noncombatants in Iraq and Afghanistan by the United States and its allies
does not simply harm Iraqis and Afghans; the deaths and maiming at US hands are
increasingly understood as an element in turning opinion against the United States
and in growing support for insurgents. This argument was framed very clearly in the
2009 Command Guidance given by Generals Michael Hall and Stanley McChrystal
in Afghanistan.

> From a conventional standpoint, the killing of two insurgents in a group of
> ten leaves eight remaining: 10-2-8. From the insurgent standpoint, those
> two killed were likely related to many others who will want vengeance. If
> civilian casualties occurred, that number will be much higher. Therefore
> the death of two creates more willing recruits: 10 minus 2 equals 20 (or
> more) rather than 8. This is part of the reason why eight years of individu-
> ally successful kinetic actions have resulted in more violence. The math
> works against an attrition mind-set.[77]

In mid-2012, the pragmatic reasons for reducing civilian casualties were underscored in an Army document on civilian casualty mitigation that the Army intends
to guide its conduct in current and future wars.

> To the extent possible, civilians (including those loyal to the enemy) must
> be protected from the effects of combat. In addition to legal and humani-
> tarian reasons, Army units must mitigate CIVCASs because they create
> lasting repercussions that impair post-conflict reconstruction and rec-
> onciliation. CIVCASs lead to ill will among the host-nation population
> and political pressure that can limit freedom of action of military forces.
> If Army units fail to protect civilians, for whatever reason, the legitimacy
> of U.S. operations is likely to be questioned by the host nation and other
> partners.... The population's support for counterinsurgency operations is
> often a center of gravity, and CIVCASs potentially jeopardize such support
> if civilians conclude that Army units and their partners (such as host-nation
> security forces or security contractors) are their greatest threats.[78]

The history of US warfare suggests that when concern to minimize noncombatant death has become part of the operational understanding of military necessity,

---

[77] General Michael T. Hall and General Stanley A. McChrystal, ISAF Commanders
Counterinsurgency Guidance, International Security Assistance Force, Kabul Afghanistan,
August 2009.

[78] Army, *Civilian Casualty Mitigation*, p. 1-5.

the military loses its fatalism and takes responsibility for minimizing noncombatant death. The US military has recognized this problem but has been only marginally successful in reducing the damage. Indeed, the United States has been losing the war of perceptions despite its efforts to turn those perceptions around with strategies to "inform and influence." Surveys of Afghan civilians, for example, undertaken in late 2008 and 2009, showed declining support of the United States and NATO, and that civilian casualties at the hands of NATO and ISAF was an important element of their opinion of the United States. Moreover, 41 percent of respondents blamed poor targeting on the part of international forces as the cause of the civilian deaths. Some 28 percent blamed the Taliban or Al Qaeda forces in their midst for causing the deaths.[79] Those Afghans who reported that their region was bombed by international forces were much more likely to support attacking those forces. The United States is also increasingly unpopular in Pakistan due to the perception that many civilians have been hurt in the drone attacks and because of US support for Pakistani military strikes on insurgents.

The third reason to care about noncombatant deaths in the wars in Afghanistan, Iraq, Pakistan, and the global war on terror is related to the moral high ground that American leaders often assert and that many Americans believe fits with their values. The United States was attacked on September 11, 2001, and thousands of noncombatants were killed and injured. Because of this attack, and the heinous record of Sadaam Hussein's regime in Iraq, the United States claims the moral high ground in its global war against terror and in its occupation of Iraq and says that unlike the terrorists who attacked the United States, America will do its best to avoid harming noncombatants.

Scrupulous attention to the well-being of noncombatants should characterize US conduct in these and other wars whether or not it helps the United States win. Even if others do not obey the injunction to protect civilians, Americans ought to do their best; we cannot control others, but we can control ourselves. We care about what is done in our name. If the United States is thought to be careless in its military operations or has a doctrine that leads to foreseeable civilian death, it will be judged harshly. The policies and practices that lead time and again to those predictable civilian killings should be changed—and not simply because it might help "win" the wars. It was perhaps hard for Admiral Mullen to admit that "despite our best efforts we sometimes take the very lives we are trying to protect." Yet, the United States must face these facts and ask if these foreseeable and preventable

---

[79] The survey was conducted by the Afghan Center for Socio-Economic and Opinion Research in December 2008 and January 2009, and reported in Shaun Waterman, "Costs of War: The Civilian Casualty Issue," ISN Security Watch, 17 February 2009, http://www.isn.ethz.ch/isn/Current-Affairs/Security-Watch/Detail/?lng=en&id=96590. Also see Gary Langer, "Frustration with War, Problems in Daily Life Send Afghans' Support for US Efforts Tumbling," 9 February 2009, http://abcnews.go.com/PollingUnit/story?id=6787686&page=1.

deaths do represent America's best efforts, and if the United States cannot, indeed, take more care.

Indeed, the US military knows that Americans and others increasingly care about avoiding civilian casualties. Public concern shaped the way some aspects of the Vietnam War was fought. In February 1968, shortly before the My Lai incident, commanders inside Vietnam showed they were very well aware of perceptions of US behavior.

> Extensive press coverage of recent combat operations in Vietnam has afforded a fertile field for sensational photographs and war stories. Reports and photographs show flagrant disregard for human life, inhumane treatment, and brutality in handling of detainees and PW. These press stories have served to focus unfavorable world attention on the treatment of detainees and prisoners of war by both [Vietnamese and American forces].... Vigorous and immediate command action is essential.[80]

Similarly, concern for public opinion has figured in the US wars in Afghanistan and Iraq. The new US Army guidance, for example, states: "Even unavoidable and lawful CIVCASs will be publicized by the news media and critically viewed by the American people, the local population, and the international community."[81]

The fourth reason to care about noncombatant killing is that protecting noncombatants may mean that US soldiers take greater risks. The soldiers know this. And so do their commanders. This balancing of risk causes great anguish and some anger. Soldiers have taken an oath to risk their lives but they are, rightly, risk averse. If we ask soldiers, for either pragmatic reasons—because we want their hearts and minds "population centric" strategy to succeed—or for moral reasons, to protect noncombatants at potentially greater risk to themselves, then we must do so consciously, and with an understanding and acknowledgment of their potential and actual sacrifice. If protecting civilians does not have to entail increased risk to US soldiers, then soldiers should know that as well.

In sum, the questions raised by this book are difficult. I ask readers to grapple with some of the hardest issues associated with war, an already complex and morally troubling activity for all involved. And I ask readers to think about moral agency in a new way; keeping individuals in mind, but recognizing that organizations, institutions, and loose collectives, namely the political public, have moral agency and can and should exercise moral responsibility. The questions associated with collateral damage killings and injury did not begin with the US wars in Afghanistan, Iraq, and Pakistan, and will not disappear when those wars finally and completely end. As

---

[80] Communication from Military Assistance Command, Vietnam, February 1968, quoted in Martins, "Rules of Engagement for Land Forces," p. 49n.

[81] Army, *Civilian Casualty Mitigation*, p. 1-5.

long as the United States intervenes in conflicts or continues to conduct its war on terror with drone, cruise missile, or combat air strikes in Yemen, Somalia, and elsewhere, questions of collateral damage will continue to arise. My analysis is intended to help us reason through the problems of civilian killing in war and find ways to diminish foreseeable collateral damage.

PART 1

THE SCOPE AND SCALE OF COLLATERAL DAMAGE

1

Moral Grammar and Military Vocabulary

We know that victory will not come without a cost. War is ugly. It causes
misery and suffering and death, and we see that every day.
—Donald H. Rumsfeld[1]

The humanizing of war! You might as well talk about the humanizing of
Hell.... If I'm in command when war breaks out I shall issue my order—
The essence of war is violence. Moderation in War is imbecility....
—John A. Jackie Fischer[2]

The words "noncombatant immunity," "discrimination," "collateral damage,"
"military necessity," "force protection," and "risk transfer" are the vocabulary of
twenty-first-century war as conducted by the United States. Each of these terms
of art is situated in a historical and cultural context, and each has a different meaning in everyday language, military operations, and international law. They are also
associated with morality and moral responsibility; they are normative beliefs, or
"norms," in the sense of articulating our sense of what is good and right to do—
what we value.[3]

The US military discriminates between civilians and soldiers and has a
policy of "noncombatant immunity"—only combatants should be deliberately targeted by US forces in war. Yet in Afghanistan, Iraq, and Pakistan, many

---

[1] Donald H. Rumsfeld, U.S. Secretary of Defense Donald H. Rumsfeld, DoD News Briefing—
Secretary Rumsfeld and Gen. Myers, 29 October 2001. http://www.defense.gov/transcripts/transcript.
aspx?transcriptid=2226.

[2] World War I British Admiral John A. Jackie Fischer, quoted in Gary D. Solis, *The Law of Armed
Conflict: International Humanitarian Law in War* (Cambridge: Cambridge University Press, 2010),
p. 267.

[3] By "norm" social scientists mean the dominant behavior, what most often happens—the behavioral norm. A *normative belief* is about what it is good and right to do and why. One particular normative
belief can be dominant. Or, that normative belief may exist alongside other normative beliefs as an
alternative understanding of the good.

civilians—noncombatants—were unintentionally killed or gravely injured by US forces in what are officially called incidents of "collateral damage." As described more fully in chapter 2, I count more than 22,000 collateral damage deaths caused by the United States and its allies in these war zones from 2001 through 2012.

While the collateral damage killing of civilians in the cases of systemic collateral damage and double effect are not deliberate massacres, they result from bureaucratic choices and standard operating procedures, and are often treated as the necessary, if tragic, outcome of operations. Although the killing and maiming of noncombatants is considered regrettable, the fact of civilian death in war is understood as natural and unavoidable. It is what we have come to expect, despite our best intentions and best efforts. The harm is treated as a normal expected outcome, ordinary killing—foreseeable and preventable—but killing that has not been prevented.

The US military is urged to avoid what it calls in the 1976 revision of the Law of Land Warfare "unnecessary killing or devastation." The Field Manual is explicit:

> loss of life and damage to property incidental to attacks must not be excessive in relation to the concrete and direct military advantage expected to be gained. Those who plan or decide upon an attack, therefore, must take all reasonable steps to ensure not only that the objectives are identified as military objectives or defended places within the meaning of the preceding paragraph but also that these objectives may be attacked without probable losses in lives and damage to property disproportionate to the military advantage anticipated. Moreover, once a fort or defended locality has surrendered, only such further damage is permitted as is demanded by the exigencies of war, such as the removal of fortifications, demolition of military buildings, and destruction of military stores.[4]

The important words here are "unnecessary," "excessive," and "disproportionate"—terms that are not defined, but which nevertheless imply that some collateral damage deaths may be necessary, appropriate, and proportionate. However, the term "military objectives" is defined: "combatants, and those objects which by their nature, location, purpose, or use make an effective contribution to military action and whose total or partial destruction, capture or neutralization, in the circumstances ruling at the time, offers a definite military advantage."[5] The US military definition of collateral damage in 2001 was "unintentional or incidental injury or damage to persons or objects that would not be lawful military targets in the circumstances ruling at the time. Such damage is not unlawful so long as it is not excessive in light

---

[4] United States Army Field Manual 27-10, The Law of Land Warfare, July 1956, as revised July 1976, Article 41.

[5] Ibid., Article 40, respectively.

of the overall military advantage anticipated from the attack."[6] Collateral damage is often considered natural, accidental, and perhaps even ordinary. Everyone is trying their best, but given certain objectives, some innocents may die.

The key phrase here is "not unlawful so long as it is *not excessive in light of the overall advantage anticipated* from the attack." Some degree of foresight, the capacity to imagine and "anticipate" three elements—the military advantage anticipated, the potential damage to noncombatants (those who would not be considered lawful targets), and whether such anticipated damage is excessive in light of the military necessity of the operation—are implied by this conception of collateral damage. So killing or harming some number of civilians is understood to be lawful if it is not disproportionate; conversely, the damage must be in proportion to military objectives and must be militarily necessary.

The US Air Force definition of collateral damage characterizes the prevailing understanding of collateral damage and alludes to the political trouble that may arise when there is the perception of excess harm to civilians.

> Collateral damage is generally defined as unintentional or incidental damage that occurs as a result of an attack but affects facilities, equipment, or personnel that are not militarily acceptable targets. Since this kind of damage is often the focal point for national and international scrutiny, the type and level of force applied against a target must be carefully selected to avoid excessive collateral damage. International law does not prohibit attacks against military objectives even though they may cause collateral damage since incidental damage is inevitable during armed conflict; but this damage should not be excessive in relation to the military advantage anticipated.[7]

As the Air Force definition notes, collateral damage is not a war crime. It is expected and understood as "inevitable." When the harm is unintended, a military necessity, and proportional to the objective, collateral damage is considered legal. The US *Operational Law Handbook 2011*, the guide for military lawyers and judges, describes collateral damage as incidental not intentional. "Incidental damage consists of unavoidable and unintentional damage to civilian personnel and property incurred while attacking a military objective." The handbook underscores the legality of collateral damage when it is incidental and refers to the relevant international treaty law. "**Incidental damage is *not* a violation of international law.** While no LOW [Law of War] treaty defines this concept, its inherent lawfulness is implicit in treaties referencing the concept. As stated above, AP I, art. 51(5) [the Geneva

---

[6] *Joint Publication 1-02, Department of Defense Dictionary of Military and Associated Terms*, 12 April 2001 (as amended through 17 March 2009), p. 95.

[7] United States Air Force, Intelligence Targeting Guide Air Force Pamphlet 14-210 Intelligence, 1 February 1998, p. 52.

Convention Additional Protocol I] describes indiscriminate attacks as those causing '*incidental* loss of civilian life … excessive … to … the military advantage anticipated.' "[8] It might be tempting to say that if collateral damage is legal, there is just
the problem of making sure inadvertent harm to civilians meets the requirements of
humanitarian/military law.

I am not disputing the fact that the United States has increased its efforts to
avoid and minimize killing civilians, for example, by using more precise weapons.
I discuss the shift more specifically in chapters 2 and 6. It is also clear that the military and civilian leadership of the United States have wanted us to know of those
efforts. As President George W. Bush told Congress in 2002, "Afghanistan proved
that expensive precision weapons defeat the enemy and spare innocent lives, and we
need more of them."[9] The Pentagon and some civilian analysts argue that the United
States has done as well as could be expected to minimize harm to civilians. Indeed,
individual soldiers are given some training regarding the Geneva Convention prohibitions on deliberately harming noncombatants, and they are also trained in how
to avoid inadvertently killing noncombatants. Individual soldiers are punished if
they are found to have deliberately killed noncombatants. Moreover, the US military offers compensation payments in some cases to the families of victims when
noncombatants are inadvertently killed.

As I emphasized in the Introduction, incidental "collateral damage" deaths are
often understood as the tragic outcome of war—they are described as natural and
framed as inevitable and certainly not the result of deliberate choices by individuals. The United States attempts to keep harm to civilians to a minimum, but says
the killing is inevitable and reasons that the United States is not morally responsible for civilian deaths because, as Donald Rumsfeld stated at the beginning of the
US war in Afghanistan, "We did not start this war. So understand, responsibility
for every single casualty in this war, whether they're innocent Afghans or innocent
Americans, rests at the feet of the al Qaeda and the Taliban."[10] Further, by not officially tallying the deaths and by downplaying their significance, the United States
is, in another way, minimizing the harm to noncombatants. This double minimization—the attempt to reduce civilian casualties while underplaying their significance
when they do occur—has fostered fatalism, inattention, and an air of inevitability
about noncombatant deaths.

The trouble is that many of these deaths are not infrequent, inevitable, and unforeseen. Many episodes of collateral damage are foreseeable, foreseen, and preventable,

---

[8] International and Operational Law Department, *Operational Law Handbook 2011* (Charlottesville,
VA: The Judge Advocate General's Legal Center and School, 2011), p. 12, emphasis in the original.

[9] George W. Bush, "The President's State of the Union Address." The White House, 29 January
2002, http://georgewbush-whitehouse.archives.gov/news/releases/2002/01/20020129-11.html.

[10] Donald H. Rumsfeld, DoD News Briefing—Secretary Rumsfeld and Gen. Myers, December 4,
2001, http://www.defense.gov/transcripts/transcript.aspx?transcriptid=2598.

albeit strictly legal. When collateral damage occurs with great frequency in ways that are predictable and often predicted, we can no longer be surprised and say that such harm was unforeseen. Rather, the acceptance of "collateral damage" as long as it is proportionate to military objectives points to a lacuna in the moral tradition that underpins the laws of war, a corresponding inadequacy in the laws of war, and a certain gap in our understanding of how such killing occurs and where moral and causal responsibility for it resides. It is this fatalism about the unintended killing that is nevertheless foreseeable, and the relaxation of the policy of discrimination and civilian immunity that is the focus here. As the Marquis of Halifax said, "Folly is often more cruel in the consequence than malice can be in the intent."[11]

It is probably fair to say that US military doctrine is ambivalent about noncombatants. The focus on intention and bad apples—those who snap and deliberately harm civilians—combined with the way the rules of engagement allow the use of force against not only hostile action but also against perceived hostile intent or threat means that by definition the majority of civilian killing is understood as either incidental or acceptable. Thus, the US president or the Pentagon can say that 99.9 percent follow the rules. However, it is the rules that yield systemic collateral damage and allow for double effect killing.

In the "Introduction" I also argued that the broad term "collateral damage" failed to capture the range of the phenomena of unintended civilian killing in war. I suggested that there were really three types of collateral damage incidents: (1) genuine accidents or mistakes that were unforeseen and perhaps unforeseeable; (2) cases of "systemic" collateral damage, where the harm was unintended, yet foreseeable and perhaps preventable—the result of organizational choices and routines, such as rules of engagement and the choice of weapons—yet not necessarily foreseen; and (3) a category of proportionality/double effect collateral damage where leaders and soldiers know that harm to civilians is likely, but it is judged proportional under the doctrine of double effect because it is not the direct intention to harm civilians. All of these types of collateral damage killings are legal under current international law.

Indeed, one has to be very clear to distinguish between "collateral damage" (which is not a crime under international law) and war crimes and crimes against humanity. Noncombatants have sometimes been killed because soldiers have "snapped" or engaged in deliberate killing of noncombatants. War crimes and crimes against humanity are both instances of intentionally harming noncombatants, but they differ in that the former is more or less ad hoc killing, while crimes against humanity are a policy. When the suffering directed at civilians is deliberate, widespread, planned, and systematic, it is a crime against humanity under international law. The International Criminal Court defines a crime against humanity as "acts [such as murder, extermination, rape,

[11] Quoted in C. Paul Vincent, *The Politics of Hunger: The Allied Blockade of Germany, 1915-1919* (Athens: Ohio University Press, 1985), p. 124.

torture] when committed as part of a widespread or systematic attack directed against any civilian population, with knowledge of the attack."[12] Invented after the Holocaust, the term would apply to the Rwanda genocide, the Cambodian genocide, and the 9/11 attacks. War crimes are also deliberate and though they may be "large scale" they do not rise to the threshold of widespread and systematic. Intentionally directing attacks against the civilian population as such or against individual civilians not taking direct part in hostilities is a war crime.[13] There can be many war crimes (for instance, the shooting of unarmed combatants for no particular reason), but such killing may not be the strategy. In the case of war crimes, the focus is on blaming individual soldiers, or in some cases their commanders, for violations of the laws of war.

We appropriately blame individual soldiers for the deliberate murders of non-combatants that they commit. Because all types of collateral damage deaths are understood as inevitable, while the deliberate massacre of civilians is clearly intentional, there has been an official tendency until quite recently in the United States to absolve the US military of operational and moral responsibility for all types of collateral damage. Yet, unlike those cases where US soldiers deliberately kill Afghans or Iraqis, it is not appropriate to put the onus of blame on individual soldiers for incidents that are genuine accidents and systemic collateral damage. Blame, and the responsibility to change the policies that lead to these casualties, must be located at the organizational and political levels because the deaths were foreseen as militarily necessary and indeed accepted because of that perceived necessity. The sense of inevitability and unavoidability of collateral damage deaths contributes to their almost invisible quality in the minds of some—such civilian death has become ordinary. Yet once we observe a great deal of "collateral damage" in Afghanistan, Pakistan, and Iraq caused by US policy and recognize that this killing waxes and wanes as a result of strategic decisions and tactical directives, we need not accept this killing as natural and inevitable. These deaths are foreseeable, they are often foreseen, and they can sometimes, perhaps often, be prevented. The term "ordinary killing" may also be appropriate because while deliberate civilian killing is no longer acceptable, inadvertent killing ("collateral damage") has become ordinary, expected, and often excused.

The phrase "ordinary killing" also recalls the language of the 1998 Rome Statute that established the International Criminal Court, where the link between criminal responsibility and intention is defined. Specifically, the ICC statutes focus on intention and knowledge: "a person shall be criminally responsible and liable for punishment for a crime within the jurisdiction of the Court only if the material elements are committed with intent and knowledge." Intention is found where someone means to engage in particular conduct and in "relation to a consequence, that

---

[12] Rome Statute of the International Criminal Court, 1998, from Article 7. http://untreaty.un.org/cod/icc/statute/romefra.htm.

[13] Ibid., from Article 8.

person means to cause that consequence or is aware that it will occur in the *ordinary course of events.*" A person has knowledge when they are aware that "a circumstance exists or a consequence will occur in the ordinary course of events. 'Know' and 'knowingly' shall be construed accordingly."[14] But the ICC focuses on individual perpetrators. When the ordinary course of events in war—choices made at the command and organizational levels of weapons, soldiers' training, and rules of engagement—predictably causes collateral damage, and such killing and maiming can be prevented, it is no longer something to be dismissed as inevitable. My argument is that ordinary killing, systemic collateral damage, is produced more at the institutional level than at the individual level, and thus moral responsibility for it should be shared among individuals and institutions.[15] As Scott Veitch argues, the "perfectly legal ... delivery of massive harms relies also on ordinary social processes—the division of labour, hierarchies, bureaucracies—within which legal institutions are set and on the capabilities of which they draw, the cumulative effect of which is often to splinter any coherent sense of congruity between acts and consequences."[16]

The legal issue, and perhaps more importantly, the moral and political dilemmas follow from the tensions between the military goals, "military necessity," the foreseeability of harm to noncombatants, and how those involved define proportionality.[17] I argue that systemic collateral damage killing is characterized not so much by a single event, but by a pattern of unintended yet foreseeable harm. Accidents which occur on a regular and predictable basis and which are foreseen may be accidents in the sense of being unintended, but they are not necessarily unpreventable. Does foreseeability and preventability amount to intentionality? No, not in the narrow way that intention is understood in international law as a specifically desired outcome. And I agree that no one intended the outcome of collateral damage in this sense. However,

---

[14] Rome Statute of the International Criminal Court, 1998, Article 30. Emphasis added.

[15] I considered and ultimately rejected calling systemic and double effect collateral damage "ordinary atrocity." Atrocity is a strong and charged word to use for actions that were legal and whose consequences were unintended even if they were foreseen. Yet, atrocity is not, in contrast to the terms "genocide" or "crimes against humanity," a precise term of international law. Rather, it is a term of description and moral judgment. We tend to use the word atrocity for the very worst acts—from small scale but nevertheless devastating suicide bombings, to the massacres of large numbers of innocent people, to slavery, genocide, and crimes against humanity. What makes something an atrocity is our sense that the victims did not deserve the harm and that the perpetrator had moral agency and specific intention to do harm. As Claudia Card argues, "atrocities imply culpable agents, not just harmful ones." Culpability, she continues "depends on what the agent knew and could reasonably have known (whether reasonable care was exercised, for example), how much freedom the agent had to do otherwise, what scruples the agent had or lacked, and what purposes or intentions, if any, the agent had in acting." Claudia Card, *The Atrocity Paradigm: A Theory of Evil* (Oxford: Oxford University Press, 2002), p. 55.

[16] Scott Veitch, *Law and Irresponsibility: On the Legitimation of Human Suffering* (New York: Routledge, 2007), p. 11.

[17] I discuss these tensions more fully in chapter 3.

I am not focused on a single incident of inadvertent/accidental civilian killing, but rather on how the harm to noncombatants is foreseen, sometimes calculated, and "adds up" in the context of the war so that the conditions that will produce such harm are predictable and avoidable. Therefore, incidents that may be perceived as genuine accidents may actually be "normal" or routine accidents. Everyone may genuinely be trying their best, but the goals and the definitions or specific criteria of military necessity and proportionality or a failure to distinguish between combatant and noncombatant may predictably lead to civilian killing. Thus, moral and perhaps legal categories should be expanded to include moral responsibility for a pattern of unintended yet foreseeable harm.[18]

Haditha: Massacre or "Cost of Doing Business"?

In the early morning of 19 November 2005, a 20-year-old Marine, Lance Corporal T. J. Miguel Terrazas, was killed by a roadside bomb. In retaliation, a group of US Marines killed twenty-four unarmed Iraqi civilians in Haditha, including children aged 14, 10, 5, 4, 3, and 1, over the course of about four hours as members of a thirteen-man unit, the 1st Squad of Marine Company K, Third Battalion Marines, attacked people in three houses and a taxi carrying four college students.[19] When the killing of the unarmed Iraqi civilians, including women and children, was uncovered, many described the incident as a massacre and atrocity. The Marines who did the killing at first argued that the deaths were unintentional, collateral damage—that fifteen civilians died when the improvised explosive device that killed T. J. Miguel Terrazas exploded and the rest were killed in the crossfire of an engagement with insurgents.[20]

The idea that the deaths of twenty-four civilians in Haditha were collateral damage—the result of returning fire—would not have raised eyebrows. Interviews of Marines,

---

[18] Dennis Thompson makes this argument as well: "Foreseeability, then needs to be considered in ascribing responsibility, especially in the context of the organizations in which public officials and their advisors work. Many patterns of bureaucratic behavior, including practices that social scientists call pathological, are quite common in government and often could be anticipated by officials within these organizations, even if no one intends that the practices should exist, or that any harmful consequences they produce should occur. Furthermore, some of these practices and consequences are also avoidable. Yet with a theory of responsibility that relies only on the criterion of intention, or that always gives intended consequences moral precedence over merely foreseen consequences, we are less likely to hold officials responsible for doing anything about these defective organizational practices and the harmful consequences that flow from them." Dennis Thompson, "Ascribing Responsibility to Advisors in Government," *Ethics*, vol. 93, no. 3 (April 1983): 546–560, 553.

[19] Ellen Knickmeyer, "In Haditha, Memories of a Massacre," *Washington Post*, 27 May 2006, p. A1.

[20] The Marine battalion of which the soldiers involved in the Haditha massacre were a part, had been fighting earlier in Fallujah, where the rules of engagement were notably less restrictive. Indeed, for many in Kilo Company of the Third Battalion, First Marines, it was their third tour in as many years. Nancy Sherman, *The Untold War: Inside the Hearts, Minds, and Souls of Our Soldiers* (New York: W. W. Norton, 2010), p. 76.

conducted during the military's own early 2006 investigation of Haditha, showed that what happened was not considered unusual. When the Marine Commander in the region, Major General Johnson, was asked, "If it was reported at the time that 15 non-combatants were killed, however they were killed, then was that not a significant event?" he replied that he had heard of the incident. But, he said, "I didn't feel I had information at that point in time that would cause me to go back and look at it. There were other—this was November, so we had been at it since March. And examples of many civilians being killed at a given time were a precedent for that. It happened all the time. Not necessarily in MNF-West all the time but throughout the whole country."[21] Major General Johnson added, "So, you know, maybe—I guess maybe if I was sitting here at Quantico and heard that 15 civilians were killed, I would have been surprised and shocked and gone—done more to look into it. But at that point in time, I felt that that was—had been, for whatever reason, part of that engagement and felt that it was just a cost of doing business on that particular engagement." Similarly, when asked if the number of civilians killed raised alarm, Marine Colonel T. Cariker responded that he could not remember the particular incident.

> We would have civilians reported killed....when we get fire from a building and the initial reports the building is dropped and they'd estimate, you know, battle damage. But afterwards, they might find some civilians in there that they didn't know was in. But they were well within the rules of engagement proportionality of response. And I'd have to go, you know, we would, unfortunately, you would get civilian casualties. I mean, whether it's a result of our action or others actions, you know, discovering twenty bodies, throats slit, twenty bodies, you know, beheaded, twenty bodies here, twenty bodies there. Grenade attacks on a check point, and, you know, collateral with civilians. But, I can't remember if we had, I think, you know, we wouldn't see fifteen all the time, but it wasn't—it wasn't something that, would be an alarm like, "Hey, what the hell is going on down there."[22]

There were several such incidents, some of which, like Haditha, were considered potential crimes.[23] But Haditha was widely reported a few months after the

---

[21] Major General Steve Johnson, Interview transcript. http://www.nytimes.com/interactive/2011/12/15/world/middleeast/haditha-selected-documents.html?ref=middleeast#document/p1/a41194.

[22] Col. T. Cariker from interview transcript, 31 March 2006. http://www.nytimes.com/interactive/2011/12/15/world/middleeast/haditha-selected-documents.html?ref=middleeast#document/p1/a41194.

[23] Other incidents in Iraq and Afghanistan were documented in a press release by the US Army Criminal Investigation Command, "Army Criminal Investigators Outline 27 Confirmed or Suspected Detainee Homicides for Operation Iraqi Freedom, Operation Enduring Freedom," Fort Belvoir, VA, 25 March 2005.

incident, and it became symbolic of how things could and did go wrong in the Iraq war. Many Iraqis believed the attack was a deliberate massacre in revenge for the earlier deaths of Marines in Haditha. Two Marine commanders were relieved of duty in July 2006 for negligence in investigating the Haditha incident. In December 2006 four Marines were charged with "unpremeditated murder" and four officers were charged with failing to fully investigate and accurately report the incident.[24]

The case of Haditha highlights the grey zone between massacre/atrocity and collateral damage. One participant, Sergeant Sanick Dela Cruz said, "I know it was a bad thing what I've done, but I done it because I was angry TJ was dead."[25] Of the eight Marines charged for various offenses related to the killings, most charges, including those of unpremeditated murder, were dropped for all but one Marine, Frank Wuterich.

Staff Sergeant Frank Wuterich had reportedly killed five men who had surrendered and then led an assault on several houses where more were killed. When his case finally came to trial, Wuterich faced as many as 152 years in prison. In January 2012, Wuterich pleaded guilty to a lesser charge, "dereliction of duty" at his court martial and was reduced to Private.[26] Wuterich apologized at the trial for killing civilians but argued that he had not done anything wrong. "When my Marines and I cleared those houses that day, I responded to what I perceived as a threat, and my intention was to eliminate that threat in order to keep the rest of my Marines alive. So when I told my team to shoot first and ask questions later, the intent wasn't that they would shoot civilians, it was that they would not hesitate in the face of the enemy."[27]

The conditions that allow for and sometimes inadvertently encourage individuals to commit atrocities are not always local to the occasion of the harm or limited in time. Robert Jay Lifton argues that we must put incidents like Haditha in a larger context and distribute moral responsibility for deliberate killing more widely and look up the chain of command to find moral and causal responsibility.

> To attribute the likely massacre at Haditha to a "few bad apples" or to "individual failures" is poor psychology and self-serving moralism. To be sure, individual soldiers and civilians who participated in it are accountable

---

[24] Eric Schmidt and David S. Cloud, "General Faults Marine Response to Iraq Killings: Calls Officers Negligent," New York Times, 8 July 2006, p. A1; Paul von Zielbauer and Carolyn Marshall, "Marines Charge 4 with Murder of Iraqi Civilians," New York Times, 22 December 2006, p. A1.

[25] Quoted in Mark Oliver and agencies, "Haditha Marine 'Watched Superior Kill Surrendering Civilians,'" The Guardian, 10 May 2007, http://www.guardian.co.uk/world/2007/may/10/usa.iraq.

[26] Michael S. Schmidt, "Anger in Iraq after Plea Bargain over 2005 Massacre," New York Times, 24 January 2012. http://www.nytimes.com/2012/01/25/world/middleeast/anger-in-iraq-after-plea-bargain-over-haditha-killings.html.

[27] Wuterich statement, quoted in Julie Watson, "Haditha Killings: Frank Wuterich, Convicted in Killings of Iraqi Civilians, Escapes Jail Time," Huffington Post, 24 January 2012, http://www.huffingtonpost.com/2012/01/25/haditha-killings-frank-wuterich-iraq_n_1230889.html.

for their behavior, even under such pressured conditions. But the greater responsibility lies with those who planned and executed the war in Iraq and the "war on terrorism" of which it is a part, and who created in policy and attitude, the accompanying denial of the rights of captives (at Abu Ghraib and Guantanamo) and of the humanity of civilians (at Haditha).[28]

Lifton's analysis of Haditha points to the context and the systemic pressures that make a deliberate atrocity more likely. While we would like to hold individuals responsible for harm—and are offended when they "get away with murder"—the structure of a situation can make both deliberate killing and "inadvertent" killing more likely. Thus, Claudia Card notes that individual culpability is not a requirement for atrocity to have occurred. Specifically, "Injustices do not always presuppose a culpable individual.... We can be treated unjustly (dealt less than our fair share) even though no one is at fault. Likewise we can suffer evils even though culpability in individual participants, beneficiaries or others is non-existent.... One can suffer intolerable harm as the result of a practice that is indefensible (even unjust), even though no one is culpable."[29]

Civilian Immunity

Most of us—except, apparently, the perpetrators of deliberate attacks on noncombatants—know that deliberately killing civilians is morally wrong and a crime. It was not always the case that civilians were understood to be immune from attack in war. Not long ago, targeting civilians was understood by many militaries as an effective, and indeed moral, way to conduct war; it was thought that causing civilian pain could end a conflict sooner. By contrast, there is nothing essentially controversial, these days, about the wrongness of deliberately targeting noncombatant civilians. For most of us, there is nothing controversial or even morally complex about the wrongness of the September 11th attacks—the acts were condemnable, full stop. Nor is it unclear that carrying bombs into marketplaces with the intent of killing innocent people is wrong. Neither is US military doctrine unclear about the wrongness of any deliberate attacks by US soldiers on civilians in Iraq or Afghanistan. There is nothing morally puzzling here—deliberate attacks on civilians are always

---

[28] Robert Jay Lifton, "Haditha: In an 'Atrocity-Producing Situation'—Who is to Blame?" *Editor & Publisher*, 4 June 2006.

[29] Claudia Card, *Confronting Evils: Terrorism, Torture, Genocide* (Cambridge: Cambridge University Press, 2010), p. 19. Philosophers have noted how the arrangement of social rules and resources can create structural injustices and vulnerabilities. For example, see Henry Shue, "The Unavoidability of Justice," in Andrew Hurrell and Benedict Kingsbury, eds., *The International Politics of the Environment: Actors, Interests and Institutions* (Oxford: Oxford University Press, 1992), pp. 373–397.

and everywhere to be condemned.[30] These are the principles of discrimination and noncombatant immunity—soldiers must discriminate between combatants and noncombatants, and avoid harming the latter. Those who fail to recognize a distinction between combatants and civilian noncombatants and attack civilians using the argument of military necessity are using terrorist tactics. [31]

This principle of distinction and civilian immunity from deliberate attack has been codified in several religions and the understanding of who is a noncombatant has evolved over time. For example, in parts of Europe 1,000 years ago, both clergy and farmers were protected from deliberate attack. The principle of noncombatant immunity gradually became part of international law in the nineteenth century and was codified in US laws of war. For example, General Winfield's Scott's General Order 20, instructions to the American Army during the Mexican War, ordered that civilians be protected. The 1863 instructions to the Union Army, General Orders 100, also known as the Lieber Code, were even clearer. Articles 21-23 of General Orders 100 makes three arguments which are found in subsequent US and international law—distinguishing between civilians and combatants, noting that civilians will necessarily suffer in any case given the demands of war, but arguing that civilians should be spared deliberate harm.

> Art. 21. The citizen or native of a hostile country is thus an enemy, as one of the constituents of the hostile state or nation, and as such is subjected to the hardships of the war.
>
> Art. 22. Nevertheless, as civilization has advanced during the last centuries, so has likewise steadily advanced, especially in war on land, the distinction between the private individual belonging to a hostile country and the hostile country itself, with its men in arms. The principle has been more and more acknowledged that the unarmed citizen is to be spared in person, property, and honor as much as the exigencies of war will admit.
>
> Art. 23. Private citizens are no longer murdered, enslaved, or carried off to distant parts, and the inoffensive individual is as little disturbed in his private relations as the commander of the hostile troops can afford to grant in the overruling demands of a vigorous war.

---

[30] Of course, we still might ask why or under what conditions governments and nonstate belligerents choose to deliberately kill civilians. For a recent discussion, see Alexander B. Downes, *Targeting Civilians in War* (Ithaca, NY: Cornell University Press, 2008).

[31] All political organizations, including states, that do not discriminate between combatants and noncombatants in war, and aim to either punish or coerce civilians by attacking them are using terrorist tactics. Terrorists are appealing to military necessity to justify civilian killing. For example, Germany's "terror bombing" during World War II, apartheid South Africa's "raids" into neighboring states in the 1970s and 1980s that targeted civilian members of the African National Congress, and Al Qaeda's attacks on civilians 9/11 certainly qualify as terrorism.

As I discuss more fully in chapter 3, the principles of discrimination and "noncombatant immunity" were articulated in international law in the Hague Regulations of the late nineteenth and early twentieth centuries and reaffirmed in the Geneva Conventions of 1949 and in the Additional Protocols to the Geneva Conventions of 1977.[32] The Additional Protocol I of the Geneva Convention suggests a general rule of thumb for distinguishing between civilians and combatants in ambiguous cases: "In case of doubt whether a person is a civilian, that person shall be considered to be a civilian." Further, "the presence within the civilian population of individuals who do not come within the definition of civilians does not deprive the population of its civilian protection."[33] Civilian objects are also to be protected from attack: "In case of doubt whether an object which is normally dedicated to civilian purposes, such as a place of worship, a house or other dwelling or a school, is being used to make an effective contribution to military action, it shall be presumed not to be so used."[34] US military law subscribes to the principle of noncombatant immunity and US military lawyers refer to the Geneva Conventions and specifically Additional Protocol I when it defines civilians, civilian status, discrimination, and proportionality.[35] Army manuals echo the Additional Protocol I language: "In the context of CIVCAS [civilian casualty] mitigation, a civilian is any person who is not a combatant. In other words, a civilian is a person not engaged in hostilities during an armed conflict, regardless of the groups or organizations to which the person belongs. If there is any doubt, Army forces consider a person to be a civilian."[36]

The 1998 Rome Statutes of the International Criminal Court articulated the criteria for assigning individual responsibility for war crimes deliberately perpetrated against civilians. Thus, the idea of noncombatant immunity from attack has largely become taken for granted in both treaty and customary law. As Henry Shue argues, it is "reaffirmation of the morally foundational 'no-harm' principle. One ought not to harm other persons. Non-combatant immunity says one ought, most emphatically, not to harm others who are themselves not harming anyone. This is as fundamental, and as straightforward, and as nearly non-controversial, as moral principles can get."[37]

---

[32] See Solis, *The Law of Armed Conflict*, pp. 232–233. For a rich discussion of the development of the relevant international law, also see Geoffrey Best, *War and Law since 1945* (Oxford: Oxford University Press, 1994).

[33] Geneva Convention Additional Protocol I, Article 50.

[34] Ibid., Article 52.

[35] International and Operational Law Department, *Operational Law Handbook 2011* (Charlottesville, VA: The Judge Advocate General's Legal Center and School, 2011), pp. 131–133.

[36] Department of the Army, *Civilian Casualty Mitigation*, Army Tactics, Techniques and Procedures, No. 3-37.11 (Washington, DC: Department of the Army, 18 July 2012), p. 1-1.

[37] Shue, quoted in Igor Primoratz, "Civilian Immunity in War: Its Grounds, Scope, and Weight," in Igor Primoratz, ed., *Civilian Immunity in War* (Oxford: Oxford University Press, 2007), pp. 21–41, 29.

The status of "noncombatant" is almost always defined in terms of the absence of a particular quality. "Noncombatants" are not combatant soldiers—they do not carry weapons—nor are they in a chain of command. Civilians are immune from deliberate attack when and because they do not pose an actual military threat. Some noncombatants are innocent in the sense of having done nothing to directly harm their adversary or they pose no immediate threat.[38] Prisoners of war or the wounded are *hors de combat,* and thus also considered noncombatants because they are unable to fight. The fact that US treatment of "detainees" at Guantanamo, Bagram Air Base in Afghanistan, and Abu Ghraib was for several years a policy harsh treatment—torture of prisoners by another name—did not vitiate the distinction. Nor did the unsanctioned practice of "dead checking"—shooting wounded unarmed prisoners, which was witnessed in Iraq.[39] War makes civilians and noncombatants vulnerable to direct physical harm and to indirect hardship such as starvation, loss of access to medical care, and traumatic fear. Thus, part of what makes it necessary to protect noncombatants is the fact of their relative vulnerability.[40]

Not surprisingly, however, some people dispute civilian immunity or want to blur the sharp distinctions between combatant and noncombatant that were adopted in the last three centuries.[41] First, as I note below, the distinction may, in fact, not be so clear in war. All would be much simpler if the only practical, moral, and legal questions on the table revolved around discrimination, that is, determining who was a combatant or noncombatant. If civilians are deliberately targeted, there has been a war crime. Yet exercising discrimination and adherence to the principle of immunity depends on the sometimes uncertain ability to determine a person's status. But discrimination is not so simple, and indeed it may be difficult to determine whether someone is a noncombatant. First, soldiers do not always wear uniforms or carry their weapons openly. And indeed, even when they do wear uniforms, they sometimes stop soldiering for any number of reasons—for instance, they may want to take care of their crops or work in a business. Second, when war occurs in cities or other areas populated by civilians, civilians are often drawn into the conflict. Third, when states or nonstate actors hire civilians, such as private contractors, to do certain functions, civilians are drawn into war.

---

[38] As Igor Primoratz summarizes, civilians have done nothing to forfeit their presumed immunity from attack and "therefore they have it and must not be attacked. Soldiers have, by waging war on us, or on those to whose aid we have come; therefore they have forfeited this right and may be attacked." Primoratz, "Civilian Immunity in War," p. 28. For a longer discussion, see R. Charli Carpenter, '*Innocent Women and Children': Gender, Norms, and the Protection of Civilians* (Aldershot: Ashgate, 2006); Helen M. Kinsella, *The Image before the Weapon: A Critical History of the Distinction between Combatant and Civilian* (Ithaca, NY: Cornell University Press, 2011).

[39] Evan Thomas and Scott Johnson, "Probing A Bloodbath," *Newsweek,* 12 June 2006.

[40] But this is, of course, a relative vulnerability. Soldiers are certainly also vulnerable to their adversaries, the difference is that they have the capacity to fight back.

[41] See Best, *War and Law since 1945,* pp. 253–369.

Further, Michael Green argues, although the principle of noncombatant immunity is long-standing, it is outdated in the era of democracy. "In a perfect democracy each and every person would be...fundamentally responsible because if the method of consent has been in operation, each has agreed to the decision reached by that method, or if not that, to be bound by whatever decision was reached by that method." For Green, democracy entails responsibility, and he thus disputes the principle of noncombatant immunity.[42] Some US leaders have, arguably, inadvertently erased or blurred the distinction between combatants and noncombatants, on the argument that our adversaries do so. In the early days of the war in Afghanistan, the Bush administration often recalled how civilians were intentionally targeted on September 11, 2001. As Donald Rumsfeld said, "We did not start the war; the terrorists started it when they attacked the United States, murdering more than 5,000 innocent Americans. The Taliban, an illegitimate, unelected group of terrorists, started it when they invited the al Qaeda into Afghanistan and turned their country into a base from which those terrorists could strike out and kill our citizens."[43]

Most or many adults living in a state at war participate in the war to some extent. Widening civilian involvement is, in fact, what war mobilization is in large part aimed to accomplish. Yes, the soldiers muster and the weapons are sent to the war zone. But civilians play their part. The people are taxed, their children are conscripted, and their leaders exhort them to behave in ways that will support the war effort—to have more children, buy war bonds, grow more food, and show enthusiastic support for the troops. In guerrilla and insurgency war, the people are exhorted to feed the guerrillas, hide them, or at least look the other way. But none of these activities causes civilians to lose their immunity from deliberate attack.

While it is the case, as I later argue, that civilians in democracies are morally responsible for wars, this responsibility does not vitiate their immunity from attack. Only when civilians are in "direct participation" in hostilities do they lose their immunity.[44] For a civilian to be considered a direct participant in hostilities, they must be engaged in acts that are likely to cause harm to either soldiers or civilians, and that there is a direct (as opposed to an indirect) causal link between the action and the harm, and that the act is designed to contribute to the war effort of a party to the conflict.[45] The distinction between direct and indirect contribution is significant. The International Committee of the Red Cross gives the example of a civilian driving an ammunition truck. A civilian truck driver delivering ammunition to people engaged

---

[42] Green, quoted in Ewe Steinhoff, "Civilians and Soldiers," in Primoratz, ed., *Civilian Immunity in War*, pp. 42–61, 47.

[43] Donald H. Rumsfeld, U.S. Secretary of Defense Donald H. Rumsfeld, DoD News Briefing—Secretary Rumsfeld and Gen. Myers, Monday, October 29, 2001. http://www.defense.gov/transcripts/transcript.aspx?transcriptid=2226.

[44] See Geneva Convention Additional Protocol II, Article 13(1) and (3).

[45] See Nils Melzer, *Interpretive Guidance on the Notion of Direct Participation in Hostilities under International Humanitarian Law* (Geneva: International Committee of the Red Cross, 2009).

in active fighting becomes an integral part of the combat and is a direct participant. But someone driving a truck, filled with bombs, let's say from a factory to a port, where the bombs will then be shipped to a war zone, "is too remote from the use of the ammunition in specific military operations to cause ensuing harm directly." So while the truck itself is a legitimate target, the driver is not.[46] If guerrillas depend on the local population to feed and shelter them, are the men and women who produce that food and provide that shelter legitimate targets? The answer, under international law, is no, because the idea is that the contribution of the civilian is indirect. If the civilian members of a state strongly agree with a war and give their consent to their leaders to wage it, are they not guilty and therefore, not innocent? Should they be legitimate targets? Again, under international law, the answer is no.

The category "civilian" generally includes noncombatants, but it can also include those whose actions pose a threat, such as civilian leaders of a country at war who are in the chain of command or private contractors performing military functions. Civilian political leaders are thus sometimes legitimate targets, but they are not combatants.[47] Military contractors who support the military (for instance, by functioning as engineers or cooks) but do not operate weapons or take part in hostilities also retain their civilian status. Combatants are members of armed forces or guerrilla groups. When contractors who are otherwise not in the uniform of a state's armed forces operate weapons or otherwise participate in hostilities they lose their civilian protection. Combatants are armed—they pose a threat and can lawfully be attacked. Thus, although they are not exactly the same, I will use the terms "civilian" and "noncombatant" interchangeably throughout, although my focus is on the subcategory noncombatant civilian.

The noncombatant immunity norm, as a deontological value, has deep roots in just war theory and international law. But the norm with even deeper roots is military necessity, the notion that the military can and should use the means necessary to accomplish a mission. In a way, military necessity reflects simple utilitarianism (or moral consequentialism) and a belief that the reasons of state may, on occasion, justifiably trump human rights. The idea is that sometimes, some amount of inadvertent civilian death is acceptable if it means an important military goal is served. The trouble is defining and deciding the threshold of acceptable inadvertent killing and the value of the military objective.

---

[46] Ibid., p. 56.

[47] Although they should, some actors do not recognize a distinction between civilian authorities who are in a chain of command and those who are not. The Taliban in Afghanistan, for example, have attacked and killed village religious and political leaders and even local functionaries arguing that those civilian targets are collaborators with American occupation and thus legitimate targets. However, unless these people are directing attacks, they are not legitimate targets. Similarly, unarmed civilian aid workers should be immune from kidnapping and attack, although the Taliban has repeatedly targeted those people. See the Afghanistan NGO Safety Office reports, http://www.ngosafety.org/reports.html.

Military necessity has sometimes been defined to emphasize the protection of US forces. In the recent emphasis on protecting civilians, the US military has explicitly recognized the greater potential risks and costs to US soldiers. "The counterinsurgent gains ultimate success by protecting the populace, not himself."[48] The fact is, even though soldiers can defend themselves, they are also vulnerable. The protection of civilians may and often does entail increased risk to soldiers and a greater toll in lost limbs and lives.

Force Protection and Potential Risk Transfer

Much more recently than noncombatant immunity, "force protection" has emerged as a strong normative belief. Some call this a "body bag syndrome" or casualty aversion. The soldier, for centuries used as a tool whose life could be traded for victory, is increasingly respected as a human whose life must be preserved and protected. The militaries of the great powers no longer have millions of men to throw into battles by the thousands on the hope that masses of men might overwhelm the enemy. Soldiers are no longer disposable. Soldiers are, indeed, scarce in societies that have abandoned conscription in favor of volunteer forces.

Force protection has become both a normative value and a political necessity. The US military has come to respect its own soldiers' lives to the point where it is sometimes willing to put the adversary's civilians at greater risk to preserve its soldiers' lives. The technological advantages of the United States over most of its adversaries also allowed it to engage in highly lethal combat from a distance: accuracy could be obtained from higher altitudes, and soldiers could launch rockets from greater distances. The conduct of US war in the former Yugoslavia—bombing from relatively high altitudes and avoiding the use of ground forces—illustrates how the United States emphasized force protection.

Martin Shaw argued that casualty aversion and the greater attention to force protection led to "risk transfer war": a wish to kill from a distance but little willingness to put one's own soldiers at risk.[49] The debate among defense intellectuals in the 1990s, and after the 9/11 attacks, was that perhaps the United States had become too casualty averse. Jeffrey Record argues that casualty aversion is legitimate and "healthy," but that at times the US military and political leadership has demonstrated what he calls "elite casualty phobia" which he argues is rooted in the Vietnam War experience.[50] Record suggests, casualty aversion was sound policy,

---

[48] Eliot Cohen, Conrad Crane, Jon Horvath, and John Nagl, "Principles, Imperatives, and Paradoxes of Counterinsurgency," *Military Review* (March-April 2006): 49–53, 52.

[49] Martin Shaw, *The New Western Way of War* (Malden: Polity Press, 2005).

[50] Jeffrey Record, "Collapsed Countries, Casualty Dread, and the New American Way of War," *Parameters* (Summer 2002): 4–23, 10–12.

but that casualty "phobia" was disabling. "This dread of casualties is pronounced among the country's political and military leadership, and in the war over Kosovo it produced the elevation of force protection above mission accomplishment."[51] Some feared that there was a growing perception that the United States would not fight back in the face of an attack if many of its soldiers were injured or killed, but "cut and run" as it was perceived to have done after more than 200 US soldiers, mostly Marines, were killed in a truck bomb attack on barracks in Lebanon in 1983.

Conversely, after surveying public opinion, some have argued that the American public is less "casualty averse" than US elites believed.[52] Similarly, *Washington Post* columnist Charles Krauthammer suggested in 2002 that "America is allergic to casualties—but only in wars that do not matter. Our history over the last century suggests a General Theory of Casualties: America's capacity to sustain casualties is near infinite, as long as the wars are wars of necessity."[53]

The US military has been acutely aware of the tension between protecting civilians and its own forces. As described in a 2004 US Army Field Manual, "The American way of war has been to substitute firepower for manpower. As a result, US forces have frequently resorted to firepower in the form of artillery or air any time they make contact."[54] The doctrine and training in place at the outset of the wars in Afghanistan and Iraq also emphasized force protection. Specifically, the US Army was trained to call in firepower, commonly close air support, if it could not quickly overwhelm insurgents. At least in the early part of the wars in Iraq and Afghanistan the respect for the value of a soldier's life led to the devaluing of other lives.

But it was also increasingly clear that this strategy, while protecting US forces, was in some ways counterproductive in a counterinsurgency. And the military was not unaware of the potential problems of this approach. "This creates two negatives in a counterinsurgency. First, massive firepower causes collateral damage, thereby frequently driving the locals into the arms of the insurgents. Second, it allows insurgents to break contact after having inflicted casualties on friendly forces." The solution proposed was pursuit. "A more effective method is to attack with ground forces to gain and maintain contact, with the goal of completely destroying the insurgent force. This tactic dictates that military forces become skilled in pursuits. The unit that makes the

---

[51] Ibid., pp. 10–11.

[52] See, for instance, Peter D. Feaver and Christopher Gelpi, "How Many Deaths are Acceptable? A Surprising Answer," *Washington Post*, 7 November 1999; Peter D. Feaver and Christopher Gelpi, *Choosing Your Battles: American Civil-Military Relations and the Use of Force* (Princeton: Princeton University Press, 2004); and Christopher Gelpi, Peter Feaver, and Jason Reifler, *Paying the Human Costs of War: American Public Opinion and Casualties in Military Conflicts.* (Princeton: Princeton University Press. 2009).

[53] Krauthammer, quoted in Record, "Collapsed Countries, Casualty Dread, and the New American Way of War," p. 11.

[54] US Army FMI 3-07.22, "Counterinsurgency Operations," Department of the Army, October 2004, section 3.40.

initial contact with the insurgent force requires rapid augmentation to maintain pressure against the fleeing force, envelop it, and destroy it."[55]

The tensions between force protection and civilian protection can become palpable. Soldiers, who are already vulnerable, can become more vulnerable. The moral responsibility for this vulnerability is shared, I argue, by the military organization and the political actors who set the priorities. Larry May also argues that the political public is responsible for their vulnerability.

> Because soldiers are acting on behalf of the society, or the State, the society should also take an interest in trying to protect them from the worst effects of being a soldier, for harm to soldiers is also the collective responsibility of that society. The society is responsible for what the soldiers suffer because it has ordered them to put themselves in harm's way and has coerced them to remain there, steadfastly defending us from our perceived enemies. The soldiers represent their society, or State, on the battlefield; but when they are harmed, it is a personal not a collective harm—they bleed and lose limbs for us, and we are responsible for these wounds and lost limbs because it is we, collectively, who have commanded them to be put in harm's way. [56]

Because the US military now believes more fully and firmly than before that the support of the populations in counterinsurgency situations is a key to its success, the US changed its operations in order to minimize civilian killing. The problem, from the perspective of the US and allied troops who must implement these policies, is that they are often asked to and do take greater risks. So, the US military can and does succeed in "dialing down" the level of civilian killing when doing so is understood as a military necessity. And in doing so, it consciously, though not gladly, dials up the risk to US troops. US soldiers' deaths have political consequences: "As soldiers feel more restricted in using force and as friendly deaths mount, public support for a foreign deployment may fade quickly in a nation that abhors American casualties."[57]

In other words, when the strategy shifts to winning hearts and minds in a long-term counterinsurgency effort, the military increases its efforts to avoid noncombatant death. When the United States makes the effort to reduce noncombatant fatalities and injuries through new training and rules of engagement, it is often successful, at least for a time. The US military's aim, at this juncture, is not perhaps so much an increased desire to comply with international law or norms of noncombatant immunity, as to prevent civilians from turning against the United States because the US military keeps killing their family members, their neighbors, and maiming

---

[55] Ibid.

[56] Larry May, *War Crimes and Just War* (Cambridge: Cambridge University Press, 2007), pp. 37–38.

[57] Mark Martins, "Rules of Engagement for Land Forces: A Matter of Training, Not Lawyering," *Military Law Review*, vol. 143, no. 1 (Winter 1994): 1–160, 14–15.

their children. Protection of noncombatants is understood as a military necessity. However, when the emphasis shifts to protecting noncombatants, when counterinsurgency is understood to require greater restraint, the risk to US military personnel may increase and US military casualties—the dead and injured—may grow.

The idea that pursuing insurgents and protecting noncombatants sometimes entails greater risk for one's own forces is clearly understood by those who advocated the new counterinsurgency strategy articulated in 2006 that was focused on protecting populations and winning hearts and minds. Counterinsurgency (COIN), as Sarah Sewell wrote in *Military Review*, "demands that intervening forces accept greater levels of risk than they would in conventional conflicts."[58]

> COIN demands a different form of risk tolerance. In counterinsurgency there is a direct relationship between exercising restraint in the use of force and achieving long term mission success....
>
> There is no question that the restrained use of force can, certainly by individual incident and in the short term, equate to increased physical risk for counterinsurgent forces. Yet counterinsurgency demands increased acceptance of physical risks to forces in order to enhance the prospects of strategic success.
>
> This is an operational requirement—not a normative preference.[59]

US troops in Afghanistan complained that the rules of engagement were too restrictive, and indeed, the number of US soldiers killed in Afghanistan increased after the directive was operationalized. For example, in Afghanistan in July 2009, General McChrystal's tactical directive institutionalizing his emphasis on protecting noncombatants by reducing the use of airstrikes acknowledged the increased risk to troops. "I recognize that the carefully controlled and disciplined employment of force entails risks to our troops—and we must work to mitigate that risk wherever possible. But excessive use of force resulting in an alienated population will produce far greater risks. We must understand this reality at every level in our force."[60] There is some evidence to suggest that as the doctrine shifted to civilian protection, not only did the perception of risk to combatants grow, but their actual harm increased. At the same time that killing of noncombatants declined by a third—as a consequence of the new population centric strategy—the number of fatalities in US and UK forces more than doubled.

Specifically, in the first six months of 2009, the number of US military fatalities averaged about twelve per month in Afghanistan. From July through December 2009, the incidence of US military fatalities in Afghanistan averaged about 33

---

[58] Sarah Sewall, "Modernizing U.S. Counterinsurgency Practice: Rethinking Risk and Developing a National Strategy," *Military Review* (September-October 2006): 103–109, 104.

[59] Ibid.

[60] Declassified excerpt from NATO Tactical Directive, 2 July 2009, released by NATO ISAF Headquarters, 6 July 2009.

Table 1.1 **US Military and International Coalition Hostile Fatalities in Afghanistan in 2009**

	January	February	March	April	May	June	Average fatalities
US forces	12	15	11	3	9	20	11.7
Other coalition members	9	9	14	7	14	13	11.0
Coalition	21	24	25	10	23	33	22.7
	July	August	September	October	November	December	Average fatalities
US forces	39	47	33	47	15	15	32.7
Other coalition members	26	25	26	14	11	17	19.8
Coalition	65	72	59	61	26	32	52.5

Source: Icasualties, http://icasualties.org/oef/.

fatalities per month. This increase in US deaths occurred before the US "surge" in troop numbers in Afghanistan, announced in December 2009, had taken effect, and before the tempo of US military operations had dramatically increased. Thus, it was not unreasonable for soldiers to assert that their increased care for noncombatants in 2009 caused increased risk and harm to themselves. US soldiers were also now dying in greater numbers than their coalition partners after July 2009 (table 1.1).

If increased attention to civilian protection led to greater risk to US soldiers in Afghanistan, these figures also suggest that the trend to greater force protection by transferring risk to noncombatants—Shaw's "risk-transfer war"—does not apply in a counterinsurgency doctrine that defines protecting civilians as a military necessity. In Afghanistan in 2009, risk was quite consciously, transferred back to combatants.

The greater risk to US soldiers did not go unnoticed within the military and among close outside observers. As one observer noted in a pro-war website: "Let's start with a simple fact. Yes the change in Rules of Engagement (ROE) in Afghanistan was a major factor in the combat deaths of 4 US Marines recently. Unfortunately they will not be the last, but the change is designed to save US lives in the long run. Tough to swallow, but let's discuss."[61] Another officer told a reporter, "The ROE, lawyers, and bureaucrats are killing us."[62]

[61] Uncle Jimbo, "ROE in Afghanistan and U.S. Deaths," Blacksfive, posted 9 September 2009, http://www.blackfive.net/main/2009/09/roe-in-afghanistan-and-us-deaths.html.

[62] Quoted in Rowan Scarborough, "Afghan Rules Need Changes," *Human Events*, 30 June 2010, http://www.humanevents.com/article.php?id=37774.

By late 2009 and early 2010 the quiet criticism by US troops about taking greater risk had grown to the point where it could not be ignored. Soldiers complained of waiting an hour or more for a response to requests for close air support and that too often, they felt, their requests were denied. A critique of the policy was offered by defense intellectuals, such as Lara M. Dadkhah, writing in the *New York Times*, in early 2010. "So in a modern refashioning of the obvious—that war is harmful to civilian populations—the United States military has begun basing doctrine on the premise that dead civilians are harmful to the conduct of war. The trouble is that no past war has ever supplied compelling proof of that claim." Dadkhah argued, "Wars are always ugly, and always monstrous, and best avoided. Once begun, however, the goal of even a 'long war' should be victory in as short a time as possible, using every advantage you have."[63]

New York Times reporter C. J. Chivers noted in June 2010 that "the new rules have also come with costs, including a perception now frequently heard among troops that the effort to limit risks to civilians has swung too far and endangers the lives of Afghan and Western soldiers caught in firefights with insurgents who need not observe any rules at all." Chivers described disgruntlement at the enlisted level over the civilian protection policy. "Young officers and enlisted soldiers and Marines, typically speaking on the condition of anonymity to protect their jobs, speak of 'being handcuffed,' of not being trusted by their bosses and of being asked to battle a canny and vicious insurgency 'in a fair fight.' "[64] Similarly, Rowan Scarborough, a conservative columnist, described McChrystal's more restrictive rules of engagement and argued that they were unpopular among the soldiers in the field:

> First, [McChrystal] greatly restricted air strikes in support of ground troops, because mistaken bombings accounted for many civilian deaths. Then he put new limits on night operations on the theory that daytime fire fights were less likely to result in the death of innocent civilians.
>
> In another move, he discouraged attacks on homes where terrorists were holed up. Such raids can end up destroying the simply built abodes, as well as the Taliban. Again, the idea here was that sparing civilian lives and homes will help convince the average Afghan to become an ally.
>
> More galling to soldiers was a rule that they cannot shoot an unarmed man putting in place an improvised explosive device (IED)—even though such bombs kill the most NATO troops.
>
> While the rules may have lofty goals, they are hated in the field.[65]

[63] Lara M. Dadkhah, "Empty Skies over Afghanistan," *New York Times*, 18 February 2010, p. A27.

[64] C. J. Chivers, "General Faces Unease among His Own Troops Too," *New York Times*, 22 June 2010, http://www.nytimes.com/2010/06/23/world/asia/23troops.html.

[65] Scarborough, "Afghan Rules Need Change."

By mid-2010, members of the US Congress were noting dissatisfaction and resistance among soldiers to taking greater risks and they too were questioning the balance. In his June 2010 Senate confirmation hearings to become the US Commander in Afghanistan General David Petraeus was asked if the rules were too restrictive and might be rethought. Petraeus responded by talking in terms of protecting troops as a "moral imperative." He said: "I want to assure the mothers and fathers of those fighting in Afghanistan that I see it as a moral imperative to bring all assets to bear to protect our men and women in uniform and the Afghan security forces with whom ISAF troopers are fighting shoulder-to-shoulder. Those on the ground must have all the support they need when they are in a tough situation."[66] General Petraeus acknowledged these tensions in the hearings when he said, "I am keenly aware of concerns by some of our troopers on the ground about the application of our rules of engagement and the [2009] tactical directive. They should know that I will look very hard at this issue."[67]

When General Petraeus was asked upon taking Command if he would change the rules of engagement, he responded that he would not. His response highlights how the normative beliefs of noncombatant immunity, force protection, and military effectiveness have come into stark tension in the Afghanistan war.

I have reaffirmed to President Karzai, to the other Afghan officials, to the Secretary General, to my US governmental leaders and to our forces that we must maintain the commitment to reducing the loss of innocent civilian life in the course of military operations to an absolute minimum. That is a counter-insurgency imperative and one that I strongly supported as General McChrystal pursued it with his commanders. In a counter-insurgency, the human terrain is the decisive terrain and therefore you must do everything humanly possible to protect the population and indeed again to reduce the loss of innocent civilian lives. Now along with that, as I explained in my Senate testimony, was not the revision of the rules of engagement. It is rather to ensure that the application of the rules of engagement—which I believe are sound—and the application of the tactical directive which governs the use of close air support and other forms of support for our troopers when they are in a tough position, that the application of these is proper. And there are concerns among the ranks of some of our troopers on the ground that some of the processes have become a bit too bureaucratic.

Now, I have a moral imperative as a commander. Any commander has a moral imperative to bring all force that is available to bear when our

---

[66] General David Petraeus, "Opening Statement," Confirmation Hearing, Commander, ISAF/US Forces, Afghanistan, 29 June 2010.
[67] Ibid.

troopers and by the way when our Afghan troopers are in a tough position. I discussed this again with President Karzai and the two ministers. They absolutely support the intent that I explained to them which was on the one hand to maintain the focus on the reduction of loss of innocent civilian lives in the course of military operations and also to ensure that our troopers—and ours means now Afghan as well as ISAF—are supported by all means when they are in a tough position.

I think that our commanders are more than experienced enough and more than tactically expert enough to be able to accomplish both of those elements of intent. Reduction of civilian casualties which by the way has in fact worked. The last twelve weeks, when you compare with the twelve weeks of the previous year, has seen a marked reduction in the loss of civilian lives in the course of military operations. Quite marked. In fact something like a 50% reduction in civilian lives lost in the course of those operations. And that is very important given that our force numbers have expanded so significantly and therefore our operations have expanded so significantly. And that is a result of commanders and troopers who understand the context within which they are operating.

But again we must also ensure that when they are in a tough spot, that we do what it is necessary to help them get out of it. And so in that state there is no intent to change rules of engagement. It is to look very hard in how the rules and the tactical directives are implemented and to ensure that there is even implementation across all units instead of perhaps some unevenness that has crept in in some. [68]

Moral questions or, in General Petraeus's words, "moral imperatives" are found in every war from the decision to launch an attack to the years after soldiers have laid down their weapons and returned home. At the same time, the overall effectiveness of US counterinsurgency in Afghanistan remained unclear. The strategy of a counterinsurgency focused on protecting the civilian population is premised on the belief that an insurgency will lose strength and popular support and ultimately, that US forces would face fewer foes. The short-term risk to US soldiers should translate into long-term peace, at least according to the theory. So, absent hard numerical evidence, it appears that the troops used the hard evidence of experience. They felt more vulnerable, and more of their comrades seemed to be dying in ways, so they blamed the change in tactics. Journalists and politicians listened.

The question of whether there was actually a risk-transfer effect—shifting harm from civilians to soldiers—is complicated to assess for several reasons. First, at

---

[68] David Petraeus, "Press Conference," Transcript, 1 July 2010, NATO Headquarters, http://www.nato.int/cps/en/natolive/opinions_64783.htm.

about the same time that the United States began to emphasize population protection, it also increased the number of troops in Afghanistan. So, both combat and noncombat fatalities might have increased simply because more troops were in the war zone. I have attempted to focus on the effect of changed strategy on combat risk by only counting combat fatalities (ruling out nonhostile fatalities such as car accidents and heart attacks), using statistics of troop deaths due to hostile activity. Second, in 2010 and 2011, both sides in Afghanistan began to increase the intensity of their operations and also promised to ignore the traditional "winter lull" in fighting that occurs because the snow makes travel and combat extremely difficult from December through March. The US operation in Marjah in February 2010 was an example of winter operations. The number of injuries and fatalities would also be expected to increase if the soldiers were engaging in more frequent and intense combat, over more months of the year.

The role of changes in tactics—namely how restraint in the use of air power, for example, affects the rate of soldiers' deaths and injuries—would have to be assessed at a micro-level, in part because the "population centric" strategy was applied unevenly and the strictness of adherence to it varied over time in Afghanistan. For example, the US strategy in the battle for Marjah in February and March 2010 was to announce the pending invasion of that city in the hope that both civilians and Taliban would leave the city before the US assault. The hope was to minimize risk on all sides. But though Marjah was taken with relatively few casualties, the insurgency remained strong there and the Taliban increased their assaults on NATO and US forces throughout the country. The gloves came off US strategy again, and civilian killing increased as the United States increasingly used night raids and other strategies that put noncombatant Afghans at risk. Thus, when the sense of military necessity shifted, the consequences for noncombatants also shifted and civilian casualties grew again. In sum, aggregate numbers are only a crude indicator of the effect of changing tactics on risk and actual harm. The hard questions are about the causal processes at work. Specifically, does killing fewer civilians really mean that fewer insurgents are created and that ultimately fewer US soldiers die and the war ends more quickly? Absent the tactical directives and US restraint in close air support bombings, would both more US soldiers and civilians have been killed in Afghanistan?

Whether or not risk is actually transferred, there is the moral question of whether it should be and how risk should knowingly be distributed. The normative question about which way to prioritize risk is also not simple. In contrast to Michael Walzer and others' arguments, discussed more fully in chapter 3, that the greater risk should be born by combatants, Asa Kasher and Amos Yadlin, respectively an Israeli philosopher and a Major General in the Israeli Defense Force, argued that while force protection is typically "last on the list of priorities, or next to last," it should rather come before protecting civilians when soldiers are fighting terrorists in an area where they do not have effective control. Soldiers should take greater risk when they protect their own citizens, but not necessarily when they protect the citizens of other states.

> [C]onsider the situation in which persons directly involved in terror are pursued or targeted by combatants in the vicinity of persons not involved in terror. Where the state does not have effective control of the vicinity, it does not have to shoulder responsibility for the fact that persons who are involved in terror operate in the vicinity of persons who are not. Injury to bystanders is not intended and attempts are made to minimize it. However jeopardizing combatants rather than bystanders during a military act against a terrorist would mean shouldering responsibility for the mixed nature of the vicinity for no reason at all.[69]

Kasher and Yadlin's reasoning rests on a unique blurring of the distinction between combatant and noncombatant/civilian, where the combatant is understood to deserve the same protection as a civilian. They argue that "a combatant is a citizen in uniform. In Israel, quite often, he is a conscript or on reserve duty. His state ought to have a compelling reason for jeopardizing his life. The fact that a person involved in terror . . . reside[s] and act[s] in a vicinity of persons not involved in terror is not a reason for jeopardizing a combatants life in their pursuit."[70]

Moral Grammar

Whether or not moral reasoning is transparent, words do not make sense without the grammar of moral reasoning. The trouble is that sometimes, and in the case of war, more often than not, different systems of moral reasoning may be simultaneously in use. Specifically, as international legal scholar Mark Osiel observes, "military law enshrines two very different theories of morality."[71] The Kantian grammar is categorical—it consists of firm rules, including strict prohibitions, for example, on harming prisoners of war, against torture, and on deliberately attacking civilians.

---

[69] Asa Kasher and Amos Yadlin, "Assassination and Preventive Killing," *SAIS Review*, vol. 25, no. 1 (Winter-Spring, 2005), pp. 41–57, 51.

[70] Ibid., pp. 50–51.

[71] Mark J. Osiel, *Obeying Orders: Atrocity, Military Discipline, and the Law of War* (New Brunswick, NJ: Transaction Publishers, 2009), p. 101. To suggest that there are two different sets of moral reasoning at work does not yet explain how it is that they are used by decision-makers. Psychological research on moral reasoning is voluminous. See, for example, Walter Sinnott-Armstrong, *Moral Psychology*, Volume 3: *The Neuroscience of Morality: Emotion, Brain Disorders and Development* (Cambridge, MA: MIT Press, 2008); on reasoning in general, see Daniel Kahneman, *Thinking Fast and Slow* (New York: Farrar, Strauss and Giroux, 2011).

The utilitarian or consequentialist grammar is flexible: in crude terms, the ends justify the means. The ideas of military necessity, proportionality, or double effect killings articulate utilitarian moral reasoning. These two systems often clash.

Even within one moral grammar, it can be more or less difficult to engage in moral reasoning. On the one hand, it is possible for the values of military necessity, noncombatant immunity, and force protection to complement and reinforce each other. The quest for discrimination can prompt the development and use of more accurate and longer-range weapons. The more accurate weapons may enable soldiers to reduce their risk by allowing them to fire out of the range of their adversary's weapons. And it is possible that more accurate weapons could accomplish a mission more quickly and efficiently, thereby satisfying the needs of military necessity. The advocates of civilian protection as a military strategy are wagering that in the long term, if the strategy of protecting civilians succeeds, they can win the war and end the killing more quickly.

Alternatively, the values of force protection and noncombatant immunity might be in tension with military necessity. For instance, when it was believed that the way to win wars (military necessity) was to get the other side's population to capitulate, civilians were deliberately targeted. This was the logic underlying the long-standing practice of targeting civilians and the belief, articulated clearly in General Orders 100 during the US Civil War, that "the more vigorously wars are pursued the better it is for humanity. Sharp wars are brief."[72] When force protection was valued over the other sides' civilians, risk to one's own soldiers was transferred to the other sides' military and civilians. When it is believed that the way to win wars is to win hearts and minds through civilian protection, then military necessity dictates restraint and great care not to harm civilians; at the same time, one's own forces may incur a greater risk.

Meanings of Responsibility

Both liberals and realists believe that the primary responsibility of a state is to provide for the physical security of its citizens. But that is often not easily done. When the provision of security requires the use of military force and when a country decides to go to war, there are two persistent problems: how to win and how to keep the "blood and treasure" costs of war as low as possible. Winning is achieving one's political objectives, which might be defined as narrowly as defending the border from attack or, alternatively, as broadly as acquiring territory or an empire. Keeping the blood cost of war low can be defined as narrowly as keeping the loss of one's own soldiers low or as broadly as minimizing the intended and unintended killing of soldiers and civilians on all sides. War always has its costs, leaving its mark

---

[72] *General Orders 100*, 1863, Article 29.

not only on the bodies of the dead and living and in diminished treasuries but also in psychological trauma, lost infrastructure, missed opportunities, reduced political freedoms, and in the distortion of legal principles and procedures.

Thus, "war is hell" for both soldier and civilian; "war is ugly." There is no disagreeing with either statement, the first perhaps the most oft quoted aphorism of the US Civil War General William T. Sherman, the second a remark by US Secretary of Defense Donald Rumsfeld. Sherman's siege and destruction of Atlanta, and his scorched earth policy as the Union Army marched through Georgia and South Carolina, are indeed famous for their brutality. In 1864, Sherman told the Mayor of Atlanta before he burned the city that "war is cruelty and you cannot refine it.... You might as well appeal against the thunder-storm as against these terrible hardships of war. They are inevitable"[73]

For soldiers the horror of war is often unavoidable: they are deliberately attacked and their injury or death is often the immediate aim of a military operation whose ultimate ends they may not even know or understand. Yet, by military custom, the doctrines of most religions, and international law, civilians (and the definition of a civilian has not always been the same) should be protected in war. This is the norm of "noncombatant" immunity. But civilians often die in war, and many who do not die are gravely injured.

The questions at the center of this book are about the cruelty of war for civilians and the risk to soldiers. In guerilla wars, insurgencies, and counterterrorism, who is a combatant and who is not? How should we understand the accidental, incidental, or purposeful killing of civilians? Are civilian deaths in the United States' "long war" natural and inevitable? What should be done, and by whom, to prevent those deaths? Who is morally and legally responsible for the harm to civilians? How should we hold those responsible to account? If protecting civilians—as a moral duty or a tactic to win hearts and minds—means putting one's own soldiers at greater risk, who bears the moral burden of the increased risk to soldiers?

These are questions of responsibility, another element of the vocabulary of twenty-first-century warfare, although there is more than one way to understand responsibility. Specifically, the idea of responsibility is often deployed in the causal and morally neutral sense of identifying human agency.[74] For example, one might say, "Jones loaded the weapon" or "Jones was the one responsible for loading the weapon." Moving from causal to moral responsibility depends on context—in this case, how the weapon was subsequently used with or without Jones's foreknowledge. We tend not to ascribe blame for accidents that are a consequence of truly

---

[73] Letter by General William T. Sherman to the Mayor and City Council of Atlanta, 12 September 1864.

[74] Of course, we also speak of natural causes, such as when we say, icy road conditions were responsible for the accident, or drug-resistant tuberculosis was responsible for a death.

unforeseen, unforeseeable, and unintended actions. These are true accidents—the cause is clear, but the moral responsibility is absent.

Causal and moral responsibility are often intertwined, as when on September 11, 2001, President Bush said, "The search is underway for those who are behind these evil acts. I've directed the full resources for our intelligence and law enforcement communities to find those responsible and bring them to justice. We will make no distinction between the terrorists who committed these acts and those who harbor them."[75] Here responsibility is linked to blame and a call for punishment. Some, including perhaps most famously John Stuart Mill, have argued that "moral responsibility means punishment."[76]

A further understanding of responsibility is the sense of having an obligation or duty. We are responsible for something when it is our job or role to behave in a particular way and we are considered blameworthy if we fail to meet our obligations.[77] Responsibility in the sense of the prospective duty to act was invoked in the United Nations doctrine of the "Responsibility to Protect." The obligation was to prevent, respond to, and rebuild after large-scale human rights violations. Similarly, the report of a UN Secretary General panel, *A More Secure World: Our Shared Responsibility* invoked obligations to act to promote security.[78] In his 2002 State of the Union address, US President George W. Bush spoke of an axis of evil: North Korea, Iran, and Iraq. "History has called America and our allies to action, and it is both our responsibility and our privilege to fight freedom's fight."[79] Presidents Bush and Obama frequently spoke of bringing the US presence in Iraq and Afghanistan to a "responsible" conclusion.[80] US National Security Adviser Thomas Donilon described President Obama's involvement in decisions about who to target and kill in drone strikes as "His [Obama's] view is that he's responsible for the position of the United States in the world."[81]

---

[75] George W. Bush, Statement by the President in his Address to the Nation, 11 September 2001, http://www.opm.gov/guidance/09-11-01GWB.htm.

[76] Mill, quoted in Marion Smiley, *Moral Responsibility and the Boundaries of Community: Power and Accountability from a Pragmatic Point of View* (Chicago: University of Chicago Press, 1992), p. 169.

[77] The 9/11 Commission seeks to understand in part, what factors and human errors were responsible for the failure to prevent the 9/11 attacks and whether everyone performed according to their role responsibilities.

[78] See the Report of the International Commission on Intervention and State Sovereignty, *The Responsibility to Protect* (Ottawa: International Development Research Center, December 2001); Report of the Secretary General's High-level Panel on Threats, Challenges and Change, *A More Secure World: Our Shared Responsibility* (New York: United Nations, 2004).

[79] George W. Bush, "State of the Union, 2002" 29 January 2002, http://en.wikisource.org/wiki/George_W._Bush%27s_Second_State_of_the_Union_Address.

[80] For example, see Barack Obama, "Remarks by the President to the Nation on the Way Forward in Afghanistan and Pakistan," 1 December 2009. http://www.whitehouse.gov/the-press-office/remarks-president-address-nation-way-forward-afghanistan-and-pakistan.

[81] Donilon, quoted in Jo Becker and Scott Shane, "Secret 'Kill List' Proves a Test of Obama's Principles and Will," *New York Times*, 29 May 2012, p. 1.

Further, the idea of taking responsibility for the actions of subordinates is often invoked. So, commanders and platoon leaders are said to be responsible for the actions of their subordinates. When military and political leaders apologize and accept responsibility for mistakes, they are enacting the hierarchical view of responsibility where the person at the top of a chain of command assumes responsibility for the behavior of subordinates whether or not they had direct causal responsibility. In international criminal law, responsibility for subordinates is known as command or superior responsibility.[82]

Leaders sometimes make a great show of "taking full responsibility for" their subordinates' behavior. But in such cases, for instance, the making of an apology, the sending of condolences, the request for forgiveness, and the acknowledgement of tragedy sometimes becomes a punctuation mark signaling the end of the conversation, or at least a desire on the part of those apologizing to end the conversation, and the end of a search for deeper causes and other sites of moral responsibility. As Dennis Thompson argued, sometimes taking responsibility "becomes a kind of political ritual that has no negative effect on a leader.... Most significantly, the ritual often quells public debate about a controversial decision or policy, effectively blocking further inquiry into the general moral responsibility of all the officials involved, especially that of the leader."[83]

The dominant framework for understanding legal and moral responsibility for conduct in war, as in the rest of our social lives, stresses both intentionality and individual agency. The reasoning, as articulated at the Nuremberg Tribunal Trial of Major War Criminals is simply that "crimes against international law are committed by men, not by abstract entities, and only by punishing individuals who commit such crimes can the provisions of international law be enforced."[84] Similarly, Michael Walzer argues that "there can be no justice in war if there are not, ultimately, responsible men and women."[85]

As Mark Osiel argues, "the criminal law assumes a world of unencumbered individuals, independently interacting."[86] In this view, an individual's failings or criminal conspiracies lead them to deliberately harm noncombatants. When civilians are killed, it is the conduct of individual soldiers and commanders in the war that may be criminal. This framing is often appropriate. It is, after all, individuals who act or

[82] See Chantal Meloni, *Command Responsibility in International Law* (The Hague: TMC Asser Press, 2010).

[83] Dennis F. Thompson, "Moral Responsibility of Public Officials: The Problem of Many Hands," *American Political Science Review*, vol. 74, no. 4 (December 1980): 905–916, 907.

[84] Quoted in Meloni, *Command Responsibility in International Criminal Law*, p. 13.

[85] Michael Walzer, *Just and Unjust Wars: A Moral Argument with Historical Illustrations* (New York: Basic Books, 1977), p. 288.

[86] Mark Osiel, *Making Sense of Mass Atrocity* (Cambridge: Cambridge University Press, 2009), p. 187.

fail to act and we cannot turn attention completely away from individuals. By contrast, there are sometimes large coordinated actions where the killing is a purposeful policy, plan, or criminal conspiracy—as in genocides and massacres. In these cases, responsibility is said to go all the way to the top.

Military law and investigations by armed services of incidents of civilian killing focus on what happened in the event after the collateral damage or deliberate atrocity has occurred; after the fact of a potential violation of law, the system seeks to hold individuals accountable. Judgments about the lawfulness of civilian killing depend on both the intention of those who caused the harm and the proportionality of the harmful unintended outcome in comparison to the military utility of the operation. If the harm was unintentional and proportionate to military advantage, it might be considered lawful. If harm to noncombatants was intentional or disproportionate, it may be unlawful. Collateral damage is lawful if it is not intended and the anticipated military objectives outweigh the risk to civilians. The effect of law prior to a violation is to make the bounds of acceptable behavior clear and to possibly deter criminal acts. Yet, as Osiel suggests, "legalists are right to insist that law can and does influence battlefield behavior in important ways. But they are wrong to focus exclusively on threats of punishment *ex post*. Far more important in averting atrocity are the more mundane legal norms structuring day-to-day operation of combat forces. These rules achieve their effect *ex ante*, long before the soldier faces any opportunity to engage in atrocious conduct."[87]

Osiel's analysis points to a long causal and moral chain. The trouble is, as psychological research shows, it is very easy to think of the requirements of moral responsibility as simply associated with individuals who are directly and intentionally causing harm. These three features of the dominant conception of moral responsibility are cognitive short cuts, or heuristics, often used to understand moral responsibility. Individual, direct, and intentional action are, of course, part of the picture, and they do indeed point our attention to responsibility for many acts we might want to understand. But to overemphasize directness, intention, and the autonomous individual is to bias our analysis and miss important features of actions by organizations. What do I mean?

A narrow focus on direct, individual, and intentional action can obscure the causes of outcomes and the importance of foreseeability. Individuals are constrained by their roles within the military organization. A focus on direct or immediate cause and effect also has the consequence of discounting the factors that shaped the immediate context. Psychological research shows that observers tend to think that those who are closer to the action (primary agents) should get more of the blame (or praise), and those who are indirectly responsible tend to be forgiven. Thus, as Paharia et al. argue, indirect agency "may attenuate moral condemnation because it

---

[87] Osiel, *Obeying Orders*, p. 163.

is unclear whether the primary agent foresaw the resulting harm."[88] Strategies and organizational preferences can lead unintentionally, and predictably, to systemic collateral damage. Further, the concern with intentional action has the effect that unintended consequences are often ignored or forgiven. As Dennis Thompson notes, "the priority these theories give to intention distorts the nature of responsibility in bureaucratic and other government institutions, where unintended consequences are so rife they might be regarded as an occupational hazard."[89] We have few tools for understanding the causal and moral responsibility for harm that is unintended, the result of procedures that are considered legal and foreseeable. "The criminal law developed its conceptual repertoire to redress conventional deviance, to which individualistic notions readily apply—notions of responsibility, causal agency, intention. These ideas sit uneasily, however with the defining features of modern mass atrocity: officially endorsed, bureaucratically enforced, perpetrated by and against groups, often motivated as much by vocational obligation as personal inclination."[90]

There are times when the isolated individuals' intentions are the appropriate focus; at other times, there are problems with focusing on individual intention as the locus for moral responsibility. For one thing, we cannot always know what someone intended. And second, even if we do know a person's intentions, an act with negative consequences may not be intended, but it is nevertheless foreseeable and we should hold the person responsible. For example, consider the situation where someone drives a car through a red light at a busy intersection. A collision results. The driver says they did not mean to cause a collision. Rather, they meant to get to their appointment on time. When the assignment of moral responsibility is linked to specific conscious intention, it is possible to mistakenly believe that there is no moral responsibility for whole categories of action where the consequences were foreseeable, although perhaps not specifically intended.[91] As Oliver O'Donovan suggests, "the intention of an act is implied in the structure of the act, and not in some moment of psychological clarity in the actor."[92]

---

[88] Neeru Paharia, Karim S. Kassam, Joshua D. Green, and Max H. Bazerman, "Dirty Work, Clean Hands: The Moral Psychology of Indirect Agency," *Organizational Behavior and Human Decision Processes*, vol. 109, no. 2 (July 2009): 134–141, 137.

[89] Thompson, "Ascribing Responsibility to Advisors in Government," pp. 551–552.

[90] Osiel, *Making Sense of Mass Atrocity*, p. xi.

[91] It may be useful to recall the distinction made sometimes in the law between general and specific intent. A specific intention would be one where a person acts with the view to gaining a specific outcome. A general intent would be acting to gain an objective when the actor foresees that their actions will almost certainly result in another consequence. So, in the realm of torture, the relevant international law, the Convention on Torture, uses the concept of general intent while US torture law (U.S. Code 2340-2340A) uses the notion of specific intent.

[92] Oliver O'Donovan, quoted in Nigel Biggar, "Christianity and Weapons of Mass Destruction," in Sohail Hashmi and Steven P. Lee, *Ethics and Weapons of Mass Destruction: Religious and Secular Perspectives* (New York: Cambridge University Press, 2004), pp. 168–99, 177. This is similar to but not the same as the idea of a belligerent nexus. "Belligerent nexus should be distinguished from concepts such as subjective intent and hostile intent. These relate to the state of mind of the person concerned,

Humans do assign moral blame or responsibility if someone is reckless, heedless of the consequences of their actions, and whether or not they intend it, cause great harm. Further, there are sometimes situations where we know that if we do this thing, under particular circumstances, harm is likely to occur even if we do not intend that specific harm. We call it negligence when someone anticipates that harm will happen as a result of their action or inaction, but allows that harm occur when they do little or nothing to stop it. When we do not intend the expected if undesired harm, but we know it will occur at some rate because the process is high risk. Indeed, we sometimes know enough about a process or situation that although harm is not guaranteed, it is possible to calculate the expected rate or magnitude of harm. Actuaries and systems analysts can sometimes give us rather precise formulations about risk and anticipated harm. During the Gulf War, for example, "friendly fire" accounted for 24 percent of US combat fatalities.[93]

The puzzle is why this death and maiming occurs despite the best intentions of soldiers. The cause of repeated incidents of collateral damage is not individual behavior; rather, the cause of repeated incidents of collateral damage is systemic—rooted in the norms and practices of military organizations. Normative beliefs (namely about the relationship between military necessity, proportionality, civilian protection, and force protection), articulated in international law and embedded in military organizations, condition attitudes regarding the acceptability of civilian death in the context of military operations. These beliefs are an important part of the organizational knowledge that structures how militaries organize and enable institutional practices. These beliefs can lead predictably to the protection of civilians and, also predictably, to civilian death. The fact that the US Army began to see the potential for preventing civilian casualties by enlarging the time frame for causal responsibility is evident in its 2012 guidance for civilian casualty mitigation. The term of art is "tactical patience."

> If possible, commanders exercise tactical patience to develop the situation and acquire accurate information. Units and Soldiers should try to create a standoff in time or space to reduce the need for split-second decisions that might lead to unnecessary casualties. CIVCAS mitigation entails an extended cycle...that addresses much more than the moment a decision is made to engage a target. Unit actions before and after an incident are equally important.[94]

whereas belligerent nexus relates to the objective purpose of the act. The purpose is expressed in the design of the act or operation and does not depend on the mindset of every participating individual." Melzer, *Interpretive Guidance on the Notion of Direct Participation in Hostilities under International Humanitarian Law*, p. 59.

[93] U.S. Congress, Office of Technology Assessment, *Who Goes There: Friend or Foe?* OTA-ISC-537 (Washington, DC: U.S. Government Printing Office, 1993).

[94] Department of the Army, *Civilian Casualty Mitigation*, Army Tactics, Techniques, and Procedures, No. 3-37.31 (Washington, DC: Department of the Army, 18 July 2012), p. 1-11.

Related to the common, and understandable, tendency to focus ascriptions of moral responsibility on direct, individual, and intentional acts, moral responsibility for all systemic and proportionality/double effect collateral damage has also received little attention because collateral damage is not a crime under international law. The law excuses unintentional and proportionate harm to civilians as long as it is in service of a military objective. Thus, I agree with C. A. J. Coady about the "complex relation between law and ethics, but...law needs ethical reflection at its foundation....In the matter of collateral damage...the protections afforded by Geneva and its protocols seem to me clearly morally inadequate and lagging behind the realities they are designed to address."[95] If law sanctions collateral damage, is part of the problem with the law itself? If individuals are responsible for intentional killing, who is morally responsible for legal, unintended, yet foreseeable, killing? How should moral responsibility be assigned in these cases of unintentional harm?

Unintended yet foreseeable killing of civilians in war, killing that could often be prevented, is, I argue, a systemic problem because the causes of such killing generally lie in the military-political system—the organization of beliefs, including international law, resources, and procedures—that enable such a complex activity as war. I needed another term to describe the causal conditions and moral considerations that produced foreseen, but essentially legally forgiven killing of civilians that has occurred with some regularity and predictability in these wars. While to say that the law is inadequate is an important first step, it is not yet to answer the subsequent questions of moral responsibility.

The turn in philosophy and international law toward individual responsibility was itself a turn away from collective responsibility and specifically a response to the fear that collective responsibility necessarily leads to assigning blame to all the individuals in that collective. The Nuremburg Tribunal used the concept of conspiracy, but this tool has not been widely used out of the concern that it was incompatible with personal responsibility.[96] There are other tools in the law to deal with collective responsibility or corporate liability for outcomes that may not be specifically intended but may nevertheless be foreseen. They are theories of partnership, corporate liability, and enterprise participation.[97] While this is a reasonable concern,

---

[95] C. A. J. Coady, "Bombing and the Morality of War," in Yuki Tanaka and Marilyn B. Young, eds., *Bombing Civilians: A Twentieth Century History* (New York: The New Press, 2009), pp. 191–214, 192–193.

[96] Meloni, *Command Responsibility in International Law*, pp. 20–21.

[97] An example is *Prosecutor v. Dusko Tadic*. Tadic was found guilty for crimes committed in the Former Yugoslavia. When he appealed his sentence, the ICTY Tribunal reasoned, "Whoever contributes to the commission of crimes by the group of persons or some members of the group, in execution of a common criminal purpose, may be held to be criminally liable, subject to certain conditions, which are specified below.... [I]nternational criminal responsibility embraces actions perpetrated by a collectivity of persons in furtherance of a common criminal design. [One category of such behavior

collective blame and punishment are not the necessary outcome of assignments of collective moral responsibility. As Tracy Isaacs argues, "a collective can be responsible without all of its members being responsible."[98] Individuals certainly may have contributed to an outcome, but "where as a collective is responsible for a collective act, individual members are responsible for their contributions, and the degree of their responsibility will depend, in part, on the extent to which they share the collective's goals and act with a view to bringing those goals about."[99] It is, of course, still important to understand the role of the individual, but much of what is causally and morally important is situated at the organizational and political level. We need to understand how organizations create the possibilities and conditions for actions and outcomes that individuals could not, by themselves, intentionally or unintentionally, bring about.

Examining the role of military organizations in creating the context for individual acts also, conversely, illuminates the scope and limits of individual moral agency and moral responsibility in cases of deliberate killing, when soldiers "snap," and in situations of systemic collateral damage. We typically think of moral agency in individual terms— individuals have the capacity to deliberate and act. But, as I argue in my discussion of military organizations, complex collectives may also be (imperfect) moral agents to the extent that members of the organization share intentions, persist over time to enact their goals, have institutionalized decision-making procedures, the capacity to act, and the capacity to reflect on its goals, rules, knowledge, and behaviors. It is my argument that military organizations as imperfect moral agents can be both causally and morally responsible.

---

includes] cases involving a common design to pursue one course of conduct where one of the perpetrators commits an act which, while outside the common design, was nevertheless a natural and foreseeable consequence of the effecting of that common purpose. An example of this would be a common, shared intention on the part of a group to forcibly remove members of one ethnicity from their town, village or region (to effect "ethnic cleansing") with the consequence that, in the course of doing so, one or more of the victims is shot and killed. While murder may not have been explicitly acknowledged to be part of the common design, it was nevertheless foreseeable that the forcible removal of civilians at gunpoint might well result in the deaths of one or more of those civilians. Criminal responsibility may be imputed to all participants within the common enterprise where the risk of death occurring was both a predictable consequence of the execution of the common design and the accused was either reckless or indifferent to that risk. Another example is that of a common plan to forcibly evict civilians belonging to a particular ethnic group by burning their houses; if some of the participants in the plan, in carrying out this plan, kill civilians by setting their houses on fire, all the other participants in the plan are criminally responsible for the killing if these deaths were predictable." *Prosecutor v. Dusko Tadic (Appeal Judgment)*, IT-94-1-A, International Criminal Tribunal for the former Yugoslavia (ICTY), 15 July 1999, Paragraphs 190, 193, and 204. Available at: http://www.unhcr.org/refworld/docid/40277f504.html, accessed 5 January 2012, cited in Osiel, *Making Sense of Mass Atrocity*, p. 54.

[98] Tracy Isaacs, *Moral Responsibility in Collective Contexts* (New York: Oxford University Press, 2011), p. 61.

[99] Ibid., p. 62.

By focusing on both individual and systemic causes of killing (at the organizational and political level), I locate moral responsibility for those deaths not only with individual actors and commanders but also in the military organization, specific political institutions, and to some degree, in the US public. Indeed, every time the US military adjusts its rules of engagement to minimize harm to civilians, it acknowledges that such harm is not inevitable, and it is taking organizational responsibility for reducing the harm to noncombatants. As I show in chapters 2 and 6, the US military took increasing institutional moral responsibility and exercised moral agency at an institutional level. Indeed, at risk of adding even more vocabulary, I introduce the concepts of the institutionalization of moral agency and "cycles of moral agency" describing responsibility as a process. I argue that cycles of moral agency are observable in the institutionalization of the norms of noncombatant immunity and civilian protection by the US military.

Moral responsibility is thus a wider notion than strict legal culpability.[100] Although legal responsibility will be discussed, I am less concerned with finding culpability or punishing the "guilty" than with using the search for responsibility as a tool of moral analysis and the starting point for ways to reduce collateral damage. I use the term "responsibility" here in both its moral sense (where moral responsibility is the "blameworthiness and praiseworthiness of moral agents") and its causal sense.[101] Primary moral responsibility rests with those who are closest to the causal action—soldiers, commanders, and the military organization. When those with primary responsibility cannot or do not act as they should, those with secondary responsibility, the institutions, namely Congress and the Courts, charged with formal oversight of the executive branch, and the public, must act.[102]

---

[100] Indeed, when the ethical questions are clarified, the law may follow. Such is the case with other practices and institutions that were once legal and are now either illegal or viewed negatively such as slavery, forced labor, and environmental pollution. As Marion Smiley argues, "our moral judgments can themselves lead to structural changes in our community." Smiley, *Moral Responsibility and the Boundaries of Moral Community*, p. 27.

[101] Isaacs, *Moral Responsibility in Collective Contexts*, p. 15. Also see Smiley, *Moral Responsibility and the Boundaries of Community*.

[102] The scheme of primary and secondary responsibility is drawn from Robert E. Goodin, *Protecting the Vulnerable: A Reanalysis of Our Social Responsibilities* (Chicago: University of Chicago Press, 1985), pp. 151-152. Also see Paharia, Kassam, Green, and Bazerman, "Dirty Work, Clean Hands," p. 134, who distinguish between proximate or primary actors and those who are indirectly responsible.

2

How They Die

US Doctrine and Trends in Civilian Death

We are the only great power in really in the history of the world with the possible exception of Great Britain that actually puts its own troops in serious harm's way in order to defend and protect civilian lives this way. This is something that we should be bragging about and boasting about and take great pride in, the way we do war. That doesn't mean we should go too far and risk winning, because not winning looks even worse than killing civilians.

—Jonah Goldberg[1]

We had fights people were in and fragged homes inside of Fallujah and found females inside the homes....I mean throughout our time in five months in Al Qarma, I had Marines shoot children in cars and deal with the Marines individually one on one about it because they had a hard time dealing with that. The thing I would always ask them was, you know, they crossed the trigger line?...Did you use EOF [escalation of force procedures]. Good, and the deal with it was that child was still dead....Did you know the child was in the backseat? No, Sergeant Major. I hate to see but there it is. But I don't see that as your fault at the time. Because he is going to have to live with that for the rest of his life and it is a hard thing to do.

—Sergeant Major E. T. Sax[2]

On 28 November 2006, US soldiers found a roadside bomb in the Hamaniyah neighborhood of Ramadi, Iraq. US soldiers observed "two insurgents" moving away

---

[1] Jonah Goldberg, editor, *National Review Online*, interviewed on Fox News, "Panel on New Rules of Engagement for Marines in Afghanistan," 17 February 2010, http://www.foxnews.com/story/0,2933,586461,00.html.

[2] Sergeant Major E. T. Sax, US Marines, transcript of interview with military investigators. http://www.nytimes.com/interactive/2011/12/15/world/middleeast/haditha-selected-documents.html?ref=middleeast#document/p1/a41194.

from the bomb's trigger site where they "took up positions on the roof of a house and observed the coalition forces clearing the explosive device." Pentagon press reported the incident:

> As coalition forces cleared the bomb, the insurgents engaged the security element with small-arms fire. After establishing positive identification, coalition forces returned fire with small-arms and machine-gun fire. As the insurgents continued to engage the patrol, coalition forces returned fire with main-tank-gun rounds.
>
> Coalition forces conducted an extensive search of the house and found one boy and five girls, ages ranging from infant to teenaged, dead. One woman injured at the scene refused treatment. According to local residents, the house was a known insurgent safe house.[3]

No insurgents were found at the house afterwards: "Officials believe one of the insurgents was wounded and other insurgents came to remove him from the scene." A coalition spokesperson, Marine Lt. Col. Bryan Salas, said, "In a very tragic way, today reminds us that insurgents' actions throughout Iraq are felt by all. Efforts are under way to coordinate and offer available assistance to surviving family members."[4] The five dead girls ranged in age from 6 months to 10 years old. Clearly, US soldiers intended to kill the "insurgents" but did not intend to kill the children.[5] Yet, as I show below, likely about 22,000 civilians were killed by the United States and its allies in Afghanistan and Iraq from 2001 through late 2012. Adding the drone strike killing of civilians in Pakistan (400–2,300), and the killing of civilians by the Pakistani military in their counterinsurgency war, perhaps as many as 16,000 civilians have been killed in Pakistan as the United States has pursued a proxy and drone war strategy, avoiding a large commitment of US "boots on the ground" in Pakistan.[6] In addition, drone and other military strikes in Yemen have killed at least sixty to eighty-two civilians from 2002 through 2012. All told, the United States and its allies in Afghanistan, Pakistan, Iraq, and Yemen

---

[3] Armed Forces Press Service, "Coalition, Iraqi Forces Detain Terrorists; Iraqis Killed in IED Attack," *Armed Forces Information Service*, 29 November 2006, http://www.defense.gov/News/NewsArticle.aspx?ID=2247.

[4] Quoted in ibid.

[5] BBC, "Five Girls Killed in Iraqi Clash," *BBC News*, 28 November 2006, http://news.bbc.co.uk/2/hi/middle_east/6193620.stm.

[6] An arguable case could be made that civilian deaths in Pakistan caused by the Pakistani military should count as collateral damage in the US war in the AfPak conflict because of the formal and informal ties between the United States and Pakistan. Others would argue that the Pakistani military operates sufficiently independently of the United States in its war against militants and is pursuing other political-military objectives besides counterterrorism, and thus should not count. But, just as in Iraq and Afghanistan, national military forces are obviously moral agents and responsible for their own behavior.

may have killed 38,000 civilians in collateral damage from 2001 through 2012.[7] But as I discuss below, these numbers are very soft indeed. My estimate could be too high; it is more likely that it is too low. The key point to remember, and I underscore the argument several times lest it is lost in the details, is that no matter the actual incidence of collateral damage deaths and injuries, when the United States perceived the harm to civilians as posing a political-military problem, it attempted and succeeded in decreasing collateral damage deaths.

In the US wars in Afghanistan and Iraq that followed the 9/11 attack, American officials repeatedly asserted that they were making "every effort" to avoid civilian casualties. In October 2001, Pentagon spokesperson Victoria Clark said about the war in Afghanistan, "U.S. forces are intentionally striking only military and terrorist targets. We take great care in our targeting process to avoid civilian casualties."[8] Similarly, weeks before the March 2003 US invasion of Iraq, Rumsfeld said, "If force becomes necessary, it is clear that coalition forces would take great care to avoid civilian casualties."[9] When the United States invaded Iraq, President George W. Bush said, "I want Americans and all the world to know that coalition forces will make every effort to spare innocent civilians from harm."[10] President Obama repeated pledges of US effort to avoid harm to civilians. In a joint news conference in May 2009, with the presidents of Pakistan and Afghanistan, President Obama said that "the United States will work with our Afghan and international partners to make every effort to avoid civilian casualties as we help the Afghan government combat our common enemy."[11]

Donald Rumsfeld articulated a prevailing sense of inevitability about civilian casualties in war. "We know that victory will not come without a cost. War is ugly. It causes misery and suffering and death, and we see that every day. And brave people give their lives for this cause, and, needless to say, innocent bystanders can be

---

[7] Numbers can convey the scale of death, but of course the trouble with an enumeration, and with round numbers, is that even as I try to highlight the harm, those killed are rendered even more anonymous and essentially disappear. Similarly, the wounded are often undercounted or disappear from accounts of wars. Until the recording of the death and injury in war becomes more precise, I can do little better however.

[8] Quoted in U.S. Department of State, "Fact Sheet: US Military Efforts to Avoid Civilian Casualties," 25 October 2001.

[9] Rumsfeld, quoted in Kathleen T. Rhem, "U.S. Military Works to Avoid Civilian Deaths, Collateral Damage," 5 March 2003, American Forces Press Service, U.S. Department of Defense, http://www.defense.gov/news/newsarticle.aspx?id=29337.

[10] George W. Bush, "Bush Declares War," 19 March 2003, CNN, http://articles.cnn.com/2003-03-19/us/sprj.irq.int.bush.transcript_1_coalition-forces-equipment-in-civilian-areas-iraqi-troops-and-equipment?_s=PM:US.

[11] "Remarks by the President after the Trilateral Meeting with President Karzai of Afghanistan and President Zardari of Pakistan," 6 May 2011. http://www.whitehouse.gov/video/The-Presidents-Trilateral-Meeting-with-Karzai-and-Afghanistans-Presidents#transcript.

caught in crossfire." Rumsfeld also suggested that there were fewer civilian casualties caused by the United States than had been reported. "Every time General Myers and I stand before you at this podium, we're asked to respond to Taliban accusations about civilian casualties, much of it unsubstantiated propaganda." He continued, "On the other hand, there are instances where in fact there are unintended effects of this conflict, and ordnance ends up where it should not. And we all know that, and that's true of every conflict."[12] Thus, the harm to civilians was at first minimized by the administration under the argument that it was doing all it could to prevent such harm and that in any case, the enemy exaggerated the harm, and it was their fault in the first place that the United States was at war. For example, JCS Chairman General Myers said, "Though we are concerned about any number of unintended civilian casualties, to be honest, the one number that stands foremost in my mind, is the over 5,000 men, women and children that were killed on 11 September, intentionally killed by the terrorists."[13] Rumsfeld, as was his habit, was more blunt.

> So let there be no doubt; responsibility for every single casualty in this war, be they innocent Afghans or innocent Americans, rests at the feet of Taliban and al Qaeda. Their leaderships are the ones that are hiding in mosques and using Afghan civilians as human shields by placing their armor and artillery in close proximity to civilians, schools, hospitals, and the like. When the Taliban issue accusations of civilian casualties, they indict themselves.[14]

But, over the course of these wars, civilian casualties caused by the United States and its allies in the war zones of Afghanistan and Iraq became increasingly visible amid assurances that the harm was occasional and inevitable. By my conservative estimate, about 22,000 US- and allied-caused "collateral damage" deaths of all types—genuine accident, systemic, and proportionality/double effect killing— occurred from late 2001 to through 2012 in the war zones of Afghanistan and Iraq, and more in Pakistan and Yemen. An understanding of how those deaths occurred, and the overall patterns of their occurrence, is important for assessing whether they were foreseeable and for locating moral responsibility for the harm. The number seriously injured by the United States and its allies is likely also in the tens of thousands, although the data on injuries is imprecise.

---

[12] Donald H. Rumsfeld, "U.S. Secretary of Defense Donald H. Rumsfeld, DoD News Briefing—Secretary Rumsfeld and Gen. Myers," 29 October 2001. http://www.defense.gov/transcripts/transcript.aspx?transcriptid=2226.

[13] General Myers, DoD News Briefing—Secretary Rumsfeld and Gen. Myers, 25 October, 2001, http://www.defense.gov/transcripts/transcript.aspx?transcriptid=2183.

[14] Donald H. Rumsfeld, Remarks at Stakeout Outside ABC TV Studio, 28 October 2001, http://www.defense.gov/transcripts/transcript.aspx?transcriptid=2225.

Accountability for killing begins, often, with an accounting in the form of an enumeration, a narration, and an explanation. I review the change in the US understanding of the problem of civilian casualties and describe collateral damage in the war zones, focusing on direct deaths and injuries due to violence. I am primarily concerned here with combat-related collateral damage caused by US forces and their allies and how the United States has responded to that harm. The United States gradually developed a new understanding of the problem posed by "collateral damage" and, at least in Afghanistan and Iraq, I found that efforts to reduce civilian killing had measurable effects. Specifically, administration officials moved from saying the United States was making "every effort" to avoid inevitable civilian casualties, to acknowledging that there were many civilian casualties due to the military operations of US and allied forces, and that it was urgent—a strategic necessity—to prevent them. The Chairman of the Joint Chiefs of Staff Admiral Mike Mullen was blunt in a visit to Afghanistan in March 2010: "We just can't win if we keep killing the locals."[15] As Admiral Mullen's statement illustrates, US military and civilian leaders began to see "collateral damage" as a strategic problem during the wars in Afghanistan and Iraq, and this gradually led to operational changes at the organizational level. When the US military made efforts to minimize civilian killing, the incidence of collateral damage sometimes declined. However, US casualties sometimes increased when the emphasis was placed on civilian protection. The question is, of course, whether this risk transfer is inevitable or can be minimized in some way.

While there has been a great deal of attention to US-caused collateral damage in Afghanistan and Iraq, comparatively little attention has focused on civilian casualties caused by US military strikes in Pakistan and Yemen. While the United States has struggled to get the military and police in Afghanistan to take on more of the fighting against militants and remove US boots-on-the-ground, the United States has largely by-passed a boots-on-the-ground phase in Pakistan by using drones and relying on Pakistani military and paramilitary forces.

When discussing the US drone attacks, Pakistan's President Asif Ali Zardari is reported to have told CIA Director, Mike Hayden, in November 2009, "Kill the seniors. Collateral damage worries you Americans. It does not worry me."[16] But, the US drone strikes in Pakistan eventually began to pose a political problem for the United States because of the growing perception, at least in Pakistan, that there were significant numbers of civilians injured or killed by the strikes. The question of risk transfer between US soldiers and civilians has not been directly on table in either Pakistan or Yemen. Rather, the use of remotely piloted drones for strikes in Yemen and Pakistan has kept

---

[15] Mullen, quoted in Jim Garamone, "Chairman Emphasized Eliminating Civilian Casualties," American Forces Press Service, U.S. Department of Defense, 31 March 2010, http://www.defense. gov/news/newsarticle.aspx?id=58547. A study ordered by Mullen, Sarah Sewall, and Larry Lewis, "Reducing and Mitigating Civilian Casualties: Afghanistan and Beyond: Joint Civilian Casualty Final Report," 31 August 2010.

[16] Bob Woodward, *Obama's Wars* (New York: Simon and Schuster, 2010), p. 26.

US soldiers out of direct action in those war zones (although a small number of US soldiers have been killed in Pakistan). Drones are considered an ideal weapon because they can ostensibly be targeted on insurgents, keep civilian risk low, without increasing immediate risk to US forces. The main question is how many civilians have been harmed by US drone strikes in Pakistan and Yemen.[17] In the case of Yemen, in particular, the numbers of civilians killed and injured are comparatively low at the time of this writing. But also at this time, it is clear that the US Central Intelligence Agency would like to invest more in the drone technology it uses to conduct strikes in Yemen and potentially elsewhere in the Middle East and North Africa.[18] The questions raised here are not likely to go away.

In addition, the case of Pakistan raises the problem of escalation and the US responsibility for the behavior of the Pakistani military. I show below that while the Pakistani military has fought militants in the Northwest region of Pakistan for its own reasons, they have also fought militants on behalf of the United States, and with US equipment, training, advisors, and funding. A probably large, but essentially unknown, number of civilians have been killed, wounded, and displaced because of the fighting.

I also discuss the indirect death and harm in war—those who suffer because war has destroyed the material infrastructure that makes it possible for them to have access to food, safe drinking water, and medical care. Indirect harm also results from displacement, or the inability to find work in a society disrupted by war. Such indirect harm is often a significant long-term effect of war on civilians—indirect deaths usually outnumber the deaths due to violence in war and may occur years after the fighting ends. It is arguable that those civilians who are indirectly harmed are indirect collateral damage. I mention indirect deaths and other adverse health effects of war, such as increased malnutrition and disease, because they are certainly important to everyone in the war zone and the US military has begun to acknowledge the importance of indirect harm. For example, the Army's 2012 *Civilian Casualty Mitigation* manual mentions indirect effects of warfare as a concern. "Civilians are vulnerable to the direct effects of combat as well as the indirect effects of having their lifestyles, livelihoods, and infrastructure disrupted."[19] As I discuss below, however, it is not easy to attribute the direct causes of indirect harm.

---

[17] The risk of conventional military attacks on insurgents in Pakistan and Yemen is borne, respectively, by the Pakistani and Yemeni military and police. Another question, unanswered here, is whether the risk to Pakistani soldiers increases as the United States engages in drone strikes.

[18] Greg Millar, "CIA Seeks to Expand Drone Fleet, Officials Say," *Washington Post*, 19 October 2012, http://www.washingtonpost.com/world/national-security/cia-seeks-to-expand-drone-fleet-of ficials-say/2012/10/18/01149a8c-1949-11e2-bd10-5ff056538b7c_story.html?hpid=z1.

[19] Department of the Army, *Civilian Casualty Mitigation*, Army Tactics, Techniques and Procedures, No. 3-37.11 (Washington, DC: Department of the Army, 18 July 2012), p. 1-5.

Civilians and US War Fighting in the Post 9/11 Wars

It is common to talk about the "norms" of American warfare, "how we fight," or the "way we *do* war."[20] The American way of war is to try to win and so, unsurprisingly, the normative belief that long dominated US war making was that military necessity, defined expansively as shown in the next chapter, should determine operational decisions. Moreover, good intentions were often understood to be sufficient—if the US military was not deliberately killing civilians, inadvertent harm was not blameworthy. At least at the beginning of these wars, Sahr Conway-Lanz's observation about the US attitude toward collateral damage in previous wars was apt.

> The centrality of intentions has contributed to a complacent stance toward the problem of collateral damage. Intent is simply a state of mind. The intention not to harm noncombatants has no direct connection to actually keeping them from harm. An interpretation of noncombatant immunity that weighs intentions so heavily imposes only the requirement of right thinking and some evidence of that right thinking such as warnings or relief aid for civilians. It does not necessarily prevent the killing of civilians by American weapons. As a consequence, Americans have spent more time thinking about their good intentions than about how they could prevent more civilian deaths from their wars.[21]

Further, the US military has, for most of its history, subscribed to the view that killing and otherwise hurting noncombatants potentially served military necessity. As General William T. Sherman believed, if the enemy, in this case Southerners, "could not be made to love us," they should be "made to fear us and dread the passage of troops through their country." Sherman, and many generals before and after him, believed that "Fear is the beginning of wisdom."[22] Thus, in the United States' various counterinsurgency wars from the Civil War through Vietnam, and in its conventional conflicts through Korea, the policy was to make civilians feel what Sherman called the "hard hand of war."

[20] For example, see Colin H. Kahl, "How We Fight," *Foreign Affairs*, vol. 85, no. 6 (November/December 2006): 83–101; Dominic Tierney, *How We Fight: Crusades Quagmires and the American Way of War* (New York: Little Brown, 2010).

[21] Sahr Conway-Lanz, *Collateral Damage: Americans, Noncombatant Immunity, and Atrocity after World War II* (New York: Routledge, 2006), p. 230.

[22] Sherman, quoted in Andrew J. Birtle, *U.S. Army Counterinsurgency Operations Doctrine, 1860-1941* (Washington, DC: U.S. Army Center of Military History, 1998), pp. 36–37. The northern strategy was more subtle than these quotes suggest; Lincoln and others believed that they must not alienate potential supporters in the South and hence treated different groups of Southerners differently, when it was possible to tell who would be a future ally.

But US policy changed gradually in the late twentieth century, during and after the Vietnam War. American military strategists began to believe they could make the enemy "love us" through strategies variously termed "hearts and minds" or "population-centric" counterinsurgency. When the US military came to believe that protecting civilians served military necessity, it stopped deliberately targeting noncombatants for coercive pain and made an effort (for example, institutionalized in rules of engagement) to minimize "collateral damage" or "incidental killing." When the US military, again after Vietnam, came to understand that large numbers of US soldiers coming home dead, maimed, or traumatized, was unacceptable to the US public, and harmed morale within the armed forces, it prioritized "force protection."

Thus, as I discuss in the next chapter, three normative beliefs characterize the American military's understanding of what is good and right to do in war—a belief that noncombatant immunity is an important value; the belief in doing what it takes to win; and the belief that soldier's lives should not be wasted. Though military necessity is generally dominant, the beliefs in civilian protection and force protection have increasingly affected operations, and gradually been defined as an element of military necessity.

In broad outline, there was never a cavalier attitude toward civilian harm, early in both the wars in Afghanistan and Iraq, yet the US military and political leadership seemed to tolerate greater collateral damage when military necessity was believed to demand it. At the same time incidents or claims of civilian casualties caused by the United States were often dismissed as "exaggerated" or "propaganda." The US emphasis in the early phases of each war was military victory through the annihilation of their military adversaries. In that phase, there was a conscious effort to minimize collateral damage and to protect US forces, by, for example, having the Northern Alliance take on the brunt of the fighting against the Taliban in Afghanistan. After the main military forces of their adversaries were defeated, in both cases relatively quickly, the United States turned toward consolidating regime change and promoting elections. When the United States and its allies faced a growing counterinsurgency, it responded with military force. The trouble, in both cases, was that US operations caused numerous civilian casualty incidents. While civilian casualties were to be avoided, however, they were not a major concern.

Because the military resistance to outside occupation was growing in Afghanistan, and even more dramatically in Iraq, the US Army and Marines became extremely focused on how to win defeat insurgency. Articles in US military journals, such as *Parameters* and *Military Review*, and books, such as John Nagl's, *Learning to Eat Soup with a Knife: Counterinsurgency Lessons From Malaya and Vietnam* discussed lessons learned from previous counterinsurgency wars, including Vietnam and the Philippines.[23] There was a growing consensus that victory in a counterinsurgency

---

[23] See, for example, Wad Markel, "Draining the Swamp: The British Strategy of Population Control," *Parameters*, vol. 36 (Spring 2006): 35–48. John A. Nagl, *Learning to Eat Soup with a Knife: Counterinsurgency Lessons from Malaya and Vietnam* (Chicago: University of Chicago, 2005).

war depends precisely on not killing civilians. The US military repeatedly noted that the reason for minimizing civilian death in Iraq and Afghanistan was that the political and military consequence of killing civilians made the US effort more difficult. And as the US military gradually came to believe that killing civilians harmed the counterinsurgency effort in Iraq and Afghanistan—and also hurt support for the war at home—it increased its effort to reduce the harm to civilians and moved toward a doctrine of civilian protection as part of a larger shift in the mid-2000s toward counterinsurgency.

The US military was recalling lessons it had learned in previous conflicts. The US leadership learned—not for the first time—that the strongly negative moral and political reaction to civilian killing can prolong wars. Of course, this was an old insight: as Immanuel Kant argued in *Perpetual Peace* more than two hundred years ago, "No nation at war with another shall permit such acts as shall make mutual trust impossible during such future time of peace.... Some level of trust in the enemy's way of thinking must be preserved even in the midst of war, for otherwise no peace can ever be concluded."[24] Political and military leaders have long recognized that in war, perceived justice and cost are linked. If a war is perceived as undertaken for bad reasons, it will be difficult to sustain domestic political support. Further, even if the cause is perceived as just, mobilization may be unsustainable when the domestic population that must serve in the military, or pay taxes to fund the war, balk at military actions that cost too much in blood and treasure. And it is increasingly the case that killing civilians on the other side can diminish support both at home and abroad.

In Afghanistan, where the first few months of the US uses of force were dominated by the use of air power, concerns about killing civilians held at the top levels of the Bush administration rippled through all levels of the air combat operations. As Benjamin Lambeth argues, US leaders were aware of the potential political impact of too many civilian deaths. "To cite but one case in point, significant attacks against Afghan infrastructure and a high incidence of civilian fatalities could easily have caused Pakistan to withdraw its support for the war, thus denying the United States the use of Pakistani air space and possibly sparking a popular anti-American uprising."[25] Some within and outside the administration complained, however, that the concern to minimize collateral damage hindered the air campaign—slowing targeting or even causing the United States to abort strikes it could have made.[26] As the fighting in Afghanistan continued, it became clear that collateral damage was

[24] Immanuel Kant, *Perpetual Peace: A Philosophical Sketch* (1795), in Immanuel Kant, *Perpetual Peace and Other Essays*, translated by Ted Humphrey (Indianapolis: Hackett, 1983), pp.107–143, 109–110.

[25] Benjamin S. Lambeth, *Air Power against Terror: America's Conduct of Operation Enduring Freedom* (Santa Monica, CA: RAND Corporation, 2010), pp. 321–322.

[26] See William M. Arkin, "Fear of Civilian Deaths May have Undermined Effort," *Los Angeles Times*, 16 January 2002. Also see Lambeth, *Air Power against Terror*, pp. 320–324.

hurting more than relations with allies, it harmed the war and political effort in Afghanistan itself.

In Iraq, it also became clear that civilian casualties were counterproductive to the goals of US fighting. The goal was "liberation." As President Bush argued, "a liberated Iraq can show the power of freedom to transform that vital region, by bringing hope and progress into the lives of millions."[27] While there were news reports of collateral damage incidents that reached the American public, there was also a steady stream of information about civilian killing—both massacres and collateral damage killing— making its way to the top commanders. For example, in 2005 US Lieutenant General Peter Chiarelli identified the large number of civilian deaths at US checkpoints as a military problem because it created resentment and hatred that fueled the insurgency in Iraq. "We have people who were on the fence or supported us who in the last two years or three years have in fact decided to strike out against us. And you have to ask: Why is that? And I would argue in many instances we are our own worst enemy."[28] Chiarelli argued that if fewer civilians were killed in escalation of force incidents at checkpoints, "I think that will make our soldiers safer."[29]

Some years later, the same reasoning was articulated in Afghanistan by the US military. In March 2010 Admiral Mullen told reporters in Kabul that General McChrystal had shared the results of a study on civilian casualties with him during his visit there: "When we cause them, they generate a serious uptick in violence for up to five months. When the Taliban cause them, they generate an uptick in violence for about three months."[30] A working paper released in July 2010 by the National Bureau of Economic Research and funded in part by the US Air Force found that killing civilians by ISAF forces did increase insurgent recruiting and the intensity of violence in Afghanistan.[31]

The December 2006 *US Army/Marine Corps Counterinsurgency Field Manual* was the codification of a new consensus: "An operation that kills insurgents is counterproductive if collateral damage leads to the recruitment of fifty more insurgents."[32] The *Counterinsurgency Field Manual* thus stressed calibrating the use of force so as not to unleash a backlash. "Any use offeree produces many effects,

[27] President Discusses the Future of Iraq, 26 February 2003, http://georgewbush-whitehouse. archives.gov/news/releases/2003/02/20030226-11.html.

[28] Nancy Youssef, "Commander: Fewer Civilians Dying," *Philadelphia Inquirer*, 22 June 2006, http:// articles.philly.com/2006-06-22/news/25403128_1_iraqiciviliansciviliancasualties-roadsidebombing.

[29] Ibid.

[30] Mullen, quoted in Garamone, "Chairman Emphasizes Eliminating Civilian Casualties."

[31] Luke N. Condra, Joseph H. Felter, Radha K. Iyengar, and Jacob N. Shapiro, "The Effect of Civilian Casualties in Afghanistan and Iraq," NBER Working Paper Number 16152, National Bureau of Economic Research, Cambridge, MA, July 2010, http://www.nber.org/papers/w16152.

[32] United States Army and Marine Corp, *U.S. Army/Marine Corps Counterinsurgency Field Manuel*, Field Manual No. 3-24: Marine Corp Warfighting Publication No. 3-33.5 (Chicago: University of Chicago, 2007), I-141, p. 45.

not all of which can be foreseen. The more force applied, the greater the chance of collateral damage and mistakes. Using substantial force also increases the opportunity for insurgent propaganda to portray lethal military activities as brutal."[33] The concern here is pragmatic—military necessity dictates restraint. As Sarah Sewall observes in her introduction to the *Counterinsurgency Field Manual*, "The field manual directs U.S. forces to make securing the civilian, rather than destroying the enemy, their top priority." She argues that "the real battle is for civilian support for, or acquiescence to, the counterinsurgents and host nation government." Sewall warns that "killing the civilian is no longer just collateral damage. The harm cannot be easily dismissed as unintended. Civilian casualties undermine the counterinsurgents goals.... Civilian deaths create an extended family of enemies—new insurgent recruits or informants—and erode support for the host nation."[34]

The shift in perspective, from understanding collateral damage as simply an inevitable aspect of fighting to the view that minimizing civilian harm and providing protection for civilians was an urgent military necessity, was gradually internalized and institutionalized. Good intentions were no longer seen as good enough; protection of civilians had to be institutionalized for pragmatic reasons and yield results in the form of both the perception that the United States cared about civilians and the reality of a reduction in harm to civilians.

More than that, for some involved in the wars, American identity came to include preventing civilian casualties. US Colonel John Nicholson's statement in 2007 about civilian casualties in Afghanistan illustrates the linkage between a sense of American honor and pragmatism about the effects of killing noncombatants. Nicholson said, "And if they [civilian casualties] do occur, we go to great lengths to try and make it right with the people who've suffered because that is not what America stands for. They know that. They hold us to a higher standard, and they should hold us to a higher standard. And we should hold ourselves to a higher standard because we are professionals, and we can be better than that." But even Nicholson did not stray far from a pragmatic motivation for civilian protection when he said, in the next sentence, "So we work very hard to do no harm to the Afghan people and to deliver those effects that we know will achieve the buy-in by the Afghans of their own government and will help us to win this war on terror."[35] Preventing civilian casualties was linked to legitimacy and legitimacy was understood to be the key to success in counterinsurgency. Or, as the Department of Defense Report on Afghanistan

---

[33] Ibid., I-150, p. 48.

[34] Sarah Sewall, "Introduction to the University of Chicago Press Edition: A Radical Field Manual," in United States Army and Marine Corp, *U.S. Army/Marine Corps Counterinsurgency Field Manual*, pp. xxi–xlii, xxii.

[35] DoD News Briefing with Col. Nicholson from Afghanistan, 8 May 2007, http://www.defense.gov/transcripts/transcript.aspx?transcriptid=3959.

explained in January 2009, "Kinetic operations have to be carefully executed to avoid civilian casualties and collateral damage that weaken popular support for International forces" and the Afghan government.[36]

The new mantra included the terms legitimacy, trust, and security and civilian casualties were seen to undermine all that.[37] The Chairman of the United States Joint Chiefs of Staff, Mike Mullen wrote about the importance of this trust at the start of the Obama administration's shift in strategy in Afghanistan in early 2009.

> We in the U.S. military are…held to a high standard. Like the early Romans, we are expected to do the right thing, and when we don't, to make it right again.
>
> We have learned, after seven years of war, that trust is the coin of the realm—that building it takes time, losing it takes mere seconds, and maintaining it may be our most important and most difficult objective.
>
> That's why images of prisoner maltreatment at Abu Ghraib still serve as recruiting tools for al-Qaeda. And it's why each civilian casualty for which we are even remotely responsible sets back our efforts to gain the confidence of the Afghan people months, if not years.
>
> It doesn't matter how hard we try to avoid hurting the innocent, and we do try very hard. It doesn't matter how proportional the force we deploy, how precisely we strike. It doesn't even matter if the enemy hides behind civilians. What matters are the death and destruction that result and the expectation that we could have avoided it. In the end, all that matters is that, despite our best efforts, sometimes we take the very lives we are trying to protect.
>
> You cannot defeat an insurgency this way.
>
> We can send more troops. We can kill or capture all the Taliban and al-Qaeda leaders we can find—and we should. We can clear out havens and shut down the narcotics trade. But until we prove capable, with the help of our allies and Afghan partners, of safeguarding the population, we will never know a peaceful, prosperous Afghanistan.
>
> Lose the people's trust, and we lose the war.[38]

Legitimacy was the subtext of General McChrystal's confirmation hearings to become US Commander in Afghanistan in June 2009. He said that it had become

---

[36] Department of Defense, "Report on Progress Toward Security and Stability in Afghanistan," January 2009, p. 18.

[37] In this sense, US tactical changes mirror larger normative changes. See Alex J. Bellamy, *Massacres and Morality: Mass Atrocities in an Age of Civilian Immunity* (Oxford: Oxford University Press, 2012).

[38] Mike Mullen, "Building Our Best Weapon," *Washington Post*, 15 February 2009, p. B7.

essential for the United States to reduce civilian casualties in Afghanistan: "If defeating an insurgent formation produces popular resentment, the victory is hollow and unsustainable." He argued: "This is a critical point. It may be the critical point. This is a struggle for the support of the Afghan people. Our willingness to operate in ways that minimize casualties or damage—even when doing so makes our task more difficult—is essential to our credibility."[39] Thus, intentions matter in a moral sense if not a practical sense to Afghans, Iraqis, and Pakistanis. The new jargon in Afghanistan, popularized by General Stanley McChrystal in 2009 was "population centric" warfare: protect civilians and win the war.

In June 2009, outside observers, some of whom were on occasion advising the US military, also argued that protecting civilians was the key to US success in Afghanistan. "The central goal of counterinsurgency is to make the population feel secure enough to engage in peaceful politics and to marginalize insurgents and other illegal armed groups. Since killing non-combatant civilians fundamentally undermines this goal, violence against civilians—whether committed deliberately by the Taliban or carelessly by the coalition—will be the key metric."[40] The language inside was nearly identical. The April 2010 Department of Defense "Report on Progress Toward Security and Stability in Afghanistan" emphasized that "minimizing the number and magnitude of CIVCAS incidents is critically important, as is the need to effectively manage the consequence of such incidents when they do occur."[41] In his June 2010 Senate confirmation hearings to replace Stanley McChrystal as Commander in Afghanistan, General Petraeus reiterated the purpose of the American focus on protecting civilians:

> Our efforts in Afghanistan have appropriately focused on protecting the population. This is, needless to say, of considerable importance, for in counterinsurgency operations, the human terrain is the decisive terrain. The results in recent months have been notable. Indeed, over the last 12 weeks, the number of innocent civilians killed in the course of military operations has been substantially lower than it was during the same period last year. And I will continue the emphasis on reducing the loss of innocent civilian life to an absolute minimum in the course of military operations.[42]

[39] McChrystal, quoted in BBC News, "US 'Admits Afghan Raid Mistakes,'" 3 June 2009, http://news.bbc.co.uk/2/hi/south_asia/8080440.stm.

[40] Andrew Exum, Nathaniel C. Fick, Ahmed A. Humayun, and David J. Kilcullen, "Triage: The Next Twelve Months in Afghanistan and Pakistan," *Center for a New American Security*, June 2009, p. 24.

[41] Department of Defense, "Report on Progress Toward Security and Stability in Afghanistan," April 2010, p. 43.

[42] David Petraeus, "Opening Statement," Confirmation Hearing, Commander, ISAF/US Forces, Afghanistan, 29 June 2010.

Petraeus also made the same argument during the hearing using more concrete language:

> You're being engaged from a house. Let's say it may not be completely effective fire. You can break contact. You know, our predisposition is to close with and destroy the enemy. That's the motto of the infantry, to press the fight, to take the fight to the enemy. But there are cases in which you have to balance that with the recognition that if you don't know who's in that house, then taking the fight to the enemy ultimately means blowing up the house, which is sometimes what has to result.
>
> If you're going to take out those bad guys that are shooting at you, but in the course of doing that you kill a substantial number of civilians, that, quote, 'tactical success' then becomes a strategic setback of considerable proportions.[43]

In sum, the importance of preventing civilian casualties and protecting civilians became the Pentagon's new common sense. Already part of the mix, the need to reduce civilian casualties was translated (as I describe in much greater detail in the chapter on organizational responsibility) with greater urgency, into the institutionalization of collateral damage estimation and mitigation practices within the US military. The 2006 *Counterinsurgency Field Manual* underscored the importance of civilian protection, but training had already begun to emphasize civilian protection. By the time the US Army manual *Civilian Casualty Mitigation* was released in July 2012, the reasons for protecting civilians could be articulated much more succinctly than in the past. The importance of civilian protection in international law was illustrated by the inclusion of a full-page table summarizing the treaty and customary law that related to protecting civilians, and civilian protection was linked to the American soldier's identity: "Protection of civilians is at the heart of the profession of arms."[44] Civilian protection had become taken for granted. The reasoning was also bluntly pragmatic: "Focused attention on CIVCAS mitigation is an important investment to maintain legitimacy and ensure eventual success."[45] And by 2012, the urgent necessity to protect civilians had been generalized beyond counterinsurgency war: the procedures for civilian casualty mitigation were to be applied to all kinds of military operations, from major war to limited contingency operations.

---

[43] Petraeus, quoted in Rowan Scarborough, "Afghan Rules Need Changes," *Human Events*, 30 June 2010, http://www.humanevents.com/article.php?id=37774.

[44] Army, *Civilian Casualty Mitigation*, p. 1-1. On the origins of the document, see Spencer Ackerman, "Army Writes New Manual on Preventing Civilian Deaths," *Wired*, 14 June 2011, http://www.wired.com/dangerroom/2011/06/army-writes-a-new-manual-on-preventing-civilian-deaths/.

[45] Army, *Civilian Casualty Mitigation*, p. 1-5.

In their efforts to defeat enemies, Army units and their partners must ensure that they are not creating even more adversaries in the process. CIVCASs, whether caused by lethal action such as direct and indirect fires or aggressive security measures, can generate resentment and undermine popular support....

Army leaders at all levels should be aware that CIVCASs can jeopardize the strategic goals prompting such interventions.[46]

When ISAF held a conference in Kabul, Afghanistan, in January 2012, participants' statements illustrated the important shift in attitude. Air Force Colonel Clay Hall said, "Regarding precise execution, we strive for and expect perfection." Air Force Major General Tod Wolters said, "We are now at seven events. We need to go from seven to three events. Next, we'll need to go from three to one and finally, we need to go from one to zero."[47] The goal of going to "zero" civilian casualties in Afghanistan was reiterated ISAF commanders at ISAF's third conference on civilian casualties in March 2012.[48]

Estimating Civilian Death

I have emphasized the pragmatic reasons the United States moved toward increasing its emphasis on preventing civilian casualties: the perception of growing and perhaps preventable harm to civilians was seen to undermine US legitimacy and was linked to growing counterinsurgent activity. Any analysis of collateral damage begins with these questions: How often does unintended civilian killing occur? What set of circumstances leads to these deaths? What deaths count as "collateral damage?" By my conservative estimate, about 22,000 noncombatants were killed in Afghanistan, Iraq, and Pakistan from 2001 through 2012 in incidents that are described by the United States and its allies as "collateral damage."

Why is it necessary to make an estimate, much less a conservative one? Unlike the numbers for killed and wounded US forces, there is uncertainty and disagreement about how many civilians were killed and wounded by the United States and its allies. Because the data is too imprecise to give precise numbers of civilian casualties, I must necessarily examine "broad trends."[49] The number of direct civilian collateral damage

---

[46] Ibid., p. 1-6.

[47] Quoted in David Olson, "ISAF Conducts Aviation Civilian Casualty Conference," ISAF News, 19 January 2012, http://www.isaf.nato.int/article/news/isaf-conducts-aviation-civilian-casualty-conference.html.

[48] Kristopher Levasseur, "ISAF holds Third Civilian Casualty Conference," ISAF News, 4 March 2012, http://www.isaf.nato.int/article/news/isaf-holds-third-civilian-casualty-conference.html.

[49] In the interest of space, I have abbreviated what could be a much longer dissection of the sources and methods for counting and ascribing the parties responsible for civilian death. Another book could more fully explore the data and the causes for disputes between different counts and estimates.

victims is certainly higher—and may be much higher than reported or estimated. Part of the trouble, discussed more fully below, is not simply saying how many were killed, but attributing the status—whether combatant or noncombatant—of those injured or killed. While it is obvious in some cases that a person was not a combatant, the kind of data necessary to say whether the attribution of civilian versus soldier is correct is not publicly available or may not exist. Because we do not yet know the total number of civilians killed in these wars, my estimates are admittedly crude. But perhaps 5 to 15 percent of those civilians killed by violent means in the war zones of Afghanistan, Iraq, and Pakistan are collateral damage deaths attributable to the United States and its coalition partners. I also describe how the deaths occurred in these wars to illustrate the difference between the types of collateral damage—accident, systemic, or double effect—experienced in these war zones.

There are three reasons for the uncertainty and contentiousness surrounding some estimates and counts of collateral damage. The first is politics, specifically, the belief among some US policymakers, mentioned earlier, that the ultimate moral responsibility for civilian casualties lay with those who started the war or continued to resist the United States. Further, there was the concern that the numbers, especially if they were exaggerated for propaganda purposes, are too politically explosive and would potentially undermine support at home or inflame resistance abroad.

Official US reports of civilian casualties were infrequent and often incomplete during the early years of the US wars in Afghanistan and Iraq. Despite its obligations as an occupying power, it was US policy early in these wars to not make estimates or counts of civilian or enemy casualties. "You know we don't do body counts," US General Tommy Franks said early in the Afghanistan war.[50] Or, more precisely, as Donald Rumsfeld said in November 2003, "We don't do body counts on other people."[51] As Brigadier General Vincent Brooks said in April 2003 when discussing both coalition and Iraqi casualties, "It's very one-sided. In some cases we take a few wounded. In some cases we have one or two killed. But in all cases we inflict a considerable amount of destruction on whatever force that comes into contact with us. It just is not worth trying to characterize by numbers. And, frankly, if we are going to be honorable about our warfare, we are not out there trying to count up bodies. This is not the appropriate way for us to go."[52]

Some years into the Iraq war, the US Department of Defense commissioned the RAND Corporation to assess the questions and controversies related to counting casualties and Rand produced the report in 2008, *An Argument for Documenting*

[50] US General Tommy Franks, quoted in "Success in Afghan War Hard to Gage," *San Francisco Chronicle*, 23 March 2002.

[51] "Transcript: Donald Rumsfeld on 'Fox News Sunday,'" Fox News Sunday, 2 November 2003, http://www.foxnews.com/story/0,2933,101956,00.html.

[52] Central Command Briefing Transcript, 6 April 2003. http://www.iwar.org.uk/news-archive/2003/04-06.htm. The United States later began to use body counts of Iraqi insurgents as a measure of efficacy. See Bradley Graham, "Enemy Body Counts Revived: U.S. is Citing Tolls to Show Success in Iraq," *Washington Post*, 24 October 2005, p. A1.

Casualties.[53] The authors, Katherine Hall and Dale Stahl, note that it was not clear that "anyone in the U.S. military or Coalition is systematically collecting and analyzing" data on Iraqi civilian fatalities.[54] Hall and Stahl observed that "had there been a more robust effort to collect accurate information on Iraqi civilians, military strategists and political leaders might have acted more determinedly to secure the civilian population prior to the carnage of 2006."[55]

The politically sensitive issue was not simply civilian deaths, but a concern with counting any dead. As implied in the use of the phrase "body counts," the reasoning at work in the desire not to aggregate the incidents or make the count of those killed public was a reference to the Vietnam War. There was a concern that because counts of the enemy dead had been exaggerated in Vietnam by US officials, and the exaggeration—coupled with a lack of "progress" in the war—had gradually undermined US credibility. Further, there may have been the fear that making numbers of enemy killed known could be counterproductive. Specifically, US commanders were well aware that body counts had been used as a proxy measure for progress in the Vietnam War. Andrew Krepinevich argues that attention to body counts in Vietnam led to a perverse incentive to be more aggressive, ultimately undermining the goal of winning hearts and minds.

> By giving top priority to the body count, the Army gave its officers the incentive to bend the ROE [rules of engagement] in favor of killing "potential" insurgents, although in many instances they might have been innocent civilians. The availability of firepower and technology...made it easier to "send a bullet" instead of a soldier, who could have made the distinction between friend and foe.[56]

Counting enemy dead would require making a distinction between noncombatant civilians and combatants. Despite the fact that the US military increasingly grew to believe that protecting civilians was essential, the military put few resources into evaluating whether their efforts to do so were successful. Investigations of these civilian casualty incidents were not the norm and they would often occur sometime after an event. There were ad hoc measures taken to assess the civilian toll. For instance, the US Commander in Afghanistan, General David McKiernan, began to track civilian casualties systematically in Afghanistan in 2008, and in 2009, Admiral Mullen ordered a study of civilian casualties. And while the United States, its coalition partners in Iraq, and NATO International Security Assistance Forces (ISAF) in

[53] Katherine Hall and Dale Stahl, *An Argument for Documenting Casualties: Violence Against Iraqi Civilians 2006* (Santa Monica, CA: RAND Corporation, 2008).

[54] The military was collecting some data at the time, but it may not have been made available to Hall and Stahl.

[55] Hall and Stahl, *An Argument for Documenting Casualties*, p. xiii.

[56] Andrew F. Krepinevich, *The Army in Vietnam* (Baltimore: Johns Hopkins, 1986), p. 202.

Afghanistan did keep some records, the figures were not made available to the public in a systematic format on a regular basis. Only in 2012 was a systematic method of accounting proposed. The US Army guidelines for tracking and investigating incidents, released in 2012, arguably came quite late in the wars. And while there is an injunction to collate, analyze, and share the data on civilian casualties, the methods for doing so are unclear.[57]

Another side of the politics of body counts was the concern that counting civilians would feed into enemy propaganda. The United States often said in the Afghanistan and Iraq wars that the numbers of civilians killed in any one incident was exaggerated and bemoans the propaganda advantages that insurgents reap from civilian casualties caused by, or alleged to be caused by, US forces.[58] Indeed, for many years of the Afghanistan war, the pattern of statements after the killing of some number of civilians by US forces was often one of initial denial followed by subsequent clarification and apology. The 2012 Army guidelines on civilian casualty mitigation, however, highlighted the importance of public relations and acknowledging what is known to be true about civilian casualty incidents. "Army units...should respond promptly to any allegations even if they simply state that allegations will be investigated.... Immediate and broad denial of reports without complete and accurate information in hand can undermine credibility, especially if investigation finds reports are correct."[59]

Finally, in each of these countries—Iraq, Afghanistan, Pakistan, and Yemen—local and national politics has interfered with accounting for the dead. Each government has an incentive to underscore its effectiveness at both protecting its civilians and in killing insurgents or militants. No government wants to acknowledge that it has failed to provide for its people's security. This concern with legitimacy can mean that civilians deaths in the wars are unrecorded, miss-identified as combatants, or if counted as civilian deaths due to violence, that the attribution of the cause of civilian death in ambiguous cases—such as crossfire—is given to militants. On the other hand, in Afghanistan, the Karzai government has blamed the US and NATO ISAF forces for deaths that may well have been caused by its own forces or by militants.

But political sensitivity is only one reason an accounting of civilian killing is hard to come by. The second reason for uncertainty about the numbers of civilians killed and injured is a lack of non-military resources to assess civilian casualties. Because the Pentagon and international military forces in Afghanistan, Pakistan, and Iraq have not systematically made their own counts and estimates

---

[57] See Appendix B, "Reports and Investigations," Department of the Army, *Civilian Casualty Mitigation*, Army Tactics, Techniques, and Procedures, No. 3-37.31 (Washington, DC: Department of the Army, 18 July 2012), pp. B-1-B-6.

[58] "Adversaries will use information to discredit U.S. efforts, and CIVCASs are a theme they will attempt to exploit." Army, *Civilian Casualty Mitigation*, p. 1-10.

[59] Ibid., p. 2-22.

of civilians killed and wounded available, the public depended on estimates for civilian death in both wars made by the press, nongovernmental organizations (NGOs), various organs of the Afghan, Pakistani, and Iraqi governments, and United Nations agencies. Reporters are few and sometimes embedded with international forces; there is little incentive for reporters to follow-up on smaller events and reporters are often left sorting through conflicting estimates and counts in the larger incidents of civilian killing. Further, there is also a dearth of nongovernmental organization actors in these conflict zones with the capacity and resources to investigate and evaluate instances of civilian death. Human rights organizations are relatively underresourced and the resources that humanitarian NGOs do have are generally directed toward their primary missions— such as tending the wounded and displaced, providing food and medicine, and repairing infrastructure.[60] There is little money for counting casualties despite the political importance of understanding what is happening in these conflicts. Some organizations, such as Handicap International track injuries, but injuries are notoriously undercounted.

Whether or not their mission is to document civilian casualties, it is extremely dangerous for NGO and international organization personnel to travel and work in war zones. From late 2001 through 2012, more than 350 humanitarian workers were killed while doing their jobs in Afghanistan, Iraq, and Pakistan.[61] For example, Marla Ruzicka, a 28-year-old human rights advocate and the founder of the NGO organization Campaign for Innocent Victims in Conflict (CIVIC) was killed by a suicide bomber in Iraq with her colleague Faiz Ali Salim on 16 April 2005.

In addition, the process of investigating noncombatant killing can put both noncombatant and combatant witnesses at risk. Specifically, Physicians for Human Rights (PHR) uncovered a mass grave in 2002 that contained the remains of Taliban soldiers who had surrendered to US Special Forces and Northern Alliance Troops in 2001.[62] Prisoners of war are considered noncombatants under international law. A US-backed Afghan General, Abdul Rashid Dostum, allegedly had those prisoners killed and buried. Estimates of the number of those killed vary from the hundreds to several thousand, but one source gave the US State Department an estimate that

---

[60] Exceptions are the Oxford Research Group's Recording Casualty Project based in the United Kingdom and the Campaign for Innocent Victims in Conflict (CIVIC) based in the United States.

[61] Compiled from the reports of the Afghanistan NGO Safety Office (ANSO), *ANSO Quarterly Data Report*, from 2005 through June 2012; Aid Worker Security Database, https://aidworkersecurity. org/incidents. In addition, many other aid workers have been injured or kidnapped in attacks. Most victims are nationals. About 15 percent of those killed are international aid workers.

[62] Physicians for Human Rights, "Investigation Timeline," http://afghanistan.phrblog.org/ get-the-facts/chronology/. James Risen, "U.S. Inaction Seen after Taliban P.O.W.'s Died," *New York Times*, 10 July 2009, p. 1.

about 1,500 prisoners were killed. PHR estimated that about 2,000 were killed and buried.[63] In an attempted cover-up, witnesses to the killing of those Taliban prisoners were reportedly tortured or killed.[64]

And the third problem might be called one of knowledge—recording the civilian dead and wounded in war is never easy. Moreover, apart from questions of political sensitivity, it is often difficult in counterinsurgency wars to determine whether someone was a combatant or a noncombatant civilian. The "fog" of war extends to the aftermath of battles. In many incidents it is difficult to know how people were injured or killed and who they were. This uncertainty is sometimes because the bodies are in pieces or because they are buried quickly according to religious tradition. Uncertainty sometimes arises because the areas where death or injury occurred are remote and difficult to access in a timely way. This basic uncertainty is the source of much of the disagreement between casualty counts. Who died and why? Were the people killed civilians or "insurgent" military pretending to be civilians? Were those harmed the victims of factional violence? Were individuals killed by a grenade or by aerial bombing? Were they killed by "insurgents" or international military forces? How shall the cause for death be attributed in cases of "crossfire" killings? Should only armed males be considered combatants? Or should any military age males living in a combat zone be counted as a combatant? The United States may count a dead male with a shovel as an insurgent, where the family may insist that the person was simply a bystander. Should the traffic incident caused by the passage of military convoys that leads to civilian death be included as a civilian casualty? There is also a great deal of uncertainty because many deaths are the result of what appears to be single gun-shot wounds, suggesting, at least in Iraq, that criminal motives underlie much of the killing of civilians. Indeed, according to analysis by Iraq Body Count, small arms fire accounts for 20 percent of the civilians killed from 2003 to 2008.[65] Further, it is common for each source of casualty data to outline the deficiencies it sees in other estimates and to disparage the methods used for counting or estimating deaths in war.

The main purpose here is to understand the ways that noncombatants were injured or killed by the United States in Afghanistan, Iraq, Yemen, and Pakistan and the moral responsibility for the harm. Another book would be required to describe the methodological and political issues associated with counting civilian death and injury and ascribing causal responsibility for it. It hardly needs to be said that much more effort must go into counting the direct killing and indirect deaths and injury in these wars.

---

[63] Physicians for Human Rights, "Investigation Timeline."

[64] Risen, "U.S. Inaction Seen after Taliban P.O.W.'s Died."

[65] Madelyn Hsiao-Rei Hicks, Hamit Dardigan, Gabriela Guerrero Serdán, Peter M. Bagnall, John Sloboda, and Michael Spagat, "The Weapons That Kill Civilians—Deaths of Children and Noncombatants in Iraq, 2003-2008," *New England Journal of Medicine*, vol. 360 (16 April 2009): 1585–1588.

Harm due to direct violence occurs from what American soldiers call "kinetic" events—such as when a gunshot kills or a bomb explodes and its fragments take a limb or a life. Direct violence injuries and deaths also occur when a bomb blast knocks down a structure and crushes someone, or starts a fire. In these cases, although it may not always be possible to know whether the harm to civilians was intended or, in cases such as crossfire, whose weapon caused the harm, we know that the use of force caused the injury. Traffic accidents that are attributable to military vehicles that are engaged in combat-related functions, for example, transporting material or protecting those who are transporting troops and material, are also directly related to war.

Before turning to the discussion of collateral damage and US operations, I make three general observations about the numbers of civilians killed and injured in the military operations of the United States and its allies. First, if the US military had been deliberately targeting civilians as a policy, many more people could have and would have been injured and killed in these wars. Students of military history might be tempted to argue that, in comparison to previous wars, the number of civilians killed in these wars is relatively small, so we should not be too concerned. I addressed reasons to care about civilian killing in the introduction, and I will not rehearse those arguments here. I simply underscore, however, that the political effects of these deaths and injuries is enormous, particularly in the cases of systemic and proportionality/double effect collateral damage.

Further, occupying forces do not constitute the only violent threats to noncombatants. Most disturbingly, noncombatants have been deliberately put in harm's way, used as "human shields" so that US forces will not fire their weapons. "Insurgents" in Afghanistan, Pakistan, and Iraq have also strapped bombs on their bodies and blown themselves up in markets and along roads. The improvised explosive devices (IEDs) designed to destroy US and coalition military vehicles destroy civilian vehicles as well. Guerrillas and uniformed soldiers have deliberately attacked civilians as part of a policy of intimidation, coercion, and reprisal. The guerrilla/insurgent forces in Afghanistan and Iraq have done the former with increasing frequency. Further, there is also insurgent caused "collateral damage," such as when Afghan civilians living near a US military base in Kunar Province in mid-2006 were the victims of indiscriminate shelling by the insurgents that was aimed at the base. Men, women, and children died and many others lost limbs.[66] Indeed, in its 2008 and 2009 report, the United Nations urged both the Afghan and international military forces to move their bases away from civilian residential areas.[67] Although the focus of this book is on the harm the United States does, the deliberate and also

---

[66] Afghan Independent Human Rights Commission, "Insurgent Abuses Against Afghan Civilians," December 2008.

[67] United Nations Assistance Mission to Afghanistan (UNAMA), *Afghanistan: Annual Report on Protection of Civilians in Armed Conflict, 2008*, pp. 24–25; UNAMA, *Afghanistan: Annual Report on Protection of Civilians in Armed Conflict, 2009*.

the unintended but nevertheless foreseeable killing and injury of noncombatants by "insurgents" is obviously condemned.

Second, as I discuss below, perhaps none of these statistics is without actual or perceived problems, or critics. Rather than attend to each and every number, readers should focus on the trends and the causal chains. This is an instance where looking at patterns in the forest, rather than focusing on each of the trees or their leaves, will be most instructive. Even if the numbers of civilians killed in Afghanistan and Iraq are "soft" and disputed, it is still clear that the majority of violent civilian deaths were caused by insurgents who either deliberately target civilians or who also inadvertently killed civilians when their target was their military adversary.

Third, the relatively detailed discussion of civilian killing below shows how changes in rules of engagement can affect the numbers of both civilians and combatants killed. Specifically, the United States was able to reduce civilian death at checkpoints in Iraq in 2006 and due to air operations in Afghanistan in 2009 as I described above. Yet as US strategy shifted, so sometimes did the burden of killing and dying. In other words, attending to the patterns suggests that the number of US and allied soldiers deaths may fluctuate with the emphasis on noncombatant immunity. These trends illustrate the tensions between military necessity, force protection, and noncombatant immunity.

Afghanistan

In October 2001, Secretary of Defense Donald Rumsfeld said, "No nation in human history has done more to avoid civilian casualties than the United States has in this conflict."[68] Rumsfeld distributed the responsibility for civilian casualties from the air campaign in Afghanistan more broadly.

> There has never been a conflict where people have not been killed, and this is the case here. There is ordnance flying around from three different sources. It's flying around from us, from the air down; it's flying around from the al Qaeda and the Taliban up, that lands somewhere and kills somebody when it hits; and there's opposition forces and al Qaeda forces that are engaged in shooting at each other.
>
> Now in a war, that happens. There is nothing you can do about it.[69]

Although Rumsfeld's public statements suggest the attitude that civilian casualties were taken for granted, his remarks actually imply a more nuanced view within the Bush administration. While, for many years noncombatant death in Afghanistan

[68] Rumsfeld briefing, 29 October 2001.
[69] Ibid.

was taken for granted as an unfortunate price of victory, from the start, the White House was concerned about minimizing civilian casualties in Afghanistan. President Bush told the Pentagon leadership before the start of US operations in Afghanistan that "they have whatever authority they need as long as it abides by the rule of low collateral [damage]."[70] According to the journalist Bob Woodward, the procedure was that "commanders and pilots had discretion to hit targets as long as they expected it would only cause minimal damage to civilians. Anything that could cause high collateral damage or make it look or feel like a war against civilians had first to come to Rumsfeld and [Bush] for approval."[71]

It appears that no one in an official capacity was keeping a systematic count of civilian casualties in Afghanistan. Nevertheless, the first months of the war, which the United States waged primarily from the air while its Afghan allies fought on the ground, saw perhaps as many as 1,000 to 2,000 civilian casualties caused by US bombing. And as mentioned earlier, between 1,000 and 2,000 Taliban prisoners were executed in 2001 by a US ally.

Leaving aside the massacre of prisoners, how did the civilian collateral damage deaths attributable to the United States occur early in the war? One cause was simply that, although more than 60 percent of munitions were satellite or laser-guided, many bombs simply missed their targets. US military officials reported that in the first months of the war of the 22,434 bombs and missiles the United States used in Afghanistan, one in four, or more than 5,600 weapons, failed to hit their intended targets.[72]

Other civilian deaths were due to weapons choices. Specifically, the United States dropped 1,228 cluster bombs (containing 248,056 bomblets) between 7 October 2001 and 18 March 2002. In addition to those civilians who were immediately killed and injured by cluster bombs, civilians continue to be killed by those cluster bomblets that failed to detonate on impact.[73] The United States essentially stopped using cluster munitions in Afghanistan after March 2002, and many of the unexploded US cluster bomb munitions were removed or destroyed. Yet, Afghanistan remains contaminated with unexploded ordnance from both the US war and the earlier Soviet occupation.

For several years, essentially between 2002 and 2006, there was little media attention to civilian death in Afghanistan. Eyes were on Iraq, where the civilian death toll was much higher. Yet even as observers, including the United Nations Assistance Mission in Afghanistan (UNAMA) noted an intensification of the conflict in 2007

---

[70] George W. Bush, quoted in Bob Woodward, *Bush at War* (New York: Simon and Schuster, 2002), p. 208.

[71] Woodward, *Bush at War*, p. 208.

[72] Eric Schmitt, "Improved U.S. Accuracy Claimed in Afghan Air War," *New York Times*, 9 April 2002.

[73] Human Rights Watch, "Fatally Flawed: Cluster Bombs and their Use by the United States in Afghanistan," Human Rights Watch, December 2002. Handicap International, Cluster Munition Coalition, et al., *Cluster Munition Monitor 2010* (Mines Action Canada, October 2010), p. 118.

and 2008, complaints by Afghans that too many civilians were being harmed in collateral damage incidents were either minimized by coalition spokespersons, or the deaths were blamed on the Taliban and al Qaeda.[74]

Attention began to shift in 2007 and 2008 as Afghan and international NGOs pointed to what they saw as an alarming increase in civilian death. An important milestone was the release of a statement on 19 June 2007, by the Agency Coordinating Body for Afghan Relief (ACBAR) that laid the responsibility for "the deaths of a minimum of 230 civilians including at least 60 women and children" since the beginning of 2007 on "international and Afghan government forces."[75] ACBAR simply listed several examples of incidents in 2007 where Afghan civilians had been killed by NATO or US forces, inviting the world to see a pattern:

> 11th Jan, 13 killed in compound raid, Garmser, Helmand; 4th March, 19 killed in alleged force protection shooting, Nangahar; 4th March, 9 killed in air-strike, Nijrab, Kapisa; 15th March, 3 killed in airstrike, Alingare, Laghman; 20th April, 12 killed in ground fighting, Sanhin, Helmand; 29th April, 9 killed in botched house raid, Shinwar, Nangahar; 1st May, 13 killed in ground combat, Maruf, Kandahar; 8th May, 21 killed in retaliatory airstrike, Sangin, Helmand; 27th May, 19 killed in air-strikes Gereshk, Helmand; and 17th June, 7 killed in air-strike, Paktika.[76]

Timing is everything. The ACBAR statement framed the problem and called for both acknowledgement of it and a response, and almost immediately afterwards, several new incidents of civilian deaths at the hands of international and Afghanistan government forces appeared to confirm ACBAR's analysis. For instance, in Kanjakak, on 22 June 2007, the *New York Times* reported that "at least 25 civilians were killed, including nine women, three babies and an elderly village mullah, were killed in an airstrike early this morning when they were caught in a battle between Taliban and

---

[74] United Nations Assistance Mission in Afghanistan (UNAMA) *Annual Report on Protection of Civilians in Armed Conflict* (January 2009). UNAMA annual reports are hereinafter cited as UNAMA, annual *POC* report for and the relevant year(s). UNAMA introduced an electronic database to track civilian death in October 2008 and in began using it in January 2009.

[75] Agency Coordinating Body for Afghan Relief, "Protecting Afghan Civilians: Statement on the Conduct of Military Operations," 19 June 2007, p. 1.

[76] ACBAR, "Protecting Afghan Civilians," p. 1. Human Rights Watch noted that "at least 230 civilians were killed during coalition or NATO operations in 2006, some of which appear to have violated the laws of war. While there is no evidence suggesting that coalition or NATO forces have intentionally directed attacks against civilians, in a number of cases international forces have conducted indiscriminate attacks or otherwise failed to take adequate precautions to prevent harm to civilians." Human Rights Watch, "The Human Cost: The Consequences of Insurgent Attacks in Afghanistan," April 2007, p. 3, http://www.hrw.org/reports/2007/afghanistan0407/.

NATO forces in Southern Afghanistan."⁷⁷ And on 30 June 2007, though the numbers were in dispute, Afghanistan government sources said that forty-five Afghan civilians died in a US-led raid against the Taliban that killed sixty-two Taliban in the remote village Gereshk, in Helmand province.⁷⁸

Even as it appeared to some observers that the number of ISAF-caused collateral damage incidents was on the rise, NATO ISAF and US military leaders suggested that the media or victim's reports of the numbers of civilians killed or injured were wrong. For example, the ACBAR statement mentioned nineteen killed in an airstrike on Gereshk in May 2007. ISAF spokesperson Major John Thomas said of reports that many had been killed in Gereshk that "we don't mean to trivialize any of those who died but we want to make it clear that we believe the numbers are a dozen or less."⁷⁹ In any case, coalition forces do their best to avoid civilian deaths. US Brig. General Perry Wiggins, in response to a question about nongovernmental organization (NGO) reports that the number of Afghan civilians killed in 2007 by coalition forces exceeded the number killed by Taliban and Al Qaeda in Afghanistan said:

> I've seen the same reports you've seen with regard to NGOs. They're reporting those particular numbers.
>
> I can tell you that it's difficult for me to believe that you can actually capture an accurate number with regards to the terrain in Afghanistan, some of the remote areas where some of these operations go on, and the fact that you have motivations out there that are different. Not to say that all the numbers are wrong, but to absolutely say that we—when we conduct our operations, we go out and investigate thoroughly, especially when there's accusations of civilian casualties.
>
> In a number of cases in recent [sic], we've gone out and investigated where they have claimed there were civilians killed and in fact those were unfounded. And in cases—we go to great lengths as I've said in the past, in order to mitigate civilian casualties.

Later, in the same press conference, General Wiggens repeated: "On a number of those occasions, we have gone and investigated. We have found those claims to be unfounded." Then Wiggens provided what has long been the main response by US and NATO troops to the charge that they are killing Afghan civilians: "But we

⁷⁷ Barry Bearak and Taimoor Shah, "Afghans Say NATO Bombs Kill 25 Civilians," *New York Times*, 22 June 2007.

⁷⁸ "Airstrikes Kill 106, Afghan Officials Say," *USA Today*, 30 June 2007, http://www.usatoday.com/news/world/2007-06-30-afghanistan-violence_N.htm.

⁷⁹ Andrew Buncombe, "Civilian Deaths Fuel Afghan Outrage," *Independent*, 2 July 2007.

have found that in a number of occasions the Taliban uses those civilians as human shields. And in some cases when we do target, you know, and there are civilians that have been killed as a result of targeting, those are reported."[80] While standing next to Afghan President Hamid Karzai, US Secretary of Defense Robert Gates said: "Avoiding civilian casualties is very important in terms of winning the loyalty and the support of local populations. At the same time I think it is important to stress, as the NATO secretary-general did...that we not forget that the Taliban is deliberately putting civilians in harm's way. They deliberately mingle civilians with them and deliberately put civilians up front. They are the ones that murder school-teachers and so on. So we must be more careful. At the same time, it's important to realize that the Taliban are actually the ones that often create the opportunity for the risk to civilians posed by military operations."[81]

Observers noted that though the Taliban had killed more civilians in 2006, US or NATO strikes had killed more Afghan civilians by July 2007.[82] ISAF and US responses—minimizing the problem, or seeking to put the blame on the Taliban—seemed at least tone-deaf and at worst, callous to Afghans. President Karzai, reflecting on several incidents in June 2007 said: "Our innocent people are becoming victims of careless operations of NATO and international forces. We are thankful for help to Afghanistan, but that does not mean that Afghan lives have no value. Afghan life is not cheap and it should not be treated as such."[83] Former Afghan Prime Minister and Takbeer party leader Ahmad Shah Ahmadzai asked: "What does this sorry mean? They are bombarding villages because they hear the Taliban are there. But this is not the way, to bomb and kill 20 people for one Taliban. This is why people are losing hope and trust in the government and the internationals." According to *Time* magazine reporter Aryn Baker, "Like many Afghans, Ahmadzai is starting to suspect a more sinister meaning behind the recent spate of civilian deaths. 'The Americans can make a mistake once, twice, maybe three times,' he says. 'But 20, 30 times? I am not convinced that they are doing this without intention.'"[84]

Apparently, at least in part as a response to Afghan concerns, NATO ISAF reviewed its rules of engagement in Afghanistan. A NATO ISAF spokesperson told Human Rights Watch:

---

[80] DoD News Briefing with Brig. Gen. Wiggins, 3 July 2007, http://www.defense.gov/transcripts/transcript.aspx?transcriptid=4006.

[81] DoD News Briefing with Secretary Gates and President Hamid Karzai from Kabul, Afghanistan, 5 July 2007, http://www.defense.gov/transcripts/transcript.aspx?transcriptid=3978.

[82] "Civilian Bloodshed Clouds Afghan Effort," CTV.CA, 1 July 2007, http://www.ctv.ca/servlet/ArticleNews/story/CTVNews/20070701/afghan_deaths_070701/20070701?hub=TopStories.

[83] Aryn Baker, "Backlash from Afghan Civilian Deaths," *Time*, 23 June 2007, http://www.time.com/time/world/article/0,8599,1636551,00.html.

[84] Ibid.

In the summer of 2007, NATO-ISAF reviewed its tactics, techniques and procedures. We committed ourselves to undertake rigorous and constant investigations of incidents involving possible civilian casualties. In particular, the Commander of ISAF mandated that the greatest possible use be made of precision systems and that, when taking fire from an Afghan house, on-scene commanders satisfy themselves that every effort had been made to confirm that the Afghan facility did not shelter innocent civilians. In addition SACEUR [Supreme Allied Commander, Europe] mandated that enhanced and timely After Action Reviews identify lessons learned and that there be a strong system of reporting from investigations when deemed necessary.[85]

In July 2007, NATO ISAF forces in Afghanistan announced a change in tactics—for example, using house to house searches to verify who was present in the area suspending action when civilians might be hurt, and by using smaller bombs in airstrikes—to decrease collateral damage casualties.[86] And the number of deaths due to airstrikes did decline for a few months in late 2007.[87]

However, the rate of US close air support missions in support of ground forces grew in 2008 and there were a number of civilian casualty incidents that drew international attention. Again, the pattern appeared to be that when civilians were killed, the United States either blamed others or said the numbers were exaggerated. For example on 4 July 2008, US forces used close air support to attack two vehicles in Afghanistan about 30 miles from the border with Pakistan. The United States said it believed that the vehicles were carrying insurgents; a district governor said that those killed, twenty-two civilians, were fleeing a military operation against the Taliban.[88] On 6 July 2008, a US-led airstrike targeted Taliban insurgents in Eastern Afghanistan. Afghan officials said the strike killed at least twenty-two people in a wedding party—most of them women and children.[89]

---

[85] Email communication from NATO Media Operations Center to Human Rights Watch, 6 May 2008, quoted in Human Rights Watch, "'Troops in Contact': Airstrikes and Civilian Deaths in Afghanistan," September 2008, p. 22.

[86] Mark Tran, "NATO Changes Tactics to Avoid Afghan Civilian Deaths," *Guardian Unlimited*, 30 July 2007 http://www.guardian.co.uk/world/2007/jul/30/afghanistan.nato. Human Rights Watch, "'Troops in Contact,'" p. 33.

[87] Human Rights Watch, "'Troops in Contact,'" p. 6.

[88] "US Says Rebels Killed; Afghan Officials Reports Civilians Dead," Turkish Press.com, 4 July 2008, http://www.turkishpress.com/news.asp?id=239784&s=&i=&t=US_says_rebels_killed,_Afghan_official_reports_civilians_dead.

[89] "Afghan Official: Coalition Airstrike Kills Civilians in Eastern Afghanistan," Voice of America, 6 July 2008, http://voanews.com/english/archive/2008-07/2008-07-06-voa28.cfm?CFID=37349525&CFTOKEN=87885038; Carlotta Gall, "Afghan President Assails U.S. led Airstrike That He Says Killed 95," *New York Times*, 24 August 2008.

Then, in one of the most widely publicized episodes in that period, on 22 August 2008, the United States attacked insurgents in Azizabad, in the Shindand District in the western part of the country, in an attempt to kill Mullah Sadiq, a senior Taliban commander. The joint Afghan and US raid, which began around 1 A.M. with a ground assault, was concluded by an American airstrike using an AC-130 gunship, firing cannons and howitzers. The US military said that twenty-five Taliban were killed, including Mullah Sadiq, and said that five civilians (two women and three children) had been killed as well. Afghan officials reported that fifteen houses were destroyed and other homes were damaged. The villagers, Afghan officials, and United Nations investigators, said that more than ninety civilians—including sixty children—were killed. A few days after the raid a man claiming to be Mullah Sadiq called Radio Liberty to say that he was alive and said that he had not been in Azizabad during the raid. General James Conway, commandant of the US Marine Corp, told reporters five days after the raid, that, "if the reports of the Afghan civilian casualties are accurate—and sometimes that is a big 'if' because I think we all understand the Taliban capabilities with regard to information operations—but if that proves out, that will be truly an unfortunate incident. And we need to avoid that, certainly, at every cost."[90]

US officials ultimately acknowledged that more civilians had been killed, and noted flaws in their initial investigation and statements, but continued to suggest that Afghans were exaggerating the death toll. President Bush later called Afghanistan's President Karzai to express his regrets and General McKiernan issued orders tightening restrictions on the use force in close air support and night raids.[91] Yet, the raid in Azizabad was only the largest and most widely publicized instance where the United States killed Afghan civilians during the summer of 2008. Nearly four years later, General McKiernan recalled the incident vividly to me in a short conversation about civilian casualties in Afghanistan during his tenure as one where he spent four hours making apologies to local Afghan leaders.[92]

Air strikes were not the only cause of civilian casualties in Afghanistan: Afghan civilians were killed by US and ISAF personnel in "force protection" or "escalation of force" incidents. Escalation of force procedures are rules that dictate the steps soldiers must take before using deadly force in order to reduce the likelihood of friendly fire and civilian death scenarios such as traffic checkpoints. An escalation of force incident occurs, for instance, when civilians approach ISAF vehicles too closely on

---

[90] DoD News Briefing with Gen. Conway from the Pentagon, 27 August 2008.

[91] Carlotta Gall, "Afghan President Assails U.S. led Airstrike That He Says Killed 95," New York Times, 24 August 2008; Carlotta Gall, "U.S. Killed 90 in Afghan Village, Including 60 Children, U.N. Finds," 27 August 2008; Eric Schmitt, "U.S. Officials Describe Afghan Airstrike," New York Times, 28 August 2008; Carlotta Gall, "Trail of Evidence Points to High Civilian Toll in Afghan Raid," New York Times, 8 September 2008; Eric Schmitt, "30 Civilians Died in Afghanistan Raid, U.S. Inquiry Finds," New York Times, 7 October 2008, http://www.nytimes.com/2008/10/08/washington/08inquiry.html.

[92] Conversation with General McKiernan at Boston University, 27 April 2012.

the roads, or when civilians fail to stop quickly enough (perhaps because they fail to see the signal to stop) at checkpoints. In about half of the incidents where British soldiers were involved in killing or wounding civilians from late 2006 to late 2009, the incidents involved "warning" shots to people in cars, on motorcycles, or on foot (for example, when British Royal Marines in Helmand Province fired warning shots at a car in 2006 killing two civilians and wounding two others, including a child).[93]

In response to concerns that the United States was killing too many civilians in Afghanistan, the United States again reviewed its policies. On 2 September and 30 December 2008, the US Commander in Afghanistan, General McKiernan issued tactical directives that changed US procedures with the goal of reducing civilian casualties. A key element of the new procedures was to include more Afghan security forces in raids. McKiernan also created a special unit within the ISAF, the "Civilian Casualty Tracking Cell" in August 2008 to compile basic information on combat-related civilian deaths and injuries caused by both "insurgents" and "ISAF/OEF" activity.

But Afghans remained skeptical of US and NATO ISAF promises and most Afghans were against NATO and US airstrikes in particular. A survey of Afghan civilians conducted in late 2008 and early 2009 showed that 77 percent of Afghans said the airstrikes were unacceptable because they posed such a great risk to Afghan civilians. Further, overall Afghan approval of the US operations had declined to 32 percent, a reduction from 68 percent approval in 2005. The belief that NATO ISAF was performing well had also declined.[94] The international humanitarian assistance community was also critical of ISAF, and international aid organizations publicly urged greater transparency and accountability by the international forces.[95]

The perception that the US and NATO ISAF forces were failing to protect Afghan civilians from collateral damage was reinforced in January 2009 when the United Nations reported that of the 2,118 Afghan civilians who were killed in the conflict in 2008, 39 percent—828 civilians—were killed by international forces, and of those, the majority, 552 civilians, were killed by airstrikes.[96] This was a 31 percent increase in the number of deaths caused by ISAF and US forces over the previous year.

---

[93] Wikileaks data as interpreted by *The Guardian*, "Afghanistan War Logs: List of Civilian Shootings by British Troops," 25 July 2010, http://www.guardian.co.uk/world/2010/jul/25/british-shootings-afghan-civilians-list.

[94] Afghan Center for Socio-Economic and Opinion Research poll cited in Shaun Waterman, "Costs of War: The Civilian Casualty Issue," *ISN Security Watch*, 17 February 2009, http://www.isn.ethz.ch/Digital-Library/Articles/Detail/?ord538=grp2&size538=10&lng=en&id=96590.

[95] "Caught in the Conflict—Civilians and the International Security Strategy in Afghanistan," A Briefing Paper by Eleven NGOs Operating in Afghanistan for the NATO Heads of State and Government Summit, 3-4 April 2009. ActionAid, Afghanaid, CARE Afghanistan, Christian Aid, Cordaid, DACAAR, Interchurch Organisation for Development Cooperation, International Rescue Committee, Marie Stopes International, Oxfam International, Save the Children UK. Downloaded from http://reliefweb.int/node/303325.

[96] UNAMA, annual *POC* report for 2008 (UNAMA, 2009), p. 16.

Moreover, the UN report highlighted the fact that the "increase occurred notwith-standing various measures introduced by IMF [International Military Forces] to reduce the impact of the war on civilians, including internal as well as independent external investigations, after-action reviews, the creation of mechanisms geared to reviewing trends and reducing the impact of the war on civilians, and the issuance of new tactical directives regarding the use of air-strikes."[97] Even though it highlighted the fact that the Taliban were deliberately targeting Afghan civilians or in some cases inadvertently harming them, the UN report was another public relations blow for the United States.

In February 2009, the US military conducted another review of its policies and the American and Afghan forces agreed to increase their coordination and coop-eration to reduce civilian casualties. Chairman of the US Joint Chiefs of Staff Mike Mullen's op-ed, quoted above, appeared in the *Washington Post* and was intended to underscore the US commitment to Afghan civilians.[98] Further, the *New York Times* reported that beginning in mid-February 2009 the United States halted Special Operations commando raids for two weeks.[99] Yet, there were more civilian casual-ties when the raids resumed. On 22 March 2009, a raid by US Special Forces led to another disputed incident where the United States said it attacked a compound and killed five men that the United States said were part of a "terrorist network." Local Afghan officials said that the dead were civilians.[100] American apologies continued as more incidents occurred. Yet, General McKiernan noted, "Apologies are not suf-ficient, so we do try to compensate families and communities where we've made mistakes. But that's not sufficient either. In fact, there is nothing I could do or say that would replace the loss of a loved one. There's not enough money in the world to replace the loss of a family member."[101]

In late June 2009, as described in the introduction, the new ISAF commander General Stanley McChrystal again changed the rules of engagement, limiting the use of airstrikes. McChrystal's directive said, "I expect leaders at all levels to scru-tinize and limit the use of force like close air support (CAS) against residential compounds and other locations likely to produce civilian casualties in accordance with the guidance. Commanders must weigh the gain of using CAS against the cost of civilian casualties, which in the long run make mission success more difficult and turn the Afghan people against us.... The use of air-to-ground munitions and

[97] UNAMA, annual *POC* report for 2008.

[98] Mullen, "Building our Best Weapon."

[99] Mark Mazzetti and Eric Schmitt, "U.S. Halted Some Afghan Raids Over Concern on Civilian Deaths," *New York Times*, 10 March 2009, p. A1.

[100] Abdul Waheed Wafa and Carlotta Gall, "U.S. Kills 5 Afghans in Raid on House," *New York Times*, 23 March 2009, p. A5.

[101] Quoted in Jason Straziuso, "McKiernan Speaks Out on Afghan Civilian Deaths," *Military Times*, 19 April 2009, http://www.militarytimes.com/print/article/20090419/NEWS/904190301/McKiernan-speaks-out-Afghan-civilian-deaths.

indirect fires against residential compounds is only authorized under very limited and prescribed conditions."[102] US and ISAF soldiers would take greater risks in the hopes that this would reduce civilian casualties. This was a "civilian protection" strategy. All pre-planned air-to-ground operations were supposed to implement collateral damage estimation and mitigation procedures and all operations were to be pre-planned "unless troops were in an emergency situation requiring close air support (CAS) or close combat attack (CCA). In both CAS and CCA in Afghanistan, the pilot may not deploy a weapon without ground commander direction.... The pilot's only discretion is to elect not to release a weapon."[103]

Did the tactical directive lead to the reduction of civilian casualties due to US air strikes? According to official ISAF data, the effort worked. In early 2011, NATO ISAF released Civilian Casualty Tracking Cell data in Afghanistan for January 2008 through December 2010 to *Science*, which then made that data public in spreadsheet form (table 2.1). The United Nations and Afghanistan Rights Monitor also released some of their data in spreadsheet form at that time.[104] The ISAF data includes tallies of both the killed and the wounded for the period of 2008 to 2010 where the "killed" column indicates "civilian deaths confirmed by ISAF." Wounded are "survivors following injuries received as a result of ISAF, ANSF or insurgent actions. The term encompasses all kinds of wounds. There are no specifics regarding thresholds for counting the injury, according to our data practitioners."[105]

How accurate is the ISAF data? Table 2.2 summarizes ISAF data on deaths due to two types of air operations (close air support and close combat air) released by NATO in early 2011.[106] Data on civilian deaths due to air operations is instructive for two reasons. First, we can be confident that because the Taliban and other anti-government forces do not operate fixed wing aircraft or helicopters, the attribution of the causes of incidents of civilian killing is less difficult, for instance, in comparison to the attribution of deaths of civilians, due to crossfire. We know, with more or less certainty, how someone was killed. The question is determining who was killed—whether a civilian or combatant. And second, this data suggests whether and how much the ISAF change in the rules of engagement to reduce deaths from air operations in mid-2009 made a difference in the number of civilians

---

[102] Declassified excerpt from NATO Tactical Directive, 2 July 2009, released by NATO ISAF Headquarters, 6 July 2009.

[103] Gregory S. McNeal, "The U.S. Practice of Collateral Damage Estimation and Mitigation," 9 November 2011, p. 2, http://papers.ssrn.com/sol3/papers.cfm?abstract_id=1819583.

[104] The Wikileaks release of US data in 2010 overlaps with and adds to other data sets but is essentially limited to US sources and is certainly also an undercount of total civilians killed by either NATO or anti-government forces.

[105] International Security Assistance Force (ISAF), CIVCAS, 13 January 2011; as referred to in J. Bohannon, "Counting the Dead in Afghanistan," *Science*, vol. 331 (2011): 1256-1260.

[106] Ibid.

Table 2.1 **NATO ISAF Data on Total Number of Civilians Killed and Wounded, 2008–2010, by Perpetrator**

Killed	ISAF	Anti-Government	Total
2008	258	973	1231
2009	181	976	1157
2010	202	1178	1380
Total	641	3127	3768
Wounded	ISAF	Anti-Government	Total
2008	365		
2009	335	2383	2718
2010	269	2607	2876
Total	969	4990	5959

Source: NATO International Security Assistance Force (ISAF), CIVCAS, 13 January 2011; as referred to in J. Bohannon, *Science*, 331, 1256 (2011).

Table 2.2 **NATO ISAF Tally of Civilian Deaths, 2008–2010, Due to Air Operations**

	2008	2009	2010
Close Air Support	177	62	20
Close Combat Air	unknown	10	44
Total	> 177	72	64

Source: NATO International Security Assistance Force (ISAF), CIVCAS, 13 January 2011, released with J. Bohannon, *Science*, 331, 1256 (2011).

killed. The June 2009 tactical directive was intended to reduce civilian casualties due to close air support. Assuming that NATO ISAF tracking of civilian casualties was accurate, or at least unbiased, it could be used to help ISAF commanders and the public assess whether they had reduced civilian killing by air operations.

The ISAF provided data suggests that ISAF was relatively successful in reducing civilian casualties due to close air support operations. Table 2.3 compares the NATO Civilian Casualty Tracking Unit data for 2009 civilian deaths due to air operations to the UN figures for that same period. Comparing the first and the second half of the year, the NATO ISAF CIVCAS data suggests a dramatic decline in deaths due to air operations (a 50 percent reduction in deaths due to NATO air

Table 2.3 **Comparison of NATO ISAF and UN Tallies of Deaths Due to Air Operations in 2009**

	January-June	July-December	Total for 2009
CIVCAS Data	48	24	72
UN Data	191	168	359

Source: NATO International Security Assistance Force (ISAF), CIVCAS, 13 January 2011, released with J. Bohannon, *Science*, 331, 1256 (2011). UN Data from United Nations Assistance Mission to Afghanistan (UNAMA).

operations).[107] The steady increase in US and ISAF caused civilian deaths abated in the latter part of 2009. General McChrystal's tactical directive was credited with the reduction in civilian deaths due to airstrike.

The UNAMA data for 2009 suggests a more modest reduction in civilian death due to ISAF airstrikes from 2008 when more than 550 civilians were killed by NATO ISAF air operations. Yet, the UN recorded five times more civilian deaths due to air power than the ISAF CIVCAS tracking cell.

Both the UN and ISAF suggest that there was a decline in civilian casualties due to air strikes in 2009 after the July Tactical Directive. When ISAF focused on reducing civilian casualties by air operations it was able to do so, at least for a time. Nevertheless, some other types of operations, namely force protection and raids, continued to kill civilians at about the same level. Figure 2.1 shows the United Nations Mission in Afghanistan (UNAMA) record of civilians killed by pro-government forces (PGF) and anti-government elements (AGE) from 2007 to 2012 in all types of operations.

A second observation concerns the quality of the databases. There is evidence that the ISAF data compiled by the Civilian Casualty Tracking Cell is, at a minimum, incomplete. UNAMA consistently records a higher number of civilians killed by all parties than the ISAF Civilian Casualty Tracking Cell. And the CIVCAS Tracking Cell figures are, in at least some important cases, inconsistent with NATO's own actions and statements. The NATO ISAF civilian casualty database does not appear to record all, or in some incidents any, of the deaths of civilians due to either close air support or close combat air operations.

For example, it was widely reported in the press that on 4 September 2009 more than 100 people had gathered around two fuel tankers that had been attacked earlier that day by the Taliban in Kunduz Province of northern Afghanistan. The

[107] Human Rights Watch (HRW) found that 116 civilians were killed by NATO and US airstrikes in 2006 and 321 were killed by NATO and US airstrikes in 2007. HRW, "Troops in Contact: Airstrikes and Civilian Deaths in Afghanistan" (New York: HRW, 2008), pp. 13–14.

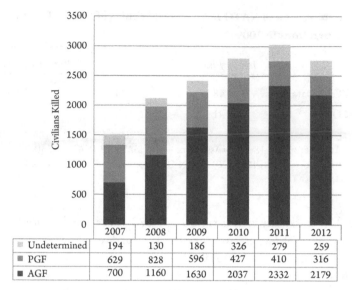

	2007	2008	2009	2010	2011	2012
Undetermined	194	130	186	326	279	259
PGF	629	828	596	427	410	316
AGF	700	1160	1630	2037	2332	2179

AGE: Anti-Government Elements

PGF: Pro-Government Forces, including International Military and Afghan Forces

Figure 2.1 Civilians killed in Afghanistan: UNAMA attribution of responsibility 2007–2011.

Source: UNAMA annual *POC* reports for 2008–2012.

people surrounding the vehicles were attempting to siphon the fuel from the tankers. Under the orders of German officer, Col. George Klein, a US F-15 dropped two 500-pound bombs.[108] ISAF initially suggested that all those killed in the blast, up to 130 people, had been Taliban fighters, though ISAF said it would immediately investigate the incident. Later in September an ISAF investigation said that seventy of those killed were Taliban and thirty were civilians.[109] Subsequent NATO ISAF investigation found the actions of the German officer at fault and called his orders to bomb the gathering a violation of the rules of engagement.[110] The German Army's Chief of Staff, Wolfgang Schneiderhan, resigned over the attack. The NATO

[108] Rajiv Chandrasekaran, "NATO Orders Probe of Afghan Airstrike Alleged to Have Killed Many Civilians," *Washington Post*, 5 September 2009, http://www.washingtonpost.com/wp-dyn/content/article/2009/09/04/AR2009090400543.html.

[109] Yochi J. Dreazen, "NATO Says U.S. Airstrike in Kunduz Killed 30 Civilians," *Wall Street Journal*, 17 September 2009, http://online.wsj.com/article/SB125315261757418561.html.

[110] John Goetz, Konstantin von Hammerstein, and Holger Stark, "NATO's Secret Findings: Kunduz Affair Report Puts German Defense Minister under Pressure," *Der Spiegel*, 19 January 2010, http://www.spiegel.de/international/germany/0,1518,672468,00.html.

ISAF report said 142 people were killed.[111] ISAF forces eventually acknowledged that most of those killed were civilians, and Germany made condolence payments amounting to $500,000 to the families of ninety-one civilians killed and the families of eleven wounded.[112] The United Nations notes these deaths in their database. The ISAF CIVCAS database does not record any civilian deaths due to close air support for September 2009 in northern Afghanistan, and only eight deaths in the South West despite the fact that this is one of the most well-known incidents of civilian killing by ISAF forces in the war.[113]

Similarly, there is no report of civilians killed or injured in the CIVCAS database published by *Science* for the August 2008 incident that corresponds to the deaths of as many as ninety people in Azizabad during an American raid with an AC-130 gunship, firing cannons and howitzers. The relevant columns in the data say either 0 or "No Data." The Azizabad incident is, however, discussed in the January 2009 Department of Defense Report on Afghanistan, where the "33 civilians were killed by an airstrike to defend U.S. ground forces under fire from the Taliban, has resulted in a change in operating procedures to prevent civilian casualties whenever possible."[114] Another example of incomplete coverage is that while the NATO ISAF database published in *Science* records more than twenty-five deaths in western Afghanistan in May 2009 that could correspond with the Garani strike, where B-1 aircraft dropped 500- and 2,000-pound bombs, human rights observers suggested that many more than 100 civilians were reported to have been killed by the bombing.

The August 2008 incident in Azizabad, the May 2009 incident in Garani where the village was bombed by B-1s, and the September 2009 airstrike against people gathered at a fuel tanker in Kunduz, followed a familiar pattern little changed from the 30 June 2007 incident in Gereshk. After the US or NATO ISAF forces use force in an attempt to kill the enemy in Afghanistan, they are accused of killing many Afghan civilians; Afghan officials protest American carelessness and urge greater caution, while at the same time suggesting they want the United States to remain; US officials deny the charges of killing any civilians or discount the Afghan count of the dead and injured. Later, in some cases after there are protests of the deaths, the United States investigates and acknowledges the civilian dead and makes an apology for the tragic loss of life when they revise their estimate. US and/or NATO

[111] "Germany's Army Chief of Staff Resigns over NATO Airstrike in Kunduz," 26 November 2009, *DW-World.de*, http://www.dw-world.de/dw/article/0,,4930694,00.html.

[112] Matthias Gebauer, "Germany to Pay $500,000 for Civilian Bombing Victims," *Der Spiegel,* 6 August 2010, http://www.spiegel.de/international/germany/0,1518,710439,00.html.

[113] S. Carran, A. Ravindar, S. Y. Lau, J. Bohannon, Afghanistan Casualty Timeline (2008–2010), 11 March 2011; as referred to in Bohannon, "Counting the Dead in Afghanistan."

[114] It is described as the "Shindand incident in Helmand Province." Department of Defense, "Report on Progress toward Security and Stability in Afghanistan," January 2009, p. 9.

ISAF announce that they will take greater care to avoid civilian deaths, and rules of engagement and escalation of force procedures may be modified. Another incident occurs and the Afghan government protests.[115]

Finally, the UNAMA human rights team acknowledges that their data is incomplete because they do not include incidents where they are not satisfied with the quality of information. "Where UNAMA is not satisfied with information concerning an incident, it will not be reported. In some instances, investigations may take several weeks before conclusions can be drawn....Where information is unclear, conclusions will not be drawn until more satisfactory evidence is obtained, or the case will be closed without conclusion and will not be included in the statistical reporting." Further, UNAMA notes, "This may mean that conclusions on civilian casualties from an incident may be revised as more information becomes available and is incorporated into the analysis." Indeed, the numbers do occasionally change. Further, UNAMA does not presume all military age males are combatants.

> In some incidents the non-combatant status of the reported victims cannot be conclusively established or is disputed. In such cases, UNAMA is guided by the applicable standards of international humanitarian law and does not presume fighting age males are either civilians or fighters. Rather, such claims are assessed on the facts available on the incident in question. If the status of one or more victim(s) remains uncertain, such deaths are not included in the overall number of civilian casualties.[116]

The irony, from the US military's perspective, is that while they took significant political heat and have observed an increase in violence directed toward ISAF forces after incidents of civilian casualties, the majority of Afghan civilians killed or injured by direct violence were harmed by insurgent forces. When ISAF kills civilians, anti-occupation sentiment and violence increases; when insurgents kill civilians,

---

[115] Hundreds of civilians have been killed by Afghan National Army and Afghan National Police forces. Although Afghan civilians have expressed concern about the accountability of Afghan police and military forces, the incidence of civilian killing by ANA and Police has not been consistently tracked. In 2010, of the at least 2,777 civilians killed by all combatants that year, the Afghan security forces killed about 10 percent of all the victims, a third of those killed by "pro-government" forces. In recent years, the ANA and ANP may well have killed about third of all the civilians killed by pro-government forces including ISAF. Campaign for Innocent Victims in Conflict (CIVIC), Human Rights Research and Advocacy Consortium (HRRAC), and Oxfam, "No Time to Lose: Promoting Accountability of the Afghan National Security Forces," Joint Briefing Paper, 10 May 2011, http://www.oxfamamerica.org/publications/no-time-to-lose. Afghanistan Rights Monitor, which records fewer civilian deaths than the United Nations, attributed 520 civilian deaths in 2008 and 239 civilian deaths in 2010 to Afghan forces of a total of 1,620 and 790 civilian deaths attributed to both the Afghan and international forces fighting the insurgency. Afghanistan Rights Monitor, "The Crisis of Afghan Civilians in 2008," and http://www.arm.org.af/index.php.

[116] UNAMA, annual POC report for 2011, p. i.

there is less reaction. In most years, the various insurgent groups in Afghanistan harm more civilians than does the pro-government forces of the US, NATO ISAF, and the Afghan Police and Army.[117]

One reason for the great ire directed at ISAF and the US forces after collateral damage incidents may be the pattern of civilian killing: ISAF and insurgent forces kill equal numbers of women and children. In other words, "as a *proportion* of all civilian casualties, ISAF kills and injures many more women and/or children."[118] On the other hand, a key difference between ISAF and insurgent forces is that while insurgents unintentionally kill civilians, the Taliban's military forces have also deliberately and systematically targeted civilians. Indiscriminate killing of civilians caused by improvised explosive devices alone caused between 41 and 47 percent of all civilian deaths from 2009 through 2011. But deliberate attacks (targeted killings and suicide attacks) by insurgents killed more than 2,100 Afghans in that same period. In fact, the number and proportion of civilians killed deliberately by insurgents has grown as the Taliban increased their attacks on civilians perceived to be collaborating with foreign and government forces or at least tolerating the NATO and US forces and the unintentional killing of civilians. Targeted killings by insurgents alone more than doubled, from 225 deaths in such attacks documented by UNAMA in 2009 to 495 deaths in 2011.[119]

The growing number of deliberate attacks on civilians by insurgents illustrates overall changes in the pattern and means of civilian death caused by the Taliban and other anti-government forces (including the Haqqani network and Hizb-l-Islami) over the course of the war. In the early years of the war, the Taliban focused their fire on the Northern Alliance forces, the United States, and other international forces. Later, the Taliban began to target the Afghan National Security Forces, including the Afghan National Army (ANA) and Afghan National Police (ANP) as well as the border patrol. Civilians died in the crossfire of fighting, or as Taliban rockets fired at ISAF operating bases fell in neighborhoods near bases. In addition, Taliban weapons intended to kill NATO ISAF forces, such as improvised explosive devices, have often killed noncombatants. Indeed, roadside improvised explosive devices have become the single greatest way civilians are killed and injured in Afghanistan.

When the Taliban increased the level of their military activity in 2005, their forces began to more systematically target civilians who were perceived as collaborators, sometimes beheading or hanging suspected spies. Women and female children were also attacked as the Taliban enforced their strict view of women's roles. Taliban strikes also killed noncombatant Afghans who were simply located near NATO ISAF bases. The United Nations repeatedly called for both the NATO and

---

[117] In every year, some number of civilian deaths cannot be attributed to either side.

[118] Condra, Felter, Iyengar, and Shapiro, "The Effect of Civilian Casualties in Afghanistan and Iraq," p. 10. UNAMA reported 1,023 children killed by all parties from 2009-2011. UNAMA annual *POC* reports, 2009-2011.

[119] Calculated from UNAMA figures, UNAMA annual *POC* reports, 2009-2011.

Taliban forces to move their combatants away from noncombatants, indeed urging NATO to close bases located in residential areas and has urged the Taliban to abide by international law.

Apparently taking a page from the US analysis, in mid-2009 the Afghan commander of the Taliban, Mullah Mohammed Omar, ordered Taliban forces to take greater care to protect civilian life: "The utmost steps must be taken to avoid civilian human loss in martyrdom operations."[120] Contained in a 61-page "Rule Book for the Mujahedin of the Islamic Emirate of Afghanistan" published in May 2009, the caution to protect Afghan civilians was stronger than a 9-page set of directives issued in 2006 by the Taliban.[121] The Layha was again updated in 2010 and reiterated in a statement by the Taliban leadership council in August 2011.[122] According to a report in the *New York Times*, the Taliban's new approach is believed by some in NATO to have made the insurgency more effective.[123] According to Kate Clark, "the fact that winning the support of the local population is crucial appears also to have led to some changes since 2006. For example, orders in the 2006 Code to beat and (eventually) kill recalcitrant teachers, burn schools and have nothing to do with NGOs—which were described as "tools of the infidels"—have been quietly dropped in 2009 and 2010."[124] Yet attacks by the Taliban on noncombatants continued through 2010 and 2011. Clark also notes that "when UNAMA reported in mid-2010 that most civilian casualties were due to insurgent attacks and criticized the Taliban for violating their own Code, it hit a raw nerve. The Taliban reacted strongly, with denial, indignation, *and* a call for the setting up of a joint commission on civilian casualties. A small scrap of common ground was opened up in the stated desire by all parties to protect Afghan civilians."[125] Clark has argued that the code of conduct is an important opening that could allow for outsiders to call the Taliban to account.

In its report on civilians in 2011, UNAMA simply recalled the Taliban statements that year and said, "UNAMA welcomes any public pronouncements of Taliban policy on reducing civilian casualties but asserts that such rules are only

---

[120] Quoted in Dexter Filkins, "'09 Deadliest Year for Afghans, U.N. Says," *New York Times*, 14 January 2010, p. A6.

[121] Radio Free Europe, Radio Liberty, "New Taliban Rule Book Aims to Win Afghan Hearts and Minds," http://www.rferl.org/content/New_Taliban_Rule_Book_Aims_To_Win_Afghan_Hearts_And_Minds/1790002.html. Christopher Dickey, "Afghanistan: The Taliban's Book of Rules," MSNBC, 12 December 2006, http://www.msnbc.msn.com/id/16169421/site/newsweek/print/1/displaymode/1098.

[122] Kate Clark, "Calling the Taliban to Account," 6 July 2011, *Foreign Policy*, http://afpak.foreignpolicy.com/posts/2011/07/06/calling_the_taliban_to_account_0.

[123] Alissa Rubin, "Taliban Using Lighter Touch to Win Allies," *New York Times*, 21 January 2010, p. A1.

[124] Clark, "Calling the Taliban to Account."

[125] Ibid.

meaningful if implemented on the ground. Despite the Taliban's improved messaging on protection of civilians in 2011, UNAMA did not document improved compliance with international humanitarian law by the Taliban or a reduction in civilian casualties caused by them. The Taliban continued to directly target civilians and use indiscriminate weapons such as pressure plated IEDs."[126] In fact, UNAMA found that "in incidents where intended targets appeared to be military, those responsible for placing IEDs showed no regard for the presence of civilians and no evidence of distinguishing between civilian and military targets in violation of the international humanitarian law principles of distinction, precaution and proportionality."[127]

Figure 2.1, showing direct civilian death in Afghanistan from 2007 through 2012, illustrates the total number of civilians killed and the UNAMA attribution of responsibility for civilian death. In any year, some portion of deaths cannot be attributed to a specific belligerent party. Overall, United Nations data suggest that in the most recent years of the war in Afghanistan, roughly 10 percent of the civilian killing in Afghanistan cannot be attributed to either insurgent or pro-government forces, which includes the International Security Assistance Forces and the Afghan military and police forces. While the total number of civilians killed in the war has grown in recent years, the percentage of the total number of civilians killed by international and Afghan forces has declined from a high of 41 percent in 2008 to 14 percent in 2011 according to UN data.[128]

But the understanding of the number of civilians killed, and the responsibility for their deaths, can vary by source. For instance, figure 2.2 compares the UNAMA data for civilians killed by different forces to the Afghanistan Rights Monitor (ARM) figures for the same year, 2010. ARM distinguishes among pro-government forces, by counting deaths caused by international forces and Afghan security forces in separate categories, suggesting that the majority of deaths that year caused by pro-government forces are attributable to the operations of the international forces. The UN classifies pro- government forces (PGF) and anti-government elements (AGE), while the ARM call insurgents "armed opposition groups" (AOG). UNAMA reports 2,790 civilian deaths in 2010, attributing 427 to "pro-government forces"; ARM reports 2,421 civilian deaths and attributes 512 deaths to international military forces and another 278 to the Afghan national forces. Finally, while for 2010, the UNAMA says that in the case of about 250 deaths, they were unable to attribute responsibility for the violent death. Afghanistan Rights Monitor said 100 deaths could not be attributed to either side.[129]

---

[126] UNAMA, annual *POC* report for 2011, p. 4.

[127] UNAMA, annual *POC* report for 2011, p. 10.

[128] UNAMA, annual *POC* reports, 2008, 2009, 2010, 2011, 2012.

[129] Afghanistan Rights Monitor, *ARM Annual Report, Civilian Casualties of War, January–December 2010* (Kabul, February 2011).

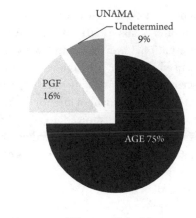

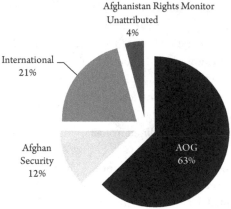

AOG: Armed Opposition Groups

Figure 2.2 Alternative attributions of civilian casualty counts in 2010 by the UN and Afghanistan Rights Monitor.
Source: UNAMA annual *POC* report for 2010. Afghanistan Rights Monitor, *ARM Annual Report, Civilian Casualties of War, January–December 2010* (Kabul, February 2011).

Figure 2.3 summarizes the trends in the causes of collateral damage deaths attributed to pro-government forces from 2008 to 2012 by UNAMA. The figure shows, first, as noted above, that total collateral damage deaths due to the operations of pro-government forces have declined. The overall decline in civilian death occurred at the same time that the number and the frequency of pro-government international and Afghan forces coming into contact with enemy forces increased as the United States pressed its operations against militants, beginning with its operation in February 2010 in Marjah. Thus, even as the United States pressed its fight, it was able to reduce harm to civilians. The idea that civilian casualties are an inevitable consequence of the fighting can thus be questioned. These data also suggest that

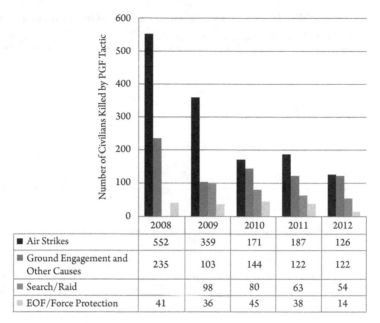

	2008	2009	2010	2011	2012
■ Air Strikes	552	359	171	187	126
■ Ground Engagement and Other Causes	235	103	144	122	122
■ Search/Raid		98	80	63	54
▨ EOF/Force Protection	41	36	45	38	14

Figure 2.3 UNAMA attribution of civilian deaths to pro-government forces by type of operation, 2008–2012.
Source: UNAMA, annual *POC* reports for 2008, 2009, 2010, 2011, 2012.

NATO ISAF's development and implementation of tactical directives aimed at reducing civilian killing in ISAF air operations seem to have paid off in reduced death. Specifically, NATO ISAF tactical directives on air power and escalation of force have resulted in fewer civilian casualties.

Afghans have paid particular attention to deaths caused by the air operations of international forces, and the numbers suggest that they have had good reason to be concerned with the NATO ISAF use of airpower. There can be little confusion about which side causes the death from the air, since the international forces and more recently the Afghan military are the only belligerents flying in Afghanistan. The attribution of cause is thus often quite clear. Further, the numbers of civilians killed by any single use of air power can be quite large, compared to the many more civilians killed in crossfire, or by the improvised explosive devices planted by insurgent forces. As General McKiernan described to me in April 2012 when the ISAF close air support bombings hurt civilians, a local person almost immediately used a cell phone to call officials in Kabul, which increased the pressure for Afghan officials to do something to stop the killing. So, for example, on 28 May 2011, when an airstrike killed another group of between nine and fourteen civilians, President Karzai protested, saying that "from this moment, airstrikes on the houses of people are not allowed." Karzai was adamant that "the Afghan people can no longer tolerate these

Table 2.4 **Causes of Civilian Casualties Attributed to Pro-Government Forces in Afghanistan, 2009-2010**

Tactic	2009	2010
Air attacks	358	171
Ground engagement	12	20
Mortar and rocket	27	51
Shooting	32	64
Other	30	9
Search raid	98	80
Escalation of force	39	45
Total	596	440

Sources: UN Monthly data, January-June 2010: UNAMA, Civilian Casualty Data, 24 February 2011, as released in J. Bohannon, *Science*, 331, 1256 (2011); UNAMA, annual *POC* reports for 2009 and 2010.

attacks."[130] An ISAF spokesperson, Major Sunset Belinski said in response that ISAF would coordinate with Karzai and that "coalition forces constantly strive to reduce the chance of civilian casualties and damage to structures, but when the insurgents use civilians as a shield and put our forces in a position where their only option is to use airstrikes, then they will take that option."[131]

Civilian casualties caused by air strikes will likely remain an issue however. First, there are still incidents of civilian killing during pre-planned airstrikes, such as when, on 16 September 2012, five NATO ISAF airstrikes killed eight civilians, four of them children. Second, the use of drone aircraft in strikes in Afghanistan has increased in recent years. In 2011, the United States launched 294 weapons from drones; in 2012, the United States launched 506 weapons from drones, resulting in sixteen civilian deaths.

Table 2.4, also based on United Nations data, shows a finer grained breakdown of the causes of civilian killing by pro-government forces in 2009 and 2010, where "other" causes of death are identified with more specificity.

There is some evidence for the concern that US forces took relatively greater risk when NATO ISAF was more conservative in the use of air power. This can be seen in the following diagram where the cause of civilian killing by pro-government forces is broken down by tactic each month for the period of January 2009 to June 2010. Recall, as I noted in chapter 1, that in mid-2009, as civilian collateral damage

---

[130] Karzai, quoted in Heidi Vogt and Rahim Faiez, "Afghan President Seeks to Limit NATO Airstrikes," 31 May 2011 http://www.armytimes.com/news/2011/05/ap-afghan-president-seeks-to-limit-NATO-airstrikes-053111/.

[131] Belinski, quoted in Vogt and Faiez, "Afghan President Seeks to Limit NATO Airstrikes."

death declined due to changes in ISAF rules of engagement, US and coalition military fatalities increased in Afghanistan. The tensions between civilian protection, force protection, and military necessity became evident to US soldiers. In the first six months of 2009, the number of US military fatalities averaged about twelve per month in Afghanistan. From July through December 2009, the incidence of US military fatalities in Afghanistan averaged about thirty-three per month.[132] The spike in both civilian airstrike death and US military deaths in February 2010 corresponds to the pro-government force offensive in Marjah (figure 2.4).

In sum, though number of civilian casualties in US and allied collateral damage incidents in the earlier years of the war are essentially unknown, I estimate that between a minimum of 17,000 to 19,000 civilians were killed in direct war-related violence from the invasion in 2001 through 2012 by all parties (figure 2.5).[133] Those concerned with civilian casualties caused by the United States and its allies want to know how many of those deaths can be attributed to pro-government forces. Using the (extremely thin) data for the early years of the war, and the much better work by the United Nations as described above for the period of 2008 through 2012, I estimate that more than 5,000 of the civilians killed by direct war violence can be attributed to US and allied/pro-government forces.[134] This is a conservative figure

[132] The June 2009 tactical directive would, of course, appear to have had a greater impact on civilian casualties due to airstrikes if the September 2009 Kunduz attack on the tankers, which killed more than 90 civilians had been avoided.

[133] For 2001-2006, I approximate as follows. In 2001, the Northern Alliance massacre of surrendered Taliban accounts for, at a minimum 1,500 noncombatant deaths. There were likely a minimum of additional 1,000-1,300 civilian deaths according to Conetta of the PDA and Zucchino of the *LA Times* due to allied bombing. Carl Conetta, "Operation Enduring Freedom: Why a Higher Rate of Civilian Bombing Casualties," Project on Defense Alternatives (PDA), *Briefing Report # 13*, 18 January 2002, revised 24 January 2002, http://www.comw.org/pda/0201oef.html. Also Human Rights Watch, *"Troops in Contact": Airstrikes and Civilian Deaths in Afghanistan* (New York: Human Rights Watch, 2008). Afghanistan NGO Safety Office, "ANSO Quarterly Data Report," Kabul, Afghanistan data from 2007, 2008, 2009, 2010 quarterly reports.

[134] My estimate is conservative and crude; its main virtue is transparency and consistency. For 2001, leaving aside the at least 1,500 soldiers killed in the Northern Alliance massacre, I assume that 1,000 collateral damage deaths were caused by the pro-government forces, specifically US airstrikes. See Conetta, "Operation Enduring Freedom"; Global Exchange, "Afghan Portraits of Grief: The Civilian/Innocent Victims of U.S. Bombing in Afghanistan" (San Francisco: Global Exchange, September 2002) http://peacefultomorrows.org/downloads/apogreport.pdf. The GE "survey [found] at least 824 Afghan civilians were killed between October 7 and January 2002 by the US-led bombing campaign"; David Zucchino, "The Untold War: 'The Americans...They Just Drop Their Bombs and Leave,'" *Los Angeles Times*, 2 June 2002; Chris Wilson and Jeremy Singer-Vine, "Afghanistan's Census of the Dead," *Slate*, 27 July 2010. http://www.slate.com/id/2261911/. For the years 2002-2006, for which there are almost no estimates, and a period when the fighting was much less intense, I use the assumption that pro-government forces (PGF) may be responsible for 40 percent of those civilian casualty deaths (PGF caused about 40 percent of the deaths in 2007 and 2008). For 2007-2011, I use annual *POC* reports, 2008-2011, for the actual numbers killed by PGF.

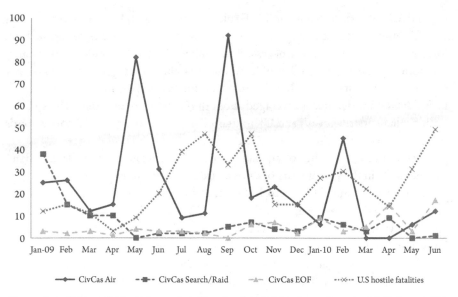

Figure 2.4 US hostile fatalities and civilian death in Afghanistan, January 2009–June 2010.
Source: UN Monthly data January–June 2010: United Nations Assistance Mission in Afghanistan (UNAMA), Civilian Casualty Data, 24 February 2011; as referred to in J. Bohannon, *Science* 331, 1256 (2011) and Icasualties, http://icasualties.org/oef/, accessed 1 May 2012.

for at least three reasons: first, in every year, there are some number of the total killed which be attributed to either side—between 6 and 13 percent of the total number killed. Second, the Afghanistan National Security Forces and local police generally refuse to acknowledge their responsibility for any civilian deaths and the UNAMA suggests that "it is highly likely that civilian casualties from ANSF are under-reported."[135] And third, when doubt exists about whether someone is a combatant or noncombatant, there may be a tendency to identify males as combatants.

But regardless of the exact number, the overall trends are clear. When the United States and the forces it either commands or has trained and operates alongside— namely NATO ISAF forces and Afghan National Security Forces—began to focus on reducing civilian casualties in Afghanistan, the number and percentage of civilian casualties attributable to those forces declined. The decline is associated with a series of tactical directives aimed at reducing civilian casualties.

Pakistan

If the number of civilians killed in Afghanistan was blurred by politics and the fog of war, the scene in Pakistan is much more difficult to decipher. Pakistan

---

[135] UNAMA, *Protection of Civilian in Armed Conflict* (Kabul: UNAMA, 2013), p. 38.

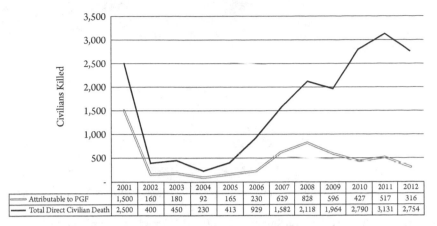

	2001	2002	2003	2004	2005	2006	2007	2008	2009	2010	2011	2012
Attributable to PGF	1,500	160	180	92	165	230	629	828	596	427	517	316
Total Direct Civilian Death	2,500	400	450	230	413	929	1,582	2,118	1,964	2,790	3,131	2,754

Figure 2.5 Estimated civilian casualties attributable to pro-government forces (PGF), Afghanistan 2001–2012.

Note that "Total Direct Civilian Death" included those deaths caused by all parties and those deaths that could not be attributed to any party to the conflict.

Sources: For 2008 through 2012, UNAMA, annual *POC* reports, 2008 to mid-year report 2012. For 2001–2007, see notes 122 and 123 in text.

was immediately entangled in the US war against the Taliban and al Qaeda in Afghanistan, first as a ground line of communication to Afghanistan for transit of war materiel, and later as an emerging front in the war. Specifically, much of the fuel, military equipment, and other supplies (about 70–80 percent at its peak) that the United States has used to wage war in Afghanistan has been transported overland through Pakistan from the port in Karachi.[136] Further, because the territorial boundary between Afghanistan and Pakistan does not mark a cultural divide for the Pashtun people who live in northwest Pakistan and southern Afghanistan, the border has never been a hard barrier. Indeed, many of the Taliban and al Qaeda militants the United States sought to kill after the 9/11 attacks fled Afghanistan, entering the northwest border region of Pakistan in late 2001 and early 2002. These militants, and other militant organizations, began operating training camps and organizing raids into Afghanistan from Pakistan, while their leaders plotted and organized further terrorist attacks. Militants also increasingly attacked US and NATO ISAF fuel tankers and other supplies destined for Afghanistan, as they moved through Pakistan. The US relationship with Pakistan has been complicated by the knowledge that at least some in the Pakistani security forces have tolerated and supported the very militants the United States sought to target.

After 2001 the United States increased military and economic monetary aid to Pakistan, sold and provided free weapons to Pakistan's military, and trained

---

[136] Other US fuel and materiel for the war in Afghanistan has been transported through Uzbekistan.

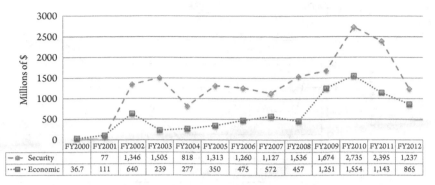

	FY2000	FY2001	FY2002	FY2003	FY2004	FY2005	FY2006	FY2007	FY2008	FY2009	FY2010	FY2011	FY2012
Security		77	1,346	1,505	818	1,313	1,260	1,127	1,536	1,674	2,735	2,395	1,237
Economic	36.7	111	640	239	277	350	475	572	457	1,251	1,554	1,143	865

Figure 2.6 US security and economic assistance to Pakistan, FY2000-FY2012, in current millions of $ US.
Source: Susan B. Epstein and K. Alan Kronstadt, "Pakistan: U.S. Foreign Assistance," 7 June 2011, Congressional Research Service, pp. 18–20; and Susan B. Epstein and K. Alan Kronstadt, "Pakistan: U.S. Foreign Assistance," 4 October 2012, Congressional Research Service, pp. 20–22.

Pakistan's military and paramilitary forces. Increased monetary assistance began just one week after the 9/11 attacks. On the same day that the US Congress voted to authorize the use of military force against terrorists, the Congress authorized emergency appropriations to Pakistan, and on 15 November 2001, the United States gave Pakistan $600 million in a cash transfer. From 2001 through 2012, the United States provided Pakistan about $17 billion in military assistance and almost $8 billion in economic assistance. Of this, the largest single item in the military assistance to Pakistan, about $10 billion, has been the Coalition Support Funds, used to compensate Pakistan for the use of airfields and seaports, and to keep more than 100,000 Pakistani military in the northwest of the country (figure 2.6).[137]

In addition to urging Pakistan, with US military equipment and training, to directly attack militants inside their country (discussed further below), the Bush and Obama administrations conducted direct attacks inside Pakistan in three ways that have led to civilian injuries and deaths.

First, apparently beginning in 2003, the United States conducted several covert special operations forces raids into Pakistan. US Special Forces have operated in northwestern Pakistan since 2008 either alongside the Pakistani military or by themselves.[138] For example, in late 2008, US Special Operations forces attacked three houses in South Waziristan, killing fifteen people. US officials said the

---

[137] Susan B. Epstein and K. Alan Kronstadt, "Pakistan: U.S. Foreign Assistance," Congressional Research Service Report, 4 October 2012, pp. 13 and 20.

[138] Declan Walsh, "WikiLeaks Cables: U.S. Special Forces Working Inside Pakistan," *The Guardian*, 30 November 2011, http://www.guardian.co.uk/world/2010/nov/30/wikileaks-cables-us-forces-embedded-pakistan.

targets were members of al Qaeda, but acknowledged that several civilians were killed, including women and at least one child.[139] Most well-known, of course, was the 2011 raid in which Special Forces attacked and killed Osama bin Laden. The Navy Seals who attacked the Bin Laden compound were under CIA command. Further, the US Central Intelligence Agency has, according to a November 2009 report in the *Los Angeles Times*, "funneled hundreds of millions of dollars" since the 11 September 2001 attacks to Pakistan's Inter-Services Intelligence (ISI) agency for help in tracking, capturing or killing militants in Pakistan, accounting for as much as a third of ISI's annual budget.[140] By early 2011, the United States had deployed about 150 Special Operations Forces as trainers in Pakistan, but about twenty-five to thirty trainers were "told to leave" according to a US military official, in late spring 2011, before the raid that killed Osama bin Laden.[141] In addition, although its operations are secret, it appears that the US Central Intelligence Agency is involved in targeted killing in Pakistan, which may also result in civilian casualties.[142]

Second, the US military and NATO ISAF forces operating in southern Afghanistan have pursued militants across the border into Pakistan. The Pak Institute for Peace Studies (PIPS) has found that many of those killed in the ISAF and Afghan military cross-border raids and clashes along the Afghanistan-Pakistan border are civilians.[143] But militants also target civilians and the Pakistani military along the border. From 2007 through 2012, PIPS reported 212 cross-border incidents where more than 906 Pakistani soldiers, civilians, and militants were killed and nearly 700 total were injured. Clashes in 2008 were particularly lethal: of the forty-seven clashes and cross-border attacks, ten incidents were between Pakistani

---

[139] Farhan Bokhari, Sami Ysafzai, and Tucker Reals, "U.S. Special Forces Strike in Pakistan," *CBS News*, 3 September 2008, http://www.cbsnews.com/stories/2008/09/03/terror/main4409288.shtml.

[140] Greg Miller, "CIA Pays for Support in Pakistan: It has Spent Millions Funding the ISI Spy Agency despite Fears of Corruption. But Some Say It Is Worth It," *Los Angeles Times*, 15 November 2009, http://articles.latimes.com/2009/nov/15/world/fg-cia-pakistan15.

[141] Karen DeYoung and Karin Brulliard, "Pakistan Ordered about a Fifth of U.S. Special Forces Trainers to Leave the Country as Relations Deteriorated," *Washington Post*, 20 May 2011, http://www.washingtonpost.com/world/bomb-targeted-at-us-vehicles-injures-13-in-pakistan-city/2011/05/20/AFryUb7G_story.html. Also see Rob Crilly and Toby Harnden, "US to Reduce Special Forces Presence in Pakistan," *The Telegraph*, 26 May 2011, http://www.telegraph.co.uk/news/worldnews/asia/pakistan/8538976/US-to-reduce-Special-Forces-presence-in-Pakistan.html.

[142] For example, although the circumstances are still unclear, Raymond Davis, a CIA employee, killed two Pakistanis in early 2010. US embassy personnel driving a car to remove Davis from the scene inadvertently killed a Pakistani civilian. CBS/AP, "Pakistan Judge Orders Arrest of U.S. Car's Driver," *CBS News*, 18 February 2011, http://www.cbsnews.com/stories/2011/02/18/501364/main20033286.shtml.

[143] Pak Institute for Peace Studies, *Pakistan Security Report*, for 2007, 2008, 2009, 2010, 2011, and 2012 (PIPS, Islamabad). Available at http://www.san-pips.com/index.php?action=reports&id=psr_list_1.

and NATO ISAF or Afghan forces; in that year, of the 388 people killed, 120 were civilians.[144]

Pakistani soldiers have also been harmed in these clashes, including when US and NATO ISAF forces cross the Pakistan border. There were sixteen such cross-border attacks in 2012. In one incident, in September 2010, NATO helicopters, crossing the border from Afghanistan into northwest Pakistan in pursuit of insurgents, killed three Pakistani soldiers. The incident caused Pakistan to close the border for more than a week, leading immediately to the backup of fuel tankers and trucks attempting to move supplies and fuel into Afghanistan. More than 150 trucks were then destroyed when they were forced to sit on the roads or in parking lots.[145] In May 2011, two Pakistani soldiers were injured in a firefight with ISAF forces that had crossed the border.[146] A November 2011 incident, when twenty-four Pakistani security forces were killed by NATO ISAF forces, prompted Pakistan to halt NATO ISAF transit into Afghanistan between November 2011 and early July 2012.

Finally, the United States has launched Predator and Reaper "drone" (unmanned, remotely piloted) aircraft attacks on militants leaders of Al Qaeda, the Haqqani network, and the Taliban in northwest Pakistan, and these attacks cause the majority of collateral damage deaths directly attributable to the United States.[147] US officials aim to kill militant leaders, and minimize the collateral damage, in drone strikes, but there are

[144] Pak Institute for Peace Studies, *Pakistan Security Report 2008* (Islamabad, PIPS, 2009), p. 13.

[145] Chris Brummit and Deb Riechman, "Pakistan Cuts NATO Supply Line after Border Firing," *Washington Post*, 30 September 2010, http://www.washingtonpost.com/wp-dyn/content/article/2010/09/30/AR2010093000491.html. Associated Press, "Pakistan Reopens Key Afghan Border Crossing to NATO Convoys," *The Guardian*, 10 October 2010, http://www.guardian.co.uk/world/2010/oct/10/pakistan-reopens-key-border-crossing-to-nato.

[146] Haris Anwar and James Rupert, "NATO Helicopters Cross into Pakistan, Spark Firefight with Border Guards," Bloomberg, 17 May 2011, http://www.bloomberg.com/news/2011-05-17/pakistan-troops-clash-with-nato-helicopters-in-afghanistan-border-region.html.

[147] Begun under the Bush administration there are actually two organizational lines of authority for the drone aircraft strikes under the US Central Intelligence Agency and the US military's Joint Special Operations Command (JSOC). The drones offer live high tech electro-optical and infrared real time video, and the ability to hover over a potential target for many hours. The drone cameras may transmit video feeds to US intelligence headquarters in the region, and to the United States, where the drone strike program is overseen by the US Central Intelligence Agency. The first use of US drones to target members of Al Qaeda and the Taliban occurred in Afghanistan in October 2001, when the United States struck against Mohammed Atef. Drones cost about 30 times less than a fighter aircraft and do not put US pilots at physical risk. Their pilots are located at Nellis Air Base in Nevada. The United States uses two kinds of drones for military strikes in Pakistan, the remotely piloted Predator and Reaper drones, which require a 2,000 foot length for takeoff and landing, and thus can be launched from small airfields to perform surveillance or airstrikes. Predator drones, originally meant simply for surveillance, have been modified to carry lightweight laser guided Hellfire missiles. The newer Reaper drone, which is different can operate from a much higher altitude and may be armed with an internal payload of up to 800 pounds and an external payload of 3,000 pounds. The Reaper can thus be armed with up to sixteen Hellfire missiles, although it usually carries four Hellfire IIs, and two

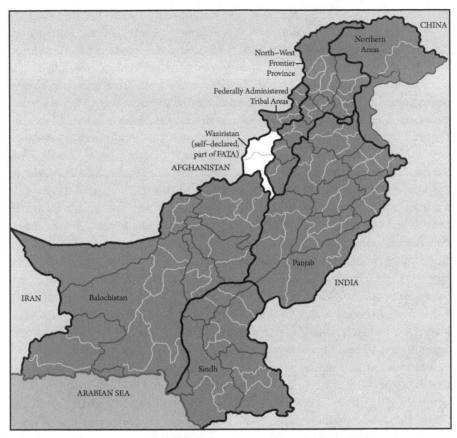

Figure 2.7 Map of Pakistan, highlighting the location of most US drone strikes (in white).

disputes about the identity of those killed. If the drone strikes kill relatively few civilians in comparison to the number of militant leaders or combatant, then the United States can argue that its drone strikes met the criteria of proportionality.[148] Both the Bush and Obama administrations have claimed that the drone strikes are surgical—killing militant leaders and harming relatively few others.

The first US drone attack in Pakistan's Waziristan region, in the northwest of the country (figure 2.7), against a member of the Taliban Nek Muhammad occurred on 18

500-pound laser-guided bombs. The ability of the newer Predator drone to loiter varies depending on payload—between 14 hours with weapons, and as much as 24-30 hours without external weapons or fuel stores. See Winslow T. Wheeler, "Revisiting the Reaper Revolution," *Time*, 27 February 2012, http://battleland.blogs.time.com/2012/02/27/1-the-reaper-revolution-revisited/, and Winslow T. Wheeler, "The MQ-9's Cost and Performance," *Time*, 28 February 2012, http://battleland.blogs.time.com/2012/02/28/2-the-mq-9s-cost-and-performance/.

[148] The idea that these strikes target the leadership of militant organizations is still, however, subject to the criticism that they violate the law against assassination.

June 2004.[149] A report in the *New York Times* described the event: "Residents said Mr. Muhammad was sitting in a courtyard with four other men eating dinner at 10 p.m. on Thursday when the missile struck. They said it hit the middle of where Mr. Muhammad and the men were sitting, leaving a crater 6 feet by 6 feet. All five men were killed."[150] In a lack of clarity that would come to characterize reporting on drone strikes, there were different accounts of who was killed in this strike. Several sources suggest that only combatants were killed. The *New York Times* says simply that Mohammad, a "27-year-old former Taliban fighter," was sitting with "four other men"; the New America Foundation counted four militants and one militant leader killed.[151] Other sources, located inside Pakistan, suggest that both civilians and militants were killed in the strike. For example, Pakistan Body Count tallies one militant and four civilians killed. The report in *Dawn*, a Pakistan newspaper describes those killed as Mohammad, and "four other militants" in the title and says "four other tribal militants" were killed. "Also killed were two sons of Nek's two mujahideen [sic] friends and his hosts, Fakhar Zaman and Azmat Khan."[152]

For many years, even as the Pakistani government cooperated with the US military and Central Intelligence Agency in identifying and locating Taliban and Al Qaeda targets, Pakistani officials denied that they gave permission for the drone strikes.[153] However, a Pakistani Major General, Ghayur Mehmood, acknowledged Pakistani involvement when he defended it to reporters in 2011: "Most of the targets are hardcore militants. The number of innocent people being killed is relatively low."[154]

But it is just that question—whether the number of civilians killed by drone strikes is low—which became a concern in Pakistan and may eventually come to constrain US military operations there. Indeed, Gregory McNeal argues that, in part, "the Obama administration was worried about collateral damage," when it chose to use Special Forces in April 2011—not drones—to attack the compound where Osama bin Laden was suspected to be hiding.[155] Nevertheless, the US Special

---

[149] Pakistani officials took credit for the killing, denying US involvement, although witnesses reported that they heard a drone flying overhead in the moments before the attack.

[150] David Rohde and Mohammed Khan, "Ex-Fighter for Taliban Dies in Strike in Pakistan," *New York Times*, 19 June 2004.

[151] New American Foundation, "2004-2007: The Year of the Drone," http://counterterrorism. newamerica.net/drones/2007; Scott Shane, "C.I.A. to Expand Use of Drones in Pakistan," *New York Times*, 3 December 2009, http://www.nytimes.com/2009/12/04/world/asia/04drones.html.

[152] Ismail Khan and Dilawar Khan Wazir, "Night Raid Kills Nek, Four Other Militants: Wana Operation," *Dawn*, 19 June 2004, http://archives.dawn.com/2004/06/19/top1.htm.

[153] Mark Mazzetti, "The Downside of Letting Robots Do the Bombing," *New York Times*, 22 March 2009, p. WK4.

[154] CNN Wire Staff, "Pakistan Acknowledges U.S. Drone Strikes Targeting Militants," CNN World, 10 March 2011, http://articles.cnn.com/2011-03-10/world/pakistan.drone. attacks_1_drone-strikes-militants-on-pakistani-soil-north-waziristan?_s=PM:WORLD.

[155] Gregory S. McNeal, "The bin Laden Aftermath: Why Obama Chose SEALS, Not Drones," *Foreign Policy.com*, http://blog.gsmcneal.com/2011/05/05/the-bin-laden-aftermath-why-obama-chose-seals-not-drones/.

Forces attack on bin Laden did prompt a rejection of US drone strikes. The Pakistani Parliament resolved on 14 May 2011 that "such drone attacks must be stopped forthwith, failing which the government will be constrained to consider taking necessary steps including withdrawal of (the) transit facility allowed to Nato."[156] On 21 May 2011, thousands of Pakistani civilians protested the strikes in Karachi, Pakistan. In late November 2011, in response to the border incident where the US killed twenty-four Pakistani soldiers, when Pakistan cut off NATO ISAF transport through the country to Afghanistan, the US drone strikes were temporarily halted.

From 2002 to early 2011, the United States hardly commented on the drone strikes in Pakistan and released little information about the effects of the drone strike program in Pakistan. But on occasion the Obama administration, through mostly unnamed sources, gave the number of civilians killed in drone strikes. For example, in May 2011, an administration official said that thirty noncombatants had been killed from the beginning of 2009 to that point, and none had been killed since the summer of 2010.

On the other hand, there were media reports and analysis of civilian death during this period that contradicted official accounts. For example, research by a nongovernmental organization, the US-based Campaign for Innocent Victims in Conflict (CIVIC) published in 2010, questioned US government claims that few civilians were harmed by drone strikes in Pakistan. "CIVIC's research and that of other independent nongovernment organizations indicates that the number of civilians killed and injured by drones is higher than the US admits."[157] CIVIC reported in 2010 that "since 2009, over 120 strikes have killed between an estimated 804-1367 people. The US government claims a civilian death toll of around 20 total, much lower than most other independent estimates." CIVIC found that "one strike alone in June 2009 killed 45-60 people, including up to 18 civilians." CIVIC reported that interviews in Pakistan with drone strike victims and others from the areas where drone strikes occurred "confirms that drones have struck civilians with no connection to militancy. Indeed, CIVIC uncovered more than 30 alleged civilian deaths in only nine cases investigated, all of which took place since January 2009."[158] CIVIC also noted that the US criteria for distinguishing between civilians and combatants were not available to the public, making it difficult to evaluate US claims. Similarly, a group of lawyers reviewed the evidence and conducted research in 2012 Pakistan and found evidence of many more civilian casualties than acknowledged by the US government.[159]

---

[156] AFP, "No Repeat of bin Laden Raid: Parliament," *Dawn*, 14 May 2011, http://www.dawn.com/2011/05/14/no-repeat-of-bin-laden-raid-parliament.html.

[157] Christopher Rogers, *Civilians in Armed Conflict: Civilian Harm and Conflict in Northwest Pakistan*, Campaign for Innocent Victims in Conflict (CIVIC), 2010, p. 2.

[158] Ibid., p. 15.

[159] Stanford Law School, International Human Rights and Conflict Resolution Clinic, and NYU School of Law Global Justice Clinic, "Living under Drones: Death, Injury and Trauma to Civilians from US Drone Practices in Pakistan," September 2012, http://livingunderdrones.org/.

If it were possible to pronounce with any degree of confidence that x number of civilians were killed by drone strikes, I would do so. But that is not possible. Most drone strikes in Pakistan occur in a remote and difficult to access region—in the areas of North and South Waziristan, part of the Federally Administered Tribal Areas (FATA). Residents of FATA have fewer civil rights protections than elsewhere in Pakistan, and the Pakistani courts have no jurisdiction there. The FATA region is governed under different laws (the Frontier Crimes Regulation) than the rest of Pakistan. Outside access to FATA is tightly controlled by the Pakistani government, few reporters have had access to the areas in northwest Pakistan, and there is a small NGO presence in the area. Thus, there is little or no opportunity for independent organizations or journalists to confirm police and other reports of drone strikes in FATA, making it difficult for NGOs to consistently assess the impact of the drone strikes and the fighting.[160] In addition, the movement of people who reside within the FATA region is controlled by curfews and Pakistani government restrictions on leaving the region. Finally, the Pakistani military and intelligence services, as well as the Taliban, practice intimidation and kill journalists reporting on the conflict there.

Given the difficulty in accessing FATA, how is it possible to describe the drone strikes and their effects? Several nongovernmental organizations collate information about drone strikes, regularly reporting the number and location of the strikes, and of how many and who were killed. The level of transparency and comprehensiveness of these sources varies. They rely on local police and news accounts supplemented by official statements.[161] On occasion, independent investigators visit the North and South Waziristan regions of FATA, but on occasion so much time has passed between the strike and the visit that it is difficult for investigators to determine what happened. The Stanford Law School, International Human Rights and Conflict Resolution Clinic, and the New York University School of Law Global Justice Clinic have sent investigators and compared several of the major public databases, discussed below, namely the Long War Journal (LWJ), the New America Foundation (NAF), and the Bureau of Investigative Journalism (BIJ).[162] I have included additional sources in my survey of the data, namely Pakistan Body Count (PBC), the Pak Institute for Peace

---

[160] The New America Foundation maps the strikes that it reports. See http://maps.google.com/maps/ms?ie=UTF8&hl=en&msa=0&msid=111611283754323549630.00047e8cdfc55d220dee7&ll=33.100745,70.444336&spn=4.41699,7.03125&t=p&z=7&source=embed.

[161] For a thorough discussion of the qualities of data gathering on drone strikes for 2010, see Jacob Beswick, "The Drone Wars and Pakistan's Conflict Casualties, 2010," Oxford Research Group, Working Paper, May 2011. http://oxfordresearchgroup.org.uk/publications/briefing_papers_and_reports/working_paper_drone_wars_and_pakistan%E2%80%99s_conflict_casualties.

[162] See, for instance, "Living under Drones."

Studies (PIPS), the Conflict Monitoring Center (CMC), all based in Pakistan, and the South Asia Terrorism Portal (SATP) database, kept by the Institute for Conflict Management in Delhi, India.[163]

There is relatively close agreement among the organizations that track US drone strikes about the number and trends of US drone strikes since 2004 in Pakistan. For example, observers agree that the number US drone strikes in Pakistan increased in 2008, and then more than doubled from 2009 to 2010. Table 2.5 shows the aggregate total of drone strikes for the period 2004-2012 recorded by several sources. The South Asia Terrorism Portal (SATP) records far fewer drone strikes than the other sources and as will be seen below, a lower number of persons killed. In sum, the nongovernmental organizations that track drone strikes in Pakistan are in general agreement about the number of drone strikes, each year.

The increase in CIA strikes in early 2010 are understood by some to be a response to the attack on a CIA base in Khost, Afghanistan, on 30 December 2009 that killed seven US personnel.[164] But the tempo of strikes had already increased before that assault.

General agreement on the number of strikes is about the only convergence among those organizations that attempt to keep aggregate figures about the strikes. Specifically, there are three key areas of disagreement. First, observers disagree about the total number of people killed in the strikes. For example, figure 2.8 illustrates the range of estimates for the number of people killed each year in the US drone strikes in Pakistan since 2004.[165] Because the aggregate counts of those killed are uncertain, some observers report a "low" or "minimum" estimate, and a "high" or "maximum" estimate, to indicate the range of uncertainty. Among these, the Bureau of Investigative Journalism, New America

---

[163] BIJ: Bureau of Investigative Journalism, http://www.thebureauinvestigates.com/category/projects/drone-data/; LWJ: Long War Journal, "Charting the Data for US Airstrikes in Pakistan, 2004–2013," http://www.longwarjournal.org/pakistan-strikes.php; NAF: New America Foundation, "The Year of the Drone," http://counterterrorism.newamerica.net/drones/; PBC: Pakistan Body Count, http://www.pakistanbodycount.org/ including data provided by PBC site administrator Zeeshan-ul-hassan Usmani, October 2012; SATP: South Asia Terrorism Portal, "Drone Attack in Pakistan: 2005-2013," http://www.satp.org/satporgtp/countries/pakistan/database/Droneattack. htm. Conflict Monitoring Center, "Drone Attacks in Pakistan," http://cmcpk.wordpress.com/drone-attacks-in-pakistan/; PIPS: Pak Institute for Peace Studies, Timeline, http://san-pips.com/index.php?action=reports&id=tml3. Updated 6 May 2012.

[164] Scott Shane and Eric Schmitt, "CIA Deaths Prompt Surge in Drone War," *New York Times*, 23 January 2010, p. A1.

[165] Pakistan Body Count has another category, "foreigners" killed. PBC also notes that when news sources are imprecise, it translates the word "many," to 8 casualties, and "several" to 4 casualties. http://www.pakistanbodycount.org/dattacks.php.

Table 2.5 **Comparing Sources Counts of Drone Strikes in Pakistan, 2004–2012**

	2004	2005	2006	2007	2008	2009	2010	2011	2012	Total
BIJ	1	3	3	5	38	55	128	75	48	356
CMC*				9	34	53	132	75	38	341
LWJ	1	1	3	5	35	53	117	64	46	325
NAF	1	3	2	4	36	54	122	72	48	342
PBC	1	2	3	4	36	50	109	73	51	329
PIPS	1	2	2	1	34	51	135	75	26	327
SATP		1	0	1	19	46	90	59	46	262

*CMC gives a total of nine drone strikes for 2004-2007, without disaggregating by year.

Sources: BIJ, The Bureau of Investigative Journalism; CMC, Conflict Monitoring Center; LWJ, Long War Journal; NAF, New America Foundation; PBC, Pakistan Body Count; PIPS, Pak Institute for Peace Studies; SATP, South Asia Terrorism Portal.

Foundation, and Pakistan Body Count are the most transparent and comprehensive in their sourcing.[166]

Figure 2.9 shows the total number of people each source reports killed from 2004 through 2012.

Second, there is significant disagreement about the number and proportion of civilians killed in US drone strikes. Figure 2.10 illustrates the counts and estimates for the number of civilians killed by the drone attacks in Pakistan compared to the total number of others killed. Most often sources describe those others as unknown, militants or members of specific groups such as Al Qaeda, Taliban, or even "foreigners." The comparison suggests a wide range of estimates of civilians versus combatants killed.

Why do these organizations disagree about the number of civilians killed? Which set of figures is more credible?[167] The divergence between these organizations counts

---

[166] Each strike has one or more often several sources with live links.

[167] Two of the most widely cited US sources of data on drone strikes, Long War Journal (LWJ) and New America Foundation (NAF), have been criticized as biased, either by their connection to a pro-war agenda or because of their reliance on limited media reporting in Pakistan. Specifically, a recent opinion piece in *Al Jazeera* by Mohammed Idrees Ahmad, for example, stated, "Like the LWJ, the NAF also relies on media reports and errs conspicuously on the side of official claims. For example, its data shows that, of the 287 Pakistanis killed so far this year, 251 were militants. This of course cannot be true, since a single incident—the March 17 killing of 38 pro-government tribal elders at a gathering in Datta Khel, North Waziristan—undermines these calculations." Ahmad concludes that "these civilian deaths were only acknowledged because the victims were known notables with favourable relations with the Pakistani government." Muhammad Idrees Amhad, "The Magical Realism of Body Counts," *Al Jazeera*, 13 June 2011, http://english.aljazeera.net/indepth/opinion/2011/06/2011613931606455. html. There are other differences in reporting that illustrate both the range of information available and

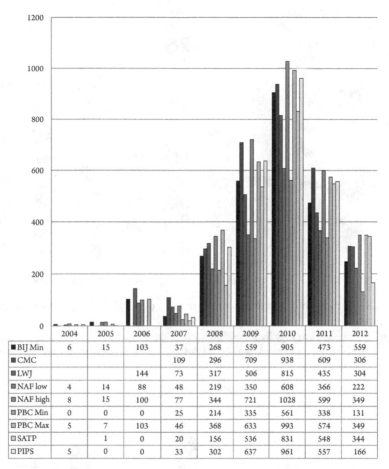

	2004	2005	2006	2007	2008	2009	2010	2011	2012
■ BIJ Min	6	15	103	37	268	559	905	473	559
■ CMC				109	296	709	938	609	306
■ LWJ			144	73	317	506	815	435	304
■ NAF low	4	14	88	48	219	350	608	366	222
■ NAF high	8	15	100	77	344	721	1028	599	349
▣ PBC Min	0	0	0	25	214	335	561	338	131
▣ PBC Max	5	7	103	46	368	633	993	574	349
▣ SATP		1	0	20	156	536	831	548	344
▢ PIPS	5	0	0	33	302	637	961	557	166

Figure 2.8 Estimates of total killed by US drone strikes in Pakistan, 2004–2012.
*NAF does not include a strike on 30 October 2006 in their total that may have killed "up to 80"militants.
Sources: BIJ: Bureau of Investigative Journalism; CMC: Conflict Monitoring Center; LWJ: Long War Journal; NAF: New America Foundation; PBC: Pakistan Body Count; SATP: South Asia Terrorism Portal; PIPS, Pak Institute for Peace Studies.Sources updated February 2013.

is rooted, in part, on how they define a civilian versus a combatant. Under the relevant international law, a civilian is defined as any person who is not a combatant; in case of doubt, a person shall be regarded as a civilian.[168] In 2012, members of the Obama administration, interviewed by reporters, indicated that the administration counts all military age males in the zone of a drone strike as combatants "unless

the divergence among sources in their understanding of the consequences of the US drone strikes. For instance, both the Bureau of Investigative Journalism and Pakistan Body Count report whether women and children are killed in strikes. Further those sources, as well as SATP and PIPS provide figures for the number injured in drone strikes.

[168] Geneva Convention IV Relative to the Protection of Civilian Persons in Time of War (1949) and Additional Protocols I and II to the Geneva Convention (1977).

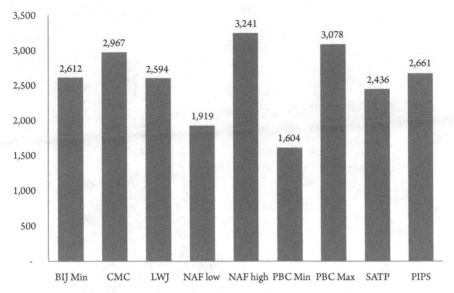

Figure 2.9 Comparison of estimates of total number of people killed by US drone strikes, 2004–2012.

Sources: BIJ: Bureau of Investigative Journalism; CMC: Conflict Monitoring Center; LWJ: Long War Journal; NAF: New America Foundation; PBC: Pakistan Body Count; Pak Institute for Peace Studies. SATP: South Asia Terrorism Portal; PIPS, Pak Institute for Peace Studies.

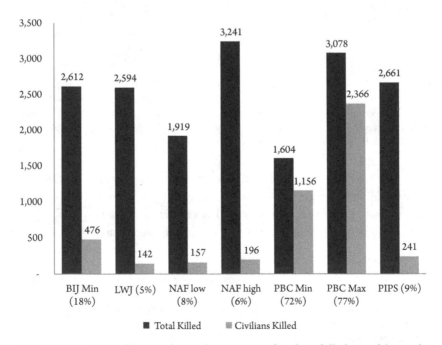

Figure 2.10 Estimates of the number and percentage of civilians killed out of the total killed by drone strikes in Pakistan, 2004–2012.

there is explicit intelligence posthumously proving them innocent." One Obama administration official told the reporters: "It bothers me when they say there were seven guys, so they must all be militants. They count the corpses and they're not really sure who they are."[169]

At the low end the Long War Journal (LWJ) counts civilians as about 5 percent of the total victims of drone attacks. The coordinators of the Long War Journal said in 2009 that "it is possible to get a rough estimate of civilian casualties by adding up the number of civilians reported killed from the media accounts of each attack. While our number is undoubtedly a low estimate, this extremely small percentage suggests that the accuracy and precision of these strikes have improved along with the increased pace of these strikes over the past few years."[170]

At the high end, the Pakistan Body Count estimates that about 77 percent of the victims of US drone strikes are civilians. The coordinator of Pakistan Body Count (PBC), Dr. Zeeshan Usmani said, "We classify all killed and injured as civilians, until it is clearly mentioned that they belonged to Taliban... Al-Qaeda, or any other terrorist group." The category " 'Suspected Fighters' is too vague a term to classify in any category." Usmani argues that "while the West like to call everyone 'Terrorist,' we take the opposite approach to classify everyone as 'Civilians' until proven otherwise." Usmani also said that when they receive more information "we change our counts accordingly."[171] The Pakistan Body Count rules more closely reflect the categories of civilian and combatant operative in international law.

Third, there are disagreements about the number of high-level militants killed in the strikes. The coordinators of the New America Foundation (NAF) dataset on drones give a range of "militants killed" and a range of "unknown" killed. NAF estimates are thus more nuanced, admitting that they simply cannot ascribe an identity to a large number of people killed in the US drone strikes from 2004 through 2012. This is shown in table 2.6.

At the same time that it increased the number of drone strikes, according to media reports, the criteria for targeting was loosened by the Obama administration.[172] David Cloud of the *Los Angeles Times*, reported his interviews of current and former counterterrorism officials that late in the Bush administration it was decided that the CIA would no longer be restricted to targeting individuals whose names are on an approved list. The Obama administration has apparently continued this policy. This means that more people may be killed, but it is uncertain that they

[169] Jo Becker and Scott Shane, "Secret 'Kill List' Proves a Test of Obama's Principles and Will," *New York Times*, 29 May 2012, p. 1.

[170] Bill Roggio and Alexander Mayer, "Analysis: U.S. Air Campaign in Pakistan Heats Up," 5 January 2010, http://www.longwarjournal.org/archives/2010/01/analysis_us_air_camp.php#ixzz1NvwWSOFH.

[171] Email communication, 31 May 2011.

[172] David S. Cloud, "CIA Drones have Broader List of Targets," *Los Angeles Times*, 5 May 2010. http://www.latimes.com/news/nationworld/world/la-fg-drone-targets-20100506,0,57614.story.

Table 2.6 **New America Foundation Estimates of People Killed in Drone Strikes, 2004–2012**

	2004	2005	2006	2007	2008	2009	2010	2011	2012
Low civilian	2	6	87	0	20	23	11	3	5
High civilian	2	6	99	0	32	27	16	9	5
Low unknown	1	4	0	0	21	59	16	27	23
High unknown	2	4	0	0	22	158	20	58	39
Low militant	1	4	1	48	176	266	570	336	194
High militant	5	5	1	77	289	538	991	535	317

Source: NAF.

are high- or even mid-level militant leaders. Obama assured the public that there were criteria for inclusion on the kill list, but those criteria remain largely secret. The US Department of Justice White Paper, drafted in November 2011, restricted discussion of criteria for targeted killing of US citizens who were senior leaders in al Qaeda.[173]

Regardless of the legal criteria for inclusion on the "kill list," the question remains of whether those killed qualify as senior operational leaders of militant organizations. In other words, have the strikes killed the senior leaders that the Bush and Obama administration set as their targets? The lack of transparency about drone strikes means it is difficult to determine how many high-level militant leaders, as opposed to foot-soldiers, have been killed.

Further, there is the question of proportionality. It took perhaps sixteen attempts from June 2008 to August 2009 with Hellfire missile strikes to kill one high-level militant in Pakistan, Baitullah Mehsood and several of his aides. In October 2009, Jane Mayer noted in these attempts to kill Mehsood, "between two hundred and seven and three hundred twenty-one additional people were killed, depending on which news accounts you rely upon."[174] David Kilcullen and Andrew Exum reported in May 2009 that "over the last three years drone strikes have killed about 14 terrorist leaders" in Pakistan. Kilcullen who served in the Australian armed forces and was an advisor to US General Petraeus from 2006 to 2008, and Exum, who served in the US Army in Iraq and Afghanistan, argued that the kills were not worth the

---

[173] U.S. Department of Justice White Paper, "Lawfulness of a Lethal Operation Directed Against a U.S. Citizen Who is a Senior Operational Lader of Al-Qa'ida or An Associated Force," Draft 8 November 2011.

[174] Jane Mayer, "The Predator War," *The New Yorker*, 26 October 2009, p. 45.

costs: "according to Pakistani sources, they [the drone strikes] have also killed some 700 civilians. This is 50 civilians for every militant killed, a hit rate of 2 percent— hardly 'precision.'" Kilcullen and Exum conceded that their own numbers may be less than precise, but "nevertheless, every one of these dead noncombatants represents an alienated family, a new desire for revenge, and more recruits for a militant movement that has grown exponentially even as drone strikes have increased."[175] Similarly, Peter Bergen and Katherine Tiedman of the New America Foundation said in late 2010: "US officials continue to claim (anonymously, of course) that only 1 or 2 percent of those killed by the strikes are civilians, and other estimates of civilian deaths range from a high of 98 percent down to 10 percent of the total fatalities." Bergen and Tiedman continue, "The majority of those killed appear to be lower or midlevel militants; of the some 1,260 militants reported killed in the strikes since 2004, only 36, or around 2 percent, have been leaders of al Qaeda, the Taliban, or other militant groups."[176]

Below are two unofficial counts of the number of those killed who are the targets of the US drone killing program, what the New America Foundation calls "militant leaders" and what the Pak Institute for Peace Studies calls "reportedly high value targets" killed in US drone strikes from 2004 to 2012.[177] If these counts are right, only 1.6 percent of the 3,241 total killed in the NAF analysis, and 2.6 percent of the total 2,661 killed according to the Pak Institute for Peace Studies, killed by US drone strikes from 2004 to 2012 were militant leaders. These figures raise questions about whether the drone strikes have been "surgical" as claimed by the United States.

Reports about specific incidents illustrate the difficulties in coming to an assessment of effects of drone strikes. A strike on 3 September 2008 by US forces against Al Qaeda in Pakistan produced a dispute about the number and identities of civilian casualties. While the Pakistani military said that about twenty people were killed, including seven villagers, the United States said one child and several women were killed.[178] On 23 June 2009, a drone attack targeting militants during a funeral outside the village of Makeen, reportedly killed between two and six militants and dozens, "possibly as many as eighty six," civilians.[179] Associated Press reported eighty

[175] David Kilcullen and Andrew McDonald Exum, "Death From Above, Outrage Down Below," *New York Times*, 17 May 2009. Also see Andrew Exum, Nathaniel C. Fick, Ahmed A. Humayun, and David J. Kilcullen, "Triage: The Next Twelve Months in Afghanistan and Pakistan," *Center for a New American Security*, June 2009; Amir Mir, "60 Drone Hits Kill 14 Al-Qaeda Men, 687 Civilians," 10 April 2009, *The News*, http://web.archive.org/web/20090610204750/http://www.thenews.com.pk/top_story_detail.asp?Id=21440.

[176] Peter Bergen and Katherine Tiedemann, "The Hidden War," *Foreign Policy*, 21 December 2010, http://www.foreignpolicy.com/articles/2010/12/21/the_hidden_war?page=0,5.

[177] See NAF, "The Year of the Drone: Leaders Killed," http://counterterrorism.newamerica.net/about/militants.

[178] Pir Zubair Shah, Eric Schmitt, and Jane Perlez, "NATO Accused of Civilian Deaths inside Pakistan," *New York Times*, 4 September 2008.

[179] Mayer, "The Predator War," p. 45.

Table 2.7 **Estimates of the Number of Militant Leaders Killed by US Drone Strikes**

	2004	2005	2006	2007	2008	2009	2010	2011	2012	total
NAF	1	2	0	0	14	10	8	10	6	51
PIPS	1	1	2	0	19	16	19	7	3	68

deaths in that strike.[180] A witness described one attack in January 2010 on the village of Sanzalai as a first and then second strike that killed and wounded more villagers: "Just when people gather at the scene to retrieve the bodies and pull out the wounded, another missile struck an hour later."[181]

Exum told the journalist Jane Mayer: "We're not saying that drones are not part of the strategy. But we are saying they are part of the problem. If we use tactics that are killing people's brothers and sons, not to mention their sisters and wives, we can work at cross-purposes with insuring that the tribal population doesn't side with the militants. Using Predator is a tactic, not a strategy."[182] Some Pakistani civilians have apparently come to fear the drones more than they fear the Taliban and al Qaeda.[183] Indeed, while many Pakistanis remained unaware of the drone strike program, a survey conducted by the Pew Research Center in May 2011 found that among those who knew about the strikes almost 90 percent believed that the drone attacks "kill too many innocent people."[184]

Directly caused US collateral damage harm in the northwestern region of Pakistan is a small part of the harm to civilians in Pakistan due to war since 2001. The Pak Institute for Peace Studies counts nearly about 13,500 killed and more than 25,000 injured in armed conflicts in Pakistan from 2007 to early 2012.[185] Civilians are caught in the crossfire of a war between the Pakistani military and militants. Anti-government militant organizations, including the Taliban in Pakistan, have killed and injured many thousands of civilians and police inadvertently, in the crossfire with Pakistani security forces. Further, Pakistani militants target US fuel tankers and other trucks en route through Pakistan to the war in Afghanistan. Between

---

[180] Rohan Sullivan, "US Drone Attack Claims 80 Lives in Pakistan," *The Guardian*, 24 June 2009, http://www.guardian.co.uk/world/feedarticle/8575556.

[181] Ismail Khan and Salman Masood, "U.S. Drone Strikes Reported in Pakistan's Tribal Region," *New York Times*, 7 January 2010, p. A18.

[182] Exum, quoted in Mayer, "The Predator War," p. 45.

[183] Exum, Fick, Humayun, and Kilcullen, "Triage," p. 19.

[184] Pew Research Center, Pew Global Attitudes Project, "U.S. Image in Pakistan Falls No Further Following bin Laden Killing," 21 June 2011, p. 20.

[185] Pak Institute for Peace Studies, "PIPS Digital Database on Conflict and Security," http://san-pips.com/app/database/index.php?action=main&id=2, accessed 7 May 2012.

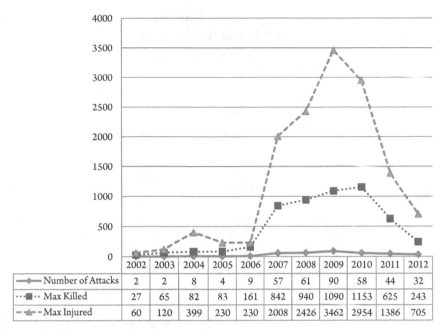

	2002	2003	2004	2005	2006	2007	2008	2009	2010	2011	2012
Number of Attacks	2	2	8	4	9	57	61	90	58	44	32
Max Killed	27	65	82	83	161	842	940	1090	1153	625	243
Max Injured	60	120	399	230	230	2008	2426	3462	2954	1386	705

Figure 2.11 Militant suicide attacks in Pakistan, 2002–2012.
Source: PBC, http://www.pakistanbodycount.org/.

January 2007 and December 2012 there were more than 330 such attacks, causing eighty civilian deaths. In 2012, twenty-seven attacks on NATO supplies in 2012 led to five civilian deaths.[186]

Pakistani insurgents have also deliberately attacked civilians. For instance, as figure 2.11 shows, 355 suicide attacks by insurgents killed a maximum estimated 5,200 and injured a maximum of about 13,600 Pakistani civilians in the period between 2002 and late October 2012.

The Pakistani military has also killed civilians in their counterinsurgency and counterterrorism operations in the northwest and elsewhere in Pakistan. The Pakistani security forces' operations (including military and paramilitary forces) have included the use of significant military force using F-16 strikes, mortar attacks, and raids on militant camps. In June 2009, the chief of the Pakistani Armed Forces, General Ashfaq Parvez Kayani described the dilemma Pakistan's armed forces faced. "Terrorists are the enemies of Pakistan and enemies of Islam. We have to eliminate them." Yet, Kayani acknowledged, "in the present circumstances…it is difficult to differentiate between friend and enemy." He said, "The problem is that you have to separate black from

---

[186] Pak Institute for Peace Studies database and "Pakistan Security Report 2012," p. 29. SATP records 266 such attacks from 2008 through 2012. http://www.satp.org/satporgtp/countries/pakistan/database/natoattack.htm, accessed March 2013.

Table 2.8 "People" Killed and Injured
by Pakistani Security Force
Operational Attacks, 2008–2012

Year	Killed	Injured
2008	3182	2267
2009	6329	3181
2010	2631	1495
2011	1046	384
2012	960	469
Total	14148	7796

Source: Pak Institute for Peace Studies (PIPS)
Security Reports for 2008-2012.

white...to avoid collateral damage."[187] Some attribute a share of moral responsibility to the United States for the Pakistani military's collateral damage harm to civilians. Whether the United States, which has supplied some of the military equipment, training, and money for Pakistan to conduct these counterinsurgency operations, is morally responsible for Pakistani collateral damage to civilians is of course debatable.

However one attributes accountability for this killing, Pakistani counterinsurgency operations have taken a toll on civilians—though the scale of destruction is unclear. Most civilians killed and injured by Pakistani military forces are harmed by artillery and mortar fire. Others are killed when fixed wing aircraft and helicopters use bombs or open fire with heavy guns. In 2008, according to the Pak Institute for Peace Studies, Pakistani security forces killed 3,182 people, more than the number killed by terrorists attacks. Table 2.8 provides the Pak Institute for Peace Studies counts for "people" killed by the Pakistani security forces for 2008–2012.

Paramilitary forces account for some of the harm to Pakistanis. For instance, a 400-person paramilitary commando unit, part of the Frontier Corps, trained by US Special Forces to operate in the tribal areas, has also hurt civilians.[188] Pakistanis were shocked in May 2011 when the Frontier Corp killed five unarmed people in Quetta, Balochistan. But, according to the Pak Institute for Peace Studies, operational attacks have killed about 14,100 people in Pakistan from 2008 through 2012. Some of these are undoubtedly militants, but an unknown portion of this number is civilians. Pak Institute for Peace Studies records a total of 17,000 civilian deaths by all parties for the period of 2002-2012.[189]

[187] Kayani, quoted in Associated Press, "Pakistan Chief Warns against Civilian Deaths," MSNBC, 15 June 2009, http://www.msnbc.msn.com/id/31374284#storyContinued.

[188] See Eric Schmitt and Jane Perlez, "U.S. Secretly in Pakistan Lends Ally Support," New York Times, 22 February 2009, http://www.nytimes.com/2009/02/23/world/asia/23terror.html.

[189] Pak Institute for Peace Studies database, accessed 20 March 2013.

Further, Pakistan, which governs its northwest region under British colonial era law, has been accused of collective punishment and extrajudicial killings of suspected militants, their relatives, and potential supporters of militants. Human Rights Watch reported that "since September 2009, when the Pakistani military re-established control over the [Swat] valley, Human Rights Watch has received numerous credible reports of collective punishment, including arbitrary detention, forced evictions, and house demolitions by the military and police. Human Rights Watch has investigated these allegations on the ground in Swat since February 2010, and documented scores of abuses."[190] Further, Human Rights Watch investigated reports of extrajudicial killing in the Swat Valley in February 2010. They researched "alleged human rights violations in Swat based on an initial list of 238 suspicious killings provided by local sources and the independent Human Rights Commission of Pakistan. Human Rights Watch has corroborated about 50 of these cases."[191] Finally, the Pakistani Army has also enlisted or coerced, depending perhaps on perspective, some local tribesmen in Khyber to fight the Taliban; they were told to fight or leave the area in April 2011. Some chose to stay and fight, but thousands left the region, becoming internally displaced.

In sum, I have emphasized that there is significant variation in the estimates and counts of Pakistani civilians directly harmed by US operations. However, I suggest that if one uses moderate estimates of civilians killed by the US drone strikes and NATO-ISAF cross-border raids, between 500 and 2,300 civilians have been killed directly by US and allied forces from 2004 to mid-October 2012. Beyond that, the number of civilians killed by the Pakistani military forces allied with the United States in the counterinsurgency is extremely difficult to grasp. If we subtract approximately 5,200 civilians killed by militants in suicide attacks from the total 17,000 civilians killed between 2002 and 2012, it is plausible to argue that the Pakistani counterinsurgency has directly cost more than 10,000 civilian lives.

Iraq

The United States was at great pains to underscore its commitment to avoid harming civilians in Iraq during the invasion in 2003 and its subsequent occupation of Iraq

---

[190] Human Rights Watch, "Pakistan: End Collective Punishment in Swat," 22 July 2010, http://www.hrw.org/en/news/2010/07/21/pakistan-end-collective-punishment-swat.

[191] "In no case examined by Human Rights Watch was a killing falsely reported, suggesting that the total number of killings is as high as or greater than those reported. The information for each case includes names or numbers of victims, place names, and dates. To date, the Pakistani military has not held any of the perpetrators accountable for these killings." Human Rights Watch, "Pakistan: Extrajudicial Executions by Army in Swat," 16 July 2010, http://www.hrw.org/en/news/2010/07/16/pakistan-extrajudicial-executions-army-swat.

through 2011. Before the invasion, the Pentagon invited reporters to hear how civilian casualties would be minimized in the air war.[192] Chairman of the Joint Chiefs of Staff Richard Myers emphasized that in US "targeting, we'll go to extraordinary lengths to protect non-combatants and civilians and—and facilities that should not be struck. And we always do that."[193] The use of precision weapons was highlighted by US officials; when civilians were killed, the US military spokespersons tended to emphasize the great care that had been taken to minimize effects on civilians. American leaders did not predict a swift military victory, but neither did they plan for a prolonged war, the following insurgency and counterinsurgency, or the sectarian violence and criminality that raged for many years. As promised, the United States did go to some lengths to keep collateral damage to a minimum. However, collateral damage and, much more rarely, deliberate killing of civilians occurred during the US war and occupation.

Given the high level of prewar economic development and the presence of many reporters, the potential for gauging the scale of harm to civilians in Iraq was comparatively good. The war and occupation produced large numbers of the kinds of casualties associated with war—direct deaths and injuries due to combat-related violence (including the three kinds of collateral damage); violent deaths and injuries due to lawlessness—such as military atrocity and revenge killing; deaths and injuries due to accidents related to military occupation, such as traffic accidents; and the indirect harm to health that results from the destruction of infrastructure and the lingering environmental effects of war.

The focus here is on deaths due to war violence. The Iraq Body Count (IBC) records more than 116,900 civilian deaths due to armed violence between the March 2003 invasion and December 2011, when the United States formally exited Iraq.[194] Figure 2.12 shows the figures for Iraqi civilian death from Iraq Body Count and the Brooking Institution, "Iraq Index." As the figure shows, the peak of civilian death occurred between 2004 and 2008. The war's violence diminished after 2008, although it certainly did not end for civilians. In addition to the civilian toll through December 2011, when the United States completed its military withdrawal, more than 4,400 US soldiers were killed in the war, more than 10,000 Iraqi police and Iraqi military forces

---

[192] Senior Defense Official, "Background Briefing on Targeting," 5 March 2003, http://www. defense.gov/transcripts/transcript.aspx?transcriptid=2007.

[193] Matt Lauer and Katie Couric, "General Richard Myers, chairman, Joint Chiefs of Staff, Discusses Preparing for a Possible War with Iraq," Today Show, NBC-TV, 27 February 2003, 7:00 A.M.

[194] The Brookings Institution's "Iraq Index" gives a similar number. The Brookings data was, for some years, derivative of the Iraq Body Count Data and their close correspondence should not be a surprise. Brookings uses IBC data as a starting point for 2003 to 2005 and then increased those counts by a rate of 1.75 to reflect the fact that "estimates for civilian casualties from the Iraqi Ministry of the Interior were 75 percent higher than those of our Iraq Body Count-based estimate over the aggregate May 2004-December 2005 period." In May 2010, Brookings began using Iraqi government figures. Michael E. O'Hanlon and Ian Livingston, "Iraq Index: Tracking Variables of Reconstruction and Security in Post-Saddam Iraq," Brookings, 29 May 2011, pp. 3 and 32.

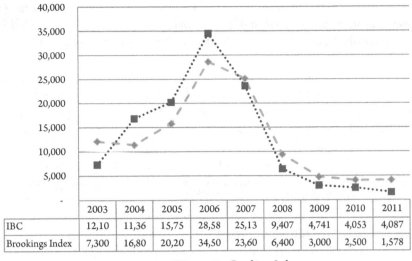

	2003	2004	2005	2006	2007	2008	2009	2010	2011
IBC	12,10	11,36	15,75	28,58	25,13	9,407	4,741	4,053	4,087
Brookings Index	7,300	16,80	20,20	34,50	23,60	6,400	3,000	2,500	1,578

—◆— IBC   ··■·· Brookings Index

Figure 2.12 Brookings Iraq Index and Iraq Body Count record of Iraqi civilian deaths from violence, 2003-2011.
Source: Brookings, "Iraq Index," http://www.brookings.edu/iraqindex; Iraq Body Count, http://www. iraqbodycount.org/database/. Iraq Body Count, Documented Civilian Deaths from Violence, Monthly table, http://www.iraqbodycount.org/database/, accessed 14 May 2012. Note that IBC includes five deaths from January–February 2003; IBC also notes that a full analysis of the WikiLeaks War Logs may add more than 13,000 deaths besides those they have already incorporated from the Wikileaks data.

were killed by insurgents or in friendly fire incidents from June 2003 through July 2011.[195] But these are only the recorded deaths—methods using cluster sampling suggests that the *unrecorded* violent war deaths may be a multiple of recorded number.[196] However, we may never know. Despite the fact that the numbers are low, I am only confident drawing conclusions about the pattern of "collateral damage" civilian killing using recorded war deaths.

[195] More than 4,480 US soldiers were killed in Operations Iraqi Freedom and New Dawn, from 2003 to 2011. More than 32,000 were wounded according to the US Department of Defense, though this number is almost certainly an undercount. The number of Iraqi Military and Police killed is from Brookings Institution, Michael E. O'Hanlon and Ian Livingston, "Iraq Index: Tracking Variables of Reconstruction and Security in Post-Saddam Iraq," Brookings Institution, February 2012, p. 4. In addition, more than 10,100 Iraqi Security Forces were killed from June 2003 through July 2011. See http://www.icasualties.org/Iraq/IraqiDeaths.aspx, accessed 14 May 2012.

[196] See Barry S. Levy and Victor Sidel, "Adverse Health Consequences of the Iraq War," *The Lancet*, vol. 381 (16 March 2013): 949–948; Frederick Burkle, Jr. and Richard Garfield, "Civilian Mortality after the 2003 Invasion of Iraq," *The Lancet*, vol. 381 (16 March 2013): 877–879. Also see Christine Tapp, Frederick M. Burkle, Jr., Kumanan Wilson, Tim Takaro, Gordon H. Guyatt, Hani Amad, and Edward J. Mills, "Iraq War Mortality Estimates: A Systematic Review," *Conflict and Health*, vol. 2 (7 March 2008), http://www.ncbi.nlm.nih.gov/pmc/articles/PMC2322964/.

Despite enormous media attention to incidents where soldiers violate the laws of war, a small portion of civilian deaths at coalition hands occurred when soldiers deliberately killed Iraqi civilians—perhaps about 1 percent.[197] Rather, the majority of the civilians killed by the United States and other coalition members were "collateral damage"—accidents, systemic collateral damage, and proportionality/double effect killing. There is no good count of traffic accident death caused by US and coalition forces, though the compensation records of the Foreign Claims Act program in Iraq, when fully available, may suggest how many died in noncombat-related incidents.[198]

Of the total number or Iraqi civilians killed in the war, Iraq Body Count documented 14,781 violent deaths caused by the US coalition during the US war and occupation.[199] This is 13 percent of all recorded violent deaths during that period. Almost half of the US- and coalition-caused collateral damage deaths occurred during the first 12 months of the fighting and occupation. IBC also noted in early 2013 that a full analysis of the WikiLeaks War Logs, which are the US military's own records, may add more than 12,000 deaths besides those they have already incorporated from the Wikileaks data. If so, and if the ratio of 13 percent holds, an additional 1,560 deaths could be attributed to the United States, bringing the total of recorded US-caused civilian deaths to more than 16,300.[200]

Again, there is the problem of recording. The US military apparently did not make a systematic account of Iraqi casualties in the early weeks of the war, nor did it make public many estimates or detailed accounts of civilian death unless in response to an undeniable tragedy. The US Department of Defense began to make more of its data public over the years, but the releases were periodic, often incomplete, and did not include all the years of the war.[201] The Pentagon often said it did not have good data. In late 2005, the *New York Times* noted the "first public disclosure that the United States military is tracking some of the deaths of Iraqi civilians." The figures were partial, tracking only those civilians killed or wounded by insurgents and observers suggested that those numbers were low.[202] Another US estimate

---

[197] Based on figures for short duration events, in Madelyn Hsiao-Rei Hicks, Hamit Dardagan, Gabriela Guerrero Serdan, Peter Bagnall, John Sloboda, Michael Spagat, "Violent Deaths of Iraqi Civilians: Analysis by Perpetrator, Weapon, Time and Location," *PLOS Medicine*, vol. 8, no. 2 (February 2011): 5.

[198] For a discussion, see John Fabian Witt, "Form and Substance in the Law of Counterinsurgency Damages," *Loyola of Los Angeles Law Review*, vol. 41 (2007-2008): 1455–1481.

[199] Iraq Body Count, "Iraq Deaths from Violence 2003-2011," 2 January 2012, http://www.iraqbodycount.org/analysis/numbers/2011/, accessed 14 May 2012. As of this writing, IBC had not yet completed its research and expected to add to this count based on new released materials.

[200] Of course, the ratio may not hold—there may be a bias in the war deaths that were unrecorded.

[201] See "Measuring Security and Stability in Iraq," http://www.defense.gov/home/features/iraq_reports/index.html.

[202] Sabrina Tavernise, "U.S. Quietly Issues Estimate of Iraqi Civilian Casualties," *New York Times*, 30 October 2005, http://www.nytimes.com/2005/10/30/international/middleeast/30civilians. html?pagewanted=2&_r=2&&fta=y;pagewanted=all.

for Iraqi casualties, given in late 2010 by the US Central Command, is 76,939 total Iraqi security and civilians killed, and 121,649 wounded for the period of January 2004 to August 2008.[203]

Official Iraqi reporting was also intermittent and incomplete. Iraq's Ministry of Health's statistics department was ordered to stop counting the civilian dead in late 2003, by some reports at the insistence of the US-led Coalition Provisional Authority. Reporting has been intermittent since that time.[204] In October 2009, the Iraqi Ministry of Human Rights gave an estimate of 85,694 people killed and 147,195 wounded for the period January 2004 to 31 October 2008.[205] Hannah Fischer of the Congressional Research Service suggested that the Ministry figures only included those who died as a result of insurgent attacks or displacement, suggesting that they did not include deaths due to fighting between groups within Iraq or due to the United States and other coalition forces occupation of Iraq.[206]

Second, as I have demonstrated with respect to Afghanistan and Pakistan, the way one counts the dead, tallies public records, or estimates the human toll can produce what appear to be, and sometimes are, dramatically different figures. To a certain extent, the uncertainties associated with counting casualties and the disputes between advocates of different approaches has focused attention on the methods and controversies associated with the studies, rather than on the dead and wounded in Iraq.

The most widely cited source on Iraqi civilian deaths, Iraq Body Count, as described above, tallies publicly recorded deaths of civilians by violent means. It relies on cross-checking media reports and supplementing those reports with morgue and hospital accounts. Since the beginning of the war, IBC regularly scanned more than two hundred media sources, mostly English language or translations, and cross-checked their data. IBC does not count the deaths of insurgents and security forces or the excess or indirect nonviolent deaths that are attributable to war.[207] IBC has acknowledged that their numbers are likely an undercount and noted that the new information on civilian deaths contained in WikiLeaks releases

[203] Lara Jakes, Associated Press, "U.S. Says Iraq War led to 77k Deaths over 5 Years," Salon.com, 14 October 2010. Associated Press, "U.S. Military Tallies Deaths of Iraqi Civilians," *New York Times*, 14 October 2010.

[204] Associated Press, "Iraq's Health Ministry Ordered to Stop Counting Civilian Dead from War," *USA Today*, 10 December 2003, http://www.usatoday.com/news/world/iraq/2003-12-10-iraq-civilians_x.htm.

[205] Michael Todd, "Iraq's Official Death Toll Supports Unofficial Tally," *Miller-McCune*, 15 October 2009, http://www.miller-mccune.com/politics/iraq-official-death-toll-supports-unoffici al-tally-3406/.

[206] Hannah Fischer, "Iraq Casualties: U.S. Military Forces and Iraqi Civilians, Police, and Security Forces," Congressional Research Service, 7 October 2010, p. 2.

[207] The Brookings Institution made estimates based on the Iraq Body Count, but later adjusted them to reflect figures released by the Iraqi and US governments. "Information for May 2003-December 2005 is based upon data from Iraq Body Count. The data for war-related fatalities was calculated at 1.75 times

would increase their total by more than 12,000 civilian deaths. Further, Iraq Body Count acknowledges that not all violent deaths have been reported and that because their data set counts only publicly reported data, they are an undercount of violent war death in Iraq.[208] In addition, IBC notes that there is often uncertainty about whether someone is a combatant or noncombatant. As John Tirman notes, the problem of identification may be a significant cause of undercounting civilian death. Sources that count civilian dead rely on a determination of who is a civilian and who is a combatant: "But who is the source of such an identification? It was often coalition forces, which frequently overstated the number of 'insurgents' killed in their operations."[209]

Supplementing the IBC numbers with Wikileaks data and official Iraqi reports will still produce a number for civilian direct death that is too low. Iraqi officials at the Ministry of Health may have been systematically encouraged to underreport deaths. One person who worked at the Baghdad central morgue statistics office told National Public Radio: "By orders of the minister's office, we cannot talk about the real numbers of deaths. This has been the case since 2004.... I would go home and look at the news. The minister would say 10 people got killed all over Iraq, while I had received in that day more than 50 dead bodies just in Baghdad. It's always been like that—they would say one thing, but the reality was much worse."[210]

Passive recording of civilian deaths, as reported by the media, and even by morgues, may be inadequate, but much of the criticism of civilian casualty counting in the Iraq war has focused on one particular form of research, public health surveys that use cluster sampling methods. For example, three studies of the effects of war on Iraqi civilians employed the household cluster sample survey method commonly used in public health research. The first, published in 2004 in the British medical journal *The Lancet*, and commonly referred to as the *Lancet* study, estimated that about 98,000 excess deaths (over the number that would have occurred in Iraq without war) in Iraq from 19 March 2003 to 16 September 2004. The second, a 2006, study also published in, the *Lancet*, gives a range of between

our IBC-based numbers, reflecting the fact that estimates for civilian casualties from the Iraqi Ministry of the Interior were 75 percent higher than those of our Iraq Body Count-based estimate over the aggregate May 2003–December 2005 period. During this time, we separately studied the crime rate in Iraq, and on that basis estimated 23,000 murders throughout the country. In order to add these back in to our estimate, we used estimated monthly murder rates for Baghdad as a guide in proportionally allocating these 23,000 additional fatalities. CENTCOM, Unclassified briefing slides (monthly through April 2010)." Michael E. O'Hanlon, and Ian Livingston, "Iraq Index: Tracking Variables of Reconstruction & Security in Post-Saddam Iraq," Brookings Institution, 9 December 2010, pp. 3 and 44.

[208] Iraq Body Count, http://www.iraqbodycount.org/about/.

[209] John Tirman, *The Deaths of Others: The Fate of Civilians in America's Wars* (Oxford: Oxford University Press, 2011), p. 332.

[210] Lourdes Garcia-Navarro, "Iraq: Though Numbers Unclear, Iraqi Deaths Touch Many," National Public Radio, 24 February 2009, http://www.npr.org/templates/story/story.php?storyID=100145401.

426,000 and 793,000 killed after the invasion through July 2006.[211] More specifically, the authors estimated about 655,000 excess deaths, of which they suggested some 601,000 were due to violent causes. A study published in *The New England Journal of Medicine*, conducted by the Iraq Family Health Survey Study Group, surveyed a larger number of household clusters than the *Lancet* published studies, but found a lower number of violent deaths; they estimated 151,000 deaths from March 2003 to June 2006.[212] An even higher figure for violent death—more than 1 million killed—was given in 2007 by the Opinion Research Bureau (ORB), based in Britain.[213]

Although cluster sampling may ultimately provide the best estimate of war caused mortality, the ORB and *Lancet* studies were criticized on methodological grounds. Specifically, critics questioned whether the samples were random and whether there were too few clusters analyzed.[214] Because of the problems associated with random sample surveys in a war zone, some scholars have concluded that it may be that the *Lancet* study was the best that could be done given the extreme violence in Iraq at the time.[215] Whether or not the resulting numbers from these particular cluster sample surveys are valid, cluster sampling from Iraq and other conflicts shows that reliance on media reports of death undercount the number of those killed.[216]

As inadequate as the data on recorded death is, and despite the uncertainty associated with the various counts and estimates, it is possible to outline the causes of collateral damage deaths in Iraq at US and coalition hands. Combat-related deaths and injuries to civilians in Iraq were caused in several ways: when bombs missed their intended targets, in crossfire, and when insurgents used suicide bombs and improvised explosive devices. In the first year of the war, as figure 2.13 shows, the majority of civilian deaths were caused by US coalition forces. Specifically, about 52 percent of recorded violent deaths could

[211] Gilbert Burnham, Riyadh Lafta, Shannon Doocy, and Les Roberts. "Mortality after the 2003 Invasion of Iraq: A Cross-Sectional Cluster Sample Survey," *Lancet*, vol. 368, no. 9545 (11 October 2006): 1421–1428.

[212] Iraq Family Health Survey Study Group, "Violence Related Mortality in Iraq from 2002 to 2006," *New England Journal of Medicine*, vol. 358, no. 5 (31 January 2008): 484–493.

[213] National Public Radio, "Survey puts Iraqi War Dead above One Million," 18 September 2007, http://www.npr.org/templates/story/story.php?storyId=14501232.

[214] See, for example, John Bohannan, "Iraqi Death Estimates Called Too High; Methods Faulted," *Science*, vol. 16, no. 314 (20 October 2006): 396–397; Michael Spagat and Josh Dougherty, "Conflict Deaths in Iraq: A Methodological Critique," *Survey Research Methods*, vol. 4, no. 1 (2010): 3–15; and Tapp et al., "Iraq War Mortality Estimates."

[215] Beth Osborne Daponte, "Wartime Estimates of Iraqi Civilian Casualties," International Review of the Red Cross, vol. 89, no 868 (2007) pp. 943–957.

[216] Aldo A. Benini and Lawrence H. Moulton, "Civilian Victims in an Asymmetrical Conflict: Operation Enduring Freedom, Afghanistan," *Journal of Peace Research*, vol. 41, no. 4 (July 2004): 403–422. Tapp et al., "Iraq War Mortality Estimates," p. 12.

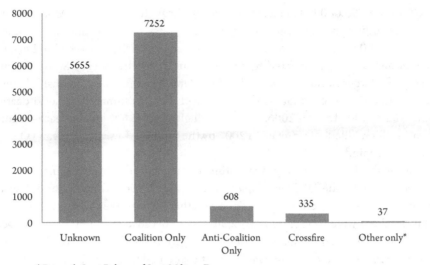

* Primarily Iraqi Police and Iraqi Military Forces

Figure 2.13 Reported perpetrators of civilian deaths by armed violence in Iraq from 20 March 2003–19 March 2004.
Source: Madelyn Hsiao-Rei Hicks, Hamit Dardagan, Gabriela Guerrero Serdan, Peter Bagnall, John Sloboda, and Michael Spagat, "Violent Deaths of Iraqi Civilians: Analysis by Perpetrator, Weapon, Time and Location," *PLOS Medicine*, February 2011, vol. 8, no. 2. www.plosmedicine.org.

be attributed to coalition forces, and of those, most of the coalition-caused deaths in that period occurred in air attacks. Unknown perpetrators accounted for 41 percent of recorded violent deaths, while anti-coalition forces accounted for about 4 percent of recorded deaths.

The pattern of the killing changed over the course of the war. As is well known, after the initial, rather quick victory over Iraq's conventional military forces, the war became an insurgency and civil conflict. The first five years of war in Iraq were the most violent, with more than 92,000 people killed in armed violence according to Iraq Body Count. Most violent Iraqi deaths during the war occurred as a result of the lawlessness that was endemic from 2003 to 2008 in Iraq.[217] A reflection of the lawlessness and sectarian violence that developed in the mid-2000s in Iraq following the invasion (as revenge killings and clashes between Sunni, Shia, and Kurdish groups escalated) is that by the end of the first five years of fighting in March 2008, unknown perpetrators caused the most (74 percent) violent deaths recorded by

[217] Armed violence, including executions, during and after major combat ends occurs in many wars. Geneva Declaration Secretariat, "Global Burden of Armed Conflict" (Geneva: Geneva Declaration Secretariat, 2008).

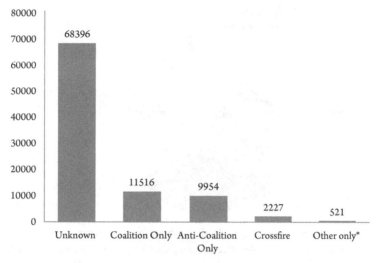

* Primarily Iraqi Police and Iraqi Military Forces

Figure 2.14 Reported perpetrators of civilian deaths by armed violence in Iraq from 20 March 2003–19 March 2008.
Source: Hicks et al., "Violent Deaths of Iraqi Civilians," see source note for figure 2.13.

Iraq Body Count. Unknown perpetrators executed their victims or tortured them and then executed them. Figure 2.14 shows an analysis of recorded civilian death by perpetrator for the first five years of the war in Iraq.

Not surprisingly, in some cases of crossfire, it was impossible to say whether coalition or anti-coalition forces had caused the deaths. When coalition forces were identified as responsible for killing civilians, 12 percent of the total deaths could be attributed to coalition forces during the first five years of the war. The use of airpower continued to be the main cause of coalition-caused civilian death—65 percent of coalition collateral damage over the first five years. Anti-coalition forces killed about 11 percent of the civilians during this period. When anti-coalition forces killed civilians, it was primarily by suicide bombs, vehicle bombs, and roadside bombs. Unknown perpetrators killed the majority of their victims by execution and small arms fire.[218] Figure 2.15 shows the way Iraqi civilians were being killed during the first five years of the war in a subset of civilian casualty incidents—short duration events (lasting two days or less).

In sum, using the Iraq Body Count documented 14,781 violent deaths caused by the US coalition from 2003 to 2011 during the US war and occupation, and the additional number likely to be added by including Wikileaks data, the total number

[218] Hicks et al., "Violent Deaths of Iraqi Civilians."

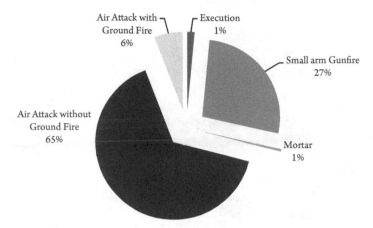

Figure 2.15 Coalition-caused civilian deaths in short duration events in Iraq, 2003–2008.
Source: From data in Hicks et al., "Violent Deaths of Iraqi Civilians," see source note for figure 2.13, table 2, p. 5.

of recorded US-caused collateral damage deaths may be about 16,300 civilians.[219] But, again, this is almost certainly an undercount.

Yemen

Yemen was an early site of US counterterror operations after the 9/11 attacks, but for many years the war zone was relatively quiet. In November 2001, the United States began military cooperation with Yemen, opening a training facility that included CIA and Special Operations forces, and in April 2002, the United States designated Yemen a combat zone to support Operation Enduring Freedom (OEF) in Afghanistan. Yemen's political stability was, at the time, fragile, and the government welcomed US military assistance, which it used to fight dissidents as well as Al Qaeda affiliated organizations.

The political context and the US role in Yemen are not dissimilar from the situation in Pakistan. Under the authoritarian government of President Salah from 1990 to 2011, disaffection with the government grew. Yemen's growing political instability attracted militants and terrorists, who fed on local discontent and used the unrest to hide. The United States began direct military operations in Yemen in 2002, in cooperation with the government of Yemen, consisting of drone strikes, other air strikes, and Special Forces operations. The purpose of US operations was to kill Al

---

[219] Iraq Body Count, "Iraq Deaths from Violence 2003-2011," 2 January 2012, http://www.iraq-bodycount.org/analysis/numbers/2011/, accessed 14 May 2012. As of this writing, IBC had not yet completed its research and expected to add to this count based on new released materials.

Qaeda leaders and engage in broader counterterrorism. However, as in Pakistan, the United States encouraged and supported the Yemeni military to take the lead in counterterrorism operations. In January 2009, two al Qaeda related organizations merged to form Al Qaeda in the Arabian Peninsula (AQAP) and promised to train in Yemen for attacks. Others, also protesting Yemen's close ties to the United States and the Yemeni forces attacks on civilians, took up arms against the Yemeni government.

The Obama administration reviewed its strategy in Yemen in 2009 and initiated a comprehensive program that included increased economic and military assistance to the Yemeni government and direct US military strikes. In September 2009, President Ali Abdullah Saleh of Yemen promised the US deputy National Security Adviser, John Brennan, "unfettered access to Yemen's national territory for US counterterrorism operations."[220]

In line with the shift in policy, direct US military operations in Yemen and US support to the government Yemen through the Department of Defense (section 1206 funding) and Department of State (Foreign Military Financing) for military purposes dramatically increased. Indeed, Yemen became the largest recipient of the Congress's newly authorized counterterrorism 1206 funding between FY2006 and FY2011, receiving more than $250 million over that period. Pakistan received $203 million over the same period.[221] The majority of US funding went to purchase and support upgrades of the Yemeni Air Force's helicopters and fixed wing aircraft. Yemen used the US military assistance funding, equipment, and training, against AQAP but also against other dissidents and pro-democracy protestors, which concerned some members of the US Congress.[222]

As in Pakistan, most civilians and members of insurgent organizations die at government hands, not as a result of direct US strikes. But, in contrast to Pakistan where drones are the primary instrument of intervention, the US strikes in Yemen involve a number of different weapons platforms—drone aircraft, cruise missiles, and piloted aircraft. The first targeted US drone missile strike in Yemen occurred in November 2002 when the United States used a Predator drone to kill Al Qaeda leader Qa'id Salim Sinan, al-Harithi who was involve in the attack on the *U.S.S. Cole* in December 2000, and Abu Ahmad al-Hijazi. Four other militants were killed in the strike.

After more than seven years, the next major US military operations in Yemen were attacks on suspected Al Qaeda training camps in Sana' and Abyan provinces

---

[220] U.S. Diplomatic Cable, 15 September 2009, Wikileaks, *The Guardian*, http://www.guardian.co.uk/world/us-embassy-cables-documents/225085.

[221] Nina M. Serafino, "Security Assistance Reform: 'Section 1206' Background and Issues for Congress," 13 January 2012, Congressional Research Service, pp. 25–26 and 28–29.

[222] See Jeremy M. Sharp, "Yemen: Background and U.S. Relations," Congressional Research Service, 22 March 2011, RL34170, p. 38.

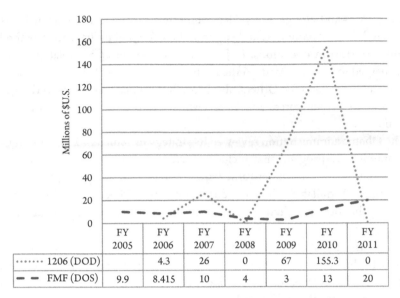

	FY 2005	FY 2006	FY 2007	FY 2008	FY 2009	FY 2010	FY 2011
······· 1206 (DOD)		4.3	26	0	67	155.3	0
─ ─ FMF (DOS)	9.9	8.415	10	4	3	13	20

Figure 2.16 Major US Congressional Authorizations for Yemen, FY2005–FY2011.
Sources: Alfred B. Prados and Jeremy M. Sharp, "Yemen: Current Conditions and U.S. Relations,"
CRS Report for Congress, RS21808, 4 January 2007. Jeremy M. Sharp, "Yemen: Background
and U.S. Relations," Congressional Research Service, CRS, 22 March 2011; Jeremy M. Sharp,
"Yemen: Background and U.S. Relations," Congressional Research Service, CRS, 10 April 2012.

in late 2009. The strike in Abyan was originally reported in the West as conducted
by the government of Yemen. It later emerged that the United States had launched
a cruise missile carrying cluster bombs in the village of al-Majala on 17 December
2009.[223] In a meeting with David Petraeus shortly after the strikes, President Saleh
said that Yemen would conceal the US role: "We'll continue saying the bombs are
ours, not yours." The deputy prime minister, Rashid al-Alimi said, "U.S. munitions
found at the sites could be explained away as equipment purchased from the U.S."[224]
The local authorities in Yemen, and a parliamentary commission investigation,
found that of the fifty-eight people killed, forty-four were civilians. The parliamentary commission described the effects of the attack, which it said killed "*14 members
of the al-Haidra family in one settlement and 27 members of the al-Anbour family in the
other. The sole survivor from the al-Haidra family, a 13-year-old girl was reported to have*

[223] Amnesty International, "Images of Missile and Cluster Munitions Point to US Role
in Fatal Attack in Yemen," 7 June 2010, http://www.amnesty.org/en/news-and-updates/
yemen-images-missile-and-cluster-munitions-point-us-role-fatal-attack-2010-06-04. Robert Booth
and Ian Black, "WikiLeaks Cables: Yemen Offered US 'Open Door' to Attack al-Qaida on its Soil,"
The Guardian, 3 December 2010, http://www.guardian.co.uk/world/2010/dec/03/wikileaks-yemen-
us-attack-al-qaida.

[224] Scott Shane, "Yemen Sets Terms of a War on Al Qaeda," *New York Times*, 3 December 2010, http://
www.nytimes.com/2010/12/04/world/middleeast/04wikileaks-yemen.html?pagewanted=all.

been sent abroad to receive medical treatment for her injuries."[225] Cluster bombs later killed three and wounded nine others who stepped on bomblets remaining from the attack. Those killed ranged in age from 1 to 67 years old.[226] The United States waged a second strike that day, but it is unclear who was killed. An airstrike reportedly made by the Yemeni military with US assistance, against a US citizen working with Al Qaeda in Yemen, Anwar Al Alawki, on 24 December, killed about thirty members of AQAP.[227] On 25 December, a man who had trained in Yemen tried to blow up a US airliner over Detroit, underscoring the threat emanating from Yemen. The December 2009 strikes were the beginning of increased drone and cruise missile air strikes in Yemen. A strike on 14 March 2010 killed an Al Qaeda leader, but the next US strike, on 25 May 2010, killed a top civilian official, the deputy governor of Marib Province, and some of his bodyguards.[228]

But there is some uncertainty about both the number of US strikes and the platforms being used. For example, the Bureau of Investigative Journalism (BIJ) publishes short narratives of each confirmed strike, and other possible strikes, as well as its sources, and they count more strikes in Yemen than the Long War Journal (LWJ). Figure 2.17 illustrates the difference in the two counts of strikes. As in Pakistan, few outside reporters have had access to Yemen, and the government was, for many years not honest about the source of the attacks, over when they were made, and how many and the identities of those who are killed or injured.

There is thus, unsurprisingly, uncertainty about the death toll of US military strikes in Yemen. For example, the Long War Journal reports no civilian deaths in Yemen due to US military strikes in 2011. By contrast, other sources report civilian deaths due to US strikes. *Wired* noted contradictory reports of an incident on a US strike on 14 July 2011 on a police station in Yemen that had been taken over by militants. While the Long War Journal did not report any civilian deaths for the entire year, the *New York Times* reported eight militant deaths in the strike, and *CNN* reported witness statements that "at least" thirty civilians were killed along with about twenty militants.[229]

---

[225] Quoted in The Bureau of Investigative Journalism, Drones Team, "Yemen: Reported U.S. Covert Actions 2011-2011," 29 March 2012, http://www.thebureauinvestigates.com/2012/03/29/yemen-reported-us-covert-actions-since-2001/.

[226] The Long War Journal counts forty-one dead, perhaps not including the later victims of cluster munitions.

[227] Sudarsan Raghavan and Michael D. Shear, "U.S.-Aided Attack in Yemen Thought to Have Killed Aulaqi, 2 Al Qaeda Leaders," *Washington Post*, 25 December 2009, http://www.washingtonpost.com/wp-dyn/content/article/2009/12/24/AR2009122400536.html.

[228] Scott Shane, Mark Mazzetti, and Robert F. Worth, "Secret Assault on Terrorism Widens on Two Continents," *New York Times*, 14 August 2010, http://www.nytimes.com/2010/08/15/world/15shadowwar.html?_r=1.

[229] Spencer Ackerman, "Massive Drone Strike Hits Qaida Cop Station in Yemen," *Wired*, 15 July 2011, http://www.wired.com/dangerroom/2011/07/massive-drone-strike-hits-qaida-cop-station-in-yemen/#more-51982. Hakim Almasmari, "Massive Demonstrations Turn Deadly in Yemen," CNN, 17 July 2011, http://edition.cnn.com/2011/WORLD/meast/07/15/yemen.drone.strike/.

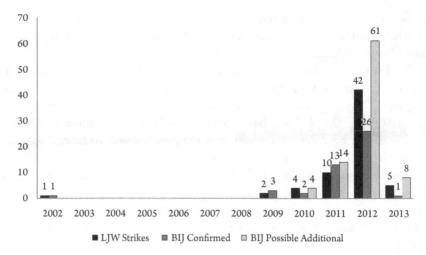

Figure 2.17 Comparison of counts of US strikes in Yemen, 2002–March 2013.
Sources: LWJ, http://www.longwarjournal.org/multimedia/Yemen/code/Yemen-strike.php.
BIJ: Bureau of Investigative Journalism, Drones Team, "Yemen Strikes Visualized," http://www.
thebureauinvestigates.com/2012/07/02/yemen-strikes-visualised/; BIJ and LWJ, accessed 20
March 2013.

The most famous drone strike in Yemen occurred on 30 September 2011 when
the United States killed a US citizen Anwar al-Alawki and three others. The Obama
administration ordered that al-Alawki, a member of AQAP who endorsed and
advocated violence against the United States, including civilians, be put on a terrorist "capture or kill" list in 2010 and several attempts had been made to kill him.
Killed with al-Alawki that day was another US citizen, Samir Kahn, the editor of a
pro-Al Qaeda magazine, *Inspire*. Two weeks later, Al-Alawki's 16-year-old son, and
17-year-old nephew were killed in US drone strikes. By almost any definition, the
editor and the two boys were civilians.

In late November 2011, after eleven months of intensive protests by
pro-democracy activists, the government agreed to elections, which occurred in
February 2012. The new government, led by President Abed Rabbo Mansour Hadi
acknowledged the US strikes publicly for the first time in October 2012. Hadi told
reporters that he personally approved "every operation" by the US Joint Special
Operations Command and the CIA in Yemen and had visited the US command
facility near the Sanaa.[230]

[230] Hadi, quoted in Greg Miller, "In Interview, Yemeni President Acknowledges Approving U.S. Drone
Strikes," *Washington Post*, 29 September 2012, http://www.washingtonpost.com/world/national-security/
yemeni-president-acknowledges-approving-us-drone-strikes/2012/09/29/09bec2ae-0a56-11e2-afff-
d6c7f20a83bf_story.html.

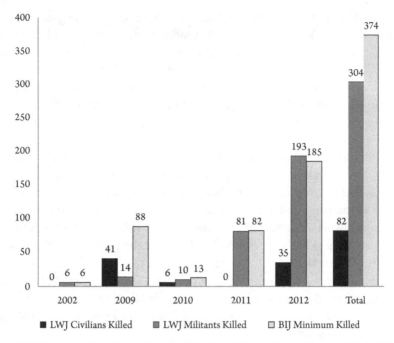

Figure 2.18 Estimated number of people killed by US airstrikes in Yemen, 2002–2012.

In sum, the number of US strikes in Yemen in 2012 increased dramatically over previous years. Thus, BIJ minimum number of deaths due to US strikes during this period was similar the LWJ total for the same period.[231] Overall, in the period from 2008 to 2012, Long War Journal documented eighty-two civilians killed out of a total of 386 killed in strikes from 2002. If this conservative figure is correct, 27 percent of the targeted killing deaths in Yemen are civilians. The Bureau of Investigative Journalism appears to count a minimum of sixty civilian deaths to US strikes from 2002 to late 2012, with a minimum number of total deaths of 374 during this period or 16 percent of those killed.

Indirect Harm and Structural Violence

In addition to direct violence, war also causes indirect, nonviolent death and injury as the effects of the destruction of infrastructure and objects essential for human survival, as a consequence of war and military occupation, ripple through a society

[231] Drones Team, "Yemen: Reported U.S. Covert Action 2012," The Bureau of Investigative Journalism, 8 May 2012, http://www.thebureauinvestigates.com/2012/05/08/yemen-reported-us-covert-action-2012/, accessed 17 May 2012.

and population like an enormous tidal wave, causing cascades of negative effects on health. As the Army's *Civilian Casualty Mitigation* manual notes, "In addition to the inherent risks from combat, a society disrupted by armed conflict will have other vulnerabilities, particularly if large numbers of civilians lack food, water, shelter, medical care, and security. Disease, starvation, dehydration, and the climate may be more threatening to civilians than casualties from Army operations."[232]

In previous centuries, deliberate destruction of infrastructure and other objects was the norm; orchards, food stores, and farms were burned, and dams were destroyed with the intention of denying sustenance to the military and causing pain to the civilian population. Today, when a bomb destroys a water treatment facility, and a man, woman, or child later dies from cholera, spread by now untreated water, the harm to humans is indirect. We know that the cholera killed the person, but the cause of the presence of cholera in the water, or the lack of antibiotics to treat the illness, was most likely the bomb that destroyed the water treatment facility or perhaps the destruction of the hospital or the road to take someone to a hospital. Wars also lead to mass displacement, as people flee the fighting, and to the creation of refugee camps. The excess morbidity (illness, disease, and injury) and mortality due to the destruction of infrastructure or the hardships of displacement is a form of structural violence.

This indirect death and injury to civilians is foreseen in the laws of armed combat and its' intentional infliction is to be avoided. Specifically, Additional Protocol I of the Geneva Conventions requires the "protection of objects indispensable to the survival of the civilian population" such as foodstuffs, agricultural areas, and drinking water supplies.[233] That the focus of the prohibition is on intentionally harming civilians is clear in the Treaty language: "It is prohibited to attack, destroy, remove or render useless objects indispensable to the survival of the civilian population…for the specific purpose of denying them for their sustenance value to the civilian population or to the adverse party, whatever the motive, whether in order to starve out civilians, to cause them to move away, or for any other motive."[234] The treaty also requires the "protection of the natural environment" including the "prohibition of the use of methods or means of warfare which are intended or may be expected to cause such damage to the natural environment and thereby prejudice the health or survival of the population."[235]

In a formulation that parallels the legality of collateral damage killing, attacks on infrastructure are legal under international law if such an attack will contribute to a military objective and the attack will not foreseeably harm civilians. The law allows attacks on objects used by the enemy for sustenance, or "if not as sustenance, then

[232] Army, *Civilian Casualty Mitigation*, p. 1-9.
[233] Geneva Convention Additional Protocol I (1977), Article 54.
[234] Ibid., Article 54.
[235] Ibid., Article 55.

in direct support of military action, provided, however that in no event shall actions against these object be taken which may be expected to leave the civilian population with such inadequate food or water as to cause its starvation or force its movement."[236] The principles of intention and proportionality also allow the destruction of foodstuffs and infrastructure, for example, if they are used in direct support of an adversary's military action. In sum, harm to civilians may result from the effects of war on the "objects" indispensable for their survival, but such harm is legal as long as it is militarily necessary and not intentional.

The logic is thus the same as already discussed; a principle of distinction between military and civilian applies, and civilians are to be protected, in this case, against indirect harm. Thus, the civilians who die or become ill because of the indirect consequences of military operations, namely that the infrastructure that is essential to their lives and health has been damaged or destroyed may also be considered collateral damage: the harm was not intentional but it may have been an unforeseen and genuine accident, an unintentional foreseeable consequence of an operation, that was judged necessary to achieve a given a military objective.

Beth Osborne Daponte found that "in modern warfare, postwar deaths from adverse health effects account for a large fraction of total deaths from war."[237] Societies with stressed or rudimentary public health systems or where the civilian population was weakened by previous wars or economic sanctions will likely have a higher incidence of war-related indirect death. Yet the indirect health impact of war can be ameliorated or exacerbated by the robustness of the existing public health infrastructure. It may also be that a war coincides with or exacerbates an environmental disaster, such as prolonged droughts or flooding. "Loss of livelihood, poor diets, lack of food, displacement, poor sanitation, and countless other factors are often treated as the underlying determinants of [indirect] mortality within a conflict."[238]

Although it is difficult to estimate, indirect deaths tend to outnumber direct deaths. Research has yielded an extremely crude rule of thumb: "between three and 15 times as many people die indirectly for every person who dies violently."[239] The question is how to tell which conflicts are associated with which scale of indirect death. The Geneva Declaration Secretariat, which closely examined data from armed conflicts occurring in the period of 2004-2007, suggests that "a reasonable average estimate would be a ratio of four indirect deaths to one direct death in

---

[236] Ibid., Article 54.

[237] Beth Osborne Daponte, "A Case Study in Estimating Casualties from War and Its Aftermath: The 1991 Persian Gulf War," *Physicians for Social Responsibility Quarterly*, vol. 3 (1993): 57–66. Archived at *Medicine and Global Survival*, http://www.ippnw.org/pdf/mgs/psr-3-2-daponte.pdf.

[238] Geneva Declaration Secretariat, "Global Burden of Armed Conflict," p. 35.

[239] Ibid., pp. 4 and 32.

contemporary conflicts."[240] Beth Osborne Daponte estimated in 1993 that of the total deaths from the 1991 Gulf War in Iraq, violent civilian wartime deaths comprised less than 2 percent of all deaths due to the war: "In the Gulf war, far more persons died from postwar health effects than from direct war effects."[241] Similarly, in the Congo, from 1998 to 2001, 350,000 were killed violently, and of those, 145,000 died in combat, but an additional 2.5 million were indirectly killed in that time, primarily from disease. In other conflicts in Africa, battle deaths accounted for between 2 percent and 30 percent of total war deaths.[242] However, the data on excess death and indirect harm for African conflicts is poor and contested.

Some of the nonviolent deaths that occur in a country at war would have occurred anyway. As Lacina and Gleditch note, "measuring war related deaths involves comparing the number of deaths that occurred due to a conflict against the counterfactual scenario of peace."[243] But what would "peace" have looked like? In countries like Afghanistan, Iraq, and Pakistan, there was little peace prior to the conflicts. In other words, as Michael Spagat emphasizes, "the key to any excess death estimate is to establish a plausible baseline mortality rate to serve as a counterfactual."[244] Unfortunately, for the purpose of understanding the likely indirect health impact of wars, the quality and reliability of prewar data in Afghanistan, Pakistan, and Iraq is probably not very high. In this respect, Afghanistan, Pakistan, and Iraq are little different from other poor countries at war. Health information systems, such as hospital and clinic records, and death certificates, are "almost universally weak in conflict-affected areas, and between two-thirds and three quarters of the world's population are not covered by any type of health surveillance."[245] Current mortality rates can be estimated, but while violence is ongoing in Iraq, Afghanistan, and the border region of Pakistan, it is very difficult to assess the indirect health effects of these wars. Neither Afghanistan nor Iraq had a census in the years immediately prior to the onset of the US wars in 2001 and 2003, respectively.

Further, it is difficult to disentangle the causal effects of the most recent wars from the damage caused by previous decades of fighting and sanctions. Afghanistan and Iraq have been at war or under sanctions for the better part of the last thirty years. And, it is sometimes impossible to disentangle the effects of war from other environmental, economic, or political events. "It is necessary to judge whether certain events—such as a famine or riot—would not have happened at all if peace had

---

[240] Ibid., p. 32.

[241] Daponte, "A Case Study in Estimating Casualties from War and Its Aftermath."

[242] Bethany Lacina and Nils Petter Gleditsch, "Monitoring Trends in Global Combat: A New Dataset of Battle Deaths," *European Journal of Population*, vol. 21, no. 2/3 (2005): 145–166, 159.

[243] Ibid., pp. 148–149.

[244] Michael Spagat, "Estimating the Human Costs of War: The Sample Survey Approach," *Households in Conflict Network, HiCN Research Design Note 14*, May 2010, p. 8.

[245] Geneva Declaration Secretariat, "Global Burden of Armed Conflict," p. 37.

prevailed, and to measure the degree of elevation (or depression) in peacetime risks of mortality from factors like crime or malnutrition."[246] In addition, there is the issue of estimating the future long-term and lagged effects of war. We might say that a war ends with a ceasefire, but the indirect effects of war will ripple and linger for years after the end of conflict. Thus, the conflict researchers Lacina and Gleditsch rightly ask, "How many years of elevated mortality due to, for instance, depressed economic performance, environmental degradation, or the spread of sexually transmitted diseases should be attached to the terminated war and can those impacts be measured in a reliable way?"[247]

Environmental disasters, such as earthquakes, can stress or ruin the infrastructure and support system that would otherwise be used to help the victims of war. In Afghanistan, Iraq, and Pakistan, droughts and floods have turned these war zones into cases of "complex emergency." As Beth Daponte argues, "disentangling deaths due to the war from those due to other factors can be impossible and beyond expertise of most statisticians and demographers. Perhaps the best that the statisticians and demographers can do is to provide estimates of the mortality levels of civilians at different time periods, and let the political scientists argue about the proportion of the increase in mortality that should be attributed to different parties and policies."[248]

In sum, research from recent wars and armed conflicts suggests that battle deaths are sometimes a fraction of the total deaths attributable to war.[249] But quantifying the ratio of direct to indirect deaths is not an exact science given the limits of existing data. As the Geneva Declaration Secretariat noted, "it is not possible to give a precise estimate of the indirect burden" of war although "an order of magnitude can be offered."[250] In cases where the populations' health was already low and perhaps taxed by previous conflicts and concurrent natural disasters, it may be both difficult to disentangle the previous indirect effects of war and the ongoing disasters from the indirect effects of the current war. Rather, these conditions amplify each other and no one-size-fits-all rule about the ratio of direct to indirect death will apply. The Geneva Secretariat suggests that "a conservative ratio of 4:1 indirect to direct death" is a good rule of thumb.[251]

Public health studies of Iraq and Afghanistan, and analysis of press reports show increased mortality due to war. In both Afghanistan and Iraq, the prewar infrastructure was not robust.[252] Afghanistan was already experiencing low life

[246] Lacina and Gleditsch, "Monitoring Trends in Global Combat," p. 149.

[247] Ibid.

[248] Daponte, "Wartime Estimates of Iraqi Civilian Casualties," p. 945.

[249] Geneva Declaration Secretariat, "Global Burden of Armed Conflict," p. 42.

[250] Ibid.

[251] Ibid.

[252] United Nations sanctions, in place from the 1991 Gulf War, had helped to cripple Iraqi infrastructure. Further, because the prewar regimes in both Iraq and Afghanistan had not invested sufficient in public health and infrastructure, the populations of both countries were already vulnerable.

expectancy and high infant mortality rates prior to the US invasion in 2001. A survey of 600 war-affected communities conducted from early to mid-2002 found that in 211 of those affected some or all of their residents had fled the violence.[253] Defense analyst Carl Conetta argues that the US bombing campaign exacerbated the already existing humanitarian crisis in Afghanistan by causing people to flee their homes, frustrating or halting humanitarian relief efforts already underway, disrupting winter planting, and in further degrading Afghanistan's infrastructure. Thus, Conetta estimates indirect deaths of between 8,000 and 18,000 Afghans from mid-September 2001 to mid-January 2002 "due to starvation, exposure, associated illnesses, or injury sustained while in flight from war zones," in addition to those who were killed by direct violence.[254] Of this Conetta argues that "at least 40 percent of the deaths (3,300+) are attributed to the effects of the crisis and war."[255]

Similarly, Iraq's infrastructure had been devastated by its wars against Iran in the 1980s and the United States in 1991, and by UN sanctions from 1991 to 2003. On the one hand, the war made Iraq a more dangerous place to live: "Many injuries to Iraqis such as injuries from electric shock, unintentional explosions, unintentional gunshot wounds, and falls resulted from the breakdown of the infrastructure in Iraq."[256] Overall health suffered greatly because of the effects of the breakdown of infrastructure. For instance, malnutrition and stunting were a problem for children: 26 percent of Iraqi children in the mid-2000s had moderate or severe stunting. Outbreaks of cholera and hepatitis and other diseases occurred. The public health infrastructure was devastated: hospitals and clinics were destroyed and nearly 20,000 doctors fled Iraq after 2003 and many failed to return. "The destruction and looting of health facilities that followed the invasion resulted in heavy loss of equipment and pharmaceutical stocks. Quality of care continued to deteriorate and shortages were widespread. Major loss of health staff from tertiary hospitals had an effect on teaching of trainees and care of patients."[257]

There is a long tradition of deliberately targeting infrastructure. For example, in World War II the British firebombed German railway junctions as a deliberate targeting of infrastructure. Sanctions that cut off the material necessary to grow food, produce medicines, or to treat water can also hurt or kill civilians. Infrastructure

---

[253] Aldo A. Bernini, "Civilian Victims in Asymmetrical Conflict: Operation Enduring Freedom, Afghanistan," *Journal of Peace Research*, vol. 41, no. 4 (July 2004): 403–422, 409.

[254] Carl Conetta, *Strange Victory: A Critical Appraisal of Operation Enduring Freedom and the Afghanistan War*, Project on Defense Alternatives Research Monograph 6 (Cambridge: Commonwealth Institute, 2002), pp. 36 and 37.

[255] Conetta, *Strange Victory*, p. 36.

[256] Levy and Sidel, "Adverse Health Consequences of the Iraq War," p. 950.

[257] Thamer Kadum Al Hilfi, Riadh Lafta, and Gilbert Burnham, "Health Services in Iraq," *The Lancet*, vol. 381 (16 March 2013): 939–948, 939. Also see Burnham, Lafta, Doocy, and Roberts, "Mortality after the 2003 Invasion of Iraq: A Cross-Sectional Cluster Sample Survey," p. 1421.

has been targeted in the wars in Afghanistan and Iraq. In deliberately targeting infrastructure, the idea is to hurt civilians who might be aiding insurgents and to directly diminish the insurgent's military potential. So, some battles in Iraq, notably Fallujah, began to resemble ancient sieges—towns were surrounded, the women and children were encouraged to leave, and the flow of vital materials, such as water and food were cut off. The modern twist is of course that the electricity might be shut off as well. Infrastructure can also be inadvertently destroyed, for example, by inaccurate bombs, or by a large fire that is ignited as a result of a bombing. In this case, the idea was not necessarily to hurt civilians, but they are nevertheless harmed later, if not immediately.

The 2012 *Civilian Casualty Mitigation* manual acknowledges that destruction of infrastructure may cause harm, but implies a proportionality calculus in decisions about whether to attack infrastructure. Both the short-term risk of collateral damage and the longer term, indirect, harm are to be considered. "During operations, it may be desirable to attack key infrastructure targets such as bridges, power plants, and office buildings. The military benefit of should [*sic*] be balanced against the possibility that the targets are occupied by or in close proximity to civilians, that destroying such targets will unduly harm civilians, or that their destruction will create long-term effects such as contaminating the environment."[258] Interestingly, the *Civilian Casualty Mitigation* notes that "if left unrepaired, damaged infrastructure such as buildings, bridges and roads increase the risk of CIVCASs." The potential for long-term harm is also noted: "For example, risk increases if a structure could collapse, if contaminated materials such as asbestos or polychlorinated biphenyls might be released, or if accidents more likely."[259] Finally, the Army manual notes that "the population may blame Army units for hardships and decreased human security resulting from a lack of infrastructure or diminished essential services."[260]

Although civilians may die due to displacement and the denial of essentials such as food, water, and medicine, it is arguable whether the modern equivalent of siege warfare is a war crime. The Geneva Convention prohibits an occupying power from hindering the transfer of food and medicine to noncombatants.[261] On the other hand, forcing people to leave a city may occur "if the security of the population or *imperative military reasons* so demand."[262] Still, in cases of occupation, when the occupier effectively controls the distribution of food, water, and medicines, by their ability to deny access to those essentials, a strong case can be made that "if a person is 'in the hands of a party to the conflict or Occupying Power' ... then not providing

---

[258] Army, *Civilian Casualty Mitigation*, p. 1-10.
[259] Ibid., p. 1-11.
[260] Ibid., p. 2-17.
[261] Geneva Convention IV, Articles 23 and 50.
[262] Ibid., Article 49, emphasis added.

food, water and medical supplies would constitute a war crime on the basis of the Fourth Geneva Convention."[263]

I have refrained from attempting to quantify the indirect death and illness in Afghanistan, Iraq, Pakistan, and Yemen, but war-caused destruction of infrastructure has caused increased morbidity and mortality. Moreover, indirect death and injury that will last beyond the fighting itself. It always does. In Iraq, for example, life expectancy and child immunization rates have fallen, infant mortality has increased, and mental health has declined. About half of Iraq's physicians, fled Iraq during the US war and occupation, and many failed to return.[264]

The causal responsibility for indirect death and injury to civilians cannot be traced to the actions of the belligerents in the current war alone. The question from the perspective of international law is how much of the harm that was inflicted in the wars under discussion here was intended or foreseeable. Obviously, as in other forms of harm to civilians, parties should not dismiss the importance of the harm simply because it was unintentional. Parties to war should refrain from causing damage to important infrastructure and provide assistance as quickly and effectively as possible when infrastructure is damaged. The reconstruction efforts of the United States, the United Nations, and many nongovernmental organizations have ameliorated some of the indirect health effects of the wars in Afghanistan and Iraq. These efforts, for example, in repairing infrastructure, immunizing children and adults, and in providing basic medical care, have led to improvements in some regions of the war-affected countries.

Summary

The US military increasingly emphasized civilian protection during the wars in Afghanistan and Iraq at rhetorical, doctrinal, and operational levels. Minimizing collateral damage went from one concern among several, to an imperative that was institutionalized to a degree that it had never been before. The fact is, that despite the increased emphasis on civilian protection during the US fighting in Afghanistan and Iraq, and its air and Special Forces strikes in Pakistan and Yemen, collateral damage incidents occurred. By my admittedly incomplete and conservative estimate, the United States and its allies or coalition partners have directly caused about 22,000 violent civilian deaths in Afghanistan and Iraq. Target killing deaths in Pakistan and Yemen since 2001, and deaths, most commonly by drone strike, have caused an additional estimated 500-2,000 deaths. If we include

---

[263] Larry May, *War Crimes and Just War* (Cambridge: Cambridge University Press, 2007), p. 45.

[264] Paul C. Webster, "Iraq's Health System Yet to Heal from Ravages of War," *The Lancet*, vol. 378 (3 September 2011): 863–866.

the ambiguous category of killing of civilians in Pakistan by Pakistani security forces—on the argument that the United States has encouraged, equipped, and trained Pakistani forces in their counterinsurgency and paid for a good portion of the effort we might add about 14,000 to the toll.[265] Direct collateral damage deaths could total well over 38,000 in these wars since 2001. Of this, only a small number of civilians killed—about 1 percent of the total—if IBC data from Iraq is representative, were executed by US soldiers who either "snapped" or acted with criminal intent. The rest of those deaths were certainly genuine accidents (including traffic accidents), some, probably more than we think, were foreseeable systemic collateral damage, and some were foreseen proportionality/double effect collateral damage.

It is difficult to know the relative share of the different types of collateral damage, but using some data a very rough estimate may be made. When the political pressure to reduce this killing mounted, the attention to reducing civilian casualties translated into the institutionalization of collateral damage estimation (CDE) and mitigation practices within the US military. A recently published account of US collateral damage estimation and mitigation practices reports that, of the pre-planned air to surface and artillery operations where collateral damage estimation and mitigation practices were used, less than 1 percent resulted in collateral damage. Of those incidents where collateral damage occurred, 8 percent were "attributable to proportionality balancing—e.g. a conscious decision that anticipated military advantage outweighed collateral damage."[266]

As the data above show, in both Afghanistan and Iraq, the majority of collateral damage deaths are from the air. Pre-planned air strikes are subject to collateral damage estimation and mitigation although many strikes are not pre-planned. According to the June 2009 tactical directive in Afghanistan, all airstrikes, except for those cases where troops were in danger of being overrun, were to be pre-planned and when it was possible, pre-planned operations were to use the collateral damage methodology.[267]

The argument that "civcas" were inevitable and unforeseeable is belied by the fact that when US rules of engagement or procedures changed, the incidence of civilian killing waxed and waned. Further, while I cannot make a definitive causal argument without more data, it also appears that when civilian protection was emphasized and successfully increased, risk to US soldiers and indeed the number of US casualties also followed the path predicted by many inside and outside the military—they went up.

---

[265] The individual country estimates and counts are described below. This total does not include indirect deaths, for reasons discussed below.

[266] Gregory S. McNeal, "The U.S. Practice of Collateral Damage Estimation and Mitigation," 9 November 2011, p. 2, http://works.bepress.com/gregorymcneal/22/.

[267] Ibid., p. 5.

My focus on US- and coalition-caused civilian casualties does not tell the entire story of course. There are arguably two other categories of death that should concern us. The US allies in Pakistan and Yemen have also harmed civilians in their counterterror and counterinsurgency operations. In the case of Pakistan, this harm has led to the deaths of tens of thousands and the displacement of many more. Similarly, the US-funded Yemeni counterterror operations have killed Yemeni civilians. The United States is not obviously directly responsible for these collateral civilian deaths. But the United States does bear some moral responsibility for continuing to fund governments that, in pursuit of terrorists and militants, show too little regard for the lives of civilians.

‖ 3 ‖

Norms in Tension

Military Necessity, Proportionality, and Double Effect

Moral argument is especially important in wartime because ... the laws of war are radically incomplete.

—Michael Walzer[1]

[In the United States, practices of resettlement and destruction of villages in Vietnam,] the rules of engagement and the policy they embodied could hardly be defended. It seems to violate even the principle of proportionality—which is by no means easy to do, as we have seen again and again, since the values against which destruction and suffering are to be measured are so readily inflated.

—Michael Walzer[2]

When many Afghan civilians were being killed by close air support (CAS) strikes in high-profile incidents in 2008 and early 2009, the US military reacted by changing tactics. In late 2008, NATO ISAF Commander General David McKiernan ordered that civilian deaths be tracked and issued tactical directives to try to reduce the killing. Then, as civilian deaths continued to mount, the new ISAF Commander, General Stanley McChrystal, gave a tactical directive ordering in June 2009 that CAS strikes be restricted to cases where US forces might be overrun, so that civilian casualties could be minimized. Air power could be called in to support ground operations when it was judged by forces on the ground to be needed because US forces were at high risk. In those instances, civilians might be unintentionally killed but US forces might be saved.

---

[1] Michael Walzer, *Just and Unjust Wars: A Moral Argument with Historical Illustrations* (New York: Basic Books, 1977), p. 288.

[2] Ibid., p. 192.

These US generals' responses to collateral damage, and specifically the issuance of new tactical directives, illustrate the differences and the overlap between genuine accidents, foreseeable systemic collateral damage, and double effect/proportionality killing. Inadvertent killing of civilians is legal. When civilians died in these incidents, the problem was not that the laws of war were being broken. The law was not violated. The problem was that those deaths were, in many cases, predictable and could have been avoided, and when they occurred, they prompted a backlash against the United States. The new orders implicitly acknowledged that the deaths were foreseeable and preventable. The cause of the killing was in part systemic—an unintended result of choices made at the organizational level—and changing tactics could reduce the harm.

Cicero wrote that "in time of war, law is silent." It is, and it isn't. As international legal scholar Kenneth Watkin notes, "Humanitarian law requires the balancing of humanity with military necessity."[3] But the idea of balancing is perhaps misleading. The 2009 tactical directive, and other orders like it, embodies deep tensions among the values of civilian protection, force protection, and military necessity in US military strategy, international law, and the older Just War tradition. In other words, the laws of war offer clear protection of civilians against deliberate killing but can allow and excuse a great deal of "collateral damage," essentially forgiving civilian killing that is unintended if it is not disproportionate to military objectives. Indeed, a great deal of inadvertent harm may be legal, accepted, and excused under the contemporary understanding of military necessity, proportionality, double effect, and due care.

This paradox is the result of three closely related factors. First, the law of war privileges military necessity. When military necessity is understood to require noncombatant death, such killing is permissible and legal if it is proportionate to the expected military advantage of an operation. An elastic conception of military necessity and proportionality that depends on the eye of the beholder may, legally, trump civilian protection, and collateral damage that is the result of proportionality/double effect calculations is attributable to the valuing of military necessity above civilian protection. In other words, just war theory and international humanitarian law allow for and legitimize the unintentional killing of potentially large numbers of people if the harm is both unintended and proportional to some military objective under the doctrine of double effect. The abstract *rights* of noncombatants to protection are put at grave risk by the logic of military necessity and a failure to attend to the foreseeable consequences of operations.

Second, movements in philosophy and law over the last several hundred years stressed individual moral responsibility and intentionality, and the assumptions underlying the laws of war have, unsurprisingly, also been shaped by this paradigm.

---

[3] Kenneth Watkin, "Controlling the Use of Force: A Role for Human Rights Norms in Contemporary Armed Conflict," *American Journal of International Law*, vol. 98, no. 1 (January 2004): 1–34, 9.

Yet, assumptions of individual moral responsibility and intentionality can be misleading. War is a collective activity, sometimes requiring years of preparation and mobilization that both enables and limits the agency of individuals. The stress on individual action and intentionality tends to deemphasize outcomes that are the result of many actors working together and also to deemphasize the foreseeability of unintended outcomes. Ironically, at the time that social organizations and institutions, including the military and law, have become more complex and powerful, we have tended to focus more precisely on individual agency and capacity. As a consequence, our understanding of both the causal and moral responsibility for large-scale processes can be limited, or at least blinkered, in those circumstances where the power and effects of organizations are most acute and individual agency is constrained.

A focus on individual moral agency also tends to highlight intentionality; thus unintended outcomes and synergies are often invisible or excused. The emphasis on intentionality is found in the Just War tradition and in international law in the principle of "double effect," where in attempting to achieve one goal, I inadvertently cause something else to happen. Because the second effect was not my intention and, as long as it is not "disproportionate," I may be forgiven for this unintentional side effect of my action. This is the key logical support for excusing both systemic and proportionality/double effect "collateral damage." However, if we put more weight on foreseeability, then the excusing power of invoking intentionality and double effect is weakened.

Third, even as humans have gradually come to believe that the deliberate killing of civilians in war is abhorrent, weapons have become much more destructive in their effects, and the organization of contemporary warfare makes inadvertent killing more likely. While significant improvements in guidance have occurred, most weapons are still not so accurate that discrimination between combatant and noncombatant is guaranteed. In any case, precision delivery is overwhelmed by a weapon of such size that it can destroy an area of several hundred square yards in a village or city. This is an example of systemic collateral damage, where the likelihood of harm to civilians is foreseeable.

In sum, contemporary international law privileges an expansive understanding of military necessity and focuses on individual intention, not on harm that is foreseeable and unintended as it brought about by organizations, in a context where the destructive power of weapons has grown and discrimination has become more difficult. In the chapter on moral grammar and military vocabulary, I outlined the norms and the law. In what follows here, I make the moral and legal reasoning that underlies the relevant international laws explicit and discuss their evolution. I then describe the ways that the tensions between norms of noncombatant immunity, force protection, and military necessity have become institutionalized in US military law and operations in US planning and at specific turning points including the Vietnam War and the 1991 Gulf War.

Tensions in the Just War Tradition

Tensions between military necessity, proportionality, and noncombatant immunity are rooted in the Just War tradition, which assumes that war is an evil that ought to be avoided, if possible. War may sometimes be just or justified (*jus ad bellum*) and if war is justified, its conduct must be just (*jus in bello*). The Just War tradition is itself rooted in a "natural law" framework, where the law is determined by nature or given by God. Contemporary international law uses the terms of traditional Just War thinking but from the contemporary "positive" law tradition, where law is made by humans through legislatures, courts, or treaties, which tends to put more distance between morality and the law. Even though the contemporary law of war is historically embedded in and dependent on the Just War tradition, the shift to positive law means that international lawyers tend to read international treaty and domestic law literally, and the discourse is concerned with narrowly defining what is legal.[4]

Very briefly, Just War tradition reasoning about whether a war is justified (*jus ad bellum*) focuses on several factors, including whether the war is undertaken for a just cause (self-defense and defense of another), whether war is the last resort after other methods have been tried and failed, and whether war is required or necessary, in the sense of being the only action that can accomplish the objective.[5] The war should be proportionate in the sense that "the good of the war will outweigh the evil of the harm inflicted."[6] There must also be a probability of success. A legitimate or "right authority" weighs proportionality of ends and means and evaluates the other *jus ad bellum* concerns, and if war is deemed justified, wages the war.

Ethical considerations about conduct in war, *jus in bello*, are traditionally understood to have two elements: proportionality and distinction between combatants and noncombatants, or discrimination. Both the Just War tradition and international law articulate the principle of distinction in what appear to be categorical terms: noncombatant civilians cannot be intentionally targeted. But the principle of proportionality allows for unintended killing of civilians.

Specifically, the idea of proportionality is that harm should not be out of proportion to the anticipated military advantage.[7] And, as Kateri Carmola suggests,

---

[4] See James Turner Johnson, *Morality and Contemporary Warfare* (New Haven: Yale University Press, 1999).

[5] My attention to *jus ad bellum* questions is brief here because the focus of the book is on the conduct of war. I take up questions of the justice of war later, however, when I consider the moral responsibility of the public.

[6] Kateri Carmola, "The Concept of Proportionality: Old Questions and New Ambiguities," in Mark Evans, ed., *Just War Theory: A Reappraisal* (Edinburgh: Edinburgh University Press, 2005), pp. 93–113, 98.

[7] See Antonio Cassese, *International Law*, 2d ed. (Oxford: Oxford University Press, 2005), p. 417. Also see A. V. P. Rogers, "The Principle of Proportionality," in Howard M. Hensel, ed., *The Legitimate Use of Military Force: The Just War Tradition and the Customary Law of Armed Conflict* (Aldershot: Ashgate Publishing, 2008), pp. 189–218.

proportionality in decisions about going to war and proportionality in the conduct of war (*jus in bello*) are linked: "We can only judge acceptable levels of collateral damage, or the unintended harms of warfare, if we assume that the war itself, and the specific battle in particular, are just: either that the mistakes made are worth the short term 'military objective', or the long-term benefit, or, more nefariously, that the other side 'deserves' the harms inflicted upon it, either because they have lost their right of protection, or because they have never had it in the first place."[8] The level of damage or harm to noncombatants that might be acceptable is linked to two ideas: (1) that the resort to force be necessary; and (2) that there be some sense of the worth of both the objective of the war and of the lives and property that may be destroyed in achieving the objective of the war.

While the Just War tradition stresses that deliberate harm to noncombatants should be avoided, actions might have more than one consequence—intended and unintended—a double effect. In articulating the doctrine of double effect in the thirteenth century, Thomas Aquinas argued that we judge the morality of an action by the actors' intention: if intentions are good, we need not be too concerned with bad side effects. While self-defense might be my intention, I could unintentionally kill someone who is not a threat to me (as long as their death is not the means to my preservation). This narrow understanding of intention, which minimizes the importance of foreseeability if the harm is not out of proportion to the anticipated military gains of an operation, is still dominant.

When the doctrine of double effect is applied to the problem of civilian casualties in war, the moral problem of unintended, yet foreseeable, harm is resolved under certain conditions, namely that if soldiers kill noncombatants, the resulting deaths might be excused if the harm was an unintended consequence of a necessary military operation and if some effort was made to "minimize" civilian casualties. Further, the operation must be proportionate; the good of the military operation must outweigh the negative consequences of the operation; the "goodness of hitting the legitimate military target is 'worth', or proportional to, the badness of the collateral civilian casualties."[9] Put another way, Colm McKeogh summarizes, "The principle of double effect, then, permits killing where it is the foreseen but unintended side-effect of doing good, where the bad does not lead to the good, and where the good outweighs the bad."[10] Michael Walzer similarly argues that double effect excuses one from blame for civilian casualties if the operation that caused noncombatant deaths was legitimate, if the soldier did not intend to kill noncombatants, and if the positive military result could be said to "compensate" for the harm to noncombatants.[11]

[8] Carmola, "The Concept of Proportionality," pp. 98–99.

[9] Brian Orend, *The Morality of War* (Peterborough, Ontario: Broadview Press, 2006), p. 118.

[10] Colm McKeogh, *Innocent Civilians: The Morality of Killing in War* (New York: Palgrave, 2002), p. 65.

[11] Walzer, *Just and Unjust Wars*, p. 153.

McKeogh suggests that double effect reasoning is "injurious to the health of noncombatants. For in later hands, it was to make their deaths, though a foreseen consequence of a military act, morally permissible as long as they are not intended, not directly productive of the military goal, and proportionate to the good sought."[12] The trouble is that the emphasis on intention undermines the constraint that the foreseeability of civilian harm should provide, and the slippery notion of proportionality trades potential military value, almost always described as "military necessity," for more or less certain harm to civilians. Similarly, Walzer cautions that commanders and soldiers can be too generous in their calculations of military necessity and proportionality: "We have to worry about all those unintended but foreseeable deaths, for their number can be large; and subject only to the proportionality rule—a weak constraint—double effect provides a blanket justification."[13]

Brian Orend also finds the doctrine of double effect difficult, raising the question of the proportionality of the war itself. He asks: "Can one refer to the ultimate 'worth' of hitting a military target to justify collateral civilian casualties *without* referring to the substantive justice of one's involvement in the war to begin with?" Orend then expresses a serious reservation about the reasoning that justifies civilian casualties in an unjust war. "Personally, I fail to grasp how it can be morally justified to foreseeably kill innocent civilians in order to hit a target which only serves the final end of an aggressive war." For Orend, then, "The *only* justification sufficient, in my mind, for the collateral civilian casualties would be that the target is materially connected to victory in an otherwise *just* war."[14] But if the actor believes that their cause is just, then presumably this concern would fade. Frederik Kaufman is also skeptical of the reasoning that allows for foreseeable killing of civilians. "It is striking that permissible infringements of a right to life are so blithely accepted as more extensive in war than in peace." Kaufman argues that:

> Peacetime actions by the state that might kill one's own citizens, such as a dam construction or medical testing, would never be excused by a hand-waiving appeal to unintended consequences, insisting that those deaths, though clearly foreseen and useful, were, in any case proportional to the ends sought. It is not that innocent people may never be unintentionally killed by state actions in peacetime, but what counts as exercising due care to avoid those deaths in peace is much more stringent than during war (and typically involves one's own citizens). Evidently, the exigency of war changes what in peacetime would be negligent violations of a right to life to permissible infringements of the right.[15]

[12] McKeogh, *Innocent Civilians*, p. 65.

[13] Walzer, *Just and Unjust Wars*, p. 153.

[14] Orend, *The Morality of War*, p. 118.

[15] Frederik Kaufman, "Just War Thinking and Killing the Innocent," in Michael W. Brough, John W. Lango, and Harry van der Linden, eds., *Rethinking the Just War Tradition* (Albany: State University of New York Press, 2007), pp. 99–114, 101.

It is the combatant who makes these judgments: they must determine whether a military operation that may, or will certainly, kill noncombatants is necessary, that the deaths are not intended, and that the beneficial effects of the necessary action are proportionate, outweighing the harm to noncombatants. Commanders may believe that the likelihood of achieving an important military objective is high, while the likelihood of harm to civilians is low, when just the opposite is the case. Are commanders to be faulted for a wrong guess or calculation?

Walzer does not require commanders to be omniscient, but they must at least consider the potential harm to civilians of their actions and use "due care" in planning and executing their operations. "Simply not to intend the death of civilians is too easy; most often, under battle conditions, the intentions of soldiers are focused narrowly on the enemy."[16] Walzer continues:

> What we look for in such cases is some sign of a positive commitment to save civilian lives. Not merely to apply the rule of proportionality and kill no more civilians than is militarily necessary—that rule applies to soldiers as well; no one can be killed for trivial purposes. Civilians have a right to something more. And if saving civilian lives means risking soldier's lives, the risk must be accepted.[17]

When Walzer says, "And if saving civilian lives means risking soldier's lives, the risk must be accepted," he is not simply asking individual "common soldiers" to make the calculations but also asking "their immediate superiors" to take care with civilian lives.[18] In exercising due care, the military planner or commander should attempt to reduce the risk to noncombatants or may forgo the attack altogether. The military commander must exercise due care not only for civilian lives but also for soldiers, the imperative for "force protection." Walzer argues that: "Strategists and planners will for reasons of their own weigh the importance of their target against the importance of their soldiers' lives. But even if the target is very important, and the number of innocent people threatened relatively small, they must risk soldiers before they kill civilians."[19]

Thus, in Walzer's formulation of the doctrines of double effect and due care, there is a delicate balancing act. Even though Walzer appears to suggest that protecting civilians is to be weighted more heavily, he is also clear to admit that balancing risks to soldiers against risks to civilians is a difficult task.

> Once again, I have to say that I cannot specify the precise point at which the requirements of "due care" have been met. How much attention is

---

[16] Walzer, *Just and Unjust Wars*, p. 155.
[17] Ibid., pp. 155–156.
[18] Ibid., p. 319.
[19] Ibid., p. 157.

required? How much risk must be accepted? The line isn't clear. But it is clear enough that most campaigns are planned and carried out well below the line; and one can blame commanders who don't make minimal efforts, even if one doesn't know exactly what a maximal effort would entail.[20]

But, to reduce the risk to noncombatants, or to wait, may mean that the risk to one's own soldiers will increase. Walzer recognizes this and suggests that the "limits of risk are fixed, then, roughly at that point where any further risk taking would almost certainly doom the military venture or make it so costly that it could not be repeated."[21] C.A.J. Coady also acknowledges that increased care to avoid collateral damage may mean that greater risks for one's own side are taken. But he takes a more restrictive perspective. "The degree of risk to one's own troops or one's cause that is involved in avoiding collateral damage certainly needs to be factored into the understanding of [entirely avoiding incidental injury or damage] 'where possible,' but some risks need to be taken where the lives of innocent people are at stake."[22] There is a limit to what we can expect the military to do to protect civilian lives; commanders have a duty to their soldiers not to take undue risks with their lives.

On the other hand, in the same paragraph where Walzer emphasizes a "positive commitment to save civilian lives" and says that "if saving civilian lives means risking soldier's lives, the risk must be accepted," he also seems to weigh military necessity and force protection more heavily than civilian protection. Specifically, when Walzer argues that concern for risk for civilians has the potential to "doom the military venture," he then suggests that when the military objective is important or civilian protection may impose too great a burden on soldiers then greater risk to civilians must be accepted. Specifically, Walzer says that "there is a limit to the risks that we require" soldiers bear to protect civilians. Walzer's reasoning rests on the excusing power of the distinction between intended and unintended harm in the doctrine of double effect. "These are after all unintended deaths and legitimate military operations, and the absolute rule against attacking civilians does not apply. War necessarily places civilians in danger: that is another aspect of its hellishness. We can only ask soldiers to minimize the dangers they impose."[23]

Lex Lata: International Humanitarian Law

The tensions in Just War theory are also found in international humanitarian law, but the Just War tradition and international law are not the same. Starting in the

[20] Ibid., p. 319.

[21] Ibid., p. 157.

[22] C. A. J. Coady, "Bombing and the Morality of War," in Yuki Tanaka and Marilyn B. Young, eds., *Bombing Civilians: A Twentieth Century History* (New York: The New Press, 2009), pp. 191–214, 209.

[23] Walzer, *Just and Unjust Wars*, p. 156.

mid-nineteenth century, the term *military necessity* became understood by law of war specialists as a third element of *jus in bello* decisions about the use of force within war. In the Just War tradition, the term *necessity* is most often associated with the criteria for *jus ad bellum*, decisions to go to war and is only implied as a consideration in determining proportionality in the conduct of war. Under the interpretation of the laws of war now dominant, military necessity has come to mean having a military objective, doing something that is useful to win the war. The excusing power of "double effect" reasoning depends on the action being one of military necessity, understood as expansively as an action that contributes broadly to the success of the operation or the war, and a narrow reading of intention that minimizes foreseeable harm. An expansive definition of military necessity, as general utility, weakens the constraint of proportionality and widens the allowance for legal civilian killing. The exigency of war excuses the deaths of the other sides' civilians precisely because of the way that military necessity and proportionality are understood in international law.[24] How did this happen?

One of the seminal documents of international humanitarian law, and also a foundational document for US laws of war, is the US General Orders 100 (or the "Lieber Code" after its primary author, Frances Lieber), written for the North in 1863 to govern its conduct in the US Civil War. The definition of military necessity in General Orders 100 articulates the now dominant view: noncombatants ought to be protected, but they may also be killed in cases of military "necessity" defined both in terms of lawfulness and utility. In other words, while respect for noncombatants is to be assumed, military necessity can trump, or override, respect for noncombatants. "Military necessity, as understood by modern civilized nations, consists in the necessity of those measures which are indispensable for securing the ends of the war, and which are lawful according to the modern law and usages of war."[25] The General Orders continue, "Military necessity admits of all direct destruction of life or limb of armed enemies, and of other persons whose destruction is incidentally unavoidable in the armed contests of the war."[26] The use of the word "unavoidable" is important here: by prioritizing military utility, and equating it with military necessity, achieving the military objective becomes unquestionable, and the civilian casualties become unavoidable. General Orders 100 specifies the kinds of acts allowed as military necessity:

> it allows of the capturing of every armed enemy, and every enemy of importance to the hostile government, or of peculiar danger to the captor; it allows of all destruction of property, and obstruction of the ways

---

[24] Of course, it is the other side's civilians who are being put at risk and harmed. It is unlikely that a state would accept comparable risk to its own civilians, even in war.

[25] United States, *Laws of War: General Orders 100*, Article 14.

[26] Ibid., Article 15.

and channels of traffic, travel, or communication, and of all withholding of sustenance or means of life from the enemy; of the appropriation of whatever an enemy's country affords necessary for the subsistence and safety of the army, and of such deception as does not involve the breaking of good faith either positively pledged, regarding agreements entered into during the war, or supposed by the modern law of war to exist.[27]

In this way, "whatever" is necessary/useful is allowed. These acts are not unavoidable, but, rather, the result of tactical and strategic decisions about what may be useful.

Not surprisingly, given the use of the word "unavoidable," General Orders 100 implies the inevitability of killing civilians in war. But agency disappears— the cause is the "misfortune", "exigency," and/or "hardship" of "war." Article 156 says: "Common justice and plain expediency require that the military commander protect the manifestly loyal citizens, in revolted territories, against the hardships of the war as much as the common misfortune of all war admits."[28] While care can and should be taken to limit harm to noncombatants, there is a sense of fatalism about the inevitability of harm to civilians. "The principle has been more and more acknowledged that the unarmed citizen is to be spared in person, property, and honor as much as the exigencies of war will admit."[29] General Orders 100 also says: "The citizen or native of a hostile country is thus an enemy, as one of the constituents of the hostile state or nation, and as such is subjected to the hardships of the war."[30] The misfortune and exigency of war becomes a license in the General Orders to harm civilians when such harm is deemed necessary. This is also seen in the Articles that mention when it is lawful to starve or forcibly move or bombard noncombatants.

Art. 17.

War is not carried on by arms alone. It is lawful to starve the hostile belligerent, armed or unarmed, so that it leads to the speedier subjection of the enemy.

Art. 18.

When a commander of a besieged place expels the noncombatants, in order to lessen the number of those who consume his stock of provisions, it is lawful, though an extreme measure, to drive them back, so as to hasten on the surrender.

---

[27] Ibid., Article 15.
[28] Ibid., Article 156.
[29] Ibid., Article 22.
[30] Ibid., Article 21.

Art. 19.

Commanders, whenever admissible, inform the enemy of their intention to bombard a place, so that the noncombatants, and especially the women and children, may be removed before the bombardment commences. But it is no infraction of the common law of war to omit thus to inform the enemy. Surprise may be a necessity.[31]

International law scholar Gary Solis argues that "Lieber's embrace of the then-nebulous concept raised military necessity to a general legal principle and a commander's requirement."[32] Indeed, the privileging of military necessity, understood to mean utility, continued through the nineteenth- and early twentieth-century attempts to regulate conduct toward both combatants and noncombatants. The 1949 Geneva Conventions use language that is consistent with the Lieber Code: noncombatants are always to be treated "humanely" except when it is "necessary" not to do so. Article 27 of the 1949 Geneva Convention IV states: "Protected persons...shall at all times be humanely treated, and shall be protected especially against all acts of violence or threats thereof and against insults and public curiosity....However, the Parties to the conflict may take such measures of control and security in regard to protected persons as may be necessary as a result of the war."[33]

The 1977 Additional Protocols to the Geneva Convention ostensibly establish a bright line between combatant and noncombatant and resolve the issue of indeterminacy in favor of protecting potential noncombatants. Additional Protocol I defines civilians and civilian protection and prohibits indiscriminate attacks.[34] The language in Protocol I acknowledges that it is sometimes difficult to distinguish between combatants and noncombatants, but Protocol I is clear that the presumption should be for civilian status: "In case of doubt whether a person is a civilian, that person shall be considered to be a civilian."[35]

Article 85 of Geneva Convention's Additional Protocol I (AP I) labels the launching of large-scale, indiscriminate attacks against civilians with the knowledge that it will cause "excessive loss of life, injury to civilians and damage to civilian objects" a crime.

> ...the following acts shall be regarded as grave breaches of this Protocol, when committed willfully, in violation of the relevant provisions of this Protocol, and causing death or serious injury to body or health:

[31] Ibid., Articles 16–18.

[32] Gary D. Solis, *The Law of Armed Conflict: International Humanitarian Law in War* (Cambridge: Cambridge University Press, 2010), p. 260.

[33] Geneva Convention IV, Article 27.

[34] The Geneva Convention Additional Protocol I focuses on the protection of civilians during international conflict; Protocol II concerns civil conflicts.

[35] Geneva Convention Additional Protocol I, Article 50,

(a) Making the civilian population or individual civilians the object of attack;

(b) Launching an indiscriminate attack affecting the civilian population or civilian objects in the knowledge that such attack will cause excessive loss of life, injury to civilians or damage to civilian objects, as defined in Article 57, paragraph 2 (a) (iii);

(c) Launching an attack against works or installations containing dangerous forces in the knowledge that such attack will cause excessive loss of life, injury to civilians or damage to civilian objects, as defined in Article 57, paragraph 2 (a) (iii);

(d) Making non-defended localities and demilitarized zones the object of attack;

(e) Making a person the object of attack in the knowledge that he is *hors de combat*.[36]

But the bright line is not so bright, and the allowance of proportionality/double effect collateral damage is also in the Additional Protocol I, which permits actions that could be anticipated to harm civilians if it is not "excessive in relation to the concrete and direct military advantage anticipated."[37] As international law expert Judith Gardam notes, key to the determination of military advantage is the perceived "importance of the target for achieving a particular military objective. The more integral the proposed target is to the military strategy, the higher the level of likely civilian casualties and damage to civilian objects that will be acceptable."[38]

In this way, civilian protection is abandoned as an absolute value: it becomes a matter of a calculation about proportionality and military necessity. The precise meaning of *excessive* casualties is ambiguous in the Additional Protocol I; it depends on balancing between military necessity and likely casualties. Protocol I does not specify how to calculate the balance. Thus, while the AP I language says that "indiscriminate attacks are prohibited," it simultaneously gives permission to override the prohibition. An indiscriminate attack is defined in AP I, as one that "may be expected to cause incidental loss of civilian life, injury to civilians, damage to civilian objects, or a combination thereof, which would be excessive in relation to the concrete and direct military advantage anticipated."[39] Proportionality can thus override the prohibition on indiscriminate attacks.

Even the most specific international treaty prohibitions are ambiguous, but resolve the balancing of considerations in favor of military advantage. For instance, the 1980 "Convention on Prohibitions or Restrictions on the Use of Certain

---

[36] Ibid., Article 85, paragraph 3.

[37] Ibid., Article 51, paragraph 5b. In general, see Articles 48 to 51.

[38] Judith Gardam, *Necessity, Proportionality and the Use of Force by States* (Cambridge: Cambridge University Press, 2004), p. 100.

[39] Geneva Convention Additional Protocol I, Article 51.

Conventional Weapons Which May be Deemed to be Excessively Injurious or to Have Indiscriminate Effects" does not define excessive.[40] After *"further recalling* the general principle of the protection of the civilian population against the effects of hostilities," the treaty provisions use the phrases "superfluous injury" and "unnecessary suffering" in the preamble: *"Basing themselves* on the principle of international law that the right of the parties to an armed conflict to choose methods or means of warfare is not unlimited, and on the principle that prohibits the employment in armed conflicts of weapons, projectiles and material and methods of warfare of a nature to cause superfluous injury or unnecessary suffering." However, the treaty does deal more directly with the responsibility for acts that are not only intended but also the unintended, albeit nevertheless foreseeable result of using particular weapons: "it is prohibited to employ methods or means of warfare which are intended, or may be expected, to cause widespread, long-term and severe damage to the natural environment."[41]

The exceptions to this indeterminacy in the law of war are two recent treaties that build on the 1980 Conventional Weapons Convention where particular weapons have been defined as causing excessive and indiscriminate harm. The "Mine Ban Treaty" of 1997 and the "Convention on Cluster Munitions" of 2008, respectively, ban antipersonnel land mines and cluster munitions on the argument that by their "nature" those weapons are likely to cause excessive and indiscriminate harm. The preamble to the 1997 Land Mine Treaty repeats verbatim the language of the 1980 convention: "the right of the parties to an armed conflict to choose methods or means of warfare is not unlimited on the principle that prohibits the employment in armed conflicts of weapons, projectiles and materials and methods of warfare of a nature to cause superfluous injury or unnecessary suffering" and extends the logic to a prohibition of indiscriminate weapons "on the principle that a distinction must be made between civilians and combatants."[42]

While it may be disputable that some conventional weapons are more or less indiscriminate in their effects, there is little dispute about the indiscriminate effects of nuclear weapons. Nuclear weapons have four major types of effects: electromagnetic pulse; blast overpressure spread over a wide zone, that causes greater than hurricane force winds and can knock down or damage even steel reinforced buildings; high heat (enough to ignite large cities ablaze); and nuclear radiation

---

[40] "Convention on Prohibitions or Restrictions on the Use of Certain Conventional Weapons Which May be Deemed to be Excessively Injurious or to Have Indiscriminate Effects," 10 October 1980, http://www.icrc.org/ihl/INTRO/500.

[41] Preamble, "Convention on Prohibitions or Restrictions on the Use of Certain Conventional Weapons Which May be Deemed to be Excessively Injurious or to Have Indiscriminate Effects," 10 October 1980.

[42] "Convention on the Prohibition of the Use, Stockpiling, Production and Transfer of Anti-Personnel Mines and on Their Destruction," 18 September 1997, http://www.un.org/Depts/mine/UNDocs/ban_trty.htm.

that is "prompt" and "delayed" over the long-term of many years. The long-term radiation effects of nuclear use will span generations, while the use of many nuclear weapons would pose a threat to global environment and the sustainability of life on earth.

The 1996 International Court of Justice (ICJ) Advisory opinion on the legality of nuclear weapons threats and use described these effects in dramatic terms: "nuclear weapons as they exist today, releases not only immense quantities of heat and energy, but also powerful and prolonged radiation. According to the material before the Court, the first two causes of damage are vastly more powerful than the damage caused by other weapons, while the phenomenon of radiation is said to be peculiar to nuclear weapons. These characteristics render the nuclear weapon potentially catastrophic." Nuclear weapons use would thus be indiscriminate.

> The destructive power of nuclear weapons cannot be contained in either space or time. They have the potential to destroy all civilization and the entire ecosystem of the planet. The radiation released by a nuclear explosion would affect health, agriculture, natural resources and demography over a very wide area. Further, the use of nuclear weapons would be a serious danger to future generations. Ionizing radiation has the potential to damage the future environment, food and marine ecosystem, and to cause genetic defects and illness in future generations.[43]

Yet, even in the case of nuclear weapons, considerations of military necessity and proportionality trump the foreseeable effects of the weapons on noncombatants and future generations according to the majority opinion of the ICJ on the legality of the threat or use of nuclear weapons. The reasoning was that because states have the right to self-defense under the United Nations Charter, nuclear weapons use may be legitimate as long as it is "necessary" and "proportionate." According to the majority opinion, "The submission of the exercise of the right of self-defence to the conditions of necessity and proportionality is a rule of customary international law." The legal norm of proportionality is the constraining factor.

> The proportionality principle may thus not in itself exclude the use of nuclear weapons in self-defence in all circumstances. But at the same time, a use of force that is proportionate under the law of self-defence, must, in order to be lawful, also meet the requirements of the law applicable in armed conflict which comprise in particular the principles and rules of humanitarian law.[44]

---

[43] International Court of Justice (ICJ), "Threat or Use of Nuclear Weapons (Advisory Opinion)," 8 July 1996, excerpts from paragraph 35.

[44] ICJ, "Threat or Use of Nuclear Weapons (Advisory Opinion)," excerpt from paragraph 41.

And, even though the killing of many noncombatants would occur due to nuclear weapons use, the ICJ found, using current treaty and customary international law, that only the intent to do so could rise to a crime, such as genocide. "The Court would point out in that regard that the prohibition of genocide would be pertinent in this case if the recourse to nuclear weapons did indeed entail the element of intent, towards a group as such, required by the provision [of the 1949 Genocide Convention] quoted above." Moreover, the ICJ does not allow *foreseeable* and *unintended* harm to count as a crime. Only retrospective judgment is possible. "In the view of the Court, it would only be possible to arrive at such a conclusion after having taken due account of the circumstances specific to each case."[45] But who is to judge necessity and on what grounds?

> The Court does not find it necessary to embark upon the quantification of such risks; nor does it need to enquire into the question whether tactical nuclear weapons exist which are sufficiently precise to limit those risks: it suffices for the Court to note that the very nature of all nuclear weapons and the profound risks associated therewith are further considerations to be borne in mind by States believing they can exercise a nuclear response in self-defence in accordance with the requirements of proportionality.[46]

The users of nuclear weapons are to inform the United Nations Security Council after the fact of their use, where the questions of military necessity, proportionality, and intention would be assessed.

Restrictive and Permissive Interpretations of Military Necessity

International humanitarian law articulates an ambiguous understanding of military necessity that is descendent from the Just War tradition. As Asa Kasher and Amos Yadlin note, "Although the notion of 'military necessity' is ubiquitous in evaluations of military activities, legal deliberations and philosophical analyses have failed to establish a commonly held meaning of the term."[47] The law leaves each belligerent to be the judge in its own cause with regard to whether its choice of targets, weapons,

---

[45] ICJ, "Threat or Use of Nuclear Weapons (Advisory Opinion)," excerpt from paragraph 26. By contrast, both the majority and minority reports of the General Advisory Committee of the Atomic Energy Commission, a committee composed entirely of scientists, was that thermonuclear weapons use was "genocidal." "General Advisory Committee's Majority and Minority Report on Building the H-Bomb," 30 October 1949, http://www.atomicarchive.com/Docs/Hydrogen/GACReport.shtml.

[46] ICJ, "Threat or Use of Nuclear Weapons (Advisory Opinion)," excerpt from paragraph 43.

[47] Asa Kasher and Amos Yadlin, "Assassination and Preventive Killing," *SAIS Review*, vol. 25, no. 1 (Winter-Spring, 2005): 41–57, 47.

and rules of engagement protect noncombatants and do not cause excessive harm.[48] The fact that combatants are also to determine the military necessity and proportionality of their own plans and actions means that it matters just how they define military necessity, since military necessity will more than likely be the dominant consideration—if only because it is the job of soldiers and their commanders to win the battles and the war. However, military necessity can be understood in at least two different ways, one restrictive, and the other expansive or permissive.[49]

The restrictive interpretation of military necessity, which is closest to the Just War tradition's *jus ad bellum* understanding of necessary, is that force is the only way to achieve a particular objective and one uses only so much force as required. If some alternative means could achieve the result, without risk of harm to civilians, then that course of action should be pursued. An act is necessary if it is required to achieve some objective; it is indispensible in the sense that absent that action, the objective cannot be achieved. Military necessity then authorizes, as General Orders 100 suggests, "those measures which are *indispensible* for securing the ends of war."[50] The Hague Convention of 1899 articulates this usage of necessity when it prohibits destroying or seizing an enemy's property "unless such destruction or seizure be *imperatively* demanded by the *necessities* of war."[51]

This restrictive interpretation of military necessity functions as a limit or ceiling to guard against excessive or unnecessary uses of force: only that force which is necessary or required may be employed, and nothing "excessive" beyond that which is necessary should be used. For example, the US General Orders 100 says what is not allowed: "Military necessity does not admit of cruelty—that is, the infliction of suffering for the sake of suffering or for revenge, nor of maiming or wounding except in fight, nor of torture to extort confessions. It does not admit of the use of poison in any way, nor of the wanton devastation of a district."[52] Similarly, the 1907 Hague Convention states that "the right of belligerents to adopt means of injuring the enemy is not unlimited"—and it forbid weapons "calculated to cause unnecessary suffering."[53] Nearly verbatim language appears in later treaties, for example, "the

---

[48] Judgments of the decisions of individual commanders, after the fact, may be made a criminal court.

[49] If it is helpful, one might think of these two interpretations as corresponding to deontological and consequentialist forms of reasoning.

[50] United States, *Laws of War: General Orders 100*, Article 14, emphasis added.

[51] Emphasis added, Hague Convention with Respect to the Laws and Customs of War on Land (Hague II), 29 July 1899, Article 23 and also Hague Convention with Respect to the Laws and Customs of War on Land 1907, Article 23.

[52] United States, *Laws of War: General Orders 100*, Article 15. Similarly, Napoleon said, "My great maxim has always been, in politics and war alike, that every injury done to an enemy, even though permitted by the rules, is excusable only in so far as it is absolutely necessary; everything beyond that is criminal." Quoted in Geoffrey Best, *War and Law Since 1945* (Oxford: Oxford University Press, 1994), p. 242.

[53] Hague Convention with Respect to the Laws and Customs of War on Land (Hague IV), 18 October 1907, 22 and 23.

right of the parties to an armed conflict to choose methods or means of warfare is not unlimited."[54] Under this view, the justification for the acknowledged harm of collateral damage is that while some noncombatants may be harmed, *no more will be harmed than is necessary* to accomplish the military objective and the harm is only justified because the act is necessary. Thus, the Geneva Convention Additional Protocol I says, "When a choice is possible between several military objectives for obtaining a similar military advantage, the objective to be selected shall be that the attack on which may be expected to cause the least danger to civilian lives and to civilian objects."[55]

Some contemporary students of the Just War tradition take a restrictive view. For example, Larry May defines necessity as: "only that use of force that can accomplish the military objective is justified."[56] Similarly, C. A. J. Coady takes the restrictive view of necessity when he argues for "the requirement that we should not embark upon actions involving collateral damage, and hence should not resort to the DDE [doctrine of double effect], unless we have first examined other feasible ways of achieving the good end that do not involve the harmful side effects or involve fewer or less grave such effects."[57] May and Coady follow the sixteenth-century scholar Francisco de Vitoria, who advised that "it is never lawful to kill innocent people, even accidentally and unintentionally, except when it advances a just war which cannot be won any other way."[58] Yet, even when adopting the restrictive view of necessity, one still has the very concrete problem of distinguishing what is minimally necessary and what is excessive.

By contrast, in interpretations of military necessity that are permissive or expansive, necessity is a synonym for military utility and functions as a license to override prohibitions on harm to noncombatants when doing so would be useful. "For example, an analysis of 'military necessity' as 'what facilitates victory' would allow killing prisoners of war. Another analysis in terms of 'what is needed to secure a victory over enemy troops' specifies what should be maximized, that is what is to be accomplished 'most efficiently' although it fails to specify what should be minimized and thus accomplished 'at least cost.' "[59] An action considered militarily necessary can excuse a breach in the law of war or is defined so that it is legal. On this reading of necessity, bright-line prohibitions fade, and the choice is a matter of calculating the degree of advantage to be gained from using force in a particular

---

[54] "Convention on Prohibitions or Restrictions on the Use of Certain Conventional Weapons Which May be Deemed to be Excessively Injurious or to Have Indiscriminate Effects," 10 October 1980.

[55] Geneva Convention Additional Protocol I, Article 57, paragraph 3.

[56] Larry May, *War Crimes and Just War* (Cambridge: Cambridge University Press, 2007), p. 21.

[57] C. A. J. Coady, "Bombing and the Morality of War," in Yuki Tanaka and Marilyn B. Young, eds., *Bombing Civilians: A Twentieth Century History* (New York: The New Press, 2009), pp. 191–214, 209.

[58] Quoted in Coady, "Bombing and the Morality of War," p. 209.

[59] Kasher and Yadlin, "Assassination and Preventive Killing," p. 47.

way and weighing the advantages against the costs to noncombatants. Necessity, according to one Marine Lieutenant Colonel, thus becomes a "moral allowance."[60] Or as Yoram Dinstein argues, "Even extensive civilian casualties may be acceptable, if they are not excessive in light of the concrete and direct military advantage anticipated."[61]

Although some, including the American military historian and legal expert W. Hays Parks cautioned against an expansive understanding of necessity as utility—*"Military convenience* must not be mistaken for *military necessity"*—there is conceptual room to interpret military necessity as military convenience in international law.[62] The Hague Convention of 1899 articulates this understanding of necessity in the preamble: the provisions of the treaty were "inspired by the desire to diminish the evils of war so far as military necessities permit."[63] Similarly, the 1899 and 1907 Hague Conventions forbid belligerents to "destroy or seize the enemy's property, unless such destruction or seizure be imperatively demanded by the necessities of war."[64] In other words, there are limits to conduct in war, but humanitarian considerations may be overridden by military necessity. Although never ratified, the 1923 Hague Rules of Air Warfare similarly stress the immunity of noncombatants from aerial attack, while simultaneously allowing for the attack of the areas where noncombatants reside: "In the immediate neighborhood of the operations of land forces, the bombardment of cities, towns, villages, dwellings, or buildings is legitimate provided that there exists a reasonable presumption that the military concentration is sufficiently important to justify such bombardment, having regard to the danger thus caused to the civilian population."[65]

An extreme version of the permissive view of military necessity holds that necessity trumps law altogether, or that the law is a valid guide to action only when it suits necessity. In the nineteenth and early twentieth century some German strategists believed that *kriegsraison*, reason of war, trumped the law of war: when particular means were understood as necessary to achieve victory, they were justified.[66] A 1915 German text described the logic this way: "By steeping himself in military history an officer will be able to guard himself against excessive humanitarian notions, it

---

[60] Lt. Col. Ian Houck, at the conference on "Civilian Devastation" at George Mason University, Fairfax, VA, March 2009.

[61] Yoram Dinstein, "Collateral Damage and the Principle of Proportionality," in David Wippman and Mathew Evangelista, eds., *New Wars, New Laws? Applying the Laws of War in the 21st Century* (Ardsley, NY: Transnational Publishers, 2005), pp. 211–224, 214.

[62] Quoted in Solis, *The Law of Armed Conflict*, p. 269.

[63] Hague Convention with Respect to the Laws and Customs of War on Land (Hague II), 29 July 1899, preamble.

[64] Hague Convention with Respect to the Laws and Customs of War on Land (Hague IV), 18 October 1907, Article 23.

[65] Hague Rules of Air Warfare, 1923, Article XXIV.

[66] See Mika Nishmura Hayashi, "The Martens Clause and Military Necessity," in Hensel, ed., *The Legitimate Use of Military Force*, pp. 135–159; Walzer, *Just and Unjust Wars*, p. 144.

will teach him that certain severities are indispensible to war, nay more that the only true humanity very often lies in a ruthless application of them."[67] This extreme view is generally derided, although there is sometimes a tendency to define necessity too broadly, perhaps legitimating a desire to take shortcuts.

Thus, the first route to an expansive definition of military necessity is to equate it with military utility. A second route to a permissive conception of military necessity is to say that the threat is so extreme as to legitimize any means. Winston Churchill employed such an expansive understanding of military necessity in World War II on the belief that civilization was at stake if the Nazis were to win. Britain was faced with a "supreme emergency," he argued, "Our defeat would mean an age of barbaric violence, and would be fatal, not only to ourselves but to the independent life of every small country in Europe.... The letter of the law must not in supreme emergency obstruct those who are charged with its protection and enforcement." The law must yield to military advantage according to Churchill. "It would not be right or rational that the aggressive Power should gain one set of advantages by tearing up all laws, and another set by sheltering behind the innate respect for law of its opponents. Humanity, rather than legality, must be our guide."[68]

On the one hand, the threat really is so grave it could justify extraordinary measures. On the other hand, as many have noted, the logic of supreme emergency (used to justify or give permission to violations of the laws of war) is often at work in cases where there is no such extreme danger, but it rather functions to bolster the assertion of military necessity as permission by asserting that there is no alternative.[69] In discussing the reasoning of "supreme emergency," which could allow for deliberately killing civilians, as during the allied terror bombing of World War II, Walzer argues that there must really be such a supreme emergency (which he suggests is not as common as wartime rhetoric often supposes), and that there must be no other alternative to using extreme measures, such as bombing that would certainly harm civilians and might make a significant military contribution. Walzer's reasoning underscores how the assertion of supreme emergency can be used to trump the protections of the rules of war, and he rejects such a path except in *true* supreme emergencies when there is no other alternative. Ultimately, Walzer concludes:

> These, then are the limits of military necessity. Utilitarian calculation can force us to violate the rules of war only when we are face-to-face not merely with defeat but with a defeat likely to bring disaster to a political community. But these calculations have no similar effects when what is at stake is

---

[67] Quoted in Solis, *The Law of Armed Conflict*, p. 266.

[68] Quoted in Walzer, *Just and Unjust Wars*, p. 245

[69] I do not have space here to fully consider the criteria for calling a situation a supreme emergency, nor to discuss whether and what kinds of force such a framing of the situation would permit. That is a much larger discussion. See Orend, *The Morality of War*, pp. 140–159; Walzer, *Just and Unjust Wars*, pp. 251–268; Kaufman, "Just War Theory and Killing the Innocent."

only the speed or the scope of victory. They are relevant only to the conflict between winning and fighting well, not to the internal problems of combat itself. Whenever that conflict is absent, calculation is stopped short by the rules of war and the rights they are designed to protect. Confronted by these rights, we are not able to calculate consequences, or figure relative risks, or compute probable casualties, but simply stop short and turn aside.[70]

Walzer thus appears to want to rein in the expansive conception of military necessity and return to a restrictive formulation. In this way, the important distinction between military necessity (which is applied by decision-makers to both tactical and strategic situations) and supreme emergency (which ought to be applied only to extreme cases) is blurred or lost.

When the distinction between supreme emergency and military necessity is blurred, the already ambiguous concept of military necessity, defined as utility or even convenience, is given more weight than risk to noncombatants or even one's own forces. Blurring the distinction between military necessity and supreme emergency may then diminish the strong inhibiting effect of the principle of noncombatant immunity and elevate the importance of the military objective in a particular operation, thus permitting and justifying the inadvertent and foreseeable killing or harm of civilians.

The Intentional versus the Foreseeable

The excusing power of double effect rests on two logical pillars: military necessity, understood either restrictively or permissively, and intention. As with military necessity, different interpretations of intention can be accommodated within traditions of ethics and international law. Commanders may foresee civilian death but not intend it. Intention is not simply what is in the commander's mind to be described after the fact, but evident in how the commander acted.

The law of war conception of intention generally minimizes foreseeability; unintentional acts are not of great concern, regardless of whether they can be or have been foreseen. Most law of war experts interpret intention this way, perhaps because the question of intentions (whether there is *mens rea*) is at the heart of criminal liability; if someone intends to do something that is wrong, they may be criminally responsible. As Hannah Arendt argued, this is the prevailing "assumption current in all modern legal systems that intent to do wrong is necessary for the commission of a crime.... Where this intent is absent... we feel no crime has been committed."[71] If

[70] Walzer, *Just and Unjust Wars*, p. 268.

[71] Hannah Arendt, *Eichmann in Jerusalem: A Report on the Banality of Evil* (New York: Penguin Books, 1963), p. 277.

intentions are good then, it seems, much can be forgiven. Similarly, Yoram Dinstein, who is concerned with questions of when someone should be charged with a crime, argues that a person is criminally liable when they intend harm to civilians, whether or not they actually harm the civilians, and an "absence of intention to attack civilians or civilian objects relieves the actor of criminal accountability for the targeting of civilians."[72] According to this view, intention is more important than the foreseeable or actual result of the action.

What about those cases where collateral harm to civilians is not intended but may be both incidental and anticipated? In these cases, it may not be our intention to harm the other, but we know we are likely to do so. Harm was foreseen as a reasonably likely or even certain, outcome. Specifically, as Dinstein says, "a belligerent may fully realize in advance that the destruction of a particular military objective can be accomplished only by injuring civilians or damaging a civilian object." Dinstein then asks, "Is it mandatory to abort the attack under these circumstances?"[73] Dinstein's answer is, basically, that it depends on the situation. If anticipated military utility is high, the attack is lawful even if we know civilians are likely to be killed and that attack need not be aborted. What is important for Dinstein, and many others, is the specific and immediate intention of the actor. "Just as the absence of intention to attack civilians or civilian objects relieves the actor of criminal accountability for the targeting of civilians, presence of such an intention should tilt the balance in the opposite direction" even in the case where no harm to civilians occurred.[74]

The focus on the specific intentions of individual actors—as more important than unintended and foreseeable consequences, and as a moral allowance—helps determine whether civilian killing is collateral damage or a crime. If we accept the view that what matters is what someone intended, then determinations of whether the consequences of an act are intentional or unintentional will have legal and normative effects—defining and determining right from wrong. Or, as Scott Veitch argues, "Intention, and particularly 'good intentions'—or at least not 'bad intentions—have a potent legitimation function in the disavowal of actions that knowingly and foreseeably result in harms. The search for intentions...accounts for an important way in which immunity from attributions of responsibilities occurs; when intention is built into a legal definition, not finding it is one important way of making responsibility disappear."[75] This has the consequence, as Veitch says, that, "a lack of intention covers a multitude of killings."[76] When the harm is unintended, it may be lawful.

[72] Yoram Dinstein, *The Conduct of Hostilities under the Law of International Armed Conflict*, 2d ed. (Cambridge: Cambridge University Press, 2010), p. 125.

[73] Dinstein, "Collateral Damage and the Principle of Proportionality," p. 212.

[74] Dinstein, *The Conduct of Hostilities under the Law of International Armed Conflict*, p. 125.

[75] Scott Veitch, *Law and Irresponsibility: On the Legitimation of Human Suffering* (New York: Routledge, 2007), p. 108.

[76] Ibid., p. 109.

But, one may not only be concerned with determining whether an individual intentionally broke the law, or was criminally negligent. An act may be perfectly legal, and nevertheless, morally troubling.[77] As Brian Orend suggests, the "core moral problem" here is that "even if soldiers intentionally aim *only* at legitimate targets, they can often *foresee* that taking out some of these targets will still involve *collateral* civilian casualties. And if civilians do nothing to lose their human rights, doesn't it follow that such acts will be unjust, since civilians will predictably suffer some harm or even death?"[78] Orend has identified the problem—what is the difference between intentional and foreseeable if we accept foreseeable consequences as necessary, *sine qua non*, to our ends even without specifically having the foreseeable consequence as an immediate intention?

The alternative to a legalist weighting of intentions is to give more weight to foreseeability; that is, to be as concerned with what can be foreseen as with an actor's clear intention.[79] In other words, there is more on the mind of an attacker or the commander who sends them, than their intentions; they have, or ought to have, a number of considerations in view, including likely foreseeable unintended consequences. To weigh foreseeability on par with intentions has the consequence that the doctrine of double effect is pushed aside; unintentional consequences matter as much as intended ones. Even if the military objective is met, saying for the moment nothing about whether the objective is a military necessity, if a pattern of civilian death emerges where harm is foreseeable and perhaps even foreseen, the lawfulness of the individual commander's orders is beside the point. The core issue is that the harm to noncombatants was, in this scenario, reasonably foreseeable, even if unintentional. To ask about what is foreseeable is to ask about the larger patterns of operations and their effects.

At times, international lawyers and soldiers do weigh the foreseeability of harm to civilians on par with intention and sometimes fault actors for failing to attend to the foreseeable consequences of their actions. For example, classifying indiscriminate attack as a crime implies that foreseeable unintended consequences are as important as intended consequences. Thus, Dinstein argues: "The indiscriminate character of an attack is not a by-product of 'body count' (i.e. the ensuing number

---

[77] A focus on intentionality from a criminal liability perspective exemplifies the potential consequences of "legalism," the "ethical attitude that holds moral conduct to be a matter of rule following." Judith N. Shklar, *Legalism: Law, Morals and Political Trials* (Cambridge, MA: Harvard University Press, 1964), p. 1.

[78] Brian Orend, *The Morality of War* (Peterborough, Ontario: Broadview Press, 2006), p. 115, emphasis in the original.

[79] It is to take something like the view that the "intention of an act is implied in the structure of the act, and not in some moment of psychological clarity in the actor." Oliver O'Donovan, quoted in Nigel Biggar, "Christianity and Weapons of Mass Destruction," in Sohail Hashmi and Steven P. Lee, eds., *Ethics and Weapons of Mass Destruction: Religious and Secular Perspectives* (New York: Cambridge University Press, 2004), pp. 168–99, 177.

of civilian fatalities). The key to a finding that a certain attack has been indiscriminate is the nonchalant state of mind of the attacker."[80] In other words, if the attacker showed no concern for the effect of an attack on civilians, they may be criminally liable. "Nonchalance" is not evidence of good faith intention.

In defining an indiscriminate attack, Judith Gardam places foreseeability more squarely into the frame of reference. "Indiscriminate attacks...strictly speaking delineate the situations in which the international community has decided *on the basis of prior experience* that the level of civilian casualties and damage to civilian objects is more than likely to be unacceptable."[81] Gardam argues that the issue of criminal liability for indiscriminate attacks, absent an intention to harm, turns on whether the attack was indiscriminate due to a lack of care—the actor knew unintended negative consequences were possible, or even likely, but proceeded anyway.

Foresight and unintended consequences are also taken into account under provisions of international law that stress taking "reasonable precautions" to reduce or avoid harm to civilians. Specifically, Article 57 of the Geneva Convention Additional Protocol I uses terms such as "constant care" and "precautions" to suggest that planners look to the foreseeable unintended consequences of operations.

> In the conduct of military operations, constant care shall be taken to spare the civilian population, civilians and civilian objects." And, those who "plan or decided upon an attack shall....
>
>   (ii) take all feasible precautions in the choice of means and methods of attack with a view to avoiding, and in any event to minimizing, incidental loss or civilian life, injury to civilians and damage to civilian objects." Further, the Article stresses the importance of foreseeability by suggesting attackers either refrain from deciding to launch an attack that will yield "incidental loss of life" or abort such attack. Planners and decision-makers should:
> (iii) refrain from deciding to launch any attack which may be expected to cause incidental loss of civilian life, injury to civilians, damage to civilian objects, or a combination thereof, which would be excessive in relation to the concrete and direct military advantage anticipated;
>
>   (b) an attack shall be cancelled or suspended if it becomes apparent that the objective is not a military one or is subject to special protection or that the attack may be expected to cause incidental loss of civilian life, injury to civilians, damage to civilian objects, or a combination thereof, which would be excessive in relation to the concrete and direct military advantage anticipated;

[80] Dinstein, *The Conduct of Hostilities under the Law of International Armed Conflict*, p. 127.
[81] Gardam, *Necessity, Proportionality and the Use of Force by States*, p. 95, emphasis added.

However, even in cases where harm is foreseeable and precautions are required, military necessity and proportionality are weighted more heavily in the Geneva Convention Additional Protocol I than concern for civilian life or civilian objects. Actors "shall...take all *reasonable* precautions to avoid losses of civilian lives and damage to civilian objects" but must only refrain from, cancel, or suspend an attack if "damage to civilian objects, or a combination thereof, which would be excessive in relation to the concrete and direct military advantage anticipated."[82] As if to balance the permission to cause some degree of harm that is implicit in the idea of reasonable precautions and proportionality—avoiding excessive harm but allowing some proportionate harm—the idea of precaution is later underscored: "No provision of this article may be construed as authorizing any attacks against the civilian population, civilians or civilian objects."[83]

The foreseeability of long-term harm to civilians also arises in the discussion of targeting of objects "indispensible to the survival of the civilian population." Specifically, Article 54 of AP I prohibits starvation as a method of war and prohibits the attack, destruction, removal, or rendering useless of objects "such as foodstuffs, agricultural areas, crops, livestock, drinking water installations and supplies, irrigation works, for the specific purpose of denying them for their sustenance value to the civilian population, whatever the motive."[84] That attacks on dual use objects will harm civilians is acknowledged when the Article suggests that such attacks are permissible "provided, however, that in no event shall actions against these objects be taken which may be expected to leave the civilian population with such inadequate food or water as to cause its starvation or force its movement."[85]

The question then arises whether the potential negative consequences for civilians were not simply foreseeable but were foreseen. The law of war deals with anticipation in terms of the competence and the intentions of the commander in specific cases. The trouble is that too often in war, events are seen as unique incidents, and thus the patterns that develop in war, for instance, of weapons failures or procedures that routinely produce collateral damage, are too often not recognized. If they were, one might shift the framing of an incident from tragic accident to systemic collateral damage. The importance of stressing foreseeability of the harm to civilians (which had been almost erased from the calculation because of the forgiving power of the principle of double effect), rather than intention, is that it gives greater weight to anticipating harm, putting

[82] Geneva Convention Additional Protocol I, Article 57, paragraph 4, emphasis added.

[83] Geneva Convention Additional Protocol I, Article 57, paragraph 5.

[84] The exceptions are objects that provide resources "solely" for the military and objects that are "dual use," which are used in "direct support of military action."

[85] Article 55 also prohibits attacks on the natural environment that would cause harm to health. Article 56 prohibits attacks on works or installations containing dangerous forces that could be released unless it is used for military functions and such an attack is the "only feasible way to terminate such support."

the protection of civilian life on more equal footing with the anticipated military advantage, which itself is also "foreseen," not certain.

Indeed, the 1998 Rome Statute of the International Criminal Court both preserves the focus on military necessity and military advantage while highlighting foreknowledge of incidental harm to civilians. Such foreknowledge of incidental harm to noncombatants may be criminal even if that harm is unintended. The relevant text of the ICC Statute suggests an individual may have committed a war crime of: "Intentionally launching an attack in the knowledge that such attack will cause incidental loss of life or injury to civilians or damage to civilian objects or widespread, long-term and severe damage to the natural environment which would be clearly excessive in relation to the concrete and direct overall military advantage anticipated."[86] Not surprisingly, US military lawyers (Judge Advocates or judge advocate generals (JAGs)) resist a conception of intention that includes foreseeability because the framework for understanding moral and legal responsibility changes once one considers the foreseeability of the consequences of an act. One US military lawyer argues that this ICC statute goes too far, that the provision is "sufficiently vague to allow and perhaps invite, prosecutions for almost any collateral damage incident."[87]

Returning to Proportionality

In war zones, soldiers and civilians share risk and vulnerability, but not usually to the same degree or level of consent. International humanitarian law clearly stipulates that states ought to protect civilians from ("unnecessary" or "excess") harm.[88] Yet, the laws of war seem to privilege military necessity or military advantage, yielding to an expansive conception of military necessity and a narrow understanding of individual commander's intention. Even those parts of the Geneva Convention Additional Protocol I concerned with foreseeable unintended harm, weight military necessity very heavily. The question for commanders and observers then becomes one of proportionality: "damage to civilian objects, or a combination thereof, which would be excessive in relation to the concrete and direct military advantage anticipated." The trouble in calculating proportionality is how to compare and weigh different values: the value of a military objective, the value of soldiers' lives, and the value of civilian lives.

[86] Article 8(2)(b)(iv) of Rome Statute of International Criminal Court, adopted 1998. http://untreaty.un.org/cod/icc/statute/romefra.htm.

[87] Jefferson D. Reynolds, "Collateral Damage on the 21st Century Battlefield: Enemy Exploitation of the Law of Armed Conflict, and the Struggle for the Moral High Ground," *Air Force Law Review*, vol. 56 (2005): 1–108, 69.

[88] Sometimes protecting one's own forces is a military necessity while at other times, one's own soldiers are considered expendable. As I argued earlier, force protection, valuing the life and limb of soldiers as more than expendable assets and minimizing risk to soldiers, is a relatively new concern when compared to the value of civilian protection.

The weighing of necessity and proportionality are likely to be biased toward state interests and not those of the potential civilian victims. States, and in the moment, commanders, are the judge in their own cause and, as US military lawyers make clear, they do not apply international humanitarian law, but the "laws of war." As the philosopher Jeff McMahan observes, "one can always claim that one's goals are so important, and one's situation is so precarious, that what may seem like an inconsequential military advantage is in fact vital to the security of one's people."[89]

The line between acceptable collateral damage (those unintended killings of noncombatants which are to be excused under the doctrine of double effect), and excessive harm or even atrocity is unclear. Indeed, as Thomas Nagel argues, "It is not easy to keep a firm grip on the idea of what is not permissible in warfare, because while some military actions are obvious atrocities, other cases are more difficult to assess, and the general principles underlying these judgments remain obscure."[90] The problem of determining whether some action is necessary and the potential military gain is proportionate to the potential loss of civilian life does not go away even if we underscore the idea that military necessity must be interpreted restrictively and that foreseeable consequences cannot be excused simply because they were unintended. We are left with the issue of what is acceptable versus unacceptable harm, and from whose perspective. Dinstein argues that there is no simple way to determine proportionality in the abstract: it must be "calculated in relation to a given attack."[91] But that is too narrow. We must necessarily be concerned with the proportionality of a particular attack, but also with overall proportionality of harm in war.

In the introduction, I quoted US Major General William Caldwell's argument that we should not think of one particular incident of collateral damage in Iraq as typical of a pattern. While the "temptation exists to lump all these incidents together," General Caldwell argued, "each case needs to be examined individually."[92] Yes, each case deserves its own analysis. Yet, understanding the effects of restrictive versus permissive interpretations of military necessity requires "adding up" individual instances of collateral damage and evaluating whether they are the predictable and foreseeable result of specific choices of doctrine, weapons, tactics, or rules engagement. Civilian lives have been discounted in proportionality/double effect calculations that use permissive definitions of military necessity and a narrow emphasis on intended outcomes in isolated cases. When this happens repeatedly, individual collateral damage incidents may well be legal but can nevertheless "add up" to a great deal of harm to civilians. If a restrictive interpretation of military necessity is used, and the intended and unintended but nevertheless foreseeable, consequences of an attack are considered to be equally

---

[89] Jeff McMahan, *Killing in War* (Oxford: Oxford University Press, 2009), pp. 30–31.

[90] Thomas Nagel, "War and Massacre," *Philosophy and Public Affairs*, 1 (Winter 1972): 123–144, 124.

[91] Dinstein, "Collateral Damage and the Principle of Proportionality," p. 217.

[92] Caldwell, quoted in John D. Banusiewicz, "Probe Clears Coalition Forces of Wrongdoing in March 15 Raid," American Forces Information Services New Articles, US Department of Defense, 3 June 2006. http://www.defense.gov/News/NewsArticle.aspx?ID=16139.

important, then concerns about civilian casualties would be more heavily weighted. The excusing power of double effect would thus be limited in the cases where we suspect some number of civilian casualties may occur, and in those where we are making a conscious trade-off of military advantage against innocent lives. And we must not forget that there are genuine accidents.[93]

Although the hold of the permissive and intention-oriented understanding of military necessity and double effect is strong, the historical trend in the United States has gradually moved toward a more restrictive understanding of military necessity and toward a greater concern for unintended effects. I suggest that this gradual change is driven in part by a strategic and political concern for the consequences of collateral damage—collateral damage prompts a negative reaction that can make military operations more difficult and diminish political support. My reason for making these tensions and the logic explicit is to strengthen the movement toward a more restrictive understanding of military necessity.

The ambiguous understanding of the norms of military necessity, proportionality, and the duties to reduce risk to both combatants and noncombatants are evident in US doctrine, operations, and laws of war during the twentieth century. When push comes to shove—that is when political leaders or soldiers feel that their backs are against the wall—there are still many who prefer the more expansive understanding of military necessity which may too easily become an "anything goes" as long as it helps logic. When military necessity is privileged over concern for civilians, there is less attention to reducing risk to civilians and a tendency to focus only the most grievous acts of intentional harm to civilians—those cases of massive destruction or instances when soldiers "snap."

Evolution of US Views of Necessity, Proportionality, and Due Care

During World War I, World War II, and the Korean War, civilians were deliberately targeted on the view that doing so would hasten the end of the war by breaking the enemy's will or reducing their contribution to the war effort. However, there were often arguments about both the morality and efficacy of targeting civilians, and the

---

[93] There is a further problem. Combatants sometimes hope to take advantage of international law by putting civilians in harm's way, by for instance putting bases near civilian areas or by sheltering near civilians, to forestall attack. Or combatants may put civilians in harm's way by preventing or discouraging civilians from leaving an area. But to do so is clearly a crime under Article 51 of Additional Protocol I. Further, Article 58 of Geneva Convention Additional Protocol I notes that parties to a conflict should protect civilians by limiting their vulnerability to attack. Again, whether or not the civilians functioning as shields were there voluntarily or their presence was involuntary, military necessity seems to trump their protected status in most cases. See Dinstein, *The Conduct of Hostilities under the Law of International Armed Conflict*, pp. 152–155.

interpretation of relevant international law reflected the tensions between the normative beliefs of military necessity, civilian protection, and force protection.

For example, in World War II, tensions surrounding the "moral issue," as it was then called, were clearly articulated with respect to strategic bombing. Ronald Schaffer, a historian of American bombing in World War II, found that "virtually every major figure concerned with American bombing expressed some views about the moral issue—a phrase that usually meant to them the bombing of cities and civilians, though it also referred to air attacks on artifacts of civilization." American commanders faced competing virtues, namely the desire for a speedy victory and growing discomfort with killing civilians. Thus, Schaffer found that the Americans "who conducted the air war and those who advised them were divided among themselves and sometimes divided within themselves about moral questions that bombing raised.... while moral constraints almost invariably bowed to what people described as military necessity, there was substantial dispute over what military necessity meant"[94]

In its major wars since World War II and Korea, the United States' understanding of the balance between military necessity, force protection, and noncombatant immunity has evolved. When the idea of noncombatant immunity was gradually institutionalized in the middle of the twentieth century, the prohibition on killing civilians and the exceptions created by military necessity and double effect created a tension that has not been resolved. The evolution of US military doctrine is reflected in the relevant US military field manuals and legal documents, which themselves refer to the 1949 Geneva Conventions as a source of US military law.[95]

The US Law of Land Warfare of 1956 is clear that the purpose of the law is "to diminish the evils of war by: a. Protecting both combatants and non-combatants from unnecessary suffering; b. Safeguarding certain fundamental human rights of persons."[96] As with the earlier Lieber Code, the aim is to avoid "unnecessary" suffering, but military necessity does not vitiate the force of international law. The question obviously becomes, what is militarily "necessary" and what is unnecessary suffering. The air and ground forces began to use specific rules of engagement in the Korean War to impart instructions and rules of thumb.[97] Further, the United States signed the 1977 Geneva Convention Additional Protocols I and II, and although the Senate has never ratified these treaties, for the most part, the United States observes their provisions.

[94] Ronald Schaffer, *Wings of Judgment: American Bombing in World War II* (Oxford: Oxford University Press: 1985), p. xii.

[95] See United States "The Uniform Code of Military Justice," Preamble on the sources of military jurisdiction, p. A21-3.

[96] U.S. Army Field Manuel (27-10) *The Law of Land Warfare* of 1956 (revised in 1976), paragraph 2.

[97] Mark Martins, "Rules of Engagement for Land Forces: A Matter of Training, Not Lawyering," *Military Law Review*, vol. 143, no. 1 (Winter 1994): 1–160, 34–35.

The Vietnam War marks the beginning of a turning point in the US treatment of civilians. In Vietnam, W. Hays Parks suggests, the rules for assessing the balance between military necessity and civilian protection, depended on the political calculations of the president, and, Parks believes, the president tipped too far in avoiding civilian death at the expense of military necessity. The tensions were acute during the "Rolling Thunder" bombing campaign, when the military services, the Office of the Secretary of Defense, and the State Department selected targets and the White House approved them. Rolling Thunder, which began in March 1965, was initially conceived as an eight-week effort; it lasted forty-four months and became the subject of intense debate within the Johnson administration and between the military and civilians.[98] Each Tuesday during and after lunch, President Johnson, Secretary of Defense Robert McNamara, and other military advisors met to discuss the details of the campaign and the list of potential targets supplied by the Pentagon. Potential bombing targets were categorized according to four criteria: military advantage, risk to US aircraft and pilots, estimated civilian casualties, and danger to third country nationals.[99] The president and others at the lunch would then choose the targets. This sort of intimate knowledge and control over targeting by the White House was both unprecedented and generally resented in the Pentagon.

Parks argues that during Rolling Thunder, the United States misread the balance between military necessity and concern for noncombatants by choosing targets with an eye toward minimizing casualties. This led, he contends, to avoiding targets that the American civilian and military leadership thought could lead to too many civilian casualties. In Parks's view, when the US leaders paid too much attention to the potential for collateral damage, they ignored the fact that the law of war recognizes that civilian casualties will occur and that what is prohibited is excessive collateral damage.[100] Parks argued that operations during Rolling Thunder were in part impeded by a "paranoiac fixation with regard to any civilian casualties" and the restrictions resulted in "unreasonable burdens" that the North Vietnamese were quick to exploit. In Parks's view, the restrictions in the later Vietnam War "Linebacker" bombing campaign were more reasonable.[101]

US Secretary of Defense Robert McNamara told Johnson in 1966 that "to bomb the North sufficiently to make a radical impact upon Hanoi's political, economic, and social structure, would require an effort which we could make but which would

[98] On the internal politics of Rolling Thunder, see W. Hays Parks, "Rolling Thunder and the Law of War," *Air University Review*, vol. 33, no. 2 (January-February 1982): 2–21, and Earl H. Tilford, Jr., *Crosswinds: The Air Force's Setup in Vietnam* (College Station: Texas A & M University Press, 1993), pp. 59–103.

[99] Parks, "Rolling Thunder and the Law of War," pp. 13–14.

[100] Parks, "Rolling Thunder and the Law of War," pp. 2–21.

[101] W. Hays Parks, "Linebacker and the Law of War," *Air University Review*, vol. 34, no. 2 (January-February 1983): 2–30.

not be stomached either by our own people or by world opinion, and it would involve a serious risk of drawing us into open war with China."[102] The United States was killing many soldiers, but McNamara noted, *"there is no sign of an impending break in enemy morale."*[103] On the other hand, the military felt that restricted bombing would increase US vulnerability in the air and diminish military effectiveness. Secretary of the Air Force Harold Brown said in March 1968 that he wanted the restrictions eased "so as to permit bombing of military targets without the present scrupulous concern for collateral civilian damage and casualties."[104] When the bombing ended in October 1968, the Rolling Thunder operation had killed an estimated 52,000 North Vietnamese.[105] The Air Force denied that it deliberately targeted civilians. General William Momyer, who commanded the Air Force in the theater, put the blame for some civilian deaths on the enemy, saying that "many of the North Vietnamese claims of civilian damage came about because their own anti-aircraft rounds and SAMs missed their mark and impacted the ground."[106]

After Vietnam the US Air Force gradually codified and institutionalized what had been more or less ad hoc procedures for minimizing collateral damage. A key milestone in the institutionalization of civilian protection occurred in 1976, when the Air Force published its understanding of the relationship between airpower and international humanitarian law in Air Force Pamphlet 110-31, *International Law— The Conduct of Armed Conflict and Air Operations.* Most of the language adheres closely to then current international law. There are exceptions and asides however. For instance, the distinction between civilians and combatants is made but also muddied. Specifically, the document states that since World War II, "several trends have tended to blur the distinctions between combatants and noncombatants, including civilians" and the document suggests that this includes "the rise of totalitarian states such as Nazi Germany."[107] The chapter on aerial bombardment discusses the rationale for US bombing practices in World War II, Korea, and Vietnam, and argues that US practices in those wars were justified.

---

[102] Quoted in Ward Thomas, *Ethics of Destruction: Norms and Force in International Relations* (Ithaca, NY: Cornell University Press, 2001), p. 156.

[103] Quoted in Andrew Krepinevich, *The Army and Vietnam* (Baltimore: Johns Hopkins, 1986), p. 184, emphasis in the original.

[104] Quoted in Thomas, *The Ethics of Destruction*, pp. 157–158.

[105] United States National Security Study Memorandum estimate quoted in Robert Pape, *Bombing to Win: Airpower and Coercion in War* (Ithaca, NY: Cornell University Press, 1996), p. 190. Clodfelter notes that the CIA estimated that by 1967, the 200,000 tons of bombs dropped had caused 29,600 deaths. Mark Clodfelter, *The Limits of Air Power: The American Bombing of North Vietnam* (New York: The Free Press, 1989), p. 136.

[106] William W. Momyer, *Air Power in Three Wars* (Washington, DC: Air Force, 1979), pp. 179–180.

[107] United States Department of the Air Force, Air Forces Pamphlet 110-31, *International Law—The Conduct of Armed Conflict and Air Operations*, 1976 (Washington, DC: Government Printing Office, 1976), paragraph 3-5, p. 3-4. Hereinafter AFP 110-31, 1976.

Tensions between military necessity and civilian protection were articulated in the 1976 pamphlet. The Air Force defined military necessity, as "measures of regulated force not forbidden by international law which are indispensible for securing the prompt submission of the enemy, with the least possible expenditures of economic and human resources."[108] The rule of thumb was that under the principle of necessity, everything not forbidden is acceptable if it is needed for victory. Yet, the document also clearly states: "The principle of military necessity is not the 19th Century German doctrine, *Kriegsraison*, asserting that military necessity could justify any measures—even in violation of the laws of war—when the necessities of the situation purportedly justified it. War crimes trials after World War II clearly rejected this view."[109]

An expansive interpretation of necessity is thus both asserted and rejected. The ways military necessity is further specified then becomes important. The idea of a military objective and direct military advantage is understood to mean the use value of an object or location. If an object makes an effective contribution to the adversary's military capacities, it is understood as a legitimate target. There is nothing inherent that makes an object a military objective, but rather its ability to make an "effective contribution" to the adversary's military effort.[110] Clearly then, whether a target was legitimate, regardless of civilian casualties, depended on the military's understanding of "effective contribution." Further, while the Air Force acknowledges that the laws of war prohibit "unnecessary suffering" and the deliberate targeting of civilians, it also states that the law "does not preclude unavoidable incidental casualties which may occur during the course of attacks against military objectives, and which are not excessive in relation to the concrete and direct military advantage anticipated."[111] The Air Force recognizes a "careful balancing of interests is required between potential military advantage and the degree of incidental injury or damage in order to preclude situations raising issues of indiscriminate attacks violating general civilian protections."[112]

The Rolling Thunder campaign in the Vietnam War signaled the institutionalization of concern for civilian casualties in bombing, albeit with many necessity and proportionality decisions taken at the White House rather than in the Pentagon, and the post-Vietnam 1976 Air Force guidance marked another level of institutionalization, albeit with the tensions between necessity and civilian protection

---

[108] AFP 110-31, 1976, pp. 1-5 and 1-6.

[109] AFP 110-31, 1976, p. 1-6.

[110] AFP 110-31, 1976, pp. 5-8 and 5-9. Also see Parks, "Linebacker and the Law of War" and George N. Walne, "AFP-110-1: *International Law—the Conduct of Armed Conflict and Air Operations* and the Linebacker Bombing Campaigns of the Vietnam War," Center for Naval Analysis, Professional Paper 487, November 1987, pp. 5 and 12.

[111] AFP 110-31, 1976, p. 1-6.

[112] AFP 110-31, 1976, paragraph 5-3(c)(2)(b), p. 5-10.

still evident. From the mid-1970s to the invasion of Afghanistan, the United Stated avoided long and intense ground combat, and thus attitudes and procedures regarding civilian casualties are perhaps well illustrated by looking at air force doctrine and procedures.[113] In the next section, I discuss the institutionalization of measures to reduce collateral damage during air operations in the 1991 Gulf War.

The 1991 Gulf War

While it is said that militaries often fight the last war, major wars just as often spark military innovation and institutionalization of new procedures. The August 1990 invasion and occupation of Kuwait by Iraq, which killed many Kuwaiti civilians, was an act of blatant aggression. Iraq's occupation was reversed in early 1991 by a US led counter-assault begun on 17 January 1991 and concluded in a ceasefire on 28 February 1991. The 1991 Gulf War is an important milestone in the institutionalization of concern for noncombatants, but at the same time illustrates how military necessity was understood permissively to allow for collateral damage.

Three points about US-caused collateral damage in the 1991 Iraq war are emphasized here. First, although not long before the start of the war, fatalism about civilian casualties was articulated in Air Force doctrine, while the United States took care not to directly target Iraqi civilians (compared to other US wars). The Lieber Code's mid-nineteenth century language and reasoning—specifically that some civilian killing may be necessary, "incidental," and inevitable—are echoed in a 1990 US Air Force guidance for targeting: "In spite of precautions, such incidental casualties are inevitable during armed conflict."[114] Yet, far from seeing civilian casualties as inevitable, the concern for civilian casualties and civilian casualty mitigation procedures were institutionalized to an unprecedented extent and engaged military lawyers as never before. The staff Judge Advocate for Central Command in the Gulf War, Col. Raymond Ruppert said, "Desert Storm was the most legalistic war we've ever fought."[115] As a consequence, compared to how many could have been killed if the United States had not taken care to avoid civilian casualties, relatively few Iraqis became US-caused collateral damage during the short "hot" phase of the war. This is in part because US procedures were successful in reducing both systemic and double effect/proportionality collateral damage. It was also because the military

---

[113] US ground operations did require attention to civilian casualties in this era. For instance, the members of the Marine Corps used rules of engagement in Lebanon during 1983 that included the instructions to respect civilian property and "protect innocent civilian lives from harm." White card instructions for Multinational Forces in Lebanon, quoted in Martins, "Rules of Engagement for Land Forces," p. 12n.

[114] Air Force Pamphlet (AFP) 200-18, vol. 1, *Target Intelligence Handbook: Unclassified Targeting Principles* (October 1990), p. 97.

[115] Quoted in Steven Keeva, "Lawyers in the War Room," *ABA Journal* (December 1991): 52–59, 52.

objectives of the war were limited: the aims were to free Kuwait, to destroy Iraq's weapons of mass destruction program, and weaken the Iraqi military.

On the other hand, one of the political objectives was more ambitious: to promote a coup or popular uprising in Iraq that would overthrow Saddam Hussein. This objective arguably led to a second consequence of the way the war was fought, that the long-term effects of bombing Iraqi infrastructure during the invasion arguably killed many more Iraqi civilians after the war than during the hot phase. The attacks on Iraqi infrastructure were aimed not simply at military objectives but at the morale of Iraqi civilians. These deaths and effects on health are an indirect effect of the bombing.

Third, because the US led an effort to weaken and isolate Iraq after the war through sanctions, many more civilians suffered after the war. The sanctions functioned as a blockade. While the consequences of the sanctions were certainly not collateral damage, their scale demands that they at least be acknowledged. Although the United States conduct was legal in important respects, the devastating toll of the economic sanctions on Iraq's civilians in the aftermath of the hot war was foreseeable and foreseen. Or, as two scholars writing in the wake of the 1991 Gulf War argued, the "laws of war thus helped to legitimate the very atrocities that they were supposed to deter, leading to the 'legal' slaughter of civilians."[116]

To the first point: the United States took unprecedented care to avoid immediate direct harm to Iraqi civilians in the 1991 Gulf War. Indeed, Operation Desert Storm was the first large-scale military operation since Vietnam where the United States had an opportunity to put in practice the mechanisms it had developed to minimize harm to civilians. The care taken by the United States to minimize harm to civilians is illustrated in the rules of engagement given to US soldiers prior to deployment: "1. Fight only combatants. 2. Attack only military targets. 3. Spare civilian persons and objects. 4. Restrict destruction to what our mission requires."[117] The institutionalization of the norm of minimizing noncombatant harm is most evident in the planning and conduct of air operations. I focus here on the air war where it is perhaps easiest to see how the tensions between military necessity, force protection, and noncombatant immunity played out and led, foreseeably, to what were at first understood as minimal levels of "collateral damage" but were ultimately high levels of in some ways slow motion civilian killing.

The priorities for the air war were Iraq's political/military leadership and its military and industrial assets. The order from President George H. W. Bush was to minimize harm to civilians: the target was the regime. Military targets included: Iraq's

---

[116] Christopher af Jochnick and Roger Normand, "The Role of Law in the Gulf War: Protection of Civilians or Legitimation of Violence," in Tom O'Loughlin, Tom Mayer, and Edward S. Greenberg, eds., *War and Its Consequences: Lessons from the Persian Gulf War* (New York: Harper Collins, 1994), pp. 59–76, 67.

[117] "1991 Operation Desert Storm, U.S. Rules of Engagement: Pocket Card," quoted in May, *War Crimes and Just War*, p. 94.

nuclear, chemical, and biological weapons facilities; its SCUD air-defense missile sites, and radar for its strategic air defenses; and the elite component of Iraq's military, known as the Republican Guard. Other targets were military support, production, and research facilities; and command, control, and communications. The industrial targets were: electrical power generation, oil facilities, railroad and bridges, airfields, and naval ports.[118] If the objective had been to occupy Iraq and remake its political system, civilian casualties would have been much higher, in line with the high level of casualties seen in the 2003 invasion.

Nevertheless, because damaging civilian infrastructure was an objective of the air campaign, civilians did suffer enormously after the 1991 invasion, though not immediately. How and why did this occur? Immediate and direct civilian harm was avoided by civilian casualty mitigation efforts, but civilian suffering occurred over the long run because military necessity was defined to include "dual use" facilities (such as electrical generating, which provided power for both civilian and military purposes) and to also include the larger economic infrastructure of Iraq and the will of the Iraqi people.

The core of the plan for the air war against Iraq was conceived along the lines of Air Force Colonel John Warden's theory of coercive air power. Colonel Warden and the "Checkmate" planning group based in the Pentagon believed a strategic strike against the Iraqi regime could obviate the need for a land war.[119] In Warden's model, the enemy's strengths (and vulnerabilities) should be understood as a system that included five core functions: command leadership, organic essentials such as petroleum, transportation infrastructure, civilian population and agriculture, and fielded forces. Of these, leadership was the most important: if the target state's leadership could be neutralized or immobilized, their war effort would fall apart.

But, Warden did not think of the leadership in isolation: he saw "the enemy as a system" where each element in the system should be "under rapid—or parallel—attack."[120] Enemy leadership could be compelled to submit if they were squeezed hard enough in all areas. If all went as planned, a costly ground war could be avoided or shortened, potentially saving thousands of US soldier's lives. In Warden's plan, harm and hardship for civilians, explicitly Baathists and the "middle class," was thus part of the plan for both the immediate objective and the long-term vision of a postwar Iraq without Saddam Hussein.[121]

---

[118] Michael W. Lewis, "The Law of Aerial Bombardment in the 1991 Gulf War," *American Journal of International Law*, vol. 97 (2003): 481–509, 488. Also see Thomas Keaney and Eliot A. Cohen, *Gulf War Air Power Survey Summary Report* (Washington, DC: GPO, 1993). The entire survey was five volumes.

[119] Keaney and Cohen, *Gulf War Air Power Survey Summary Report*, p. 69. The name "Instant Thunder" was a deliberate reaction to Johnson's Vietnam air war campaign of gradually ratcheting up the pressure: "That's exactly it: it's not Rolling Thunder—it's Instant Thunder!" John Warden, quoted in John Andreas Olsen, *John Warden and the Renaissance of American Air Power* (Washington: Potomac Books, 2007), p. 148.

[120] John A. Warden, *The Air Campaign* (New York: toExcel Press, 2000), p. 147.

[121] Ibid., pp. 146, and 150–151.

Because Iraq was a totalitarian state, there appears to be some blurring of distinctions between combatant and noncombatant, not unlike that described in the 1976 Air Force guidance. As one senior Air Force officer said in 1991, many Iraqis supported the invasion of Kuwait: "The definition of innocents gets to be unclear. They do live there, and ultimately the people have some control over what goes on in their country."[122] Iraqi civilian support for the regime, civilian morale, was thus a target. These views echoed arguments that had been made about bombing Germany, Japan, and North Korea, but in the case of the Gulf War, the effects on morale were to be rendered psychologically, rather than by directly killing civilians.[123] While the Air Force believed that civilian casualties were to be "kept to a minimum," US planners felt that it was important to put pressure on the Iraqi population. Early in the planning process for the Gulf War, Air Force plans stressed the "psychological impact on the Iraqi populace of being open to unremitting air attacks will be a powerful reminder of the bankruptcy and impotence of the Saddam Hussein regime."[124] Although Warden's general plan for striking deep into Iraq had support at high levels, theater commanders stressed the need to attack Iraq's military forces at a tactical level and Warden's plans were not adopted without modification. Yet most of the targets Warden advocated survived the planning process and were hit during the war.

The Operational Orders approved by the commander of air operations, Lieutenant General Charles Horner, on 2 September 1990, stated that "civilian casualties and collateral damages will be kept to a minimum. The target is Saddam Hussein's regime, not the Iraqi populace." [125] Yet the idea that airstrikes would spark a rebellion or coup that would lead to the overthrow of Saddam Hussein's

---

[122] Quoted in Barton Gellman, "Allied Air War Struck Broadly in Iraq," *Washington Post*, 23 June 1991.

[123] During the US Civil War, General William T. Sherman's view, apparently shared by Generals Grant, Sheridan, and their commander Halleck, was that if southern property could be destroyed, it would not only decrease the material support available to the Confederate Army, but it would also break the Southerners' will to fight. General Sheridan wrote that "death is popularly considered the maximum punishment in war; but it is not; reduction to poverty brings prayers for peace more surely and more quickly than does the destruction of human life as the selfishness of man has demonstrated in more than one great conflict." Similarly, General Halleck wrote to General Sherman in December 1864, "Should you capture Charleston, I hope by some accident the place may be destroyed, and if a little salt should be sown upon its site it may prevent the growth of future crops of nullification and secession." Sheridan, quoted in Mark E. Neely, Jr., *The Civil War and the Limits of Destruction* (Cambridge, MA: Harvard University Press, 2007), p. 138. Halleck, quoted in Lance Janda, "Shutting the Gates of Mercy: The American Origins of Total War, 1860-1880," *Journal of Military History*, 59 (January 1995): 7–26, 18.

[124] "Strategic Air Campaign against Iraq to Accomplish NCA Objectives," 16 August 1990, p. 3 as quoted by Pape, *Bombing to Win*, p. 222.

[125] John Andreas Olsen, *John Warden and the Renaissance of American Air Power* (Washington, DC: Potomac Books, 2007), p. 187.

government and the installation of a government more friendly to US interests was never abandoned.[126] The air campaign, lasting forty-three days, used a strategy that was a compromise between US theater commanders, who foresaw an integrated air and land battle, and Warden's vision that strategic air power could force the Iraqi's to capitulate. The Bush administration approved the overall plan, leaving the details to the military.[127]

International law and the US laws of war were considered at every phase of the air campaign, and concern for civilian casualties affected the planning of the air war at several junctures during the Gulf War. Specifically, the lawyer for each air wing reviewed the targets from the perspective of necessity, proportionality, and discrimination. The military lawyers, or JAGs, who worked for Central Command and all the services in Iraq, were not only in headquarters but also deployed with fielded troops. The Army alone deployed 200 lawyers.[128] During the planning phase, each target was assessed by a military lawyer for its potential to cause collateral damage. One such lawyer, Major Harry Heintzelman, said that as he understood it, his job in evaluating targets was "balancing the importance of the target to the enemy against the potential collateral damage which might result from the attack."[129]

JAGs were able to, and did, make recommendations during the air campaign that aim points or some other aspect of a strike, such as timing or height of burst, be changed to avoid harming civilians. In addition, the US Air Force was instructed to call off strikes during the war if they might cause collateral damage. The US military emphasized that it dropped warnings to Iraqi civilians to announce pending attacks and warned civilians to avoid the Iraqi military. The choice of weapons was affected by concern for civilian casualties as well, and the weapons used near concentrations of civilians were precision laser guided bombs or cruise missiles, which use a terrain mapping system of guidance. In discussing the air campaign, US officials emphasized the precision of the air attacks. Precision-guided weapons hit their targets 90 percent of the time, and the US military was impressed with the performance of laser guided and GPS guided bombs against Iraq's bridges, tanks, air defenses, and command and control facilities. Of the total ordnance dropped (88,500 tons), precision guided munitions accounted for less than 10 percent (6,250 tons). The bulk of the unguided ordnance dropped by airplane was targeted on military assets. Yet, unguided bombs were accurate only 25 percent of the time.[130]

The bombing of Baghdad, the location of the bulk of Saddam Hussein's command and control assets, was a key feature of the air war. A total of 330 weapons,

[126] Pape, Bombing to Win, p. 222.

[127] Gellman, "Allied Air War Struck Broadly in Iraq."

[128] Keeva, "Lawyers in the War Room," p. 54.

[129] Quoted Lewis, "The Law of Aerial Bombardment in the 1991 Gulf War," p. 487.

[130] Conrad Crane, Bombs, Cities, & Civilians: American Airpower Strategy in World War II (Lawrence: University Press of Kansas, 1993), p. 156.

amounting to 287 tons, were used against targets in Baghdad, which included air defense, airfields, government and intelligence sites, and presidential buildings. The strikes on leadership included targets such as bunkers where, according to the final plan drawn up by General Horner, the aim was to decapitate the Iraqi leadership. Although none of Iraq's top leadership was killed, air strikes did damage eighteen of the twenty-six leadership targets.

The single largest episode of civilian killing by the United States during the war occurred in an attempted strike on Iraqi leadership. On 13 February 1991, by two 2,000-pound bombs, delivered by two F-117 "Stealth" fighters, struck a shelter, the Al Firdos bunker, that, although some civilians were at risk, US targeters had concluded was a legitimate target sheltering high-level Iraqi officials.[131] In the event, the strike killed an estimated 200-400 people, and no top Iraqi officials. The United States apologized for the attack, saying the shelter would not have been attacked had US intelligence shown it housed civilians.[132] At this juncture, the authorization to destroy targets in Baghdad became a matter for much greater scrutiny by the area commander, General Norman Schwartzkopf and Chairman of the Joint Chiefs of Staff, General Colin Powell. The targeting of Baghdad was halted for five days after the incident and only a handful of other targets were struck inside the city after that.[133]

Military lawyers use the bombing of the Al Firdos bunker as an example of how to understand the laws of war in the case of "incidental" or inadvertent killing of civilians.

> There may be situations where, because of incomplete intelligence or the failure of the enemy to abide by the [Laws of War] LOW, civilian casualties occur. Example: Al Firdus Bunker. During the first Persian Gulf War (1991), U.S. military planners identified this Baghdad bunker as an Iraqi military command and control center. Barbed wire surrounded the complex, it was camouflaged, armed sentries guarded its entrance and exit points, and electronic intelligence identified its activation. Unknown to coalition planners, however, some Iraqi civilians used upper levels of the facility as nighttime sleeping quarters. The bunker was bombed, allegedly resulting in 300 civilian casualties. Was there a violation of the LOW? No, at least not by the U.S. forces (there was, however, a clear violation of the principle of distinction and discrimination (discussed *infra*) by Iraqi forces). Based upon information gathered by Coalition planners, the commander made an assessment that the target was a military objective. Although the attack may have resulted in

---

[131] William M. Arkin, "Baghdad: The Urban Sanctuary in Desert Storm?" *Airpower Journal*, vol. 11, no. 1 (Spring 1997): 4–21, 5 and 7.

[132] Lewis, "The Law of Aerial Bombardment in the 1991 Gulf War," p. 503.

[133] Thomas, *The Ethics of Destruction*, p. 88.

unfortunate civilian deaths, there was no LOW violation because the attackers acted in good faith based upon the information reasonably available at the time the decision to attack was made.[134]

This legal interpretation underscores how the United States used the law to absolve itself of legal responsibility for the direct killing of Iraqi civilians—US planners acted in "good faith," not with the intention to harm civilians. And the interpretation is correct. No laws of war were violated. The United States did not intend to kill civilians. Indeed, it is fair to say that the United States acted within the laws of war throughout the air campaign in the 1991 Gulf War. It does seem, however, that the excusing power of double effect—that lack of intention absolves even foreseeable and in some cases avoidable harm—was deployed during and after the war. The military's interpretation of the episode as legal, but nevertheless limiting, underscores the ambivalent relationship the US military has with the law. As observers noted, the Air Force interpreted the military consequences of the episode as unduly constraining: "The political fallout from the Al Firdos raid had accomplished what the Iraqi air defenses could not: downtown Baghdad was to be attacked sparingly, if at all."[135]

About 3,000 to 3,500 Iraqi civilians died immediately as a consequence of US airstrikes during the Gulf War, although, as is usually the case, the numbers killed and injured are disputed.[136] Further, civilians continued to die in the immediate aftermath of the war, as unexploded cluster bombs (delivered by air or rocket) detonated. Some of the cluster bombs used in the Gulf War were stock from the Vietnam War era. Between the start of the war and 28 February 1991, the United States and its allies used a total of 61,000 air-dropped cluster munitions accounting for the release of twenty million sub-munitions. An estimated 400 Iraqis (and 1,200 Kuwaitis) were killed by cluster bombs in the first two years after the conclusion of the war. More than a decade after the war "dud" cluster bombs were still being found in Kuwait and Iraq.[137] Further, hundreds more civilians were killed and injured by airstrikes from 1992 to early 2003 in continued bombing of Iraqi air defenses in "no-fly zones."[138]

---

[134] International and Operational Law Department, *Operational Law Handbook 2009*, p. 11.

[135] Michael R. Gordon and Bernard E. Trainor, *The General's War: The Inside Story of the Conflict in the Gulf* (Boston: Little Brown, 1995), p. 326.

[136] See Thomas, *Ethics of Destruction*, p. 169. Frank Hobbs, "Population Estimates for Iraq," Population Studies Branch, Center for International Research, U.S. Bureau of the Census, January 1992, cited in Pape, *Bombing to Win*, p. 357. Beth Osborne Daponte estimates 3,500 civilian deaths from direct war effects before the ceasefire. Beth Osborne Daponte, "A Case Study in Estimating Casualties from War and its Aftermath: The 1991 Persian Gulf War," *PSR Quarterly*, vol. 3, no. 2 (1993): 57–66. Also see Niko Price, "Tallying Civilian Death Toll in Iraq War is Daunting," *Philadelphia Inquirer*, 11 June 2003.

[137] Human Rights Watch, "Ticking Time Bombs: NATO's Use of Cluster Munitions in Yugoslavia," June 1999, http://www.hrw.org/legacy/reports/1999/nato2/, accessed 24 November 2002. Human Rights Watch Briefing Paper, "Cluster Munitions a Foreseeable Hazard in Iraq," March 2003.

[138] The "no-fly zones" were implemented by Coalition forces in 1992 and maintained until 2003 to prevent Iraq from attacking its own civilians. The BBC reported February 2001 that Iraq claimed 300

Yet, many more noncombatants could have died during the war if the US strategy had been, as in past wars such as Korea and World War II, to deliberately target civilians and civilian morale.[139] For example, the United States killed 3,000 in one night during World War II in an attack on Berlin, and tens of thousands in the fire-bombing of Tokyo.

Some of the responsibility for collateral damage rests with the Iraqi government. Specifically, as US officials repeatedly emphasized, the Iraqi military had a "strategy to conceal military assets with civilian objects, wear civilian clothes, and comingle with the civilian population."[140] Discrimination is very difficult in such circumstances. Further, the Iraqi government was responsible for the deliberate killing tens of thousands of Iraqis, in the immediate aftermath of the war, when Saddam Hussein ordered antigovernment uprisings in the north and south of Iraq crushed. Demographer Beth Osborne Daponte estimates that 30,000 civilians may have died in the uprisings in Iraq that began immediately after the US-led war ended.[141]

The focus of this book is on the immediate result of the use of force, the direct killing caused by bombs and bullets, flying debris, and fire. The effects of the strikes on infrastructure are also important. As noted in chapter 2, when attacks destroy or damage infrastructure, deaths and injury may occur months, sometimes years after the use of force damages infrastructure and diminishes, for example, access to safe drinking water or food. Often that hardship and killing is foreseeable and foreseen.[142]

civilians had been killed in the zones, which were maintained in the northern and southern areas of Iraq. BBC, "No-fly Zones: The Legal Position," 19 February 2001, http://news.bbc.co.uk/2/hi/middle_east/1175950.stm. Susan Taylor Martin, "'No-fly' Zone Perils were for Iraqis, Not Allied Pilots," *St. Petersburg Times*, 29 October 2004, http://www.sptimes.com/2004/10/29/Columns/_No_fly__zone_perils_.shtml, accessed 23 November 2009. Jeremy Scahill reported in 2002 that "Baghdad says over the last decade more than 1,400 civilians have been killed in the US and British attacks in the no fly zones. While this cannot be independently verified, UN statistics say that more than 300 civilians have been killed in the raids since December 1998." Scahill, "No-Fly Zones over Iraq," *CounterPunch*, 4 December 2002, http://www.counterpunch.org/scahill1204.html.

[139] Thomas, *Ethics of Destruction*, p. 158.

[140] Reynolds, "Collateral Damage on the 21st Century Battlefield," p. 51.

[141] Daponte, "A Case Study Estimating Casualties from War and Its Aftermath, pp. 57–66.

[142] Such long-term harm was, for example, the point of the Romans sowing the land with salt when they destroyed Carthage. The Roman policy in 146 B.C.E. was to destroy Carthage and it did so even after the city had formally surrendered. After a three-year siege, during which the population of Carthage was greatly reduced by starvation, the Romans entered the city and moved from house to house, killing thousands of residents. Accounts vary, but hundreds of thousands may have immediately died during the course of the siege and the massacre. The city was set on fire and burned for more than two weeks, and the farmland was, it is said, sown with salt. The survivors were sold into slavery. As John Keegan argues: "So ferocious were the Romans of the later first millennium BC that, in broad historical perspective, their behavior bears comparison only with the Mongols or Timorids 1500 years later. Like the Mongols, they took resistance, particularly that of besieged cities, as a pretext justifying wholesale slaughter of the defeated." John Keegan, *A History of Warfare* (New York: Knopf: 1993), p. 265.

The question is sometimes simply how long the hardship will go on and how many indirect deaths and illnesses are attributable to the damaged infrastructure.

In the 1991 Gulf War, there was debate over whether the US damage to Iraq's water supply, and its subsequent impact on civilians, was intentional.[143] Specifically, the US air war plan included attacks on the electrical infrastructure of Iraq. Electricity was key to Iraqi leadership communications inside the capital. More than 200 sorties using guided and unguided weapons were directed at twenty-five key electrical sites, including boilers, generators, and transformers. Electricity in Baghdad was cut, as Colonel Warden said, "within minutes" of the start of the war.[144] The Gulf War Air Power Survey reported that by the end of the air campaign 88 percent of Iraq's electrical generation capacity was damaged or destroyed.[145]

There is some dispute about whether the aim was to cripple Iraq's postwar electrical generating capacity. The Gulf War Air Power Survey suggested that planners wanted to avoid causing significant postwar damage. Rather, the attacks on electrical generators were not intentional. Local commanders found generators were "convenient aim points," and flying units "were not aware that operational planners in Riyadh were attempting to limit long-term damage."[146]

The evidence shows that the United States planned the attacks on electrical infrastructure to have both short-term military effects and longer term political effects. The short-term effect was, of course, to make command and communication difficult, and as General Horner said, the fact that the lights went out for civilians was a "side-benefit" in terms of psychological warfare.[147] Warden argues, "Although it has much more important effects, shutting off electricity is rather like pouring a layer of molasses over the whole country; people can still move, but they move slower and they spend energy they would otherwise have put to more profitable uses. Attacks on electricity were exceptionally valuable in creating the system wide strategic paralysis that we wanted to impose on Iraq."[148]

Planners also foresaw long-term effects of crippling Iraq's capacity for electricity generation and intended those effects: either Saddam Hussein would yield to United Nations demands in the postwar era as a condition for receiving help to restore electricity, or the Iraqi people would overthrow their government if they felt enough pain. According to Colonel Warden, the aim of attacks on infrastructure was

---

[143] Lewis, "The Law of Aerial Bombardment in the 1991 Gulf War," pp. 504–507.

[144] Warden, The Air Campaign, p. 149.

[145] Thomas Keaney and Elliot Cohen, Gulf War Air Power Survey Summary Report, pp. 72 and 73. Further, attacks on thirty key bridges and petroleum facilities impeded military transportation including the transportation of oil to backup generators.

[146] Keaney and Cohen, Gulf War Air Power Survey Summary Report, p. 72.

[147] See Gellman, "Allied Air War Struck Broadly in Iraq" and Olsen, John Warden and the Renaissance of American Air Power, pp. 149–150.

[148] Warden, The Air Campaign, p. 155.

to amplify the long-term effect of sanctions and increase the leverage of the United Nations. Destroying the electrical grid, Warden argued, "imposed a long-term problem on the leadership that has to deal with it sometime. Saddam Hussein cannot restore his own electricity. He needs help. If there are political objectives that the U.N. coalition has, it can say, 'Saddam, when you agree to do these things, we will allow people to come in and fix your electricity.' It gives us long-term leverage."[149] After the war, an Air Force planner told Barton Gellman of *The Washington Post*, "Big picture, we wanted to let people know, 'Get rid of this guy and we'll be more than happy to assist in rebuilding. We're not going to tolerate Saddam Hussein or his regime. Fix that and we'll fix your electricity.' "[150]

The military acknowledged that damage to Iraqi infrastructure as a result of the attacks in 1991 was substantial. Most important from the perspective of civilians was the disruption of electricity by air attacks on transformers and the subsequent closure of water purification and sewage treatment facilities, which depended on electricity to operate.[151] Power was cut off within one minute of the start of the air campaign in Baghdad and was not restored until the end of the war. The supply of water to homes was halted within hours of the start of the air war. Some hospitals and clinics were damaged by bombs and rendered less effective by shortages of electricity and water. In February 1991, the World Health Organization and Unicef found the water supply to Baghdad at 5 percent of its prewar level.[152]

In March 1991 the United Nation's Special Envoy Martti Ahtissari found that "most means of modern life support had been destroyed or rendered tenuous."[153] A second UN special envoy Sadruddin Agha Khan found similar conditions in July 1991. The attacks on Iraqi infrastructure and the war immediately led to greater child and infant mortality due to disease, including cholera and typhoid, according to research conducted in August and September 1991 and published in the *New England Journal of Medicine*. But, as the research showed, the causes of civilian suffering cannot be simply and directly tied to the US bombing alone. "Our data demonstrate the link between the events that occurred in 1991 (war, civilian uprising, and economic embargo) and the subsequent increase in mortality." Overall, they estimated 46,900 excess deaths among children under age 5 in Iraq for the first eight months of 1991. They found:

---

[149] Warden, quoted in Gellman, "Allied Air War Struck Broadly in Iraq."

[150] Gellman, "Allied Air War Struck Broadly in Iraq."

[151] Lewis, "The Law of Aerial Bombardment in the 1991 Gulf War," p. 504.

[152] Eric Hoskins, "Humanitarian Impact of Economic Sanctions and War in Iraq," in Thomas G. Weiss, David Cortright, George A. Lopez, and Larry Minear, eds. *Political Gain and Civilian Pain: Humanitarian Impacts of Economic Sanctions* (Boulder, CO: Rowman and Littlefield, 1997), pp. 91–147, 116.

[153] Quoted in Joy Gordon, *Invisible War: The United States and the Iraq Sanctions* (Cambridge, MA: Harvard University Press, 2010), p. 22.

The destruction of the supply of electric power at the beginning of the war, with the subsequent disruption of the electricity-dependent water and sewage systems, was probably responsible for the reported epidemics of gastrointestinal and other infections. These epidemics were worsened by the reduced accessibility of health services and decreased ability to treat severely ill children. Increased malnutrition, partly related to the rising prices of food, may also have contributed to the increased risk of death among infants and children. The effect of the war has been greater among groups that had higher base-line mortality rates, suggesting that poverty and lower educational level increased children's vulnerability to the crisis. In northern and southern Iraq, the situation was exacerbated by the civilian uprisings and the subsequent flight of 2 million Kurds and Shiites into mountains and marshes at a climatically inhospitable time.[154]

Others have suggested that these estimates are conservative. Daponte estimated approximately 111,000 excess Iraqi deaths in 1991 due to war-induced adverse health effects, for all age groups. Children under 15 accounted for 70,000 of those excess deaths. The Gulf War Air Power Survey argues that these and other estimates are too large, not taking into account how quickly the regime was able to restore electricity.[155]

Even if the estimates are too high by a factor of ten, the devastation to Iraq's infrastructure wrought in a few weeks by the US air campaign eventually killed many thousands of Iraqis through indirect effects. Regardless of whether the killing was intentional, the deaths and illnesses were foreseeable and probably foreseen. Lt. General Charles Horner, who directed the air campaign, said the effect on civilians was "terrifying and certainly saddening." But, Horner emphasized US restraint and the effort to minimize civilian killing and put the blame for the effects of war elsewhere. "To say it's the fault of the United States for fighting and winning a war, that's ludicrous. War's the problem. It's not how we fought it or didn't fight it. I think war's the disaster."[156] Coady argues that targeting dual purpose facilities, as occurred during the Balkan and Iraq wars, can harm noncombatants too much and may not be justified: "The mere existence of a dual purpose is not itself enough to legitimate an attack and thereby count the damage to noncombatants as permissible 'incidental' injury."[157] Coady continues:

---

[154] Alberto Ascherio, Robert Chase, Tim Coté, Godelieave Dehaes, Eric Hoskins, Jilali Laaouej, Megan Passey, Saleh Qaderi, Saher Shuqaidef, Mary C. Smith, and Sarah Zaidi, "Effect of the Gulf War on Infant and Child Mortality in Iraq," *New England Journal of Medicine*, vol. 327 (24 September 1992): 931–936.

[155] Keaney and Cohen, *Gulf War Air Power Survey Summary Report*, p. 75.

[156] Quoted in Gellman, "Allied Air War Struck Broadly in Iraq."

[157] Coady, "Bombing and the Morality of War," p. 210.

The destruction of water supplies by bombing and the noncombatant deaths from thirst and disease that ensue cannot be justified by the mere fact that enemy soldiers use the same water supplies as enemy civilians. Casual attitudes about the destruction of power supplies, oil reserves, bridges, communications networks, and media facilities need more careful scrutiny lest they really display a disregard for the rights and protections that should be accorded noncombatants.[158]

But in this case, the damage to civilians was not inadvertent or the result of negligence. It was central to the US political aims in the war—to gain leverage over the Saddam Hussein regime—although the magnitude of the harm to civilians, and its duration, may have been underestimated.

If these were the indirect effects of the use of military force, it must also be said that in the aftermath of the 1991 Gulf War sanctions were much more devastating for civilians in Iraq than the war itself, and the sanctions exacerbated the effects of targeting electrical infrastructure. The initial United Nations sanctions (Resolution 661) against Iraq were intended to coerce the regime into leaving Kuwait before the war. Sanctions under the United Nations essentially cut off Iraq from the rest of the world—forbidding any trade and ultimately reducing both imports and exports by more than 90 percent. Food imports and medical supplies were allowed, but they were soon restricted as well. After Iraq pulled out of Kuwait, UN Resolution 687 continued the trade embargo in April 1991 in an effort to force Iraq to pay reparations to Kuwait, recognize the border between the two countries, and frustrate the development of weapons of mass destruction. The restrictions exacerbated the damage to Iraq's infrastructure done by the bombs—without spare parts, it was difficult if not impossible to repair damaged infrastructure. Indeed, it is probably impossible to completely disentangle the effects of sanctions and the effects of damage to infrastructure.

The effect of sanctions on Iraq's civilian population was devastating—more devastating than the immediate collateral damage caused by the war. Not surprisingly, the numbers killed and harmed by the sanctions were in dispute at the time, and the blame for the sanctions-related deaths is disputed. In August 1991, the oil for food program was proposed, but rejected by Iraq. Iraq could sell oil to purchase food and other humanitarian goods. In April 1995 the oil for food program passed the Security Council and Iraq agreed to its terms. By then, the standard of living for Iraqi civilians had deteriorated markedly.[159] For example, in 1995, the water supply levels for the entire country were at 50 percent of their prewar levels. Prior to the war, 72 percent of rural dwellers had access to clean water; by 1995 that had dropped to 50 percent.

---

[158] Ibid.

[159] Hoskins, "Humanitarian Impact of Economic Sanctions and War in Iraq," p. 116.

Some argue that the UN sanctions were still too restrictive even after they were modified as a result of public pressure to allow "oil for food." In her study of the sanctions regime, Joy Gordon argues that the UN sanctions led to a humanitarian disaster in slow motion for over a decade, causing perhaps as many as 500,000 excess deaths from 1990 to 2003.[160] So, even when electricity for running water treatment plants was restored, the restrictions imposed by the sanctions committee at the United Nations meant that the spare parts and chemicals necessary to keep the plants functioning were in short supply or unavailable. All of these restrictions, which led over the course of thirteen years to what became predictable and foreseeable deaths, were legally authorized by the UN committee that ran the sanctions program. Others argue that it was the Hussein regime's intransigence that hurt the Iraqi people. The effects of attacks on infrastructure, though exacerbated by sanctions and the brutal Iraqi regime, and the indirect death that followed, should arguably be considered "collateral damage."

In sum, the values of military necessity, force protection, and noncombatant immunity were on the table every time a target was considered and an attack was approved both in the planning stages and in the operational command center for the 1991 war in Saudi Arabia. Civilian casualties were to be minimized, but calculated risks were taken in the air war in the effort to decapitate the Iraqi leadership. The civilian hardship that resulted from damage to the electrical infrastructure was also foreseen and deliberately planned.

Developments after the Gulf War

There was a consistent understanding of collateral damage in the period following the 1991 Gulf War as inevitable but nevertheless political. Recall that the 1998 Air Force targeting guide says: "Collateral damage is generally defined as unintentional or incidental damage that occurs as a result of an attack but affects facilities, equipment, or personnel that are not militarily acceptable targets." Interestingly, the definition also emphasizes public "scrutiny" of collateral damage deaths. "Since this kind of damage is often the focal point for national and international scrutiny, the type and level of force applied against a target must be carefully selected to avoid excessive collateral damage."[161]

In this period, the US military also began defining military necessity more broadly and permissively. The emergence of a doctrine of "effects-based" war during the Gulf War, where the focus was on undermining the sources of government

---

[160] See Gordon, *Invisible War*, p. 37. Alexander B. Downes, *Targeting Civilians in War* (Ithaca, NY: Cornell University Press, 2008), pp. 227–232; and Thomas, *Ethics of Destruction*, p. 166.

[161] USAF Intelligence Targeting Guide Air Force Pamphlet 14- 210 Intelligence, 1 February 1998, p. 52.

power as a way to victory, was applied in later wars, including Kosovo, Afghanistan, and Iraq in 2003. Military objectives were understood broadly to be those that "effectively contribute to the enemy's war-fighting or war-sustaining capability and whose total or partial destruction, capture, or neutralization would constitute a definite military advantage to the attacker."[162] As Adam Roberts and Henry Shue separately note, this entailed a blurring of civilian and military objects and led to a weakening of the prohibition of attacks on civilian objects.[163] Almost any economic asset could be considered war sustaining. As Shue argues, the US "accounts of what qualifies as a military objective are becoming looser and departing further from international law."[164]

The January 2000 US Standing Rules of Engagement (SROE), which articulates the conditions under which commanders and individual soldiers are authorized to use force, defines necessity broadly. Necessity "exists when a hostile act occurs or when a force or terrorist(s) exhibits hostile intent." Necessity is understood as permission to override legal and moral limits on the use of force. The understanding of military necessity in current US operational law is less a limit than a license or a threshold for permission to use force. Under the US SROE, "necessity" is not a condition where the use of force is a last resort or the only effective way to defend oneself. Nor is there a sense that the threat must be significant. Proportionality is also required for self-defense under the January 2000 SROE. The definition of proportionality is: "Force used to counter a hostile act or demonstrated hostile intent must be reasonable in intensity, duration, and magnitude to the perceived or demonstrated threat based on all facts known to the commander at the time."[165] In this context, proportionality functions as a potential limit on the use of force even as it can be used to override limits.

Thus, from the Civil War to Kosovo, the United States has been fairly consistent in its assertion of a permissive conception of military necessity and the forgiving power of double effect. The military should do what is required or necessary to win its military objectives, on the one hand, and it should strive to "avoid *excessive* collateral damage." But, while US doctrine stresses a permissive understanding of military necessity as military objectives which can include a wide range of "war sustaining" objects and activities, it has also increasingly institutionalized measures for civilian protection within that permissive understanding.

---

[162] "Annotated Supplement to the Commander's Handbook on the Law of Naval Operations" (Newport, RI, 1997), paragraph 8.1.1.

[163] Adam Roberts, "The Civilian in Modern War," in Hew Strachan and Sibylle Schieppers, eds., *The Changing Character of War* (Oxford: Oxford University Press, 2011), pp. 357–380; Henry Shue, "Target-Selection Norms, Torture Norms, and Growing U.S. Permissiveness," in Strachan and Schieppers, eds., *The Changing Character of War*, pp. 464–483.

[164] Shue, "Target-Selection Norms, Torture Norms, and Growing U.S. Permissiveness," p. 470.

[165] United States, Chairman of the Joint Chiefs of Staff Instruction, CJCSI 3121.01A, 15 January 2000, "Standing Rules of Engagement for US Forces," Enclosure A paragraph 5f, p. A-4.

This is clearest perhaps in the discussions of the laws of war by US military lawyers who must advise soldiers in the field before the fact of target selection and weapons use, and after the fact to determine whether the laws of war have been observed. The JAGs understanding of the intersection between the law of war (LOW) and operations, "operational law," can be illustrated, for example, in the 2009 *Operational Law Handbook.* This handbook for JAGs interprets military necessity as *not* vitiating the rights of noncombatants to protection. Further, the US view of the laws of war contains a conception of due care: civilians can never be deliberately targeted; care must be taken not to inadvertently but knowingly harm civilians. "**The principle of military necessity authorizes that use of force required to accomplish the mission. Military necessity does not authorize acts otherwise prohibited by the LOW**. This principle must be applied in conjunction with other LOW principles... as well as other, more specific legal constraints set forth in LOW treaties to which the United States is a party."[166]

Consistent with international humanitarian law, the US military's interpretation of collateral damage focuses on intentionality in understanding culpability and is thus relying on the principle of double effect to excuse the unintentional killing of noncombatants. US military lawyers are clear that "under the principle of distinction, the civilian population as such, as well as individual civilians, may not be made the object of attack."[167] On the other hand, collateral damage, called "incidental damage," is understood as within the law of war under the principle of proportionality. "Incidental damage consists of unavoidable and unintentional damage to civilian personnel and property incurred while attacking a military objective." The key finding is emphasized in bold print in the *Operational Law* manual. "**Incidental damage is *not* a violation of international law.** While no LOW treaty defines this concept, its inherent lawfulness is implicit in treaties referencing the concept. As stated above, [the Geneva Convention] AP I, art. 51(5) describes indiscriminate attacks as those causing 'incidental loss of civilian life... excessive... to... the military advantage anticipated.' "[168]

The decision thus involves a balancing act, conceived within a utilitarian framework, where the "anticipated" and sufficiently compelling ends may justify the "incidental" or "inevitable" consequences of the means used. This is the justification, in other words, of proportionality/double effect collateral damage. The prohibition on killing civilians, either intentionally or inadvertently, is seriously eroded by a utilitarian logic, which we can find stated rather boldly in the words of the philosopher R. B Brandt: "Substantial destruction of lives and property of enemy civilians is

---

[166] International and Operational Law Department, *Operational Law Handbook 2009* (Charlottesville, VA: The Judge Advocate General's Legal Center and School, 2009), p. 10, emphasis in the original.

[167] Ibid., p. 12.

[168] Ibid., p. 12, emphasis in the original.

permissible only when there is good evidence that it will significantly enhance the prospect of victory."[169]

In this respect, the American military is like all other militaries that tend to put "necessity" and efficiency above protection of noncombatants. In this way international humanitarian law, understood as the law of war to be interpreted by each belligerent as the judge in its own cause, becomes part of the legitimation of operations in war. The trouble in applying the doctrine of double effect and military necessity comes when the distinction between combatants and noncombatants is lost or denied or when military necessity is defined permissively to include deliberate or at least a high tolerance for inadvertent harm to civilians.

The evolution of US military views about collateral damage accelerated during the Afghanistan and Iraq wars and occupations. Civilian protection became a priority when it was understood as a strategic necessity for the counterinsurgency strategy. The 2012 manual on tactics, techniques, and procedures, *Civilian Casualty Mitigation*, makes explicit reference to balancing and trade-offs. And unlike previous manuals, the scales of the balance are not so clearly tipped in favor of short-term military necessity. "An Army leader must balance the need to defeat an ill-defined enemy with the need to protect civilians and minimize their casualties, while at the same time preserving the force."[170]

The fact that the tensions have been clearly articulated in Army guidance and will be more explicit in training means that decisions about the use of force are more difficult. This fact is also acknowledged in the guidance. "The impact of this guidance on the unit's ability to mitigate CIVCASs and carry out their mission should not be underestimated. Army units must balance the necessity of using force with its likely effects."[171] What is new, in the 2012 guidance, is the option to back off. "The rules of engagement indicate when the use of force is authorized. However, not all permissible force is necessary in every case, and leaders must consider second-order effects as well. In other words, even if Soldiers or units are permitted to use lethal action, they should not necessarily do so."[172]

> Commanders apply judgment to determine how to accomplish missions while—
>
> • Defeating the enemy.
> • Preserving the force.
> • Protecting civilians.

[169] R. B. Brandt, "Utilitarianism and the Rules of War," *Philosophy and Public Affairs*, vol. 1 (1972): 156, quoted in Richard Norman, *Ethics, Killing and War* (Cambridge: Cambridge University Press, 1995), p. 165.

[170] Department of the Army, *Civilian Casualty Mitigation*, Army Tactics, Techniques and Procedures, No. 3-37.11 (Washington, DC: Department of the Army, 18 July 2012), p. 1-5.

[171] Ibid., p. 1-7.

[172] Ibid., p. 1-7.

These imperatives can require tradeoffs; for example, a high force protection condition may increase the chances of accidental harm to civilians. Commanders prioritize these imperatives based on short- and long-term mission objectives.[173]

The idea of trade-offs and tensions and balances to be found appears several times in the *Civilian Casualty Mitigation* manual.

Commanders and staffs should develop an appreciation of the tensions and tradeoffs related to CIVCAS mitigation, which may include—

- Short-term security versus long-term stability.
- Short-term population expectations versus long-term expectations.
- Protection of Army forces versus protection of the population.
- The risk of CIVCASs versus long-term legitimacy of the operation or host nation.[174]

The Exceptional Case: Drones and Targeted Killing

The targeted killing program begun under the Bush administration in 2002 also balances the norms of military necessity, discrimination, and proportionality. The drone strikes in Pakistan and Yemen operate ostensibly under the same rationale that has come to characterize the counterinsurgency strategy—a concern to minimize civilian death by precision—but in practice, the logic of the drone program's implementation has allowed for significant numbers of systemic collateral damage and proportionality/double effect deaths. Much of the focus of discussion concerning drones has focused on the lack of transparency of the targeted drone strike program. Indeed, the fact that the Bush administration did not discuss the program allowed the critics to make argument against US drone strikes on three grounds—concerning the legality of targeted killings, whether the actual strikes meet the criteria of discrimination and proportionality, and whether the program is prudent. It was only when the Obama administration accelerated the use of drones in Pakistan and Yemen that the United States began to discuss the drone strike program in relatively more detail in response to criticism.

First, on the question of legality, some international lawyers suggest the strikes in Pakistan are illegal because the United States is not in an armed conflict in

---

[173] Ibid., p. 1-7.
[174] Ibid., pp. 2–7-8.

Pakistan.[175] Under international law, resort to force is only legal and justified in cases of self-defense against "armed attacks" (Article 51 of the UN Charter) or when the UN Security Council has authorized the use of force (Chapter VII). Mary Ellen O'Connell argues that "there is no Security Council authorization for drone attacks nor does the U.S. have a basis in the law of self-defense for attacking inside Pakistan."[176]

The Obama administration has argued that the United States is in an armed conflict with Al Qaeda and the Taliban, and that the Authorization for Use of Military Force made by Congress on 18 September 2001 permits the use of force in self-defense.[177] State Department Legal Advisor Harold Koh has argued specifically that:

> As a matter of international law, the United States is in an armed conflict with al-Qaeda, as well as the Taliban and associated forces, in response to the horrific 9/11 attacks, and may use force consistent with its inherent right to self-defense under international law. As a matter of domestic law, Congress authorized the use of all necessary and appropriate force through the 2001 Authorization for Use of Military Force (AUMF). These domestic and international legal authorities continue to this day.

---

[175] "To put the matter simply," Kenneth Anderson summarized, "the international law community does not accept targeted killings even against al Qaeda, even in a struggle directly devolving from September 11, even when that struggle is backed by U.N. Security Council resolutions authorizing force, even in the presence of a near-declaration of war by Congress in the form of the AUMF [September 2001], and even given the widespread agreement that the U.S. was both within its inherent rights and authorized to undertake military action against the perpetrators of the attacks." Kenneth Anderson, "Targeted Killing in U.S. Counterterrorism Strategy and Law," A Working Paper of the Series on Counterterrorism and American Statutory Law, A joint project of the Brookings Institution, The Georgetown University Law Center and the Hoover Institution, May 2009, p. 16.

[176] Mary Ellen O'Connell, "Unlawful Killing with Combat Drones: A Case Study of Pakistan, 2004-2009," *University of Notre Dame Law School*, Legal Studies Research Paper, No. 09-43, July 2010, p. 26.

[177] The U.S. Congress, 18 September 2001, Authorization for Use of Military Force says, "Whereas, on September 11, 2001, acts of treacherous violence were committed against the United States and its citizens; and Whereas, such acts render it both necessary and appropriate that the United States exercise its rights to self-defense and to protect United States citizens both at home and abroad; and Whereas, in light of the threat to the national security and foreign policy of the United States posed by these grave acts of violence; and Whereas, such acts continue to pose an unusual and extraordinary threat to the national security and foreign policy of the United States; and Whereas, the President has authority under the Constitution to take action to deter and prevent acts of international terrorism against the United States." Text of Resolution, http://www.gpo.gov/fdsys/pkg/PLAW-107publ40/pdf/PLAW-107publ40.pdf.

Further, Koh argued, the threat has not disappeared:

> As recent events have shown, al-Qaeda has not abandoned its intent to attack the United States, and indeed continues to attack us. Thus, in this ongoing armed conflict, the United States has the authority under international law, and the responsibility to its citizens, to use force, including lethal force, to defend itself, including by targeting persons such as high-level al-Qaeda leaders who are planning attacks.[178]

The argument about whether drone killings are legal thus turns on whether the United States is, in fact, in an armed conflict against terrorist organizations and whether the use of drones can be considered a case of self-defense. Lawyers such as O'Connell argue that the right to self-defense is triggered in only cases of armed attack. "An armed response to a terrorist attack will almost never meet these parameters for the lawful exercise of self-defense. Terrorist attacks are generally treated as criminal acts because they have all the hallmarks of crimes, not armed attacks that can give rise to the right of self-defense."[179]

Indeed, while the United States was attacked on 9/11, the argument justifying self-defense use of force against individuals who may be members of the terrorist organizations must be that the terrorist threat is always imminent and that members of terrorist organizations always pose a threat because they intend, plan, and organize to carry out armed attacks against the United States. This is why Koh argues that the threat is "ongoing" and that the United States targets "specific high-level belligerent leaders."[180] Similarly, US Attorney General Eric Holder argued in March 2012 that the drone strike program against "enemy belligerents" was consistent with the US Constitution, which he argued, "empowers the President to protect the nation from any imminent threat of violent attack...international law [which] recognizes the inherent right to national self-defense."[181]

The second line of criticism questions the necessity, proportionality, and discrimination of the drone strikes.[182] Attorney General Holder argued that drones met the main criteria for the use of force.

---

[178] Harold Hongju Koh, "The Obama Administration and International Law," Annual Meeting of the American Society of International Law, 25 March 2010. http://www.state.gov/s/l/releases/remarks/139119.htm.

[179] O'Connell, "Unlawful Killing with Combat Drones," p. 14.

[180] Koh, "The Obama Administration and International Law."

[181] Eric Holder, "Attorney General Eric Holder Speaks at Northwestern University School of Law," 5 March 2012, http://www.justice.gov/iso/opa/ag/speeches/2012/ag-speech-1203051.html.

[182] The necessity argument works on two levels: first that there is no other way to stop the threat than by killing members of al Qaeda, and second, that drones are the only way (because the local military cannot or will not target these individuals) to reach the targets.

Of course, any such use of lethal force by the United States will comply with the four fundamental law of war principles governing the use of force. The principle of necessity requires that the target have definite military value. The principle of distinction requires that only lawful targets—such as combatants, civilians directly participating in hostilities, and military objectives—may be targeted intentionally. Under the principle of proportionality, the anticipated collateral damage must not be excessive in relation to the anticipated military advantage. Finally, the principle of humanity requires us to use weapons that will not inflict unnecessary suffering."[183]

By contrast, Daniel Byman of the Brookings Institution argued in 2009, "Sourcing on civilian deaths is weak and the numbers are often exaggerated, but...for every militant killed, 10 or so civilians also died."[184] Mary Ellen O'Connell has also argued that: "Drones kill many unintended victims for each intended one, raising questions of proportionality....Nor has the U.S. apparently taken the necessary precautions to protect civilian lives."[185] Koh, acknowledged that the drone strikes do occur among civilians. "As you know, this is a conflict with an organized terrorist enemy that does not have conventional forces, but that plans and executes its attacks against us and our allies while hiding among civilian populations. That behavior simultaneously makes the application of international law more difficult and more critical for the protection of innocent civilians."[186] A study by Stanford and NYU Law Schools that included 130 interviews and two trips to Pakistan to investigate drone strikes stated simply: "In the United States, the dominant narrative about the use of drones in Pakistan is of a surgically precise and effective tool that makes the US safer by enabling 'targeted killing' of terrorists, with minimal downsides or collateral impacts. This narrative is false."[187]

Some critics have questioned whether those killed by drone are actually the leaders of al Qaeda and the Taliban, or rather, more often, the ones killed may be low-level members of the organization, or rather "foot soldiers" and civilians who happen to be near the strike. Indeed, In May 2010, Reuters reported US intelligence estimates that of the 500 militants killed in the drone strikes between the summer of 2008 and May 2010, only fourteen were in the top-tier of targets and twenty-five

---

[183] Holder, "Attorney General Eric Holder Speaks at Northwestern University School of Law."

[184] Daniel L. Byman, "Do Targeted Killings Work?" Brookings, 14 July 2009, http://www.brookings.edu/opinions/2009/0714_targeted_killings_byman.aspx.

[185] O'Connell, "Unlawful Killing with Combat Drones," p. 26.

[186] Koh, "The Obama Administration and International Law."

[187] Stanford Law School, International Human Rights and Conflict Resolution Clinic, and NYU School of Law Global Justice Clinic, "Living under Drones: Death, Injury and Trauma to Civilians from US Drone Practices in Pakistan," September 2012, http://livingunderdrones.org/, p. v.

were mid- to high-level organizers. [188] The remaining 460 or so militants killed must be lower level in the organization. If most of the militants killed are "low-level" operatives, then one cannot easily argue that the majority of those killed in the strikes pose a serious imminent threat.

Overall, the Obama administration has maintained the position that drone strikes kill few civilians. Reuters reported intelligence estimates that no more than 30 noncombatants had been killed at the same time as the 500 militants killed between summer 2008 and May 2010.[189] Conversely, O'Connell argues that the drone strikes are far from surgical. "Most serious of all, perhaps, is the disproportionate impact of drone attacks. Fifty civilians killed for one suspected combatant killed is a textbook example of a violation of the proportionality principle. Even in cases with fewer unintended victims, it makes a difference whether the victims are children, elderly people, in a home, and so on. Proportionality is not just a matter of numbers."[190] Without more information about just who has been killed, it is difficult to evaluate whether the drone strikes kill enough high-level militants to justify the risk to civilians, or even if so, whether those killings are legal. What is clear, however, is that the Bush and Obama administrations have understood the inadvertent killing of civilians as a proportionality/double effect case of collateral damage.

The third criticism of drone strikes is that their use is imprudent and counterproductive.[191] As David Kilcullen argued before the US House of Representatives, "I realize that they [drone strikes] do damage to al Qaeda leadership. Since 2006 we've killed 14 senior al Qaeda leaders using drone strikes. In the same time period we've killed 700 Pakistani civilians in the same area." Thus, he said, "The drone strikes are highly unpopular" in Pakistan. "They are deeply aggravating to the population. And they've given rise to a feeling of anger that coalesces the population around the extremists and leads to spikes of extremism well outside the parts of the country where we are mounting those attacks."[192] Similarly, O'Connell says, "If... drone attacks in Pakistan are fueling interest in fighting against the United States rather than suppressing it, using drones is difficult to justify under the principle of necessity."[193]

In late April 2012, John Brennan, the Obama administration's chief of counterterrorism, gave a fuller description and arguments justifying the drone strike program. Brennan underscored the administration's arguments that the strikes were legal, but his key point seemed to be the contention that "targeted strikes are

---

[188] Adam Entous, "Special Report: How the White House Learned to Love the Drone," Reuters, 18 May 2010, http://www.reuters.com/article/2010/05/18/us-pakistan-drones-idUSTRE64H5SL20100518.

[189] Ibid.

[190] O'Connell, "Unlawful Killing with Combat Drones," p. 24.

[191] A fourth criticism is that killing suspected militants without due process is equivalent to murder.

[192] David Kilcullen, testimony Hearing of the House Armed Services Committee, "Effective Counterinsurgency: The Future of the U.S. Pakistan Military Partnership," 23 April 2009.

[193] O'Connell, "Unlawful Killing with Combat Drones," p. 24.

ethical."[194] Specifically, Brennan amplified Holder's arguments about distinction, necessity, and proportionality.

> Targeted strikes conform to the principles of distinction....With the unprecedented ability of remotely piloted aircraft to precisely target a military objective while minimizing collateral damage, one could argue that never before has there been a weapon that allows us to distinguish more effectively between an al-Qaida terrorist and innocent civilians.
>
> Targeted strikes conform to the principle of proportionality, the notion that the anticipated collateral damage of an action cannot be excessive in relation to the anticipated military advantage. By targeting an individual terrorist or small numbers of terrorists with ordnance that can be adapted to avoid harming others in the immediate vicinity, it is hard to imagine a tool that can better minimize the risk to civilians than remotely piloted aircraft.
>
> For the same reason, targeted strikes conform to the principle of humanity which requires us to use weapons that will not inflict unnecessary suffering. For all these reasons, I suggest to you that these targeted strikes against al-Qaida terrorists are indeed ethical and just.

Brennan then argued that the drone strike program was militarily prudent in the current context. "Remotely piloted aircraft in particular can be a wise choice because of geography, with their ability to fly hundreds of miles over the most treacherous terrain, strike their targets with astonishing precision, and then return to base. They can be a wise choice because of time, when windows of opportunity can close quickly and there just may be only minutes to act." Brennan observed that drone strikes "dramatically reduce the danger to U.S. personnel, even eliminating the danger altogether" and argued that drone strikes "dramatically reduce the danger to innocent civilians, especially considered against massive ordnance that can cause injury and death far beyond their intended target." Brennan argued that the technology allowed drone pilots to act more calmly and with the benefit of greater information than if they were in the field: "compared against other options, a pilot operating this aircraft remotely, with the benefit of technology and with the safety of distance, might actually have a clearer picture of the target and its surroundings, including the presence of innocent civilians." Further, "the unprecedented advances we have made in technology provide us greater proximity to target for a longer period of time, and as a result allow us to

---

[194] John Brennan, "The Efficacy and Ethics of U.S. Counterterrorism Strategy," 30 April 2012, Woodrow Wilson International Center for Scholars, http://www.wilsoncenter.org/event/the-efficacy-and-ethics-us-counterterrorism-strategy.

better understand what is happening in real time on the ground in ways that were previously impossible."

As I noted in the introduction, Brennan also describes balancing military necessity with the concern to avoid civilian casualties: "We only authorize a strike if we have a high degree of confidence that innocent civilians will not be injured or killed, except in the rarest of circumstances." Brennan explicitly stated that with drone strikes, "We can be much more discriminating and we can make more informed judgments about factors that might contribute to collateral damage."

> I can tell you today that there have indeed been occasions when we decided against conducting a strike in order to avoid the injury or death of innocent civilians. This reflects our commitment to doing everything in our power to avoid civilian casualties, even if it means having to come back another day to take out that terrorist, as we have done previously. And I would note that these standards, for identifying a target and avoiding the loss of innocent—the loss of lives of innocent civilians, exceed what is required as a matter of international law on a typical battlefield. That's another example of the high standards to which we hold ourselves.
>
> Our commitment to ensuring accuracy and effectiveness continues even after a strike. In the wake of a strike, we harness the full range of our intelligence capabilities to assess whether the mission in fact achieved its objective. We try to determine whether there was any collateral damage, including civilian deaths. There is, of course, no such thing as a perfect weapon, and remotely piloted aircraft are no exception.

The key contention is that drone strikes are a surgical tool with little collateral damage of the accidental sort. John Brennan argued, "It's this surgical precision, the ability, with laser-like focus, to eliminate the cancerous tumor called an al-Qaida terrorist while limiting damage to the tissue around it, that makes this counterterrorism tool so essential."[195] Yet, because it appears that the drone strikes are taken with the knowledge that there are or may be some number of civilians in the vicinity, who are likely to be harmed, the strikes also fall into the category of a proportionality/double effect collateral damage. An anonymous US government official told the New York Times in 2009 that "We Believe the number of civilian casualties is just over 20, and those were people who were either at the side of major terrorists or were at facilities used by terrorists."[196] An official told the New York Times in May 2012 that the number of civilians killed by the Obama administration's drone strikes in Pakistan was in the "single digits."[197]

---

[195] Ibid.

[196] Shane, "C.I.A. to Expand Use of Drones in Pakistan."

[197] Jo Becker and Scott Shane, "Secret 'Kill List' Proves a Test of Obama's Principles and Will," *New York Times*, 29 May 2012.

In one of his few direct statements about the drone program, President Obama underscored that the drone attacks were not being conducted "willy-nilly" but were discriminating. "I want to make sure that people understand, actually, drones have not caused a huge number of civilian casualties. For the most part they have been very precise precision strikes against Al-Qaeda and their affiliates. And we are very careful in terms of how its been applied.... This is a targeted, focused effort at people who are on a list of active terrorists."[198]

As I showed in chapter 2, however, the aspiration of precision is not the same as implementation. Even the May 2013 presidential requirement for "near certainty" that no civilians are at risk in drone strikes must be implemented through procedures that involve an interpretation of "near" and also clearly depends on the operational definition and identification of "civilians."

Summary and a Proposal

The tensions and operational trade-offs between noncombatant immunity, force protection, proportionality, and military necessity in US military doctrine are long-standing and rooted in the Just War tradition and international law. Further, combatants' perception of the appropriate balance of these values may change in any particular war and during the course of a war. The Just War doctrine of double effect is often less a constraint than a way to understand, justify, and forgive harm to civilians, while the notion of "due care" too often gives way to ideas of military necessity understood as the permission to override the prohibition on harming noncombatants.

Historical perspective highlights the essential arbitrariness of war conventions that make some kinds of killing in war legal and others illegal. The virtue of a prohibition on intentionally harming noncombatants is its ostensible clarity. Yet, our very embeddedness in the legal framework and military landscape of proportionality, the avoidance of "excessive" harm, and the acceptance of incidental foreseeable albeit unintended killing makes it difficult to gain perspective on just how the law allows for systemic collateral damage and double effect/proportionality killing. Philosopher Frederick Kaufman says: "We are told that innocent deaths in war are wrongful when disproportional, useless, or when due care is not exercised by attackers in pursuit of legitimate military targets. But when due care is exercised there is no violation of the innocent victim's right to life; such deaths are tragic, not wrong, making them permissible infringements of the right to life." As Kaufman notes, "An official military spokesperson sometimes even expresses regret for the loss of

---

[198] David E. Sanger, *Confront and Conceal: Obama's Secret Wars and Surprising Use of American Power* (New York: Crown Publishers, 2012), p. 251.

innocent life caused by its action, but nevertheless defends the attack as a permissible military operation."[199]

Indeed, as the Just War scholar William O'Brien suggests, the notion of noncombatant immunity itself can be compromised by a certain definition of military necessity: "A literal interpretation of the principle of discrimination is incompatible with the conduct of modern war at all levels." Yet, as O'Brien argues, in "nuclear war, conventional war, and revolutionary/counter-insurgency unconventional war it becomes necessary to use means that by any fair interpretation involve the direct intentional attacking of noncombatants and nonmilitary targets."[200] The tensions, incompatibilities, and contortions are often resolved by appeal to military necessity.

In sum, US doctrine and laws of war place priority on the value of military necessity understood as a permission to override prohibitions. Thus, it is possible to unintentionally but foreseeably kill many noncombatants and to believe that such killing is not only warranted by "military necessity" but allowed under international law. This, albeit reluctant, permission to harm civilians as a means to the accomplishment of a military objective creates the context within which systemic collateral damage can occur and why this killing is so difficult to observe as systemic. Proportionality/double effect collateral damage, and a certain (undefined) amount of systemic collateral damage, is perfectly legal within a frame of reasoning that prioritizes military necessity. The idea that foreseeable, albeit unintended, noncombatant killing is accepted—as inevitable, or incidental, or as a proportionate trade-off, or as military necessity, or as double effect—is what make systemic collateral damage in some sense "ordinary." The very ordinariness of systemic collateral damage has contributed to its essential political and moral invisibility and an acceptance of its inevitability. That such killing can be understood as legal under international law does not make it any more acceptable.

If the law allows wide latitude with respect to unintended killing, and forgives what our conscience may find morally troubling, then the law must be reexamined. It may be that the law is appropriately balanced among military necessity, force protection, and noncombatant immunity and protection. Or it may be that because the law is written by legal experts working for states or with states in mind, and then interpreted and judged mostly by military lawyers, with military interests in mind, the scales are tipped too far toward a permissive view of military necessity. I do not propose changes in international law. My objective here is first to show how the law currently frames norms of military necessity, noncombatant immunity, and force protection. I argued that the laws of war permit and excuse collateral damage, even when collateral damage becomes something that is quite morally troubling, namely

---

[199] Kaufman, "Just War Theory and Killing the Innocent," p. 101.
[200] William O'Brien, *The Conduct of Just and Limited War* (New York: Praeger, 1981), p. 340.

systemic collateral damage and proportionality/double effect killing.[201] Those individuals who make the decisions about the use of force must do so wisely and must be held to account when they fail. Yet, as I have shown, these individuals may have no legal liability for individual incidents that have caused collateral damage, for they have done nothing wrong under the law. However, the moral responsibility and political accountability for collateral damage when it is systemic should be understood and examined.

The fact is that the US military changed its views about civilian casualties during the course of the wars in Afghanistan and Iraq. The impetus has been a sense that a new view of military necessity demanded the shift; quite simply, killing too many civilians hurt the war effort. That re-visioning of the strategic imperative has been highly motivating of organizational change, as I show in chapter 6. On the other hand, as the previous discussion of drone strikes suggests, the revisioning of necessity has not extended to the question of targeted killings in Pakistan and Yemen. Thus, there is a deep tension between the norms of war, military necessity, force protection and civilian protection that must be rethought.

What does it mean to rethink these norms and their relationship? Is there a way out of this seemingly insoluble set of tensions and paradoxes? Should civilian immunity be on par with, or above, calculations of the difficult assess values of military necessity and proportionality? Is it appropriate to think of force protection as equally valuable as civilian protection? If not, why not? And should intentionality really trump foreseeability to the point where foreseeable but unintentional harm should be less of a concern than intentional harm?

I suggest three ways to address these dilemmas and give more weight to civilian protection in the context of current international law. The first step is to erase, or at least blur, the sharp distinction between foreseeability and intention. In other words, the excusing power of double effect should be weakened. If harm is foreseeable and foreseen, I argue, the commanders' intentions become less important than the fact of the foreseeability of harm. Foreseeable is not the same as intentional, but if we can foresee harm, we would be negligent not to take precautions to avoid the harm even if such harm is not our intention. As I show in the chapters on command and organizational responsibility, increasing the regard for the foreseeable

---

[201] Immanuel Kant wrote about this distinction in a discussion of the "right of necessity." "The motto of the right of necessity is 'Necessity has no law' (*neccissitas non habet legem*); but there still cannot be any necessity that will make what is unjust legal.... the equivocation arises from a confusion of the objective with the subjective grounds of the exercise of justice (before reason and before a court). Thus, on the one hand, what one himself recognizes on good grounds to be just will not receive confirmation in a court of justice, and on the other hand, what he must judge unjust in itself will be treated with indulgence by the court. This is a consequence of the fact that the term 'justice' [or right] is not used with the same meaning in the two cases." Immanuel Kant, *The Metaphysical Elements of Justice*, translated with an introduction by John Ladd (Indianapolis: Bobbs-Merrill, 1965), p. 42.

consequences of action, anticipating outcomes, is increasingly the view held among strategists.

Second, I argue, we need to recall that military necessity and proportionality may be satisfied in many ways. Harm to civilians should not be accepted too readily in the name of military necessity. In other words, before commanders think about precautions and limiting harm to civilians, commanders must think creatively about avoiding it altogether. Perhaps more often than we think, there is more than one way to achieve a military objective. Moreover, killing civilians may in fact run counter to the larger military objectives, as US military planners have more recently come to believe. This suggestion is not simply wishful thinking; commanders have already made such choices (foregoing what they believe to be short-term military advantage) to good effect. The 2012 *Civilian Casualty Mitigation* calls for such a reevaluation.

Third, I suggest that the questions of balancing risk to combatants and civilians, and risk transfer, be addressed differently. As Walzer acknowledges and international law prescribes, the exercise of due care may mean that the risks to combatants in an operation increase, or that an attack has to be abandoned and taken up elsewhere, entailing a potential delay. But if an attack is to go forward, and protecting civilians means increased risks to soldiers, how could we justify that increased risk? The argument cannot be that the life of a soldier is worth less than the life of a civilian. Both lives are valuable. However, while the lives and limbs of civilians and soldiers are both equally valuable, the civilian is, on the whole, more vulnerable. But isn't that a circular argument? After all, the definition of a civilian is that they pose no threat and that they are vulnerable. My argument is that the civilian deserves greater protection because although both soldiers and civilians are vulnerable in war, the greater relative vulnerability of civilians means that those who are relatively less vulnerable come second in our evaluation. In other words, the relatively less vulnerable soldier owes it to the relatively more vulnerable civilian to take care with their lives, even if those civilians "belong to" the other side. It is this same reasoning that protects other noncombatants, namely the sick, the wounded, and the disarmed prisoner.[202]

---

[202] Robert Goodin makes a similar argument with respect to other vulnerabilities. Robert E. Goodin, *Protecting the Vulnerable: A Reanalysis of Our Social Responsibilities* (Chicago: University of Chicago Press, 1985), pp. 118–119.

PART II

PRIMARY MORAL RESPONSIBILITY

4

When Soldiers "Snap"

Bad Apples, Mad Apples, and Individual Moral Responsibility

> Most of us thought that we were there to do something good. I don't
> think anybody joins an army or goes off to war thinking they are going
> to do evil.
>
> —Charlie Anderson[1]

> Why, man, he doth bestride the narrow world
> Like a Colossus, and we petty men
> Walk under his huge legs and peep about
> To find ourselves dishonourable graves.
> Men at some time are masters of their fates:
> The fault, dear Brutus, is not in our stars,
> But in ourselves, that we are underlings.
>
> — William Shakespear's Cassius[2]

In March 2006, Mahmudiya, Iraq, about 20 miles south of Baghdad, was part of
what American soldiers called the "triangle of death," the heart of the Sunni resistance to the US occupation. The US soldiers stationed there, the 502nd Infantry
Regiment of the 101st Airborne, were dying at a rate of one per week. The soldiers'
base was regularly attacked and an electrical fire had recently destroyed their living
quarters. Like many Iraqis in Mahmudiya, Abheer Qasim Hamza, a 15-year-old girl,
passed through US checkpoints on a nearly daily basis. Abheer described her fear of
the US soldiers who were making advances toward her and to her mother.

On 12 March 2006, Private Steven D. Green was manning a checkpoint in
Mahmoudiya when he and four other men, who had been drinking Iraqi whisky,

---

[1] Charlie Anderson, US Marine, quoted in Matthew Guttman and Catherine Lutz, *Breaking
Ranks: Iraq Veterans Speak Out against the War* (Berkeley: University of California Press, 2010), p. 5.

[2] Cassius to Brutus in William Shakespeare, *Julius Caesar*.

decided to rape Abheer Qasim Hamza, whose home was a few hundred yards from the checkpoint. The rape was apparently Specialist James Barker's idea, but the participants discussed the plan over the course of several hours. Believing they could not leave any witnesses alive, Barker asked Green if he would kill everyone in the house. An 18-year-old private, Bryan Howard, was told to stay and man the radio, and to warn the men if a US patrol was nearby. Two of the soldiers then changed into long black underwear, what Green described as "ninja suits." Green remained in uniform.

At Abheer's home, the four soldiers subdued Abheer, her mother Fakhrihah Taha Muhsin, her father, Qasim Hamza Raheem, and her 7-year-old sister, Hadeel Qazim Hamza. Green then shot and killed Abheer's mother, father, and sister, while Barker and another soldier, Sergeant Paul Cortez raped Abheer in a separate room. Green entered the room and said: "They're all dead. I killed them all." Green then raped Abheer. Next Green shot Abheer in the head. Barker doused the girl with kerosene and set her body on fire. The soldiers then returned to their checkpoint.

Abheer's two brothers escaped death because they were at school at the time. When the boys returned from school, they found the bodies in a smoking house. Abheer's body was still smoldering. Called on by Iraqi forces to investigate, US soldiers, including some of the participants in the murders, went to the scene. The US investigators eventually surrounded the house and told neighbors that the family had been killed by Sunni insurgents. In June 2006, two US soldiers revealed the rape and killing to US authorities.[3]

In the interval between Abheer's rape and the four murders and their disclosure, Private Green was given an honorable discharge for a personality disorder. No longer subject to prosecution for his crimes under military law, Green was arrested in the United States by civilian authorities. The three other soldiers were investigated in Iraq and found guilty by military courts. James Barker and Paul Cortez were sentenced to 90 and 100 years in military prison, respectively. Private First Class Jesse Spielman was sentenced to life in prison, though his sentence was reduced to 90 years. The lookout, Bryan Howard, was sentenced to 27 months in prison and released after 17 months. Green, tried in civilian court, was found guilty of sixteen felonies including premeditated murder in May 2009. The federal prosecutor, Brian Skarat sought the death penalty for Green, arguing at his sentencing hearing that: "They have tried to paint Mr. Green as a victim, but we know who the real victims are. This is not about leadership. This is not about the stress of warfare. This is about heinous crimes inflicted on innocent civilians."[4]

---

[3] Robert F. Worth, "U.S. Military Braces for Flurry of Criminal Cases in Iraq," *New York Times*, 9 July 2006, p. 10; Ellen Knickmeyer, "Details Emerge in Alleged Army Rape, Killings," *Washington Post*, 3 July 2006, http://www.washingtonpost.com/wp-dyn/content/article/2006/07/02/AR2006070200673. html.

[4] Quoted in Jim Frederick, "When a Soldier Murders: Steven Green Gets Life," *Time*, 21 May 2009, http://www.time.com/time/nation/article/0,8599,1900389,00.html.

Indeed, Green had told a reporter from *Stars and Stripes* in February 2006, "I came over here because I wanted to kill people." Over dinner with the reporter, Green said, "I shot a guy who wouldn't stop when we were out at a traffic checkpoint and it was like nothing." Green said, "Over here, killing people is like squashing an ant. I mean you kill somebody and its like, all right, let's go and get some pizza."[5]

The defense argued that Green was a troubled person before he entered the military and that he deserved mercy. Evidence was given that Green was essentially a damaged man operating in a damaged unit that had been deemed "combat incapable" before the incident by Lieutenant Colonel Karen Marrs.[6] Marrs had visited Green's platoon and assessed it in her role as a psychiatric nurse. In Marrs's interview of Green at Mahmudiya in December 2005, he described being abused as a child and reported his homicidal feelings toward Iraqis. Marrs diagnosed Green with "combat and operational stress reaction"[7] and prescribed medication to help him sleep. It is not surprising that Green remained with his unit with a diagnosis of combat stress: the US system for treating combat stress emphasizes keeping soldiers in the field, and near their combat units, for emotional support.[8] Green was also not alone in using prescription and nonprescription drugs in Iraq: many soldiers were prescribed or somehow found drugs. "My partner got us some pills to keep us awake. Then pills for us to sleep. It was just constant pills."[9] Marrs also suggested in a report that someone conduct a psychiatric follow up with Green. Green was seen again on 20 March 2006, a week after the murders.

Dr. Ruben Gur examined Green's brain using an MRI and testified at Green's civilian trial. "Green has frontal lobe damage. This means Green has difficulty making decisions and does not work well under disorganization or without being told what to do. He is happy to follow a leader, he doesn't want to be pressured. He works well in a structured environment, but in a chaotic environment, he behaves chaotically."[10] Green's lawyer, Scott Wendelsdorf, pleaded for Green's life at the sentencing hearing: "The United States of America failed Steven Green." He concluded by

[5] Green, quoted in Andrew Tilghman, "Encountering Steven Green—'I came over here because I wanted to kill people,'" *Washington Post*, 30 July 2006, http://www.washingtonpost.com/wp-dyn/content/article/2006/07/28/AR2006072801492.html.

[6] Evan Bright, "Steven Green Sentencing Trial: Platoon Had Dire Mental Health Status," *Huffington Post*, 18 May 2009.

[7] Jim Frederick, *Black Hearts: One Platoon's Descent into Madness in Iraq's Triangle of Death* (New York: Harmony Books, 2010), p. 158.

[8] On the US Army's Combat and Operational Stress Control program, see Erin P. Finley, *Fields of Combat: Understanding PTSD among Veterans of Iraq and Afghanistan* (Ithaca, NY: Cornell University Press, 2011). The Army method for treating combat stress is modeled on programs developed in World Wars I and II. By contrast, when soldiers receive serious physical wounds, they are almost immediately evacuated to a field hospital and then flown to the United States, often within days of their injury.

[9] Iraq war army veteran Tina Gernanez, quoted in Guttman and Lutz, *Breaking Ranks*, p. 99.

[10] Bright, "Steven Green Sentencing Trial."

saying, "America does not kill its broken warriors! Spare this boy. For God's sake, spare him."[11] Green was sentenced to life in prison without parole.

The US wars in Iraq and Afghanistan have had their share of American soldiers killing outside the law or harming noncombatants. When they come to light, these acts, and others like them, are condemned, and US political and military leaders argue that incidents of deliberate killing are both "abhorrent" and aberrant. These cases are said to be exceptional. The rule, we are told, is that most US forces behave within the law and with honor. Asked for comment about the case of murder and rape in Mahmudiya, Iraq, in 2006, White House spokeswoman, Dana Perino, said: "The president has full confidence in the military to investigate alleged crimes and to punish anyone convicted of abhorrent behavior that dishonors the proud traditions of our military. He will not comment on ongoing investigations so as not to prejudice the outcome; however, he believes that 99.9 percent of our men and women in uniform are performing their jobs honorably and skillfully and they deserve our full appreciation and gratitude."[12] At a briefing in Baghdad, Brigadier General Donald Campbell made a similar argument. "While the bulk of our forces, 99.9 percent, serve with honor, there are a small number of individuals who sometimes choose the wrong path. While we understand the stresses and pressures inherent in combat operations, we cannot and will not accept behavior that is legally, morally, or ethically questionable."[13]

But, by US soldiers' own reporting, a certain level of brutality is acknowledged. For example, a 2007 Army Mental Health Advisory Team survey found that "approximately 10 percent of Soldiers and Marines report mistreating non-combatants (damaged/destroyed Iraqi property when not necessary or hit/kicked a non-combatant when not necessary)."[14] In several high-profile cases, US soldiers in Iraq were investigated, prosecuted, and disciplined.

For example, in Ramadi, Iraq, on 15 February 2006, Specialist Nathan Lynn of the Pennsylvania National Guard shot and killed an unarmed Iraqi man. A rifle was placed near his body to suggest that the victim was an insurgent. Lynn and Sergeant Milton Ortiz were charged with voluntary manslaughter and with obstructing justice. The manslaughter charge was dropped against Lynn when investigators found he acted within the rules of engagement, but Ortiz pled guilty to planting the

---

[11] Quoted in Frederick, "When a Soldier Murders."

[12] David S. Cloud and Kirk Semple, "Ex-G.I. Held in 4 Slayings and Rape in Iraq," *New York Times*, 4 July 2006, p. 1; David Stout and Kirk Semple, "U.S. Veteran Charged in Rape-Killing in Iraq," *International Herald Tribune*, 4 July 2006, p. 5.

[13] DoD News Briefing with Brig. Gen. Campbell from Baghdad, Iraq, http://www.defense.gov/transcripts/transcript.aspx?transcriptid=6.

[14] Jerry Harben, "Mental Health Advisory Team IV Findings Released," US Army Medical Department, Army Medicine, Press Release, 4 May 2007, http://www.armymedicine.army.mil/news/releases/20070504mhat.cfm.

weapon and was reduced in rank.[15] In Hamandia, on 26 April 2006, a 52-year-old Iraqi man, Hashim Ibrahim Awad, was kidnapped from his home and bound by his hands and feet before being shot. After his death, an automatic weapon and shovel were placed next to his body in attempt to make it appear as if Awad was planting a roadside bomb. Seven Marines and a Navy corpsman were charged under the US Uniform Code of Military Justice with murder, conspiracy, and kidnapping.[16]

At Thar Thar Canal, Iraq, on 9 May 2006, soldiers of the 101st Airborne Division raided a suspected insurgent training camp. Lieutenant Justin Wehreim said: "We were going to hit the ground shooting and kill all the al-Qaeda and Iraqi insurgents. We were to positively identify and kill any military-age male on the island."[17] Staff Sergeant Raymond L. Girouard described their orders as, "Hit the first house, kill all military-age males, hit any secondary houses, then stand by for follow-on missions."[18] One Iraqi man was shot and killed and three unarmed Iraqi men, found in the second house, were detained, bound, and blindfolded.[19] The plastic "zip-tie" restraints were cut by the soldiers and according to Private Corey Clagett's testimony in his own trial for the murders, Private William "Hunsaker told them to run. I told them 'Yalla,' to get them to run faster. They didn't run faster, so I raised my weapon. Hunsaker raised his. He shot, then I shot."[20] Four US soldiers were charged with premeditated murder, conspiracy, and obstruction of justice: the two privates, Clagget and Hunsaker, pled guilty and received 18-year sentences; Sergeant Girouard was sentenced to 10 years for negligent homicide; and Specialist Juston Graber, who pled guilty to aggravated assault for shooting an already wounded Iraqi on the order of Sergeant Girouard "to put him out of his misery" was sentenced to 9 months in prison. While the soldiers had initially maintained that they only killed the men as they attempted to escape, the US soldiers accused, and later convicted, of killing the detainees argued that they were ordered by superiors to kill all Iraqi males of military age.[21] The commander, Colonel Michael Steele, who distributed

[15] J. Michael Kennedy, "Two GIs Charged in Iraq Death," *Los Angeles Times*, 26 June 2006, http://articles.latimes.com/2006/jun/26/world/fg-charges26. Josh White, "Killing by Guardsman in Iraq Called Appropriate," *Washington Post*, 22 July 2006, p. A2.

[16] Robert F. Worth, "U.S. Military Braces for Flurry of Criminal Cases in Iraq," *New York Times*, 9 July 2006, p. 10; Teri Figueroa and William Finn Bennett, "Military Justice under Spotlight in Hamdania Case," *U-T San Diego*, http://www.utsandiego.com/news/2006/Jun/25/military-justice-under-spotlight-in-hamdania-case/?#article-copy.

[17] Bo Petersen, "Murder at Thar Thar," *The Post and Courier*, 21 June 2009, http://www.postandcourier.com/news/2009/jun/21/murderat_thar_thar86727/.

[18] Quoted in Paul von Zielbauer, "Accounts of 4 G.I.'s Accused of Killing Civilians, Tell of How Iraqi Raid Went Wrong," *New York Times*, 7 August 2006, p. A9.

[19] Brian Bender, "Army Says 3 Soldiers Shot 3 Iraqis Execution Style," *Boston Globe*, 20 June 2006; Paul Von Zielbauer, "Accounts of 4 G.I.'s Accused of Killing Civilians, Tell of How Iraqi Raid Went Wrong," *New York Times*, 7 August 2006, p. A9.

[20] Petersen, "Murder at Thar Thar."

[21] Associated Press, "Accused GIs: We had Orders To Kill," CBS News, 11 February 2009, http://www.cbsnews.com/2100-500257_162-1826706.html. Peterson, "Murder at Thar Thar."

knives to soldiers who killed insurgents and reportedly stressed "kill counts," was later reprimanded and reassigned out of Iraq.[22] An investigation by the 101st Airborne of the incident concluded that "although clearly unintentional, confusion regarding the R.O.E. was the proximate cause of the death of at least four unarmed individuals, none of whom committed a hostile act or displayed hostile intent."[23]

In Afghanistan, in March 2012, Staff Sergeant Robert Bales left his base and killed seventeen Afghan civilians. A year earlier, "trophy" photographs taken by US Army soldiers in Afghanistan, who called themselves a "kill team," showed the soldiers posing with their civilian victims.[24] In one case, when US Special Forces troops and Afghan forces stormed a house in February 2010, where family and friends were attending a party to celebrate the naming of a child, US forces killed five civilians, including two pregnant women and a teenage girl, and wounded several others by mistake. For some time, ISAF insisted that those killed were insurgents and that the women had been killed before the raid by others. Afghans charged that, in an attempt to cover up the killings, US Special Forces used knives to remove the bullets from the bodies of their victims. Survivors argued that two of the injured, who died of their wounds, a police commander and his teenaged niece, might have survived had they been taken for medical treatment earlier.[25]

When events such as these occur, many suppose that soldiers "snapped" or "cracked under the pressure of a war fought on a battlefield with no front lines, no easy way to tell civilians from insurgents, and no end in sight."[26] What can turn soldiers, trained to kill only other soldiers under orders, into wanton murderers of civilians? What could lead soldiers to abuse captives or desecrate the bodies of their enemies? If a soldier's training stresses both discipline and the distinction between combatants and noncombatants, who is to blame when soldiers deliberately kill or harm noncombatants in violation of the law? How is it that soldiers can become

---

[22] Borzou Daragahi and Julian E. Barnes, "Officers Allegedly Pushed 'Kill Counts,'" Los Angeles Times, 3 August 2006, http://articles.latimes.com/2006/aug/03/world/fg-probes3.

[23] Paul von Zielbauer, "Army Says Improper Orders by Colonel Led to 4 Deaths," New York Times, 21 January 2007, http://www.nytimes.com/2007/01/21/world/middleeast/21abuse.html?_r=1.

[24] See Matthias Gebauer and Hanain Kazim, "US Army Apologizes for Horrific Photos from Afghanistan," Der Spiegel, 21 March 2011, http://www.spiegel.de/international/world/0,1518,752310,00.html; Jon Boon, "Photos Show US Soldiers in Afghanistan Posing with Dead Civilians," The Guardian, 21 March 2011, http://www.guardian.co.uk/world/2011/mar/21/afghanistan-trophy-photos-us-soldier.

[25] Jerome Starkey, "UN Report Criticises Covert Troops who Committed Afghan Killings," The Times, 16 March 2010, http://www.timesonline.co.uk/tol/news/world/afghanistan/article7063184. ece, Jerome Starkey, "US Special Forces 'Tried to Cover-Up' Botched Khataba Raid in Afghanistan," The Times, 5 April 2010, http://www.timesonline.co.uk/tol/news/world/afghanistan/article7087637. ece; Richard A. Oppel and Abdhul Waheed Wafa, "Afghan Investigators Say U.S. Troops Tried to Cover Up Evidence in Botched Raid," New York Times, 5 April 2010, http://www.nytimes.com/2010/04/06/world/asia/06afghan.html.

[26] Evan Thomas and Scott Johnson, "Probing a Bloodbath," Newsweek, 12 June 2006.

negligent in war so that their actions lead to unintentional killing? These are the questions at stake here. What are the limits of the soldiers' responsibility? How much moral agency do soldiers have while they are at war? Where does individual moral responsibility begin and end?

The standard answer to these questions, where soldiers are understood to be autonomous moral agents, is that individual soldiers are, and should be, held solely responsible for their behavior in war. By definition an autonomous moral agent is "free," with the capacity to make decisions and to act voluntarily. Thus, the age old debate about the limits of free will—whether we are truly and fully free or alternatively captive to beliefs and social structures—recurs in the context of war crimes.

Michael Walzer argues that while responsibility for the justice of the war itself rests with political leaders, responsibility for conduct in war rests with the soldier: "The atrocities he commits are his own; the war is not. It is conceived, both in international law and in ordinary moral judgment, as the king's business—a matter of state policy, not of individual volition, except when the individual is the king."[27] The state chooses the war and "the state decrees that an army of a certain size be raised."[28] In this sense, the soldier has limited moral agency: "The battles are no longer theirs. They are political instruments, they obey orders, and the practice of war is shaped at a higher level."[29] The need to seek a soldier's consent before going to war would "surely limit the occasions of war"[30] because soldiers would take care not to waste their own lives, even if a political leader might do so.[31] In sum, according to Walzer, the state is responsible for the initiation of war while moral responsibility for battlefield conduct belongs to the soldier, "at least within their own sphere of activity."[32] Indeed, even in extreme situations, soldiers are responsible for their conduct: "War is a world of duress, of threat and counter-threat.... Soldiers are attacked and forced to fight, but neither aggression nor enemy onslaught forces them to kill innocent people." Walzer is emphatic: "But constricted and frightening as their situation is, we still say that they choose freely and are responsible for what they do. Only a man with a gun to his head is not responsible."[33]

While the focus of this book is not the deliberate killing of civilians by either insurgents or US forces, there is something to learn about collateral damage, and the lines between individual and collective moral responsibility, by examining cases where soldiers deliberately kill civilians. I argue here that the dominant paradigm of individual responsibility for both deliberate killing and "collateral damage"

---

[27] Michael Walzer, *Just and Unjust Wars: A Moral Argument with Historical Illustrations*, 3d ed. (New York: Basic Books, 2000), p. 39.

[28] Ibid., p. 28.

[29] Ibid., p. 29.

[30] Ibid.

[31] Ibid., p. 38.

[32] Ibid., pp. 38–39.

[33] Ibid., p. 314.

needs to be revisited in the light of a deeper understanding of both the constraints on individual agency within military organizations and the effects of combat on the brain. Individual agency is constrained by military training, the rules of engagement, and the deference to command authority that is required of soldiers, at the same time that the fear and fatigue that characterize war degrade human capacities for reason and restraint. As Mark Osiel argues, "the social forces of military life and the experience of combat have fostered atrocities in several ways: (1) by stimulating violent passions among the troops ('from below'); (2) through organized, directed campaigns of terror ('from above'); (3) by tacit connivance between higher and lower echelons, each with its own motives; and (4) by brutalization of subordinates to foster aggressiveness in combat."[34] The line between intentional killing and unintended killing, ostensibly clear in the case of individual soldiers is not so clear after all. There may be some level of organizational responsibility for cases of deliberate killing. Moreover, some of the remedies proposed and implemented by commanders and military organizations for the problem of deliberate killing by individuals have been or can be applied to the problem of collateral damage.

Why Soldiers "Snap"

Combat soldiers are trained, as the military likes to say, in the employment of "kinetic force" to break things and kill people. The individual combat soldier is a trained killer. The claim that there are only a few who choose the wrong path articulates a commonsense understanding of atrocity which assumes that soldiers are autonomous moral agents, able to understand the laws of war, make decisions about their conduct, and act with restraint. The soldiers who "do the right thing even when no one is watching" observe a long-standing distinction between combatants and noncombatants: they do not deliberately target or unnecessarily endanger noncombatants, and they treat prisoners of war decently. It is an atrocity to deliberately target noncombatants or to treat noncombatants with such carelessness that they are gravely injured or killed by accident. It is an atrocity to harm soldiers who have surrendered or to treat prisoners of war cruelly.

Prior to training, a soldier is probably no more or less violent than the average person in a given society. Indeed, as Douglass MacArthur argued, "the soldier above all other people prays for peace, for he must suffer and bear the deepest wounds and scars of war."[35] The soldiers' understanding of war—what war is, how they are to act in it, and who the "enemy" is and why the enemy acts as they do—is formed well

[34] Mark Osiel, *Obeying Orders: Atrocity, Military Discipline, and the Law of War* (New Brunswick, NJ: Transaction Publishers, 2009), p. 173.

[35] Douglas MacArthur, Farewell to West Point, 12 May 1962.

before they arrive in a battlefield and that understanding is at least reforged twice more—in their military training and again on the "battlefield."

The young men and women who engage the "enemy" are told to perform their missions in the service of larger military and political goals. "Basic training" teaches the skills a soldier will need to follow orders, survive, and kill on a battlefield. Training emphasizes specific skills, obedience, and unit cohesion. Soldiers are trained to protect each other. They are obliged to obey lawful orders and to ignore unlawful commands. As Walzer argues, "the War convention requires soldiers to accept personal risks rather than kill innocent people."[36] Soldiers learn to discriminate between combatants and noncombatants and to only kill combatants in specific circumstances. Soldiers are taught to make these determinations in an instant. "There, a flash of motion. Is that a weapon? Is that a child? Is that a child with a weapon? Is that someone aiming at my buddy?" Discrimination is hard. As Specialist Jabbar Magruder said of his time in Iraq, "The enemy doesn't wear uniforms.... You almost have to assume that everybody is hostile."[37] Thomas Nagel argues, "We must distinguish combatants from noncombatants on the basis of their immediate threat or harmfulness."[38] Soldiers must also learn to stop killing when it is no longer necessary.

There is no doubt that in Afghanistan, Pakistan, and Iraq various militant or "insurgent" organizations including the Taliban and Al Qaeda have killed and injured civilians as part of their military or political strategy.[39] As the United States has correctly emphasized, militants may put noncombatants in the middle of a battle with outside forces to provide "human shields" for insurgents. But noncombatants are also deliberately targeted by these organizations for other reasons: to eliminate "moderate" voices or those who may support the United States; to intimidate those who are noncooperative or who have different religious views; and to extort protection payments or taxes. This killing and maiming, along with the private revenge killings that have little or nothing to do with either of the larger political-military conflicts, have yielded many thousands of deaths and injuries in Afghanistan, Pakistan, and Iraq. These are the incidents we hear about: marketplace bombings in Iraq, the mutilation and killing of girls who attend school in Afghanistan, and the guerilla fighters hiding in homes and

---

[36] Walzer, *Just and Unjust Wars*, p. 305.

[37] Quoted in Chris Hedges and Laila Al-Arian, *Collateral Damage: America's War against Iraqi Civilians* (New York: Nation Books, 2008), p. 21.

[38] Thomas Nagel, "War and Massacre," *Philosophy and Public Affairs*, 1 (Winter 1972): 123–144, 140.

[39] An overview of insurgent-instigated violence in Iraq is Human Rights Watch, "A Face and a Name: Civilian Victims of Insurgent Groups in Iraq" (New York: Human Rights Watch, October 2005). In Afghanistan, the Afghanistan NGO Safety Office (ANSO) provides a quarterly compilation of statistics, which includes insurgent-instigated violence. Also see Human Rights Watch, *The Human Cost: The Consequences of Insurgent Attacks in Afghanistan* (New York: Human Rights Watch, 2007).

villages, putting noncombatants who live there at risk. For these groups, deliberately killing civilians is still considered an acceptable strategic choice in some instances. In those instances, there was no question, as Cicero put it, that "in time of war the law is silent."[40]

It is not US policy to deliberately target civilians in war. Indeed, US policy in Afghanistan, Pakistan, and Iraq is just the opposite: civilian protection. Deliberate killing of civilians is no longer acceptable under contemporary domestic and international law; soldiers are to kill only in particular ways and in specific circumstances as governed by the rules of engagement and the laws of war. International law regards noncombatants as off-limits because they pose no immediate threat. Deliberate killing of civilians in war is a war crime or a crime against humanity.

When individuals or groups of soldiers deliberately break the rules, engaging in wanton destruction, they act outside the laws of war and the rules of engagement. Much of the sustained press attention to civilian death at the hands of US forces in Iraq and Afghanistan has focused on this sort of deliberate killing—cases where US soldiers and Marines "snap," clearly violating the laws of armed combat and the rules of engagement. Two explanations are commonly given for why these soldiers kill, rape, kidnap, or torture civilians.

In the first view, the problem is a lack of discipline and the response, as Osiel notes, is typically to tighten discipline.[41] Former Army prosecutor Michael Newton described a video of four Marines urinating on the bodies of dead Afghans presumed to be Taliban accordingly: "Some people will look at this and say all Marines are animals. But that's not true. That instance was undisciplined and unprofessional. And that is why it's a war crime. The law exists to instill professionalism. But it is also there to create a humanitarian imperative, even in combat."[42] This is the "bad apple" view of war crimes, where the bad apples are fully autonomous moral agents who are no longer exercising discipline. They are failing to control their anger and other emotions, such as the desire for revenge. War unleashes our natural passions. Ultimately, it is the job of the soldiers themselves, and their commanders, to keep control, and so, the reasoning goes, these malevolent passions are unleashed in war if the soldier or commander loses control.

A second common theory suggests that deliberate killing or harm of unarmed civilians, when it is not the explicit strategy of the government, is sometimes so awful that the person who does so must be out of their right mind in some way—at least for the moment, literally insane. In this view, the soldier is not the problem; war is the problem because it breaks people. And multiple tours do break people. Indeed, more than 100,000 US soldiers had already been on three or more tours of

---

[40] *Inter arma enim silent leges.*

[41] Osiel, *Obeying Orders*, pp. 176–180.

[42] Quoted in James Dao, "Reprehensible Behavior is a Risk in Combat, Experts Say," *New York Times*, 14 January 2012, p. A5.

duty from 2001 to March 2012.[43] Those who described the killing spree of Robert Bales in Afghanistan in March 2012 emphasized that he had already been on multiple tours of duty in Iraq and that he was arguably suffering from post-traumatic stress. When otherwise sane and law-abiding soldiers snap or deliberately commit crimes in combat, something has gone terribly wrong. In this case, mad apples commit atrocities where the moral agency of the mad apples is compromised and diminished by the stress of war. Thus, the assignment of moral responsibility to soldiers for their actions that violate the laws of war depends on the soldiers' capacity to make decisions and their freedom to act—their agency.

There is a fine line between these theories, and both the mad apple and the bad apple view are implied in the US military response to several incidents of deliberate killing of Iraqis in 2005 and 2006. In June 2006, although the military emphasized that the soldiers' behavior in the high-profile incidents was an anomaly, the Commander of Multi-National Core in Iraq, Lieutenant General Peter Chiarelli announced that the US would retrain every soldiers in Iraq in "core warrior values."

> Of the nearly 150,000 Coalition forces presently in Iraq, 99.9 percent of them perform their jobs magnificently every day. They do their duty with honor under difficult circumstances. They exhibit sound judgment, honesty and integrity. They display patience, professionalism and restraint in the face of a treacherous enemy. And they do the right thing even when no one is watching. Unfortunately, there are a few individuals who sometimes choose the wrong path. As military professionals, it is important that we take time to reflect on the values that separate us from our enemies. The challenge for us is to make sure the actions of a few do not tarnish the good work of the many.[44]

When Chiarelli argued that "as military professionals, it is important that we take time to reflect on the values that separate us from our enemies" he underscored his belief the moral agency of American soldiers.[45] The training, which included a two-to-three hour slide presentation, was designed to reinforce training

[43] Anna Mulrine, "Sgt. Robert Bales and Multiple Tours of Duty: How Many is Too Many?" *Christian Science Monitor*, 23 March 2012, http://www.csmonitor.com/USA/Military/2012/0323/Sgt.-Robert-Bales-and-multiple-tours-of-duty-How-many-is-too-many.

[44] Lt. General Peter Chiarelli, quoted in Armed Forces Press Service, "Operational Commander in Iraq Orders Core Values Training," 1 June 2006, http://www.defense.gov/News/NewsArticle.aspx?ID=16154.

Core Warrior Values Training, Multinational Forces, Iraq, http://www.atsc.army.mil/crc/core_warrior_values_training.pdf.pdf. Chiarelli's statement is repeated almost verbatim as points in the slide presentation.

[45] Quoted in Armed Forces Press Service, "Operational Commander in Iraq Orders Core Values Training."

combatants received prior to deployment in Iraq. One slide emphasized the Geneva Conventions.

Core Warrior Values Training, Slide 15

The Laws Applicable to Military Personnel also Reflect Our Values

Example: Geneva Convention Requirements

- Treat prisoners of war humanely.
- Engage only combatants with deadly force.
- Respect and protect noncombatants.
- Allow the enemy to surrender.
- Collect and care for the wounded.
- Desecration of dead bodies prohibited.
- Don't cause unnecessary suffering.

The Core Warrior Values training[46] suggested that several factors could lead to what was labeled "bad behavior." The slides emphasized the psychological status of individual soldiers. "This behavior may be based on:—Stress, fear, or fatigue.—Loneliness or a feeling of isolation.—Peer pressure.—Contempt for the enemy or their conduct." Again, there is something wrong with individuals: "Some simply fail to do the right thing, even when they know they should. Often this is a result of fear, stress, or peer pressure."[47]

The training in "core warrior values" emphasized the belief that war drives some people to extremes, or that some kinds of war drive people to extremes. Soldiers "snap" or suffer a mental "breakdown" and kill enemy soldiers that are no threat to them, harm civilians, or even sometimes attack members of their own military in the field. In the heat of battle, the rage, the fear, and the hostility that has kept the soldier going cannot be shut off. Something, or rather, many things, happen in war that make it hard for soldiers to maintain their discipline and refrain from harming either civilians or soldiers who are no longer a threat to them. War is extreme—soldiers "snap" or "lose it" because they just can't take it any more. They are no longer capable of distinguishing combatants from noncombatants, or they just don't care to do so any longer. Everyone is perceived as a potential threat. "In addition, there is the instilled hatred and anger that cloud our judgment about the actions of others and what is their due for so acting, as well as the seeming need to respond right

---

[46] Core Warrior Values Training, Multinational Forces, Iraq.
[47] Ibid.

away lest our own safety be jeopardized."[48] Soldiers sometimes thus act as if there were a gun to their head. The metaphorical "gun" in this case is socialization, social pressure, and the hardship of war—the extreme fatigue, the heat, the cold, the loud sounds, the blood, and more than anything else, the fear.

Both civilian experts and Pentagon officials have argued that atrocities in Iraq and Afghanistan were understandable and, perhaps, to be expected due to the nature of combat itself. Brigadier General Donald Campbell argues that "obviously, when you're in the combat theater dealing with enemy combatants who don't abide by the law of war, who do acts of indecency, soldiers become stressed, they become fearful." Further, Campbell says, "It is very difficult to determine on the battlefield who is a combatant and who is a civilian." Thus, in those contexts, the implication is that mistakes could occur; civilians could accidentally be killed. But, Campbell is quick to say that, whatever the reason, "it doesn't excuse the acts that have occurred, and we're going to look into them." Campbell suggests that the atrocities were an emotional reaction caused by extreme conditions. "But I would say it is stress, fear, isolation, and in some cases they're just upset. They see their buddies getting blown up on occasion and they could snap."[49] Similarly, sociologist Charles Moskos, suggests that individual soldiers who feel frustrated and powerless can and do "lose" it in certain combat circumstances and experience "temporary insanity." Moskos said, "If they feel that a local town is covertly involved in the killing of G.I.'s, that's when people lose their sense of right and wrong."[50] The soldier's restraint has broken. A soldier, Staff Sergeant Calvin Gibbs, convicted and sentenced to life in prison for organizing the killing of civilians in Afghanistan in 2010 over a period of several months, insisted that those he killed were a threat and that he took fingers and a tooth from the bodies of those he killed because he had "disassociated" and no longer saw the bodies as human.[51]

Further, just as it is no longer US policy to deliberately attack civilians, the attitude toward wanton violence by individual soldiers who "snap" has also changed. Not long ago, when soldiers snapped and killed civilians, this was seen as an inevitable, if regrettable and rare occurrence. Today, although the individuals are often forgiven for "losing it," the military goes to great length to evaluate its soldiers' mental health. Still, as Ronald Smith, the director of psychiatry at Walter Reed National Military Center admitted, the tools for evaluating soldiers are not reliable. When someone

---

[48] Larry May, *War Crimes and Just War* (Cambridge: Cambridge University Press, 2007), p. 11.

[49] DoD News Briefing with Brig. Gen. Campbell from Baghdad, Iraq, http://www.defense.gov/transcripts/transcript.aspx?transcriptid=6.

[50] Mark Mazzetti, "Military Memo: War's Risks Include Toll on Training Values," *New York Times*, 4 June 2006.

[51] William Yardley, "American Soldier is Convicted of Killing Afghan Civilians for Sport," *New York Times*, 11 November 2011, p. A15.

does fall apart, "there's going to be lots of soul-searching and teeth-gnashing, but the reality is that we can't tell when somebody is going to snap."[52]

The Paradigm Bad Apple: My Lai

The "bad apple" explanation of military atrocity is often given by US military officials and outside observers. For instance, Andrew Krepinevich observes that "in cases where you fail to defeat the insurgency, you sometimes adopt out of frustration increasingly ruthless methods to try to defeat the insurgents."[53] When he ordered training in "core warrior values" in 2006, General Chiarelli implied a bad apple understanding of the cause of atrocity by stressing the idea that the bulk of US forces were behaving according to law, while "there are a few individuals who sometimes choose the wrong path."[54] The solution to the problem of bad apples, according to Dick Couch, is to get them out of the barrel before they affect an entire unit.

> Morally the troops *know* what is expected of them. Ongoing sustainment and reinforcement training can keep those issues and values current within the course of their physical and professional battlefield preparation. But when bad conduct becomes part of the small-unit culture, that culture is broken, and very little can be done in the way of lectures or punishments or reasoning to get the 'unit train' back on acceptable 'moral rails.' This is not an issue of training time, it's an issue of moral will. Leaders and instigators of wrong or dysfunctional conduct need to be publicly humiliated and sent away.[55]

The paradigmatic bad apples in American military history include Jacob "Howling Wilderness" Smith, the perpetrator of atrocities in the Philippines more than one hundred years ago. Smith was court-martialed, yet, in his day, he was also considered a hero to many in the US military.

More recently, First Lieutenant William Calley of the My Lai Massacre has come to exemplify a bad apple. On 15 March 1968, Task Force Barker, made up of several Army infantry battalions, was given the order by the commander Colonel Oran Henderson of the 11th Brigade to attack Son My village in Vietnam on the

---

[52] Anna Mulrine, "Sgt. Robert Bales and Multiple Tours of Duty: How Many is Too Many?" *Christian Science Monitor*, 23 March 2012.

[53] Andrew Krepinevich, quoted in Mazzetti, "Military Memo," p. A10.

[54] CBC News, "U.S. Troops in Iraq to Get Refresher in Battlefield Morality," CBC News, http://www.cbc.ca/news/world/story/2006/06/01/warrior-classes060601.html.

[55] Dick Couch, *A Tactical Ethic: Moral Conduct in the Insurgent Battlespace* (Annapolis: Naval Institute Press, 2010), p. 109.

assumption that a Viet Cong battalion was located in and near the village. The commander of Task Force Barker, Lieutenant Colonel Frank Barker, told the infantry commanders to burn the houses, kill the livestock, and destroy the food. The company commanders then told their platoon leaders that only enemy soldiers would be in and around the village.

On 16 March 1968, after 25 minutes of artillery and helicopter gunship operations to "prepare" the area, US soldiers landed just before 8 A.M. in the village of My Lai. They met no resistance. In a scene that was repeated for several hours that morning and afternoon, both large and small groups of villagers were rounded up by the US military and shot. Nearby villages were also attacked. Houses were burned, the livestock were killed, and the wells closed. Helicopter pilot, Warrant Officer Hugh Thompson witnessed the killing of civilians and landed his helicopter several times in the morning to attempt to halt the killing and rescue Vietnamese civilians. Thompson returned to base shortly before noon and reported what he had witnessed. A second report of civilian killing came in to the Brigade Commander's office later in the afternoon. By the end of the day, having met no resistance, US soldiers killed between 200 and 500 Vietnamese noncombatants, men, women, and children. Many of the dead had been tortured, raped, or mutilated. An army photographer, Ronald Haeberle, documented the massacre that day with his personal camera.

Early on the day of the massacre, reports of events went up the chain of command but were not investigated. At the conclusion of the operation, Colonel Henderson praised his troops for killing Viet Cong. Over the next few days and months, officers sought to control perceptions of My Lai within the military, cover up the massacre, and evade responsibility for civilian deaths. In this way, the My Lai massacre remained essentially unknown outside the US military for a year. News of the killing at My Lai trickled out in letters and eventually investigative reporting. Once the massacre became more widely known, a military investigation and subsequent court martial sought to establish causal, legal, and moral responsibility for what happened. The main question was who gave the orders that led to the massacre. The next questions were about why members of Charlie Company, 1st Battalion, 20th Infantry Regiment, acted as they did.

Military courts found Calley guilty and sentenced him for the murder of dozens of Vietnamese. The investigation and prosecution of the men who committed or concealed the My Lai massacre was thus a milestone, albeit not a complete turning point. Journalist Luke Mogelson summarized the response to Lieutenant Calley's conviction this way:

> In 1971, when Lt. William Calley Jr., who had led his platoon in the massacre of hundreds of unarmed civilians, including women, children and the elderly in the Vietnamese village of My Lai, was found guilty of premeditated murder and sentenced to life in prison, public outrage erupted across

the country. Thousands of telegrams advocating clemency were sent to
the White House, mass protests were held nationwide, a popular folk song
was written and Georgia's governor, Jimmy Carter, instituted American
Fighting Man's Day in solidarity with the convicted war criminal. President
Nixon immediately ordered Calley released to house arrest, just three and
a half years of which he would serve before being freed entirely by a federal
judge. Aubrey Daniel, the Army lawyer who prosecuted Calley, and who
wrote a letter of protest rebuking Nixon for his involvement, would later
say of the reaction: "It was a country that wanted this war to end and a
country that didn't want to believe that this had happened. But if it did, it
wanted to say that it's our fault collectively, and not his fault."[56]

At the Nuremburg Tribunals, the United States had articulated and implemented a doctrine of individual responsibility for war crimes. But it is in the
aftermath of My Lai that the lessons are internalized. No longer were men who
committed massacres heroes: they were held to be criminally responsible as
individuals for their conduct, even if the American culture was not yet ready to
internalize the new norms. The trial was also notable for reinforcing the idea of
individual responsibility.

Of the four officers and two enlisted soldiers who were court-martialed for My
Lai, William Calley was the only one convicted. However, the Army investigation in 1970, known as the Peers Commission Report, after Lt. General William
Peers, found thirty members of Task Force Barker culpable for either acts of commission—killing, raping, and maiming noncombatants, and lying about what happened—and omission, namely failing to stop the massacre or failing to report it.
The report named and described the actions and inaction of these individual soldiers but also described a climate that had developed "prior to the incident" within
the 11th Brigade. Specifically, the Peers Report noted that "a permissive attitude
toward the treatment and safeguarding of non-combatants which contributed to the
mistreatment of such persons" during the operation which was "on 16-19 March
1968, exemplified by an almost total disregard for the lives and property of the civilian population of Son My Village on the part of the commanders and key staff officers of TF Barker."[57] Further, though many rules of engagement cards, which had
specific instructions to protect civilians, had been distributed, many of the soldiers,

---

[56] Luke Mogelson, "A Beast in the Heart of Every Fighting Man," *New York Times Magazine*, 1 May
2011, http://www.nytimes.com/2011/05/01/magazine/mag-01KillTeam-t.html?_r=1&emc=eta1&
pagewanted=all.

[57] Peers Commission Report, in Joseph Goldstein, Burke Marshall, and Jack Schwartz, eds., *The My
Lai Massacre and Its Cover-up: Beyond the Reach of the Law?* (New York: Free Press, 1976), pp. 314–
315. Michael Walzer similarly blames commanders for the failings that led to My Lai. See Walzer, *Just
and Unjust Wars*, p. 322.

General Peers noted, "had put the card in their pockets unread and never had any idea of their contents." Peers thus put some of blame for My Lai on what he called "lackadaisical" training. But Peers also said, "Even accepting these training deficiencies... there were some things a soldier did not have to be told were wrong—such as rounding up women and children and them mowing them down, shooting babies out of mothers' arms, and raping."[58]

Official Rules of Engagement

I accept that the top military and political leadership of the United States and its allies abhor the deliberate killing of civilians in war. Efforts are taken to train soldiers in how to avoid harming or killing civilians. Nor is it a high-level US policy to condone the behavior of "bad apples" or to look the other way when soldiers snap. And, though it is difficult to know the numbers, I accept the assertion that—given the duration and scale of US operations in Iraq and Afghanistan—the instances where soldiers snap or when "bad apples" commit war crimes has been relatively rare in historical terms.

Analyst Colin Kahl correctly argued that the US has killed a lower proportion of civilians in Iraq and Afghanistan than in previous US wars. In late 2006, Kahl argued that "U.S. compliance with non-combatant immunity in Iraq is relatively high by historical standards [and] ... it has been improving since the beginning of the war."[59] That may be true, but Kahl goes even further: "All told, the number of civilian deaths per ton of air-delivered munitions during major combat in Iraq was about 19 times lower than that in Dresden and 162 times lower than that in Tokyo."[60] But this comparison is inappropriate: as Kahl acknowledges, it was deliberate policy in previous US wars to attack civilians. It was not US policy to kill civilians in Iraq and Afghanistan and those wars in Afghanistan and Iraq exemplify a relatively recent transition in US policy.

The doctrine of the US military has at times—through most of its history until the Vietnam War—directly targeted noncombatants in either the belief that there is no significant distinction between combatants and noncombatants, or the belief that targeting noncombatants was militarily useful and necessary. In the not too distant past it was explicit US policy to deliberately target civilians in the hope that it would hasten the capitulation of US adversaries. On occasion, the US military has deliberately targeted civilians in acts of reprisal. That is no longer the case.

Basic training gives soldiers the skills to survive and is the place where they first learn guidelines for the legitimate use of force. Then, prior to deployment, enlisted

---

[58] W. R. Peers, *The My Lai Inquiry* (New York: Norton, 1979), p. 230.
[59] Colin H. Kahl, "How We Fight," *Foreign Affairs*, vol. 85, no. 6 (November/December 2006): 84.
[60] Ibid.

personnel and officers are instructed in the laws of war. Soldiers may not read the Geneva conventions verbatim, but they are taught the combatant/noncombatant distinction and that there are limits to when the soldier may kill—the rules of engagement or ROE. These rules are the ways that military necessity, force protection, proportionality, and noncombatant immunity are translated and transmitted to the individual soldier. Mark Martins observes that ROE, and in particular, their interpretation and application in the field must avoid two extremes—either fostering "over-tentativeness" which leaves the soldier potentially vulnerable to aggressors, or "undisciplined fire" which can lead to civilian casualties or even friendly fire.[61]

US soldiers have long been issued instructions about when and who to kill. During the Korean War, these instructions became more explicit and afterward became known as "rules of engagement." While the rules of engagement, which emphasized avoiding harm to noncombatants, were widely distributed in Vietnam, Martins observes that "few senior leaders in Vietnam felt that soldiers understood the ROE well before the My Lai massacre and even fewer believed that soldiers adhered carefully to the ROE."[62] Martins argues that during the Vietnam War soldiers believed that the "restrictions designed to avoid noncombatant casualties unduly tied their hands, United States soldiers engaged in 'creative application' of the ROE."[63]

Since Vietnam, the "Standing Rules of Engagement" (SROE)—the conditions under which a soldier may use deadly force—are given by the head of the uniformed military, the Chairman of the Joint Chiefs of Staff, and approved by the Secretary of Defense. The SROE, which are translated into specific orders at various levels of command, emphasize that soldiers have an "inherent right of self-defense." Specifically, "US forces always retain the right to use necessary and proportional force for unit and individual self-defense in response to a hostile act or demonstrated hostile intent."[64] The Standing Rules of Engagement then define these terms, giving the authority and obligation to commanders to use "all necessary means" for self-defense.

> a. *Inherent Right of Self-Defense.* A commander has the authority and obligation to use all necessary means available and to take all appropriate actions to defend that commander's unit and other US forces in the vicinity from a hostile act or demonstration of hostile intent. Neither these rules, nor

---

[61] Mark Martins, "Rules of Engagement for Land Forces: A Matter of Training, Not Lawyering," *Military Law Review*, vol. 143, no. 1 (Winter 1994): 1–160.

[62] Ibid., p. 19.

[63] Ibid., pp. 19–20.

[64] United States, Chairman of the Joint Chiefs of Staff Instruction, CJCSI 3121.01A, 15 January 2000, "Standing Rules of Engagement for US Forces," Enclosure A, paragraph 1 c. (1), p. A-1.

the supplemental measures activated to augment these rules, limit this inherent right and obligation. At all times, the requirements of necessity and proportionality, as amplified in these SROE, will form the basis for the judgment of the on-scene commander (OSC) or individual as to what constitutes an appropriate response to a particular hostile act or demonstration of hostile intent.[65]

The standing rules appear to limit collective and unit self-defense to "an observed hostile act or demonstrated hostile intent."[66] A hostile act is: "An attack or other use of force against the United States, US forces, and, in certain circumstances, US nationals, their property, US commercial assets, and/or other designated non-US forces, foreign nationals and their property. It is also force used directly to preclude or impede the mission and/or duties of US forces, including the recovery of US personnel and vital US Government property." Hostile intent is understood as the: "threat of imminent use of force against the United States, US forces, and in certain circumstances, US nationals, their property, US commercial assets, and/ or other designated non-US forces, foreign nationals and their property. Also, the threat of force to preclude or impede the mission and/or duties of US forces, including the recovery of US personnel or vital USG property."[67]

But demonstrated hostile acts and hostile intent may not be required in some instances. National self-defense "may be exercised by designated authority declaring a foreign force or terrorist(s) hostile."[68] Specifically, "Once a force is declared hostile by appropriate authority, US units need not observe a hostile act or a demonstration of hostile intent before engaging that force."[69] The definition of hostile force includes civilians: "Any civilian, paramilitary, or military force or terrorist(s), with or without national designation, that has committed a hostile act, exhibited hostile intent, or has been declared hostile by appropriate US authority."[70]

---

[65] Ibid., Enclosure A, paragraph 5a, p. A-3.

[66] Martins notes that the precise definition of hostile acts and hostile are restricted. Martins, "Rules of Engagement for Land Forces," pp. 29–30.

[67] "Standing Rules of Engagement for US Forces," CJCSI 3121.01A, Enclosure A paragraph 5g and h.

[68] Ibid., Enclosure A, paragraph 5b, p. A-4.

[69] Ibid., Enclosure A, paragraph 6, p. A-5. The rest of the paragraph reads: "The responsibility for exercising the right and obligation of national self-defense and as necessary declaring a force hostile is a matter of the utmost importance. All available intelligence, the status of international relationships, the requirements of international law, an appreciation of the political situation, and the potential consequences for the United States must be carefully weighed. The exercise of the right and obligation of national self-defense by competent authority is separate from and in no way limits the commander's right and obligation to exercise unit self-defense."

[70] Ibid., Enclosure A, paragraph 5i, p. A-5.

The soldier is concerned with their individual right to self-defense, which is defined as: "The inherent right to use all necessary means available and to take all appropriate actions to defend oneself and US forces in one's vicinity from a hostile act or demonstrated hostile intent is a unit of self-defense."[71] The SROE further define two "elements of Self-Defense."

(1) *Necessity.* Exists when a hostile act occurs or when a force or terrorist(s) exhibits hostile intent.

(2) *Proportionality.* Force used to counter a hostile act or demonstrated hostile intent must be reasonable in intensity, duration, and magnitude to the perceived or demonstrated threat based on all facts known to the commander at the time.[72]

The standing rules of engagement are reiterated and specified in each situation. In other words, commanders give every soldier the specific rules of engagement (ROEs) that apply to their particular mission. These rules are given orally and often summarized on the equivalent of a 3 by 5 card that a soldier may carry with them. A summary of the US military's Rules of Engagement for Iraq, given to all US Army and Marine personnel by the US Central Command in 2003 read, in part: 1. "c) Do not target or strike any of the following except in self-defense to protect yourself, your unit, friendly forces, and designated persons or property under your control:—civilians—Hospitals, mosques, national monuments, and any other historical and cultural sites. d) Do not fire into civilian populated areas or buildings unless the enemy is using them for military purposes or if necessary for your self-defense. Minimize collateral damage."

The question of when it is legitimate to use force has long been a source of tension in Iraq and Afghanistan. First Lieutenant Wade Zirkle described the problem clearly: "You got a guy trying to kill me but he's firing from houses...with civilians around him, women and children. You know, what do you do? You don't want to risk shooting at him and shooting children at the same time. But at the same time, you don't want to die either."[73] In January 2007, retired Navy Admiral James A. Lyons described the then current Rules of Engagement for Baghdad as too restrictive.

> The current ROEs for Baghdad—including Sadr City, home of the Mahdi Army—have seven incremental steps that must be satisfied before our troops can take the gloves off and engage the enemy with appropriate violence of action.

---

[71] Ibid., Enclosure A, paragraph 5e, p. A-4.
[72] Ibid., Enclosure A, paragraph 5f, p. A-4.
[73] Zirkle, quoted in Hedges and Al-Arian, *Collateral Damage*, pp. 25–26.

(1) You must feel a direct threat to you or your team.

(2) You must clearly see a threat.

(3) That threat must be identified.

(4) The team leader must concur that there is an identified threat.

(5) The team leader must feel that the situation is one of life or death.

(6) There must be minimal or no collateral risk.

(7) Only then can the team leader clear the engagement.

These ROEs might sound fine to academics gathering at some esoteric seminar on how to avoid civilian casualties in a war zone. But they do absolutely nothing to protect our combat troops who have to respond in an instant to a life or death situation.

If our soldiers or Marines see someone about to level an AK-47 in their direction or start to are [*sic*] receive hostile fire from a rooftop or mosque, there is no time to go through a seven-point checklist before reacting. Indeed, the very fact that they see a weapon, or begin to receive hostile fire should be sufficient justification to respond with deadly force.

Lyons argued that Iraqi insurgents used the United States' "restrictive" ROEs to "to their advantage" by deliberately putting civilians in the way and targeting civilians themselves. Lyons said this showed that the enemy has "no regard for human life." Protecting civilians was thus unrealistic. "We cannot, therefore, afford to keep our combat troops shackled by a naive, legalistic disadvantage that takes no note of the real world, or the real battlefield."[74]

"Ground Truth": Written and Unwritten Rules of Engagement

In rapidly evolving situations, the rules of engagement are verbal instructions, issued by local commanders before a soldier enters an area. Sometimes the "rules" evolve, much the way many customs do—as improvised local acts, with local names. In a place, like Fallujah, where a cell phone can be used to detonate an improvised explosive device, the language can be as simple as, "If you see someone with a cell phone, put a bullet in their f—ing head."[75] As Lieutenant Colonel Nathan Sassaman recalled, during his command in Iraq, "anyone found digging by the side of the road

---

[74] James A. Lyons, Jr. "Untie Military Hands," *Washington Times*, 25 January 2007, http://www.washingtontimes.com/news/2007/jan/25/20070125-091730-8692r/.

[75] A US commander in Fallujah, quoted in Nancy Sherman, *The Untold War: Inside the Hearts, Minds, and Souls of Our Soldiers* (New York: W. W. Norton, 2010), p. 76. Thomas and Johnson, "Probing a Bloodbath."

or highway, at night, under the cover of darkness, was considered to be engaged in nefarious activity—in all likelihood, this person was in the process of burying an IDE, the purpose of which was to ambush and kill American soldiers. Therefore, soldiers were under standing orders to eliminate these targets." Sassaman acknowledges that, "this means that the rules of engagement allowed for the execution of Iraqi insurgents under certain conditions, regardless of whether insurgents were actively engaged in battle." [76]

Marine Sergeant Jason Wayne Lemieux describes unwritten rules of the US deployment in Iraq: "In January 2004, I remember attending a formation where we were given our mission for the second deployment. I was sitting there like a good marine with my pen and paper, and our commander told us that our mission was to 'kill those who need to be killed, and save those who need to be saved.' "

For Lemieux's unit, those who needed to be killed changed. "During the April offensive of 2004, in which attacks erupted all over Anbar province, my unit was involved in a two day firefight. Shortly after the firefight was underway, the same commander who had given us the mission ordered that everyone wearing a black dishdasha and a red headscarf were displaying 'hostile intent' and a 'hostile action' and was to be shot." Lemieux said that later, that same commander "ordered that *everyone* in the streets was an enemy combatant." A few weeks later, Lemieux says, "the standing Rules of Engagement for my unit were changed so that marines didn't need to identify a hostile action in order to use deadly force. They just had to identify hostile intent." Lemieux recalled,

> The rules also explicitly stated that carrying a shovel, standing on a rooftop while speaking on a cell phone, or holding binoculars or being out after curfew constituted hostile intent, and we were authorized to use deadly force.
>
> On my third tour [September 2005-March 2006], the Rules of Engagement were stricter, but they only existed so that the commander could say there were Rules of Engagement that were being followed. In reality, my officers explicitly told me and my fellow marines that if we felt threatened by an Iraqi's presence, we "should shoot them," and *the officers* would "take care of us." [77]

Marine Corporal Jason Washburn said that during his three tours in Iraq, the rules of engagement were frequently revised: "It seemed like every time we turned around we had different rules of engagement. For example, during the invasion, we

[76] Nathan Sassaman, with Joe Layden, *Warrior King: The Triumph and Betrayal of an American Commander in Iraq* (New York: St. Martin's Press, 2008), p. 142.

[77] Lemieux's testimony in Iraq Veterans Against the War (IVAW) and Aaron Glantz, *Winter Soldier Iraq and Afghanistan: Eyewitness Accounts of the Occupations* (Chicago: Haymarket Books, 2008), pp. 17–19: 17–18, emphasis in the original.

were told to use target identification before engaging anyone, but if the town or city that we were approaching was a known threat, if the unit in the area before us took a high number of casualties, we were allowed to shoot whatever we wanted. It was deemed to be a free fire zone, so we opened fire on everything, and there really were no rules governing the amount of force we were allowed to use on targets during the invasion."[78]

Private Clifton Hicks also describes what he also called a free-fire zone in southern Baghdad in April 2004. "During Operation Blackjack, I was instructed by our troop commander, a captain, that one sector was now a free-fire zone. He told us there were 'no friendlies in the area.' He said, 'Game on. All weapons free.'"[79] Hicks said that the "majority of those so-called KIAs [killed in action] were civilians attempting to flee the battlefield." Hicks argued that the reason for civilians being killed was in part simply the difficulty of discriminating between combatants and noncombatants.

> This is what happens when a conventional force such as the US military attacks a heavily populated urban area. We are not bad people. We were there because we thought that we were gonna make things better, because these people wanted us to be there. We showed up and realized that there's a whole bunch of people that wanted to kill us. Guess what? They look just like the folks who don't want to kill us. How were we gonna sort them out? The only way to ensure our survival was to make sure that we put them in the dirt before they put us in the dirt, to put it bluntly.[80]

But the difficulty of discriminating between combatants and noncombatants could be used as a "claim" for legitimacy too. As Lieutenant Van Engelen recalled of his time in Iraq, " 'Cover your own butt' was the first rule of engagement. Someone could look at me the wrong way and I could claim my safety was in threat."[81]

Military organizations need supplies: soldiers need food, water, weapons, ammunition, medical equipment, places to sleep and shower, fuel, and entertainment for their periods of rest. Nearly all of those supplies are moved by trucks in large convoys driven by other soldiers or contractors. Each convoy is protected by soldiers driving armed and, sometimes, armored vehicles. Every time a convoy drives from one point to the next, it is vulnerable to ambush or buried improvised explosive devices. Soldiers drive quickly through the streets; the faster one drives, the less time on the road and the less vulnerable to attack. Soldiers often shoot at oncoming vehicles or cars that are traveling in the same direction that do not leave the

---

[78] Washburn's testimony, in IVAW and Glantz, *Winter Soldier Iraq and Afghanistan*, pp. 20–22, 20.

[79] Clifton Hicks testimony in IVAW and Glantz, *Winter Soldier Iraq and Afghanistan*, pp. 28–32, 28.

[80] Hicks testimony in IVAW and Glantz, *Winter Soldier Iraq and Afghanistan*, p. 29.

[81] Quoted in Hedges and Al-Arian, *Collateral Damage*, p. 40.

road when a speeding convoy approaches. Many cars and pedestrians are run off the road and pedestrians who do not get out of the way are often simply run over. As Sergeant Geoffrey Millard explained: "You don't put American lives in danger by stopping a whole convoy for one kid. You run the kid over."[82]

War as an "Atrocity-Producing Situation"

Michael Walzer observed that the soldier "is not indeed a machine that can just be turned off, and it would be inhumanly righteous not to look with sympathy on his plight."[83] Yet, Walzer suggests, we cannot allow that the "killing frenzy that begins in combat and ends in murder, the line between the two being lost to the mind of the individual soldier," be simply excused.[84] Neither, Walzer argues, ought we excuse soldiers for "following orders."

But it is not so easy to say how individuals should be judged in war when they ostensibly "lose control." Psychiatrist Robert Jay Lifton argues that soldiers do horrible things when they are placed in horrible contexts. Counterinsurgency war, in particular, Lifton suggests, leads to brutality and sometimes to an "atrocity producing situation—one so structured, psychologically and militarily, that ordinary people, men or women no better or worse than you or I, can commit atrocities."[85]

Lifton's concept of an atrocity-producing situation was initially formulated when he worked with Vietnam veterans, and, in particular, sought to make sense of the My Lai massacre through interviews with participants. The context for an atrocity-producing situation is a "counterinsurgency war undertaken by an advanced industrial society against a revolutionary movement of an underdeveloped country, in which revolutionary guerrillas are inseparable from the population."[86] This leads, Lifton argues, to:

> the draconian military policies in Vietnam: the "free-fire zone" (where every civilian is a target), and the "search and destroy mission" (on which everyone and everything can be killed, or as the expression has it, "wasted"); the extensive use of defoliants that not only destroy the overall ecology of Vietnam but, if encountered in sufficient concentration by pregnant women, human embryos as well; and the almost random saturation

[82] Ibid., p. 13.

[83] Walzer, *Just and Unjust Wars*, p. 307.

[84] Ibid.

[85] Robert Jay Lifton, "Haditha: In an 'Atrocity-Producing Situation'—Who is to Blame?" *Editor & Publisher*, 4 June 2006.

[86] Robert Jay Lifton, *Home from the War: Learning from Vietnam Veterans* (New York: Simon and Schuster, 1973), p. 41.

of a small country with an unprecedented level of technological destruction and firepower from both the air and the ground.[87]

Lifton found that "external factors and military policies" changed the internal psychological capacities of individuals as they "internalized and then act[ed] upon an image of slaughter."[88]

Lifton argues, with respect to US atrocities in Iraq, "A major factor in all of these events was the emotional state of US soldiers as they struggled with angry grief over buddies killed by invisible adversaries, with a desperate need to identify the 'enemy.'" Like Vietnam, "Iraq is also a counterinsurgency war in which US soldiers, despite their extraordinary firepower, feel extremely vulnerable in a hostile environment, and in which high-ranking officers and war planners are frustrated by the great difficulty of tracking down or even recognizing the enemy."[89] Lifton noted profound psychological changes in the soldiers who commit atrocity.

> Recognizing that atrocity is a group activity, one must ask how individual soldiers can so readily join in? I believe they undergo a type of dissociation that I call doubling—the formation of a second self. The individual psyche can adapt to an atrocity-producing environment by means of a sub-self that behaves as if it is autonomous and thereby joins in activities that would otherwise seem repugnant.
>
> In environments where sanctioned brutality becomes the norm, sadistic impulses, dormant in all of us, are likely to be expressed. The group's violent energy becomes such that an individual soldier who questions it could be turned upon.... To resist such pressure requires an unusual combination of conscience and courage.[90]

While he focuses on individual reactions, Lifton emphasizes that soldiers do not randomly come upon an atrocity-producing situation but are put there by their political leadership. At root, he suggests, an ideological vision provides the conditions for an atrocity-producing situation: "What ultimately drives the dynamic is an ideological vision that equates Iraqi resisters with 'terrorists' and seeks to further justify almost any action against them." Counterinsurgency wars and wars of occupation are "particularly prone to sustained atrocity" when the conflicts are "driven by profound ideological distortions."[91]

What happened in Haditha, Iraq, in 2005, was the killing of two dozen unarmed civilians by US Marines who were grieving the death of a comrade to a roadside

[87] Ibid.
[88] Ibid., pp. 41–42.
[89] Lifton, "Haditha."
[90] Ibid.
[91] Ibid.

bomb. More than grieving, the Marines wanted revenge for the death of T. J. Miguel Terrazas. As Nancy Sherman notes: "Those responsible for the killing may have been the initial target, but the objects of payback becomes fungible. The point is retribution not discrimination. Retribution often falls on those who are easier targets."[92]

The Iraq war produced much smaller scale war crimes, many not so clearly related to immediate feelings of grief, anger, or a desire for revenge, such as when in May 2007, US Army snipers killed an unarmed vegetable farmer, Genei Nesir Khudair al-Janabi, who had stumbled upon a sniper hideout. Staff Sergeant Mike Hensley ordered Sergeant Evan Vela to kill the man, who was lying face down in the dirt at the time under Vela. Hensley put an AK-47 next to the body of Khudair. Out of eight people killed by the snipers between 7 April and 11 May 2007, the farmer was the fourth unarmed Iraqi to be killed. In two of the incidents, it appears that soldiers placed evidence on the dead civilians to show they were insurgents. The soldiers of the 1st Battalion of the 25th Infantry Division's 501st Regiment were tired, dehydrated, and they felt they were under pressure from their superiors Lieutenant Colonel Robert Balcavage and Command Sergeant Major Bernie Knight to kill Iraqi insurgents. At a hearing one sniper in the battalion, Alexander Flores said he was given the message, "Get more bodies. Raise the morale of the battalion."[93] Another said he felt similar pressure: Specialist. Joshua Michaud said Balcavage and Knight "constantly pushed for 'If you feel threatened, you know, obviously eliminate the threat.' But they kind of said it in a manner in which a lot of us took it like, 'Hey, you need to go out there and you guys gotta start getting kills.'" Staff Sergeant Hensley was charged with three murders. Sergeant Anthony Murphy later said, "You hear that we were pressured to get more kills." He admitted, "Well, what's not politically correct is that we *wanted* more kills. I mean, why would we not want to kill the enemy that's killing us? Yeah, of course we want to kill them. Legitimate targets, man."[94] Reporters who reviewed the hearings and documents associated with the snipers' killing of unarmed Iraqis said, "The words 'hostile intent' would show up again and again in thousands of pages of sworn testimony about the incidents."[95]

Hensley was reduced in rank to Sergeant and convicted of planting the AK-47 on Khudair. He served about six weeks in prison. Vela was convicted of Khudair's murder and sentenced to ten years in prison. Hensley later told a reporter from *Esquire* magazine, "In the end, it comes down to, when that guy walked in my hide site, I made a decision. It was my decision. Nobody else made it, nobody else could make it, because nobody else had the whole picture. Evan Vela killed that guy because

[92] Sherman, *The Untold War*, pp. 76–77.

[93] Quoted in Mark Benjamin and Christopher Weaver, "Killing by the Numbers," *Salon*, 9 May 2008, http://www.salon.com/news/feature/2008/05/09/snipers.

[94] Murphy, quoted in Tom Junod, "The Six Letter Word that Changes Everything," *Esquire*, 11 June 2008, http://www.esquire.com/features/michael-hensley-0708.

[95] Benjamin and Weaver, "Killing by the Numbers."

I ordered him to and because he had no reason not to. Was it a good kill? It's a good kill because I *say* it's a good kill. That's why I was there. That's why the battalion put me there."[96]

Mixed Agency, Limited Responsibility

Evil personified as a demon or reified as a force is not something to be reasoned with or understood....Demons are monolithic, malevolent through and through, never ambivalent or changeable. They are literally inhuman....Atrocities are perpetrated by agents who have epistemological limitations and emotional attachments. They are ambivalent, deluded, changeable, fickle. "No moral excuse" does not mean "no humanly understandable reasons."[97]

Lifton's belief that some environments are atrocity-producing situations recalls the question of moral agency. The dominant legal framework, formulated in the Enlightenment and in place since the nineteenth century, assumes individual liability for deliberate criminal acts in war. Soldiers failing to respect noncombatants are held individually accountable under the laws of war. This understanding of responsibility was in place in the US military during the Mexican-American War and can be seen in the orders for conduct, promulgated by General Winfield Scott, and later in the Lieber Codes of the Civil War, which clearly blamed individuals for lapses such as rape or pillaging. Violations, of Scott's General Orders 20, which prohibited such rape, murder, and the burning of Mexican homes and churches, could be punished by imprisonment or execution. Following World War II, the individual responsibility paradigm held: individual soldiers are held to account for deliberate atrocities because they are understood to be autonomous moral agents. In this view, soldiers are responsible moral actors. As Walzer says, "we regard soldiers as moral agents...even if we regard them as coerced moral agents. They are not mere instruments....It is precisely because they do (sometimes) choose to kill or not, to impose risks or accept them, that we require them to choose in a certain way."[98] Here Walzer is assuming that individuals can understand what they do, why they act, and refuse to do something wrong if their life is not at immediate risk.

Contemporary international law and US military law are in line with this view of individual moral responsibility. The United States participated in the United Nations International Criminal Tribunals for Yugoslavia and Rwanda, established

---

[96] Hensley, quoted in Junod, "The Six Letter Word that Changes Everything."

[97] Claudia Card, *Confronting Evils: Terrorism, Torture, Genocide* (Cambridge: Cambridge University Press, 2010), p. 16.

[98] Walzer, *Just and Unjust Wars*, p. 306.

in the 1990s, and in the drafting of the Rome Statutes of the International Criminal Court (ICC) completed in 1998. The ICC Statutes identified specific crimes for which individual perpetrators and commanders could be held responsible, which include crimes identified in the Hague Conventions of 1899 and 1907, and in the Geneva Conventions of 1929 and 1949 and the two Geneva Protocols of 1977.[99] Although the United States is not currently a signatory to the treaty for the International Criminal Court, the United States is bound by the 1949 Geneva Conventions, which it has signed and ratified. After briefly becoming a signatory, the United States withdrew from the International Criminal Court on the argument that its domestic courts, and military justice system, were sufficient to find and assign criminal responsibility for war crimes.

In recent cases in Iraq and Afghanistan, the individual responsibility framework has held. Individuals are tried (or not) for crimes they commit in war. When Iraq's Prime Minister, Nuri Kamal al-Maliki addressed the Mahmudiya rape and murder case, he assumed a framework of individual responsibility but pointed to higher levels of moral responsibility. "We believe that the immunity granted to international forces has emboldened them to commit such crimes in cold blood."[100]

Of course, there is much about the context of war that renders a simple view of individual agency and autonomy inadequate. Recall that moral agents must have the capacity to deliberate and act. Four conditions diminish the capacity of soldiers to make moral deliberations: the soldier's objective status as servants of the state; the soldier's socialization in obedience; the tendency, often cultivated by officers, to dehumanize the enemy; and the pressure of war itself, which can literally change the biology of a soldier and make it difficult for soldiers to control their emotional responses.

First, the soldier's status as a servant of the state limits their objective and legal agency. In modern (bureaucratic) states individuals rarely decide or act alone and with full autonomy. Soldiers are commanded by the state to be where they are and to do the things they do, and soldiers who do not follow lawful orders may be informally disciplined, or formally court-martialed and imprisoned. "Soldiers rarely engage in behavior that has not been commanded, or at least sanctioned, by higher ups. For this reason, it is usually a mistake to treat soldiers as if they were acting entirely on their own when they commit harms against others."[101] Soldiers are agents in a principal-agent relationship where the principal, the "commander," calls the shots and the soldier may have little idea of the larger political, strategic, or operational context. Soldiers are treated as tools: "It was as though we were totally

---

[99] Rome Statute (for the establishment) of the International Criminal Court, 17 July 1998, UN Doc. A/Conf.183/9.

[100] Kirk Semple, "Iraqi Says Immunity for Soldiers Fosters Crime," *New York Times*, 6 July 2006, p. A8.

[101] May, *War Crimes and Just War*, p. 171.

expendable."[102] As Jeff McMahan observes, although they have some training in the law of war, "soldiers are discouraged from thinking about the morality of war, and especially about whether wars are just or unjust. On that issue, they are expected to defer to the judgment of their government."[103] Moreover, deference to civilian authority is the norm.

Second, soldiers are socialized to obey orders and to conform. This pressure for conformity, the simple desire to go with the flow and not to stand out begins during basic training and continues throughout a soldier's service. Military instruction reduces the sense of individual agency even as the soldier is given a powerful weapon and trained in its use. "The grueling experience 'denudes,' as one observer puts it: It strips civilian and personal identity and socializes individuals into members of a cadre. It cuts down in order to build up."[104] Soldiers are trained to overcome the fear that could cause a person to flee the danger inherent in battle and the aversion most humans have to killing other humans, even the ones they consider their enemies. "The history of warfare can be seen as a history of increasingly more effective mechanisms for enabling and conditioning men to overcome their innate resistance to killing their fellow human beings."[105]

How is the fear that causes soldiers to flee or freeze and the aversion toward killing others that might prevent a soldier from firing their weapon overcome in combat training? J. Glenn Gray, a combat veteran of World War II noted: "The routine of military life, the repetition, drill, and uniformity of response, works to dampen and dull any individual intensity of awareness. Even the civilian soldier who finds the military way quite alien and strange can learn to hold fast to the few simple rules, to be a proper cog in the vast machine, and to suspend thoughts that might unfit him for his appointed mission. He learns to expect orders from above and to pass them along to those under his control. Thinking tends to become not only painful but more and more unnecessary."[106]

The elements of training that increase the propensity of soldiers to kill—simple practice (drill) so that using one's weapon and following orders become habits, and the cultivation of a sense of duty and love for fellow soldiers—at the same time decrease the soldier's sense of agency. Army Specialist Garett Reppenhagen found that training in the Geneva Convention faded after a period of deployment in Iraq. "Once you get into the situation and you're surrounded by people that have been there for a year, that have been dealing with that for a year, those slip away, you

---

[102] Iraq war veteran, Charlie Anderson, quoted in Guttman and Lutz, *Breaking Ranks*, p. 53.

[103] Jeff McMahan, *Killing in War* (Oxford: Oxford University Press, 2009), p. 120.

[104] Sherman, *The Untold War*, p. 12.

[105] Dave Grossman, *On Killing: The Psychological Cost of Learning to Kill in War and Society* (Boston: Little Brown and Company, 1995), p. 13.

[106] J. Glenn Gray, *The Warriors: Reflections on Men in Battle* (Lincoln: University of Nebraska Press, 1959), p. 103.

know? You're like, you're like just one gear in this huge machine, and you can't not choose to spin, you know? You just spin with the whole thing."[107]

Training so that the soldier is tough enough to face combat is also accomplished by essentially brutalizing the recruit—toughening the soldier so that they are accustomed to violence and inured to its consequences. Thus, one Marine described a form of military discipline practiced at Parris Island known as "quarter decking" (exercises that are performed when a Marine does not perform their assignment as well as they should) as "torture" and another Marine suggested that "there was this undercurrent of abuse" in the Marines.[108] The training is potentially traumatizing the soldier before battle and may encouraging brutal attitudes and a loss of empathy for enemy civilians.[109]

A third factor, the inculcation of dehumanizing attitudes of hostility and contempt for the enemy, lowers the soldier's resistance to killing and limits the soldier's capacity to judge whether their actions are justified. Gray noted that "the basic aim of a nation at war in establishing an image of the enemy is to distinguish as sharply as possible the act of killing from the act of murder by making the former into one deserving of all honor and praise."[110] When a contemptuous hatred of the enemy is cultivated in boot camp and in the field, it is the obverse of the love of and loyalty to fellow soldiers that is called "unit cohesion." These attitudes were encouraged openly in Vietnam, as was the coupling of rage with grief, leading to violent revenge or "berserking," but they are also not absent in the military that went to Iraq and Afghanistan.[111]

Ben Flanders, who served in Iraq, said: "I felt like there was this enormous reduction in my compassion for people. The only thing that wound up mattering is myself and the guys that I was with. And everybody else be damned."[112] Army Specialist Josh Middleton said of his fellow soldiers, "A lot of guys really supported that whole concept that, you know, if they don't speak English and they have darker skin, they're not has human as us, so we can do what we want."[113] The Iraqis were called "towel heads," "dune coons," "hajjis," "camel jockeys," and "sand niggers."[114] As Specialist Mike Harmon argued: "By calling them names, they're not people

[107] Quoted in Guttman and Lutz, *Breaking Ranks*, p. 92.

[108] Chris Magaoay and Charlie Anderson quoted, respectively, in Guttman and Lutz, *Breaking Ranks*, pp. 48 and 66.

[109] Jonathan Shay noted that "humiliation and degradation as techniques of motivation" were viewed as effective during the Vietnam War. He argues that instead, these techniques "should be seen as signs of leadership failure." Jonathan Shay, *Achilles in Vietnam: Combat Trauma and the Undoing of Character* (New York: Touchstone Books, 1994), p. 202.

[110] Gray, *The Warriors*, pp. 131–132.

[111] On Vietnam, see Shay, *Achilles in Vietnam*, chapter 5.

[112] Quoted in Hedges and Al-Arian, *Collateral Damage*, p. xv.

[113] Ibid., p. xix.

[114] See ibid., pp. 94–95; Guttman and Lutz, *Breaking Ranks*, p. 83.

any more. They're just objects."[115] Specialist Steve Mortillo said: "You start, you just form this deep, deep hatred for the people you're fighting against. You become capable of doing things you would never have thought done."[116] The 2012 Army *Civilian Casualty Mitigation* manual explicitly links derogatory terms with negative attitudes toward civilians and potentially with a cavalier attitude toward civilian harm. "Negative attitudes, such as perceiving host-nation civilians as inferior, must be avoided because they lead to thinking that CIVCASs are not too regrettable. Leader emphasis on the importance of all human life and cultural respect will help reinforce desired attitudes. For example, Soldiers should not refer to civilians in disparaging slang terms."[117]

The fourth condition that diminishes a soldier's capacity to act as a moral agent is the biological and psychological effects of war itself. This is the duress that soldiers often describe and sometimes allows us to excuse their actions. It is the lack of food, water, and sleep; it is extreme temperatures; it is the injury and death of comrades.[118] And above all, war, one's life is often at risk, or at least a soldier might reasonably believe so, instilling a not unreasonable fear response. Indeed, it is the sort of fear that diminishes the capacity to distinguish between neutral actions and threats, and that, in turn, increases the pressure to conformity. Gray saw that in World War II.

> In mortal danger, numerous soldiers enter into a dazed condition in which all sharpness of conscience is lost. When in this state, they can be caught up into the fire of communal ecstasy and forget about death by losing their individuality, or they can function like cells in a military organism, doing what is expected of them because it has become automatic. It is astonishing how much of the business of warfare can still be carried on by men who act as automatons, behaving almost as mechanically as the machines they operate.[119]

The effects of prolonged fear can change the underlying biology of individuals and, important for this context, their ability to make complex and discriminating decisions that demand both speed and restraint. When a person perceives a threat—such as a smell or a stimulus that they have learned is associated with pain (e.g., electrodes or a gun), that signal might travel directly to the place in our brain

---

[115] Quoted in Hedges and Al-Arian, *Collateral Damage*, p. 95.

[116] Ibid., p. 103

[117] Department of the Army, *Civilian Casualty Mitigation*, Army Tactics, Techniques and Procedures, No. 3-37.11 (Washington, DC: Department of the Army, 18 July 2012), p. 2-3.

[118] See Shay, *Achilles in Vietnam*. Shay also emphasizes the feelings of grief and the sense of betrayal that soldiers may feel.

[119] Gray, *The Warriors*, p. 102.

that processes fear, the amygdala (fastest). The amygdala sends signals to other areas of the brain which tell the body to react. Other neurochemicals act to inhibit the response if the stimulus is nonthreatening so that the amygdala's neurons are not constantly firing. But when the stimulus causes a flood of fear response that overwhelms the inhibitory neurochemicals, a cascade of other biochemical events occurs within seconds, as neurons in the amygdala fire, sending messages to the hippocampus, affecting memory, the locus coeruleus (in the brain stem), affecting alertness and the hypothalamus (located just in front of the thalamus). The hypothalamus, pituitary, and adrenal (HPA) axis is engaged.

> The hypothalamus releases a hormone (within seconds) that stimulates the pituitary to release another (within 15 seconds) which acts on the adrenal glands to release *cortisol* (hydrocortisone) and other glucocorticoids (within a few minutes) that regulate metabolism and blood pressure, among other things. At the same time, the nervous system directly triggers the middle of the adrenal gland (not the cortex) to produce adrenaline (also called epinephrine), as well as related hormones and some other biochemicals such as endorphins to kill pain.
>
> The outcome of these rapid responses is an 'adrenaline rush' from the immediate release of sugar in the blood stream, along with faster breathing, rapid heartbeat, higher blood pressure, and related changes. These effects make maximum energy available to muscles as quickly as possible.[120]

Or, a signal may be routed through the thalamus (very fast) or the prefrontal cortex (comparatively slow). The prefrontal cortex is the place where we process information more deliberatively, and for fully developed adults, it is the seat of our moral reasoning. The prefrontal cortex is important for both reducing responsiveness to fear and to inhibiting violence.[121] When we are confronted with signals that we interpret as threats, the amygdala essentially takes over, at least for a time, and the other areas in our brain take a back seat, no longer driving our actions.

For the fear system to function correctly, that is, help us react in a timely and effective way, but prevent us from overreacting, three conditions must obtain. First, the system has to "fire" when faced with threat—and, for that to happen, all the elements of the system must work. Second, it has to shut off when the threat has passed. After the stressful situation has been resolved (for instance, by retreat or confrontation), the nervous system should relax—heart rate and blood pressure should lower, and digestion should return to normal. In situations of chronic stress,

---

[120] Joshua S. Goldstein, *War and Gender* (Cambridge: Cambridge University Press, 2001), p. 158.

[121] See Donald W. Pfaff, *The Neuroscience of Fair Play: Why We (Usually) Follow the Golden Rule* (New York: Dana Press, 2007), pp. 142 and 151.

however, a person's physiology does not return to normal.[122] "The stress response is costly in the long run. It shuts down reproductive physiology, inhibits the storage of energy, slows down digestion, diverts blood flow to muscles at the expense of other parts of the body, and turns off the immune system along with the inflammation of injuries (which helps them heal) and perception of pain."[123] Third, humans must be able to distinguish between stimuli that are threats and those that are not, one of the jobs of the prefrontal cortex.

Long-term fear or even a single particularly traumatic event may change human brains at a chemical level. The human amygdala can literally be reshaped by the chemistry of fear as cortisol etches a traumatic trace on physical structures.[124] In other words, long-term potentiation occurs—neurons respond more strongly to stimuli having once, or more than once, experienced fear. Over time, our biology, perceptions, and cognitions will become primed for perceiving threat (hyper-vigilance) and overreactive. In sum, stress and fear change our brans.[125] Nurture becomes nature. Repeated stress caused by real or anticipated threats can initiate a spiral of consequences. If we cannot turn off our fear response, we will be unable to distinguish non-threats from threats; if we cannot distinguish threats from non-threats, we will find it hard to turn off our fear response. The brains of people with Post-Traumatic Stress Disorder (PTSD) show abnormal activation of both the amygdala and prefrontal cortex and atrophy of the hippocampus. The effects of fear on memory and reasoning are not confined to those with PTSD.

> Repeated stress affects brain function, especially of the hippocampus, which has high concentrations of cortisol receptors. The hippocampus participates in verbal memory and is particularly important for the memory of "context," the time and place of events that have strong emotional bias.... Impairment of the hippocampus decreases the reliability and accuracy of contextual memories. This may exacerbate stress by preventing access to the information needed to decide that a situation is not a threat. The hippocampus also regulates the stress response and acts to inhibit the response of the HPA axis to stress.[126]

---

[122] Bruce S. McEwen, "Protective and Damaging Effects of Stress Mediators," in John T. Cacioppo et al., eds., *Foundations in Social Neuroscience* (Cambridge, MA: MIT Press, 2002), pp. 1127–1140.

[123] Goldstein, *War and Gender*, p. 158.

[124] "If the ability of GABA to keep meaningless stimuli from turning on the amygdala is compromised for some reason (either because the projection cells come to fire more easily or because the GABA cells fire less easily), stimuli that are not dangerous come to be responded to as though they were." Joseph LeDoux, *Synaptic Self: How Our Brains Become Who We Are* (New York: Penguin, 2002), p. 63.

[125] Richard J. Davidson and Bruce S. McEwen, "Social Influences on Neuroplasticity: Stress and Interventions to Promote Well-Being," *Nature Neuroscience*, vol. 15, no. 5 (May 2012): 689–695.

[126] McEwen, "Protective and Damaging Effects of Stress Mediators," pp. 1132–1133.

Because stress hormones affect our ability to store memory, memories associated with strong emotion are often vivid, though not necessarily entirely accurate. Further, situations that evoke similar emotions will likely bring to mind those historical events that deeply affected the participants. This is analogical reasoning triggered by emotions, not a coldly cognitive assessment—suggesting that a past event where we were afraid is like the current situation (regardless of whether the historical event is similar in important respects). Just as there are cognitive cues for priming our brain to look for certain kinds of patterns, there are sometimes emotional cues, for example, in the case of fear when, "as part of interrelated memory systems, memorial representations of moods or emotional responses may prime memory areas focused on threat."[127] In other words, fear changes what we look for and, therefore, what we see, and thus the way we think.

Fear affects the ability to engage in complex cognition. The prefrontal cortex can override fear, but the amygdala can shut down the prefrontal cortex. Fearful experiences understandably prompt individuals to focus on potential future threats. The fearful are often less able to see how their defensive behavior might be seen by others as threatening, enhancing what is already a cognitive bias. The fearful also have a decreased ability to calculate the costs, risks, and benefits of options. An individual's emotions and emotional states can be the basis of categorization: "Things that evoke fear, for example, may be categorized together and be treated as the same kind of thing, even when they are otherwise perceptually, functionally, and theoretically diverse."[128] Further, an individual that has firsthand or bystander experience with a highly emotionally charged event will likely have strong emotional memories of that event. Brain research also demonstrates what we know historically: "Conditioned fear reactions are notoriously difficult to extinguish and once extinguished they can recur spontaneously or can be reinstated by stressful experiences."[129] Once bitten, twice shy. The information we gain from our cognitions and memory is both affected by our amygdalas and not unbiased: our brains are biased to give more weight to negative information.

I have, so far, emphasized how fear can influence memories and cognitions. But the amygdala can be moderated by inputs from areas that are involved in cognition and memory (the frontal cortex and hippocampus). These inputs affect the amygdala more slowly than direct sensory input or input from the thalamus, but speed of arrival does not necessarily determine response. In sum, cognition and memory can

[127] Arne Öhman, "Fear and Anxiety as Emotional Phenomena: Clinical Phenomenology, Evolutionary Perspectives, and Information Processing Mechanisms," in Michael Lewis and Jeannette M. Haviland, eds., *The Handbook of Emotions* (New York: Guilford Press, 1993), pp. 511–536, 526.

[128] Paula M. Niedenthal, Jamin B. Halberstadt, and Åse H. Innes-Ker, "Emotional Response Categorization," *Psychological Review*, vol. 106, no. 2 (April 1999): 337–361, 338. See also Daniel L. Schacter, "The Seven Sins of Memory: Insights from Psychology and Cognitive Neuroscience," *American Psychologist*, vol. 54, no. 3 (March 1999): 182–203, 195–196.

[129] Joseph LeDoux, "Emotion: Clues from the Brain," in Cacioppo et al., eds., *Foundations in Social Neuroscience*, pp. 389–410, 396.

either enhance or diminish the amygdala's activation. Humans are neither rational nor irrational—"the neural circuitry of emotion and cognition interact from early perception to decision making and reasoning."[130] Further, the part of the brain, the prefrontal cortex, that helps us reason through complex moral dilemmas and exercise restraint is generally not fully developed until humans are in their early twenties. This is precisely the part of the brain that the hormones associated with fear may override.

There is also the fear that is internally generated within military organizations: the fear of not fitting in, the fear of sanctions for disobeying an order, and the fear of being abandoned by one's peers. "Although combatants are now required to disobey a manifestly unlawful order, it required considerable courage and composure to do this when a doubtful order is accompanied by an implicit or explicit threat of sanctions for noncompliance.... This kind of threat from superiors may combine with fear of the enemy to overwhelm a combatant's will."[131]

Trauma

Unsurprisingly, the longer a soldier is exposed to combat, the more likely that individual will suffer psychological trauma. During World War I, the British Army rotated their soldiers out for four days of rest after about twelve days of combat. Nevertheless, "shell shock" afflicted many soldiers on all sides who had been in the front lines and trenches. As many as 40 percent of British casualties in World War I may have been mental breakdowns.[132] "During World War I, the probability of a soldier becoming a psychiatric casualty was greater than that of his being killed by enemy fire."[133] World War II was similarly traumatic. Two psychiatrists studying the effects of combat during World War II found that 200-240 days could break a soldier. "There is no such thing as 'getting used to combat'.... Each moment of combat imposes a strain so great that men will break down in direct relation to the intensity and duration of their exposure. Thus, psychiatric casualties are as inevitable as gunshot and shrapnel wounds in warfare."[134]

Combat breaks soldiers in the current wars but, as with past wars, the causes and rates of trauma vary. In 2008, the RAND Corporation published results from the first nongovernmental organization study of returning US soldiers from Iraq

[130] Elizabeth A. Phelps, "Emotion and Cognition: Insights from Studies of the Human Amygdala," *Annual Review of Psychology*, 57 (2006): 27–53, 28; Also see, Joseph P. Forgas, ed., *Thinking and Feeling: The Role of Affect in Social Cognition* (Cambridge: Cambridge University Press, 2000).

[131] McMahan, *Killing in War*, p. 127.

[132] Grossman, *On Killing*, p. 44. Judith Herman, *Trauma and Recovery: The Aftermath of Violence from Domestic Abuse to Political Power* (New York: Basic Books, 1992), p. 43.

[133] Grossman, *On Killing*, p. 55.

[134] J. W. Appel and G. W. Beebe, "Preventive Psychiatry: An Epidemiological Approach," *Journal of the American Medical Association*, 131 (1946): 1468–1471, 1470. Quoted in Herman, *Trauma and Recovery*, p. 25. See also Shay, *Achilles in Vietnam*.

and Afghanistan, finding rates of depression and post-traumatic stress of about 18.5 percent. This meant that about 300,000 veterans suffered from PTSD at the time. RAND also found 320,000 veterans had traumatic brain injuries. Moreover, RAND found that only half of the soldiers suffering were receiving care.[135] That is not surprising since the Department of Defense believes that much lower numbers suffer from PTSD and Traumatic Brain injury. Tables 4.1 and 4.2 were compiled by Hannah Fischer for the Congressional Research Service.

US soldiers have tours that last between twelve and fifteen months, and many soldiers in these wars are on their second, third, or fourth deployment. British soldiers, who serve six-month tours, have been found to have a lower rate, 4 percent, of post-traumatic stress.[136] Many argue that the official US military rates of PTSD undercount the real rates of post-combat stress. In July 2010, the Obama administration moved to streamline the process for veterans to obtain services for post-traumatic stress disorder.[137] But service members who are on active duty or deployed in war zones do not always have access to the mental health care they need.

But fear is not the only emotion at play. Many soldiers experience anger, which, tends to decrease the perception of a threat and to heighten risk-taking behaviors.[138] Recent work by the Army Mental Health Advisory Team has, unsurprisingly, found a link between the distress soldiers feel and their conduct in the field. "Soldiers that have high levels of anger, experienced high levels of combat or screened positive for a mental-health problem were nearly twice as likely to mistreat non-combatants as those who had low levels of anger or combat or screened negative for a mental health problem."[139] High levels of combat exposure and PTSD are correlated with unethical conduct.[140]

---

[135] Terri Tanielian and Lisa H. Jaycox, eds., *Invisible Wounds of War: Psychological and Cognitive Injuries, Their Consequences and Services to Assist Recovery* (Santa Monica, CA: RAND Corporation, 2008). David Morgan, "Study Says 300,000 Troops Have Mental Problems," Reuters, 17 April 2008, http://www.reuters.com/article/idUSN1728241320080417.

[136] Benedict Carey, "U.S. Troops Suffer More Stress Than Britons, Study Says," *New York Times*, 17 May 2010, p. A10.

[137] Brad Knickerbocker, "PTSD: New Regs will Make It Easier for Vets to Get Help," *Christian Science Monitor*, 10 July 2010, http://www.csmonitor.com/USA/Military/2010/0710/PTSD-New-r egs-will-make-it-easier-for-war-vets-to-get-help.

[138] Leonie Huddy, Stanley Feldman, and Erin Cassese, "On the Distinct Political Effects of Anxiety and Anger," in Russell W. Neuman, George E. Marcus, Ann N. Crigler, and Michael MacKuen, *The Affect Effect: Dynamics of Emotion in Political Thinking and Behavior* (Chicago: University of Chicago, 2007), pp. 202–230.

[139] Jerry Harben, "Mental Health Advisory Team IV Findings Released," US Army Medical Department, Army Medicine, Press Release, 4 May 2007, http://www.armymedicine.army.mil/news/ releases/20070504mhat.cfm. The Mental Health Advisory Team Survey released in November 2009 does not include a discussion of how soldiers treat noncombatants.

[140] Christopher H. Warner, George N. Appenzeller, Angela Mobbs, Jessica R. Parker, Carolynn M. Warner, Thomas Grieger, and Charles W. Hoge, "Effectiveness of Battlefield-ethics Training during Combat Deployment: A Programme Assessment," *The Lancet*, vol. 378, no. 3 (September 2011): 915–924, 915 and 921–922.

Table 4.1 **Annual New Post-Traumatic Stress Disorder Diagnoses in All Services as of 3 December 2012**

Year	Not Deployed	Deployed
2000	1,610	0
2001	1,694	0
2002	1,697	133
2003	1,609	1,100
2004	1,777	3,095
2005	1,912	7,015
2006	1,893	7,745
2007	2,272	11,763
2008	2,589	14,405
2009	2,676	13,975
2010	2,638	14,828
2011	2,806	15,702
2012	2,376	14,031
Total	27,549	103,792

Sources: Hannah Fischer, "U.S. Military Casualty Statistics: Operation New Dawn, Operation Iraqi Freedom, and Operation Enduring Freedom," Congressional Research Service, RS22452, 5 February 2013, p. 2. Fischer gives as her source "personal communication with Dr. Michael Carino, Army Office of the Surgeon General, December 13, 2012. Data source is the Defense Medical Surveillance System (DMSS)."

As Garret Reppenhagen said of his own combat experience:

It's hard when you're going in as a soldier being told by your command and your leaders that you're there to liberate those people and bring them democracy, and then those people that you're supposed to be liberating are killing you.... So there becomes a rift, and the soldiers start, they stop trusting the Iraqi people and start hating them, and you can generally get degraded to the point where if you have to kill somebody, you have to almost dehumanize your enemy. And that starts to spread into, you know, the Iraqi people, and instead of blaming your own command for putting you in that situation, you start blaming the Iraqi people because you can't abuse your own chain of command and your superiors, but you do have complete power over the average Iraqi person. And a lot of times it's too much power for like an eighteen-year-old kid straight out of high school and put in a fearful war situation to be able to handle and compute,

Table 4.2 **Traumatic Brain Injuries in the US Military, 2000 to 2011**

Year	Severe or Penetrating TBI	ModerateTBI	Mild TBI	Not Classifiable*	Total Incident Diagnoses
2000	450	4,150	6,326	37	10,963
2001	478	3,553	7,760	39	11,830
2002	380	3,077	8,974	39	12,470
2003	449	2,643	9,770	36	12,898
2004	463	2,281	10,536	32	13,312
2005	407	1,906	9,857	41	12,211
2006	521	2,466	13,919	52	16,958
2007	591	3,708	18,665	210	23,174
2008	686	3,343	21,859	2,679	28,567
2009	809	3,751	22,673	2,022	29,255
2010	553	4,294	24,989	1,571	31,407
2011	401	3,771	23,633	2,575	31,380
Total	6,188	38,943	178,961	9,333	233,425

* "Requires additional incident information and further investigation prior to TBI categorization."

Source: Hannah Fischer, "U.S. Military Casualty Statistics: Operation New Dawn, Operation Iraqi Freedom, and Operation Enduring Freedom," Congressional Research Service, RS22452, 12 June 2012, p. 4. Fischer's sources are Dr. Michael Carino, Army Office of the Surgeon General, and the Defense Medical Surveillance System (DMSS) Defense and Veterans Brain Injury Center, http://www.dvbic.org/TBI-Numbers.aspx, updated as of 10 February 2012.

materially process. So it's a constant psychological battle to try to keep— stay humane and treat the Iraqi in a justifiable way.[141]

While duress may explain some of the maltreatment of civilians, does duress also excuse behavior we would normally condemn? What, precisely, is it about the realities of war that could diminish the moral agency of the soldier beyond that of their already structurally diminished agency? "The situations of war," Larry May argues, "and the institutions created during war...change the normal moral situation."[142] In May's view, "the circumstances of war make all of us different people than we would be otherwise. Especially in the case of soldiers, these men and women become trained killers, when in their previous lives such behavior would have been

[141] Quoted in Hedges and Al-Arian, *Collateral Damage*, pp. 102–103.
[142] May, *War Crimes and Just War*, p. 11.

anathema."[143] Similarly, Jeff McMahan notes that "the stresses of battlefield conditions are frequently so severe as to impair a combatants capacity for rationality, creating a state of genuinely diminished responsibility."[144]

War pushes individuals to an extreme—the conditions of battle may erode or destroy inhibitions, reduce empathy, and diminish the capacity for judgment. A soldier's subordinate position, socialization to conformity, a narrative and climate of dehumanization, and the physical and psychological pressure of combat combine to create intense stress for some soldiers. When soldiers are sent on patrol in unarmored or inadequate vehicles, when they are pushed by commanders to act beyond their physical or mental endurance, when they are treated as tools and given medication so that they can continue to fight, we can hardly be surprised that soldiers have contempt for noncombatants or that even the most well-intentioned soldier will find it difficult to discriminate between combatants and noncombatants.[145]

For many soldiers the stress is too much to bear. Despite close supervision and the deployment of hundreds of mental health workers and chaplains in Afghanistan and Iraq and in the United States, soldiers kill themselves at what the US Army considers an alarming rate. The number of suicides among active duty soldiers, National Guard, and Reserves has grown steadily since 2003.[146] General Peter Chiarelli said in 2009 that "there is no doubt in my mind that stress is a factor in this trend we are seeing."[147] In early 2009, the US Army ordered a "stand-down" to put new material about suicide prevention in the hands of troops.

In July 2010, the Army announced that at 20.2 per 100,000 in the population, the suicide rates among active duty soldiers from 1 October 2008 to 30 September 2009 had exceeded suicide rates (19.2 per 100,000) in the civilian population.[148] Military suicide rates are usually lower than the rates in the overall US population. However, while suicide rates in the overall civilian population were essentially steady or slightly rising, by 2010 suicide rates in all branches of the US military had

---

[143] Ibid.

[144] McMahan, *Killing in War*, p. 127.

[145] Gregg Zoroya, "U.S. Deploys More than 43,000 Unfit for Combat," *USA Today*, 8 May 2008, http://www.usatoday.com/news/military/2008-05-07-nondeploy_N.htm.

[146] Associated Press, "U.S. Army Suicide Rate at Highest Level since 1993," *Fox News*, 21 April 2006. http://www.foxnews.com/story/0,2933,192683,00.html; CNN, "Concern Mounts over Rising Troop Suicides," CNN.Com, 3 February 2008, http://edition.cnn.com/2008/US/02/01/military.suicides/index.html.

[147] C. Todd Lopez, "Army Addresses Rising Suicide Rate, Highest in Four Years," Army.mil, 29 January 2009, http://www.army.mil/-news/2009/01/29/16230-army-addresses-rising-suicide-rate-highest-in-four-years/.

[148] Elisabeth Bumiller, "As Military Suicides Hit Record High, Pentagon Report Faults Commanders," *New York Times*, 30 July 2010, p. A10; Anna Fifield, "US Army Suicide Rate Exceeds National Average," *Financial Times*, 30 July 2010, http://www.ft.com/cms/s/0/2c662840-9b74-11df-8239-00144feab49a.html.

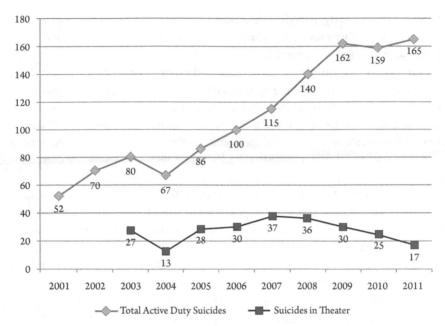

Figure 4.1 Number of Active Duty Army Suicides, 2001–2011.

Sources: US Army, *Army 2020: Generating Health and Discipline in the Force Ahead of the Strategic Reset: Report 2012* (Virginia: Prepared by the Army Suicide Prevention Task Force, Headquarters, Department of the Army, 2012), 54; Rajeev Ramchand, Joie Acosta, Rachel M. Burns, Lisa H. Jaycox, and Christopher G. Perrin, *The War Within: Preventing Suicide in the U.S. Military*, Prepared for the Office of the Secretary of Defense (Santa Monica, CA: RAND Center for Military Health Policy Research, 2011), 10. "Army Releases July Suicide Data," 16 August 2012, http://www.defense.gov/releases/release.aspx?releaseid=15517.

roughly doubled since 2001. In 2010, more soldiers committed suicide than died in combat. As General Chiarelli said of the suicide rate, "I think you have to have your head buried in the sand to not think a lot of them [the suicides] come out of 8 1/2 years of war."[149] In 2011, there were more than 1,000 recorded suicide attempts by members of the active duty Army and 162 suicides.[150] The graph in figure 4.1 shows the rise in the number of active duty Army suicides.[151]

---

[149] Quoted in Jaime Tarabay, "Suicide Rivals the Battlefield in Toll on US Military," *National Public Radio*, 17 June 2010, http://www.npr.org/templates/story/story.php?storyId=127860466.

[150] United States Army, *Army 2020: Generating Health and Discipline in the Force Ahead of the Strategic Reset: Report 2012*, Prepared by the Army Suicide Prevention Task Force (Washington, DC: Headquarters, Department of the Army, 2012), p. 6.

[151] Suicides among active duty members of the Air Force, Navy, and Marines have also increased since 2001. Rajeev Ramchand, Joie Acosta, Rachel M. Burns, Lisa H. Jaycox, and Christopher G. Perrin, *The War Within: Preventing Suicide in the U.S. Military*, Prepared for the Office of the Secretary of Defense (Santa Monica, CA: RAND Center for Military Health Policy Research, 2011), p. 10.

The number of successful suicides only begins to suggest the anguish. In 2002, 350 soldiers attempted suicide. In 2007, 2,100 soldiers attempted suicide. In response to the increasing number of suicides, violence, and other high-risk behavior of active duty, reserve, national guard, and veterans, the military has gone from treating mental health as a private problem indicating personal weakness to an organizational problem with remedies.[152] The US Army, in particular, has invested heavily in suicide prevention and in the counseling for risk factors such as drug and alcohol abuse. As part of that effort the Army engaged in data collection and analysis to assess the scope of the problem of active duty suicide and its causes.[153] In discussing some of the data released in a 2012 report, US Army General Peter W. Chiarelli took the same attitude to suicides and other high-risk and aggressive behaviors that he took to the problem of civilian deaths at checkpoints in Iraq in 2005 and 2006. About one statistic, an almost 30 percent increase in violent sex crimes among active duty soldiers in 2011, he said, simply: "This is unacceptable. We have zero tolerance for this."[154]

The Army's efforts to reduce suicides among active duty soldiers have borne some fruit. On the other hand, despite some success in reducing suicides, the leading cause of death among soldiers outside of combat is since 2010 had been suicide. Suicide numbers again grew in 2012, averaging one per day, and a study of those who had attempted suicide found that the "top reason... these guys are trying to kill themselves is because they have this intense psychological suffering and pain."[155]

Withdrawal and Resistance

Yet, not everyone snaps under these conditions, nor do all soldiers conform. Some potential soldiers simply refuse to go to war. For instance, many sought draft deferments and conscientious objector status to avoid serving in Vietnam. Some filed for conscientious objector status once they were enlisted in the military. In Fiscal

---

[152] See Terri Tanielian and Lisa Jaycox, eds., *Invisible Wounds of War: Psychological and Cognitive Injuries, Their Consequences, and Services to Assist Recovery* (Santa Monica, CA: RAND, 2008); Ramchand, Acosta, Burns, Jaycox, and Perrin, *The War Within*.

[153] United States Army, *Army Health Promotion, Risk Reduction, Suicide Prevention Report 2010*, Prepared by the Army Suicide Prevention Task Force (Washington, DC: Headquarters, Department of the Army, 2010) and United States Army, *Army 2020*.

[154] Quoted in Elisabeth Bumiller, "Active-Duty Soldiers Take their Own Lives at Record Rate," *New York Times*, 19 January 2012, http://www.nytimes.com/2012/01/20/us/active-duty-army-suicides-reach-record-high.html.

[155] Craig Bryan, researcher at the National Center for Veterans Studies, quoted in Gregg Zoroya, "Study Reveals Top Reason Behind Soldiers' Suicides," *USA TODAY*, 11 July 2012, http://www.usatoday.com/news/military/story/2012-07-10/army-study-soldiers-suicides/56136192/1.

Year 1971 (October through September) during the Vietnam War, for example, 125,000 individuals applied for conscientious objector status, and 61,000 quali-fied as conscientious objectors. The number of soldiers and Marines filing for con-scientious objector status grew nearly 400 percent and 200 percent, respectively, from 1967 to mid-1971, during the most intense period of ground conflict in the Vietnam.[156]

Further, some soldiers go absent without leave (AWOL) and after thirty days are considered deserters. It is not always clear why soldiers desert, but there are deserters in every war. For instance, in World War II, the desertion rate was 63 per thousand in 1944. During the Vietnam War, Army desertion rates were 14.9 per thousand in 1966 but had risen to 73.5 per thousand in 1971.[157] Army deser-tion during Vietnam, in the period 1968 to 1971, averaged 5 percent of the overall enlisted force. In Fiscal Years 2000 and 2001, Army desertion rates were less than 1 percent.[158] An Associated Press report in 2007 that received widespread attention noted that desertion rates in the US Army had risen by 80 percent since 2003.[159] And, as in the Vietnam era, some deserters from the wars in Afghanistan and Iraq fled to Canada.

Others resist orders or refuse to participate in specific operations while in the field. In Vietnam and again in Iraq, some US soldiers sent on search and destroy missions instead performed what they called "search and avoid." In Vietnam, David Cortright describes how patrols began "intentionally skirting potential enemy clashes or halting a few yards beyond the defense perimeter for a three-day pot party."[160] Similarly, in the Afghanistan and Iraq wars, some US soldiers admit that would pretend to be on a combat mission but were actually avoiding contact.[161] In some cases, soldiers may have been acting out of a sense of moral duty. Dennis Thompson argues that such actions are excusable: "committing some lesser inten-tional wrong (breaking a promise to one's superior) may sometimes be necessary to prevent some greater wrong that would result from permitting the bureaucratic process to proceed as usual."[162]

---

[156] David Cortright, *Soldiers in Revolt: GI Resistance during the Vietnam War* (Chicago: Haymarket Books, [1975] 2005), pp. 5 and 16.

[157] Ibid., p. 10.

[158] Peter F. Ramsberger and D. Bruce Bell, *What We Know about AWOL and Desertion: A Review of the Professional Literature for Policy Makers and Commanders*, U.S. Army Research Institute for the Behavioral and Social Sciences, ARI Special Report 51 August 2002, p. 4.

[159] Lolita C. Baldor, "Army Desertion Rates Rise 80 percent since Invasion of Iraq in 2003," *"The Boston Globe,* 17 November 2007, http://www.boston.com/news/nation/washington/articles/2007/11/17/army_desertion_rate_up_80_since_2003/?page=full.

[160] Cortright, *Soldiers in Revolt*, p. 28.

[161] Jamail, *The Will to Resist*, p. 36.

[162] Dennis Thompson, "Ascribing Responsibility to Advisors in Government," *Ethics*, vol. 93, no. 3 (April 1983): 546–560, 553–554.

Still others speak out while in the service. During the Vietnam War, for example, Hugh Thompson, the helicopter pilot who intervened to halt the My Lai massacre did so at some personal risk, by confronting soldiers who were shooting wounded Vietnamese. A number of active duty soldiers formed antiwar organizations on their bases, such as GIs for Peace. The Reservist Committee to Stop the War obtained more than 2,200 signatures in 1970 on a petition demanding that the US withdraw from Vietnam.[163] Many veterans' organizations opposed the Vietnam War and staged protests throughout the United States. Most famously, Vietnam Veterans against the War organized the "Winter Soldier Investigation" in 1971, three days of public testimony of Vietnam War veterans who described their combat experience.[164] At the beginning of the Winter Soldier hearings, William Crandell read an opening statement:

> We went to preserve the peace and our testimony will show that we have set all of Indochina aflame. We went to defend the Vietnamese people and our testimony will show that we are committing genocide against them. We went to fight for freedom and our testimony will show that we have turned Vietnam into a series of concentration camps.... In the bleak winter of 1776 when the men who had enlisted in the summer were going home because the way was hard and their enlistments were over, Tom Paine wrote, "Those are the times that try men's souls. The summer soldier and the sunshine patriot will in this crisis shrink from the service of his country, but he that stands it now deserves the love and thanks of man and woman." Like the winter soldiers of 1776 who stayed after they had served their time, we veterans of Vietnam know that America is in grave danger. What threatens our country is not Redcoats or even Reds; it is our crimes that are destroying our national unity by separating those of our countrymen who deplore these acts from those of our countrymen who refuse to examine what is being done in America's name....
>
> We intend to tell who it was that gave us those orders; that created that policy; that set that standard of war bordering on full and final genocide. We intend to demonstrate that My Lai was no unusual occurrence, other than, perhaps, the number of victims killed all in one place, all at one time, all by one platoon of us. We intend to show that the policies of Americal Division which inevitably resulted in My Lai were the policies of other Army and Marine Divisions as well. We intend to show that war crimes in Vietnam did not start in March 1968, or in the village of Son My or with

---

[163] Cortright, *Soldiers in Revolt*, p. 166.

[164] See Andrew E. Hunt, *The Turning: A History of Vietnam Veterans against the War* (New York: New York University Press, 1999).

one Lt. William Calley. We intend to indict those really responsible for My Lai, for Vietnam.[165]

As in previous wars, some veterans have spoken against the US wars in Iraq and Afghanistan. Iraq Veterans Against the War and other antiwar veterans' organizations have formed in the since 2001, some protesting the lack of equipment, such as body armor, during their deployment, and others protesting poor veterans' services and the failure to follow through with promised enlistment bonuses and education benefits. But as with the Vietnam War, many Iraq and Afghanistan War Veterans have testified to their shame and distress at harming noncombatants.[166]

Agency and Mercy

While soldiers bear moral responsibility when they act outside their orders, their agency has been compromised by their status as tools of the state, by the pressure of combat, and the desire to conform and, quite frankly, by their urgent need not to be seen as cowards. As Aristotle suggests in the *Nicomachean Ethics*, some acts are "mixed"—both voluntary and involuntary, such as when someone throws goods overboard in a storm: "for in the abstract no one throws goods away voluntarily, but on condition of securing the safety of himself and his crew any sensible man does so." Therefore "on some actions praise indeed is not bestowed, but pardon is, when one does a wrongful act under pressure which overstrains human nature and which no one could withstand."[167] And so, Larry May argues: "It might make sense to punish the leaders of a State based on what they deserve. But it might also make sense to relieve from punishment the soldiers who followed the orders of these leaders, even if the soldiers in some sense also deserve to be punished."[168]

However, when a soldier looked at a person who was not a threat and attacked them anyway, they made a choice. We must blame those individuals who break the laws of war. It is not appropriate to simply excuse deliberate killing or abuse of noncombatants or prisoners of war. These acts are criminal. Those soldiers who refused

---

[165] Excerpt of Bill Crandall's statement at Winter Soldier Investigation, 31 January 1971, http://www2.iath.virginia.edu/sixties/HTML_docs/Resources/Primary/Winter_Soldier/WS_02_opening.html.

[166] Nancy Sherman, who interviewed veterans in several wars, including the wars in Iraq and Afghanistan, describes a constant, and often internal, moral questioning: "the debate goes on largely inside, as a soulful struggle with conscience." Sherman, *The Untold War*, p. 45.

[167] Aristotle, Book III of *The Nicomachean Ethics*, translated and with an introduction by David Ross (Oxford: Oxford University Press, 1980), pp. 48–49.

[168] May, *War Crimes and Just War*, p. 171.

to participate in war or in particular atrocities suggest that it was a capacity to see the other as a human, to empathize with Iraqis or Afghans that helped them find a critical perspective.[169] In that fact—that not everyone succumbs to madness or brutality—lies the impulse to blame individuals.

But, the soldiers who commit crimes also deserve that we look carefully at what happened to make them break those laws and consider the "facts about his character and suffering which may not be revealed simply by looking at his offense."[170] We must examine how it is that some soldiers are themselves unintentionally broken or made criminals by military organizations during their training or through their deployment. "The basic point of mercy seems to lie in the recognition that, in the absence of 'cosmic justice,' some of those to whom a socially just community would have the right to punish may be unusually more 'sinned against than sinning,' either by other persons or, metaphorically speaking by fate."[171] The hard reality is that even while many officers and training manuals stress the law of war, training also stresses obedience and dehumanization of the enemy; military culture and the demands of commanders emphasize military virtues that often tax soldiers beyond their endurance.

We ask a lot of soldiers. We ask them to leave their homes, face physical hardship in training, and then travel to distant lands to kill or be killed. We ask them to maintain their calm and to remember the line between killing as an act of war and murder and assault as a private act of hatred or vengeance. We expect young people who, simply by virtue of their very youth and relatively limited experiences, have limited capacities for moral judgment to make complex moral judgments in life-threatening situations. We ask them to do this day after day, month after month, and sometimes deployment after deployment, stretching out over years. We ask them to miss the birth or first steps of a child, the illness of a parent, and the everyday love of a spouse. We expect them to witness the mutilation or death of a comrade and then not to fire in anger. Thus, another reading of William Sherman's threat to Atlanta is possible. "War is cruelty and you cannot refine it.... You might as well appeal against the thunder-storm as against these terrible hardships of war. They are inevitable."[172] Or as US Army Specialist Steven Casey who served in Iraq in 2003 and 2004 said: "We were all good people. We were just in a bad situation and we did what we had to [to] get through."[173] Garett Reppenhagen said: "It's just the nature of the situation you're in. That's what's wrong. It's not individual

[169] See Guttman and Lutz, *Breaking Ranks*, pp. 116, 127, and 146.

[170] Claudia Card, "On Mercy," *Philosophical Review*, vol. 18, no. 2 (1972): 182–207, 191. Quoted in May, *War Crimes and Just War*, p. 80.

[171] Card, "On Mercy," p. 185. Quoted in May, *War Crimes and Just War*, p. 80.

[172] Letter by General William T. Sherman to the Mayor and City Council of Atlanta, 12 September 1864.

[173] Casey testimony in IVAW and Glantz, *Winter Soldier Iraq and Afghanistan*, pp. 33–35, 35.

atrocity. It's the fact that the entire war is the atrocity."[174] Reppenhagen was honest about his own abusive behavior in Iraq.

> Even though I understood and respected the Iraq people and culture, I still couldn't help but do my job. Even if I tried not to, you know?...And you know, here I was, like the least likely person to want to abuse anyone. I just wanted this guy [who was screaming] to be quiet. And here I was just kicking a detained, handcuffed Iraqi person. I was like...if you could get me to do these kinds of things, you can get anybody to do it. It doesn't take a type of person to be out there and to commit atrocities. It's just circumstance. So, I don't know, I always think back to that and I'm amazed. The ease at which an individual person can have control and power over another individual human.[175]

We tell soldiers to obey authority, yet to disobey "manifestly illegal" orders. Yet, as Mark Osiel observes, "Virtually everywhere, the law requires soldiers to presume the lawfulness of their orders."[176] Most soldiers are not trained in the laws of war, and the orders that lead to systemic collateral damage or proportionality/double effect killing are phrased as rules of engagement that hardly seem illegal because they are not illegal.

Soldiers who follow orders that lead to both proportionality/double effect killing and systemic collateral damage should be judged under the relevant law, and by their peers and the general public, with a measure of mercy that takes the immediate and larger structural context into account. Their actions were legal. They followed orders.

> To expect a soldier in combat to evaluate whether his superior's order is justified, on pain of severe punishment if mistaken, would often be unfair. Such evaluation will frequently require knowledge of considerations beyond his awareness. If the law requires him to make independent legal judgment whenever he receives an order, it risks eliciting his disobedience to orders that appear wrongful from the soldier's restricted perspective but which are actually justified by larger operational circumstances.[177]

---

[174] Quoted in Hedges and Al-Arian, *Collateral Damage*, p. 48.

[175] Quoted in Guttman and Lutz, *Breaking Ranks*, p. 103. Reppenhagen also told Guttman and Lutz, that he doesn't want to be thought of as a victim because the war was traumatic. "I'm not necessarily a victim in this scenario." US soldiers are not generally the victims. "He's the victimizer. And I think he feels like a criminal honestly. He feels like the killer and the rapist and the thief, and then comes back to America and its 'Thank you for your service.' But we're like, 'You have no idea what you are thanking me for. You don't know what I did.'" Guttman and Lutz, *Breaking Ranks*, pp. 144–145.

[176] Osiel, *Obeying Orders*, pp. 54–55.

[177] Ibid., p. 64.

If the laws of war and the norms of military necessity, force protection, double effect sanction practices that lead to predictable albeit unintended killing, how can an individual soldier be expected say that what is legal is, nevertheless, morally troubling? So much of what a soldier faces at the instant of contact, including their perception about the scope of their own agency, is decided well before that soldier arrived at the encounter, and often in fact decided by others or made possible or impossible by institutions. Those other actors, and those institutions, and the time before contact, before the killing, are the subjects of the next chapters.

5

Command Responsibility, Due Care, and Moral Courage

Psychologically and ethically, responsibility for the crimes at Haditha extends to top commanders, the secretary of defense, and the White House.

Robert J. Lifton[1]

You stop war crimes by coming down on the commanding officer.

Ian Cuthbertson[2]

No officer is going to be criminally charged for killing too many people if he does not actually massacre them. But the moral responsibility is clear, and it cannot be located anywhere else than in the office of commander.

Michael Walzer, *Just and Unjust Wars*[3]

US military field manuals and officer training emphasize that the responsibility for instilling moral virtues and cultivating ethical conduct rests in the hands of military commanders. The 2006 Counterinsurgency Field Manual acknowledges that this is easier at some times than others: "Ethically speaking, COIN environments can be much more complex than conventional ones." Nevertheless, "those in leadership positions must provide the moral compass for their subordinates as they navigate this complex environment."[4]

[1] Robert Jay Lifton, "Haditha: In an 'Atrocity-Producing Situation'—Who is to Blame?" *Editor & Publisher*, 4 June 2006.

[2] Ian Cuthbertson, a military historian commenting on the massacre at Haditha, quoted in Frida Berrigan, "The Fog of War Crimes: Whose to Blame When 'Just Following Orders' Means Murder?" *In These Times*, 7 January 2008.

[3] Michael Walzer, *Just and Unjust Wars: A Moral Argument with Historical Illustrations* (New York: Basic Books, 1977), p. 317.

[4] United States Army and Marine Corp, *U.S. Army/Marine Corps Counterinsurgency Field Manual*, Field Manual No. 3-24: Marine Corp Warfighting Publication No. 3-33.5 (Chicago: University of Chicago, 2007), pp. 245 and 237.

In three separate episodes in Afghanistan in 2010 Army soldiers from the Fifth Stryker Brigade, under the command of Colonel Harry D. Tunnell, IV, attacked Afghan civilians while on patrol near Kandahar. The soldiers portrayed the deaths as combat related and justified—weapons were planted next to the victims or grenades were detonated to make it appear that the person killed had posed a threat. Most of the soldiers involved later admitted to murder and manslaughter of civilians, and some acknowledged taking body parts from the victims as trophies. The focus of the court-martials and media attention was understandably on the behavior of the individual soldiers involved. The official Army investigation led by Brigadier General Stephen Twitty found that "while the alleged criminal acts may have been identified earlier or perhaps prevented with stronger leader presence, I found nothing to indicate that the alleged criminal acts occurred as a result of the command climate set by the leaders above them."[5]

By contrast, the prosecutor in the court martial of one of those accused in the incidents described the platoon as "out of control."[6] Colonel Tunnell was removed from command. When Human Rights First director Gabor Rona commented on the conviction of Staff Sergeant Calvin Gibbs, the leader of the killings, he argued that accountability for the crimes should not stop there. "Command responsibility is the most important feature of military culture. It draws the line between honorable conduct and the brutality and chaos into which war will otherwise descend. Command's enforcement of the laws of war serves the national interest. Violations place our forces at greater risk."[7]

The roles of the military commander are ostensibly clear. In *On War*, Carl von Clausewitz notes that it is commanders who ought to and do take care of what happens on the battlefield. The soldiers or Marines who throw a grenade, call in an airstrike, drop a bomb, or assault a civilian or a prisoner, are as they say, "at the pointy end of the spear," making an immediate decision at the moment of contact that could lead to their own or someone else's injury, life, or death. Yet it is the commanders who in the weeks, months, and years before the moment of contact that prepare soldiers for war, shape their attitudes, set the rules of engagement, and give the orders to engage the "enemy."

It is also commanders who speak to the survivors of those civilians killed and wounded in collateral damage incidents. In so doing, they frame the incident and

---

[5] Quoted in Luke Mogelson, "A Beast in the Heart of Every Fighting Man," *The New York Times*, 27 April 2011, http://www.nytimes.com/2011/05/01/magazine/mag-01KillTeam-t. html?_r=1&emc=eta1&pagewanted=all.

[6] Major Robert Stelle, quoted in Brad Knickerbocker, "Sergeant Seen as 'Kill Team' Leader Found Guilty in Afghanistan Atrocities," *Christian Science Monitor*, 10 November 2011, http://www.csmonitor.com/USA/Military/2011/1110/Sergeant-seen-as-kill-team-leader-found-guilty-in-Afghanistan-atrocities.

[7] Human Rights First, "'Kill Team' Sentence Only One Step in Full Accountability for Civilian Murders," 11 November 2011, http://www.humanrightsfirst.org/2011/11/11/%E2%80%9Ckill-team%E2%80%9D-sentence-only-one-step-in-full-accountability-for-civilian-murders/.

sometimes take causal and moral responsibility for the killing. For example, Vice Admiral William McRaven gave an apology to members of an Afghan household in April 2010 for the killing of five members of their family in a night raid. Those killed included an Afghan police chief, a prosecutor, and three women, including two who were pregnant. Although the laws of war only identify command responsibility for deliberate war crimes, McRaven took command responsibility for what he called a mistake.

> I am the commander of the men who accidentally killed your loved ones. I came here to send my condolences to you and to your family and to your friends. I also came today to ask for your forgiveness for these terrible tragedies.... We did not come here to do any harm. The American soldiers came here to protect the Afghan people not to hurt them. This was a terrible mistake.[8]

Political leaders give general instructions about the political objectives, but it is the military command that is responsible for determining the specific means that the military will use to achieve the political ends. Commanders must understand the coming battle, tell soldiers how to prosecute it, and give good advice to civilian leaders when they are asked for their views. Commanders must also ensure that their forces are not wasted and that they and their troops obey the laws of war, taking care to respect the rights of prisoners of war and noncombatants. There is the period during and after the contact and the killing when military commanders assess the consequences of the choices they have made and the orders given to use certain weapons or tactics. They must also choose whether to prosecute soldiers who are reckless or violate the laws of war.

For all this, Clausewitz says that soldiers and commanders need "courage in the face of personal danger, and courage to accept responsibility, either before the tribunal of some outside power or before the court of one's own conscience."[9] Unfortunately, Clausewitz only considers the first type of courage in any detail. We are left with the idea that there is something to be concerned about with respect to being judged for action in war, but Clausewitz has not, directly at least, helped us

---

[8] McRaven, quoted in Julius Cavendish, "U.S. Special Forces Apologize for Botched Night Raid," *The Independent*, 9 April 2010, http://www.independent.co.uk/news/world/asia/us-special-forces-apologise-for-botched-night-raid-1939880.html. The night raid occurred on 12 February 2010. Special Forces troops were accused of removing the bullets from the dead in attempt to cover-up the killing and to put blame on insurgents for the deaths. Richard A. Oppel, Jr. and Abdul Waheed Wafa, "Afghan Investigators Say U.S. Troops Tried to Cover Up Evidence in Botched Raid," *New York Times*, 5 April 2010, http://www.nytimes.com/2010/04/06/world/asia/06afghan.html?adxnnl=1&adxnnlx=1311853564-Ze4VfOp8GC0X88+9raKTfA.

[9] Carl Von Clausewitz, *On War*, edited and translated by Michael Howard and Peter Paret (Princeton: Princeton University Press, 1976), p. 101.

reason about the moral responsibility of command. I argue that the moral responsibility for both deliberate killing and collateral damage of all types rests only in part on the shoulders of commanders. Just as there are limits to the moral agency and responsibility of individual soldiers at the tip of the spear, there are limits to the moral agency and responsibility of commanders. In this chapter I explore the role responsibility of commanders for collateral damage, and in the next chapter I examine the ways that commanders' beliefs and agency are constrained within the military organization.

International Law of Command Responsibility

The modern law of command responsibility dates to the trials that followed World War II, where the primary concern was assigning blame and criminal responsibility for deliberate atrocity as ordered by commanders. The Nuremberg and Tokyo trials of German and Japanese perpetrators of atrocity recognized both the responsibility of individual perpetrators for crimes, as well as the legal responsibility of commanders for their own actions and the actions of their subordinates. The Nuremberg Charter states specifically that "the official position of defendants, whether as Heads of State or responsible officials in Government Departments, shall not be considered as freeing them from responsibility or mitigating punishment."[10] The post-World War II war crimes tribunals went further to identify negligence as blameworthy and to focus on what commanders should and must know about the conduct of their troops.

The case against Japanese General Tomoyuki Yamashita articulated the paradigm of command responsibility. Yamashita's troops committed hundreds of atrocities against Filipinos during Japan's occupation. Tried by a US Military Commission in 1946, General Yamashita was charged not with personally perpetrating the crimes in question, but of having failed to act: in cases where "there is no effective attempt by a commander to discover and control the criminal acts, such a commander may be held responsible, even criminally liable."[11] Yamashita either knew or should have known about the crimes of his soldiers and prevented those acts. At a minimum Yamashita was judged to be negligent. That Yamashita should have known about "widespread offenses" is the standard of "constructive knowledge."

> This accused is an officer of long years of experience, broad in its scope, who had extensive command and staff duty in the Imperial Japanese Army in peace as well as war. Clearly, assignment to command military troops is

---

[10] Quoted in Leslie C. Green, "War Crimes, Crimes against Humanity, and Command Responsibility," *Naval War College Review*, vol. 50 (April 1997): 26–68.

[11] *Re: Yamashita*, 327 U.S. 1, at 13–14 (1946).

accompanied by broad authority and heavy responsibility. This has been true of all armies throughout recorded history. It is absurd, however, to consider a commander a murderer or a rapist because one of his soldiers commits a murder or a rape. Nevertheless where murder and rape and vicious, revengeful actions are widespread offences, and there is no effective attempt by a commander to discover and control the criminal acts, such a commander may be held responsible, even criminally liable, for the lawless acts of his troops, depending upon their nature and the circumstances surrounding them. Should a commander issue orders which lead directly to lawless acts, the criminal responsibility is definite and has always been so understood.[12]

The Eichmann trial also dealt with command, albeit by a bureaucratic functionary for the machinery of killing Jews by the Nazi regime. Adolf Eichmann did not kill a single Jewish person with his own hands. Nor did he personally order the killing. He was, Eichmann argued, simply an obedient servant of the German government. Rather, the judgment against him found that his actions were "an enormous and complicated crime...wherein many people participated, on various levels and in various modes of activity—the planners, the organizers, and those executing the deeds, according to their various ranks." Further, "these crimes were committed en mass, not only in regard to the number of victims, but also in regard to the numbers of those who perpetrated the crime, and the extent to which any of the many criminals was close or remote from the actual killer of the victim means nothing as far as the measure of his responsibility is concerned." The conclusion was that in such a highly organized system of killing, "in general, the degree of responsibility increases as we draw further away from the man who uses the fatal instrument with his own hands."[13]

The doctrine of command responsibility is also articulated in the 1977 Additional Protocol I of the Geneva Convention: "The fact that a breach of the Conventions or of this Protocol was committed by a subordinate does not absolve his superiors from penal or disciplinary responsibility, as the case may be, if they knew, or had information which should have enabled them to conclude in the circumstances at the time, that he was committing or was going to commit such a breach and if they did not take all feasible measures within their power to prevent or repress the breach."[14] In addition, the parties to the treaty "shall require any commander who is aware that subordinates or other persons under his control are going to commit or have committed a breach of the Conventions or of this Protocol, to initiate

---

[12] Ibid.

[13] Judgment quoted in Hannah Arendt, *Eichmann in Jerusalem: A Report on the Banality of Evil* (New York: Penguin Books, 1963), pp. 246–247.

[14] Geneva Convention Additional Protocol I (1977), Article 86, paragraph 2.

such steps as are necessary to prevent such violations of the Conventions or this Protocol, and, where appropriate, to initiate disciplinary or penal action against violators thereof."[15]

Current international criminal law follows the previous formulations. Specifically, the International Criminal Tribunal for the Former Yugoslavia (ICTY) assumes the standard of constructive knowledge articulated in the Yamashita case. Superiors do not have to be given a specific command to be held responsible for the actions of subordinates. "The fact that any of the [prohibited] acts was committed by a subordinate does not relieve his superior of criminal responsibility if he knew or had reason to know that the subordinate was about to commit such acts or had done so and the superior failed to take the necessary and reasonable measures to prevent such acts or to punish perpetrators thereof."[16] Thus, superiors are also responsible for orders that lead to actions by subordinates with foreseeable criminal consequences. The US *Counterinsurgency Field Manual* similarly defines command responsibility for disciplining forces.

> Commanders are also responsible if they have actual knowledge, or should have knowledge, through reports received or other means, that troops or other persons subject to their control are about to commit or have committed a crime, and they fail to take the necessary and reasonable steps to ensure compliance with the law or to punish violators.[17]

The laws of command responsibility, unsurprisingly, stress individual agency and intention. This becomes clear in the 1998 Rome Statute establishing the International Criminal Court where the link between individual criminal responsibility and intention is defined: "A person shall be criminally responsible and liable for punishment for a crime within the jurisdiction of the Court only if the material elements are committed with intent and knowledge." Here knowledge can include foreknowledge of the likely consequences of an action.

2. For the purposes of this article, a person has intent where:

   (a) In relation to conduct, that person means to engage in the conduct;
   (b) In relation to a consequence, that person means to cause that consequence or is aware that it will occur in the ordinary course of events.

---

[15] Ibid., Article 87, paragraph 3.

[16] Statute of the International Criminal Tribunal for the Former Yugoslavia, Article 7(3), 25 May 1993.

[17] United States Army and Marine Corp, *U.S. Army/Marine Corps Counterinsurgency Field Manual*, D-24, p. 356.

3. For the purposes of this article, "knowledge" means awareness that a circumstance exists or a consequence will occur in the ordinary course of events. "Know" and "knowingly" shall be construed accordingly.[18]

This formulation of criminal responsibility is meant to address the problems of both a malevolent commander and a commander's negligence and willful blindness with respect to the behavior of subordinates executing specific or implied orders. The assumption here is that the negative consequences, the crime, committed by the subordinate or the commander were intentional or that crimes were *foreseeable* by the commander.

As Mark Osiel notes, "criminal law assumes a world of unencumbered individuals, independently interacting." Further, he emphasizes, "criminal law is inherently about the punishment of individuals for their culpable acts."[19] Yet, commanders do not create all, or even the majority of conditions, that yield the unintentional consequences that will foreseeably occur in the ordinary course of events. There is room here to prosecute negligence, but with the focus on deliberate intention, the bar is set very high. The problem of harm to noncombatants is that it is an unintended yet foreseeable consequence of larger forces, outside of an individual commander's immediate control and is thus, for practical purposes, outside international criminal law, with its focus on individual moral and legal responsibility. In fact, as I argued in the discussion of military necessity, double effect, and due care, international law seems to both admit the potential and forgive commanders for systemic collateral damage and proportionality/double effect killing.

The Moral Responsibilities of Command

Philosophers see the moral responsibilities of command differently than military lawyers, although they start with the assumption articulated by Michael Walzer, and Clausewitz, that the responsible agents in war are soldiers and commanders. Commanders ought to prospectively evaluate risks to noncombatants and seek to minimize them. "With reference to specific and small scale military actions... the people required to take care are common soldiers and their immediate superiors."[20] We have seen earlier that Walzer expects the common soldier to generally defer to the judgment of commanders in going to war. While Walzer does not require commanders to be omniscient, they must at least consider the potential harm of their actions for civilians. Recall that Walzer says, "Simply not to intend the death of

---

[18] Rome Statute of the International Criminal Court, 1998, Article 30.

[19] Mark Osiel, *Making Sense of Mass Atrocity* (Cambridge: Cambridge University Press, 2009), p. 187.

[20] Walzer, *Just and Unjust Wars*, p. 319.

civilians is too easy; most often, under battle conditions, the intentions of soldiers are focused narrowly on the enemy."

> What we look for in such cases is some sign of a positive commitment to save civilian lives. Not merely to apply the rule of proportionality and kill no more civilians than is militarily necessary—that rule applies to soldiers as well; no one can be killed for trivial purposes. Civilians have a right to something more.[21]

In the next sentence, when Walzer says, "And if saving civilian lives means risking soldier's lives, the risk must be accepted,"[22] he is not simply asking individual soldiers to make the calculation of risk, but implying that commanders—"the relevant individuals stand higher in the hierarchy"—or perhaps organizations must make the calculations and make the commitment to save civilian lives.[23] Walzer is thus very clear about the balance of risk on the battlefield. It might be that in protecting civilians, commanders place soldiers at greater risk or that in protecting the lives of soldiers, commanders place noncombatants at greater risk.[24] The military leader must exercise due care for civilian lives and for the soldiers.

There is, Walzer argues, a limit to what we can expect the military to do to protect civilians because commanders also have a duty to their soldiers—not to take undue risks with their lives and he calls the duty of commanders not to waste the lives of soldiers under them "hierarchical" command responsibility. "Whenever I read about trench warfare in World War I, I can hardly avoid the sense that the officers who sent so many soldiers to their deaths for so little gain in one attack after another were literally mad."[25] Walzer goes further in assigning responsibility for wasting soldiers' lives up the chain of command. "But if that is so, the madness [of the officers] was reiterated at every level of the hierarchy—up to the level where political leaders stubbornly refused every compromise that might have ended the war."[26]

Thus, it is the commander's role to manage the delicate balancing among the imperatives of military necessity, force protection, and the protection of noncombatants. If commanders fail to assess the costs of military operations for not just their own soldiers, but for civilian bystanders, they are morally responsible. Walzer is very clear that this is a difficult task.

[21] Ibid., pp. 155–156.

[22] Ibid.

[23] Ibid., p. 319.

[24] Michael Walzer, "Two Kinds of Moral Responsibility," in Michael Walzer, *Arguing about War* (New Haven: Yale University Press, 2004), pp. 29–30.

[25] Ibid., p. 25.

[26] Ibid.

Once again, I have to say that I cannot specify the precise point at which the requirements of 'due care' have been met. How much attention is required? How much risk must be accepted? The line isn't clear. But it is clear enough that most campaigns are planned and carried out well below the line; and one can blame commanders who don't make minimal efforts, even if one doesn't know exactly what a maximal effort would entail.[27]

But, when Walzer suggests, "The limits of risk are fixed, then, roughly at that point where any further risk-taking would almost certainly doom the military venture or make it so costly [in soldiers lives] that it could not be repeated," he implies that commanders must privilege military necessity.[28] In sum, Walzer moves very close here to what I called a permissive interpretation of military necessity, where when military commanders make an assessment of the military necessity and likely strategic and tactical consequences of their actions, as well as the likely effects of their attacks on noncombatants, they are apparently to weight the "military venture" more heavily.

Commanders may foresee civilian death but not intend it. In his discussion of command responsibility, Walzer writes that "in planning their campaigns, they [military commanders] must take positive steps to limit even unintended civilian deaths (and they must make sure that the numbers killed are not disproportionate to the military benefits they expect)." But again, what are the limits to the "positive steps"? As Walzer writes, "Here the laws of war are of little help; no officer is going to be criminally charged for killing too many people if he does not actually massacre them."[29] Commanders know more than their subordinates, they have more power due to their position in the chain of command, and their explicit role is to make judgments about the costs, risks, and benefits of particular decisions. In sum, commanders should be held to account for failing to perform their roles.

However, commanders can hardly be expected to be omniscient and omnipotent. A commander may sincerely believe that the likelihood of achieving an important military goal is high, while the likelihood of harm to civilians is low when it is just the opposite. Are commanders to be faulted for guessing wrong before the fact? Further, should commanders be held morally responsibility retrospectively for failing to take due care with the lives of noncombatants or for failing to make adjustments so that the actions that led to foreseeable harm are not repeated? Here is where the assignment of moral and potential legal responsibility must be shared among actors and institutions.

[27] Walzer, *Just and Unjust Wars*, p. 319.
[28] Ibid., p. 157. Given Walzer's other statements about the doctrine of double effect, I also take it that Walzer is prioritizing the minimization of risk to civilians over the minimization of risk to military personnel.
[29] Ibid., p. 317.

Specifically, I agree with Walzer that in cases of the foreseeable but unintentional killing of large numbers of noncombatants, that "the laws of war are of little help; no officer is going to be criminally charged for killing too many people if he does not actually massacre them." But, I do not believe that the next sentence—that "the moral responsibility is clear, and it cannot be located anywhere else than in the office of commander"—is the only or even the best understanding of moral responsibility for cases of systemic collateral damage and proportionality/double effect killing. Commanders should be faulted for deliberate harm and for negligence—knowing the risks and the likely harm, but choosing to act without sufficiently mitigating the risk or choosing not to act. But commanders should not necessarily be faulted for the conditions that made the risks high to begin with or made the risk difficult to assess. Like the subordinates who implement their orders, military commanders fight with the weapons that have already been purchased, under the laws of war and standard operating procedures as they found them, within the culture of a larger military organization and for political objectives determined by others. Despite their awesome power to order killing, the agency of military commanders is limited.

So if, as Walzer argues, the standards for holding Yamashita guilty for failures of command responsibility were perhaps too high, and if we accept that Yamashita could not monitor his troops to prohibit civilian killing and still effectively fight a war, and agree that Yamashita in fact had imperfect control over his subordinates, then Walzer concludes that we must exonerate Yamashita. But, Walzer then suggests, if the arguments about a trade-off between military effectiveness and imperfect control of subordinates are accepted, "they also leave us with no clear standards at all." Walzer laments: "In fact there is no philosophical or theoretical way of fixing such standards. That is also true with the planning and organization of military campaigns."[30]

I disagree. While it is difficult to "fix" standards in advance, we can do a lot better by widening the focus of responsibility from commanders as individual agents to commanders in their roles within military organizations. We can find those standards in the way that Walzer suggests by examining several cases and searching for the standards implicit in them.[31] The current way that command responsibility is understood and regulated in the US military suggests how the agency of commanders, and the military organization within which they are embedded, can be defined and organized so that the scope and limits of the "positive steps" that a commander can take to protect one's own forces and civilians can be outlined, if not "fixed."

In what follows, I focus on how the military organization understands command responsibility for preventing deliberate atrocities, cases where soldier's snap,

---

[30] Ibid., p. 321.

[31] "The appropriate standards can emerge only through a long process of casuistic reasoning, that is, by attending to one case after another, morally or legally.... Only by making such specifications, again and again, can we draw the lines that the war convention requires." Ibid., p. 322.

and in incidents of collateral damage. Drawing from these cases, I then suggest six ways that commanders can and should act to reduce and limit deliberate killing of civilians as well as accidental collateral damage, systemic collateral damage, and proportionality/double effect killing. The emphasis here is on increasing and using the moral agency of military commanders, and I show ways that this moral agency has been used in some cases and can be institutionalized. In the next chapter I explore the ways the commander's role, moral agency, and capacities are shaped and constrained within a larger organizational environment and argue that there is also organizational responsibility. But before turning to the scope of organizational responsibility, it is important to be more specific about the scope and limits of individual command responsibility for "collateral damage."

Command Responsibility in the United States

The duties of US military commanders at every level, to establish the rules of engagement stating when the use of force is authorized, are articulated in a document known as the Standing Rules of Engagement (SROE) and in officer training. Force protection and military necessity are given equal weight in US Standing Rules of Engagement: "The SROE differentiate between the use of force for self-defense and for mission accomplishment."[32] Self-defense is an absolute right in the Standing Rules of Engagement and is defined in a way that makes self-defense a military necessity. "Commanders have the inherent authority and obligation to use all necessary means available and to take all appropriate actions in the self-defense of their unit and other US forces in the vicinity. *ROE supplemental measures apply only to the use of force for mission accomplishment and do not limit a commander's use of force in self-defense.*"[33] It is the commander's responsibility to ensure that soldiers understand the rules of engagement. "Commanders have the obligation to ensure that individuals within their respective units understand and are trained on when and how to use force in self-defense.[34]

There is no doubt that like international law, US military law assumes individual and command responsibility for military operations, including cases of deliberate harm and killing of noncombatants. "Commanders must take steps to ensure that members of their commands do not violate the LOW." Those directly responsible for clear violations of the law should be both morally blamed and punished as criminals if they are found to have deliberately killed noncombatants, or failed in their duties as commanders to investigate or discipline soldiers who have done so. The

---

[32] United States, Chairman of the Joint Chiefs of Staff Instruction, CJCSI 3121.01A, 15 January 2000, "Standing Rules of Engagement for US Forces" paragraph 6b, p. 2.

[33] Ibid., paragraph 6b, p. 2, emphasis in the original.

[34] Ibid., Attachment A, paragraph 5e, p. A-4.

emphasis is clearly on preventing deliberate violations of the laws of war: "The two principal means of affecting this goal are to recognize the factors which may lead to the commission of war crimes, and to train subordinate commanders and troops to standard concerning compliance with the LOW and proper responses to orders that violate the LOW."

1. Awareness of the factors that have historically led to the commission of war crimes allows the commander to take preventive action. The following is a list of some of the factors that the commander and the judge advocate should monitor in subordinate units.

   a. High friendly losses.
   b. High turnover rate in the chain of command.
   c. Dehumanization of the enemy (derogatory names or epithets).
   d. Poorly trained or inexperienced troops.
   e. The lack of a clearly defined enemy.
   f. Unclear orders.
   g. High frustration level among the troops.

2. Clear, unambiguous orders are a responsibility of good leadership.[35]

But, according to US military lawyers, who use an *Operational Law Handbook* as their guide, the commander does not bear all the moral responsibility. Military lawyers and commanders are to instruct soldiers in the laws of war and then individual soldiers must exercise moral judgment and agency. "Soldiers who receive ambiguous orders or who receive orders that clearly violate the LOW must understand how to react to such orders." In those cases,

> Troops who receive unclear orders must insist on clarification. Normally, the superior issuing the unclear directive will make it clear, when queried, that it was not his intent to commit a war crime. If the superior insists that his illegal order be obeyed, however, the soldier has an affirmative legal obligation to disobey the order and report the incident to the next superior commander, military police, CID, nearest judge advocate, or local inspector general.[36]

By insisting that individual soldiers be the judge of the lawfulness of an order, the *Operational Law Handbook* reaffirms the paradigm of individual moral agency and responsibility. On the other hand, in ordering that commanders and judge

---

[35] International and Operational Law Department, *Operational Law Handbook* (Charlottesville, VA: The Judge Advocate General's Legal Center and School, 2011), p. 37.
[36] Ibid.

advocates train soldiers in making judgments about the legality of orders, the SROE also implicitly emphasizes the role of training and the culture of the larger military institution in socializing soldiers. Commanders are often blamed when soldiers deliberately and systematically abuse civilians or prisoners of war.[37] What is not so clear is who is morally responsible for the inadvertent killing of noncombatants. In the next chapter I explore how the larger, organizational/structural context shapes and constrains individual agency. At this juncture, the focus is on the role of commanders.

Two cases illustrate the scope and the limits of commanders' moral responsibility for collateral damage. In the first case, the US air campaign in Bosnia, commanders not only stressed the importance of protecting noncombatants, they were personally engaged in operations to ensure that civilian protection was institutionalized and operationalized. By contrast, in the second case, the battle for Fallujah, there was a degree of concern for minimizing civilian casualties, which affected the planning of the air portion of the military operations. But features of the ground siege and conquest of Fallujah illustrates the consequences when minimizing civilian casualties becomes a lower priority than military necessity.

Bosnia 1995: Deliberate Force

To simplify a great deal, and focus primarily on the US military role, the war in Bosnia began when Bosnian Serbs in the former Yugoslavia attacked Bosnian Muslims, in a campaign of "ethnic cleansing" in the early 1990s. International forces attempted to protect Muslims from the assault by establishing "safe areas" protected by UN troops. The United States armed and encouraged Serbia's opponents, the militaries of Bosnia and Croatia, but initially stayed out of direct military involvement despite a widespread outcry in the United States and Europe for humanitarian intervention. But the attack on Bosnian civilians was relentless and when Srebrenica fell to Bosnian Serbs, on 11 July 1995, thousands were killed. Other attacks, such as the shelling of a civilian marketplace in Sarajevo on 28 August 1995 that caused more than three dozen civilian deaths, made media headlines worldwide. US and NATO leaders felt compelled by public opinion to intervene in Bosnia by late 1995, when UN "safe areas," Gorazde, Bihac, Srebrenica, and Sarajevo, were under attack, and Muslim civilians were systematically being killed, raped, and driven from their homes in the three-quarters of Bosnia that had been occupied.

The war began to turn against Serbian forces when the Croatian military attacked Serbs in a major offensive, Operation Storm, in Krajina in August 1995. General

---

[37] See, for instance, Mark Moyer, *A Question of Command: Counterinsurgency from the Civil War to Iraq* (New Haven: Yale University Press, 2009).

Charles Boyd, deputy commander of the US European Command said, "Croatia would not have taken the military offensives... without explicit approval of the US government."[38] Several hundred Serbians were killed, and about 150,000 Serbians fled the Croatian assault. NATO forces directly joined in the rollback of Serbs in late August 1995. On 30 August 1995, NATO forces began a series of air attacks on Bosnian Serb forces in the former Yugoslavia. The aim of NATO action in Bosnia, Operation Deliberate Force, was to force the Serbs to halt their aggression and agree to a peace treaty. The air campaign lasted two weeks, excluding a three-day pause, with air strikes occurring during 11 days. The bombing ended on 14 September. While the Bosnian and Croatian forces continued to assault the Serbs on the ground, with apparently little concern for civilian casualties, NATO aircraft assaulted Serbian military targets.

The US and NATO air strikes in Bosnia in August 1995 were designed to achieve their political aim of halting Serbian aggression while minimizing risk to US forces and to civilians in Bosnia. The risk of confronting the Serbian forces on the ground was not borne by the NATO troops. Rather, the risk to ground forces was largely borne by Bosnian and Croatian forces whose offensive against Serbian forces had begun four weeks before the NATO air assault and continued through October 1995. In fact, the Croatian ground assault, and a barrage of artillery ordnance fired by British, French, and Dutch troops had a substantial impact on Serbian forces. Many believe it was the combined effects of the air assault and the ground offensive that pushed Milošević to end the war.

The US Air Force emphasized the political impact of the bombing on the Serbian leader, Slobodan Milošević, and its low cost in civilian casualties, and many civilian and military leaders in the United States drew the lesson from the short intervention in Bosnia that precision guided weapons and air power could force concessions at the bargaining table while at the same time minimizing the risk to US and allied forces. The role of the Bosnian and Croatian forces ground offensive against Serb forces was downplayed by the advocates of air power. But no matter the relative importance of ground versus air assault, the joint Bosnian-Croatian ground offensive resulted in several thousand Serbian civilians being killed and tens of thousands of Bosnian and Serbian civilians becoming refugees.[39] By contrast, the US led NATO air assault on Serbian forces caused few casualties.

In February 1996 the US Secretary of Defense William Perry described the US role in Deliberate Force as effective. "Every target that had been designated was destroyed and there was zero collateral damage. This was a rare instance where by combination of exclusive use of precision guided ammunitions and very strict rules of engagement we conducted this massive campaign with no damage, no damage to civilians, no collateral

[38] Quoted in David N. Gibbs, *Humanitarian Intervention and the Destruction of Yugoslavia* (Nashville, TN: Vanderbilt University Press, 2009), p. 164.

[39] Ibid., pp. 162–165. Ivo H. Daalder and Michael E. O'Hanlon, *Winning Ugly: NATO's War to Save Kosovo* (Washington, DC: Brookings Institution Press, 2000), pp. 92–93.

damage of any kind."[40] Indeed, the overall perception was that the campaign had shown the effectiveness of coercive airpower in conjunction with precision guided munitions. The Clinton administration assumed air power would get similar results—changing the political situation with low risk to own forces while minimizing civilian casual-ties—during the later Kosovo campaign. But there were civilian casualties caused by NATO airstrikes, including one inadvertent bombing of a farm house near a targeted bridge. The numbers are disputed, but there were perhaps fewer than thirty civilians killed by US and NATO military action in Bosnia.[41]

How is it that NATO's punishing air attacks caused relatively few direct non-combatant deaths? Three factors helped keep NATO caused civilian casualties low. First, and perhaps most important, for political reasons, the prevention of civilian casualties was given top priority by NATO's political leaders. NATO intervention to halt a potential genocide would not be understood as legitimate if, in the effort to save civilian lives, NATO were to kill large numbers of civilians. (Although it was understood by US political and military leaders that Bosnian and Croatian Forces might, and indeed did, kill large numbers of civilians in their operations.) The US and NATO commanders thus internalized the political imperative and made it a priority to avoid killing civilians.

Second, the commitment to avoiding collateral damage was institutionalized—turned from a rhetorical statement to a set of routines and operational consider-ations—from the planning stages to the day-to-day execution of the air campaign. Military leaders internalized the belief that it was essential to keep casualties low in Bosnia. "The concepts of proportionality, military necessity, and collateral dam-age dominated the thought process surrounding the development and execution of ROE for each air strike. The single most defining element of every planning and execution decision was the overriding need to avoid collateral damage and esca-latory force."[42] The process for determining targets and rules of engagement was decided at a high level by NATO and UN officials before the operation began, and command for Deliberate Force was delegated to Lieutenant General Michael Ryan. The operational orders for Deliberate Force required that "target planning and weapon delivery will include considerations to minimize collateral damage."[43] In improving and elaborating on methods used to minimize collateral damage by air power developed in the Gulf War, Operation Deliberate Force was one of the first

---

[40] Quoted in Ronald M. Reed, "Chariots of Fire: Rules of Engagement in Operation Deliberate Force," in Robert C. Owen, ed., *Deliberate Force: A Case Study in Effective Air Campaigning* (Maxwell Air Force Base, Air University Press, 2000), pp. 381–429, 420–421.

[41] International Committee of the Red Cross, "ICRC Report on Certain Aspects of the Conduct of Hostilities and the Consequences from a Humanitarian Point of View of NATO Air Strikes," November 1994, cited in Robert C. Owen, "Summary," in Owen, ed., *Deliberate Force*, pp. 455–522, 522.

[42] Reed, "Chariots of Fire," p. 405.

[43] Operational Orders, quoted in Reed, "Chariots of Fire," p. 411.

US military operations to use collateral damage estimation and mitigation software and procedures.

The plans for Deliberate Force were developed slowly and evolved from the previous NATO efforts to enforce a UN no-fly-zone over Bosnia and to support United Nation's peacekeeping troops (Operations Sky Monitor and Deny Flight) starting in October 1992. As Colonel Charles Wald, commander of the 7490th Wing at Aviano Air Base said, "The pilots are operating under a zero tolerance policy for collateral damage. We have the technology to do it, but it can be difficult, particularly at night, in weather, while getting shot at."[44] Yet, despite the difficulty, much of the bombing was scheduled for nighttime, when it was supposed that civilians would be less likely to be near targeted infrastructure. The weapons were also chosen to minimize civilian casualties. For instance, the United States, which flew 65 percent of all sorties, chose not to employ cluster bombs (although some were inadvertently used).[45] Most of the weapons used by the United States in the air campaign—98 percent—were precision guided, while 28 percent of the bombs dropped by non-US NATO countries were precision guided.[46] NATO dropped 1,026 bombs total: 708 precision-guided weapons and 318 "dumb" or nonprecision weapons. Thus, of the total number of bombs dropped by NATO, 69 percent were precision guided, although one-third of the precision-guided weapons missed their targets.[47] NATO also avoided putting its aircraft at risk and there were relatively few incidents of NATO force combatant injury or death in either the air operations or the subsequent peacekeeping effort.

Third, and my focus here, key individual commanders—including the top US commander Lieutenant General Ryan, in charge of Air Forces Southern Europe and the Combined Air Operations Center, Colonel Daniel Zoerb, and Major General Hal Hornberg—made it their business to be closely engaged in the details of the execution of the Deliberate Force campaign.[48] High-level involvement in the details of planning and execution of air operations was not the norm. Rather, the norm is that political leaders and top-level commanders determine the overall rules of engagement in line with political objectives. Then large campaigns are designed at

[44] Quoted in Patrick M. Shaw, "Collateral Damage and the United States Air Force," Thesis, School of Advanced Airpower Studies, Air University Maxwell Air Force Base, June 1997, p. 92.

[45] Richard L. Sargent, "Weapons Used in Deliberate Force," in Owen, ed., *Deliberate Force*, pp. 257–277, 265.

[46] Of the 622 precision-guided weapons used by the United States, 567 were laser-guided bombs.

[47] Richard P. Hallion, *Precision Guided Munitions and the New Era of Warfare*, Air Power Studies Centre Paper Number 53 (RAAF Australia: Air Power Studies Centre, 1995); Global Security.org, "Operation Deliberate Force," http://globalsecurity.org/military/ops/deliberate_force.htm, accessed 28 July 2007. Shaw, "Collateral Damage and the United States Air Force," p. 92.

[48] John C. Orndorff, "Aspects of Leading and Following: The Human Factors of Deliberate Force," in Robert C. Owen, ed., *Deliberate Force: A Case Study in Effective Air Campaigning* (Maxwell Air Force Base, Air University Press, 2000), pp. 351–378; Reed, "Chariots of Fire," pp. 381–429.

the top and the details are determined and executed by subordinates. As one goes lower in the ranks of command, the rules of engagement become more specific as they are specified into operational plans and operational orders. At the next level, special instructions may be given for each day's mission and specific rules of engagement may be given in an air tasking message. Thus, as a rule, generals do not determine the targets, or which weapons go on particular aircraft.

General Ryan was personally involved in selecting every target in the Bosnia air campaign, and within that, in selecting every aim point (desired mean point of impact or DMPI). "Ryan directed his staff to evaluate all proposed targets and DMPIs for their military significance and their potential for high, medium or low assessments of collateral damage."[49] General Ryan was also engaged in the selection of weapons and battle damage assessment. Ryan interpreted the operational orders emphasis on minimizing collateral damage to require the selection of precision-guided munitions. Over the two weeks of the air campaign, eight members of NATO flew more than 3,500 sorties and dropped 1,026 munitions of which, about 70 percent were precision guided. Within that total, the United States flew 65 percent of the sorties and used more than 98 percent precision-guided munitions.[50] Although cluster bombs (CBUs) were available, and indeed the standard ordnance on several NATO and US aircraft, "Planners decided not to use CBUs during Deliberate Force because their inaccuracy and wide dispersion pattern made them likely to cause collateral damage."[51]

This unusually high level of commander involvement was perceived by some within headquarters, and sometimes by aircrews, as complicating or slowing decision making. Further, some officers were frustrated with the flow of information from the general and his staff. For example, Ryan did not authorize the release of battle damage assessments to his pilots. One observer, Benjamin Lambeth, argued that some of the restrictions on targeting during Deliberate Force were too limiting: "Even after Operation Deliberate Force was underway, signs of Vietnam-think continued to raise their head on occasion."[52]

By "Vietnam-think," Lambeth was specifically referring to the restrictions on attacking Serbian air defenses. Indeed, as in Vietnam, when for much of the war there were strict limits on attacking North Vietnamese surface-to-air missile sites, there were restrictions on the occasions when aircraft could attempt to destroy the

---

[49] Reed, "Chariots of Fire," pp. 410–411. Note, this is the same Michael Ryan who I quoted in the first chapter as cautioning that civilian casualties are inevitable.

[50] Reed, "Chariots of Fire," p. 427 and Gibbs, First Do No Harm, p. 166.

[51] Richard L. Sargent, "Weapons Used in Deliberate Force," in Owen, Deliberate Force, pp. 257–277, 265.

[52] Benjamin S. Lambeth, The Transformation of American Air Power (Ithaca, NY: Cornell University Press, 2000), p. 180.

Serb integrated air defense systems in an effort to minimize both the risk of fratricide (friendly-fire) and collateral damage. Preventive attack of Serbian air defenses was only allowed with high-level approval, in cases of a confirmed hostile act (e.g., a missile attack by Serbian air defenses) or when "dual correlation of positive indications of hostile intent" was confirmed. The "dual correlation" requirement for determining hostile intent meant that NATO aircraft had to either have two independent on board systems indicate that they had been targeted, or the aircraft under attack and another system (e.g., a second aircraft), had confirmed that the aircraft had been targeted. Absent "dual correlation" the aircraft under threat had to leave the area.[53] However, if aircraft detecting hostile intent could not escape the area, they could use any measure for self-defense. These "reactive" rules of engagement were sometimes frustrating for pilots.

As Ronald Reed notes in his description of the rules of engagement for Deliberate Force, "The restrictions placed on targeting remind one of those used in Vietnam. Unlike the political restrictions placed on military operations in Vietnam, however, in Deliberate Force the military's own restraint limited operations.... Rather than the politicians tying the hands of the military, the military may now be tying its own hands."[54]

In sum, the United States used a great deal of force in Bosnia with relatively few civilians killed or injured because commanders made protecting civilians a high priority, redefining military necessity to include civilian protection. Commanders then took personal responsibility to institutionalize civilian protection in the rules of engagement, weapon selection, and operational considerations. Finally, high-level US and NATO commanders oversaw day to day operations, and the institutionalization of collateral damage prevention, personally engaging in battle damage assessment so that tactics could be refined as needed.

Fallujah, Iraq 2004

> The enemy has a face. It is Satan's. He is in Fallujah, and we are going to destroy him.[55]

Fallujah, a city of approximately 300,000 people before the March 2003 US invasion of Iraq, was easily occupied in April 2003 by the US military. On 28 April 2003, just a few days before President Bush's "Mission Accomplished" speech, about 200 protesters gathered at a school in Fallujah, demanding that the school,

---

[53] Lambeth, *The Transformation of American Air Power*, p. 180 and Reed, "Chariots of Fire," pp. 412–413.

[54] Reed, "Chariots of Fire," pp. 416–417.

[55] Marine Lt. Col. Gareth F. Brandl, quoted in Dick Camp, *Operation Phantom Fury: The Assault and Capture of Fallujah, Iraq* (Minneapolis: Zenith Press, 2009), p. 157.

occupied by US forces, be reopened. Iraqi protesters shouted at the soldiers to leave and threw rocks at them. US soldiers, who said that they saw AK-47 weapons and that they were shot at by protestors, opened fire, killing seventeen civilians and wounding seventy-four. An investigation by Human Rights Watch found "no compelling evidence" that the school building had been fired upon by protesters, although there were signs of rock throwing. A protest of US actions two days later resulted in three more killings of civilians by the US military, who again said they were under attack.[56]

Over the next several months, resistance to US occupation increased in Fallujah and more broadly in the area known as the Sunni Triangle. Major General James Mattis, commander of the Marines in Fallujah, ordered that the US forces gain control through sustained infantry pressure on the insurgents. Mattis said he was "determined to demonstrate respect to the Iraqi people." He said: "Keep your soldiers, sailors and Marines focused on the mission and resistant to adversarial relationships with the Iraqi people...we obey the Geneva Convention even while the enemy does not. We will destroy the enemy without losing our humanity."[57]

On 31 March 2004, four Blackwater USA private military contractors driving through Fallujah were killed by gunmen. A crowd gathered, gasoline was poured into one of the vehicles, and it was set ablaze. The charred and dismembered remains of two of the men were then hung over a bridge. Photographs of the dead contractors' mutilation and their remains on the bridge were broadcast worldwide and prompted outrage in the United States. The US Ambassador to Iraq, Paul Bremmer said, the "events are a dramatic example of the ongoing struggle between human dignity and barbarism."[58]

Despite the fact that the Marine Commander of the area, General Mattis was not in favor of an attack, President Bush ordered an assault on Fallujah. Mattis cautioned that the Marines were preparing a different strategy in Fallujah to deal with the insurgency, focused less on breaking down doors and more on building trust.[59] Although the United States was dragged into Fallujah by the death of the contractors, American leaders were now fully engaged and enraged, and Mattis's strategy was set aside. US Secretary of Defense Donald Rumsfeld reportedly said, "We have got to pound these guys." Brigadier General Mark Kimmet said: "We will hunt down the criminals. We will kill them or we will capture them...and we will pacify Fallujah."[60] During a briefing by the US commander in Iraq, Lieutenant General

---

[56] Human Rights Watch, "Violent Response: The U.S. Army in Al-Faluja," Human Rights Watch Reports, Iraq, vol. 15, no. 7 (June 2003).

[57] Mattis quoted Camp, *Operation Phantom Fury*, p. 50.

[58] Quoted in Camp, *Operation Phantom Fury*, p. 7.

[59] Camp, *Operation Phantom Fury*, pp. 33–38, 58.

[60] Quoted in Camp, *Operation Phantom Fury*, p. 7.

Ricardo Sanchez, President George Bush told Sanchez to "Kick ass!" in Fallujah. "If somebody tries to stop the march of democracy, we will seek them out and kill them! We must be tougher than hell!... Our will is being tested, but we are resolute.... Stay strong! Stay the course! Kill them! Be confident! Prevail! We are going to wipe them out! We are not blinking!"[61]

On 5 April, Operation Vigilant Resolve, meant to pacify Fallujah in a few days, began with a Marine assault. The battle turned into a bloody stalemate and a public relations fiasco for the American forces. After the bombing of a mosque and other incidents that were politically sensitive, the offensive was halted and control of the city was given to Iraqi forces on 28 April on the understanding that insurgents would be kept out of the city. But insurgents remained and a decision was made to attack again.

Public pressure, specifically concern for civilian casualties, caused the Americans to withdraw from Fallujah in April. US commanders felt they had lost the information operations (media public relations) war to critical coverage by Arab television and other news media. Or as Lieutenant General Conway said, "Al Jazeera kicked our butts."[62] But there were not only Arab language news reports of civilian casualties. An Iraqi doctor, Dr. Abdul Jabbar working in Fallujah Hospital told a reporter in May that he could not keep track of how many wounded people he treated. "Many people were injured and killed by cluster bombs. Of course they used cluster bombs. We heard them as well as treated people who had been hit by them!"[63] The doctor estimated that at least 700 people died. *USA Today* estimated that the death toll of Iraqis in Fallujah for operations in April was around 600, although the number of civilians killed within that total was unclear.[64]

But the US halt to operations was temporary. In May 2004 military operations—air, artillery, and special forces—began to "shape" the environment and to prepare the news media for a renewed assault. According to Major Sean Tracy, the idea for the slower operations was to avoid "watching this on TV and you see all these bombs dropping, and somebody's going to throw up their hands and say, 'Hey, isn't this enough?'.... Reporters and the world would become accustomed to artillery and air attack." Although the "shaping" of the battlefield began in the summer months, the order to officially plan for the attack came in September 2004.

[61] Quoted in Camp, *Operation Phantom Fury*, p. 73.

[62] Quoted in Bing West, *No True Glory: A Frontline Account of the Battle of Fallujah* (New York: Bantam Books, 2005), p. 322.

[63] Quoted in Dahr Jamail, "Iraq: The Devastation," 7 January 2005, http://www.tomdispatch.com/post/2109/.

[64] "Fallujah Death Toll for Week More than 600," *USA Today*, 4 April 2004, http://www.usatoday.com/news/world/iraq/2004-04-11-fallujah-casualties_x.htm. The journalist Dahr Jamail said he witnessed US snipers shooting civilians in April 2004 and that doctors told him that of the 736 deaths, more than 60 percent were civilians. Jamail, *Beyond the Green Zone: Dispatches from an Unembedded Journalist in Occupied Iraq* (Chicago: Haymarket Books: 2007).

The next operations were to include US Army and Marines, as well as British and Iraqi forces. The Marines were to assault the city along three entry points and then go from building to building to kill insurgents. Pilots of marine aircraft used maps and scale models to memorize their plans of attack. An area of the desert was used to practice the procedures that would be used in the assault. The United States wanted to avoid large number of civilian casualties. Marine Colonel Earl Wederbrook said, "Fallujah was mapped out to the foot. Every visible enemy roadblock, stronghold, suspected weapon cache, safe house, rat hole or storage bunker was located, identified and labeled. Pilots spent untold hours studying the maps." Wederbrook said, "Nearly every building was identified with a name or a number." Wederbrook added: "The rules of engagement were very explicit...do not drop unless you are absolutely sure of your target. And then only use munitions that would minimize collateral damage." Certain buildings were labeled as off limits and "pilots memorized the collateral damage estimates and danger close distances of all their available ordnance."[65]

The 1st Marine Division's official rules of engagement for the upcoming Operation Phantom Fury, to control Fallujah were that "no forces are declared hostile. However, individuals within the Fallujah AO who are carrying arms openly are demonstrating hostile act/intent unless there is evidence to the contrary; pose an imminent threat to Coalition Forces, and may be attacked subject to the following restrictions." The ROE then specified that Marines should "minimize collateral damage to innocent persons and property." Marines should "not target or strike any of the following except in self-defense to protect yourself, your unit, friendly forces and designated persons or property under your control."

1. Noncombatant civilians
2. Hospitals, mosques, churches, shrines, schools, museums and other historical and cultural sites
3. Civilian populated areas or buildings unless the enemy is using them for military purposes. [66]

Although the numbers were unclear, it was estimated at the outset of the operation that there were about 1,000 "hard core" insurgents and 2,000 "part-timers" in Fallujah.[67] In the days prior to the assault, the city was surrounded by US and other coalition forces and residents were told by the Marines to leave through checkpoints, or, if they remained, to stay inside their homes. At these checkpoints, males between the ages 15 and 45 were turned back in to the city, or detained. The UN-coordinated Emergency Working Group estimated on 11 November that approximately 200,000

---

[65] Quoted in Camp, *Operation Phantom Fury*, p. 136.

[66] Quoted in Camp, *Operation Phantom Fury*, p. 150.

[67] See West, *No True Glory*, p. 256 and Nicholas J. Davies, *Blood on Our Hands: The American Invasion and Destruction of Fallujah* (Ann Arbor: Nimble Books, 2010), p. 211.

people left Fallujah and were dispersed throughout Iraq while approximately 50,000 civilians remained in the city.[68]

UN Secretary General Kofi Annan wrote President George Bush and British Prime Minister Tony Blair on 31 October to express his concerns about the potential negative political effects of the impending operation. Annan favored a diplomatic solution to the crisis. Further, he said, "I wish to express to you my particular concern about the safety and protection of civilians. Fighting is likely to take place mostly in densely populated urban areas, with an obvious risk of civilian casualties."[69] Although Secretary of State Colin Powell called Annan, the concerns about civilian casualties were generally either ignored or dismissed by officials in the United States, United Kingdom, and Iraq.[70]

The second assault by US and Iraqi forces on Fallujah, Operation Phantom Fury, officially began on 7 November 2004. The assumption was that anyone who remained in the city was an insurgent. The initial breach of the city through three corridors occurred at night; the Marines preferred to fight in the dark because they could use infrared to see suspected insurgents, while the insurgents could not see them well enough to direct their fire. In their first operation, Marines secured Fallujah General Hospital by force and one of the two remaining health clinics was also destroyed that night. The press and humanitarian organizations were denied access to Fallujah, the entry of medical supplies and food were severely restricted, and electricity and water were cut by Multinational Forces. Only ambulances operated by Multinational Forces Iraq were allowed passage in and out of Fallujah.

The UN Emergency Working Group stated on 11 November, "It is reported that the water and electricity systems in Falluja have been cut off by the IIG/MNF-I. This action directly affects civilians (approximately 50,000 people inside Falluja) for whom water is a basic need and a fundamental human right."[71] Over the next few days, those residents of Fallujah who had been displaced by the operation began to face food, water, and medical shortages in the places where they took shelter. On 19 December, the Emergency Working Group noted that "monitors report there is sporadic access to the various IDP [internally displaced persons] locations due to military activities/ checkpoints and insecurity; whereas Falluja itself remains strictly inaccessible due to

---

[68] Emergency Working Group—Fallujah Crisis (EWG), "Update Note," 11 November 2004, p. 1. http://www.uniraq.org/documents/Falluja%20Bulletin%2011%20November.pdf. "The Emergency Working Group (EWG) comprises humanitarian organizations UN; NGO; Red Cross/Crescent Organizations (RCO) and relevant IIG Ministries. The most recent meeting was an IIG emergency coordination meeting on Falluja, hosted by the Ministry of Displacement and Migration (MoDM) on 9 November. This meeting, which took place in Baghdad, was linked by teleconference to the EWG in Amman and UNAMI Baghdad" (p. 1).

[69] "Kofi Annan's Letter, Fallujah Warning," BBC News, 6 November 2004, http://news.bbc. co.uk/2/hi/middle_east/3987641.stm.

[70] Dafna Linzer, "Annan's Warning on Fallujah Dismissed," *Washington Post*, 6 November 2004, p. A19.

[71] EWG, "Update Note," 11 November 2004, p. 2.

the ongoing conflict. IOM monitors report that clinics at the IDP areas are experiencing shortages of some drugs and that many IDPs have not received their food rations."[72]

The fighting in Fallujah was intense both day and night, moving house to house over the course of four weeks, though sporadic fighting continued for several more weeks after the city was opened for the return of its residents on 23 December. As the journalist Bing West observed, "With scant civilians in the city, the usual tactic was to throw grenades over the courtyard wall, blow the lock on the metal gate, rush a four-man fire team into the courtyard, and shout and bang on the windows of the house to draw fire.... If nothing happened, then the most risky step followed: smashing through the doors and searching room by room down narrow, gloomy corridors."[73] The process was quick. If the Marines received fire "the line held up while tanks moved forward, sending shell after shell into the house."[74] The Marines used air strikes from helicopters and drone aircraft, cannon from M1 Abrams tanks, and bulldozers. The US also used M825 "felt wedge" 155 mm shells, which burn white phosphorus for up to 15 minutes for illumination, to mark an area for a strike, or to provide cover.[75]

Colonel Michael Shupp thought the Rules of Engagement for Fallujah were too restrictive: "We had very, very rigid ROEs, almost to the point of being too demanding on engaging."[76] Major General Richard Natonski, commander of the operation in Fallujah, said, "there were many times that my regiments had targets they wanted to engage, but because of the rules of engagement and the amount of collateral damage, we were precluded from hitting certain sites in the city."[77] Natonski explained the procedure:

> We tried to use a progression of force in our operations. If there was a rifleman in a building we would use small arms. If there was more than one person and they were firing RPGs then maybe we'd shoot a Hellfire into the building. As the battle progressed, because of the intensity of the resistance and if we knew there were insurgents in buildings, in some cases we'd drop the structure before we'd risk soldiers' or Marines' lives by sending them into the buildings. We used everything from tanks at close range to D9 armored bulldozers to 500-pound joint direct attack munitions (JDAMs). But we'd try to isolate that one specific building rather than damaging the entire neighborhood. It is important to safeguard the Marines, soldiers

---

[72] EWG, "Bulletin Update," 19 December 2004, http://www.uniraq.org/documents/EWGFallujaBulletin-19Dec.doc, p. 1.

[73] West, *No True Glory*, p. 270.

[74] Ibid., p. 274.

[75] Camp, *Operation Phantom Fury*, p. 211.

[76] Quoted in Camp, *Operation Phantom Fury*, p. 149.

[77] Quoted in Camp, *Operation Phantom Fury*, p. 152.

and civilians in the city; you can always rebuild a house, you can't rebuild a life.[78]

By contrast, Marine Corporal Michael Leduc described his briefing on the rules of engagement for Fallujah in 2004 as including the assumption that everyone in the city was hostile.

> The battalion JAG officer wrapped up by sort of going, "Okay, Marines, you see an individual with a weapon, what do you do?"
>
> We mutter in silence for a minute, waiting for somebody else to answer, and one guy said, "Shoot him?"
>
> "No. Shooting at a target, putting rounds down range and suppressing a target, is one thing. Sighting and killing a target is another. So again, you see an individual with a weapon, what do you do?"
>
> "Kill him."
>
> "You see an individual with a pair of binoculars, what do you do?"
>
> "Kill him."
>
> "You see an individual with a cell phone out, what do you do?"
>
> "Kill him."
>
> "You see an individual, who although may not be actually carrying any-thing or displaying any specific hostile action or intent running from, say, one building to another, running across the street or even running away from you, assume that he is maneuvering against you and kill him. You see an individual with a white flag and he does anything but approach you slowly and obey commands, assume it's a trick and kill him."[79]

A Lebanese Broadcasting Corporation journalist, Burhan Fasa'a who entered Fallujah during the siege reported that he personally witnessed many civilians killed and injured. Interviewed by the independent journalist Dahr Jamail in December 2004, Burhan Fasa'a said that "the dead were buried in gardens because people couldn't leave their homes. There were so many people wounded, and with no medical supplies, people died from their wounds. Everyone in the street was a target for the Americans; even I saw so many civilians shot by them." He witnessed the house to house searches.

> Americans did not have interpreters with them, so they entered houses and killed people because they didn't speak English! They entered the

---

[78] Quoted in Camp, *Operation Phantom Fury*, p. 152.

[79] Michael Leduc testimony in Iraq Veterans Against the War (IVAW) and Aaron Glantz, *Winter Soldier Iraq and Afghanistan: Eyewitness Accounts of the Occupations* (Chicago: Haymarket Books, 2008), pp. 67–69, 67–68.

house where I was with 26 people, and shot people because they didn't obey their orders, even just because the people couldn't understand a word of English. Ninety-five percent of the people killed in the houses that I saw were killed because they couldn't speak English. Soldiers thought the people were rejecting their orders, so they shot them. But the people just couldn't understand them!

Fasa'a described American snipers shooting civilians trying to flee the city by swimming across the Euphrates River. He also said, "I saw cluster bombs everywhere, and so many bodies that were burned, dead with no bullets in them. So they definitely used fire weapons, especially in Julan district. I watched American snipers shoot civilians so many times. I saw an American sniper in a minaret of a mosque shooting everyone that moved."[80]

Corporal Leduc described a tactic called "reconnaissance by fire, which meant if for any reason we felt unsafe or unsure going into clear a house or a building, we were granted the ability to do anything we wanted to that house before we entered it....we were operating under the assumption that everyone was hostile."[81] The press travelling with troops and soldiers in Fallujah reported that, in some cases, US soldiers were told that they could fire at anything they considered hostile. NBC news correspondent Kevin Sites reported that he heard Staff Sergeant Sam Mortimer give the permission "Everything to the west is weapons-free."[82] Thus, the Vietnam era term "free-fire zone" was exchanged for the phrase "weapons-free."[83] Marine Sergeant Adam Kokesh said that "during the siege of Fallujah, we changed Rules of Engagement more often than we changed our underwear. At first it was, 'You follow the Rules of Engagement. You do what you're supposed to do.' Then there were times when it was, 'You can shoot any suspicious observer.'...At one point we imposed a curfew on Fallujah, and then we were allowed to shoot anything after dark."[84] One Marine described how his battalion operated in Fallujah.

When we would go through houses, we would burn them down. The ones that were stone and stuff like that, we'd bring in bulldozers and bulldoze them. You could look at satellite images of Fallujah now and there's a road that runs north and south and everything between that and the river was

---

[80] Quoted in Dahr Jamail, "An Eyewitness Account of Fallujah," 4 December 2004, http://dahrja-mailiraq.com/an-eyewitness-account-of-fallujah.

[81] Leduc testimony in IVAW and Glantz, *Winter Soldier Iraq and Afghanistan*, p. 67.

[82] Kevin Sites, "Marines Let Loose on the Streets of Fallujah," NBC News, 10 November 2004, http://www.msnbc.msn.com/id/6450268/ns/world_news-mideast/n_africa.

[83] Clifton Hicks testimony in IVAW and Glantz, *Winter Soldier Iraq and Afghanistan*, pp. 28–32, 28. Of course, in other contexts a "weapons-free" zone is an area where weapons are absent.

[84] Kokesh testimony in IVAW and Glantz, *Winter Soldier Iraq and Afghanistan*, pp. 42–46, 42–43.

ours and it is flat. We just flattened it. Because the enemy...we would push south and the enemy would move back and around and would try to rebuild behind us and flank us and do all that. So...we dropped bombs on it, and whatever we didn't flatten we bulldozed or did whatever we had to do.[85]

Concerns were raised during the assault that US forces were not taking due care with prisoners and civilians. For instance, an NBC news video of a US soldier killing an unarmed prisoner in a Mosque on 13 November, raised questions about whether the practice of "dead checking"—where the wounded are killed—was widespread in Fallujah. The Marine Corp investigated but chose not to prosecute the corporal filmed killing the wounded prisoner.[86] Louise Arbour, the UN Human Rights High Commissioner, and former prosecutor for the International Criminal Court, raised concerns about civilian casualties in Fallujah and called for an investigation of the practices of both sides: "the deliberate targeting of civilians, indiscriminate and disproportionate attacks, the killing of injured persons and the use of human shields."[87]

The worst of the fighting ended by late December. In January 2005, the UN Emergency Working Group reported that although refugees had begun to return to Fallujah, access to food and medical care was limited. Further, the Emergency Working Group reported estimates that Fallujah itself had 40% of buildings and homes that were "significantly damaged" while another 20% sustained "major damage," and that the remainder were "completely destroyed."[88]

The use of white phosphorus shells caused some controversy in the United States and the United Kingdom. A Pentagon spokesperson, Lieutenant Colonel Barry Venable told the BBC in a 2005 interview that the use of white phosphorus in Fallujah was legal: "White phosphorus is a conventional munition. It is not a chemical weapon. They are not outlawed or illegal. We use them primarily as obscurants, for smokescreens or target marking in some cases. However it is an incendiary weapon and may be used against enemy combatants." Venable argued that the white phosphorus shells were militarily useful. "When you have enemy forces that are in covered positions that your high explosive artillery rounds are not having an impact on and you wish to get them out of those positions, one technique is to

---

[85] Quoted in Erin P. Finley, *Fields of Combat: Understanding PTSD among Veterans of Iraq and Afghanistan* (Ithaca, NY: Cornell University Press, 2011), p. 34.

[86] Alex Chadwick, "No Court-Martial for Marine Taped Killing Unarmed Iraqi," 10 May 2005, http://www.npr.org/templates/story/story.php?storyId=4646406.

[87] "UN Rights Boss Urges Fallujah 'Abuses' Probe," ABC News Online, 17 November 2004. http://www.abc.net.au/news/2004-11-17/un-rights-boss-urges-fallujah-abuses-probe/586736. United Nations, "Situation of Civilians in Fallujah, Iraq," 16 November 2004, http://www.unhchr.ch/huricane/huricane.nsf/view01/7472316E3570A216C1256F4E0046EDC6.

[88] EWG, "Fallujah Bulletin Update," 18 January 2005, http://www.uniraq.org/documents/EWGFallujaBulletin-18Jan.doc, p. 3.

fire a white phosphorus round into the position because the combined effects of the fire and smoke—and in some case the terror brought about by the explosion on the ground—will drive them out of the holes so that you can kill them with high explosives."[89] An after action review article in the military journal *Field Artillery* described the munitions used in "fire support" by the US Army in Fallujah including high explosives (HE) and white phosphorus: *"White Phosphorous.* WP proved to be an effective and versatile munition. We used it for screening missions at two breeches and, later in the fight, as a potent psychological weapon against the insurgents in trench lines and spider holes when we could not get effects on them with HE. We fired 'shake and bake' missions at the insurgents, using WP to flush them out and HE to take them out."[90]

Other research suggests that there may be a much longer term legacy of the assault on Fallujah, in part due to the use of white phosphorus. A report published in Iraq in 2008 noted higher rates of birth defects in children and more illnesses related to exposure to toxic chemicals in the years following the Fallujah attack.[91] A later survey, undertaken to assess the validity of previous reports was published in the *International Journal of Environmental Research and Public Health* in 2010. Researchers admitted that though their survey of Fallujah households had potential shortcomings, "the results confirm the reported increases in cancer and infant mortality which are alarmingly high. The remarkable reduction in the sex ratio in the cohort born one year after the fighting in 2004 identifies that year as the time of the environmental contamination."[92]

There are relatively few estimates of the number of insurgents and civilians killed in the April and November Fallujah assaults, and disagreement about the numbers. Iraq Body Count recorded 1,874 civilian deaths in Fallujah for the period of 19 March 2003 to 19 March 2005.[93] A UN agency reported in January 2005 that head of the Fallujah General Hospital, Dr Rafa'ah al-Iyssaue described how hospital workers had recovered 700 bodies from nine of twenty-seven neighborhoods in Fallujah;

---

[89] Quoted in "US Forces Used Chemical Weapon in Iraq," *The Independent*, 16 November 2005, http://www.independent.co.uk/news/world/americas/us-forces-used-chemical-weapon-in-iraq-515551.html.

[90] James T. Cobb, Christopher A. LaCour, and William H. Hight, "TF 2-2 in FSE AAR: Indirect Fires in the Battle of Fallujah," *Field Artillery* (March-April 2005), pp. 23–28.

[91] Monitoring Net of Human Rights in Iraq and Conservation Center of Environmental and Reserves in Fallujah, "Prohibited Weapon's Crisis: The Effect of Pollution on Public Health in Fallujah," 2008; Patrick Cockburn, "Toxic Legacy of US Assault on Fallujah 'Worse than Hiroshima,'" *The Independent*, 24 July 2010, http://www.independent.co.uk/news/world/middle-east/toxic-legacy-of-us-assault-on-fallujah-worse-than-hiroshima-2034065.html.

[92] Chris Busby, Malak Hamdan, and Entesar Ariabi, "Cancer, Infant Mortality and Birth Sex-Ratio in Fallujah, 2005-2009," *International Journal of Environmental Research and Public Health*, vol. 7 (2010), pp. 2828–2837, 2836.

[93] Iraq Body Count, "A Dossier of Civilian Casualties 2003-2005," July 2005. http://www.iraqbodycount.org/analysis/reference/press-releases/12/.

550 were women and children. Many others had already been buried according to Dr Rafa'ah al-Iyssaue.[94] Other accounts of the November 2004 Operation rarely mention the presence of civilians and make no effort to count the toll. Bing West does say:

> In the month of April, 150 air strikes had destroyed 75 to 100 buildings. In November the damage was vastly greater. There were 540 air strikes and 14,000 artillery and mortar shells fired, as well as 2,500 main tank gun rounds. Eighteen thousand of Fallujah's 39,000 buildings were damaged or destroyed. In the November attack 70 Americans were killed and 609 wounded.[95]

Elsewhere in his account of Fallujah, West describes a "high ranking" US General who drove through Fallujah in late November 2004 to view the city. "After several minutes he told the driver to stop. He got out and looked up and down the streets, at the drooping telephone poles, gutted storefronts, heaps of concrete, twisted skeletons of burnt-out cars, demolished roofs, and sagging walls. 'Holy shit,' he said."[96]

The Difference Command Makes

The comparison of the relatively short US air campaign in Bosnia with the two assaults on Fallujah may seem inappropriate. After all, the Bosnia operation was an air campaign, not intended to take and hold territory, but to create the conditions for a political solution, while the battles for Fallujah were essentially infantry assaults, intended to establish on the ground control of an urban area. Despite their dissimilarities, a comparison between the two cases highlights the importance of six factors about the role of commanders that make a difference in whether noncombatants become "collateral damage."

The first factor is whether commanders emphasize the distinction between combatants and noncombatants. Though Additional Protocol I acknowledges that it is sometimes difficult to distinguish between combatants and noncombatants, Protocol I is clear that, when uncertain, the presumption should be for civilian status. "In case of doubt whether a person is a civilian, that person shall be considered to be a civilian."[97] The 2012 Army manual on civilian casualty mitigation makes this

---

[94] "Iraq: Death Toll in Fallujah Rising, Doctors Say," *IRIN*, 4 January 2005. http://www.irinnews.org/report.aspx?reportid=24527.

[95] West, *No True Glory*, pp. 315–316.

[96] Ibid., p. 316.

[97] Geneva Convention Additional Protocol I, Article 50.

point on the first page: "If there is any doubt, Army forces consider a person to be a civilian."[98]

But the distinction between noncombatants and combatants can be eroded if not consciously abandoned or ignored. Distinction may be set aside or lost. This can occur in one of two situations. Soldiers may be told that anyone who remains in a particular area must be presumed to be a combatant because noncombatants should have fled the area. Or it might be presumed that noncombatants are so politically close to combatants—in terms of providing material support or safe haven—that they are combatants. A May 2007 survey by the Pentagon found that 17 percent of US soldiers and Marines agreed or strongly agreed with the statement that, "all noncombatants should be treated as insurgents."[99] As Marine Sergio Kochergin said, "Before being deployed to Iraq, we were told that we needed to be prepared to have little kids and women shoot at us.... We were constantly told everybody there wants to kill you, everybody wants to get you."[100]

The assumption that the only people who are in a location must be enemy combatants is common in war. During the American occupation of the Philippines, and again during the Vietnam War, the United States cleared areas of the countryside, placing civilians in the case of the Philippines in "protected zones," and in Vietnam, in "strategic hamlets." Those outside the protected zones and strategic hamlets could be and were killed. Similarly, at times during the Iraq war, US soldiers believed that only an enemy combatant could be in a particular place. "We were operating under the assumption that everyone was hostile."[101] Turning back all males over the age of 14 in Fallujah is a failure to discriminate between combatants and noncombatants: "At one point during the siege of Fallujah we decided to let women and children out of the city...I went out on the northern bridge over the Euphrates on the western side of Fallujah, and our guidelines were that males had to be under fourteen years old. If they were old enough to be in your fighting hole, they were too old to get out of the city."[102]

James N. Mattis, the Marine Commander who had initially urged restraint in Fallujah and who expressed disdain for those soldiers who abused of prisoners in Abu Ghraib, also said, "There are some assholes in the world that just need to be shot."[103] Promoted to three star Lieutenant General, Mattis told an audience in San Diego in February 2005, "Actually it's quite fun to fight them, you know. It's a hell of a hoot.... You go into Afghanistan, you got guys who slap women around for five years because they didn't wear a veil. You know guys like that ain't got no manhood left anyway. So it's a hell of

[98] Department of the Army, *Civilian Casualty Mitigation*, Army Tactics, Techniques, and Procedures, No. 3-37.31 (Washington, DC: Department of the Army, 18 July 2012), p. 1-1.

[99] Unclassified briefing General James T. Conway, "Mental Health Advisory Team (MHAT) IV Brief," 18 April 2007, p. 21.

[100] Quoted in Dahr Jamail, *The Will to Resist: Soldiers Who Refuse to Fight in Iraq and Afghanistan* (Chicago: Haymarket Books, 2009), pp. 119–120.

[101] Michael Leduc testimony in IVAW and Glantz, *Winter Soldier Iraq and Afghanistan*, pp. 67–69, 67.

[102] Adam Kokesh testimony in IVAW and Glantz, *Winter Soldier Iraq and Afghanistan*, pp. 42–46, 44.

[103] Mattis, quoted in Camp, *Operation Phantom Fury*, p. 63.

a lot of fun to shoot them."[104] The fact that Afghan males had a reputation for sexism seemed to blur the line between combatant and noncombatant males in Afghanistan in Mattis's narrative. But, as I describe in the chapter on political responsibility, it was US civilian officials who first blurred the distinctions after the 9/11 attacks.

The second factor affecting whether due care is taken with civilian life, as high-lighted by military lawyers, is whether the command environment encourages dehumanization of enemy noncombatants or respect for noncombatants. In a sense, dehumanization of enemy soldiers is what makes killing in any war possible.[105] Dehumanization of noncombatants is also a prerequisite for war crimes and is arguably associated with the gratuitous mutilation of the dead. A Pentagon survey in 2007 of soldiers and Marines fighting in Iraq found that "only 47 percent of sol-diers and 38 percent of Marines agreed that noncombatants should be treated with dignity and respect."[106]

The third factor in whether due care is observed is whether commanders con-sider civilian casualties to be inevitable. Donald Rumsfeld set a tone of fatalism about killing civilians after the 9/11 attacks. "On occasion, there will be people hurt that one wished had not been. I don't think there's any way in the world to avoid that and defend the United States from the kinds of terrorist attacks which we've experienced."[107] Fatalism about the inevitability of noncombatant killing yields far different results than a determination to minimize or avoid civilian casualties that is associated with vigilant planning and review of operations. When civilians were injured or killed by military convoys driving quickly to avoid hidden explosives or ambush in Iraq and Afghanistan, there was a reluctance to report these traffic deaths. Army Colonel William Rochelle said of the killing of one family, two parents and two children, "If these fucking hajis learned to drive, this shit wouldn't happen."[108] When civilians were killed at checkpoints because they failed to stop, the response by commanders reviewing the incidents was often to see the killings as justified. By

[104] CNN, "General: It's 'fun to shoot some people,'" 4 February 2005, http://www.cnn.com/2005/US/02/03/general.shoot/. Promoted to four-star General, Mattis was tapped to replace David Petraeus as head of the Central Command in July 2010. Defense Secretary Gates said Mattis, though disciplined for his comments five years earlier, was "one of our military's outstanding combat leaders and strategic thinkers, bringing an essential mix of judgment and perspective to this important post." Thom Shanker, "Blunt General Appointed to Lead Forces in Mideast," *New York Times,* 9 July 2010, p. A8.

[105] Dave Grossman, *On Killing: The Psychological Cost of Learning to Kill in War and Society* (Boston: Little Brown and Company, 1995).

[106] Sara Wood, "Defense Department Releases Findings of Mental Health Assessment," Armed Forces Press Service, 4 May 2007, Department of Defense, http://www.defense.gov/news/newsar-ticle.aspx?id=33055.

[107] Julian Borger, "Rumsfeld Blames Regime for Civilian Deaths," *The Guardian,* 15 October 2001, http://www.guardian.co.uk/world/2001/oct/16/afghanistan.terrorism8.

[108] Geoffry Millard testimony in IVAW and Glantz, *Winter Soldier Iraq and Afghanistan,* pp. 96–97, 97.

contrast, in the 1995 Bosnia bombing campaign, the US Commander General Ryan made both force protection and minimizing collateral damage top priorities and institutionalized the concern to limit civilian casualties in the planning process. The collateral damage estimation and mitigation procedures institutionalized by the Air Force, described in the chapter on institutional responsibility, are a reminder that civilian casualties are not inevitable.

The fourth factor is the level of monitoring and oversight exercised by commanders high in the chain of command, specifically, the monitoring and assessment of civilian casualty incidents, and oversight over the choice of weapons and tactics. A fatalistic attitude about civilian casualties can make monitoring them seem like a poor utilization of resources. But, as we have seen, some commanders monitor the consequences of ongoing operations more closely than others. High-level commanders are often situated far from the action and may not grasp what is happening in the field unless they make it their business to know. Yet, as the *Operational Law Handbook* suggests, monitoring by commanders is essential. A high turnover rate of commanders can be a factor in negligence or setting the conditions for war crimes.[109]

The failure to conduct an analysis of how civilians are dying also delays the recognition that a pattern of practices is leading to predictable civilian harm. Recall that in discussing the killing of as many as thirteen civilians in Ishaqi, Iraq, in 2006, Major General William Caldwell said the investigation had found that the soldiers had followed rules of engagement: "As the enemy fire persisted, the ground force commander appropriately reacted by incrementally escalating the use of force from small arms fire to rotary wing aviation, and then to close air support, ultimately eliminating the threat." He said, "Temptation exists to lump all these incidents together. However, each case needs to be examined individually."[110] Each case does need to be examined individually. But if commanders do add up individual cases of civilian killing, a pattern may emerge; the rules of engagement may need modification. General McKiernan made just such monitoring possible in Afghanistan in 2008 when he set up the Civilian Casualty Tracking Cell.

But more than toting up numbers, an analysis of the causes of civilian killing is necessary. Recall that although cluster bombs, which have the potential to cause indiscriminate harm, were inadvertently used in Bosnia, a high levels decision had been made not to use them for just that reason. As a consequence of that decision, only two cluster bomb units were used during the first day of air operations

---

[109] See International and Operational Law Department, *Operational Law Handbook 2011* (Charlottesville, VA: The Judge Advocate General's Legal Center and School, 2011), p. 37.

[110] Caldwell, quoted in John D. Banusiewicz, "Probe Clears Coalition Forces of Wrongdoing in March 15 Raid," American Forces Information Services New Articles, US Department of Defense, 3 June 2006. http://www.defense.gov/News/NewsArticle.aspx?ID=16139.

in Bosnia, and thereafter, cluster bombs were not used.[111] However, cluster bombs were used in both Afghanistan and Iraq. Moreover, white phosphorus was also used in Iraq and Afghanistan. These weapons—which are extremely difficult to use with discrimination and which may have long-term health consequences—are in the US arsenal and soldiers are trained in their use. Commanders must make the affirmative choice not to deploy the weapons or to remove them.

The fifth factor, often highlighted by US military lawyers, is whether deliberate violations of the laws of war or "accidents" and carelessness that lead to civilian harm are tolerated by commanders or are investigated and punished. Indifference or willful blindness to civilian harm or prisoner abuse amounts to a permissive climate and discourages bystanders from intervening to stop abuse by other soldiers. When commanders say, "we don't do body counts" of civilians, they express an attitude of indifference. The *Operational Law Handbook* stresses the importance of reporting and investigating possible violations of the law of war: "WHEN IN DOUBT, REPORT."[112]

Many active duty US soldiers and Marines surveyed by the military in 2007 who had served in Iraq said they were reluctant to report abuse or even killing of a noncombatant by a unit member: 40 percent of Marines and 55 percent of soldiers said they would report a unit member for injuring or killing "an innocent noncombatant." Lower percentages of those surveyed said they would report mistreatment of or stealing from a noncombatant or violating rules of engagement.[113] Indeed, there was a widespread assumption that killing innocents would be unreported or portrayed as the killing of an insurgent.

Many soldiers in Iraq and Afghanistan learned to keep "drop weapons" or other signs of enemy combatant status on hand. A Marine who fought in Iraq said, "Something else we were encouraged to do, almost with a wink and a nudge, was to carry drop weapons, or by my third tour, drop shovels."[114] Garett Reppenhagen said that he learned in his army deployment in Iraq to "Keep AK-47s, or shovels, that you find in raids in your vehicle so if you accidently kill someone that was innocent, you can throw down a shovel, or the AK-47, on him, and you call him an insurgent. You say 'he was digging for an IED' or 'He had an AK-47,' you know? So this was kind of the world I entered in."[115]

[111] Mark J. Conversino, "Executing Deliberate Force, 30 August-14 September 1995," in Owen, ed., *Deliberate Force*, pp. 131–175, 160; Sargent, "Weapons Used in Deliberate Force," in Owen, ed., *Deliberate Force*, pp. 265–266.

[112] International and Operational Law Department, *Operational Law Handbook 2011*, p. 37.

[113] Unclassified briefing General James T. Conway, "Mental Health Advisory Team (MHAT) IV Brief," 18 April 2007, p. 23.

[114] Jason Washburn testimony in IVAW and Glantz, *Winter Soldier Iraq and Afghanistan*, pp. 20–22, 22.

[115] Garett Reppenhagen, quoted in Matthew Guttman and Catherine Lutz, *Breaking Ranks: Iraq Veterans Speak Out against the War* (Berkeley: University of California Press, 2010), p. 93.

Finally, commanders encourage respect for noncombatants when they respect their own troops. Humiliation and abuse is a feature of military training and often of the relationship between soldiers and their commanders. The idea is to harden the soldier and to increase their readiness. Jonathan Shay notes that a "belief that rage at superiors is usefully channeled into rage at the enemy is quite ancient and is acknowledged in the *Iliad*." Shay believes that the idea that "humiliation and degradation" motivates soldiers peaked during the Vietnam War. However, war is difficult enough for soldiers, and Shay argues that abuse by commanders and fellow soldiers does not inure soldiers to hardship. It simply breaks them. "Humiliation and degradation as techniques of motivation should be seen as signs of leadership failure and should result in swift, massive, and visible damage to an officer's career."[116]

The denial of combat trauma, the belief that those who claim post-traumatic stress may simply be malingering, means that those soldiers who are no longer fit to fight, through no fault of their own, are left in place. And there is no doubt that many soldiers who in the field are in distress. In 2007, an army mental health survey found both that approximately 13 percent of soldiers in Afghanistan were taking sleep medication by their third deployment. Further, the survey found that the rate of medication for mental health problems increased with the number of deployments: 3.5 percent of soldiers who were on their first deployment were taking medication. Soldiers on their second and third deployment were taking medication for mental health at rates of 4.5 and 9.8 percent, respectively.[117]

The Duty to Protest or Withdraw Participation

In exploring how military commanders may create conditions that minimize collateral damage or that allow it to occur and continue, I have emphasized a commander's role as commonly understood and articulated in international law and in ethics. Everything about military discipline stresses duty defined as obedience to civilian authority and to superior commanders. But soldiers and officers are also professionals and citizens. In the case of systemic collateral damage and proportionality/double effect killing, these role responsibilities may seem to conflict. The duty of the enlisted soldier is first to follow orders but also to judge the legality of orders and to question commanders for clarification. The soldier or commander may legitimately decide that conscientious

---

[116] Jonathan Shay, *Achilles in Vietnam: Combat Trauma and the Undoing of Character* (New York: Simon and Schuster, 1994), pp. 201–202.

[117] Office of the Command Surgeon US Forces Afghanistan and Office of the Surgeon General, United States Army, "Mental Health Advisor Team (MHAT) 6 Operation Enduring Freedom," 6 November 2009, p. 31. Tens of thousands of US soldiers who were found to be medically unfit for combat in physicals prior to deployment were nevertheless deployed to Iraq and Afghanistan from 2001 to 2008. While some were declared unfit because they needed dental work or eyeglasses, some were unfit for mental health reasons.

performance of their role as a citizen requires that they will question orders, disobey orders, or resign their commission.[118]

Indeed, just as we expect the common soldier to refuse to follow a "manifestly illegal" order, we should expect commanders to refuse to participate in actions that they know or foresee to be illegal or unethical. That is the difference that command makes. As Nathan Sassaman stresses: the difference between an officer and an enlisted man is the many more hours of "values" training the officer receives.[119] Indeed, commanders have more opportunities, education in military law and ethics to judge the nature of commands that they are given and that they give to subordinates, and commanders have greater agency. Commanders have more education about war, more time to think for themselves, and more distance from a battlefield than the soldier who is in regular contact with the enemy. In fact, it is part of the professional responsibility of commanders to examine the morality of their actions and orders; commanders in every branch in every major military are given military ethics training with an emphasis on the laws of war. Military ethics education in the US military also stresses personal virtue and trust, but that trust cannot be blind. Military discipline stresses obedience, but that too cannot be blind. Thus, even when the civilian casualty estimation and mitigation procedures suggest that there will be "minimal" civilian casualties, and the law sanctions their actions, they must still ask whether foreseeable and foreseen killing is morally justified.

Questioning will be hardest at the junior officer level and become relatively easier with increasing rank. We know "the unique position the young lieutenant occupies in the organizational hierarchy, where the youngest and least experienced officers are charged with the most demanding leadership challenges" is also the most vulnerable.[120] Commanders must be more willing to question orders. Higher ranking commanders have the duty to question up the chain of command and to question civilian leaders. It is often difficult for commanders to rethink their understanding of military discipline, duty, and honor. Yet it is less difficult, and less consequential, for a commander to challenge a superior or to refuse to follow an order.

Questioning is only a first step. If a commander questions and still draws the conclusion that the policy is indeed a violation of the laws of war or moral duty to protect noncombatants, they must pass that information up the chain of command. If superiors fail to see that something is very wrong, the commanders charged with supervising and executing a superior's military order may take the next step and

---

[118] This argument does not necessarily challenge the fundamental subordination of military commanders to civilian authority. Again, I am not concerned here so much with the justice of the war, though military commanders ought to be concerned with the overall justice of any war. I am focused on the conduct of war, in particular with respect to how conduct affects the fortunes of noncombatants.

[119] Nathan Sassaman, with Joe Layden, *Warrior King: The Triumph and Betrayal of an American Commander in Iraq* (New York: St. Martin's Press, 2008), p. 36.

[120] Jeffrey Wilson, "An Ethics Curriculum for an Evolving Army," in Paul Robinson, Nigel De Lee, and Don Carrick, eds., *Ethics Education in the Military* (Aldershot: Ashgate, 2008), pp. 31–41, 33.

refuse to give commands that they know to be wrong. The difficulty, of course, is that lieutenant colonels and even colonels fear, rightfully, that their careers will be harmed or even ruined by asking such questions. But such thinking and questioning must be rewarded at least as much as obedience is prized.

The next least personally disruptive form of withdrawal of consent or participation by commanders is to refuse to use ordnance that cannot be used discriminately. This may mean that an officer orders their subordinates to refuse to load or carry a specific weapon or that an officer refuses to command a mission where such weapons are used. As Anthony Hartle, a scholar of military ethics, observed, "the existing laws of war appear to be regrettably incomplete in terms of providing guidance for the use of modern weapons" and US military manuals do not entirely remove ambiguity.[121] Thus, it is commanders who must exercise discrimination. Similarly, certain operations may predictably lead to civilian death, such as night raids, where discrimination is much more difficult. On the other hand, night raids may give soldiers an advantage. Hartle acknowledges that these dilemmas are not easily resolved: "Duty requires adherence to law and regulations; it also requires mission accomplishment and protection of one's soldiers."[122] In sum, mid-level commanders (for example, from captains, to first lieutenants and lieutenant colonels) must evaluate whether a standard operating procedure is consistently and predictably causing harm to or killing of noncombatants, they must pass that knowledge up the chain of command, and must refuse, if necessary, to continue that operation with those weapons.

Further, higher ranking commanders, and also lower ranked commanders, may refuse an order or may resign their commission. Some soldiers who come to believe that all war is wrong file for conscientious objector status, which must be approved before they can separate their service from the military. In a tragedy that one hopes is not repeated, at least one high ranking Army officer committed suicide while deployed in 2005 to end what he said, in his suicide note, was his dishonorable participation in the Iraq war.[123]

---

[121] Anthony E. Hartle, *Moral Issues in Military Decision Making*, 2d ed. (Lawrence: University of Kansas, 2004), p. 113.

[122] Ibid., p. 184.

[123] Col. Ted Westhusing, committed suicide in Iraq in 2005 rather than continue his service there. Robert Bryce, "'I am Sullied—No More': Col. Ted Westhusing Chose Death over Dishonor in Iraq," *The Austin Chronicle*, 27 April 2007. http://www.austinchronicle.com/gyrobase/Issue/story?oid=469141. His suicide note read: "Thanks for telling me it was a good day *until* I briefed you. [Redacted name]—You are only interested in your career and provide no support to your staff—no msn [mission] support and you don't care. I cannot support a msn that leads to corruption, human right abuses and liars. I am sullied—no more. I didn't volunteer to support corrupt, money grubbing contractors, nor work for commanders only interested in themselves. I came to serve honorably and feel dishonored. I trust no Iraqi. I cannot live this way. All my love to my family, my wife and my precious children. I love you and trust you only. Death before being dishonored any more. Trust is essential—I don't know who [to] trust anymore. Why serve when you cannot accomplish the mission, when you no longer believe in the cause, when your every effort and breath to succeed meets with lies, lack

Others have refused to fight in particular wars, such as Army First Lieutenant Ehren Watada, who had served a deployment in South Korea before receiving orders to deploy to Iraq. Watada argued that "as the order to take part in an illegal act is ultimately unlawful as well, I must refuse that order."[124] Watada offered to serve in Afghanistan instead of Iraq, but this was not accepted. Watada, who believed the Iraq war was unjust and that its conduct violated the army's rules of land warfare, then attempted to resign his commission in January 2006 but his resignation was not accepted.[125] Watada then began to organize other soldiers to refuse to deploy.

The idea is this: that to stop an illegal and unjust war, the soldiers can choose to stop fighting it.

Now it is not an easy task for the soldier. For he or she must be aware that they are being used for ill-gain. They must hold themselves responsible for individual action. They must remember duty to the Constitution and the people supersedes the ideologies of their leadership. The soldier must be willing to face ostracism by their peers, worry over the survival of their families, and of course the loss of personal freedom. They must know that resisting an authoritarian government at home is equally important to fighting a foreign aggressor on the battlefield. Finally, those wearing the uniform must know beyond any shadow of a doubt that by refusing immoral and illegal orders they will be supported by the people not with mere words but by action.

The American soldier must rise above the socialization that tells them authority should always be obeyed without question. Rank should be respected but never blindly followed. Awareness of the history of atrocities and destruction committed in the name of America—either through direct military intervention or by proxy war—is crucial....

Enlisting in the military does not relinquish one's right to seek the truth—neither does it excuse one from rational thought nor the ability to distinguish between right and wrong. "I was only following orders" is never an excuse.[126]

---

of support, and selfishness? *No more.* Reevaluate yourselves, cdrs [commanders]. You are not what you think you are and *I* know it.

COL Ted Westhusing. Life needs trust. Trust is no more for me here in Iraq." Westhusing Suicide note, in " 'Life Needs Trust' Ted Westhusing's Last Note to His Superior Officers," *The Austin Chronicle*, 27 April 2007, http://www.austinchronicle.com/news/2007-04-27/469142/.

[124] Quoted in Jamail, *The Will to Resist*, p. 215.

[125] William F. Felice, *How Do I Save My Honor: War, Moral Integrity, and Principled Resignation* (New York: Rowman and Littlefield, 2009), pp. 126–129.

[126] Quoted in Dahr Jamail, "Ehren Watada: 'Soldiers can Choose to Stop Fighting," http://www.truth-out.org/article/dahr-jamail-ehren-watada-soldiers-can-choose-stop-fighting.

The logic underlying refusal is one of personal responsibility within institutions. The person who resigns or refuses to participate has done so on the view that their participation, even if it only indirectly causes harm, would enable the harm. In this view, it would be, at a minimum, a form of moral negligence to participate by continuing to perform one's assigned roles in such an institution. We know it is difficult for the common soldier to disobey or refuse an order, not least because it feels wrong for a soldier to break the rule and habits of obedience to the chain of command. Commanders are relatively safer than enlisted personnel in refusing commands and in withdrawing from combat altogether. This is not to say that commanders at all levels will feel safe to challenge commands in war or to withdraw their participation in certain operations, but questioning and withdrawal is possible. Thus, to resign a commission in the context of immoral or unlawful acts by that organization is not to behave with negligence toward the military institution, but to behave with moral integrity.

In 2009, in a commencement address at West Point, US Secretary of Defense Robert Gates talked about the courage required of commanders. Gates first addressed courage in the face of personal danger.

> Courage comes in different forms. There is the physical courage of the battlefield, which this institution and this army possess beyond measure. Consider, for example, the story of Lieutenant Nicholas Eslinger, Class of 2007. He was leading his platoon through Samarra, Iraq, when an enemy fighter threw a grenade in their midst. Eslinger jumped on the grenade to shield his men. When the grenade didn't go off, the platoon leader threw it back across the wall. And then it exploded. At the time of this incident, then-Second Lieutenant Eslinger was only 16 months out of West Point. He would later receive the Silver Star.[127]

Gates continued,

> But, in addition to battlefield bravery, there is also moral courage, often harder to find. In business, in universities, in the military, in any big institution, there is a heavy emphasis on teamwork. And, in fact, the higher up you go, the stronger the pressure to smooth off the rough edges, paper over problems, close the proverbial ranks and stay on message. The hardest thing you may ever be called upon to do is stand alone among your peers and superior officers. To stick your neck out after discussion becomes consensus, and consensus ossifies into groupthink.

[127] Robert Gates, "U.S. Military Academy Commencement," 23 May 2009, http://www.defense. gov/Speeches/Speech.aspx?SpeechID=1354.

One of my greatest heroes is George Marshall, whose portrait hangs over my desk in the Pentagon. As I said here last April, Marshall was probably the exemplar of combining unshakeable loyalty with having the courage and integrity to tell superiors things they didn't want to hear— from "Black Jack" Pershing to Franklin Delano Roosevelt. As it turns out, Marshall's integrity and courage were ultimately rewarded professionally. In a perfect world, that should always happen. Sadly, it does not, and I will not pretend there is not risk. But that does not make taking that stand any less necessary for the sake of our Army and our country.[128]

Promoting Moral Courage and Moral Responsibility

As commanders move from the war zone toward headquarters the physical courage required to fight a war diminishes while the necessity for moral courage grows. Commanders should be held, on some level, morally responsible for deliberate acts of killing civilians by their subordinates and for negligence when they could have prevented incidents of large-scale civilian killing. But commanders also need to take more responsibility for ameliorating the conditions that could lead to collateral damage. This responsibility must be taken at three junctures: before war, during war, and after combat.

Specifically, before war, commanders must say whether force can reasonably be expected to achieve the political objectives set by civilian leaders. As Clausewitz noted, some objectives cannot be served by war and, in fact, may be "alien to its nature."[129] Further, before war, commanders must evaluate whether the tools in their arsenal can be used within the law of war. If a weapon cannot, in all probability, be used discriminately, a commander should say so and remove the weapon from the arsenal. But beyond the letter of the law of war—which stresses intention— commanders must evaluate the potential for weapons and rules of engagement to inadvertently kill civilians. To hew to the letter of the law without attention to foreseeable unintended consequences is a form of negligence.

During wars, commanders must fulfill the duties of command to both their own soldiers and to the other side. Specifically, international law is clear that civilians must be respected and protected in war. Commanders, I argued, must do so in several specific ways. First, although there may be great pressure to erase distinctions between combatants and noncombatants, commanders must reinforce that distinction and emphasize the duty to protect civilians. Second, although it is not their primary duty, commanders must work to humanize the civilians of the enemy, or at least work to combat the dehumanization of the "other" that is so often a part

---

[128] Ibid.
[129] Clausewitz, *On War*, p. 88.

of the psychological reality of war. Third, commanders must work to overcome the fatalism about the inevitability of civilian casualties that often develops in war. Fourth, commanders should monitor the effects of rules of engagement, weapons, and tactics on the incidence of civilian killing and on own force protection. Closer monitoring will facilitate timely changes in operations that can save lives. Fifth, commanders should encourage compliance with the laws of war at lower levels and prosecute violations of the laws of war. Finally, commanders should respect their own troops for not only the sake of the troops themselves, but because a lack of respect for one's own soldiers is often passed from combatants to noncombatants.

I also argued that military officers must consider their role not only to be simple obedience to political authority, but also to consist, at times of disagreement with civilian authorities, in protest and withdrawal of participation. The moral courage required to speak out against the use of certain weapons or tactics, to go against the tide in time of war, may feel enormous. It will, at times, actually be enormous. But, the burden of conscience may require less courage if the military organization, political leaders, and the public become more attuned to the necessity for protecting civilians and for robust debate about the cause and conduct of war.

Like individual soldiers, the commander's moral agency is not unconstrained. The constraints on moral agency that come from operating within a military organization, and the imperfect moral agency of military organizations themselves, are described in the following discussion of organizational responsibility for systemic collateral damage.

6

Organizational Responsibility

Military Institutions as Moral Agents

Being confronted only with unjust options is commonly a result of someone's prior wrongdoing.

—Claudia Card, *The Atrocity Paradigm*[1]

When a car doesn't stop, it crosses the trigger line, Marines engage and,
yes, sir there are people inside the car that are killed that have nothing to
do with it.

— Testimony of Sergeant Major E. T. Sax[2]

The situations of war and the institutions created during war... change
the normal moral situation. This is mainly because the circumstances of
war make all of us different people than we would be otherwise.

—Larry May, *War Crimes and Just War*[3]

Operation Together, Afghanistan 2010

In February 2010, the United States and other NATO ISAF forces in Helmand
Province, Afghanistan, opened a much anticipated and widely announced offensive, called "Operation Moshtarak" (translated "Together") against the Taliban
in Marjah and Nad Ali, Afghanistan. The assault was a joint effort of 15,000 US,
British, and Afghan forces to root out and kill an estimated 400 to 1,000 militant

---

[1] Claudia Card, *The Atrocity Paradigm: A Theory of Evil* (Oxford: Oxford University Press, 2002), p. 18.

[2] Testimony of Sergeant Major E. T. Sax, from interview transcript, published 14 December 2011, http://www.nytimes.com/interactive/2011/12/15/world/middleeast/haditha-selected-documents.html?ref=middleeast#document/p1/a41194.

[3] Larry May, *War Crimes and Just War* (Cambridge: Cambridge University Press, 2007), p. 11.

fighters in the area. It was, at the time, the largest operation that the United States had undertaken in Afghanistan since the 2001 invasion. Two vignettes from that period illustrate the ways that military organizations are seen to have moral agency and take moral responsibility. In the first vignette, the US military was blamed for US deaths; and in the second, the US military took responsibility for Afghan deaths.

By the time Operation Moshtarak began, a number of observers had already argued that the US military was taking unwarranted risks with the lives of US soldiers by instituting restrictive rules of engagement. Specifically, critics argued that General Stanley McChrystal's June 2009 order that close air support could only be used when troops were in danger of being overrun meant that the United States was fighting with one hand behind its back. For example, in an op-ed published on 18 February 2010 in the *New York Times*, the intelligence analyst Lara M. Dadkhah stated that "air support to American and Afghan forces has been all but grounded by concerns about civilian casualties." Dadkhah argued that while US forces had nearly doubled from 2008 to early 2010, "close air support sorties, which in Afghanistan are almost always unplanned and in aid of troops on the ground who are under intense fire, increased by just 27 percent during that time period."[4]

And the United States did take a greater number of casualties during February and March 2010, the operation's peak period of fighting, when compared to previous periods of the war. More would die, but the US Marines took what seemed like many casualties in a short period, with eight Marines killed in combat from 18 to 21 February. In the entire month of February 2010, twenty-nine US soldiers were killed and in March, twenty-two US soldiers were killed. In the same months in the previous year, February and March 2009, respectively, when operations were less intense, fifteen and eleven US soldiers were killed. In June 2009, before the new tactical directive took effect, twenty US soldiers were killed in action or died of wounds.[5]

Still, the claim that US forces were fighting without adequate air support, under General McChrystal's population centric counterinsurgency doctrine and the

---

[4] Lara M. Dadkhah, "Empty Skies Over Afghanistan," *New York Times*, 18 February 2010, p. A27. There were civilians killed early in the offensive by ground operations. For instance, two artillery rockets, which "veered 300 yards (meters) off target and blasted a house," killed twelve civilians. CBS/AP, "Civilian Deaths Mar Marjah Offensive," CBS News, 14 February 2010, http://www.cbsnews.com/stories/2010/02/14/world/main6208526.shtml. The *Christian Science Monitor* reports that three other civilians were killed—two in escalation of force incidents, and one in crossfire in the operation a few days later. Kristen Chick, "Civilian Deaths Mounting in Marjah Offensive," *Christian Science Monitor*, 16 February 2011, http://www.csmonitor.com/World/terrorism-security/2010/0216/Civilian-deaths-mounting-in-Marjah-offensive. On 23 February 2010, the Afghanistan Independent Human Rights Commission reported sixty-three civilians killed in the operation, the majority by pro-government forces. Afghanistan Independent Human Rights Commission, Press Release, "63 Civilians Killed in Afghanistan in the Last Two Weeks," 23 February 2010.

[5] Data from the Department of Defense, "US Military Casualties, Operation Enduring Freedom, by Month," http://siadapp.dmdc.osd.mil/personnel/CASUALTY/castop.htm. These are numbers for killed inaction or died of wounds.

June 2009 tactical directive restricting the use of airpower, was perhaps exaggerated. Forces that felt under threat could and did call in air support. They did so, for instance, on 21 February 2010, when US Special Operations forces were tracking insurgents in Uruzgan Province just north of Helmand Province and west of Kabul, an area essentially dominated by the Taliban. The US objective was to engage insurgents in Khod, a village known as an insurgent stronghold. Some miles away, US remotely piloted surveillance aircraft, Predator drones, spotted three vehicles—a pick-up truck and two other vehicles—traveling by road in what appeared to be a path that could allow them to support the insurgents. The three vehicles were tracked for about 3 1/2 hours by the drone aircraft operators based in Nevada who reported the location and composition of the "convoy" to local US commanders. When they were initially observed, the vehicles were about 5 km from the US forces. The US ground force commander thought that the vehicles could be engaged in a flanking maneuver. After several hours the commander decided the threat from the "convoy" to US forces was imminent and ordered a Kiowa helicopter using Hellfire missiles and rockets, to attack the convoy. The US attack occurred when the convoy was some 12 km away from US forces.[6]

When the helicopter personnel noted bright clothing after the initial salvo, they halted the attack. In the end, twenty-three people were killed and twelve were injured. All were apparently civilians. The Afghan government called the strike, "unjustifiable." The NATO commander in Afghanistan, US General McChrystal immediately apologized for injuring and killing civilians.[7] Condolence payments were made to the families of those killed and medical care was provided to eight men, one woman, and three children.[8]

Two major US investigations of the Uruzgan incident, the first released in May 2010, and the second in September 2010, outlined the events and highlighted problems. The first US report, a US Army investigation headed by Major General Timothy McHale, blamed the incident on "inaccurate and unprofessional reporting by the Predator crew." McHale also found that the "tragic loss of life was compounded by a failure of the commands involved to timely report the incident."[9] The key failure in reporting that led to the killing itself was in the communication from

---

[6] The dead and wounded of Khod appear in the ISAF civilian casualty database released in 2011.

[7] Associated Press, "General McChrystal Apologizes to Afghans," *Washington Post*, 23 February 2010, http://www.washingtonpost.com/wp-dyn/content/video/2010/02/23/VI2010022302514.html.

[8] BBC, "Afghanistan Condemns Deadly NATO Airstrike in Uruzgan," BBC News, 22 February, 2010, http://news.bbc.co.uk/2/hi/8528715.stm. NATO, "Afghanistan: U.S. Releases Uruzgan Investigation Findings," *Relief Web*, 28 May 2010, http://www.reliefweb.int/rw/rwb.nsf/db900SID/MUMA-85X7WG?OpenDocument.

[9] Major General Timothy McHale, "Executive Summary for AR 15-6 Investigation, 21 February 2010 CIVCAS Incident in Uruzgan Province," Memorandum for Commander, United States Forces-Afghanistan/International Security Assistance Force, Afghanistan, Headquarters, United States Forces Afghanistan, Kabul USFOR-A DCDR-S. Unclassified and redacted.

Nevada about just who was in the group of vehicles. Immediately upon receipt of the first investigation McChrystal ordered changes in training and procedures both inside and outside Afghanistan.

Communication was also highlighted in the later Air Force investigation. Air Force General Robert Otto noted that, "the Predator crew's faulty communication clouded the picture on adolescents and allowed them to be transformed into military aged males."[10] Indeed, both the Army and Air Force investigations note that film from the Predator showed both women and children were present, but those facts were not communicated to the ground force commander. The communication errors were cumulative and "contributed to Kirk 97 downgrading the initial confirmed call of *children* to *possible children*." Specifically, the Air Force report notes that, "*adolescents* became *teenagers* and *teenagers* became *military aged males*." At the same time that positive reporting of the presence of children was transformed into reports of possible children, reports of "possible" weapons were transformed into reports that weapons had been identified. Ultimately, the report found that "the lack of procedures, doctrine, and training were causal factors in this incident."[11] The Air Force investigation also showed that there was confusion between the ground forces in Afghanistan and the crew at Creech Air Force Base in Nevada about roles and responsibilities.

Several points about this incident and the responses to it bear underscoring. First, a key finding of the investigations was that "the Ground Force Commander decided to engage the convoy when it was not an immediate threat."[12] Indeed, despite the Ground Force Commander's express concerns of an immediate threat, there was no evidence of threat to the US forces. The drone operators had not reported that the group of vehicles was moving toward the US forces. Rather, the drone operators reported that at the time the civilians were attacked, the three vehicles had been moving away from US forces and were then 12 km from US forces.[13]

Second, attention to individual failures overshadowed the emphasis on procedures, doctrine, and training, even though the majority of the findings and the recommendations in the US military investigations, and in the orders by General Stanley McChrystal that followed the Army investigation, focused on organizational problems and responses. Typically, although the news accounts themselves were sometimes more nuanced, headlines such as, "Operators of Drones are Faulted

---

[10] Robert P. Otto, "Executive Summary, Uruzghan Province CIVCAS Incident, 21 February 2010," Commander Directed Investigation, Creech Air Force Base, Nevada. Released 10 September 2010. Julian Barnes, "Air Force Report Faults Crew in Afghan Strike Killing 23 Civilians," *Wall Street Journal*, 11 September 2010; Christopher Drew, "Study Cites Drone Crew in Attack on Afghans," 11 September 2010, *New York Times*, p. A6.

[11] Otto, "Executive Summary, Uruzghan Province CIVCAS Incident."

[12] Ibid.

[13] Robert P. Otto, "Statement of Opinion," paragraphs C(5) and D, declassified with Otto, "Executive Summary, Uruzghan Province CIVCAS Incident."

in Afghan Deaths," in the *New York Times,* and "Air Force Report Faults Crew in Afghan Strike Killing 23 Civilians," in the *Wall Street Journal* focused on the drone crew errors.[14] In the Uruzgan incident, it is notable that nowhere in the early press accounts or in the later unclassified sections of the Army and Air Force reports were the officers involved in the 21 February attack named. Yet, it is no wonder that the media focus is on individuals; four officers were reprimanded for their role in the incident.[15] Because there was no finding of threat, there were potentially violations of law for which individuals might be held to account.

Third, the US response illustrates a change in military attitudes toward noncombatant death. Just a few months earlier, when similar incidents occurred, it was common practice to deny any civilian death or injury, or to minimize the harm. In this case, the apology was immediate, the investigations were prompt, and there was no projection of an air of fatalism about harm to civilians. Rather, the US military's organizational reaction was one of taking responsibility. As Marc Garlasco, who worked on high-value targeting for the US Joint Chiefs of Staff during the early months of 2003, said, "When I was picking targets for the Iraq invasion as chief of high-value targeting for the Pentagon, collateral damage was a side issue. We treated civilian deaths like a fire drill: When they happened, it was seen as a media problem to be dealt with, not a sign we might need to change our procedures." Garlasco believes that a change in US attitudes and procedures led to decreased killing in Afghanistan in 2009 and 2010. "Today, however, protecting civilians is taken as seriously as killing the target. When civilians are killed, Afghanistan commanding Gen. Stanley McChrystal apologizes on Afghan national television and the military investigates. Casualties in this latest offensive in Marja[h] [in early 2010] were down nearly 30 percent from previous operations as a result."[16] In this sense, the US military's implicit understanding of itself as a moral agent—and its assumption of the responsibilities of moral agency—perhaps surprisingly, exceeds the academic, legal, and wider social and political understanding of moral responsibility in war. What changed was not the foreseeability of harm (it was foreseen in 2003 as well as later) but the sense of responsibility for it. The military took responsibility, the deaths were acknowledged, and tactical changes were made in the war zone.

And finally, during "Operation Moshtarak," both the organization and the news media directed more of their resources to understanding the then more novel problem of civilian killing by drone strikes, while the more common and perhaps

---

[14] Dexter Filkins, "Operators of Drones are Faulted in Afghan Deaths," *New York Times,* 30 May 2010, p. A6; Barnes, "Air Force Report Faults Crew in Afghan Strike Killing 23 Civilians"; Drew, "Study Cites Drone Crew in Attack on Afghans."

[15] Robert H. Reid, Associated Press, "Investigation Faults Crew in Deadly February Air Strike," *Marine Times,* 1 June 2010.

[16] Marc Garlasco, "How to Cut Collateral Damage in Afghanistan," *Foreign Policy,* 3 March 2010, http://www.foreignpolicy.com/articles/2010/03/03/how_to_cut_collateral_damage_in_afghanistan?page=0,1.

routine civilian deaths caused by other means were noted, but not as extensively investigated. The toll of civilian death in southern Afghanistan in February and March 2010, according to the NATO ISAF database, was fifty-two civilians killed and sixty wounded in the Southern Region. The ISAF database tracked deaths by Close Air Support and Close Combat Air operations, escalation of force incidents at checkpoints, direct and indirect ground force fire, and road traffic accidents.[17] While the single drone incident killed twenty-three civilians, according to the database, the majority killed and wounded by ISAF operations in February and March were harmed in other ways.[18] For example, on 14 February 2010, NATO ISAF fired two rockets at insurgents in the town of Nad Ali that according to a NATO spokesman landed 300 meters off their target, and destroyed a house containing civilians. Twelve civilians were killed. In response, General McChrystal said, "We deeply regret this tragic loss of life. It is regrettable that in the course of our joint efforts, innocent lives were lost."[19]

Responsibility at My Lai

The focus of moral blame after the March 1968 My Lai massacre in Vietnam was on individual perpetrators, most notably Lieutenant William Calley and a few others. Yet even in this case, there was the question of how high in the chain of command to place responsibility, and whether and how the military, as an organization, was responsible for civilian killing and may need to change. So, in his analysis of My Lai, Michael Walzer focuses on individual commanders who were higher in the chain of command than the primary perpetrators. "If we are to fully assign blame for the [My Lai] massacre, then, there are a large number of officers whom we would have to condemn. I cannot put together a list here, and I doubt that all of them could have been or ought to have been legally charged and tried." Walzer is clear: "The officers are presumptively guilty."[20]

My Lai was also understood as symptomatic of a larger problem. For example, Walzer suggested that "the strategy of the American war in Vietnam...tended to put civilians at risk in unacceptable ways, and ordinary soldiers could hardly ignore

---

[17] International Security Assistance Force (ISAF), CIVCAS, 13 January 2011; as referred to in J. Bohannon, "Counting the Dead in Afghanistan," *Science* 331 (11 March 2011): 1256.

[18] ISAF Close Combat air operations killed twenty-three and wounded twenty civilians total in February and March 2010 according to the ISAF database.

[19] Quoted in Declan Walsh and Stephen Bates, "NATO Rockets Kill 12 Afghan Civilians," *The Guardian*, 14 February 2010, http://www.guardian.co.uk/world/2010/feb/14/nato-rockets-kill-afghan-civilians.

[20] Michael Walzer, *Just and Unjust Wars: A Moral Argument with Historical Illustrations* (New York: Basic Books, 1977), p. 322.

the implications of that strategy."[21] When US Army Captain Robert Johnson testified in Congress in 1971, he first identified higher-ranking officers and civilians for the My Lai massacre. "If we are going to prosecute Lieutenant Calley, then I think we ought to prosecute a number of generals, and a number of civilians." But then Johnson said,

> I think Lieutenant Calley should be freed and that a massive investigation into the institutional causes that in my judgment led to My Lai is the only solution. Retribution is no answer. Again the idea of guilt, there were so many GIs that served in Vietnam, that they were guilty on their part is kind of absurd because they never thought about guilt, anything like that. They just did what they were told in Vietnam, and they followed the policy set at the highest level.[22]

Johnson is thus pointing also to political responsibility for My Lai.

Captain Johnson's exchange at the hearing with member of Congress Bella Abzug began with Abzug asking about the aims of the war itself: "Many people believe that the nature of the war in Vietnam itself is war against the people of Vietnam." Abzug then asks Johnson about his individual moral responsibility.

> Mrs. [Bella] Abzug: Within the acts of individuals, there are moral judgments that are made. . . . I wonder if you, in the course of your service, made any moral judgment to kill innocent children, women, old men, as did Lieutenant Calley?
>
> Mr. Johnson: My hands are clean, you see, because I had a radio and could call in napalm strikes.
>
> Mrs. Abzug: You mean you instructed other people to do it?
>
> Mr. Johnson: I just called in air artillery strikes and they did it. That was part of the policy.
>
> Mrs. Abzug: You see, I am not in complete agreement with you, I am not in agreement with you. I think that we all know that those responsible for killing innocent civilians probably go up very high on the ladder of the chain of command, but in the testimony and in the activity of men in the Army are those who made a moral judgment to kill innocent victims, and those who made a moral judgment not to, and I don't quite understand whether you treat all acts or not all acts the same or whether you are suggesting that we do apparently?. . .

[21] Ibid.

[22] Citizen's Commission of Inquiry, ed., *The Dellums Committee Hearings on War Crimes in Vietnam: An Inquiry into Command Responsibility in Southeast Asia* (New York: Vintage, 1972), p. 54.

Mr. Johnson: I think, given the framework of genocide in Indochina, where we have killed millions of Vietnamese and there are five million refugees, it is somewhat absurd to focus on the guilt of any particular individual. When talks about guilt and innocence, it must be from a kind of moral civil righteous position, perhaps with a lack of understanding of the atmosphere that exists, the moral frame of reference that exists in Vietnam, and that if one can say waste dinks, there no longer is a moral frame of reference, there no longer is a moral judgment.

. . .

I see Lieutenant Calley as the ultimate institutional victim in this country, the man thought the whole methodology hook, line and sinker—the man who believed that the only good gook was a dead gook.[23]

Captain Johnson's reply to Abzug suggests just how an individual can feel and be constrained in their individual agency by a wider moral context: "that if one can say waste dinks, there no longer is a moral frame of reference, there no longer is a moral judgment." Johnson moves to an implicit articulation of organizational responsibility and suggests a powerful organizational frame, where the "only good gook was a dead gook." There was also, in Johnson's response to Abzug, ambivalence about his own role: he did not have blood on his hands as someone who ordered strikes because of the moral "frame of reference" he operated in while stationed in Vietnam.

Johnson said that he did not favor war crimes trials for top US generals because "We would learn nothing from it. Again, we would be focusing on the guilt of [commanding General] Westmoreland. Westmoreland doesn't know what guilt means. Westmoreland is in to killing Communists and accomplishing his mission and getting a lot of medals. He didn't say to himself it is wrong to saturation bomb these people. . . . His framework was simply, it is right to win this war, it is wrong to lose it. That is all."[24] Thus, Captain

---

[23] Ibid., pp. 55–57.

[24] Ibid., p. 57. Lt. John Kerry, in testimony to the Senate Foreign Relations Committee on 22 April 1971, said in response to a question about Lt. Calley from Senator Claiborne Pell,

My feeling, Senator, on Lieutenant Calley is what he did quite obviously was a horrible, horrible, horrible thing and I have no bone to pick with the fact that he was prosecuted. But I think that in this question you have to separate guilt from responsibility, and I think clearly the responsibility for what has happened there lies elsewhere.

I think it lies with the men who designed free fire zones. I think it lies with the men who encouraged body counts. I think it lies in large part with this country, which allows a young child before he reaches the age of 14 to see 12,500 deaths on television, which glorifies the John Wayne syndrome, which puts out fighting man comic books on the stands, which allows us in training to do calisthenics to four counts, on the fourth count of which we stand up and shout "kill" in unison, which has posters in barracks in this country with a crucified Vietnamese, blood on him, and underneath it says "kill the gook," and I think that clearly the responsibility for all of this is what has produced this horrible aberration.

Johnson's exchange with Abzug suggests that it may help to approach the issues of moral responsibility by stepping back from specific incidents of deliberate or inadvertent killing within wars to think about the nature of military institutions and of the organization of war, how the moral frame of reference is created and how it operates to shape and constrain individual agency. Johnson's analysis suggests that the moral responsibility for both systemic collateral damage and deliberate atrocity is rooted in organizations and political institutions.

The observers of My Lai were struggling with this question: How shall we understand the moral responsibility for atrocity? Walzer's analysis of My Lai and Johnson's testimony go back and forth between a focus on individual responsibility, and a sense that something larger is at work, illustrating both the embeddedness of the framework of individual responsibility and the comparative lack of a framework for understanding institutional and political responsibility. As Walzer and others noted—My Lai was an extreme outcome of a routine practice—clearing villages where guerillas were known, or thought to be, sheltering. There were rules to be followed before attacking a village, but sometimes the rules were not followed. Walzer says, "None of this, of course, would reflect on the value of the rules themselves, unless the ineffectiveness were somehow intrinsic to them or to the situation in which they were applied. This was clearly the case in Vietnam."[25]

Some believed that the doctrine was not the problem: the issue was adherence to the rules. A message from a senior officer in Vietnam in 1966 emphasized the lack of adherence to the rules.

> Another potentially serious trend reflected in recent reports pertains to disparaging comments concerning restraints on application of firepower. Comments such as "the only good village is a burned village," are indicative of the trend. Hence again, renewed command emphasis on troop indoctrination is necessary to insure that newly arrive [sic] personnel in particular are thoroughly conversant with need for minimizing noncombatant battle casualties, and understand the rationale behind the current instructions on the subject.[26]

> Now, I think if you are going to try Lieutenant Calley then you must at the same time, if this country is going to demand respect for the law, you must at the same time try all those other people who have responsibility, and any aversion that we may have to the verdict as veterans is not to say that Calley should be freed, not to say that he is innocent, but to say that you can't just take him alone, and that would be my response to that. http://www.wintersoldier.com/index. php?topic=Testimony.

[25] Walzer, *Just and Unjust Wars*, p. 190.
[26] Quoted in Mark Martins, "Rules of Engagement for Land Forces: A Matter of Training, Not Lawyering," *Military Law Review*, vol. 143, no. 1 (Winter 1994): 1–160, 47n.

Indeed, only 29 percent of US Army generals who served in Vietnam "felt that the ROE were well understood prior to the My Lai massacre, and only 19 percent claimed that they were carefully adhered to."[27] Prosecutions or discipline for violations of the ROE in Vietnam were rare.[28]

But the rules of engagement and doctrine were contradictory in Vietnam: avoid harming civilians, yet clear entire areas and kill the enemy. US Army doctrine, which emphasized firepower and maneuver to clear areas of resistance quickly while minimizing risk to US soldiers, when correctly applied, was almost guaranteed to produce a great deal of civilian death. Discrimination was not emphasized, nor could it be. As Andrew Krepinevich notes, "by placing the [enemy] body count above population security in its list of priorities, the Army provided the incentive for its commanders to shoot first and worry about the hearts and minds later."[29] Indeed, US Army Chief of Staff, General Harold Johnson, told Krepinevich in an interview that firepower was used "on a relatively random basis" and that the United States "just sort of devastated the countryside."[30]

What Organizations Add

If Napoleon Bonaparte could still master and coordinate the operations of many thousands of men at the turn of the nineteenth century, in the two centuries since his drive to control all of Europe the requirements of logistics for mass armies, the increased complexity and destructiveness of weapons, and the mobilization of industrial capacity for war has come to require increased specialization and coordination. Organization (communication, the mobilization of material resources, training, and the division of labor), always important for military success, has become essential.

Yet, the dominant framework for understanding responsibility focuses on individuals and intentional actions. As Mark Osiel argues, "The criminal law assumes a world of unencumbered individuals, independently interacting."[31] Although it is meaningful to examine individual moral agency and responsibility, individual capacities to do both good and ill are enabled, enhanced, and constrained by the features of organizations: individual moral agency cannot be understood outside the institutional contexts within which individuals act. While individuals certainly pull the triggers or drop the bombs, the underlying causes of a large portion of collateral damage deaths and injuries may lie at the organizational level.

[27] Andrew F. Krepinevich, *The Army in Vietnam* (Baltimore: Johns Hopkins, 1986), p. 199.

[28] Krepinevich, *The Army in Vietnam*, and Martins, "Rules of Engagement for Land Forces," p. 67.

[29] Krepinevich, *The Army in Vietnam*, pp. 198–199.

[30] General Johnson, quoted in Krepinevich, *The Army in Vietnam*, p. 199.

[31] Mark Osiel, *Making Sense of Mass Atrocities* (Cambridge: Cambridge University Press, 2009), p. 187.

The importance of organization and organizations is certainly not unique to war. Humans form and join organizations to achieve a significant goal because organizations can almost always do more than a single individual, or many uncoordinated individuals. As Kay Mathiesen suggests,

> Our lives are intertwined with and our agency is expressed through social groups. Aside from whatever comfort or enjoyment we get from being with and working together with other human beings, social groups allow us to extend our agency. We can do together things that we could never do alone. Even many of the activities we consider most individual are made possible by the heavy lifting of social groups.[32]

Organizations are not simply an aggregation or magnification of individual power and material resources. They are also more than social groups. Organizations are the coordinated action of many individuals, bound together by their knowledge of particular beliefs and structured routines. Organizations are *collective* or *corporate moral agents* in the sense that they have the capacity to act, albeit under constraints, and in the sense they have the capacity to deliberate about both the ends and the means of action.

In the most superficial sense, military organizations constrain individual action simply because individual soldiers follow orders. Yet, the autonomy of individual soldiers in a chain of command, and even the autonomy of the military itself, is limited; individual soldiers are not permitted to question orders unless those orders are patently unlawful. But, much more subtly, the preparation for and waging of war is enabled and enacted by institutions. The fact of individual obedience is an artifact of processes of military socialization for the habit of (normally) unquestioned rule following. Further, military organizations coordinate action and institutionalize the knowledge (about tactics and strategies) necessary to fight effectively and the practices that will allow the deployment of force. An individual might change their behavior, but the organization—the attitudes and beliefs of majority of its members, the standard operating procedures of the institution, and the resources and tools available for action—reduces the effectiveness of individual action unless it is in concert with the organization.

As Major Mark Martins argued, "Whether deployed as peacekeepers, counterinsurgents, peace enforcers, or conventional warriors, United States ground troops sometimes make poor decisions about whether to fire their weapons. Far from justifying criticism of individual soldiers at the trigger, this fact provides the proper focus for systemic improvements."[33] Individual agency is constituted and constrained by

---

[32] Kay Mathiesen, "We're All in This Together: Responsibility of Collective Agents and Their Members," in Peter A. French and Howard K. Wettstein, eds., *Midwest Studies in Philosophy*, Volume 30: *Shared Intentions and Collective Responsibility* (Boston: Blackwell, 2006), pp. 240–255, 240.

[33] Martins, "Rules of Engagement for Land Forces," p. 10.

organizational structures and choices made at the collective level. The structure of prior policy choices to an important extent (e.g., the choice of purchasing one weapon over another, whether to deploy that weapon, which strategies to use) constitutes and constrains individual human agency. And, one of the most important organizational effects results from the institutionalization of rules of engagement. "The unpredictability of armed engagements and the inherent cognitive limitations of humans under stress define the role ROE [rules of engagement] can play in guiding individual soldiers toward appropriate decisions about when to fire. That role, although potentially decisive, is extremely narrow and must play itself out mostly before the shooting starts. For when the shooting starts, soldiers follow those principles that repetitive or potent experiences have etched into their minds."[34]

I argue that it is necessary to rethink many of the dominant assumptions about individual agency, intention, the conduct of war, and the function and capacities of organizations in order to fully comprehend the causes of collateral damage in war. Military organizations, which procure the weapons that increase the chance of indiscriminate killing, or which approve strategies or rules of engagement that can be foreseen to cause great civilian harm, and which shape the moral atmosphere and frames of reference for soldiers, are organizationally responsible for setting up the conditions for the killing of innocents or for protecting them. It is perhaps ironic, though not surprising, that military organizations can and often do monitor and hold individual soldiers to account for violations of the laws of war. The organization can be more or less well structured to prevent deliberate violations of the law and to identify patterns of cause and effect that result in significant unintended consequences. When individual or small group violations of the law of war occur, military organizations should and very often do discipline soldiers and prosecute them as is appropriate to the particular case. Until recently, however, the military has been less adept at seeing its own role in creating the conditions for systemic collateral damage killing.

Systemic collateral damage killings are not intended and programmatic; they are unintended albeit often foreseeable and sometimes foreseen. These are systemically produced outcomes in the sense that they result not so much from individuals exercising their individual human agency, but are a consequence of actions taken under the constraints of a larger social structure. In the situation of systemic collateral damage, a system-wide, organizational, remedy is required. Military organizations must pay greater attention to how their policies can lead to large-scale, albeit inadvertent harm to civilians. The wars in Afghanistan and Iraq have pushed the Army and the Air Force in that direction and led to increased institutionalization of civilian casualty mitigation efforts. The incidents described above from Operation Moshtarak illustrate how the US military, as an organization, either assigned responsibility or

---

[34] Ibid., p. 6.

took responsibility for increased risk to US soldiers and unintended civilian deaths. The excusing power of intention—no one wanted to increase the risk to US soldiers or to kill civilians—was diminished in comparison to the foreseeability of harm and the ability to take greater precautions. In other words, the foreseeability of harm began to matter more to the calculations of military necessity and proportionality.

This change in perspective was gradually institutionalized—at first in the field, in tactical directives—and increasingly, at the organizational level from the mid-2000s on, in doctrine. By mid-2012, these changes were explicitly codified in a US Army tactical manual.[35] In changing its rules, doctrine, and training, from bottom to top, the US military acts as an organization to assume moral responsibility for collateral damage through the institutionalization of practices to identify and reduce likely harm. Practices of collateral damage estimation and mitigation illustrate the ways that the US military has already acted as an imperfect moral agent. Thus, this chapter is as much about how the US military learned about collateral damage and changed its behavior in the post- 9/11 wars (and whether this learning is slow or fast depends on one's perspective) as it is about questions of moral responsibility.

Characteristic Features of Organizations

Militaries are often said to be a paradigm of efficient and effective organizations, with enormous resources, well articulated lines of authority, and an emphasis on routine and training. Perhaps only in matters of procurement—where equipment from toilet seats, to hammers, to jet aircraft can be both overpriced and flawed—does the military have a reputation for inefficiency and waste. Procurement aside, as I argue here, military organizations are moral agents with a primary moral responsibility that is both related to, and different from, the responsibility of individual soldiers and commanders for two reasons, both having to do with the emergent structural properties of this complex bureaucracy.[36]

First, and most simply, the military is a complex bureaucracy: the chain of beliefs and actions is both so long and complex that it is often difficult to isolate particular individuals who could be held responsible for either causing or identifying the problem of systemic collateral damage, and because no single individual can fix the problem. This first emergent property of bureaucracy—the difficulty for individuals to make anything happen by themselves—yields what has been called the problem of "many hands." If many hands make light work, it also makes for diffuse

---

[35] Department of the Army, *Civilian Casualty Mitigation*, Army Tactics, Techniques, and Procedures, No. 3-37.31 (Washington, DC: Department of the Army, 18 July 2012).

[36] My phrase on "emergent structural properties" focuses on intended and unintended structural and procedural consequences of the institutionalization of organizational knowledge. I am not arguing that organizations have metaphysical properties.

moral responsibility. As much as we might want in every case to say that a particular individual has sole responsibility for an outcome, it is often the case that many are involved and those individuals are working under the constraints of their roles and resources.

The second emergent property of complex organizations is the capacity to make decisions and act, which constitutes what I call here imperfect moral agency. In other words, organizations, such as military forces, should be considered imperfect moral agents because their organizational structures enable them to deliberate and act in ways that are analogous to individual moral agents. It is possible to understand some of the intended, and unintended, outcomes of organizational activities, and to appropriately assign moral responsibility for the actions of organizations, by considering organizations as imperfect moral agents.[37] Dennis Thompson alludes to such a structural cause which mitigates individual responsibility for harm when he says, "perhaps more common than orders from a superior, however implicit, is that of various practices and procedures established by other officials who may not be identifiable, or, for that matter, may no longer be alive. Such practices circumscribe an officials' range of choices, and thus mitigate his or her responsibility."[38]

On the one hand, military organizations may come to accept the outcome of foreseen proportionality/double effect collateral damage as the "cost of doing business." On the other hand, some foreseeable outcomes, in this case, systemic collateral damage remain unforeseen because organizational beliefs and practices make it difficult to conduct the analysis or understand the information that would alert actors to likely outcomes.

How is it that the military organizations' own framework for understanding causal responsibility began to shift to include, at least potentially, an understanding of organizational responsibility? Does that causal responsibility extend to moral responsibility? To make a convincing argument about how it is that military

[37] The standard way of understanding social outcomes—as finding the causal weight of individual agents versus social structures—is thus reformulated here. Organizations should be understood as both collective agents/actors and structures that constrain individual agents For reasons of space, I will not rehearse the complex arguments about whether organizations are "persons." Rather, while I will not argue that organizations are persons (with intentions and so on), it is analytically and practically useful to understand the ways that organizations, as imperfect moral agents, produce both intended and unintended outcomes that constrain and enable individual agents. I will also not suggest whether and how collectives should be found legally liable and punishable. To ascribe guilt to organizations and then to suggest that the organization should be punished creates two problems. First, a focus on punishment could distract from the analysis of how unintended harm is produced and how it might be ameliorated at the organizational level. And second it violates an important principle of discriminating between those who are causally responsible and those who are not. We need to keep individual responsibility in the frame at the same time as we think about organizational responsibility.

[38] Dennis F. Thompson, "Moral Responsibility of Public of Public Officials: The Problem of Many Hands," *American Political Science Review*, vol. 74, no. 4 (December 1980): 905–916, 913.

organizations should be considered imperfect moral agents, and should thus be understood as having primary moral responsibility for collateral damage, I must show how the concepts of moral agency and moral responsibility can be applied to organizations. Complex collectives—organizations and institutions—are more than a collection of individuals independently moving in the same direction for private reasons to the extent that their members communicate and coordinate their action to achieve specific outcomes. Complex organizations thus have emergent properties that shape, enable, and constrain the options of individual actors, while they also shape, enable, and limit both the intended and unintended effects of the organization's actions.

Organizational Frames and Institutionalization

How is it that military organizations, or any organization for that matter, can simultaneously harness and magnify individual power and yet, with such potentially enormous capacity to gather information and act, miss or misread important pieces of information, or act to produce consequences counter to the intentions and interests of the organization? Part of the answer lies in understanding how large systems "think"—how organizations, or people within certain scientific or practical disciplines, make sense of the world they are in and organize their actions.[39]

Sociologist Lynn Eden illuminates the causes of the paradoxical nature of organizational power through the identification of what she calls "organizational frames." Eden shows how, in the years after World War II, the relevant actors—nuclear scientists, warriors, and ultimately, military organizations within the United States—understood the effects of nuclear weapons and then structured the nuclear arsenal according to that understanding. These frames can be more or less accurate. Eden

---

[39] Much of the early work on organizational learning focused on how science produced knowledge. But, while much of that literature is relevant, military organizations are more and different than a scientific community operating from within paradigms or epistemes. The philosopher of science Thomas Kuhn noticed that scientific communities operate within paradigms—theoretical commonplaces and procedures that helped them explore complex phenomena and make sense of it. The historian Michel Foucault saw that scientists understood the world and made sense of it within what he called an episteme, or way of thinking that allowed some pieces of information in and some arguments to be considered valid, and others not. See Thomas Kuhn, *The Structure of Scientific Revolutions* (Chicago: University of Chicago Press, 1962); Michel Foucault, *The Order of Things: An Archaeology of the Human Sciences* (New York: Vintage, 1973). Others have built on this way of understanding the production of knowledge in science—as shaped by both prior beliefs and linked to organizational habits and interests—to explore how scientific organizations "think" and act to make science and technology or influence policy related to scientific questions. See, for instance: Karin Knorr Cetina, *Epistemic Cultures: How the Sciences Make Knowledge* (Cambridge, MA: Harvard University Press, 1999); Karin T. Litfin, *Ozone Discourses: Science and Politics in Global Environmental Cooperation* (New York: Columbia University Press, 1994).

demonstrates that what became the dominant understanding of nuclear weapons effects (that blast effects were both more powerful and more predictable than the thermal or fire effects) was inaccurate and yet came to be the taken for granted, the "organizational, 'common sense'" that itself structured subsequent organizational learning and understanding.[40]

Eden defines organizational frames as "what counts as a problem, how problems are represented, the strategies to be used to solve those problems, and the constraints and requirements placed on possible solutions."[41] Organizational frames rest on and are constructed with pre-existing beliefs, and then those beliefs are used to create new beliefs and knowledge. In other words, organizational frames can be powerful lenses—like corrective eyeglasses, they can clarify what was once a vast fuzzy landscape; or like a microscope they may focus our attention on minutia; or like binoculars or a telescope, organizational frames may help their users see ahead. But no matter whether they are functioning as corrective lenses, microscopes, or binoculars, organizational frames are always more or less also working as blinders and railway tracks, directing attention and steering their users toward end points and both intended and unintended consequences. Eden argues that "as those in organizations engage in problem solving, they allocate organizational attention and resources, develop and draw on expertise inside and outside the organization, and in general build organizational capacity to solve certain problems but not others."[42]

Eden also emphasizes "organizational knowledge." She shows that the organizational knowledge which shaped decisions about nuclear weapons was not of the actual physical world, but the scientists' socially constructed understanding of nuclear weapons. This knowledge consisted of "representations of the world taken by actors as reliable information." In this way, organizational knowledge is both "*explicit knowledge*—what actors think they know about the world—and *tacit knowledge*—what actors simply assume or take for granted about the world."[43]

> By *organizational knowledge*, I mean representations of the world that are articulated or assumed at the organizational level. This is the knowledge that someone first coming into an organization must be cognizant of and appear to accept if he or she wants to be credible and effective within the organization. Individual actors need not accept, or fully accept,

---

[40] Lynn Eden, *Whole World on Fire: Organizations, Knowledge, and Nuclear Weapons Devastation* (Ithaca, NY: Cornell University Press, 2004), pp. 50–51. Eden's work also has implications for the United States' understanding of the effects of nuclear weapons on noncombatants that I do not have the space to explore here.

[41] Ibid., p. 50.

[42] Ibid.

[43] Ibid.

organizational knowledge for it to exert an overriding influence on organizational action.[44]

Organizational knowledge is evident throughout the military's understanding of civilian casualties and operational routines for dealing with the problem of civilian casualties. For example, the military's understanding of conventional weapons' effects is relevant for understanding the foreseeable production of civilian casualties, as I show below. Moreover, organizational knowledge evolves—sometimes because of dramatic instances that disconfirm previously taken for granted assumptions, or sometimes because a visionary within the organization persuades others that it is time to change.

I argue that, "moral frames," "legal knowledge," and beliefs about the enemy are also aspects of organizational frames and organizational knowledge. In the case of the United States, the understanding of noncombatant immunity, force protection, and military necessity are rooted in the Just War tradition, which itself influenced international law, and in the traditions of the American military. Specifically, the normative beliefs that structured and continue to organize the military's understanding of and treatment of civilians in war are rooted, as I have emphasized, in beliefs that stress the overriding value of military necessity and the often secondary importance of force protection and noncombatant immunity. The relative emphasis on force protection, noncombatant immunity, and military necessity can change and has changed historically. As argued above, the benefits of targeting civilians were assumed by American strategists in the nineteenth century, and for most of the twentieth century. By the later twentieth century, the balance had shifted. The resources of the military were devoted, first, to winning, but also increasingly to minimizing collateral damage understood in the context of a particular understanding of the ideas of military necessity, proportionality, double effect, and due care.

Just as organizational knowledge, the standard operating procedures, and the rules that flow from them, allow certain actions, they also make other actions and outcomes less likely. "Once created, knowledge-laden routines enable actors in organizations to carry out new actions. At the same time they constrain what those in organizations can do. One way knowledge-laden routines constrain is by appearing to be sensible or inevitable."[45] The idea that civilian casualties are inevitable—or avoidable—shapes choices and the effort taken to minimize civilian casualties and to know more about how they are caused. The choice of weapons constrains and enables. So also the emphasis in individual agency turns attention away from the effects of the military institution itself.

Further, as Eden argues, "frames do more than shape organizational attention, knowledge and action. The process of identifying problems and finding solutions

[44] Ibid.
[45] Ibid.

shapes organizations themselves."[46] An organizational frame can enable an organization to see a problem or to completely miss or minimize the contours and significance of what might be later understood to have been an important issue. So, while large complex organizations can gather and process enormous quantities of information they may also miss the obvious if the organizational frame lacks a particular concept or simply, as Eden argues, because all attention and resources are directed elsewhere.

> This shaping of organizational capacity in the process of sustained problem-solving activities both enables and constrains. Available expertise, structured activities to carry out investigations, and knowledge-laden organizational routines all enable those in an organization to solve problems. At the same time, organizational capacity reinforces how actors in organizations define problems and search for solutions: certain expertise will not be brought to bear on problems, the organization will not be structured in certain ways to carry out investigations, and organizational routines will carry certain kinds of knowledge but not other kinds.[47]

Organizational frames and organizational knowledge persist when and because they are institutionalized. Institutionalization occurs when ideas are articulated and specified so that the ideas become the guidance for rules, roles, procedures, and policies. There are three levels of institutionalization in complex organizations. At the first level, what one might call meta-institutionalization, the organization institutionalizes an area of concern. For instance, a corporation may decide that it will not just sell a product, but will create a capacity to provide customer support or service and maintenance for the product. Meta-institutionalization (or to use Eden's terminology, a change in organizational frame) then implies two additional levels of institutionalization—the institutionalization of decision-making procedures and roles (which, for good or ill, is a characteristic feature of bureaucracy), and the institutionalization of knowledge about the social and natural world that structure analysis and action.

A causal idea or normative belief has been institutionalized within an organization when the standard operating procedures of organizations are formulated or changed according with the beliefs. The immediate effect of the institutionalization of an idea is to make the implementation of the belief concrete in the form of procedures. This institutionalization then helps make the beliefs, after a time, seem taken for granted and the once new procedures become routine and expected. When institutionalized beliefs are "accurate" or suit the situation, they help actors navigate the world. But the beliefs can also create blind spots or dysfunctional routines.

---

[46] Ibid., p. 55.
[47] Ibid., p. 56.

Once new missions or knowledge are institutionalized, it is hard, but not impossible to change organizations.[48] As noted above, change is generally either the result of painstaking efforts to reorient an organization by a leader or dedicated group, or, more commonly, as a response to a significant external shock that demonstrates that previous beliefs were either terribly inadequate or false. Examples of internally driven change are comparatively rare. External shocks that have led to the reorientation of US security policy include the Pearl Harbor attack, the Soviet Union's acquisition of atomic capability, and more recently, the end of the Cold War.

The public outcry associated with the My Lai massacre is an example of an external shock that led to an organizational level response, new training, and the development of the Pentagon's Law of War program. By the beginning of the war in Afghanistan, the United Stated had institutionalized, at an organizational level, several ways to reduce the likelihood of collateral damage, and those techniques were refined through the period of the wars in Afghanistan and Iraq, as I show below. Yet, in the early years of the wars in Afghanistan and Iraq, the United States did not count civilian casualties and procedures for responding to incidents were ad hoc. The local commanders gradually elaborated rules for counting civilian casualties, the Air Force institutionalized and tightened its procedures for estimating and mitigating collateral damage, and the 2012 Army manual on *Civilian Casualty Mitigation* recommends that new organizational structures be created at the command level. The Army's organizational response to the new frame includes a specification of a level of detail that is typical of organizations in a transition from one frame to another. "It may be appropriate to establish a CIVCAS mitigation working group to meet periodically, including intelligence, civil affairs, public affairs, military information support operations (MISO), staff judge advocate, and fires representatives."

> A CIVCAS mitigation working group can collect and analyze data, assist
> and monitor progress, assess mitigation activities and incorporate lessons
> learned, monitor amends made, and respond promptly to allegations of

---

[48] There is an enormous literature on the sources of stability and change within military organizations. See: Barry Posen, *The Sources of Military Doctrine: France, Britain, and Germany between the World Wars* (Ithaca, NY: Cornell University Press, 1984); Stephen P. Rosen, *Winning the Next War: Innovation and the Modern Military* (Ithaca, NY: Cornell University Press, 1991); Kimberly Martin Zisk, *Engaging the Enemy: Organization Theory and Soviet Military Innovation, 1955-1991* (Princeton: Princeton University Press, 1993); Deborah Avant, *Political Institutions and Military Change* (Ithaca, NY: Cornell University Press, 1994); Williamson Murray and Allan R. Millett, eds., *Military Innovation in the Interwar Period* (Cambridge: Cambridge University Press, 1996); and Elizabeth Kier, *Imagining War: French and British Doctrine between the Wars* (Ithaca, NY: Cornell University Press, 1997). I have written about institutionalization of normative beliefs in Neta C. Crawford, *Argument and Change in World Politics: Ethics, Decolonization and Humanitarian Intervention* (Cambridge: Cambridge University Press, 1992). On organizational change and resistance to it in the context of counterinsurgency, see Krepinevich, *The Army and Vietnam* and John A. Nagl, *Learning to Eat Soup with a Knife: Counterinsurgency Lessons From Malaya and Vietnam* (Chicago: University of Chicago, 2005).

harm. The CIVCAS mitigation working group should be established before deployment. Examples of a CIVCAS mitigation working group's responsibilities include—

- Monitor CIVCAS risks in movements and engagements, reported or alleged CIVCAS incidents, investigations and investigation reports, inform and influence activities, and the making of amends.
- Collect, maintain, analyze, and disseminate data related to CIVCASs, including lessons learned.
- Ensure other staff members and subordinate units understand the importance of CIVCAS mitigation and their responsibilities for reporting, investigating, and making amends.
- Provide frequent and accurate assessments to the commander and other key unit personnel.
- Coordinate effectively with higher, lower, and adjacent units and other partners, including the host nation, United States governmental partners, and international organizations and nongovernmental organizations (NGOs).[49]

Military Organizational Culture

The military is not simply a collection of material capabilities and individuals organized and trained to kill using specific techniques. The military has an organizational culture, one of its chief organizational frames, that is a set of normative and identity beliefs about what it means to be a soldier and what it means to be a highly effective military. The content of military culture interacts with the other military's organizational frames and organizational knowledge, so that organizational culture, organizational frames, and organizational knowledge mutually shape each other. Although I discuss the US military as if there were one organizational culture, as in all other large military organizations throughout history, it is more accurate to say there are several organizational cultures within the US military: each service branch, and specialized forces within each service, works hard to inculcate a sense collective identity, loyalty, and a sense of duty in and among its members, an *esprit de corps*. Organizational culture, which is itself institutionalized, constrains and shapes individual agency as much as material capacities, the division of labor, and organizational frames.[50] Three features of the larger military organizational culture

---

[49] Army, *Civilian Casualty Mitigation*, p. 2-4.

[50] I am here discussing mostly small unit organizational culture and the larger culture of warfighting. There are many ways to think about cultures and military organizations as well as the relationship between the larger society's cultural values and military values. For instance, Elizabeth Kier focuses on how organizational culture affects the development of military doctrine. See Kier, *Imagining War*. John Dower uses the term "culture" in a much broader sense in his, *Cultures of War: Pearl Harbor, Hiroshima, 9-11, Iraq* (New York: W. W. Norton, 2010).

can reduce the capacity of the institution, as a whole, to be reflective and change procedures that may be counterproductive.

First, military organizational culture obviously includes a strong belief in the utility of threats or the use of military force to solve problems. But belief in the utility of force is also an organizational bias that is difficult to challenge. On the other hand, recent training in counterinsurgency stresses the value of restraint in situations where the use of force may be unwise from a strategic perspective. The US military began to question the assumption of the utility of force several years into the Afghanistan and Iraq wars. The 2006 *Counterinsurgency Field Manual* argues: "Counterinsurgents that use excessive force to limit short-term risk alienate the local populace.... Sometimes lethal responses can be counterproductive. At other times it may be essential."[51] Similarly, the 2012 *Civilian Casualty Mitigation* manual suggests that "soldiers should be aware that excessive use of aggressive escalation-of-force measures may generate resentment even if civilians are not harmed."[52] Toughness and aggressiveness are prized, and yet must be turned off as the situation demands.

Thus, while military culture emphasizes proficiency in killing, it must also stress restraint in counterinsurgency situations. "The art of command includes knowing the difference and directing the appropriate action."[53] Much more than the art of command, which is certainly essential, the military culture must come to valorize restraint, or "tactical patience," as much as combat effectiveness.[54] The 2012 *Civilian Casualty Mitigation* manual asks leaders and soldiers to think about doing something the entire military culture has trained them not to do: delay or reconsider an operation.[55]

Second, consistent with the emphasis on the utility of force, the organizational culture stresses training in weapons and combat, but not in military ethics. To be clear, each service does include military ethics and law of war training that emphasizes noncombatant immunity in its basic and advanced training. But, as Mark Martins observed in 1994:

> Most ROE training when it occurs at all, is less 'training' than, 'instruction.' With few exceptions, attempts to expose soldiers to the impact of law and other external considerations on their actions consist of a small amount of formal instruction on the law of war. When training objectives involving law of war or use of force issues do find their way into field exercises or

---

[51] United States Army and Marine Corp, *U.S. Army/Marine Corps Counterinsurgency Field Manual*, Field Manual No. 3-24: Marine Corp Warfighting Publication No. 3-33.5 (Chicago: University of Chicago, 2007), p. 245.

[52] Army, *Civilian Casualty Mitigation*, p. 2-10.

[53] *Counterinsurgency Field Manual*, p. 245.

[54] Army, *Civilian Casualty Mitigation*, p. 2-12.

[55] Ibid., p. 2-11.

unit evaluations at training centers, even realistic scenarios have no base of performance-oriented, individual soldier training on which to build. Under the present approach, rules of engagement...are things to be, 'briefed,' not trained.[56]

Martins's observation about the dearth of effective training in laws of war during the 1990s does not fully apply a generation later, yet it captures the features of current ethics instruction: discrimination and respect for civilian life and property are still more briefed, than trained. All soldiers in the US military today are informed, more or less well, of the laws of war and "core warrior values." Out of 12 weeks of Marine Corp "basic" training, recruits receive 42 hours of training in values, and Marines get another 13 hours of values instruction during their infantry training. Army recruits, who spend 10 weeks in basic training, receive 22 hours of values instruction in their Basic Combat Training or 35-40 hours in One Station Unit Training. Special Operations forces receive more instruction in warrior values.

The 2006 US Army and Marine Field Manual on Counterinsurgency offers a shorthand definition of culture and emphasizes the importance of knowing the culture of the area of military operations.[57] The manual also emphasizes core elements of Army and Marine Corp culture, namely the requirement to obey the laws of armed conflict and the "highest standards of moral and ethical conduct."[58] The manual stresses that "American military values obligate Soldiers and Marines to accomplish their missions while taking measures to limit the destruction caused during military operations, particularly in terms of harm to noncombatants. It is wrong to harm innocents, regardless of their citizenship."[59]

Ethical considerations, most often framed in terms of the Just War tradition and the law of armed combat are part of the military's organizational frame. Ethics education is constant, but nowhere more explicit in the content of normative beliefs and the practice of ethical and legal reasoning taught in ethics courses at US military service academies. For example, a course in the second year at West Point introduces students to the Just War tradition. The norms are reinforced in law of war briefings and supplemental briefings in the field on the rules of engagement.

While ethics education is considered a vital part of officer training, it is considered less important at the lower ranks. "As an enlisted soldier, I wasn't taught any lessons from Vietnam and there was no discussion of the tragedy of My Lai. As an officer we were given one class on the laws of warfare. The class was called 'The Law of Land Warfare' and they did reference the My Lai massacre. But it's a whole different story in class, with a JAG (Judge Advocate General) lawyer explaining what

---

[56] Martins, "Rules of Engagement for Land Forces," p. 72.
[57] Counterinsurgency Field Manual, pp. 88–94 and 242.
[58] Ibid., p. 244.
[59] Ibid., p. 245.

the law is [versus what it is like in combat]. When you actually go to war it's all different."[60] Others agree that there is currently not enough training in the content and practices of ethical deliberation and worry that ethics education may be reduced to a series of dos and don'ts.

> Whereas it may *seem* a bit far fetched to argue that every soldier take a college level introduction to ethics and international relations during basic training, there certainly is a place for more theoretical foundation-laying at the lowest level of the military hierarchy, before soldiers become immersed in the normative prescriptions of the law of land warfare (which are often presented to soldiers in 'PowerPoint' briefings delivered without passion by lawyers or chaplains and reinforced only by handing out of Rules of Engagement cards) and (in many, perhaps most cases at the time of writing) almost immediate deployment after initial training.[61]

In most military service institutions, ethics is understood as a personal virtue. Soldiers and commanders are taught to be virtuous and disciplined individuals, using the writing of Plato and Aristotle.[62] The Cadet Leadership Development System at West Point includes a "moral ethical" domain as one of its six developmental domains. The focus is on character development. Specifically, "Character is . . . the source of officers' warrior ethos—their strength of will to persevere and prevail to accomplish the mission and meet responsibilities in a moral and ethical manner." Cadets will learn to "act morally and ethically in ordinary and fast moving, fluid, emotional, and complex situations. They discover the right thing to do and act accordingly."[63] Soldiers and commanders also internalize the "warrior ethos" which emphasizes loyalty and character virtues that are specific to the soldier's role.

> I am an American Soldier.
> I am a Warrior and a member of a team. I serve the people of the United States and live the Army Values.
> **I will always place the mission first.**
> **I will never accept defeat.**
> **I will never quit.**
> **I will never leave a fallen comrade.**

---

[60] Ehren Watada, quoted in William F. Felice, *How Do I Save My Honor? War, Moral Integrity, and Principled Resignation* (New York: Rowman and Littlefield, 2009), p. 137.

[61] Jeffrey Wilson, "An Ethics Curriculum for an Evolving Army," in Paul Robinson, Nigel De Lee, and Don Carrick, eds., *Ethics Education in the Military* (Aldershot: Ashgate, 2008), pp. 31–41, 39.

[62] Ibid.

[63] United States Military Academy, "Building Capacity to Lead: The West Point System for Leader Development," http://www.usma.edu/strategic/SiteAssets/SitePages/Home/building%20the%20 capacity%20to%20lead.pdf, pp. 11, 26.

I am disciplined, physically and mentally tough, trained and proficient in my warrior tasks and drills. I always maintain my arms, my equipment and myself.

I am an expert and I am a professional.

I stand ready to deploy, engage, and destroy the enemies of the United States of America in close combat.

I am a guardian of freedom and the American way of life.

I am an American Soldier.

The focus in military ethics training on individual character and behavior is in line with the law's tendency to focus on individual accountability and the emphasis in the armed forces "martial honor." "One of the pitfalls of the military's favoured approach to ethics training—virtue ethics—is that because the emphasis is on character development, ethical failures may well be interpreted purely in terms of the character flaws of the individuals involved."[64]

Effective ethics education, like all other education in armed forces, depends on training and retraining. Change in values thus entails changes in training; new requirements are thus institutionalized. Thus, we would expect that when noncombatant immunity and "population centric" counterinsurgency tactics are emphasized there should be an emphasis on these values in training. At a Pentagon Press briefing in February 2010 Major General John Campbell, commanding general of the 101st Airborne Division and Major General Steve Layfield, commander of the Joint Warfighting Center at Joint Forces Command discussed how training did, or did not, change to reflect the 2009-2010 emphasis on protecting civilians. In response to a question, Layfield described the "Unified Endeavor 10-1 Mission Rehearsal Exercise" in early 2010 at Fort Campbell Kentucky to prepare soldiers for deployment to Afghanistan.

> GEN. LAYFIELD: How'd the shift to populations... I think your question was how did the—General McChrystal's tactical directive and his shift towards a population-centric approach—how does that—how has that affected our [training] regime? I think that's what you said.
>
> Dramatically. It has—it has caused all of us to go back and reinforce what we were doing in that arena to begin with. We've always been population-centric and concerned about civilian casualties and concerned about what General McChrystal's directive says. This has just reinforced that ethos.

---

[64] Paul Robinson, Nigel De Lee, and Don Carrick, "Conclusion," in Paul Robinson, Nigel De Lee, and Don Carrick, eds., *Ethics Education in the Military* (Aldershot: Ashgate, 2008), pp. 199–201, 199.

And so it has caused us to go back and scrub every single training venue, every training vignette that we put on to a training audience and make sure that we're giving them the opportunity to be challenged with that sort of guidance coming from their new commander, General McChrystal.

And so yes, it has definitely not changed anything with respect to how we put on an exercise; it has clearly refocused us on what we want to present to the training audience for him to be able to produce exactly what General McChrystal's asking him to do in theater.[65]

In sum, the focus on individual virtue and a sense that the training in ethics is probably adequate suggests that there is little in addition that needs to be done on a systemic level to prevent noncombatant killing. Thus, while Paul Robinson, Nigel De Lee, and Don Carrick caution, "Nor should ethics training allow commanders to close their eyes to the systemic failings of their institutions," it is unclear how well potential "systemic failures" are understood. Adherence to the rules of engagement and warrior virtues will not necessarily reduce noncombatant killing if most of that killing is systemic or proportionality/double effect collateral damage, not the result of deliberate attack.

Although operational culture at the unit level directly affects the behavior of soldiers, core warrior values are not easily transferred from classrooms at West Point, or other officer training venues, to operational units. It is at platoon level, far from home, that more pernicious aspects of military culture that can lead to carelessness, callousness, or even atrocity on the battlefield can be found. When the soldier is deployed, even a highly trained Navy SEAL or Army Ranger, they adapt to the dominant culture of the unit. The culture can be good or bad. As one former commander of Navy SEAL training told the former Navy SEAL and counterinsurgency expert Dick Couch, "My goal was to send new SEALs to the operational teams who were uniformly stamped with a sense of honor and good moral values.... But I don't think our efforts here at training command made much difference."

Oh we shined them up like new money and sent them off to the teams, but when they got to the operational platoons, they immediately adapted to the culture of their platoon. If that SEAL team had good leadership and practiced good values, the new guys took that on as what was expected of them. But if there were bad actors or pirates...and that kind of conduct was allowed or tolerated, then the new SEALs would immediately fall in

[65] DOD News Briefing with Maj. Gen. Campbell and Maj. Gen. Layfield via Teleconference from Ft. Campbell, Ky., 4 February 2010, http://www.defense.gov/transcripts/transcript.aspx?transcriptid=4558.

with that kind of behavior. No matter what we do at training command, it's still about the culture in the operational platoons.[66]

Dick Couch argues that small unit culture is affected by the values that the new recruits bring from the larger American culture, which he worries can undermine restraint when it is too infused with "a diet of TV violence" that "tends to make adolescents immune or indifferent to violence."[67] Couch also notes the intense desire of new soldiers to "fit in," and the new soldier's admiration for those with combat experience and combat savvy. Belonging is functional—soldiers who are disliked or who don't fit in may get left behind. An Army survey in 2007 found that "many soldiers reported a desire to hear from those who had previously deployed and from their unit leaders about how they should handle ethical dilemmas."[68] Yet unit cohesion can become dysfunctional. If the experienced soldiers are what Couch calls "bad" actors, or "pirates," he suggests they can infect unit culture with the wrong values. "Two or three influential individuals in a squad or platoon can wreak havoc with the unit culture and the mission. These few can create corrosive, pirate-type subcultures."[69]

But, despite his attention to "pirates" and other bad actors, the force of Couch's argument is organizational. Specifically, he stresses socialization for restraint in training curriculum and in particular in operational training before units are deployed. Couch gives the example of the Close Quarters Defense curriculum used by Navy SEALs to argue that the restraint emphasized in CQD, specifically training in when and how to "dial" up or down the level of force, fosters the organizational culture and socialization that may help soldiers adhere to the rule of law.[70] While it is the individual soldier who benefits from such training and who must be disciplined according to Couch, I argue that it is the responsibility of the services to provide the training and in the most effective way so that the culture of small units is conducive to restraint. I return to this below when I discuss ways the US military has changed its training.

The third way that military culture may work against civilian casualty prevention is its emphasis on personal resilience and the expectation that soldiers are to be disciplined and follow orders, including orders to avoid harming civilians, even if it puts them at greater personal risk and their mental and physical capacities are

---

[66] Quoted in Dick Couch, *A Tactical Ethic: Moral Conduct in the Insurgent Battlespace* (Annapolis: Naval Institute Press, 2010), pp. 73–74.

[67] Ibid., p. 64.

[68] Christopher H. Warner, George N. Appenzeller, Angela Mobbs, Jessica R. Parker, Carolynn M. Warner, Thomas Grieger, and Charles W. Hoge, "Effectiveness of Battlefield-Ethics Training during Combat Deployment: A Programme Assessment," *The Lancet*, vol. 378 (3 September 2011): 915–924, 917–918.

[69] Couch, *A Tactical Ethic*, p. 77.

[70] Ibid., pp. 90–91.

stressed beyond endurance. "Courageous restraint" or "tactical patience"—holding fire for a longer time to see whether a situation is a threat—may be required but soldiers are simply too tired. A rapid operational tempo, and the inability of soldiers and units to reduce stress, may decrease the ability or willingness of soldiers to pause, or reflect on their rules of engagement, and may also lead to a hair trigger response and a greater likelihood of individual soldiers or groups of soldiers "loosing it," and harming civilians.

The military may also require soldiers to return to combat after a tour of duty even though soldiers may have not recovered from the stress of a prior deployment. The *Counterinsurgency Field Manual* notes these stresses and suggests that it is the able commander who must navigate the difficulties of deployment. "Leaders do not allow subordinates to fall victim to the enormous pressures associated with prolonged combat against elusive, unethical, and indiscriminate foes. The environment that fosters insurgency is characterized by violence, immorality, distrust, and deceit; nonetheless, Army and Marine Corp leaders continue to demand and embrace honor, courage and commitment to the highest standards."[71] Yet, commitment to the highest standards is difficult for soldiers and leaders who have little physical and emotional rest. Further, boredom and the desire for revenge can lead to unwarranted aggression.

The *Civilian Casualty Mitigation* manual recognizes these stresses, but again, makes the commanders responsible for dealing with them: "CIVCAS mitigation is most effective when leaders at all levels emphasize its importance at appropriate opportunities. This may require particular emphasis in units that have recently suffered casualties."[72] The *Civilian Casualty Mitigation* manual includes a recommendation for "days off for Soldiers, with local rest and recreation to relieve stress" and the explicit acknowledgment that "Soldiers involved in CIVCAS incidents may need psychiatric treatment. These needs could persist long after the incident occurred."[73] This recommendation may be one of the most important in the manual for both preventing inadvertent harm and malicious behavior, since research shows that while PTSD was associated with unethical behavior on the part of soldiers, the intensity of combat exposure was the "strongest predictor of unethical conduct."[74]

Fourth, the military and operational units emphasize "cohesion" and soldiers are expected to be loyal. That loyalty may be conceived of narrowly—so that critical reflection or reporting of a violation of the rules or even an accident that harms civilians is perceived as disloyal. Further, "groupthink"—a tendency to conformity and a diminished sense among group members that challenging decisions or actions

---

[71] *Counterinsurgency Field Manual*, p. 240.

[72] Army, *Civilian Casualty Mitigation*, p. 1-8.

[73] Ibid., pp. 2-17 and 2-19.

[74] Warner et al., "Effectiveness of Battlefield-Ethics Training during Combat Deployment," p. 922.

is possible—is heightened when group members are fearful.[75] When someone does wrong, the strong sense of loyalty cultivated in the troops and so essential for unit cohesion may cause soldiers to let something wrong go unreported. Dick Couch suggests that this effect of loyalty is understandable as he imagines how a soldier is thinking when the laws of war or rules of engagement are violated. "When someone knowingly does the wrong thing on the battlefield, who is going to stop him or report him? When my brother warrior, who has fought alongside me and has risked his life with me, gets bored and starts harassing the locals while on patrol, what do I do? I owe him a lot more than I owe some villager who may have at one time given aid and comfort to my insurgent enemy. How do I respond when, out of frustration or boredom, my battle buddy does something stupid or criminal or both?"[76] Couch argues that "if there's a single factor that allows for wrong conduct in our deployed ground combat units, it is loyalty within those very units."[77]

Complex Organizations as Imperfect Moral Agents

Philosophers are not of a single opinion about whether collectives or complex organizations qualify as moral agents. One view is that collective intentions and action do not amount to collective moral agency or collective moral responsibility: although individuals act in and through groups, the only meaningful attribution of moral responsibility is with individuals.[78] In explaining this view, David Copp reasons, "If only things that have minds can have intentions, beliefs, and desires, agency individualism is a strong position."[79] For example, many individuals fleeing a tidal wave "share" an intention in the sense that all hold the desire to escape the path of the wave, but this simultaneous action does not constitute the coordinated effort

---

[75] Irving Janis, *Groupthink: Psychological Studies of Policy Decisions and Fiascoes* (Boston: Houghton Mifflin, 1982). Also see Ramon J. Aldag and Sally Riggs Fuller, "Beyond Fiasco: A Reappraisal of the Groupthink Phenomenon and a New Model of Group Decision Processes," *Psychological Bulletin*, vol. 113, no. 2 (May 1993): 533–552; Paul 't Hart, Eric K. Stern, and Bengt Sundelius, eds., *Beyond Groupthink: Political Group Dynamics and Foreign Policy-making* (Ann Arbor: University of Michigan Press, 1997).

[76] Couch, *A Tactical Ethic*, p. 80.

[77] Ibid., p. 81.

[78] For example, see H. D. Lewis, "Collective Responsibility," *Philosophy: The Journal of the Royal Institute of Philosophy*, vol. 24, no. 83 (1948), reprinted in Larry May and Stacy Hoffman, eds., *Collective Responsibility: Five Decades of Debate in Theoretical and Applied Ethics* (New York: Rowman and Littlefield, 1991), pp. 17–33; Seamus Miller, "Collective Moral Responsibility: An Individualist Account," in French and Wettstein, eds., *Midwest Studies in Philosophy*, pp. 176–193. A concise summary of this view is found in Christian List and Philip Pettit, *Group Agency: The Possibility, Design, and Status of Corporate Agents* (Oxford: Oxford University Press, 2011).

[79] David Copp, "On the Agency of Certain Collectives," in French and Wettstein, eds., *Midwest Studies in Philosophy*, pp. 194–221, 196.

of an organized collective. Each individual is deciding to flee and acting for him or herself: it would be inappropriate to ascribe collective moral agency responsibility to this set of individuals.

Alternatively, even though collectives may not actually be moral persons in the exact same sense that it is possible for individuals to be moral persons and moral agents, it may be useful, nevertheless, to think of collectives as imperfect moral agents having moral responsibility.[80] Thus, Paul Sheehy suggests that "if a group has the practices that allow its members to reflect and deliberate upon the group's character, goals and practices, and to bring about changes in those goals and ways of being, then it is plausible to regard the members as collectively or jointly accountable for the nature and actions of the group."[81] Toni Erskine also observes that "many institutions enjoy greater capacities for deliberation and action than are enjoyed by individuals." She argues that these capacities allow actions for good or ill that "would simply be beyond the scope of individual actors" and thus "allow institutions to bear certain duties that could not be borne by any individual."[82]

Complex organizations, I argue, are imperfect moral agents to the extent that they have at least five characteristics.

- First, members have articulated shared intentions or a common purpose for which they agree to coordinate their actions. These are meta-institutional and constitute the content of the organizational frame. The normative implications of the intentions and purposes may or may not be explicit.
- Second, the entity is a persistent organization with persistent roles. Individual members may come and go, but the institution remains functional over time because members' behavior is prescribed by rules and roles, and the organization has the ability to enforce the role performance of members. Role violators may be reeducated, removed from their position, or potentially face legal sanctions.
- Third, decision-making procedures have been institutionalized: the organization has knowledge resources, the ability to process information, decision-making

---

[80] Agents, for List and Pettit, have representational states, motivational states, and the capacity to process those states. List and Pettit, *Group Agency*, p. 20. List and Pettit stress "standards of rationality" and describe "reasoning agents." List and Pettit, *Group Agency*, pp. 29–31. Because "rationality" carries assumptions about psychological states, I refer below to decision-making procedures and reason giving.

[81] Paul Sheehy, "Holding Them Responsible," in French and Wettstein, eds., *Midwest Studies in Philosophy*, pp. 74–93, 83.

[82] "Such capacities include comprehensive access to information, sophisticated means for its collection and processing, and elaborate structures for the execution of decisions." Toni Erskine, "Assigning Responsibilities to Institutional Moral Agents: The Case of States and 'Quasi-States'," in Toni Erskine, ed., *Can Institutions Have Responsibilities? Collective Moral Agency and International Relations* (New York: Palgrave, 2003), pp. 19–40, 26.

rules and roles, and deliberative capacity.[83] Ad hoc procedures may be utilized in crises or among actors new to their roles.

- Fourth, the organization has the capacity to act: the organization has mobilized the coordinated efforts of its members, and mobilized and deployed preexisting or new resources.[84] The actions in complex organizations are often based on routines, standard operating procedures, and scripted responses to expected scenarios. Organizational frames, as described above, shape all these aspects (purpose, persistent roles, decision-making resources and procedures, and capacity to act) of the organization.

- Fifth, the organization should have the institutionalized capacity to reflect upon, and evaluate its purposes, the organization of its rules and roles, its knowledge-production and decision-making procedures, and the quality of its actions and their consequences. Such evaluations may lead to revisions of the intentions, structure, or rules of the organization, although the openness of the organization to reflection and revision is again often a function of the content of its organizational frames.[85]

For institutions or collectives to operate as effective albeit imperfect, moral agents they must be able to critically reflect on their normative beliefs and the consequences of their beliefs, decisions, and actions. With regard to intended and unintended harm, this means that each collective must have the potential to foresee the consequences of its actions and the ways the causal chains linking belief and actions are likely to produce specific outcomes—whether intended or unintended.[86] This is prospective or "forward-looking" moral responsibility.[87]

The mechanisms for evaluating past actions, discerning harmful or counterproductive consequences, identifying "best practices," and assuming backward-looking (retrospective) responsibility will vary for each collective actor. Like many individuals, institutions often lack incentives to analyze how it is that they have, in the past, knowingly or unintentionally harmed others or even group members. Few seek out

---

[83] Peter French calls this a "corporate internal decision structure." See Peter A. French, "The Corporation as a Moral Person," *American Philosophical Quarterly* vol. 16, no. 3 (1979): 207–215.

[84] Membership may change, but members' roles are essentially consistent.

[85] See Mathiesen, "We're All in This Together," pp. 244–245. Sheehy, "Holding Them Responsible," pp. 85 and 92.

[86] List and Pettit offer an alternative set of conditions as the criteria of moral responsibility: the agent must face a normatively significant choice involving the potential to do something good or bad; the agent has the capacity (understanding and access to evidence) to make judgments; and the agent has the control to make a decision. List and Pettit, *Group Agency*, p. 158.

[87] Margaret Gilbert distinguishes the terms forward-looking moral responsibility about one's future obligations from backward-looking moral responsibility about one's causal responsibility for what has one has done. Margaret Gilbert, "Who is to Blame? Collective Moral Responsibility and its Implications for Group Members," in French and Wettstein, eds., *Midwest Studies in Philosophy*, pp. 94–114, 94–95.

information that may provoke feelings of guilt or shame or raise questions of legal liability. Further, collective actors will be unable to exercise either prospective or retrospective responsibility unless there is a venue and mechanism for reflecting and arguing about what is happening. Some professions and institutions have such mechanisms (such as medical review boards for understanding the causes of mortality in hospitals). Finally, because some organizations lack adequate mechanisms for exercising prospective or retrospective responsibility, there must be a mechanism for each society and government to encourage other collectives to be responsible. In other words, a responsible system includes chains of moral responsibility. I elaborate on this last point later in the chapter.

I differ from Christian List and Philip Pettit who mostly limit moral responsibility to conscious and intentional acts: "Genuine incomprehension or unavoidable ignorance is a perfectly good excuse when something bad is done."[88] My attention to organizational frames and the processes of knowledge production suggests that it is all too easy for organizations to be uncomprehending or ignorant by conscious or inadvertent design. Good organizational design, that is a structure and set of procedures that is attentive to questions of moral agency, should include both prospective and retrospective attention to unintended yet foreseeable outcomes. List and Pettit imply this much when they suggest that groups should be designed so that it is possible to make moral judgments: "groups seeking to be incorporated would thus be legally required to have procedures in place whereby they give due consideration to evaluative matters and form collectively endorsed judgments on them."[89]

Two caveats are in order. Although complex organizations are, arguably, imperfect moral agents, this does not vitiate the moral agency of the individuals who work within them or in association with them. Individual moral agency can be enhanced or diminished through organizations. The second caveat concerns the importance of resisting the impulse to reify the imperfect moral agency of institutions. Organizations are complex entities that exist because they have those characteristics described above—meta-institutional goals/purpose, roles, decision-making structures and processes, and capacities to act, as well as to evaluate and revise. But these entities are not unitary, nor are they always acting on one purpose alone. The "decisions" made by organizations are most often the result of a mix of careful private deliberation, persuasive argumentation among actors, and cultural norms, and include adherence to the rules the organization has set for making decisions, as well as less public though not necessarily less influential processes such as bargaining and negotiation within the organization. Complex organizations are enabled by larger social processes and structures and are themselves part of those larger structures.

[88] List and Pettit, *Group Agency*, p. 155.
[89] Ibid., p. 159.

Military Organizations as (Imperfect) Moral Agents

The US military (including the civilians who work for the Department of Defense and members of the various armed services) has the characteristics of an imperfect moral agent with collective moral responsibility: purpose; persistent roles; a decision-making structure characterized by rules, roles, knowledge, and decision-making procedures; a capacity to act; and the ability to reflect upon and revise its rules, roles, and procedures.

First, the shared intention of the members of military organizations, the mission, is to win wars, either through the use of force or the threat of force, for the political purposes articulated by their political leaders. The military's institutional goals—at a meta-institutional level—are not just simple victory defined as annihilation of enemy forces but can include deterrence, occupation, peacekeeping, or "nation building." Other purposes include perfecting the arts of threat assessment, organizing and mobilizing resources to meet threats, devising effective strategies, executing those tactics and strategies, and then, learning from their successes and mistakes. In a functioning democracy, military organizations serve their civilian governments, and in this sense, they may appear to have little autonomy. Military organizations do not usually choose when or who to fight, although their assessments of their own and their adversary's capacities will often strongly influence the decisions of civilian leaders. Rather, militaries manage how to fight. Specifically, military organizations are given great latitude in the training of soldiers, in the tactics and strategies used to fight wars, including the weapons made available to soldiers, and in the rules of engagement for battle.

Second, the structure of roles within the military guarantee that the organizations' legal and physical existence does not depend on the existence or participation of particular individuals.[90] Military institutions have lines of responsibility, material assets, and resources that persist beyond the lives of individual members. Each member of the military has a part to play in the collective enterprise and the fact that members perform their role makes the collective more than the sum of its parts. The military can sanction members who do not perform their roles through disciplinary letters, hearings, demotion, or imprisonment. The organization can also choose not to sanction those members who may have violated international humanitarian law. Thus, through these rules and roles, the organization has more or less control over its individual members' behavior. These roles, and the procedures for enforcing them, create what Aristotle and others describe as military virtue or martial honor.[91]

---

[90] Individual interests and incentives may run at cross-purposes to the larger mission of the collective. For example, hoarding data may yield personal advancement but slow overall progress.

[91] See Mark J. Osiel, *Obeying Orders: Atrocity, Military Discipline and the Law of War* (New Brunswick, NJ: Transaction Publishers, 1999).

Military organizations are little different than other bureaucratic organizations: they socialize their members, create organizationally useful knowledge, devise standard operating procedures to address problems, and focus resources. In other words, well before soldiers are deployed to a place where they may kill, military organizations make some things possible and others not. Individuals within organizations make morally relevant choices at all levels, from the socialization of officers and enlisted personnel, to decisions about what weapons to buy and what tactics to use. Within organizations, causal, cultural, and identity beliefs are institutionalized in practices or organizational routines. Individual roles are partly determined by cultural norms. Militaries can train their soldiers more or less well in the Geneva Conventions and can devise rules of engagement that make it more or less likely that civilian lives will be preserved.

Within the institution, military Judge Advocate Generals (JAGs) articulate what it means to protect civilians and call attention to and prosecute violation of the principle of noncombatant immunity. JAGs have an individual moral responsibility, of course, to monitor and ensure compliance with the laws of war, but the structure and operation of military lawyers in war (how many there are, where they are deployed, whether they are engaged in vetting targets and discussing rules of engagement, and whether they report to an independent chain of command) is a feature of the military organization as a moral agent. The Law of War Program, described below, is part of that structure.

Further, military organizations are complex collectives that have organizations within the larger organization and a division of labor. The organizations within the larger military organization share some goals and cooperate with each other. But they also compete with each other—a quality known as inter-service rivalry.

Third, military organizations have refined and institutionalized structures, rules, and procedures for making decisions, known in the Army, for example, as the MDMP, the Military Decision-Making Process. This capacity to make decisions entails gathering information, creating new knowledge, developing options for dealing with problems using organizational frames, and a decision-making apparatus that includes procedures and guidelines for deliberation. Military organizations solve the problem of finding appropriate strategies for winning wars by developing military doctrines, which themselves reflect prior decisions. Organizational capacity to acquire and process information is greater than an individual's capacity to perform these tasks, yet that capacity does not always translate into the desired outcome: organizations may still lose information or lack efficiency and accuracy in processing information. Or decision-making procedures may be slow, cumbersome, and inefficient.

The acquisition and processing of information used by military organizations for deliberation is filtered and shaped by organizational frames, which may or may not conflict. For example, the Standing Rules of Engagement embody both the stress on the value of military necessity as well as the values of the Just War tradition and international law that stress noncombatant immunity. The Uniform Code of Military Justice articulates the laws and values for the US military, and each branch has its own more specific version of values.[92] As Stephen Wrage notes, the US military understands the choice of precision weapons within an organizational frame that stresses efficiency and the Just War tradition and the laws of armed conflict.

> The principle option that precision-guided munitions afford is they let the targeters choose exactly where he or she wants a weapon to go. This allows the user of force to be highly effective. It also encourages others to hold that person strictly accountable.
>
> Accuracy matters in moral terms primarily because it allows one to aim narrowly at legitimate targets and carefully away from innocents and non-combatants. In this respect, the characteristics of precision weapons enable their users to conform to the standards for discrimination established in the just war tradition.
>
> Greater accuracy also means that in addition to greater discrimination, greater effectiveness can be achieved.... This means that highly accurate weapons permit one to practice an economy in the use of force, using smaller warheads, carrying out fewer strikes, putting fewer people at risk, and cutting back the number of occasions for errors and so the likelihood of unintended damage or killing. This economy of force allows users of precision weapons to conform to the standards of proportionality established in the just war tradition. In short, greater accuracy means greater care can be taken and both the *in bello* tests that are part of the just war tradition, that of discrimination and proportionality, can be more fully satisfied.[93]

The beliefs and values embodied in organizational frames help create the options used by decision-makers and are the content of the deliberative process. While deliberative procedures within an organization may be centralized or decentralized, in the case of the US military, much of the decision-making capacity is centralized in hierarchical chains of command. Decision-making rules and organizational frames coordinate and constrain decision-making to the extent that organizational procedures, values, and preferences may lead to outcomes that override individual preferences.[94] The decision-making structure and the constraints on the autonomy of

---

[92] See Anthony E. Hartle, *Moral Issues in Military Decision Making*, 2d ed., revised (Lawrence: University Press of Kansas, 2004), pp. 62–74.

[93] Stephen D. Wrage, "The Ethics of Precision Air Power," in Stephen D. Wrage, ed., *Immaculate Warfare: Participants Reflect on the Air Campaigns over Kosovo, Afghanistan, and Iraq* (Westport, CT: Praeger, 2003), pp. 85–99, 90.

[94] See Philip Pettit, "Groups with Minds of Their Own," in Frederick Schmidt, ed., *Socializing Metaphysics* (Lanham, MD: Rowman and Littlefield, 2003), pp. 167–193; Copp, "On the Agency of Certain Collectives."

individual members in that structure help constitute the organization as an imperfect moral agent. But, again, we must remember that this moral agency emerges as a concatenation or distillation of deliberations as well as a compromise within the bureaucracy or across bureaucracies within the military.

Fourth, the military has the capacity to act to achieve its goals and to implement its decisions. The military has mobilized the coordinated efforts of its members, and mobilized and deployed preexisting or new resources, based on its assessment of its needs vis-à-vis particular threats or goals, routines, standard operating procedures, and scripted responses to expected scenarios. The military's capacity to act is thus enormous, but also not infinite, or infinitely flexible. As US Secretary of Defense Donald Rumsfeld said in response to criticism from troops about the lack of equipment in Iraq, "As you know, you go to war with the Army you have. They're not the Army you might want or wish to have at a later time."[95]

To make war, members of military organizations use both material resources and what might be called ideational resources. Material resources (e.g., rifles, fuel, helicopters, and nuclear weapons) are created, mobilized, and organized to particular ends according the ideational resources of commanders. Soldiers are often mobilized and managed as a material resource. Ideational resources are beliefs: practical beliefs about how others react to threats; ethical or normative beliefs about the legitimate use of force; scientific causal beliefs about the effects of particular weapons, tactics, and strategies; and identity beliefs about the role of the soldier. These ideational and material resources allow some practices and make other practices either inconceivable or impossible. So, for example, military organizations have for centuries emphasized the importance of drills, rigid lines of authority, and the essentially unquestioning obedience of soldiers to commanders. They have stressed the production of fear in enemies and developed weapons, tactics, and strategies to produce fear. They have also been shaped by normative beliefs, such as the prohibition on harming soldiers who are *hors de combat* (that is, outside the fight).

The fact that acceptable killing in war, a situation where force appears to determine the outcome, is governed by specific laws, known as "rules of engagement" may strike readers as both ironic and paradoxical. But the fact that the rules of engagement are both developed by and followed within the organization, locates the primary responsibility for systemic collateral damage in military organization.

Fifth, the US military also exhibits moral agency when it uses a capacity to reflect on past performance to evaluate and change its goals, training, and standard operating procedures. At the points when the US military has focused on the organizational features that allow or inhibit foreseeable noncombatant killing, it has often reduced noncombatant killing. I have argued that this is because, at those

---

[95] Quoted in Thomas E. Ricks, "Rumsfeld Gets an Earful from Troops," *Washington Post*, 9 December 2004, p. A1, http://www.washingtonpost.com/wp-dyn/articles/A46508-2004Dec8.html.

junctures, the military organization, or particularly insightful commanders, came to believe that reducing noncombatant killing was a military necessity and the necessary reforms were institutionalized. The capacity to see the need for reform, make changes, and eventually institutionalize reforms in a deep way, reflects the institutionalization of procedures for evaluation and learning.

> Doctrinal changes are not the only way in which military organizations demonstrate learning, although the published nature of formalized doctrine makes it convincing evidence of change. Learning is also demonstrated in the curricula of military schools and training institutions, in the structure of military organizations, in the creation of new organizations to deal with new or changed situations, and in myriad of other responses to change. As a result of the long process required to revise, or rewrite published doctrine and ensure its approval through all of the levels of military bureaucracy through which it must pass prior to its publication, doctrinal change is in may ways a trailing indicator of institutional learning.[96]

In sum, all these attributes—shared purpose; persistent and defined roles; a decision-making structure characterized by rules, roles, knowledge and decision-making procedures; the capacity to act; and the ability to reflect upon and revise its rules, roles, and procedures—constitute the US military as an imperfect moral agent. Of course, all military organizations specialize in two functions: (1) making manifest the threat of defense and retaliation against attack; and (2) offering the specific capacity of destruction of both people and property. The fact is that while individual soldiers could engage in acts of self-defense or aggression, it is these organizational attributes that allow for large-scale, enduring, and potentially effective uses of force sufficient to make war.

The Organizational Cycle of Moral Agency and Law of War

I argued in the chapters on individual and command responsibility that moral responsibility for deliberate atrocity is correctly placed on individual perpetrators and with their commanders, when commanders ordered or could have prevented an atrocity. In this chapter, I have rather briskly argued that an organizational perspective is essential for understanding how collateral damage occurs, and more radically, that it is possible to think of organizations, including the military, as moral agents. I described the features of organizations—frames, knowledge, roles, practices, and culture—that constitute organizations and then showed how these features are

---

[96] Nagl, *Learning to Eat Soup with a Knife*, p. 7.

evident in the US military. Yet, moral agency is not simply constituted when an actor's attributes match a checklist of characteristics and behavior. Rather, moral agency is constituted by a cycle of action and conscious reflection on the institutions' goals and when necessary, alterations in the moral agents' purposes, roles, knowledge and decision-making procedures, organizational capacity, and routines. Moral agency is a cycle, as illustrated in figure 6.1, because this process is continuous, beginning again and again, with continued reflection and modification, or what might also be called organizational learning.

The US military has tended to focus on individual behavior to prevent deliberate atrocity. The military has been, I argue, less aware of the problem of systemic collateral damage. Institutions can also be more or less well designed to exercise moral agency at an institutional level. Yet, a cycle of moral agency is evident in the ways that the US military has dealt with the problem of civilian casualties and collateral damage since Vietnam.

Specifically, at the meta-institutionalization level, the military exercised moral agency in the aftermath of the My Lai massacre when the Department of Defense used the results of the investigation of the My Lai massacre not only to identify and impose sanctions on individual perpetrators but also to make institutional reforms and to modify the training of soldiers. While most attention was focused on Lieutenant Calley and other individual perpetrators, the military changed its organizational frame by prioritizing civilian immunity and identified an institutional

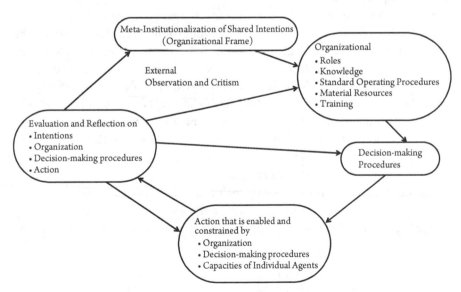

Figure 6.1 Organizations as imperfect moral agents: The cycle of moral agency.

need to stress the law of war. These reforms were codified in 1974 in what became known as the "DoD Law of War Program."[97] That directive has been renewed and modified several times—for instance in 1979, 1998, and 2006—and each military service has written regulations to specify how the Law of War directive should be implemented.

The process of institutionalization is evident from the definition of the mission through implementation. The US Department of Defense Law of War Program in 1998 defined Law of War as: "That part of international law that regulates the conduct of armed hostilities. It is often called the law of armed conflict. The law of war encompasses all international law for the conduct of hostilities binding on the United States or its individual citizens, including treaties and international agreements to which the United States is a party, and applicable customary international law."[98] The directive instructs that the relevant "Heads of the DoD Components" devise programs to "ensure that the members of their Components comply with the law of war during all armed conflicts, however such conflicts are characterized, and with the principles and spirit of the law of war during all other operations."[99] These "heads" are instructed to "institute and implement effective programs to prevent violations of the law of war, including law of war training and dissemination" of the laws of war (the 1907 Hague Convention (IV) and the 1949 Geneva Conventions) and "qualified legal advisers are immediately available at all levels of command to provide advice about law of war compliance during planning and execution of exercises and operations; and institute and implement programs to comply with the reporting requirements."[100]

The May 2006 version of the Law of War program gave a more limited definition of the law of war (there is no mention of the "spirit" of the law). Notably, the directive added explicit references to training private contractors (including their "employees and subcontractors") in the 1949 Geneva Conventions on Prisoners of War and Civilians. The 2006 Directive also expanded the authority of the Secretary of the Army to review "all reports of reportable incidents involving U.S. civilians, contractors or subcontractors assigned to or accompanying the Armed Forces...for review for prosecutory action under the criminal jurisdiction of the United States."[101] Procedures for investigation and reporting of incidents that constitute potential violations of the laws of war are much expanded.

A key element of the law of war approach taken since Vietnam is the integration of JAGs into the process of training soldiers in the laws of war, assistance in writing rules of engagement, and helping officers interpret international humanitarian law. As

---

[97] Department of Defense (DoD) Directive 5100.17, 5 November 1974.
[98] Department of Defense (DoD) Directive 5100.17, 9 December 1998, paragraph 3.1.
[99] Ibid., paragraph 5.3.1.
[100] Ibid., paragraphs 5.3.2 and 5.3.3.
[101] Department of Defense (DoD) Directive 2311.01E, 9 May 2006, paragraphs 5.7.4 and 5.8.7.

I noted in describing US air campaigns since the 1991 Gulf War, JAGs have been crucial in evaluating targets for air strikes. They also decide whether to prosecute actions that might be deliberate violations of the laws of war and thus function, as Laura Dickinson argues, as the "compliance unit within the military."[102] Indeed, it is the lawyers who interpret the norms of international law, articulate them in ways, and help devise the procedures and rules of thumb that become the institutional expression of the laws of war. Thus, the JAGs role in prosecuting violations of the laws of war is, in a way, secondary to their roles of interpretation, advise, education, and monitoring. JAGs are, in this way, the most visible expression of institutional moral agency.

The focus of the Law of War program was and is prevention and prosecution of deliberate violations of the laws of war. The program is deeply institutionalized, and we see evidence of it in the military's criminal investigations (AR-15.6) of possible deliberate harm to civilians.[103]

While it is individuals who could be investigated and potentially tried for violations of the laws of war, the military as an organization has assumed the responsibility for training soldiers in the laws of war and prosecuting them for violations of law. Indeed, in the April 2010 instructions on implementing the Law of War program, role responsibilities are carefully assigned throughout the chain of command. Specifically, combatant commanders are instructed to "institute a comprehensive program within the command to prevent law of war violations." Combatant commanders are to: "(a) Ensure that law of war training and dissemination programs of the command (including its assigned or attached subordinate units) are consistent with domestic and international law, including the law of war, and this instruction. (b) Include specific law of war scenarios in exercises to improve lawful implementation, and in cases of violations, proper reporting procedures. (c) Ensure mobilization planning includes a sufficient number of legal advisers and investigative personnel to support the commander's mission."[104] Further, the institutional role of the Joint Operations Planning and Execution System must "include appropriate guidance to ensure review of plans and rules of engagement for compliance with the laws of war."[105]

In emphasizing the importance of reviewing plans and operations for compliance with the laws of war, there is an implicit recognition that the military as an organization can create the conditions for deliberate atrocity and systemic collateral

---

[102] Laura A. Dickinson, "Military Lawyers on the Battlefield: An Empirical Account of International Law Compliance," *American Journal of International Law*, vol. 104, no. 1 (2010): 1–28, 15. Also see Michael P. Scharf, "International Law in Crisis: A Qualitative Empirical Contribution to the Compliance Debate," *Cardoso Law Review*, vol. 31 (2009): 45–97.

[103] I do not have space here to evaluate the effectiveness of the law of war program in deterring and punishing deliberate killing.

[104] Chairman of the Joint Chiefs of Staff Instruction, CJSI 5810.01D, 30 April 2010, paragraph 6 f (1).

[105] Ibid., paragraph 6 b (2).

damage, allow its occurrence, and, conversely, reduce the likelihood of both deliberate violations of the laws of war and the incidence of "collateral damage." We see this perhaps most clearly in the role of JAGs. Military lawyers articulate the importance of complying with international law's prohibition on deliberately harming noncombatants. For example, on the one hand, JAGs participate in devising rules of engagement designed to minimize collateral damage. On the other hand, when asked to participate in targeting decisions, JAGS may advise commanders about proportionality and double effect considerations where civilians are knowingly put at risk. If the adviser suggests that the risk is proportional to the anticipated military advantage, then in a sense the JAG's role is to sanction proportional collateral damage.

Prospective or "forward-looking" moral responsibility ought to comprise both the *jus ad bellum* considerations of when it is justified to make war as well as the *jus in bello* obligations to prepare to fight war justly, with discrimination and proportionality. The decisions made before wars begin, or as they continue—including the content of basic and advanced training, the selection of weapons to be procured and deployed to the battlefield, the choice of particular strategies, and the preparation of rules of engagement (when a soldier can use deadly force)—constrain and enable individual actors on the battlefield. There is no tip of the spear unless and until all these choices are made, each one with moral implications. Prospective moral responsibility at the organizational level thus entails the obligation to create an environment where both deliberate atrocity and systemic collateral damage are less likely to occur.

If, as I argue, the paradigm of individual responsibility is incomplete, and if military organizations bear some share of moral responsibility for systemic collateral damage and proportionality/double effect killing, what is the nature of that responsibility and how should it be discharged? While the individual still has moral agency, the organization set the conditions for action of individuals and made certain actions and outcomes possible. So both organizations and individuals are morally responsible.[106]

Attending to the moral agency of an organization, in fact, highlights how it is that certain outcomes were not inevitable or accidental, but created by the organization's beliefs, structures, procedures, and effect on individuals. The responsibility of relevant collective agents is forward and backward looking, rooted in their causal relationship to the structural conditions that both empower and constrain individual perpetrators. Military organizations and state institutions are thus most directly

---

[106] As List and Pettit argue, "the group agent is fit to be held responsible for ensuring that one or more of its members perform in the relevant manner. At the same time, the enacting members of the group are not absolved of their own responsibility. Other things being equal, they are still fit to be held responsible for the fact that it is they who helped get the action performed. The members have responsibility as enactors of the corporate deed so far as they could have refused to play that part and didn't. The group agent as a whole has responsibility as the source of that deed, the 'planner' at its origin." List and Pettit, *Group Agency*, p. 163.

responsible for creating the structural conditions that may, unintentionally, promote systemic collateral damage, although as I argue below, civilian institutions and publics bear some indirect responsibility. These responsibilities are also drawn from a conception of the collective agents' ideal roles, assuming they are well-functioning. Forward looking, prospective, responsibility is defined in any instance based on an understanding of how collective actors should act in their respective roles, and the attribution retrospective responsibilities is based on an understanding of how these actors have acted or failed to act.

Exercising Moral Agency for Civilian Killing

The laws of war and rules of engagement are only as effective at determining behavior and affecting outcomes to the extent that they influence the actual behavior or units on the ground and the training that soldiers get before they deploy. Choices made far from the battlefield at the Pentagon—of weapons, targets, and procedures— can lead to civilian death or diminish its likelihood. For example, I described in the last chapter how the United States chose to emphasize precision-guided munitions during the 1995 Bosnia air campaign. In that case, the directive came from political leaders and was implemented by a commander who had to take an active role because the emphasis on civilian casualty prevention was not yet deeply institutionalized.

In the wars in Afghanistan and Iraq after 9/11, the US military took both explicit and implicit responsibility for creating the conditions that could reduce the potential for systemic "collateral damage" or allow for proportionality double effect collateral damage. When systemic collateral damage occurs, the direct perpetrator did not intend the killing of particular innocents, but the killing was a foreseeable result of a military or political choice that was out of the hands of the individual "perpetrator." For example, civilians on foot or in trucks who are leaving a village may be killed by bombs because pilots are ordered to restrict their over-flight and bombings to such a high altitude that the ability to distinguish between combatants and noncombatants, or the accuracy of the weapons, was necessarily compromised. In fact, the choice to bomb from high altitudes may lead to many such incidents. There was no conspiracy to kill civilians. Indeed, the pilots and their commanders may feel great remorse over their deaths. In this case the collateral damage killing was systemic—caused by prior policy choices and institutional constraints.

In the case of systemic collateral damage, actors have created effects opposite their intention because social structure—the rules and resources created by collectives, for example, the rules of engagement, may have compromised individual knowledge and agency. The causes of systemic collateral damage are located in the social structures created and operated by collectives to the extent that social structures constrain individual choice and action, as well as psychological/cultural, in the sense that individuals possess attitudes of contempt that are widely shared and that make it difficult to see systemic collateral damage even as it is being produced. The causes of systemic collateral damage and proportionality/double effect collateral damage—the acceptance of the legitimacy of foreseeable collateral damage in case after case—are the normative beliefs about military necessity, proportionality, double effect, and intentionality that combine with the institutional incentives to downplay the value of civilian life in relation to the perceived value of a military objective. There is little incentive to think otherwise.

Conversely, because systemic collateral damage has been missing from our awareness, or even excused, the role of institutions in setting the conditions for systemic collateral damage is sometimes overlooked, while individuals are sometimes blamed for acts beyond their immediate control. Thus, the assignment of moral responsibility for systemic collateral damage has, until recently, fallen into a sort of void. States and military organizations tend to abjure their responsibility for systemic collateral damage and proportionality/double effect killing, either by excusing the deaths of noncombatants under the doctrine of double effect or by displacing responsibility on the argument that it was the other side's fault that civilians were in the way. Philosophers have tended to avoid the issue because the dominant paradigm in moral philosophy, as in criminal law, stresses individual agency and accountability.

Moral responsibility for collateral damage thus belongs at both the individual and the collective level. During and after a law of war violation we can hold individuals and collectives responsible for failing to enact their prospective moral responsibilities. In other words we can assign blame or praise. Individuals can also take retrospective responsibility to the extent that they accept blame for causing harm and enact the obligations that come from a failure to prevent harm to noncombatants. This is the duty to halt the harm and make repair. Specifically, when the conduct of war results in moral wrongs, collective actors should be held morally responsible for negligence, the failure to halt or change practices that will likely result in future wrongs. There is also arguably duty to repair after wrongs that could and should have been prevented or halted have been committed in war.[107]

In this section I examine six areas where, at the organizational level, assumptions, decision rules, training, tools, and practices either increased the likelihood of collateral damage or reduced it. In each instance, the military acted as a moral agent that is causally and morally responsible for systemic and proportionality/double effect collateral damage.[108] The first example is the understanding of how to respond

---

[107] United Nations International Law Commission (ILC) Draft Articles on "Responsibility of States for Internationally Wrongful Acts." The text can be accessed at http://www.un.org/law/ilc/, Official Records of the General Assembly, Fifty-sixth Session, Supplement No. 10 (A/56/10). Article 21 on self-defense notes that "the wrongfulness of an act of a State is precluded if the act constitutes a lawful measure of self-defence taken in conformity with the Charter of the United Nations."

[108] Whether or not an organization consciously assumes or proclaims moral agency, it is still a moral agent.

to threats, specifically the classification of noncombatants and combatants within the rules of engagement. The second is the method—the algorithms and procedures—used to estimate and minimize noncombatant harm before contact. The third example describes the training regimes used to prepare troops for encounters with combatants and noncombatants. The fourth example focuses on the choice of weapons. The fifth example involves changes in checkpoint tactics. Finally, I outline changes in attitudes about compensating civilians for harm. These examples of assumptions, rules, training, tools, and tactics illustrate the organizational awareness of, the prediction of, the normalization of collateral damage, and ultimately the understanding of collateral damage as a problem. It is clear from these mini-cases that moral agency is organizational: it is not possible, even in cases where an individual had an insight, for any individual within the military, acting alone, to enact or change the beliefs and procedures described below.

Distinction, Rules of Engagement, and Hostile Force

The key concept that determines who can be lawfully killed in war is the principle of distinction between combatant and noncombatant.[109] The institutional expression of this key organizational frame is the rules of engagement. Soldiers are permitted to use force in self-defense and against legitimate targets. Mark Martins's description of the evolution of US rules of engagement from the 1950s to the early 1990s illustrates how at times the rules of engagement were modified in response to dramatic instances, sometimes lurching from permissive to restrictive and back. So, for instance, after 241 US Marines and Sailors were killed in Beirut in 1983 by a suicide bomber, under the assumption that the ROE or their interpretation was too restrictive, the ROE were loosened. Restrictive rules of engagement were also blamed when personnel on the US frigate, the *Stark*, failed to shoot down an Iraqi Mirage Aircraft that fired missiles against it in 1987, killing thirty-seven soldiers. Alternatively, when the US Navy shot down an Iranian airliner, killing 290 civilians in a case of mistaken identification, the rules of engagement were tightened.[110]

Specific rules of engagement change from situation to situation. But these are based on a template, the peacetime rules of engagement written by the Chairman of the Joint Chiefs of Staff. Soldiers may use force in self-defense when they perceive a hostile act or hostile intention. A third category of permission exists, which can widen the authorization to use force to include civilians. According to the US Standing Rules of Engagement, "Once a force is declared hostile by appropriate

---

[109] See Helen M. Kinsella, *The Image before the Weapon: A Critical History of the Distinction between Combatant and Civilian* (Ithaca, NY: Cornell University Press, 2011) for a comparative historical discussion of distinction.

[110] Martins, "Rules of Engagement for Land Forces."

authority, US units need not observe a hostile act or a demonstration of hostile intent before engaging that force."[111] And recall that the definition of hostile force includes civilians: "Any civilian, paramilitary, or military force or terrorist(s), with or without national designation, that has committed a hostile act, exhibited hostile intent, or has been declared hostile by appropriate US authority."[112]

The reasoning surrounding the idea of a people "declared hostile" has changed little since the nineteenth century. The northern General William T. Sherman, faced with a stubborn Confederate Army in the Civil War, argued that the United States was "not only fighting hostile armies, but a hostile people." Sherman believed that the United States must "make old and young, rich and poor, feel the hard hand of war."[113] The rules of engagement that Sherman articulated discriminate according to whether the people opposed the United States: "In districts and neighborhoods where the army is unmolested, no destruction of [private] property should be permitted; but should guerrillas or bush whackers molest our march, or should the inhabitants burn bridges, obstruct roads, or otherwise manifest local hostility, then army commanders should order and enforce a devastation more or less relentless, according to the measure of hostility."[114] Or as one Specialist Jabbar Magruder said of his tour in Iraq, "The enemy doesn't wear uniforms.... You almost have to assume that everybody's hostile."[115] There is indeed a tendency in counterinsurgency situations to view everyone as a potential combatant. Not only does the one side eschew uniforms they may, as the Pentagon emphasizes, be located among noncombatants and may use noncombatants as human shields. Little has changed in this respect since the Frontier Wars. Further, civilian vehicles and women with bombs strapped to their chests may be agents of death.

In sum, the declaration of a "hostile force" can undermine the principle of distinction. More pernicious, the perception of a hostile population nearly erases the principle of distinction. Yet, while acknowledging that civilians may be "collocated" with insurgents, the 2012 *Civilian Casualty Mitigation* manual underscores distinction at

[111] "Standing Rules of Engagement for US Forces," CJCSI 3121.01A, Enclosure A, paragraph 6, p. A-5. The rest of the paragraph reads: "The responsibility for exercising the right and obligation of national self-defense and as necessary declaring a force hostile is a matter of the utmost importance. All available intelligence, the status of international relationships, the requirements of international law, an appreciation of the political situation, and the potential consequences for the United States must be carefully weighed. The exercise of the right and obligation of national self-defense by competent authority is separate from and in no way limits the commander's right and obligation to exercise unit self-defense."

[112] "Standing Rules of Engagement for US Forces," CJCSI 3121.01A, Enclosure A, paragraph 5i, p. A-5.

[113] Sherman, quoted in Andrew J. Birtle, *U.S. Army Counterinsurgency Operations Doctrine, 1860-1941* (Washington, DC: U.S. Army Center of Military History, 1998), p. 36.

[114] Sherman, quoted in ibid., p. 39.

[115] Quoted in Chris Hedges and Laila Al-Arian, *Collateral Damage: America's War against Iraqi Civilians* (New York: Nation Books, 2008), p. 21.

several junctures and reinforces the presumption of civilian status in situations of uncertainty.[116] In a near about-face of earlier attitudes in the Afghanistan and Iraq wars, which blamed civilians for being near insurgents, and excused US-caused collateral damage, the 2012 manual stresses distinction.

> The law of armed conflict, particularly the principles of proportionality and distinction, directs units not to target civilians and other noncombatants. However, because enemies may be located among civilians and may even attempt to use civilians as shields, it may be appropriate to modify or delay operations when civilians are at risk and the expected CIVCASs or damage would be excessive in relation to the concrete and direct military advantage anticipated.[117]

Balancing Risk, Calculating Harm: Algorithms and Targeting

The consideration of civilian casualties in targeting and mission planning has changed since the days of the Vietnam War when President Johnson participated in target selection over lunch with his advisers. From the end of the Vietnam War through the 1990s, most US military engagements were short and the major military actions were characterized by the use of air power as the sole or the primary instrument. The rules of engagement for ground forces in the US interventions in Grenada and Panama included protecting civilians.[118] But it was in the use of air power where civilian casualty estimation and mitigation were increasingly institutionalized. The ad hoc has been replaced by the routine and systematic, reflecting the increased understanding of the importance of civilian casualties. Some of the "back of the envelope" processes of considering civilian casualties have been replaced by computerized analysis and the algorithms used in those computer programs embody the norms and the tensions among them. With the exception of Bush and Obama administration drone strikes against high-level terrorist or insurgent targets, the military has largely taken back from the White House the role of considering targets and the problem of collateral damage.

The procedures, algorithms, and the modeling and simulation techniques of collateral damage estimation and mitigation are the institutionalization of organizational frames and organizational knowledge. While the details of contents, values, and methods of the algorithms used to estimate potential harm to noncombatants

---

[116] Army, *Civilian Casualty Mitigation*, p. 1-1.

[117] Ibid., p. 1-5.

[118] For example, see Martins, "Rules of Engagement for Land Forces."

are classified, there is a general discussion of the inputs and procedures in declassified sources and in the professional literature of policy modelers. What follows is not an exhaustive description of the process, which is quite detailed, but rather meant as illustrative of the basic procedures, and how they have evolved through the wars in Afghanistan and Iraq.

During the early part of the war in Afghanistan, the United States employed the same computer program used in previous conflicts to estimate collateral damage. During the first Gulf War, Operation Desert Storm, collateral damage estimates (CDE) were computed "using engineering estimates developed independently for each appropriate target in a very lengthy process."[119] During the subsequent years of over flights and strikes in Iraq to patrol no-fly zones, Operation Southern Watch, the Pentagon gathered data and refined the CDE process. In the next major use of US air power in 1995, the short air campaign in Bosnia, as I described in the previous chapter, high-level concern to prevent civilian casualties translated into high-level direction and monitoring of air operations in the US air campaign. During the 1999 Kosovo air war the Conventional Casualty Estimation Tool (CCET) and the Collateral Damage Estimation Tool (CDET) were used to estimate, respectively, casualties and collateral damage for over 400 targets. CDET utilized 3D modeling for "high fidelity assessment" of collateral damage. Yet, the evaluation of each target could take several hours.

Minimizing harm to civilians and civilian objects in Afghanistan was a priority; the Pentagon and the President wanted to avoid the appearance of a war with Islam. Benjamin Lambeth notes that the Central Command was given "ready access to the Joint Warfare Analysis Center and its ability to provide weaponeering support as necessary to prevent collateral damage against the most sensitive targets."[120] But Lambeth notes, "The methodology used by CENTCOM for collateral damage expectancy (CDE) assessment itself was inadequate."[121] Collateral damage estimation depends on information about both the weapons and the characteristics of the target. The early air campaign in Afghanistan relied on the data from Operation Southern Watch. Yet, the targets and surrounding structures in Afghanistan were not the same as in Iraq, and Lambeth argues, reliance on data from Southern Watch in Iraq, led to overestimating likely collateral damage. The target approval process was already slow from the perspective of commanders on the ground and the extra caution that the United States used, in Lambeth's view, was simply another factor in reducing military effectiveness. There were also

---

[119] Douglas D. Martin and Steven C. "Flash" Gordon, "Collateral Damage Estimation: Transforming Time-Sensitive Command and Control," *Interservice/Industry Training, Simulation, and Education Conference*, Paper No. 1768, 2004.

[120] Benjamin S. Lambeth, *Air Power against Terror: America's Conduct of Operation Enduring Freedom* (Santa Monica, CA: RAND Corporation, 2010), p. 320.

[121] Ibid.

several high-profile incidents of collateral damage in 2001 and 2002, which the Pentagon wanted to avoid.

Thus, in planning for the March 2003 Iraq invasion and occupation, the US Chairman of the Joint Chiefs of Staff issued a directive in September 2002 (the Combined Joint Chiefs of Staff Instructid 3160.01) that combatant commanders must estimate, evaluate, and mitigate potential collateral damage.[122] According to the directive, several algorithms, which were either already in use or newly developed for use by the services, were to be utilized for evaluating potential targets and estimating both casualties and collateral damage. The Fast Assessment Strike Tool—Collateral Damage (FAST-CD) earlier known as "BugSplat," which was developed from the CDET to be much faster, was used for the first time to "vet" about 400 targets.[123] FAST-CD uses two-dimensional images. Brigadier General Kelvin Coppock, director of intelligence for the Air Combat Command told a reporter before the United States attacked Iraq that BugSplat was "a significant advance." Coppock argued that "it will allow us to target those facilities that we want to target with confidence that we're not going to cause collateral damage."[124]

The CJSM 3160.01 of 2002 has been revised several times and become more explicit. The 2009 instruction includes lists of "no strike" targets and a description of collateral damage estimation and mitigation methods. Before analysts can conduct CDE estimates, they must complete the US Joint Forces Command Joint Targeting School collateral damage estimation course, including the use of CDE software, and a local certification program developed by the relevant combatant command. FAST-CD became the tool of choice for estimating collateral damage for "time-sensitive targets" in both Afghanistan and Iraq because it could take as little as five minutes to run the program. The software can help planners evaluate how changes in weapons or the character of the attack would affect the collateral damage estimate. Both CDET and FAST-CD software and procedures have been modified and improved so that they are now, respectively, Advanced CDET and FAST-CD 2.0.[125] Figure 6.2 is an example a two-dimensional image of a target used to estimate collateral damage.[126]

The FAST-CD program is employed as part of a more comprehensive procedure that follows a series of basic steps for preplanned operations: target identification

---

[122] Chairman of the Joint Chiefs of Staff Manual (CJCSM) 3160.01, "Joint Methodology for Estimating Collateral Damage and Casualties for Conventional Weapons: Precision, Unguided and Cluster (U)," 20 September 2002.

[123] Senior Defense Official, "Background Briefing on Targeting," 5 March 2003, http://www.defense.gov/transcripts/transcript.aspx?transcriptid=2007.

[124] Bradley Graham, "'Bugsplat' Computer Program Aims to Limit Civilian Deaths at Targets," *Washington Post*, 22 February 2003.

[125] Chairman of the Joint Chiefs of Staff Instruction, CJCSI 3160.01, "No Strike and Collateral Damage Estimation Methodology," 13 February 2009. http://www.aclu.org/files/dronefoia/dod/drone_dod_3160_01.pdf.

[126] From Martin and Gordon, "Collateral Damage Estimation."

Figure 6.2 Two-dimensional collateral damage estimation imaging.
Source: Douglas D. Martin and Steven C. "Flash" Gordon, "Collateral Damage Estimation: Transforming
Time-Sensitive Command and Control," *Interservice/Industry Training, Simulation, and Education
Conference,* Paper No. 1768, 2004.

and validation, risk assessment, risk mitigation, evaluation or proportionality balancing (military necessity and risks to civilians), and approval. In the first step, military planners determine whether a potential target is a legitimate military target.
The norm of discrimination and the laws of war prohibit strikes on civilians or civilian objects. At this point in the process, a strike may be delayed or aborted if civilians are present. Commanders and other planners, including intelligence officers,
are not expected to be perfect in this evaluation, but are judged under a standard of
"reasonableness."[127] If the target is simply a military objective, planning may proceed
without concern for civilians. The international lawyer Gregory McNeal reports,
that according to his interview sources, that in 70 percent of those instances when
collateral damage in Iraq and Afghanistan occurred, the cause was mistaken identification of the target.[128] But knowing of the presence of civilians does not mean

[127] See Geoffrey S. Corn, "Targeting, Command Judgment, and a Proposed Quantum Proof
Component: A Fourth Amendment Lesson in Contextual Reasonableness," February 2011, http://
works.bepress.com/geoffrey_corn/6, accessed 21 August 2012.

[128] Gregory S. McNeal, "The U.S. Practice of Collateral Damage Estimation and Mitigation," 9
November 2011, p. 13, http://works.bepress.com/gregorymcneal/22/.

a strike would necessarily be aborted. If the target is a military objective or is dual use, and civilians are nearby, then collateral damage estimation and mitigation procedures, including FAST-CD, would come into play. At this juncture, a civilian casualty estimate would be calculated. If civilian casualties are expected mitigation efforts are undertaken.

Assuming planners have identified a valid military target, they assess likely collateral damage. This includes information about the target, such as the population density of the area, estimated at different times of day, and information about the particular weapons that are available. Each weapon has an expected rate of reliability, level of accuracy, and "effective area" of destruction. "A Hellfire missile has only about a 40-pound warhead. So the circle that it might cause damage is relatively small: 60 or 70 feet. On the other hand, a 2,000-pound bomb will create about 90 percent of its effect out to about 600 feet of the target."[129] If the circle of damage includes civilians or civilian infrastructure, analysts will attempt to minimize the damage to civilians or civilian objects.

In the cases where significant loss of civilian life was anticipated, more often than not, something about the attack was changed so as to reduce the risk to civilians. A precision guided ("smart") weapon might be substituted for an unguided weapon ("dumb" bomb). A more accurate weapon might indeed reduce the likelihood of killing civilians. Yet, as Stephen Wrage observed in his analysis of precision weapons, "Greater discrimination also brought temptations, largely resisted by the users of precision weapons. It was tempting, for example to grow more ambitious in targeting." Wrage notes that "targeters in the Iraq [1991], Kosovo and Afghanistan campaigns began at once to work finer and finer tolerances in picking legitimate targets out of not-to-be-targeted areas." Wrage, who teaches at the US Naval Academy, cautions that "greater accuracy will not yield greater discrimination if it merely encourages more risk taking."[130]

But choosing a weapon of greater accuracy might be combined with other techniques for reducing civilian casualties. A weapon with a smaller area of destruction might be used. The aim point on a target might be changed. Or, the angle of attack (azimuth) might be altered by having the pilot come from a different direction so that the effects of a bomb (the pattern of fragmentation and blast) are directed away from civilians. The timing of an attack is sometimes shifted to avoid civilians who might be congregating in the area. For example Lieutenant General Michael Short ordered changes to NATO bombing during Operation Allied Force in Kosovo in 1999 after NATO destroyed a passenger train crossing a bridge. "The guidance for attacking bridges in the future was: You will no longer attack bridges on weekends or market days or holidays. In fact, you will only

---

[129] Senior Defense Official, "Background Briefing on Targeting," 5 March 2003, http://www.defense.gov/transcripts/transcript.aspx?transcriptid=2007.

[130] Wrage, "The Ethics of Precision Air Power," p. 93.

attack bridges between 10 o'clock at night and 4 o'clock in the morning."[131] Or a bomb might be fused differently.

> For example, if you use a bomb with an air burst, meaning it explodes some number of feet above the ground, there's nothing that absorbs the fragmentation of that bomb, so it travels farther. If you use a delay fuse that goes a millisecond or two milliseconds under the ground, in fact the explosive—the fragmentation doesn't go very far at all, and the explosive damage is created mostly straight up, as opposed to out from the target. So you can reduce the area that's affected. [132]

In this respect, and also as when the United States modified its bombing tactics in Bosnia and Kosovo to minimize harm to civilians, the US military has practiced a level of "due care."

After collateral damage estimation and mitigation steps are completed, a decision about whether to strike is made by the relevant authority. According to the now unclassified version of rules of engagement for Iraq in 2005, legitimate targets of preplanned strikes included: (1) Nonmilitary elements of former regime command and control and associated facilities, (2) WMD storage facilities, (3) Iraqi infrastructure and Iraqi economic objects, (4) Terrorists, (5) Iraqi lines of communication, and (6) Facilities (associated with Designated Terrorists or Declared Hostile Forces)."[133] The authority to strike a target depended on the "collateral damage expected: NO collateral damage, LOW collateral damage, and HIGH collateral damage."[134]

> **HIGH COLLATERAL DAMAGE TARGETS**: Those targets that, if struck, have a ten percent probability of causing collateral damage through blast debris and fragmentation and are estimated to result in significant collateral effects on noncombatant persons and structures, including: (A) Non-combatant casualties estimated at 30 or greater; (B) Significant effects on Category I No Strike protected sites in accordance with Ref D; (C) In the case of dual-use facilities, effects that significantly impact the noncombatant population, including significant effects on the environment/facilities/infrastructure not related to an adversary's

---

[131] Michael C. Short, quoted in Derek S. Reveron, "Coalition Warfare: The Commander's Role," in Stephen D. Wrage, ed., *Immaculate Warfare: Participants Reflect on the Air Campaigns over Kosovo, Afghanistan, and Iraq* (Westport, CT: Praeger, 2003), pp. 51–70, 57.

[132] Senior Defense Official, "Background Briefing on Targeting."

[133] Annex E (Consolidated ROE) SECRET//REL TO USA, IRQ, MCFI/20151003 (2005), p. E-1-9. http://wikileaks.org/wiki/US_Rules_of_Engagement_for_Iraq. This document was unclassified by a leak in 2008, as opposed to an officially declassified document.

[134] Annex E, p. E-1-11.

war making ability; or (D) Targets in close proximity to known human shields.[135]

In the first weeks of the invasion of Iraq (and until at least after the above ROE were promulgated in 2005), Defense Secretary Donald Rumsfeld or President Bush were required to authorize any airstrike where it was estimated that thirty or more civilian casualties were likely, with the standard of likely being above a 10 percent or greater chance.[136] This was certainly an effort to limit collateral damage. The ceiling of thirty potential civilian casualties did not mean that the strike would not occur, only that permission must be sought and given by a high-level commander or the president or Secretary of Defense. Authorization for strikes that risked up to thirty civilian casualties could be given at a lower, senior commander, level.

Those instances when the authorization was given in Iraq to make strikes where thirty or more civilians were at risk, and civilians were harmed, are instances of proportionality/double effect collateral damage. According to reporting published in the *New York Times*, permission was sought and given more than fifty times in the early months of the war.[137] Frequently in these cases, the United States was searching for high-level Iraqi officials. Human Rights Watch found that "many of the civilian casualties from the air war occurred during U.S. attacks on senior Iraqi leadership officials."[138] Human Rights Watch noted that "every single attack on leadership failed." Human Rights Watch also argued that "the intelligence and targeting methodologies used to identify potential leadership targets were inherently flawed and led to preventable deaths."[139] The deaths and injuries of civilians in those strikes were certainly preventable—a choice was made to risk them. And the intelligence process was also likely inadequate. But the collateral damage estimation and mitigation procedures were not necessarily flawed. What was wrong, was the relatively high "Non-Combatant Casualty Cut-Off Value" (NCV) of thirty civilians, and a proportionality/double effect calculation that weighted anticipated military necessity greater than anticipated harm to civilians.[140]

---

[135] Annex E, p. E-1-25.

[136] Annex E, p. E-1-25; McNeal, "The U.S. Practice of Collateral Damage Estimation and Mitigation," p. 3; Human Rights Watch, *Off Target: The Conduct of the War and Civilian Casualties in Iraq* (New York: Human Rights Watch, 2003), p. 19.

[137] Michael R. Gordon, "After the War: Preliminaries; U.S. Air Raids in '02 Prepared for War in Iraq," *New York Times*, 20 July 2003; Sharon Otterman, "The Calculus of Civilian Death," *New York Times*, 6 January 2009

[138] Human Rights Watch, *Off Target*, p. 22.

[139] Ibid.

[140] On the NCV, see McNeal, "The U.S. Practice of Collateral Damage Estimation and Mitigation," p. 27.

As I have argued, this weighting began to shift in Iraq and Afghanistan in the mid- and late 2000s when military necessity was redefined to require civilian protection. Specifically, in mid-2009 in Afghanistan, close air support operations were limited and placed under greater control, and all operations, except emergencies, were to be preplanned: "the pilot's only discretion is to elect not to release a weapon."[141] McNeal cites a number of reports that "current (2011) operations in Afghanistan relying on counterinsurgency doctrine employ an NCV of 1 for preplanned operations."[142] McNeal also says, citing unnamed interviewees, that when there was collateral damage in preplanned strikes, "22% of the time it was attributable to weapons malfunction, and a mere 8% of the time it was attributable to proportionality balancing—e.g. a conscious decision that anticipated military advantage outweighed collateral damage."[143] These are indeed interesting statistics. Yet, much more needs to be understood about them, as well as cut-off and the ratio of preplanned strikes.

Official and Unofficial Ethics Training

Soldiers on patrol outside their bases, or on missions, do not have the same sorts of decisions and dilemmas as those who choose the targets and the weapons used to bomb preplanned targets. Nor do they have as much time. They must take the general guidance of the rules of engagement and make immediate decisions. One early version of the Rules of Engagement for Iraq was as follows:

> 3.A.(2) (U) **MILITARY POLICY.** Commanders have the inherent authority and obligation to use all necessary means available and to take all appropriate action in self-defense of their units and other US Forces and Coalition Forces.
>   3.A.(3) (U) At all times, the requirements of necessity and proportionality will form the basis of the judgment of the on-scene commander (OSC) or individual as to what
> constitutes an appropriate response in self-defense to a particular hostile act or demonstration of hostile intent.
>   3.A.(4) (U) All personnel must ensure that, prior to any engagement, non-combatants and civilian structures are distinguished from proper military targets.
>   3.A.(5) (U) Positive Identification (PID) of all targets is required prior to engagement.

[141] Ibid., p. 5n.
[142] Ibid., p. 29.
[143] Ibid., p. 2.

PID is a reasonable certainty that the individual or object of attack is a legitimate military target in accordance with these ROE.

3.A.(6) (U) Military operations will be conducted, in so far as possible, to ensure that incidental injury to civilians and collateral damage to civilian objects are minimized. Strikes on infrastructure, lines of communication and economic objects should, to the extent possible, disable and disrupt rather than destroy.

3.A.(7) (U) Civilian structures, especially cultural and historic buildings, nonmilitary structures, civilian population centers, mosques and other religious places, hospitals and facilities displaying the red crescent or red cross, are protected structures and will not be attacked except when they are being used for military purposes. Targeting structures will be conducted in accordance with these ROE and the CDEM. US Forces will not utilize these protected structures for military purposes.

3.A.(8) (U) The use of force to accomplish authorized missions will be necessary and proportional, that is, reasonable in intensity, duration and magnitude.[144]

The rules were clear: the use of force in self-defense and against legitimate military targets was authorized while harming civilians was forbidden. Yet after several highly visible episodes of civilian massacres and the abuse of prisoners at Abu Ghraib were uncovered, the need for more training was manifest. As I noted in chapter 4, when the retraining in "core warrior values" occurred in 2006, the military and civilian leaders were asserting that the bulk, 99.9 percent of US soldiers were following the rules. That was clearly an overestimate, even after the "core warrior values" training. The military's own surveys of US military personnel in Iraq confirmed that the rules were not enough. The Mental Health Assessment Team surveys in 2006 and 2007 uncovered that, respectively, 37 and 34 percent of soldiers admitted that they insulted or cursed noncombatants and that 6 percent had hit or kicked a noncombatant. In 2006, 11 percent of those interviewed admitted to modifying the rules engagement. In both survey years, less than 50 percent of those interviewed said that they would report a unit member for mistreating, hurting, or killing a noncombatant.[145] Further, when asked, in the MHAT surveys, soldiers in Iraq said they found the Powerpoint slides ineffective.[146]

---

[144] US Rules of Engagement for Iraq, as published by Wikileaks, http://wikileaks.org/wiki/US_Iraq_Rules_of_Engagement_leaked.

[145] Results cited in Warner et al., "Effectiveness of Battlefield-Ethics Training during Combat Deployment." The MHAT surveys are found on the US Army website. http://www.armymedicine.army.mil/reports/mhat/mhat_v/MHAT_V_OIFandOEF-Redacted.pdf.

[146] Warner et al., "Effectiveness of Battlefield-Ethics Training during Combat Deployment," p. 918.

In what was a remarkable instance of organizational learning, the Army then dramatically revamped its ethics training in the war zone, leaving the Powerpoint slides behind. The analyses and briefing slides were replaced with scenario-based discussions. Leaders taught their immediate subordinates using scripts and short vignettes from films, including "Platoon," "Patriot," and "Three Kings." The scenarios included treatment of noncombatants, killing noncombatants, and reporting ethical violations. All brigades in Iraq received the training and surveys of 500 soldiers who received the training indicate that "decreased rates of unethical conduct were noted in all categories after training, with significant reductions in reports" of verbal abuse, destruction of property, and physical mistreatment of noncombatants.[147]

The commitment to training soldiers before deployment was underscored in the 2012 *Civilian Casualty Mitigation* guidance.

> CIVCAS mitigation training for Soldiers includes the law of armed conflict. CIVCAS mitigation should be incorporated into exercises.... During training and exercises, effective commanders avoid focusing exclusively on fighting against a hostile enemy, as this could reinforce a "shoot first" mentality. Exercises should include civilians who are not hostile, and units should receive training on the rules of engagement and escalation-of-force...so that Soldiers know how to engage civilians. Leaders can provide Soldiers a CIVCAS smart card [reproduced below as figure 6.3].[148]

The 2012 guidance also underscored the importance of shaping soldiers attitudes toward civilians. The reasoning was bluntly stated: "Negative attitudes, such as perceiving host-nation civilians as inferior, must be avoided because they lead to thinking that CIVCASs are not too regrettable." Further, the guidance emphasizes cultural awareness as part of pre-deployment training and simply states, "Soldiers should not refer to civilians with disparaging slang terms."[149]

The fact of a new guidance, or the occasional retraining of an entire cadre in the field, is relatively rare however. The military has institutionalized constant training and retraining in the laws of war in the battlefield using scenarios drawn from recent cases in the area. JAGs told Laura Dickinson, "We go through scenarios, we practice, and see what happens." This JAG also said, "We take a look at the circumstances in which people are getting killed," and how it may be possible to revise procedures, "how we can stop so we don't need to use deadly force but at the same time ensure that our soldiers are not attacked."[150]

---

[147] Ibid., p. 920.
[148] Army, *Civilian Casualty Mitigation*, p. 2-2.
[149] Ibid., p. 2-3.
[150] Quoted in Dickinson, "Military Lawyers on the Battlefield," p. 17.

Prevent civilian casualties:	**In case of civilian casualties:**
• Do not intentionally target civilians or civilian objects.	• Alert other Soldiers that civilians are present.
• Do not take unnecessary actions that could harm civilians.	• Continue with your mission as necessary.
• Do not abuse, degrade, or seek revenge against civilians.	**When the situation permits:**
• Protect civilians from the effects of combat when you can.	• Treat or evacuate any wounded civilians. If possible, allow a local representative to accompany any evacuated casualties.
• Know and practice the rules of engagement and escalation of force procedures	• Report the incident through your chain of command (who, what, when, where, why).
• Provide support to wounded civilians.	• Obtain names of witnesses (military and civilian).
• Treat civilians as you would want you and your family to be treated if the roles were reversed.	• Explain procedures for claims to local civilian leadership. Provide any required forms.
• Follow the Army Values when dealing with civilians.	• Maintain a respectful bearing.
	• Provide updates to the chain of command as appropriate.
Front of card	Back of card

Figure 6.3 US Army "smart card example" for civilian casualty mitigation.

Source: Reproduced from the Department of the Army, *Civilian Casualty Mitigation*, Army Tactics, Techniques, and Procedures (ATTP) No. 3-37.31 (Washington, DC: Department of the Army, 18 July 2012), figure 2-2, on page 2-3.

Weapons and Tactics

Article 85 of Geneva Protocol I describes launching large-scale attacks with "the knowledge that such attack will cause excessive loss of life, injury to civilians or damage to civilian objects" as a grave breach of international law.[151] In other words, it may not be the intention to cause indiscriminate harm, but an outcome of indiscriminate harm may be foreseeable as likely and should thus be avoided. Yet, the idea that some weapons are discriminating, and others are not, is not quite right.

[151] Article 85(3) of Geneva Protocol I states that "grave breaches" are:

(a) Making the civilian population or individual civilians the object of attack;

(b) Launching an indiscriminate attack affecting the civilian population or civilian objects in the knowledge that such attack will cause excessive loss of life, injury to civilians or damage to civilian objects, as defined in Article 57, paragraph 2(a)(iii);

(c) Launching an attack against works or installations containing dangerous forces in the knowledge that such attack will cause excessive loss of life, injury to civilians or damage to civilian objects, as defined in Article 57, paragraph 2(a)(iii);

(d) Making non-defended localities and demilitarized zones the object of attack;

(e) Making a person the object of attack in the knowledge that he is *hors de combat*.

Knives wielded by soldiers can be used in a way that is discriminating as long as soldiers are careful to discriminate between combatants and noncombatants. The farther one moves from such intimate killing, or the larger the effects of the armaments used, the effects of a weapon are potentially less discriminating. Thus, some weapons and tactics are more likely than others to produce civilian casualties. Further, there are three timelines for weapons to cause harm to noncombatants—immediate, delayed, and persistent.

The weapons that are likely to cause immediate noncombatant injury include those with large-scale effects (e.g., high explosive power) used in contexts where civilians are likely to be located. Large-scale weapons used in conjunction with civilian presence may lead to foreseeable death because despite all the precautions of soldiers, weapons effects are simply too powerful to be minimized in a given context. It is predictable that a 2,000-pound Mark-84 warhead with a damage circle of about 600 feet would kill or injure civilians as well as combatants if those weapons are deployed in urban areas or villages. General purpose unitary weapons, including those dropped from aircraft and artillery shells fired from tanks, fragment on detonation, causing blast overpressures that can knock down buildings and may begin fires.

Precision-guided munitions are not necessarily smaller than unguided weapons, only perhaps much more accurate, and they will have the same collateral damage effect as unguided munitions if they are used when civilians are present. Thus, the use of precision-guided weapons does not eliminate the potential for killing civilians from the air but can reduce the chances of doing so.

The United States has deployed systems that carry large bombs because those are the weapons that are available. The weapons procurement and training that yield a deployed military force are part of a long-term process—new equipment does not immediately materialize upon demand. When Donald Rumsfeld said, "As you know, you go to war with the Army you have. They're not the Army you might want or wish to have at a later time," he was responding to criticism that US soldiers lacked the equipment that they needed in the war zones.[152] But the statement also suggests how the pre-existing arsenal constrains and enables certain outcomes. During the initial major combat phase of the Iraq war in 2003, two-thirds of the munitions dropped from aircraft by the United States were precision-guided in some way.

In Afghanistan, and less commonly in Iraq, the United States used B-1B Lancer aircraft for close air support missions. The B-1B payload may consist of dozens of bombs, including the 2,000-lb and 500-lb bombs that can devastate a neighborhood. A B-1B bomber requires 150 people to maintain it, making it, in the words of one technician: "probably the most maintenance-intensive aircraft in the Air Force inventory. It's a technical monster. It takes the most man-hours to generate flights, so everyone who's attached to B-1B maintenance works really hard." Although it is

---

[152] Quoted in Ricks, "Rumsfeld Gets an Earful from Troops."

expensive to maintain and use, the B-1B is versatile. According to Master Sgt. Guy Matherly, "The bomber can loiter in one part of Afghanistan, and as soon as they get a call, they can be somewhere else quickly to drop weapons."[153] When one combines the use of large-scale weapons with night raids or twilight bombing, indiscriminate killing is foreseeable. For instance, at the start of the Afghanistan war, the United States had many 2,000- and 1,000-lb bombs, which destroy large areas, and a relative dearth of the smaller 250- and 500-lb bombs. The *New York Times* reported in April 2002 that "defense contractors are now looking to speed up the production of guided 500-pound and 250-pound bombs."[154]

While large weapons can leave a crater, or damage or flatten hundreds of square feet, some weapons with relatively limited blast effects may also cause large-scale, immediate, and indiscriminate harm. Specifically, incendiary weapons designed to start fires with chemical accelerants, or high-explosive bombs whose predictable effect it is to initiate fire, have long been used in war. Incendiary weapons may themselves be quite small, but their use in areas where materials are highly flammable, or their use in large numbers, can initiate indiscriminate fires or even firestorms. Protocol III of the 1980 International Convention on Certain Conventional Weapons prohibits the use of incendiary devices that are likely to harm noncombatants. Specifically, the operative provisions of Protocol III (the Protocol on Prohibitions or Restrictions on the Use of Incendiary Weapons) read:

1. It is prohibited in all circumstances to make the civilian population as such, individual civilians or civilian objects the object of attack by incendiary weapons.
2. It is prohibited in all circumstances to make any military objective located within a concentration of civilians the object of attack by air-delivered incendiary weapons.
3. It is further prohibited to make any military objective located within a concentration of civilians the object of attack by means of incendiary weapons other than air-delivered incendiary weapons, except when such military objective is clearly separated from the concentration of civilians and all feasible precautions are taken with a view to limiting the incendiary effects to the military objective and to avoiding, and in any event to minimizing, incidental loss of civilian life, injury to civilians and damage to civilian objects.

---

[153] Brok McCarthy, "Airmen Keep B-1B Ready for Bombs on Target," 3 February 2009, http://www.af.mil/news/story.asp?id=123133635.

[154] Eric Schmitt, "Improved U.S. Accuracy Claimed in Afghan Air War," *New York Times*, 9 April 2002. Schmitt also reported, "Warplanes have dropped about 6,650 Joint Direct Attack Munitions, a satellite-guided bomb that has emerged as the weapon of choice in this campaign. That has depleted the inventory so dramatically that the Boeing Company, the bombs' manufacturer, is preparing to triple production of the tail-kit device that is attached to regular gravity bombs for this purpose."

4. It is prohibited to make forests or other kinds of plant cover the object of attack by incendiary weapons except when such natural elements are used to cover, conceal or camouflage combatants or other military objectives, or are themselves military objectives.[155]

The United States submitted its intention to be bound by the protocol on incendiary weapons in January 2009. But in so doing, the United States stated a reservation that effectively allows the United States to use incendiary weapons in a way that could cause foreseeable, albeit unintentional harm to noncombatants. "The United States of America, with reference to Article 2, paragraphs 2 and 3, reserves the right to use incendiary weapons against military objectives located in concentrations of civilians where it is judged that such use would cause fewer casualties and/or less collateral damage than alternative weapons, but in so doing will take all feasible precautions with a view to limiting the incendiary effects to the military objective and to avoiding, and in any event to minimizing, incidental loss of civilian life, injury to civilians and damage to civilian objects."[156]

The US and NATO forces used white phosphorus in Iraq and Afghanistan in ground attacks. White phosphorus, launched by ground forces is used for illumination purposes although some in Afghanistan have argued that the shells have burned civilians who have come in contact with them. The United States repeatedly denied that NATO was using white phosphorus in a way that could harm noncombatants. NATO ISAF soldiers fighting in Afghanistan have also noted that white phosphorus has been used by insurgents in IED and other attacks since as early as 2003. The US military noted dozens of incidents where Taliban have used weapons including improvised explosive devices and rockets that contain white phosphorus.[157] The source of the white phosphorus is apparently both unexploded Soviet ordnance from the long Soviet war there and NATO unexploded ordnance.[158] According to

[155] Article 2, paragraphs 2 and 3, Protocol on Prohibitions or Restrictions on the Use of Incendiary Weapons (Protocol III) of the Convention on Certain Conventional Weapons

[156] "U.S. Consent to be Bound," text 21 January 2009, quoted in Jeff Abramson, "U.S. Incendiary-Weapons Policy Rebuffed," Arms Control Today, April 2010, Arms Control Association, http://www.armscontrol.org/act/2010_04/Incendiary#Sidebar1.

[157] United States Central Command, "Reported Insurgent White Phosphorus Attacks and Caches in Regional Command-East, 2003-present." Declassified for Public Release on 11 May 09, Combined Joint Task Force, 101 Press Release, http://www.centcom.mil/press-releases/reported-insurgent-white-phosphorus-attacks-and-caches; Ward Carroll, "Willy Pete in the 'Stan," Defense Tech, 22 May 2009, http://defensetech.org/2009/05/22/willy-pete-in-the-stan/. Associated Press, "U.S.: Afghan Militants Using White Phosphorus: Statement Comes Amid Probe into Coalition Strike in Farah Province," 11 May 2009, http://www.msnbc.msn.com/id/30672076/.

[158] The unexploded ordnance containing white phosphorus found in Taliban caches include 81, 82 mm, 107 mm, 120 mm rounds, 122 mm mortar rounds, all used in the NATO arsenal. United States Central Command, "Reported Insurgent White Phosphorus Attacks and Caches in Regional Command-East, 2003-present."

the US Central Command, "it is important to note that insurgent stockpiles do not necessarily derive from old Soviet-era left-behind stocks; the white phosphorus munitions found in these 38 events have their origins in a wide range of countries. Also, the vast majority of white phosphorus rounds found in listed caches were determined to be in serviceable condition."[159]

Defoliants also cause immediate collateral damage and set in chain indirect and long-term effects. For instance, the United States used the herbicide known as "agent orange" as a defoliant to damage and destroy more than 1.5 million acres of jungle and destroy more than 233,000 acres of food crops during the Vietnam War. The idea was to expose lines of communication and to deny the enemy food. A RAND study conducted for the US Department of Defense in 1967 concluded that "through 1966, crop destruction operations had not prevented the VC [Viet Cong] from feeding themselves."[160] Moreover, the study found that crop destruction led to increased hostility toward the United States at the time. RAND found that food shortages among civilians were a consequence of the crop destruction effort, and that "about 10 percent indicated cases of actual starvation."[161] The RAND study was careful to say that toxicity for humans, especially infants, from exposure to defoliants was conceivable and possible, but RAND had little data of actual harm besides the report that "70 to 80 percent of subjects" indicated that significant exposure led to harm and that some "10 percent believe that the chemicals could cause fatalities."[162]

Small weapons with relatively small-scale effects may also cause indiscriminate harm if the weapons are widely dispersed over an area where civilians are present. For example, anti-personnel land mines and cluster bombs are weapons of this sort. Anti-personnel land mines have been banned for this reason. There has been a similar movement to ban cluster munitions, but with less success. Cluster bombs remain in the US arsenal.

Cluster bombs may contain dozens or several hundred submunitions ranging in size and shape from a D-battery to a baseball or a soft-drink can. These submunitions or bomblet weapons are designed to disperse from the main munition and explode on impact over an area (footprint) of between 600 and 1,500 feet depending on the munition used.[163] The fragmentation from the exploding bomblets can injure people as far as 500 feet away.

---

[159] United States Central Command, "Reported Insurgent White Phosphorus Attacks and Caches in Regional Command-East, 2003-present."

[160] See Russell Betts and Frank Denton, "An Evaluation of Chemical Crop Destruction in Vietnam." Prepared for the Office of the Assistant Secretary of Defense/International Security Affairs and the Advanced Research Projects Agency, RAND Memo RM-5446-1-ISA/ARPA 1 (Santa Monica, CA: RAND, 1967), p. 12.

[161] Ibid., p. 15.

[162] Ibid., p. 16.

[163] The dispersal areas for CBU-103 and CBU-87, respectively.

The United States has used cluster weapons in many of its recent wars and interventions since they were first used in World War II. Thousands of cluster bomb units were used during the Vietnam War—in Laos and Cambodia as well as in Vietnam. The United States used 61,000 cluster bombs in the 1991 Gulf War to destroy tanks and Iraqi military but were also estimated by Human Rights Watch to have killed 1,600 civilians.[164] In 1995, US commanders removed cluster bombs from the NATO arsenal in Bosnia because of a concern for civilian casualties. In the 1999 Kosovo war, NATO, dropped 1,392 cluster bombs containing over 289,500 bomblets.[165] Human Rights Watch noted seven incidents where immediate collateral damage resulted from the use of cluster bombs by the United States and the United Kingdom, resulting in an estimated 90-150 civilian deaths. In one incident, a daytime attack on Nis airfield on 7 May, cluster munitions were used to target Serbian aircraft. Some bombs failed to release the bomblets over the airfield, cluster bombs fell instead on a market, the town center, a bus station, and a medical center. Human Rights Watch reported that fourteen civilians died that day in Nis, and twenty-eight were wounded.[166] Several hundred unexploded cluster bomblets reached the city center. Of the total of between 489 to 528 immediate civilian casualties, cluster bombs were responsible for between 17 and 30 percent of the deaths.

In Afghanistan, the United States dropped approximately 1,228 cluster bombs containing 248,056 submunition "bomblets" between October 2001 and March 2002. During the three weeks of major combat in the 2003 invasion of Iraq, the United States and United Kingdom used about 13,000 cluster munitions, containing about 1.8 to 2 million submunitions.[167]

In response to a global movement to ban cluster munitions and growing international support for the cluster bomb treaty, the US Department of Defense studied the issue for a year in 2007 and 2008 and announced a new policy in June 2008.[168] The United States announced in May 2008 that it had stopped using cluster bombs in Iraq and Afghanistan after 2003.[169] But, US military lawyers have argued that while cluster bombs predictably lead to civilian casualties, the weapons are legal under international law.[170] The Pentagon also reasoned that cluster bombs were

---

[164] Human Rights Watch, "United States/Afghanistan. Fatally Flawed: Cluster Bombs and their Use by The United States in Afghanistan," *Human Rights Watch*, vol. 14, no. 7 (December 2002): 2.

[165] International Committee of the Red Cross, Mines-Arms Unit, *Explosive Remnants of War* (Geneva: ICRC, August 2000, revised June 2001), p. 6.

[166] Human Rights Watch, "Civilian Deaths in the NATO Air Campaign," 1 February 2000, pp. 49–50, http://www.hrw.org/sites/default/files/reports/natbm002.pdf.

[167] Andrew Feickert and Paul K. Kerr, "Cluster Munitions: Background and Issues for Congress," Congressional Research Service, 27 June 2012 (RS22907).

[168] Secretary of Defense, "DoD Policy on Cluster Munitions and Unintended Harm to Civilians," 19 June 2008, Washington, DC. http://www.defense.gov/news/d20080709cmpolicy.pdf.

[169] Feickert and Kerr, "Cluster Munitions," p. 1.

[170] International and Operational Law Department, *Operational Law Handbook 2009* (Charlottesville, VA: The Judge Advocate General's Legal Center and School, 2009).

legitimate because they reduced risk to US forces and also "reduced unintended harm to civilians during combat, by producing less collateral damage to civilians and civilian infrastructure than unitary weapons."[171] The argument was that because "future adversaries will likely use civilian shields for military targets—for example locating a military target on the roof of an occupied building—use of unitary weapons could result in more civilian casualties and damage than cluster munitions." The Pentagon emphasized in its press release of the new policy that "blanket elimination of cluster munitions is therefore unacceptable due not only to negative military consequences but also to potential negative consequences for civilians."[172]

The second category of indiscriminate harm is the use of weapons whose effects are delayed, most often because they are faulty, and therefore, essentially random. Cluster munitions, like anti-tank and anti-personnel land mines, may persist in a war zone as unexploded munitions because some number of the thousands of cluster bombs dropped are predictably "dud" weapons that do not explode upon impact. Duds may explode minutes, days, or years after combat has ended as noncombatants come upon them. US military strategist lawyers describe cluster bombs as effective weapons against radar, aircraft, armor, artillery, and personnel.

> However, because the bomblets or submunitions are dispensed over a relatively large area and a small percentage of them typically fail to detonate, there is an unexploded ordinance (UXO) hazard associated with CEM. *Combined Effects Munitions are not mines, are acceptable under the laws of armed conflict, and are not timed to go off as anti-personnel devices.* However, if the submunitions are disturbed or disassembled, they may explode. Unfortunately, these weapons have a high 'dud' rate and as a result can cause civilian casualties if disturbed. Consequently, there is a need for early and aggressive EOD clearing efforts.[173]

The many thousands of US cluster bombs dropped in Vietnam, Laos, and Cambodia left an estimated 9 to 27 million unexploded submunitions after the wars, which are still exploding decades after that war ended. They have caused an estimated 10,000 civilian casualties.[174] As I noted earlier, about 400 Iraqis (and 1,200 Kuwaitis) were killed by cluster bombs in the first two years after the conclusion

---

[171] U.S. Department of Defense, Office of the Assistant Secretary of Defense (Public Affairs), "Cluster Munitions Policy Released," 9 July 2008, Release No. 577-08. http://www.defense.gov/releases/release.aspx?releaseid=12049.

[172] Ibid.

[173] International and Operational Law Department, *Operational Law Handbook 2009*, p. 15, emphasis in the original.

[174] Feickert and Kerr, "Cluster Munitions," p. 1.

of the 1991 Persian Gulf War.[175] NATO estimated a 10 percent dud rate for cluster bombs used during the Kosovo air campaign, although bomb clearance and disposal experts found a higher dud rate, as high as 30 percent.[176] The International Committee for the Red Cross estimated that of the ninety-eight civilians killed by the explosive remnants of NATO bombing after the conclusion of the bombing campaign (between June 1999 and May 2000), just over 50 percent were victims of cluster bombs.[177]

Cluster bombs have been improved to lower dud rates: some are set to self-destruct if they do not explode on impact. The US policy announced in 2008 was both that the US would eliminate cluster bombs in 2018 that had a dud rate greater than 1 percent, and set a higher standard of reliability for cluster bombs. And, "effective immediately through 2018, any U.S. use of cluster munitions that do not meet the one percent unexploded ordnance standard must be approved by the applicable combatant commander."[178] So, although cluster bombs, even those with an unexploded ordnance rate of greater than 1 percent, may still be used, their use must pass a higher level of scrutiny and approval.

The Convention on Cluster Munitions, an agreement negotiated in 2007 and 2008 and signed by several countries in December 2008, bans the development, production, acquisition, transfer, stockpiling, and use of "dumb" cluster munitions, those that lack a self-destruct or self-deactivation mechanism. The United States has not signed the Convention on Cluster Munitions and argues that cluster bombs are not only legal, but an essential part of the US arsenal. "Cluster munitions are available for use by every combat aircraft in the U.S. inventory, they are integral to every Army or Marine maneuver element and in some cases constitute up to 50 percent of tactical indirect fire support. U.S. forces simply cannot fight by design or by doctrine without holding out at least the possibility of using cluster munitions."[179]

Yet, the United States may greatly reduce cluster bomb use for strategic reasons out of concern for civilian casualties. The Army's Alternative Warhead Program is tasked with reducing cluster bomb failure rates. In December 2008, the United States stopped procurement of a cluster munitions with a dud rate of 5 percent. Further, the US military has begun to take greater retrospective responsibility for its unexploded ordnance, including cluster bombs. The 2012 *Civilian Casualty*

[175] Human Rights Watch, "Ticking Time Bombs: NATO's Use of Cluster Munitions in Yugoslavia," June 1999, http://www.hrw.org/legacy/reports/1999/nato2/, accessed 24 November 2002. Human Rights Watch Briefing Paper, "Cluster Munitions a Foreseeable Hazard in Iraq," March 2003.

[176] International Committee of the Red Cross, Mines-Arms Unit, *Explosive Remnants of War*, p. 8; Feickert and Kerr, "Cluster Munitions," p. 2.

[177] International Committee of the Red Cross, Mines-Arms Unit, *Explosive Remnants of War*, p. 10.

[178] Department of Defense, "Cluster Munitions Policy Released."

[179] Richard Kidd, US Department of State, quoted in Feickert and Kerr, "Cluster Munitions," p. 4.

Mitigation guidance states that unexploded ordnance poses a residual threat to civilians and then states that:

> Army units are prohibited by law from conducting humanitarian demining, but they can dispose of ordnance when there is an operational need to do so (for example, when unexploded ordnance poses a threat to Army units that operate in the area, or if the ordnance could be used by enemy forces to create IEDs). Army units can also train host-nation explosive ordnance disposal capability so that host-nation security forces can take the lead in removing unexploded ordnance that threatens civilians.[180]

Finally, legislation introduced in the US House and Senate in 2011, but not passed, was intended curb the acquisition and deployment of cluster munitions.[181]

Weapons with nonexplosive delayed effects are those that over time, perhaps decades, harm noncombatants. These weapons delayed and persistent long-term effects are carcinogenic, mutagenic, or teratogenic—causing cancers, birth defects, or other debilitating disease that may affect noncombatants who live in or enter an area where those weapons were deployed. There is no doubt that nuclear weapons and certain chemical and biological weapons have both immediate and long-term effects. But, while the long-term and persistent effects of some weapons are well understood, the effects of other weapons are not well understood or are disputed. Agent Orange, the defoliant described above, is acknowledged to have long-term toxic consequences, including irreversible nerve damage and harm to organs. White phosphorus shells, used for illumination on a battlefield or to burn combatants, may leave a chemical residue that burns those who come into contact with it shortly after a battle is over or may damage organs if inhaled or ingested.

The long-term effects of other weapons, such as depleted uranium are debated. After their service in wars in the Balkans, some NATO soldiers, calling their illnesses "Balkan Syndrome," suggested that that certain cancers were caused by the long-term effects of depleted uranium in artillery shells. NATO has disputed those effects on its soldiers and found no evidence to support a causal link between depleted uranium and diseases such as lymphoma.[182] In other cases, epidemiologists suggest that an increased incidence of birth defects, and an increase in lung cancer and lymphoma rates in Fallujah after 2004 may be traced to the use of depleted uranium in weapons.[183]

---

[180] Army, *Civilian Casualty Mitigation*, p. 2-9.

[181] Feickert and Kerr, "Cluster Munitions," p. 7.

[182] See, for example, the NATO statements on depleted uranium in http://www.nato.int/du/home. htm.

[183] Chris Busby, Malak Hamdan, and Entesar Ariabi, "Cancer, Infant Mortality and Birth Sex-Ratio in Fallujah, Iraq, 2005-2009," *International Journal of Environmental Research and Public Health*, vol. 7 (July 2010): 2828–2837.

The US civilian casualty mitigation strategies have, to the time of this writing, focused on the immediate effects of weapons, with the exception of the acknowledgment of the dangers posed by unexploded ordnance. However, the delayed and persistent effects of weapons have not been factored into most collateral damage scenarios.

Procedures: Checkpoints, Escalation of Force, and Night Raids

Some situations, procedures, and rules of engagement are more likely than not to yield civilian injury or death. I discuss two procedures here: (1) checkpoints, when civilians come to US or allied positions and must stop; and (2) night raids, when soldiers enter civilian homes in surprise raids in search of insurgents.

Military checkpoints on roads are among the most dangerous places for civilians. Civilians are required to stop at checkpoints, and US soldiers are to go through a series of steps if drivers fail to halt. At these checkpoints, and near military convoys, US soldiers order civilians to stop their vehicles using a verbal or hand signal. If the driver fails to stop, a soldier may fire a warning shot, and then shoot to disable the vehicle or kill the occupants. At several points in the post-9/11 wars, the United States recognized the dangers and modified the procedures used.

From the beginning of the US occupation in Iraq, many Iraqi civilians were being injured or killed at checkpoints.[184] In 2005, the US military documented an average of seven deaths per week at checkpoints where US soldiers had fired upon and killed Iraqi civilians, apparently mistaking them for suicide bombers.[185] As I noted in chapter 2, when Lieutenant General Peter Chiarelli identified the large number of civilian deaths at checkpoints in Iraq in 2006 as a military problem because it created resentment and hatred that fueled the insurgency in Iraq, he ordered that the procedures be reviewed and changed.

In this case, the organization recognized that its moral duty to avoid noncombatant deaths coincided with its practical interest in reducing the causes for Iraqi's to join or support insurgent activity. Organizational responsibility was exercised because it was not simply the actions of individual soldiers at checkpoints that caused the killings; soldiers were acting as instructed. The problem was the rules for escalation of force that required review, and in this case a change, at the organizational level. So, while changes in checkpoint procedures in Iraq in 2006 were an instance of a commander taking responsibility, it was the military organization that had to devise and implement a response.

---

[184] Nancy Youssef, "Commander: Fewer Civilians Dying," *Philadelphia Inquirer*, 22 June 2006, http://articles.philly.com/2006-06-22/news/25403128_1_iraqi-civilians-civilian-casualties-roadside-bombing.

[185] Alastair Macdonald, "US Troops Kill Fewer Iraqis after New Guidelines," *Boston Globe*, 25 June 2006; Thom Shanker, "New Guidelines Aim to Reduce Civilian Deaths in Iraq," *New York Times*, 21 June 2006.

The revised checkpoint procedures did indeed result in fewer Iraqi civilian deaths at checkpoints. From July through December 2005, US military sources said that 16 percent of the 3,000 escalation of force incidents led to a civilian death or injury. During the period from 1 January 2006 to 31 May 2006, fewer escalation of force incidents occurred (1,700) and a lower proportion of those incidents (12%) led to civilian death or injury.[186] A year later, however, the number of incidents at checkpoints had risen. Specifically, the US released data in July 2007 which showed an average of thirty-six injuries or deaths per month at checkpoints—a rate greater than before the new procedures were put in place.[187] Checkpoint civilian casualties probably increased because the new escalation of force procedures were not deeply institutionalized, and soldiers, who had not been systematically trained in the new procedures were rotated into Iraq.

Civilian injury and deaths at checkpoints were also a persistent problem in Afghanistan. In 2008, forty-one Afghan civilians died at NATO, US, and Afghan checkpoints. Yet, even after the 2009 tactical directives stressing the need to reduce noncombatant death were announced in mid-year, there were thirty-six checkpoint deaths in 2009. In March 2010, when it appeared that checkpoint killings were a continuing problem, then NATO commander General Stanley McChrystal acknowledged that "we have shot an amazing number of people, but to my knowledge, none has ever proven to be a threat."[188] NATO forces were told, again, to practice "courageous restraint." On 12 April 2010, NATO troops fired on a bus filled with civilians that failed to stop when instructed to do so, wounding eighteen and killing four. General McChrystal was said to be "extremely upset" by the incident, and told troops to reread the tactical directive of June 2009.[189] Indeed UN data suggested that despite the best effort at checkpoints, the pro-government force were not able to make significant improvements in reducing escalation of force deaths in Afghanistan: noted in chapter 2, UNAMA counted forty-five escalation of force deaths in 2010 and thirty-six deaths in 2011 attributable to pro-government forces.[190]

---

[186] Fischer, "Iraqi Civilian Deaths Estimates," Congressional Research Service, CRS Report, 22 November 2006, pp. 3–4, citing reporting by Nancy A. Youssef, "U.S. Strives to Curb Iraqi Deaths; Stung by an Increasingly Hostile Populace, the U.S. Military has Launched a Major Campaign to Lessen the Number of Civilian Deaths in Iraq," *Buffalo News,* 22 June 2006, p. A1.

[187] Nancy Youssef, "Pentagon: U.S. Troops Shot 429 Iraqi Civilians at Checkpoints," McClatchy Washington Bureau, 11 July 2007, http://www.mcclatchydc.com/158/story/17836.html.

[188] McChrystal, quoted in Richard A. Oppel, Jr., "Tighter Rules Fail to Stem Deaths of Innocent Afghans at Checkpoints," *New York Times,* 26 March 2010.

[189] "Officials: NATO Troops Fire on Bus, Kill 4 Civilians," 13 April 2010, http://afghanistan.blogs.cnn.com/2010/04/12/afghan-officials-nato-troops-fire-on-bus-kill-4/.

[190] UNAMA attributed forty-one and thirty-six deaths to pro-government escalation of force incidents in 2008 and 2009, respectively. United Nations Assistance Mission to Afghanistan (UNAMA), *Annual Report on Protection of Civilians in Armed Conflict, 2008* (January 2009); UNAMA, *Annual*

Because the checkpoint killing of innocent civilians persisted as a problem, the Army continued to develop equipment and procedures (including signage and loudspeakers) to facilitate communication with civilians and make these situations less likely to escalate and cause collateral damage.[191] The 2012 *Civilian Casualty Mitigation* manual notes that "positioning a checkpoint at a place of limited visibility compresses timelines for decisionmaking and determination of intent, which can contribute to faulty assumption of hostile intent. Conversely, designing a checkpoint with natural and artificial physical barriers to channel and slow down traffic buys time for decisionmaking and increases the safety of forces."[192] The tactical lessons drawn from the checkpoint experience have also been generalized into an understanding about tactical patience. The need to increase the time available for soldiers to make decisions is emphasized: "The risk of CIVCASs increases when time is short and information is incomplete or inaccurate. Risk can be mitigated if time can be bought with tactical patience, if Soldiers are afforded standoff that gives them more time to decide if they should engage a target, and if enemies are denied the ability to maneuver."[193] The standardization of procedures and their incorporation in pre-deployment training at the Army level may make for a more consistent reduction in checkpoint escalation of force incidents that lead to death or injury.

Night raids are in some senses the opposite of checkpoint situations: at checkpoints, the United States has sought to reduce the surprise in the encounters, while during night raids, soldiers seek to maximize surprise and the advantage of their night vision goggles when they enter homes at night to search, detain, or kill insurgents. Night raids have been used in both Afghanistan and Iraq. Notably, night raids have been an important tactic for international forces: in one short period, from May to the end of July 2010, the United States conducted almost 3,000 night raids in which, according to General Petraeus, 1,031 Taliban fighters were killed and 1,355 Taliban were captured.[194]

Afghan officials and civilians have increasingly protested because the night searches often lead to civilian distress, harm, and death and the detention of civilians.[195]

Report on Protection of Civilians in Armed Conflict, 2009 (New York: UN, January 2010). UNAMA and Afghanistan Independent Human Rights Commission, *Annual Report on Protection of Civilians in Armed Conflict, 2010* (Kabul: United Nations, March 2011); UNAMA and UN Office of the High Commissioner for Refugees, *Annual Report on Protection of Civilians in Armed Conflict* (Kabul: United Nations, February 2012).

[191] Army, *Civilian Casualty Mitigation*, pp. 2-6 and 2-10.

[192] Ibid., p. 2-10.

[193] Ibid., p. 2-11.

[194] UNAMA, *Protection of Civilians in Armed Conflict, Afghanistan: Annual Report 2010* (Kabul, March 2011), p. 33.

[195] While my focus is on civilians killed and injured, much of the harm to civilians is related to detentions. Thousands of civilians are detained each year in both night raids and "clearance" operations and in some cases, civilians detained are physically harmed. See Open Society Foundation, "The Cost of Kill/Capture: The Impact of the Night Raid Surge on Afghan Civilians," Kabul, Afghanistan, 19 September 2011.

In response, the United States has changed tactics for night searches several times. The 2009 McChrystal tactical directive, which famously restricted airstrikes, also mentioned entry into Afghan homes: "Any entry into an Afghan house should always be accomplished by Afghan National Security Forces (ANSF) with the support of local authorities, and account for the unique cultural sensitivities toward local women."[196] In 2010, General Petraeus released two additional tactical directives on night raid procedures, in January and August, stressing the importance of protecting civilians. Another tactical directive in December 2011 stressed the next ISAF Commander John Allen's intent that night raids occur "in a manner which minimizes disruption to Afghan civilians, protects their property, prevents civilian casualties and shares maximum information possible with local leadership and civilians before, during and after an operation."[197] Although the United Nations suggests that due to the difficulty of counting in these situations, the trend of civilian death in night raids appears to be downward in Afghanistan, from ninety-eight in 2009, to eighty in 2010, and sixty-three in 2011.[198]

Response and Compensation for Civilian Casualties

In August 2010, NATO issued a set of non-binding policy guidelines for responding to civilian casualties in its operations in Afghanistan. These guidelines are an implicit acknowledgment of organizational responsibility for reducing and minimizing the harm to civilians and the explicit assumption of responsibility to make repair, called "assistance," after the fact of civilian casualties. Notably, the rationale given for NATO doing "everything in its power to avoid harming civilians" and for making repair when civilian suffering occurs is military necessity—the "centre of gravity of NATO's mission remains the Afghan people."[199] The entire text of the guidelines and preamble are reproduced below:

---

[196] NATO Tactical Directive, 2 July 2009, released by NATO ISAF Headquarters, 6 July 2009.

[197] General John R. Allen, Commander ISAF/USF-A, COMISAF Night Operations Tactical Directive, 1 December 2011.

[198] UNAMA, reports, 2009, 2010, and 2011. The 2011 UNAMA report notes: "Accurate data on numbers of night search operations or 'night raids' and civilian casualties is difficult to obtain as such information is generally classified. Data on the total numbers of night operations carried out by a range of Afghan and international military forces, special forces, special operations forces and other government agencies and any civilian casualties resulting from all such operations is not publicly available. Given both limitations associated with the operating environment and limited access to information, UNAMA may be under-reporting the number of civilian casualties from night search operations." UNAMA, *Protection of Civilians in Armed Conflict, Afghanistan: Annual Report 2011* (Kabul, February 2012), p. 4n.

[199] NATO Nations Approve Civilian Casualty Guidelines, 6 August 2010, http://www.nato.int/cps/en/SID-9D9D8832-42250361/natolive/official_texts_65114.htm.

In an effort to find a common approach to deal with the tragedy of civilian casualties, NATO nations have agreed on a set of guidelines which have now been promulgated to the Chain of Command. These guidelines reflect the efforts NATO/ISAF is making to reduce the impact of the conflict on the people of Afghanistan. The centre of gravity of NATO's mission remains the Afghan people, and ISAF does everything within its power to avoid harming civilians. When combat-related civilian casualties or damage to civilian property occur, NATO/ISAF considers that easing civilian suffering is of tremendous importance. In Afghanistan, the pain of losing a family member can also have financial implications, which could be eased through payments. Afghans have made it clear that payments to the families of civilian casualties is a culturally-appropriate response to combat-related civilian death or damage to private property. For this reason, NATO nations have agreed on the following set of non-binding policy guidelines for when they deal with cases of civilian combat-related casualties.

1. Promptly acknowledge combat-related cases of civilian casualties or damage to civilian property.
2. Continue to fully implement the ISAF standard operating procedures for investigating possible cases of civilian casualties, or damage to civilian property, and endeavour to provide the necessary information to the ISAF civilian casualties tracking cell.
3. Proactively offer assistance for civilian casualty cases or damages to civilian property, in order to mitigate human suffering to the extent possible. Examples of assistance could include ex-gratia payments or in-kind assistance, such as medical treatment, the replacement of animals or crops, and the like.
4. Offers of such assistance, where appropriate, should be discussed with, and coordinated through, village elders or alternative tribal structures, as well as district-level government authorities, whenever possible. Assistance should also, where possible, be coordinated with other responsible civilian actors on the ground.
5. Offering and providing such assistance should take into account the best way to limit any further security risk to affected civilians and ISAF/PRT personnel.
6. Local customs and norms vary across Afghanistan and should be fully taken into account when determining the appropriate response to a particular incident, including for potential ex-gratia payments.
7. Personnel working to address cases of civilian casualties or damage to civilian property should be accessible, particularly, subject to security considerations, in conflict-affected areas, and local communities made fully aware of the investigation and payment process.

8. The system by which payments are determined and made should be as simple, prompt and transparent as possible and involve the affected civilians at all points feasible.
9. Payments are made and in-kind assistance is provided without reference to the question of legal liability.[200]

In paragraph 9, NATO sidesteps the question of legal liability. The NATO guidelines are written on the assumption that its mission requires acting as if it were organizationally responsible for civilian casualties. Further, NATO's understanding of making repair is comprehensive, so that medical assistance and economic compensation are provided, and in a way that is culturally sensitive.

The compensation for harm is not new. Neither is the fact that the timeliness and amount of compensation is frequently a bone of contention. For example, when the United States destroyed homes and farms in Kandahar province during a six-month offensive in 2010 and early 2011, Afghan officials who were members of an Afghan Presidential Commission established to investigate said that the United States had caused over $100 million in damage, destroying between 800 and 900 homes, in addition to the destruction of 100,000 trees.[201] Even as it paid compensation, US military officials denied the findings of the Afghan commission which evaluated the damage. The United States estimated the damage to be $1.4 million. General James Terry in fact argued that it really was not the fault of the United States that the homes were destroyed. "It is the insurgents who are jeopardizing the people and security forces when they use your buildings and farms to place I.E.D.'s and bombs. Further, the homes that were destroyed were abandoned, empty and wired with ingenious arrays of bombs. When the insurgents do this they threaten local civilians, particularly the children."[202]

Through its wars in Afghanistan and Iraq, the United States and its allies have made monetary payments to Afghan and Iraqi civilians for destruction of property and for injuries and deaths. Two programs are directly handled by military personnel through the Commanders Emergency Response Program (CERP).[203] Condolence payments

---

[200] Ibid.

[201] Taimoor Shah and Rod Norland, "Afghan Panel and U.S. Dispute War's Toll on Property," *New York Times*, 13 January 2011.

[202] Quoted in ibid.

[203] Other programs concerned with compensating civilians include the Department of State Claims and Condolence Payment Program and the US Agency for International Development Programs, the Marla Ruzicka Iraqi War Victims Fund, and the Afghan Civilian Assistance Program. These funds are much smaller in scale than the CERP and FCA programs. The CERP is also used for many other tasks in the war zones including funding small-scale reconstruction projects and payments to individual detainees after their release. Of the more than $41 million dispersed by the CERP in Afghanistan in 2005, for example, nearly $211,000 was used for condolence payments. U.S. Government Accountability Office, "Military Operations: The Department of Defense's Use of Solatia and Condolence Payments in Iraq and Afghanistan," GAO, May 2007.

in Iraq (from September 2003) and Afghanistan (from November 2004) are generally small may be authorized in response to death, injury, or property damage "occurs during a military operation." Also known as battle damage payments, the ceiling for these payments is $2,500, although in some instances higher awards up to $10,000 have been authorized.[204] Condolence payments are intended as "symbolic gestures" and "expressions of sympathy" and to provide urgent humanitarian relief for persons harmed by a combat operation. They are explicitly "not an acknowledgment of any moral or legal responsibility."[205] The US Government Accountability Office found that in fiscal years 2005 and 2006, the United States made more than $28 million in condolence payments in Iraq. Total reported condolence payments in Afghanistan in FY 2006 were about $211,000.[206]

The second form of compensation is the payment *solatia*, which are specifically tied to a combat action. Like the condolence payments, *solatia* payments are given as an expression of sympathy. In both Iraq and Afghanistan these payments have usually been dispersed in the field after hearings, although smaller payments can be made on the spot. The total for *solatia* payments in Afghanistan was about $141,000 in fiscal year 2006.[207] There is no program to acknowledge or express sympathy for the loss of civilian life in Pakistan caused by US action.

These two forms of compensation are considered after a determination is made that the harm is not covered under a third program, known as the Foreign Claims Act. Payments under the FCA cover harm suffered during the "routine day-to-day business" of war, which are not either directly or indirectly associated with a specific combat operation. In other words, there is a "combat exclusion" for FCA claims. Originally instituted during World War I to cover US automobile accidents in France, the FCA still covers such accidents. "For example: A coalition convoy drives through a market area and one vehicle in the convoy hits an individual on a bicycle. The convoy was not performing a specific combat operation."[208] Between 2003 and 2006, the United States settled 21,450 FCA claims in Iraq and Afghanistan at a cost of about $26 million. The primary reasons claims were paid by the US army were automobile accidents, detainee property claims or injuries, and damage resulting from negligent discharges.

Because the FCA process excludes injuries arising from combat, the determination of whether the harm claimed was combat-related is an important step

[204] Campaign for Innocent Victims in Conflict (CIVIC), "United States Military Compensation to Civilians in Armed Conflict" (Washington, DC: CIVIC May 2010); US Forces Afghanistan, *Money as a Weapon System Afghanistan* (MAAWS-USFOR-A Pub 1-06, Commanders Emergency Response Program (CERP) SOP, updated February 2011), p. 125.

[205] US Forces Afghanistan, *Money as a Weapon System Afghanistan*, p. 125.

[206] GAO, "Military Operations: The Department of Defense's Use of Solatia and Condolence Payments in Iraq and Afghanistan."

[207] Ibid.

[208] US Forces Afghanistan, *Money as a Weapon System Afghanistan*, p. 124.

in the process. In 490 cases of claims applications made in Afghanistan and Iraq for the period of January 2005 through June 2006 for which the American Civil Liberties Union acquired information through a Freedom of Information Act the majority of claims, 404 were denied. More than half of the denials were made because of a determination of combat exclusion. But the determinations of combat exclusion, according to a lawyer who reviewed the cases, have been "applied arbitrarily."[209]

There is always the question of the monetary value placed on property damage or the loss of civilian life. The US GAO has noted that the procedures and amounts given for *solatia* and condolence payments have evolved during the US wars in Iraq and Afghanistan. Although the payments have varied, CIVIC reported the amount given for different forms of harm in Afghanistan under the *solatia* and condolence programs. Payments for FCA claims can be much larger, up to 100,000. CIVIC also notes that "the valuation of life and limb under both the FCA and condolence should be examined by the relevant DOD authority, as payments seen as too low by civilians can be—and often have been—insulting and only serve to inflame anger."[210]

While there is very little data about the US compensation programs, more information is available about the amounts and the incidents where the United Kingdom's Ministry of Defence has made payments to civilians harmed in Afghanistan. A release of British data for claims suggests the sorts of harms civilians requested compensation for and how they were settled.

Table 6.1, which samples thirty incidents from claims made in July and December 2010 in Helmand Province, Afghanistan, is illustrative, not representative of all the claims made to the British in Afghanistan during 2010. Of the 1,460 claims made to the British Forces in 2010, over 400 were denied and nearly 1,000 were settled, for more than $2 million.[211]

The 2012 *Civilian Casualty Mitigation* guidelines stress immediate response to civilian casualty incidents, including medical treatment of wounded civilians. The document states that "whenever it is likely that civilians were harmed and their property damaged, Army leaders should make appropriate amends." These are separate from the formal military systems of accountability to include "apologies, *ex gratia* monetary payments (that is, paid without obligation or liability)."[212]

---

[209] Jonathan Tracy, quoted in John Fabian Witt, "Form and Substance in the Law of Counterinsurgency Damages," *Loyola of Los Angeles Law Review*, vol. 41 (2007-2008): 1455–1481, 1473.

[210] CIVIC, "United States Military Compensation to Civilians in Armed Conflict," p. 6.

[211] Ben Quinn, James Ball, and Mark Train, "MoD pays £1.3m Compensation to Afghans for Death, Injury and Damage," *The Guardian*, 28 March 2011, http://www.guardian.co.uk/world/2011/mar/28/mod-compensation-to-afghans-increases. "Afghanistan Civilian Compensation: The Sums Received from UK Forces," *The Guardian*, http://www.guardian.co.uk/world/datablog/2011/mar/28/afghanistan-civilian-compensation. Accessed 20 January 2012.

[212] Army, *Civilian Casualty Mitigation*, p. 2-21.

Table 6.1 **Maximum US Condolence and *Solatia* Payments to Iraqi and Afghan Civilians**

Harm	Solatia	Condolence/battle damage
Death	2,000 USD	2,500 USD
Serious injury	400 USD	1,600 USD
Non-serious injury	200 USD	600 USD
Serious property damage	—	2,200 USD
Non-serious property damage	200 USD	200 USD

Source: Campaign for Innocent Victims in Conflict (CIVIC), "United States Military Compensation to Civilians in Armed Conflict" (Washington, DC: CIVIC, May 2010), 4.

Taking Responsibility

As the above discussion illustrates, the US military has gradually taken prospective and retrospective organizational responsibility for civilian casualties—both deliberate killing and collateral damage—in its most recent wars. The organizational measures the United States has taken to reduce collateral damage include an effort to understand how civilians are being harmed and preventive changes at the organizational level in training, weapons procurement, and deployment, and operations. Further, some of the steps recommended by military lawyers to prevent war crimes are useful for preventing collateral damage. As Mark Osiel emphasizes, "more important in averting atrocity are the more mundane legal norms structuring day-to-day operation of combat forces. These rules achieve their effect *ex ante*, long before the soldier faces any opportunity to engage in atrocious conduct."[213] Further, the NATO guidelines and the US programs for compensation and condolence begin to address retrospective or *post hoc* organizational responsibility for civilian casualties.

The organizational measures already taken by the military underscore two of my arguments, namely that the US military, as an organization, has imperfect moral agency, and that it is possible to exercise that moral agency to reduce harm to civilians. The moral agency of the US military as an organization has been enacted with

---

[213] Osiel, *Obeying Orders*, p. 163. In *Making Sense of Mass Atrocities*, Osiel argues that the threat of collective punishment of an officer corps for atrocity might work well to prevent war crimes. Because I am focused here on both preventing and finding moral responsibility for systemic collateral damage (unintended and foreseeable), I do not address collective punishment for deliberate atrocity. My focus here is on how organizations act as agents to create structures that can lead to systemic collateral damage, and how organizations can be restructured to prevent systemic collateral damage.

Table 6.2 **Sample of Claims for Damages in Helmand Province, Afghanistan Evaluated by the British Ministry of Defence in 2010**

Date submitted in 2010	Approximate date of incident	Damages	Detail of claim	Agreed payment (US$)	Date closed	Status*
22 July	13 July 2009	Fatality	Son killed in fighting. Recorded at Role 3 as "Enemy Forces."		12 December 2010	D
22 July	1 week ago	Crop damage	Corn cut down for PB security	1,000	31 July 2010	S
22 July	1.5 months ago	Crop damage	Corn banned around PB	5,000	7 August 2010	S
24 July	18 June 2010	Fatality	Brother shot in field	8,800		U
24 July	14–16 days ago	Fatality	Son shot	1,150	7 August 2010	S
24 July	24 July 2010	Property damage	Mobile phone missing	120	31 July 2010	S
24 July	Not given	Property damage	Compound burnt	700	28 August 2010	S
24 July	August 2009	Property damage	Land used to construct Route TRIDENT	250	25 September 2010	S
24 July	11 June 2010	Property damage	Flour mill destroyed	1,020	28 August 2010	S
25 July	21 June 2010	Property damage	Compound fire	878	14 August 2010	S
25 July	17 May 2010	RTA	Taxi damaged	1,100	14 August 2010	S
26 July	2 months ago	Crop damage	5 Jerabs of wheat burnt	750	7 August 2010	S
26 July	12 months ago	Fatality	7 family members killed		26 August 2010	D
13 December	5 January 2010	Fatality	Claims husband, 2 sons and 2 daughters killed by ISAF helicopter strike	10,200	24 January 2011	S

(Continued)

Table 6.2 (Continued)

Date submitted in 2010	Approximate date of incident	Damages	Detail of claim	Agreed payment (US$)	Date closed	Status*
14 December	8 December 2010	Property damage	Damage to doors and furniture	400	18 December 2010	S
14 December	Approx. 25 August 2010	Property damage	Damage to compound and water pump	3,000	22 January 2011	S
14 December	10 October 2010	Property damage	Compound destroyed for Route	4,200	14 December 2010	S
15 December	1 March 2010	Property damage	Side road built through land	500	18 December 2010	S
15 December	10 November 2010	Property damage	Trucks set on fire whilst in the charge of ISAF		5 February 2011	D
15 December	14 November 2010	Property damage	Pumps and hut destroyed by mortars	834	18 December 2010	S
15 December	25 November 2010	Wounding	Fragmentation injuries due to UGL	1,875	14 January 2011	S
16 December	January 2010	Property damage	Claims damage to compound during Operation Moshtarak	1,200	1 January 2011	S
16 December	25 October 2010	Wounding	Claims man (cousin?) was shot during ISAF contact		16 December 2010	D
16 December	4 November 2010	Crop damage	Claimant says 3,550 kgs of harvested cotton was burned when ISAF mortars caused a fire	2,475	1 January 2011	S
20 December	20 September 2010	Property damage	Claimant says 2 goats killed, 50 fruit trees, 10 jeribs of mash and a small mosque destroyed	4,550	1 January 2011	S

Table 6.2 (Continued)

Date submitted in 2010	Approximate date of incident	Damages	Detail of claim	Agreed payment (US$)	Date closed	Status*
20-Dec	15 November 2010	Wounding	MSST confirm TIC in this location. Shrapnel wounds suffered	3,425		W
20 December	July/August 2010	Fatality	Claims wife was shot and killed when ISAF fighting with INS		14 January 2011	D
20 December	September 2010	Property damage	Wall damage confirmed by MSST, proceed to payment	750	21 February 2011	S
20 December	2 December 2010	Property damage	Warthog damage	1,000	12 February 2011	S
20 December	5 December 2010	Fatality	Claims brother caught in mortar fire and killed during fighting with INS	3,650	19 February 2011	S

*Status: D, Denied; S, Settled; U, Under investigation; W, Waiting to be paid.

Source: "Afghanistan Civilian Compensation: The Sums Received from UK Forces," The Guardian, http://www.guardian.co.uk/world/datablog/2011/mar/28/afghanistan-civilian-compensation accessed 20 January 2012.

respect to civilian casualties in reflection on the problems of collateral damage and deliberate killing of civilians. When it was understood to be necessary, the military altered its priorities, roles, decision-making knowledge and structure, organizational capacity and training, and developed procedures for reflection or organizational learning about the problem of civilian casualties. Further, the military sees civilian casualty mitigation as a learning process: "Lessons learned do not come solely from CIVCAS incidents, but also from occasions in which there was a high risk of CIVCASs but they were avoided. "'Near misses' can offer valuable lessons and illustrate best practices. Leaders should ensure that these incidents are also used for training, mentoring, and learning purposes." The Army's self-conscious understanding of the importance of institutionalization of the cycle is also evident. "Lessons learned that result in a change in CIVCAS procedures should be shared across the entire area of operations and implemented wherever appropriate, to maximize the benefit and minimize the tendency to create ad hoc or disparate solutions."[214] Nowhere is this illustrated more clearly, perhaps than in the fact that the *Civilian Casualty Mitigation* manual includes a figure, the "civilian casualty mitigation cycle" summarizing the Army's own understanding of the steps necessary for civilian casualty mitigation, which can be understood as a cycle of moral agency (figure 6.4).

Institutionalization of civilian casualty mitigation efforts has also broadened and deepened within the NATO ISAF structure in Afghanistan. In late 2010, ISAF Commander General John Allen articulated the meta-institutional goal for ISAF to reduce civilian casualties in Afghanistan to "zero." General Allen put this in bold type in a tactical directive released on 30 November 2011: **"My intent is to eliminate ISAF caused civilian casualties across Afghanistan, and minimize civilian casualties throughout the area of operations by reducing their exposure to insurgent operations."**[215]

But more important, ISAF initiated systems of accountability and review that went beyond its CIVCAS Tracking Cell. At the public level, ISAF began to hold conferences on civilian casualties in Afghanistan in 2009. At the operational level, in 2009 ISAF organized the Joint Incident Assessment Team (JIAT) for fact-finding about civilian casualty incidents if a commander requests that the team deploy. Further, in September 2012, ISAF conducted its first "senior level ANSF-ISAF joint CIVCAS board...to share our lessons learned on the mitigation of CIVCAS and to work hand-in-glove with the Afghans to set up their system for managing CIVCAS and mitigating it."[216]

---

[214] Army, *Civilian Casualty Mitigation*, p. 2-24.

[215] General John Allen, "COMISAF's Tactical Directive," 30 November 2011, ISAF Headquarters, p. 2. http://www.isaf.nato.int/images/docs/20111105%20nuc%20tactical%20directive%20revision%204%20 (releaseable%20version)%20r.pdf.

[216] Col. Robert Bradford, quoted in "Media Roundtable, 13 September 2012," 13 September 2012, *ISAF News*, http://www.isaf.nato.int/article/transcripts/media-roundtable-13-sep-2012.html.

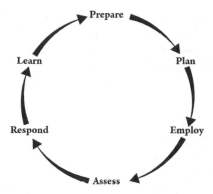

Figure 6.4 US Army Civilian Casualty Mitigation Cycle as a Cycle of Moral Agency.
Source: Department of the Army, *Civilian Casualty Mitigation*, Army Tactics, Techniques, and Procedures
(ATTP) No. 3-37.31 (Washington, DC: Department of the Army, 18 July 2012), figure 2-1, on page 2-2.

While organizational responsibility for reducing foreseeable civilian killing has grown, it could be further improved. I make recommendations below that cluster in three categories: information and analysis; immediate actions to reduce civilian casualties; changes in training, psychological support, and moral development. These recommendations are intended to support the cycle of imperfect organizational moral agency.

Information and Analysis

1. Routinely investigate instances of suspected or confirmed civilian death and regularly compare the estimates of civilian casualties made for operations with the actual number of civilian casualties. In other words, the emphasis is on collateral damage estimation and not on assessing the consequences of strikes. Much of the analysis of civilian casualty incidents has focused on large, dramatic incidents of civilian killing, such as in Garani, Afghanistan. The detailed investigation of incidents should continue, but the aggregation and analysis of civilian casualty incidents may yield greater insight into the routine, systemic collateral damage injury and killing of civilians. Further, cases where proportionality/double effect calculations were made, including estimates of possible civilian casualties, should be investigated to assess and refine the accuracy of the estimates.

    The Civilian Casualty Tracking Cell, in Afghanistan began this sort of analysis, though as I suggested in chapter 2, data collection, at least in the early years, was not systematic and comprehensive. The *Civilian Casualty Mitigation* guidelines urges the creation of standardized databases of incidents and acknowledges the usefulness of aggregating data and pattern analysis.[217] "Pattern analysis can help identify

---

[217] Army, *Civilian Casualty Mitigation*, p. 2-15.

locations where CIVCASs have greater likelihood of occurring as well as the procedures or units that may be more prone to cause such incidents. Conversely, analysis
might identify useful methods that could be emulated more widely."[218]

2. Cooperate more fully with NGOs and international organizations in their investigation of civilian casualty incidents. Current strategy emphasizes cooperation with
local governments and informing the news media of incidents, but does not stress
cooperation with investigating NGOs and IOs.

3. Make all civilian casualty data public so that lessons (e.g., about rules of engagement
at checkpoints) can be learned in a timely way by both the military and the civilian
public. The military has recently emphasized sharing information when operational
units transition but the data needs to be accessible to all. Further, the US military
should make public the data about its condolence and compensation payments for
incidental harm to civilians, including data about those who are denied payments,
and increase the quality of the records it keeps.[219]

Immediate Action

1. Remove weapons from the arsenal that are indiscriminate in the short and long
term. These weapons include cluster bombs, land mines, defoliants, and chemicals used for "illumination." Even if the United States restricts its use of cluster
munitions to those with "dud" rates of 1 percent or less, the use of thousands of
these weapons means that many hundreds of duds will remain. Similarly, while
one may intend to only use white phosphorous for illumination, its unintended
effects may include burns and contamination of areas used by civilians.

2. Reconsider the mix of weapons available in conflicts. For example, large bombs
should not be used in populated areas and thus should probably not be loaded
onto aircraft sent for close air support or close combat air operations.

3. Remove or assist in removing unexploded ordnance as soon as possible.

4. The US military has taken responsibility for killing civilians in combat through
its programs for condolence and *solatia* payments. This is an important step. The
GAO has suggested reforms to the process, as have other the nongovernmental

---

[218] Ibid., p. 2-16. JAGs are sometimes the early warning system for systemic collateral damage. One
told Laura Dickinson, that when he realized that "we weren't getting it right," he informed division headquarters that "we have a problem." Quoted in Dickinson, "Military Lawyers on the Battlefield," p. 17.

[219] The data requirements are admittedly not detailed and the GAO had to go to great lengths to
make its own assessment of the compensation programs in 2007. The military guidelines do not ask for
a great deal of information about the incidents for which payments are made. For example, US Forces
Afghanistan, *Money as a Weapon System Afghanistan* requires this information: "For condolence and
hero payments, state/confirm only that death/injury occurred during US/coalition operations (do not
detail how occurred; do not detail operation or provide names), and only state number of personnel
killed (or wounded, as applicable)" p. 111. "*For condolence payments, the name of the deceased must be
annotated on the roster.*" p. 119.

organizations, such as the American Civil Liberties Union.[220] For example, CIVIC suggests including the development of uniform guidelines for payments and better training of the personnel making the judgment of whether and how much to pay.[221]

Training, Psychological Support, and Moral Development

1. The US military has increased its emphasis on the importance of protecting noncombatants for reasons of military necessity. The military should also underscore that noncombatant immunity is a value in itself.
2. The military should evaluate and improve its programs to inculcate empathy and respect for noncombatants. Although not officially condoned, the climate at the small-unit level is often one of indifference, or even disregard and hate. Those soldiers who are hostile toward noncombatants should be disciplined.
3. The military already emphasizes training in discriminating between combatants and noncombatants. Such training should be reinforced regularly and refreshed not only after dramatic incidents of civilian killing—as in Haditha—or after the slow but nevertheless large accretion of predictable deaths—but as a routine.
4. Decrease the likelihood of soldiers "snapping" by treating soldiers with respect, decreasing the operational tempo for soldiers, and by providing prompt treatment for combat- and deployment-related stress and mental illness.
5. Move responsibility for civilian killing up the chain of command and outline criteria for positive moral responsibility and negligence. This includes disciplining commanders for failing to investigate instances of civilian killing, whether they were clearly intended or unintended.

One of the suggestions here could improve soldiers' mental health—namely decreasing the stress that soldiers face in the field. But, the overall acknowledgement that collateral damage is a systemic problem, that it is caused at the organizational level by rules of engagement and other factors outside the individual soldier's control, would perhaps alleviate the personal guilt that has plagued some soldiers.

The Relation between Individual and Collective Moral Responsibility

There are potentially significant objections to the ascription of collective moral responsibility that concern the relation between individual responsibility and

---

[220] The ACLU received some records through a Freedom of Information Act request and posted that data on its website. See: http://www.aclu.org/human-cost-civilian-casualties-iraq-afghanistan. Last accessed 20 January 2012.

[221] CIVIC, "United States Military Compensation to Civilians in Armed Conflict," p. 13.

collective responsibility. First, if we say that a group or organization was responsible for a wrong, might that let individuals avoid or evade individual responsibility? Second, an individual may not have voluntarily joined a group; can we say the individual is a morally responsible member of a collective organization? And third, assuming that someone is (whether voluntarily or involuntarily) a member of a collective, is that individual necessarily accountable for the actions of a collective? Finally, how is it that the organization can enable individual moral responsibility?

First, is it the case that if everyone is responsible, no one is responsible? Mathiesen expresses this worry: "If collective responsibility is a tool that can be used to avoid moral responsibility for our actions and fails to provide a motivation to take care lest we be open to moral sanctions, then it would be better if we reject the idea of collective responsibility."[222] This statement suggests a view of moral responsibility that is either individual or collective. But, I am not arguing that if we locate moral responsibility within organizations that individuals are no longer responsible for their individual actions within an organization. Individuals must be held responsible for what they do or do not do within organizations. Yet, the moral agency of individuals is compromised by membership and participation in an organization; individuals in organizations can thus also be said to be imperfect moral agents. This is why moral responsibility should be shared among relevant actors.

Second, who is a morally responsible member of a collective? Is everyone who is nominally a member of a collective responsible for the actions of that collective, even if their membership is not voluntary? I argue that what we do as members of a collective determines our causal and moral responsibility. Similarly, the philosopher Gregory Mellema suggests that there are "qualifying actions" that individuals perform which qualify them for membership in a collective. Mellema includes as qualifying acts: deliberate contributions, complicity in the behavior, promising to participate or uphold the ideals of an organization, and taking risks by acting to achieve a desired outcome that may lead to unintended outcomes.[223] So individuals are responsible members of an organization to the extent that they participate in these ways.[224]

---

[222] Mathiesen, "We're All in This Together," p. 250.

[223] Gregory Mellema, "Collective Responsibility and Qualifying Actions," in French and Wettstein, eds., *Midwest Studies in Philosophy*, pp. 168–175. List and Pettit suggest that "members of a jointly intentional group agent may play one or both of two roles... 'authorizing' the group agent, in the sense of accepting its claims to speak and act for the group.... [and/or] 'active'... that is acting in full awareness for the pursuit of the group's ends." List and Pettit, *Group Agency*, p. 35.

[224] I am thus against collective punishment of officers who, for example, did not order large numbers of cluster bombs moved to a war zone, but found them there. On the other hand, individual officers ought to be sanctioned for using cluster bombs in an area where civilians were present. This is a different approach than Mark Osiel who advocates collective sanctions of commanders who fail to prevent harm. Osiel argues, for example, that his approach of fining superior officers for the actions of subordinates should "harness" the self-interest of commanders by "increasing the costs and attendant risks of inaction for failing to prevent harm." See Osiel, *Making Sense of Mass Atrocity*, p. 198–199.

Third, does the ascription of collective moral agency imply that all members of a collective are equally morally responsible? Here again, we must be careful to distinguish the degree and kinds of participation of individuals. Not every member of a collective is morally responsible as an individual for the harms perpetrated by the institution. Indeed, individual humans are legal members of some collectives that they did not knowingly or intentionally join (e.g., families, states) and may not actively participate in producing the behavior of the collective. In this discussion, the focus is on complex organizations where individuals are knowledgeable and voluntary participants. Individuals who are accidental members of a loose collective, and who do not participate in actively producing or perpetrating harm, are not liable for causal or moral responsibility, unless by their membership they were in a position to avert or attenuate foreseeable harm.

While it is important not to turn aside from individual responsibility, it would be misleading to focus entirely on individual responsibility, as if individuals were completely autonomous. Indeed, we know just the opposite. Nearly all our significant endeavors occur in a connection with others, in a social and often organizational context. As Tracy Isaacs argues, "the collective perspective is significant for getting an accurate moral picture of individual actions."[225] The challenge is to understand how complex organizations shape, enlarge, and constrain individual agency and moral responsibility and how organizations themselves can be understood as morally responsible. This brings us to the question of how institutions can foster individual moral responsibility. Organizations are not only themselves morally responsible, but in part responsible for fostering individual moral responsibility. Much of this work is already done by organizations when they socialize their members as professionals who are accountable for the performance of their role. In the case of preventing deliberate atrocity and systemic collateral damage, this would be socialization in not only "warriors honor" but in the law of war.

But there is more. The military must also create and maintain the space for challenges to rules of engagement, weapons, and tactics and dissent within the organization. Jeff McMahan sees this as a vital step in preventing the initiation of unjust wars. It is also important to "enable soldiers to have both a greatly enhanced understanding of the moral character of the war in which they are commanded to fight, and certain forms of legal support if their improved moral understanding leads them to engage in conscientious refusal to fight" once the decision to go to war has been taken.[226]

We differ in part because Osiel is focused on deliberate killing and the active commander and passive bystander, whereas I am focused on inadvertent harm. I am also in this chapter emphasizing the imperfect moral agency of the military organization.

[225] Tracy Isaacs, "Collective Moral Responsibility and Collective Intention," in French and Wettstein, eds., *Midwest Studies in Philosophy*, pp. 59–73, 65.

[226] Jeff McMahan, *Killing in War* (Oxford: Oxford University Press, 2009), p. 153.

PART III

SECONDARY MORAL RESPONSIBILITY

7

Political Responsibility

When people talk, as they often do, about harmful political influence on the management of war, they are not really saying what they mean. Their quarrel should be with the policy itself, not with its influence. If the policy is right—that is, successful—any intentional effect it has on the conduct of the war can only be to the good. If it has the opposite effect the policy itself is wrong.

—Carl Von Clausewitz, *On War*[1]

Obama worries far more about collateral damage, about the precedent the United States sets when it acts. But when it's decision time about whether to order a strike or use a certain kind of weapon, he often comes out pretty close to where Bush did.

—Obama Administration official[2]

I ask here about the causal and moral responsibility of civilian institutions for conduct in war—focusing on deliberate atrocity and collateral damage. The dominant view is that Congress should authorize war and the president should act as a commander in chief of the military, setting the policies and objectives, but then leaving the day-to-day management of the war to the military and civilian professionals whose job it is to run the war.[3] The role of the courts is considered to be negligible. The practice is that political institutions set the purposes of war and authorize it,

---

[1] Carl Von Clausewitz, *On War*, edited and translated by Michael Howard and Peter Paret (Princeton: Princeton University Press, 1976), p. 608.

[2] Obama Administration official quoted in David E. Sanger, *Confront and Conceal: Obama's Secret Wars and Surprising Use of American Power* (New York: Crown Publishers, 2012), p. xvi.

[3] Most historians and legal scholars read the US Constitution this way. A prominent exception is John Yoo, who argues that the framers intended less a balance of power and clear roles with respect to making war, than a "flexible" system, where the President could initiate war on his own while the Congress might "declare" war after the fact. See John Yoo, *The Powers of War and Peace: The Constitution and Foreign Affairs After 9/11* (Chicago: University of Chicago Press, 1995).

but outside the offices of the president, National Security Council, and high civilian Pentagon and CIA leadership, other government officials, most importantly the Congress and the courts, usually do not closely direct or monitor the conduct of war. The military, and the members of the executive who are in the central national security apparatus, chafe at close supervision—as somehow questioning their competence and professionalism—and the dominant belief among civilians themselves is that the conduct of war should be left to the professionals. The role of civilian institutions in war, while formally one of oversight, has been limited to hearing reports and providing resources.

Specifically, since September 2001, the US Congress has essentially confined itself to hasty and sometimes shallow discussions about the resort to war and, to borrow a phrase from Clausewitz, frequently legislators often "assert that all available military resources should be put at the disposal of the commander" in time of war. Indeed, just three days after the 9/11 attack, the Congress gave a sweeping authorization for war against those who attacked the United States: "The President is authorized to use all necessary and appropriate force against those nations, organizations, or persons he determines planned, authorized, committed, or aided the terrorist attacks that occurred on September 11, 2001, or harbored such organizations or persons, in order to prevent any future acts of international terrorism against the United States by such nations, organizations or persons."[4]

President George W. Bush articulated the sense that Congress should acquiesce to war against Iraq when he met with members of Congress in 2002 to ask for their support. Bush said simply, "Look, I want your vote. I'm not going to debate it with you."[5] Members of Congress have often been eager to express their support of the troops and by extension of the war in Iraq. When Secretary of Defense Donald Rumsfeld and Chairman of the Joint Chiefs of Staff Richard Meyers testified before the Senate Armed Services Committee on 13 February 2003 about the impending war with Iraq, the Committee Chairman, Senator John Warner (R-Virginia) began the hearing by saying that "the troops deserve Congresses support and they well get it."[6] In 2007, during a press conference, when President Bush was asked about a push from both the Democrats and Republicans to set a deadline for withdrawal of US troops from Iraq, he articulated this view in response to this and a follow-up question. "Have you entertained the idea that at some point Congress may take some of that sole decision-making power away, through legislation? And can you

---

[4] Authorization for the Use of Military Force, Text of Resolution, http://www.gpo.gov/fdsys/pkg/PLAW-107publ40/pdf/PLAW-107publ40.pdf.

[5] Douglas Waller, Nancy Gibbs, and John F. Dickerson, "Inside the Mind of George W. Bush," *Time Magazine*, 8 September 2004, http://www.time.com/time/magazine/article/0,9171,995011-8,00.html#ixzz1565eGqDS.

[6] Quoted in Winslow T. Wheeler, *The Wastrels of Defense: How Congress Sabotages U.S. Security* (Annapolis: U.S. Naval Institute Press, 2004), p. 98.

tell us, are you still committed to vetoing any troop withdrawal deadline?" President
Bush responded:

> You mean in this interim period? Yes. I don't think Congress ought to be
> running the war. I think they ought to be funding our troops. I'm certainly
> interested in their opinion, but trying to run a war through resolution is a
> prescription for failure, as far as I'm concerned, and we can't afford to fail.
>
> I'll work with Congress; I'll listen to Congress. Congress has got all the
> right to appropriate money. But the idea of telling our military how to con-
> duct operations, for example, or how to deal with troop strength, I don't
> think it makes sense. I don't think it makes sense today, nor do I think it's a
> good precedent for the future. And so the role of the Commander-in-Chief
> is, of course, to consult with Congress.
>
> . . .
>
> Let me make sure you understand what I'm saying. Congress has all the
> right in the world to fund. That's their main involvement in this war, which
> is to provide funds for our troops. What you're asking is whether or not
> Congress ought to be basically determining how troops are positioned, or
> troop strength. And I don't think that would be good for the country.[7]

By contrast, many times during his presidency President Bush emphasized his
desire to "listen" to what the military commanders in Iraq and Afghanistan had to
say about the number of forces needed. During his press conference, the president
reiterated that view: "As the Commander-in-Chief of the greatest military ever,
I have an obligation, a sincere and serious obligation, to hear out my commander
on the ground. And I will take his recommendation." Bush would "consult" with
Congress, but the "generals" would determine the needs, and the president would
give the generals what they needed.

The US judiciary has also rarely examined the conduct of war and the treatment
of noncombatants since 2001. As William Howell and Jon Pevehouse found, "courts
during the past half century have wielded remarkably little influence over presidential
decision making during the ongoing conduct of a military adventure."[8] Exceptions to
this general rule exist, and they include investigations of the treatment of prisoners at
US military prisons and the use of torture against detainees. Specifically, in *Hamdan
v. Rumsfeld*, the Supreme Court ruled that the Bush administration had no constitutional authority to create and operate a military tribunal system.

The military now dominates decision-making at the level of operations; civilian
"oversight" of operations consists mainly in setting goals, listening to briefings, and

---

[7] Transcript, "Press Conference by the President," http://georgewbush-whitehouse.archives.gov/
news/releases/2007/07/20070712-5.html.

[8] William G. Howell and Jon C. Pevehouse, *While Dangers Gather: Congressional Checks on
Presidential War Powers* (Princeton: Princeton University Press, 2007), p. xv.

approving military timetables. During the first months of the war against al Qaeda and the Taliban in Afghanistan, Secretary of Defense, Donald Rumsfeld was deeply involved in the details of the fighting, so much so that the military leadership in the Pentagon complained of micromanagement.[9] Yet, despite these complaints, the military has enormous influence over civilian leaders within the Executive; it was as much the exceptional nature of Rumsfeld's involvement that caused offense among the uniformed military, as it was Rumsfeld's personal style. Only the occasional scandal, such as during the Iraq war when too few Humvees were armored and National Guard and Reserve troops had inadequate body armor, has prompted congressional outcry, hearings, resolutions, and appropriations.

It is not unfair to say that, for several decades, the civilian Executive's capacity to shape military operations has been essentially managed by the military's ability to frame options and capabilities to the Executive, and thus constrain their sense of possibility. The military assumed effective control of the conduct of war after Vietnam, and there has been little serious debate over the question of civilian control or oversight since Vietnam. Some argue that this is as it should be—that the prosecution of wars is the domain of the trained professional. Others note that the actual and potential power of Congress to check at least initiation and duration of war and to influence public opinion is greater than perhaps expected.[10]

On the other hand, some argue that the practice of congressional deference on war powers effectively vitiates the Congress's constitutional role in declaring war. Howell and Pevehouse argue that "in political struggles over military deployments during the past half century, Congress has ceded to the president considerable ground—so much, in fact, that its members no longer meet even basic standards of responsibility set by the Constitution."[11] In 2006, Norman Orenstein and Thomas Mann published a piece, "When Congress Checks Out," in *Foreign Affairs* arguing that "in the past six years...congressional oversight of the executive across a range of policies, but especially on foreign and national security policy, has virtually collapsed. The few exceptions, such as the tension-packed Senate hearings on the prison scandal at Abu Ghraib in 2004, only prove the rule. With little or no midcourse corrections in decision-making and implementation, policy has been largely adrift."[12] Andrew Bacevich agrees: "The problem is not that the presidency

---

[9] Benjamin S. Lambeth, *Air Power against Terror: America's Conduct of Operation Enduring Freedom* (Santa Monica, CA: Rand Corporation, 2005), pp. 316–320.

[10] See Douglas L. Kriner, *After the Rubicon: Congress, Presidents and the Politics of Waging War* (Chicago: University of Chicago, 2010); Howell and Pevehouse, *While Dangers Gather*.

[11] Howell and Pevehouse, *While Dangers Gather*, p. 6.

[12] Norman Orenstein and Thomas Mann, "When Congress Checks Out," *Foreign Affairs*, vol. 86, no. 6 (2006): 67–82, 68. Another possible exception is the Military Commissions Act of 2006, in which Congress authorized the President to conduct military tribunals of enemy combatants, after he had already instituted them, and forbade the use of "cruel, unusual, or inhumane treatment or punishment."

has become too strong. Rather the problem is that the Congress has failed egregiously—to fulfill its constitutional responsibility for deciding when and if the United States should undertake military interventions abroad."[13] Robert Buzzanco argued in 2007: "It is not hyperbolic to suggest that the military has demonstrated virtual veto power over aspects of U.S. foreign and military policy. In the aftermath of Vietnam, military leaders began to challenge openly the White House's decision-making prerogative."[14]

Above, in Part II, I argued that soldiers, commanders, and the military organization have primary causal and moral responsibility for the conduct of war. In Part III, I discuss the roles of the institutions and actors that have secondary responsibility for the conduct of war. Specifically, in this chapter, I focus on the civilian institutions of the state that must monitor those with primary responsibility and ensure that those institutions take due care. How much civilian political oversight of war is appropriate? How should civilian oversight function?

Almost all agree that civilian political authorities should determine whether and when a state goes to war. Yet, war-making is now, at least on paper, a democratic exercise, with potentially several lines of accountability. This division of labor was intentional, according to the framers of the US Constitution. Despite the formal division of authority between Congress and the president, the lines of civilian authority, oversight and responsibility for war have tended in the United States to be concentrated within the Executive branch. A second disagreement arises over the extent that political actors should affect the conduct of war. But, while the role of civilian institutions in war is debated, de facto power has shifted to the highest reaches of the Executive branch and the military.

Still, since Vietnam, some complain that civilians have inserted themselves too far into the details of war-making and want that influence reduced for reasons of expediency. During the Vietnam War, for example, Lyndon Johnson told the Joint Chiefs of Staff and Secretary of Defense McNamara in December 1967 that "some [congressional] committee chairman think they should run the strategy of the war rather than the President."[15] Barry Goldwater, ten years after the United States left Vietnam, blamed civilians, "unskilled amateurs" for the "denial of military victory."

> The real architects of the lost opportunity that doomed our undertaking in Vietnam were the civilian officials who had made a commitment large enough to risk our global position but executed it with so much hesitation as to defeat their purpose. Without derogating the principle of civilian

---

[13] Andrew J. Bacevich, *The New American Militarism: How Americans are Seduced by War* (Oxford: Oxford University Press, 2005), p. 210.

[14] Robert Buzzanco, quoted in Howell and Pevehouse, *While Dangers Gather*, p. xv.

[15] Johnson, quoted in Joseph A. Fry, *Debating Vietnam: Fulbright, Stennis, and their Senate Hearings* (Lanham, MD: Rowman and Littlefield, 2006), p. vii.

control of the military, it should be recognized that once civilian policy-makers decide on war, the result of placing military strategy and tactical operations under the day to day direction of unskilled amateurs may be greater sacrifice in blood and the denial of a military victory.[16]

If Goldwater's prescription is heeded, the "principle of civilian control of the military" is derogated and diminished. Prussian strategist Carl von Clausewitz gave some of the best reasons for civilian political control and engagement. Clausewitz argues that the statesman must judge whether war is appropriate in the first place. Clausewitz says the "first, the supreme, the most far-reaching act of judgment that the statesman and commander have to make is to establish by that test the kind of war they are embarking; neither mistaking it for, nor trying to turn it into something that is alien to its nature."[17] Clausewitz's first reason for civilian engagement is thus prudential: he cautions against the folly of using war for objectives that war, an instrument of brute force violence, cannot accomplish.

The military leader and the political leader are not one in the same for Clausewitz. Rather, Clausewitz's discussion of military leaders suggests that he sees them as specialists in the science of war. He is emphatic about the distinction. "Before continuing, we must guard against a likely misinterpretation. We are far from believing that a minister of war immersed in his files, an erudite engineer or even an experienced soldier would simply on the basis of their political experience, make the best director of policy."[18] Political leaders, in his word "statesmen," have a larger, less specialized job than soldiers. Statesmen "only" affect military operations, for the worse, he says, if they try to use war for purposes that war cannot accomplish.

Clausewitz's second reason for civilian involvement is pragmatic. Clausewitz argues that in devising the conduct of war planners should never lose sight of the political objectives and if war is to meet the political objectives, the conduct of operations should be calibrated to make that possible. "War is simply a continuation of policy with the addition of other means."[19] Specifically, political actors ought to make the decisions about when to go to war, what to fight about, how long the war shall last, and how much of the state's resources, in blood and treasure, will be devoted to the conflict, because if they do not, the political ends of war—which are not confined to military objectives—are unlikely to be met. "If we keep in mind that war springs from some political purpose, it is natural that the prime cause of its existence will remain the supreme consideration in conducting it.... War is not merely

[16] Barry Goldwater, 131 *Congressional Record*, S5431, 6 May 1985.

[17] Clausewitz, *On War*, p. 88.

[18] Ibid., p. 608. He does grant that the Prince might be in control or that the soldier and the statesman could be combined in one person. But elsewhere he seems to make it clear that there are three main roles, the people, the commander and the army, and the government. *On War*, p. 89.

[19] Clausewitz, *On War*, p. 605.

an act of policy but a true political instrument."[20] Political purpose should influence military operations: "If war is part of a policy, policy will determine its character." Clausewitz probably could not be any clearer: "The political object is the goal, war is the means of reaching it, and the means can never be considered in isolation from their purposes."[21]

At this point, careful students of Clausewitz will also recall that he said, "Policy, of course will not extend its influence to operational details. Political decisions will not determine the posting of guards or the employment of patrols."[22] Yet, in the very next sentence, Clausewitz said, "But they [policy aims] are the more influential in the planning of the war, of the campaign, and often of the battle."[23] Clausewitz is adamant, in fact, that political considerations should be in the forefront of operational concerns in war. "That the political view should wholly cease to count on the outbreak of war is hardly conceivable unless pure hatred made all wars a struggle for life and death. In fact, as we have said, they are nothing but expressions of policy itself. Subordinating the political point of view to the military would be absurd, for it is policy that has created war." Clausewitz then says, "Policy is the guiding intelligence and war only the instrument, not vice versa. No other possibility exists, then than to subordinate the military point of view to the political."[24]

> We can now see that the assertion that a major military development, or the plan for one, should be a matter for *purely military* opinion is unacceptable and can be damaging. Nor indeed is it sensible to summon soldiers, as many governments do when they are planning a war, and ask them for *purely military advice*. But it makes even less sense for theoreticians to assert that all available military resources should be put at the disposal of the commander so that on their basis he can draw up purely military plans for a war or a campaign....
>
> No major proposal required for war can be worked out in ignorance of political factors.[25]

To Clausewitz's prudential and practical considerations, I add the concern for moral responsibility. Individuals at war act as part of organizations for purposes that political institutions have presumably authorized and ordered; they act based on a social understanding of war and their particular role in that collective

---

[20] Ibid., p. 87.
[21] Ibid.
[22] Ibid., p. 606.
[23] Ibid.
[24] Ibid., p. 607.
[25] Ibid., pp. 607–608, emphasis in the original.

enterprise.[26] If war is undertaken for political purposes, those who set those purposes should monitor and manage it. Civilian oversight of military operations is
thus essential. If moral agency is constituted by a cycle of action and reflection,
then civilians must exercise their moral agency by becoming "skilled amateurs" in
their understanding of war.

Since Vietnam, the pendulum has swung too far away from effective civilian control. Presidents and presidential candidates apparently feel the need to say they will
"listen to their generals'" advice and heed it. This has the effect of simultaneously
giving too much authority and autonomy to military institutions with respect to the
conduct of war, reducing the capacity and exercise of oversight. The diminution of
oversight has also obscured the causal role of political decisions and processes in
creating the conditions on the battlefield that can lead to collateral damage. This
causal responsibility and the constitutional division of roles entail moral responsibility for the conduct of war. Thus, all the civilian political institutions in the United
States—the Legislature, the Judiciary, and the Executive—ought to understand the
conduct of war, the consequences of the use of force, and how both affect political
aims and the lives of combatants and noncombatants.

Three Cases of Civilian Institutional Weakness

I have asserted above that the US Legislature and Judiciary have not exercised adequate oversight and monitoring of the wars in Afghanistan and Iraq. In this section
I discuss two examples of inadequate involvement in the conduct of the wars and
how this has arguably led to a greater number of civilian casualties. The first case
discusses a military briefing of President Bush regarding the decision to invade Iraq.
The second example suggests how the principle of distinction was blurred early in
the war in Afghanistan with congressional approval. The third example concerns
the dearth of legislative and judicial discussion of the drone strikes and the policy
of targeted killing.

Powerpoint Analysis

Three slides from an August 2002 Pentagon Briefing by General Tommy
Franks, the Commander of US Central Command, to President Bush and the
National Security Council about a possible US invasion of Iraq are reproduced
in figures 7.1-7.3. The first slide suggests that the war would be finished within
a few months.

[26] See Mervyn Frost, "Constitutive Theory and Moral Accountability: Individuals, Institutions, and
Dispersed Practices," in Toni Erskine, ed., *Can Institutions Have Responsibilities? Collective Moral Agency
and International Relations* (New York: Palgrave, 2003), pp. 84–99.

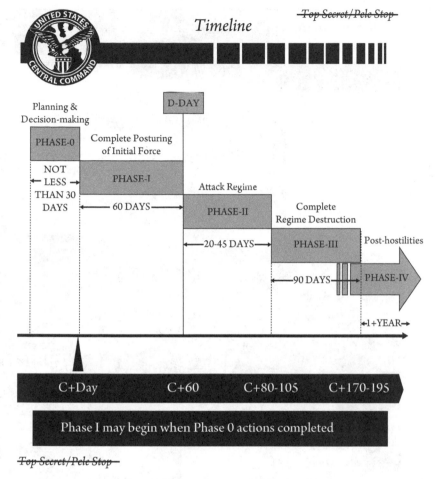

Figure 7.1 Tommy Franks August 2002 Powerpoint "Timeline" for Iraq.
Source: Declassified slide, 5 August 2002, Briefing by Tommy Franks to National Security Council,
http://www.gwu.edu/~nsarchiv/NSAEBB/NSAEBB214/index.htm.

The second slide shows how the invasion of Iraq was expected to proceed through the first 45 days. The third slide reproduced here suggests that within two to three years, US forces would be reduced to 25,000 and then 5,000 troops in a transitional role. In September 2010, when the combat mission, Operation Iraqi Freedom, ended and became Operation New Dawn, about 50,000 US troops remained deployed in Iraq. Of course, the final withdraw occurred in December 2011.

The US political leadership had decided on war at this point. There was little question, in other words, of whether the United States would try to topple the Iraqi regime. But there were many other questions that responsible political leaders could have and should have asked. The conduct of the war and the plan for the occupation

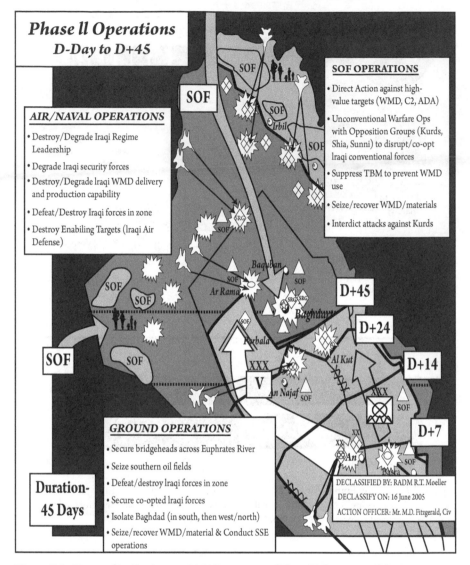

Figure 7.2 Tommy Franks August 2002 Powerpoint "Phase II Operations" for Iraq.
Source: Declassified slide, 5 August 2002, Briefing by Tommy Franks to National Security Council,
http://www.gwu.edu/~nsarchiv/NSAEBB/NSAEBB214/index.htm.

was still at issue. In fact, there was so little detail in these and other slides presented
to the president in August 2002 that it is difficult to see how they aided serious
discussion of the war's operations. These slides do not represent the totality of the
plans and timetables presented to the National Security Council and president
regarding the Iraq war. Those have not yet been declassified.

Lieutenant General David McKiernan said that in the absence of real planning,
it was difficult to continue planning or discuss alternatives in any depth. "It's quite

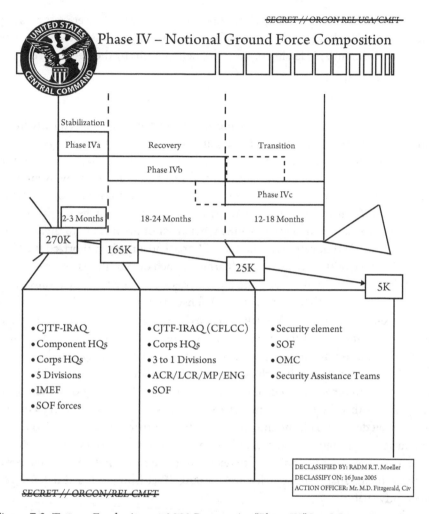

Figure 7.3 Tommy Franks August 2002 Powerpoint "Phase IV" Iraq War.
Source: Declassified slide, 5 August 2002, Briefing by Tommy Franks to National Security Council,
http://www.gwu.edu/~nsarchiv/NSAEBB/NSAEBB214/index.htm.

frustrating the way this works, but the way we do things nowadays is combatant commanders brief their products in PowerPoint up in Washington to OSD [Office of the Secretary of Defense] and Secretary of Defense.... In lieu of an order, or a frag [fragmentary] order, or plan, you get a set of PowerPoint slides.... [T]hat is frustrating, because nobody wants to plan against PowerPoint slides."[27] But as Lieutenant General McKiernan suggested, they represent a way of thinking that had taken hold in the Pentagon during this period—that detailed analysis and briefings to political

[27] McKiernan, quoted in Thomas E. Ricks, *Fiasco: The American Military Adventure in Iraq* (New York: Penguin: 2006), p. 75.

leaders, and indeed for planning, about the conduct of the wars were unnecessary. The Clausewitzian link between political aims and operations was never engaged by the Executive branch leadership or in subsequent months by the Legislature.

Loss of Distinction between Civilians and Military Targets

The distinction between combatants and noncombatants was blurred early in the response to the 9/11 attacks and repeatedly occurred during the first year of the war. This led to a broadening of the understanding of the "global war on terror" to include both people and areas of the world that had little or no involvement in the attacks on New York and Washington, D.C. Thus, there was little debate when the *National Security Strategy* proclaimed in 2002 that "we make no distinction between terrorists and those who knowingly harbor or provide aid to them."[28] The Congressional Authorization for the Use of Force had already authorized the force against both terrorists and those who "harbored such organizations or persons."

By claiming self-defense, the United States was arguing that its actions anywhere were legitimate. Similarly, Secretary of Defense Rumsfeld claimed an expanded, global, view of self-defense. "And what we are doing is going after those people, and those organizations, and those capabilities wherever we're going to find them in the world, and stop them from killing Americans."[29] Rumsfeld collapsed all action against potential terrorists into the category of legitimate self-defense on the claim that there is no other way to defend against terrorism. "I will say this, there is no question but that the United States of America has every right, as every country does, of self defense [*sic*], and the problem with terrorism is that there is no way to defend against the terrorists at every place and every time against every conceivable technique. Therefore, the only way to deal with the terrorist network is to take the battle to them. That is in fact what we're doing. That is in effect self-defense of a preemptive nature."[30]

When those who knowingly harbor terrorists are put in the category of hostile, their status is presumptively guilty. Yet those who are committed to avoiding civilian casualties must question the logic of guilt by association or co-location. How do we know who among noncombatants knowingly, and I would add, willingly harbors a terrorist or insurgent? And if a political regime harbors a terrorist, can we say that the public is liable to the indiscriminate harms of war if they merely reside in the same geographic area as a political regime that harbors terrorists? While the

---

[28] National Security Council, *The National Security Strategy of the United States of America* (Washington, DC: Office of the President, September 2002), p. 5.

[29] Donald H. Rumsfeld, Secretary Rumsfeld Interview with Wolf Blitzer, CNN, October 28, 2001, http://www.defenselink.mil/news/Oct2001/t10282001_t1028sd2.html.

[30] Donald H. Rumsfeld, Remarks at Stakeout Outside ABC TV Studio October 28, 2001, http://www.defense.gov/transcripts/transcript.aspx?transcriptid=2225.

distinction between combatant and noncombatant is not always clear, one's simple presence in the same building as a combatant certainly does not turn someone into a combatant. Only when civilians are in "direct participation" in hostilities do they lose their immunity.[31] A civilian is considered a direct participant when they are engaged in acts that are likely to cause harm to either soldiers or civilians, and there is a direct causal link between the action and the harm, and that the act is designed to contribute to the war effort of a party to the conflict.[32] Feeding a soldier, or doing their laundry is an *indirect* contribution to the war effort; if it were a direct contribution, every civilian contractor who provides meals to US soldiers, or does their laundry, at bases in war zones would be a legitimate target.

Further, the distinction was more subtly blurred when insurgents were blamed for civilian deaths caused by the United States, on the logic that the insurgents deliberately cause those casualties—either because the insurgents are barbarians, or because putting noncombatants at risk is a deliberate insurgent strategy. In this way, the burden of the causal and moral responsibility for noncombatant casualties is lifted from the United States and placed on its adversaries. On this logic, for example, members of the Bush administration argued that the "barbarism" of the Taliban and Al Qaeda released the United States from some international obligations, including provisions of the Geneva Convention. It was repeatedly emphasized that this was a "new" kind of war that demanded new tactics. For instance, John Yoo, a high-level lawyer for the Bush administration, argued: "Al-Qa'ida violates every rule and norm developed over the history of war. Flagrant breach by one side of a bargain generally releases the other side from the obligation to observe its end of the bargain."[33] As Rumsfeld stated in the early days of the war in Afghanistan:

> So let there be no doubt; responsibility for every single casualty in this war, be they innocent Afghans or innocent Americans, rests at the feet of [the] Taliban and al Qaeda. Their leaderships are the ones that are hiding in mosques and using Afghan civilians as human shields by placing their armor and artillery in close proximity to civilians, schools, hospitals, and the like. When the Taliban issue accusations of civilian casualties, they indict themselves.[34]

The belief that the use of human shields is a deliberate tactic designed to take advantage of the United States' customary restraint and respect for noncombatants is widely held. An Air Force lawyer, Jefferson Reynolds, writing in *Air Force Law Review* about

---

[31] See chapter 1, and the Geneva Convention Additional Protocol II, Article 13(1) and (3).

[32] See Nils Melzer, *Interpretive Guidance on the Notion of Direct Participation in Hostilities under International Humanitarian Law* (Geneva: International Committee of the Red Cross, 2009).

[33] John Yoo, *War by Other Means: An Insider's Account of the War on Terror* (New York: Atlantic Monthly Press, 2006), p. 23.

[34] Rumsfeld, Remarks at Stakeout.

collateral damage argued that putting civilians in harm's way was an attempt to gain "strategic advantage." Reynolds suggests that the "avoidance of collateral damage can even be determinative for nations like the United States (U.S.) who value the LOAC [law of armed conflict]." Reynolds believes that opponents of the United States "will improve methods to effectuate collateral damage in an effort to complicate attack planning, promote disinformation campaigns, deter attack, exploit humanitarian interests and, ultimately, improve survivability."[35] Reynolds proposes that the response to the tactic includes attacking targets where noncombatants are located.

> A proposed solution to this problem requires attacking target sets that are prohibited according to some humanitarian interest groups, improving awareness and understanding of collateral damage, promoting the application of emerging technology, including non-lethal technology, and the use of aggressive information campaigns designed to expose deceptive reports of collateral damage.[36]

There is no doubt that the relatively weak adversaries of the United States have sometimes used human shields or sheltered in civilian areas to take advantage of the principle of noncombatant immunity. To the extent that the Taliban and Al Qaeda, or Iraqi insurgents, have sheltered behind civilians and continue to do so, their tactics are clearly against international law.[37] This tactic is to be condemned. But, the fact that the Taliban, or any other adversary, violates international law does not vitiate the responsibility of the United States to avoid harming civilians.[38] Similarly, the

---

[35] Jefferson D. Reynolds, "Collateral Damage on the 21st Century Battlefield: Enemy Exploitation of the Law of Armed Conflict, and the Struggle for the Moral High Ground," *Air Force Law Review*, vol. 56 (2005): 1–108, 2.

[36] Ibid., pp. 2–3.

[37] Geneva Additional Protocol I, Article 58.

[38] US military lawyers recognized the legal obligation to comply with the laws of war (LOW) but also cite practical reasons for doing so.

    I. REASONS TO COMPLY WITH THE LOW—EVEN IF THE ENEMY DOES NOT

      A. Compliance ends the conflict more quickly. Mistreatment of EPWs [enemy prisoners of war] may encourage the remaining enemy soldiers to fight harder and resist capture. During OPERATION DESERT STORM, favorable treatment of Iraqi EPWs by coalition forces helped end the war quickly because reports of such treatment likely encouraged massive surrender by other Iraqi soldiers.

      B. Compliance enhances public support of our military mission; violations of the LOW seriously reduce the support that U.S. Soldiers generally receive not only from the U.S. public, but also from people in other countries (e.g., reports of misconduct in Vietnam reduced public support of the military mission).

      C. Compliance encourages reciprocal conduct by enemy soldiers. Mistreatment of EPWs by our Soldiers may encourage enemy soldiers to treat captured U.S. Soldiers in the same manner.

      D. Compliance not only accelerates termination of the conflict, but it also reduces the waste of our resources in combat and the costs of reconstruction after the conflict ends.

fact that Iraqi insurgents sheltered in hospitals and homes in Fallujah, Baghdad, or any other city in Iraq did not vitiate the principle of distinction. Yet, US commanders made statements that both blur the combatant/noncombatant distinction and suggest indifference to noncombatants.

Collateral damage is not the only consequence of a failure to discriminate between combatant and noncombatant. The loss of distinction has also been evident in the US policies of detention in Iraq and Afghanistan. For example, many thousands of Afghan civilians have been detained and eventually released in night raids and clearance operations. While being detained is usually not lethal, many of those detained are physically abused and some have suffered economic hardship after prolonged detentions.

Congress was not at fault for the way the definition of those who could be legitimately killed was expanded in the field or excused by the civilian leadership. But Congress did little or nothing to question the loss of distinction or later to rein in the administration and the military. The initial broad authorization for the use of force was also not qualified. An expansive understanding of military necessity thus became dominant with little question that it would be challenged.

The Drone War in Congress and the Judiciary

Since 2002, the US Central Intelligence Agency has "secretly" conducted several hundred air strikes into Pakistan and Yemen using drone aircraft on the mission of destroying the leadership of the Taliban and Al Qaeda located in that country. Of course, the fact of the strikes and outlines of drone technology itself are not secret. But while the total unmanned aerial vehicle inventory increased about fortyfold from 2002 to 2010 and the use of drones as offensive weapons for targeted killings constitutes a new feature of the post-9/11 wars, Congress has not yet engaged in deep deliberation on the drone strike program.[39] Nor was there, until the final months of the 2012 election, a move by the Obama administration to codify the rules for strikes.[40]

Rather the secrets include the information that might be used to evaluate the political and strategic issues associated with the drone strikes: the analysis of the

---

E. Compliance is required by law. The LOW arises in large part from treaties that are part of our national law. Violation of the LOW is a serious crime punishable by death in some cases.

International and Operational Law Department,
Operational Law Handbook 2009, p. 37.

---

[39] See Jeremiah Gertler, "U.S. Unmanned Aerial Systems," Congressional Research Service, 3 January 2012. Congress is attentive to the costs of the program. Department of Defense spending on drones increased from $284 million in FY2000 to 3.3 billion in FY2010.

[40] Scott Shane, "Election Spurred a Move to Codify U.S. Drone Policy," *New York Times*, 25 November 2012, p. 1.

legality of targeted killings, the criteria for choosing the targets of the strikes, the procedures used to ensure discrimination and the protection of noncombatants, the authority given (or not) by Pakistan and Yemen for these incursions into their air space and the launching of missiles, the effects of the strikes on civilians and the leadership of the insurgent and militant organizations, and the costs of the program which are concealed in the CIA budget. These questions were subjects of speculation during the Bush administration, but were not seriously debated at the time. When the Obama administration increased the use of the strikes, there was little political discussion of the escalation.

The secrecy about drones perhaps distracts from and adds to a deeper problem: even in the cases of relative transparency, there are questions about how much and in what ways judicial and legislative political authorities should be engaged in deliberations about the conduct of war. Specifically, assassination has been against US law since the mid-1970s, yet even officials in the Obama administration who are advocates of the drone strikes acknowledge that "it's hard to distinguish this, in a practical sense, from targeted assassination."[41] Congress and the Judiciary have not taken up the distinction, if there is one: rather, many have simply accepted the administration's assertions of the legality of the killings.

For example, consider the case of the Obama-administration-ordered killing by drone of a US citizen, Anwar al-Alawki, who the administration considered a threat because of the statements he had made. In early January 2010, it was reported that the Obama administration ordered that al-Alawki be put on a terrorist capture or kill list. Al-Alawki's father and civil liberties organizations then sued in US Federal Court to stop the order to kill his son, arguing that the order was for extrajudicial execution. The American Civil Liberties Union and the Center for Constitutional Rights argued that such an order was unlawful, an overreach of executive power. "The idea that courts should have no role whatsoever in determining the criteria by which the executive branch can kill its own citizens is unacceptable in a democracy. In matters of life and death, no executive should have a blank check."[42]

The Justice Department spokesman argued that the suit was essentially requesting an overreach of judicial power by asking "a court to take the unprecedented step of intervening in an ongoing military action to direct the President how to manage that action—all on behalf of a leader of a foreign terrorist organization."[43] In September 2010 the Obama administration filed a brief urging that the case be dismissed on the grounds of that the plaintiff lacked standing and on the grounds of "state secrets." The brief also stated that:

---

[41] Obama administration official, quoted in Sanger, *Confront and Conceal*, p. 255.

[42] The American Civil Liberties Union and Center for Constitutional Rights, quoted in Spencer Hsu, "Obama Invokes 'State Secrets' Claim to Dismiss Suit against Targeting of U.S. Citizen al-Alaqui," Washington Post, 25 September 2010.

[43] Justice Department spokesperson Matthew Miller, quoted in ibid.

The particular relief plaintiff seeks would constitute an *ex ante* command to military and intelligence officials that could interfere with lawful commands issued by the President, who is constitutionally designated as Commander-in-Chief of the armed forces and constitutionally responsible for national security. Moreover, enforcement of such an injunction would insert the Judiciary into an area of decision-making where the courts are particularly ill-equipped to venture, *i.e.*, in assessing whether a particular threat to national security is imminent and whether reasonable alternatives for the defense of the Nation exist to the use of lethal military force. Courts have neither the authority nor expertise to assume these tasks.[44]

The lawsuit was dismissed in December 2010, with the court saying that it lacked authority to override the decisions of the Executive branch in an armed conflict. Al-Alawki was killed on 30 September 2011 in Yemen along with another US citizen, Samir Khan, who was not a target, but rather collateral damage. The legal reasoning for ordering the killing was leaked in October 2011, after the killings.[45] A week later al-Alawki's 16-year-old son, also an American citizen, and another 17-year-old relative, were killed by drone attack in Yemen. There was no evidence that either Khan, killed with al-Alawki, or the 16- and 17-year-old boys killed later were high-level leaders of any terrorist organization, or even soldiers. They were, most likely, collateral damage.

The legality of the drone strike program, more generally, has been asserted. On one side, the Obama administration made specific assertions of legality. For example, in 2010 State Department Legal Advisor Harold Koh argued, "*it is the considered view of this Administration—and it has certainly been my experience during my time as Legal Adviser—that U.S. targeting practices, including lethal operations conducted with the use of unmanned aerial vehicles, comply with all applicable law, including the laws of war.*"[46] On the other side, lawyers have raised several questions about the legality of the strikes. For example, the lawyer Mary Ellen O'Connell argues that drone strikes are illegal when they are made in places where the United States is not at war.

---

[44] "Opposition to Plaintiff's Motion for Preliminary Injunction and Memorandum in Support of Defendant's Motion to Dismiss," in *Nasser al-Aulaqi v. Barack H. Obama, Robert M. Gates, and Leon E. Panetta*, Filed on 25 September 2010 in United States District Court for the District of Columbia, p. 19.

[45] Charlie Savage, "Secret U.S. Memo Made Legal Case to Kill Civilian," *New York Times*, 8 October 2011. http://www.nytimes.com/2011/10/09/world/middleeast/secret-us-memo-made-legal-c ase-to-kill-a-citizen.html?pagewanted=all.

[46] Harold Hongju Koh, "The Obama Administration and International Law," Annual Meeting of the American Society of International Law, 25 March 2010, http://www.state.gov/s/l/releases/ remarks/139119.htm, emphasis in the original.

Killing in war is justifiable morally and legally because of the extraordinary situation of real hostilities. In the limited zones on the planet where two or more contending armed groups fight for territorial control, people are on notice of the danger. In such zones, the necessity to kill without warning is understood. Still, even in combat, there are rules. Civilians may not be directly targeted; principles of necessity and humanity restrain.

Where no such intense armed fighting is occurring, killing is only justified to save a human life immediately. Peacetime human rights and criminal law prevail. The actual facts of fighting determine which rules govern killing. The president has no override authority.[47]

After arguing that the strikes meet *jus ad bellum* criteria, the administration also asserts that the strikes comply with the laws of armed conflict. So, Harold Koh argued that the strikes meet principles of distinction, proportionality, and due care.

In particular, this Administration has carefully reviewed the rules governing targeting operations to ensure that these operations are conducted consistently with law of war principles, including:

- First, the principle of *distinction*, which requires that attacks be limited to military objectives and that civilians or civilian objects shall not be the object of the attack; and
- Second, the principle of *proportionality*, which prohibits attacks that may be expected to cause incidental loss of civilian life, injury to civilians, damage to civilian objects, or a combination thereof, that would be excessive in relation to the concrete and direct military advantage anticipated.

In U.S. operations against al-Qaeda and its associated forces—including lethal operations conducted with the use of unmanned aerial vehicles—great care is taken to adhere to these principles in both planning and execution, to ensure that only legitimate objectives are targeted and that collateral damage is kept to a minimum.[48]

The legal opinions of Harold Koh were raised at the second of two congressional hearings about drones, the latter focused on the issue of targeted killings. The

---

[47] Mary Ellen O'Connell, "Killing Awlaki was Illegal, Immoral, and Dangerous," CNN, 1 October 2011, http://globalpublicsquare.blogs.cnn.com/2011/10/01/killing-awlaki-was-illegal-immoral-and-dangerous/.

[48] Koh, "The Obama Administration and International Law."

hearings were striking in several senses. First, that they occurred at all. Second, that the quality of the arguments among the expert panel was high. And third, in a setting that is often dominated by administration officials, no one in the Obama administration made an appearance. And fourth, panelists made direct reference to the respective roles and responsibilities of the Executive, Judiciary, and Legislative branches with regard to the drone targeted killing program. Finally, the question of collateral damage was hardly mentioned.

Despite the importance of these assertions, these arguments and others about the conduct of the wars have not been fully aired. The Congressional Research Service summarized some of the legal issues for Congress in May 2012, but at the time of this writing, no legislative or judicial body had pushed either the Bush or Obama administrations to defend their legal reasoning against a challenge or to specify how their procedures ensure distinction, proportionality, and due care.[49] President Obama has asserted in informal remarks, that the process of targeting terrorists by drones is legitimate: "It is important for everybody to understand that this thing is kept on a very tight leash. Its not a bunch of folks in a room somewhere just making decisions, and it is also part and parcel of our overall authority when it comes to battling al-Qaeda."[50] Details from Obama administration officials published in May 2012 gave the impression that the president was involved in approving targets on the "kill list." Obama's National Security Advisor Thomas Donilon said, "He is determined that he will make these decisions about how far and wide these operations will go.... He's determined to keep the tether pretty short."[51]

Although the president offered in his February 2013 State of the Union address to make the "legal architecture" for the drone strikes clear, it was only in late May 2013, after more than 4 years of expanding the program of targeted killing, that President Obama made a substantial case for the drone strike program. At the same time, however, the administration outlined new restrictions on its scope, contained in a classified policy guidance document. It appears that the increased sense among foreign policy decision makers that civilian deaths from the drone strikes required both a high level justification of the program, and a decrease in the number of drone strikes in Yemen and Pakistan.

Yet, the fact that a president orders a military operation, and oversees it, does not necessarily make an action legal. A former director of the Central Intelligence Agency, Michael Hayden, told a *Los Angeles Times* reporter, "This program rests on

[49] Jennifer K. Elsea, Memorandum, "Legal Issues Related to the Lethal Targeting of U.S. Citizens Suspected in Terrorist Activity," 4 May 2012, Congressional Research Service.

[50] Obama "Google Plus" interview, January 2012, quoted in Sanger, *Confront and Conceal*, pp. 251–252.

[51] Jo Becker and Scott Shane, "Secret 'Kill List' Proves a Test of Obama's Principles and Will," *New York Times*, 29 May 2012.

the personal legitimacy of the president, and that's dangerous."[52] More fundamentally, as Daniel Byman suggested, whether or not drones are used in the attacks, targeted killing is still perceived as killing outside the rule of law. Byman argues that this killing can potentially backfire politically, "because targeted killings are not widely accepted as a legitimate instrument of state, the United States risks diminishing its status as an upholder of the rule of law if it embraces them."[53]

Further, the recitation of the principles without a full description of the procedures, and evidence that the procedures are working to minimize civilian harm is not a satisfactory justification. When an opinion piece in the *New York Times* appeared in January 2012 with the title, "Do Drones Undermine Democracy?" the author, an astute observer of the use of drones, Peter W. Singer argued that drones posed a new challenge—that the Constitution's division of labor between the president and the Congress was "now under siege." Singer calls for "deep deliberation." He concludes with the argument that "America's founding fathers may not have been able to imagine robotic drones...but the Constitution did not leave war, no matter how it is waged, to the executive branch alone. In a democracy, it is an issue for all of us."[54]

Beyond questions of legality, there are questions of efficacy and proportionality that cannot be answered by those charged with oversight if they lack data. For example, when Obama administration officials stated that the secret program was an overwhelming success, there was little evidence given to back up their claim. In June 2011, the administration's chief counterterrorism official John Brennan, for example, argued that the drone strikes were "exceptionally precise and surgical in terms of addressing the terrorist threat. And by that I mean, if there are terrorists who are within an area where there are women and children or others, you know, we do not take such action that might put those innocent men, women and children in danger." Brennan further stated that in the last year, "there hasn't been a single collateral death because of the exceptional proficiency, precision of the capabilities that we've been able to develop."[55] But Pakistani officials and NGO observers have claimed otherwise—that many civilians have been killed. While the drone strikes

[52] Quoted in Doyle McManus, "Who Reviews the U.S. 'Kill List'?" *Los Angeles Times*, 5 February 2012, http://www.latimes.com/news/opinion/commentary/la-oe-mcmanus-column-drones-and-the-law-20120205,0,876903.column. On Obama's 23 May announcement of new guidance on drone strikes see, Scott Shane, "Debate Aside, Drone Strikes Drop Sharply," *New York Times*, May 22, 2013; Charlie Savage and Peter Baker, "Obama in Shift, to Limit Targets of Drone Strikes," *New York Times*, May 23, 2013

[53] Daniel Byman, "Do Targeted Killings Work?" *Foreign Affairs*, vol. 85, no. 2 (March-April 2006): 95–111, 106.

[54] Peter W. Singer, "Do Drones Undermine Democracy?" *New York Times*, 22 January 2012.

[55] Brennan, quoted in Ken Dilanian, "U.S. Counter-terrorism Strategy to Rely on Surgical Strikes, Unmanned Drones," *Los Angeles Times*, 29 June 2011. http://articles.latimes.com/2011/jun/29/news/la-pn-al-qaeda-strategy-20110629. "Remarks of John O. Brennan, Assistant to the President for Homeland Security and Counterterrorism, On Ensuring al-Qa-ida's Demise," Paul H. Nitze School of Advanced International Studies, 29 June 2011, http://www.whitehouse.gov/the-press-office/2011/06/29/remarks-john-o-brennan-assistant-president-homeland-security-and-counter.

in Pakistan have been more widely debated in policymaking circles, the strikes in Yemen have scarcely been discussed among policy analysts and legislators. David Sanger argues that the secrecy and lack of debate cannot continue. "No American president is going to be given the unchecked power to kill without some more public airing of the rules of engagement. If the use of drones is going to be preserved as a major weapon in America's arsenal, the weapon will have to be employed selectively—and each time a public case will have to be made for why it was necessary."[56]

Yet, over the course of two administrations and ten years, drones have been used without significant oversight or challenge. Senator Dianne Feinstein, Chair of the Intelligence Committee has requested that the Obama administration make its rules for the drone strikes clear. Some members of Congress are informed, either directly, or through their staffs, about the drone strikes. Senator Feinstein told the *Los Angeles Times* in May 2012 that "we receive notification with key officials shortly after every strike, and we hold regular briefings and hearings on these operations. Committee staff has held 28 monthly in-depth oversight meetings to review strike records and question every aspect of the program, including legality, effectiveness, precision, foreign policy implications and the care taken to minimize noncombatant casualties."[57] These meetings, held at CIA headquarters include viewing video footage of US drone strikes and the review of some of the intelligence information used to determine the targets.[58] Feinstein said that she believed collateral damage from the strikes had been greatly reduced.[59]

The fact that the president and national security figures have been able to assert that collateral damage is minimal and that Senator Feinstein was able to say, on the basis of access to secret information means that the features of the drone program that produce systemic collateral damage are not open to analysis, and that the criteria for double effect/proportionality killing is not on the table. How often and in what conditions do the drone strikes predictably cause civilian injury and death? What was the "Noncombatant Casualty Cut-Off Value" ceiling of risk to civilians prior to the May 2013 directive? How was that value decided? If the incidence of collateral damage has been reduced, Congress should know what it was before, what is now, and how that risk reduction was accomplished. Why has civilian political oversight on the drone program, and more generally, the operations of the wars in Afghanistan, Iraq, and Pakistan been so minimal and deferential? How did it become the case that minimal oversight seems acceptable, indeed understood as just exactly the way to be responsible, to so many parties and why did the Obama administration make the process more transparent in May 2013?

[56] Sanger, *Confront and Conceal*, p. 261.

[57] Dianne Feinstein, letter to the *Los Angeles Times*, 17 May 2012, http://www.latimes.com/news/opinion/letters/la-le-0517-thursday-feinstein-drones-20120517,0,2635114.story.

[58] Ken Dilanian, "Congress Keeps Closer Watch on CIA Drone Strikes," *Los Angeles Times*, 25 June 2012.

[59] Correspondents, "Drone Kills 12 Militants at Training Compound," *The Express Tribune*, 24 July 2012, http://tribune.com.pk/story/412308/drone-kills-12-militants-at-training-compound/.

A Short History of War Powers and Civil-Military Relations in the United States

The formal role of the US national legislature in declaring war—evaluating *jus ad bellum* concerns of right intention, last resort, just cause, necessity, and probability of success—is well established by the Constitution. The president is given the role of commander in chief under Article 2 of the Constitution. Article 1, section 8 articulates specific provisions for the role of the legislature to declare war and regulate land and naval forces.

> To define and punish Piracies and Felonies committed on the high Seas, and Offences against the Law of Nations;
>
> To declare War, grant Letters of Marque and Reprisal, and make Rules concerning Captures on Land and Water;
>
> To raise and support Armies, but no Appropriation of Money to that Use shall be for a longer Term than two Years;
>
> To provide and maintain a Navy;
>
> To make Rules for the Government and Regulation of the land and naval Forces;
>
> To provide for calling forth the Militia to execute the Laws of the Union, suppress Insurrections and repel Invasions;
>
> To provide for organizing, arming, and disciplining, the Militia, and for governing such Part of them as may be employed in the Service of the United States, reserving to the States respectively, the Appointment of the Officers, and the Authority of training the Militia according to the discipline prescribed by Congress.

In essence, while the role of civilian political institutions is nominally one of command (executive) and oversight (legislative branch), in practice the command and oversight roles are highly circumscribed by both expectations about the role of political institutions, and the structures of information flows and analysis. Arguably, the more recent aversion to oversight and advice from the legislature and judiciary builds on a much deeper deference to military authority and military expertise that has its origins in the wars of the eighteenth and nineteenth century and which was reinforced in the twentieth century.[60] For instance, during the Revolutionary War,

---

[60] See Andrew J. Bacevich, *American Empire: The Realities and Consequences of U.S. Diplomacy* (Cambridge, MA: Harvard University Press, 2002); Walter Millis, *Arms and Men: A Study in American Military History* (New Brunswick, NJ: Rutgers University Press, 1956); Michael S. Sherry, *In the Shadow of War: The United States Since the 1930s* (New Haven: Yale University Press, 1995); Catherine A. Lutz, *Homefront: A Military City and the American 20th Century* (Boston: Beacon Press, 2001); Harold Lasswell, "The Garrison State," *The American Journal of Sociology*, vol. 46, no. 4 (January

although the Continental Congress was concerned about alliances and fraud and negligence in military procurement, it left matters of strategy and the treatment of prisoners of war primarily in the hands of the military and militia. The Congress authorized and paid for the wars against Native Americans and Mexico, but did not question their conduct.

The primary exception to congressional quiescence in the nineteenth century was the Joint Committee on the Conduct of the War, formed in 1861. While Lincoln himself was quite engaged in the details of the Civil War, the Joint Committee's confrontations with President Lincoln and his commanders over strategy were legendary in their time. Indeed, the prevailing view is that the committee's activity hurt the northern war effort because it was "composed of military amateurs who attempted to influence military policy with simplistic, outmoded ideas on the art of warfare."[61] President Truman was fond of recalling that Robert E. Lee said the committee was worth about two divisions of Confederate troops.[62]

The Joint Committee on the Conduct of the War was, in general, opposed to professional military officers trained at West Point, and critical of the early efforts to reach conciliation with the South. Rather, the committee favored what northern General William Sherman and others would call the "hard hand," an aggressive approach to crushing the South.[63] Whether congressional activism during the Civil War through the Committee on the Conduct of the War made a positive or negative contribution to the war effort can be debated. What the committee did do was expose some "corruption, mismanagement, and crimes against humanity."[64]

After the Civil War, however, the tide of civilian oversight turned. First, war heroes and soldiers were ubiquitous, and respect for the soldiers grew to reverence. Indeed, in 1875, Congressman Henry Slocum, a Civil War veteran, implied an unhealthy level of military influence in the United States when he told fellow members of Congress:

> We draw on the Army for our stump orators, we call on them to preside at the polls.... If we desire to negotiate for the purchase of an island in the sea, the negotiations must be carried on by a brigadier general. If the merchants of New York wish storage for their goods they must go to a colonel

1941): 455–468; Harold Lasswell, "Does the Garrison State Threaten Civil Rights?" *Annals of the American Academy of Political and Social Science*, vol. 275 (May 1951): 111–116; Samuel Huntington, ed. *Changing Patterns of Military Politics* (New York: Free Press, 1961).

[61] Bruce Tap, *Over Lincoln's Shoulder: The Committee on the Conduct of the War* (Lawrence: University of Kansas Press, 1998), p. x.

[62] David McCullough, *Truman* (New York: Simon and Schuster, 1992), p. 258.

[63] Sherman said in 1861, "We are not only fighting hostile armies, but a hostile people, and we must make old and young, rich and poor, feel the hard hand of war, as well as the organized armies." Quoted in Lance Janda, "Shutting the Gates of Mercy: The American Origins of Total War, 1860-1880," *Journal of Military History*, vol. 59 (January 1995): 7–26, 15.

[64] Tap, *Over Lincoln's Shoulder*, p. 255.

of the staff. We can hardly pass a bill through Congress without the aid of a field officer."[65]

Deference became the norm.

And second, Congress increasingly turned its focus on military organizational and procurement issues. There are two well-known examples of the focus on organization and procurement. The Senate's Special Committee on Investigation of the Munitions Industry, more commonly known as the Nye Committee (after Gerald Nye, R-ND), begun in 1934, investigated arms production and procurement practices in World War I. Senator Harry Truman's Special Committee to Investigate National Defense, initiated in 1941, was concerned with production and defense contracting in World War II. The Nye Committee's hearings were retrospective; the Truman Committee, which held more than 400 public and more than 300 closed-door hearings and issued 51 reports, was credited with helping to streamline and make more efficient the war production process. Truman was explicit that his committee would not follow the practices of the Civil War Joint Committee on the Conduct of the War. No questions of strategy were addressed. Further, the Special Committee to Investigate National Defense stayed clear of potentially controversial domestic issues related to defense, such as race relations and the siting of military facilities.

The power to initiate war moved more fully to the president during the Cold War. Congress, as one scholar suggests, operates within a "culture of deference" to the Executive branch in matters of foreign policy, while members of the Executive defer, in turn, to members of the military in matters of the conduct of war.[66] Two key post-World War II pieces of congressional legislation of the military cemented the dominance of the military and Executive branch. The National Security Act of 1947, which reorganized the Armed Forces and established the outlines of the current national security system, and the Goldwater-Nichols Act of 1986 were both, essentially concerned with organizational and procedural issues. Congress much more rarely hears testimony or legislates on the question of the conduct of war.

After North Korea invaded South Korea on 25 June 1950, President Truman engaged the United States immediately in the United Nations effort to turn North Korea out. There was very limited discussion of what to do in the US Congress. Indeed, Truman only consulted with fourteen members of Congress from both parties on 27 June before giving General MacArthur orders on 30 June to use the forces occupying Japan to turn back the North Korean Army. Senator Robert Taft,

[65] Representative Henry W. Slocum, US Congress, House, Congressional Globe, 42nd Congress, 2nd Session, 1875, pt. 3. Quoted in Robert Wooster, The Military and United States Indian Policy 1865-1903 (New Haven: Yale University Press, 1988), p. 73.

[66] See Stephen Weissman, A Culture of Deference: Congress's Failure of Leadership in Foreign Policy (New York: Basic Books, 1995).

an isolationist leaning Republican from Ohio, said on 28 June, "There has been no pretense of consulting Congress."[67]

Congress only became active in questions of Korean War policy when the president vetoed a military strategy proposed by General MacArthur. MacArthur had pursued a bold strategy of amphibious assaults and air power, combined with hard fighting on the ground, which saw some success at pushing the North Koreans back deep into their own territory. But when the Chinese joined the North Koreans, US and UN forces were pushed back. At this juncture, MacArthur advocated attacking China itself and suggested that the United States use nuclear weapons. The political leadership and most of the military leadership rejected MacArthur's proposed escalation into China as too dangerous. Chairman of the Joint Chiefs of Staff Omar Bradley later told Congress that such an escalation would be initiating "the wrong war, at the wrong place, at the wrong time, and with the wrong enemy."[68] Yet, MacArthur persisted in pressing his case in public after he was overruled, on the belief that his duty was to the Constitution and less to the temporary occupants of the Executive branch, including the president. President Truman relieved MacArthur of command in April 1951.

MacArthur's dismissal by the president provoked more interest, hearings, and debate in the Congress than the initiation of the war. The Foreign Relations and Armed Services committees of the Senate held hearings for forty-three days in May and June 1951 on MacArthur's dismissal and the strategy in Korea. But no action was taken by Congress, and Truman retained tight control over strategy.[69]

Congressional scrutiny of the Vietnam War was arguably lax until 1966 when, in January, the Senate Foreign Relations Committee Public convened hearings to discuss the war. Chaired by Senator William Fulbright, and now known as the Fulbright hearings, the Senate Foreign Relations Committee questioned members of the Johnson and later Nixon administrations over the course of several hearings periodically through May 1971. Senator John Stennis, who believed the United States should escalate in Vietnam, also held hearings in August 1967 in the Senate Preparedness Investigating Subcommittee focused on tactics. The Fulbright Committee Hearings during April and May 1971 heard testimony about the conduct of the war from Vietnam Veterans Against the War including, famously, from Lt. John Kerry, who described on 22 April 1971 war crimes and indifference to US soldiers and Vietnam Veterans, who asked, "How do you ask a man to be the

---

[67] Quoted in Cecil V. Crabb, Jr. and Pat M. Holt, *Invitation to Struggle: Congress, The President, and Foreign Policy*, 4th ed. (Congressional Quarterly Press, 1992), p. 136.

[68] Quoted in Russell F. Weigley, *The American Way of War: A History of United States Military Strategy and Policy* (New York: Macmillan, 1973), p. 390.

[69] It has become very rare to fire Generals. US Air Force General Jack Lavelle was fired in 1972 for conducting raids against North Vietnamese air defense and radar sites against the White House prohibitions on such strikes. Mark Martins, "Rules of Engagement for Land Forces: A Matter of Training, Not Lawyering," *Military Law Review*, vol. 143, no. 1 (Winter 1994): 1–160, 38n.

last man to die for a mistake."[70] The Ad Hoc Dellums Hearings in the House of Representatives in 1971, which were convened to focus specifically on "war atrocities." Tens of thousands of US citizens protested the Vietnam War, and soldiers organized their own public "Winter Soldier" hearings on the conduct of the war. Similarly, when millions protested the nuclear strategy of the Reagan administration, Congress held hearings on nuclear policy, the freeze proposal, and passed resolutions urging arms control and reductions and the "nuclear-freeze."[71]

But, these cases are exceptional. Since the US Civil War, Congress has focused on procurement, bases, and the military budget. The Senate has focused not on conduct of war or the composition of America's military arsenal, but more on fulfilling its obligations to advise and consent on arms control and other foreign policy treaties. Both houses of Congress have debated the question of whether to initiate armed hostilities, but in recent decades, this has often been after the fact of the president committing the United States to war.

The War Powers Act of 1973, written to reign in presidential power to initiate war, is focused on the introduction of US Armed Forces into conflict. At least one Senator, Jacob Javits, believed the Act would give Congress "the responsibility for putting blood on our hands too."[72] The president may take emergency action to respond to attack, but Congress must authorize and reauthorize the use of armed force abroad at regular intervals. As a limit on the president's ability to use force without congressional authorization, the War Powers Act does require the president to report to Congress "periodically on the status of such hostilities or situation as well as on the scope and duration of such hostilities or situation."

As Douglas Kriner argues, the War Powers Act essentially conceded the president's institutional capability to start war without congressional knowledge or consent: "Recognizing this state of affairs, which perhaps was made necessary by exigencies of the Cold War and America's role as a global superpower, Congress, with the War Powers Resolution effectively delegated the power to initiate the use of force to the president and attempted to reserve, ex post facto authority to terminate an action of which it disapproved."[73] The War Powers Act was passed over President Richard Nixon's veto and since then only President Carter has recognized its constitutionality. Yet, some presidents have sought congressional approval and support for uses of force in recent decades and sent regular reports to Congress on the progress of a conflict. Other recent research has shown that Congress is far from impotent. Congress has been able to influence the duration and scale of war through the War Powers Act and other mechanisms (such as hearings and public statements

---

[70] John Kerry testimony, http://www.wintersoldier.com/index.php?topic=Testimony.

[71] See Waller, *Congress and the Nuclear Freeze: An Inside Look at the Politics of a Mass Movement* (Amherst: University of Massachusetts Press, 1987) and David S. Meyer, *A Winter of Discontent: The Nuclear Freeze and American Politics* (Westport, CT: Praeger, 1990).

[72] Javits, quoted in Crabb, Jr. and Holt, *Invitation to Struggle*, p. 145.

[73] Kriner, *After the Rubicon*, p. 8.

that affect public opinion).[74] However, Congress and the Judiciary have taken comparatively little interest in the other elements of the conduct of war—namely what weapons are used and the rules of engagement.

Whether it is a correct interpretation of the US Constitution, the Executive branch, and not the Legislative, is today firmly in control over war powers in the United States. The current argument over declaring war, to the extent that there is one, is whether the Congress has too little power and the president too much. Similarly, in the last fifty years, the Judicial branch has not been a major factor in questions of war or its conduct. US Courts have rarely assessed the legality of war or its conduct in recent decades. There were several suits brought during the Vietnam War, arguing that Congress had not authorized various escalations, but they were ineffective at curbing the war.[75] This is an extremely important debate—indeed the focus of most of the work on "civil-military relations" and "war powers"—but my focus here is the role of civilian authorities in overseeing the conduct of war.

Yet, Congress does regularly deliberate on the question of going to war and sometimes over the duration of conflict. Those deliberations can constrain or encourage executive action, and perhaps more dramatically, affect public opinion about the use of force. Further, it appears that congressional opposition to the use of force has both delayed and in cases entirely derailed US military intervention, for instance, in Vietnam in 1954 and in Nicaragua in the 1980s. In the latter case, President Reagan would have preferred to intervene directly to depose the Nicaraguan government; instead he was forced to send aid and covert support to the "contras."[76]

But Congress generally avoids probing the details of the conduct of wars once begun. This is in part because questioning the conduct of the war might be seen as questioning a wartime leader. Public support approval of and deference to political presidents grows once wars have begun.[77] For example, just before the 9/11 attacks, President George W. Bush's approval rating was just over 50 percent. Soon after the attacks and the start of the war in Afghanistan, his approval rating reached 90 percent. By October 2002 his approval had rating had fallen to 67 percent, still very strong. Similarly, President Bush's approval rating was 58 percent in the week before the start of the Iraq war in 2003. On March 22–23, just a few days into the Iraq war, Bush had risen to 71 percent approval.[78] As Kriner argues, "members of Congress

[74] Kriner, *After the Rubicon*; Howell and Pevehouse, *While Dangers Gather*.

[75] Louis Fisher, *Presidential War Powers*, 2d ed., revised (Lawrence: University Press of Kansas, 2004), pp. 139–144.

[76] Howell and Pevehouse, *While Dangers Gather*, p. 126.

[77] See, for instance, John E. Mueller, *War, Presidents and Public Opinion* (New York: Wiley, 1973) and John Mueller, *Policy and Opinion in the Gulf War* (Chicago: Chicago University Press, 1994).

[78] Gallup Poll, "Presidential Approval Ratings—George W. Bush," http://www.gallup.com/poll/116500/presidential-approval-ratings-george-bush.aspx. The bump in approval doesn't necessarily last. For instance, for Bush, through much of 2008, approval hovered around 30 percent.

who oppose the president's military policies may be reticent to attack him when his public support remains strong."[79]

Some will argue that it is responsible for the Executive and Legislative branches to remain ignorant of the details of war if that involvement leads to clumsy interference. More will perhaps argue that Congress should defer on not only the causes of war, but defer to the Executive on the conduct of war. John Yoo, a legal scholar who worked in the George W. Bush administration argues, for example, that the world is too dangerous for a rigid interpretation of the Constitution. Yoo argues that the Executive can and should take the initiative, while Congress can, ultimately, use the power of the purse to halt wars. "Congress can always cut off the funding for military adventures, which in the era of modern war, may mean simply refusing to appropriate new funds.... This effective check on the president's power renders unnecessary any formal process requirement for congressional authorization or a declaration of war before hostilities may begin."[80]

Several factors have facilitated or encouraged the relative inattention of civilian political institutions and leaders to conduct in war. First, there is an underlying culture of acceptance of the necessity and utility of using military force, and a reverence for those with the courage to do so and to face fire.[81] This fosters not only admiration for soldiers and the qualities of soldiers but also a deference to the judgments of military leaders. This deference grows in time of war unless it is eroded by a scandal within the armed forces. Indeed, the civilian leadership can often become more extreme than the military in its views about the role and efficacy of military force. The less polite terms used by soldiers during the Vietnam War, and more recently to describe those civilians who have no war experience but who are eager to send them to war and tell them how to fight, include "war wimps" and "chickenhawks." The academic terms are "civilian militarism," coined by the historian Alfred Vagts, and the "garrison state" by Harold Lasswell.[82] Lasswell stressed the effect of militarization on politics and civil liberties. Although militarization would not necessarily lead to diminished civil liberties, he argued, it might well do so gradually, through "tiny declivities."

> To militarize is to governmentalize. It is also to centralize. To centralize is to enhance the effective control of the executive over decisions, and thereby to reduce the control exercised by courts and legislatures. To centralize is to enhance the role of military in the allocation of national resources.

[79] Kriner, *After the Rubicon*, p. 236. Kriner's argument implies that the public and members of Congress see attacking the policies as attacking the president.

[80] Yoo, *The Powers of War and Peace*, p. 294.

[81] See Bacevich, *The New American Militarism*.

[82] Alfred Vagts, *A History of Militarism: Civilian and Military* (New York: Meridian Books, [1937] revised 1959); Harold Lasswell, "The Garrison State," *American Journal of Sociology*, vol. 46, no. 4 (January 1941): 455–468.

Continuing fear of external attack sustains an atmosphere of distrust that finds expression in spy hunts directed at fellow officials and fellow citizens. Outspoken criticism of official measures launched for national defense is more and more resented as unpatriotic and subversive of the common good. The community at large, therefore, acquiesces in denials of freedom that to go beyond the technical requirements of military security.[83]

Second, in the post-Vietnam era, there has been resistance to civilians "micro-managing" military operations and the military has persistently urged Congress and the Executive to stay away from the details of the conduct of war. The complaints about civilian micro-management of the Vietnam War led to both the argument that the Vietnam War could have been won if the military's hands had not been tied by civilian leaders, and to the claim that the proper role for civilians was out of the details. Scott Cooper argued, "The notion that it is inappropriate for civilian leaders to involve themselves in the details of military operations is pervasive in the military."[84] Both the Executive and Congress have internalized the belief that they interfered too much in operations during Vietnam, though as I suggest below the evidence for that argument is weak at best.

The military argument that civilians should stay out of the details of war was echoed by some in the US military. While he was preparing air campaign options for the 1991 Gulf War, Lieutenant General Charles Horner told the overall commander, General Norman Schwarzkopf, "Sir, the last thing we want is a repeat of Vietnam, where Washington picked the targets! This is the job of your Air Force commander."[85] Similarly, the Commander of tactical air operations, General Robert D. Russ, who had flown 242 combat missions in the Vietnam War invoked Vietnam when he argued against plans developed in the Pentagon for the use of air power in the 1991 Gulf War. General Russ believed that the details of plans should be left to the people who would fight the war. "What starts out as a little bit of help from the Pentagon soon leads to more and more 'help' and pretty soon you get the President in on it.... Then you have people in the White House sitting on the floor trying to figure out what targets they are going to hit. That is just the wrong way to fight a war!"[86]

[83] Harold Lasswell, "Does the Garrison State Threaten Civil Rights?" *Annals of the American Academy of Political and Social Science*, vol. 275 (May 1951): 111–116, 111.

[84] But Cooper argues that view is "misguided." Quoting Clausewitz, Cooper argues that the political objectives should determine the means of war. He concludes by arguing that "politically imposed rules of engagement and limitations on target selection will always be the servant of use of force decisions that conform to political objectives." Scott Cooper, "The Politics of Air Strikes," in Stephen D. Wrage, ed., *Immaculate Warfare: Participants Reflect on the Air Campaigns over Kosovo, Afghanistan and Iraq* (Westport, CT: Praeger, 2003), pp. 71–83, 82.

[85] Horner, quoted in John Andreas Olsen, *John Warden and the Renaissance of American Air Power* (Washington, DC: Potomac Books, 2007), p. 144.

[86] Russ, quoted in Olsen, *John Warden and the Renaissance of American Air Power*, p. 160.

During and after Operation Allied Force in 1999, the Component Commander of the air strikes, Lieutenant General Michael Short followed civilian authority but complained that "as an airman, I'd have done this a whole lot differently than I was allowed to do. We could have done this differently. We should have done this differently."[87] General Short told members of the Air Force Association in January 2000: "Our politicians need to understand that this isn't going to be clean. There is going to be collateral damage. There will be unintended civilian casualties. We will do our level best to prevent both, but they've got to grit their teeth and stay with us. We can't cut and run the first time we hit the wrong end of a bridge. We can't cut and run the first time we kill innocent people that clearly we did not intend to kill."[88] Short believed that political interference harmed the war effort. "We all understood the moral imperative to attack fielded forces that the Chief has said. But I had forces made available to me that would also strike at Belgrade. We were denied that. The incredible reaction to collateral damage and loss of civilian life, I believe, prevented us from conducting effects-based targeting. But you all need to understand that Admiral Jim Ellis and General John Jumper and myself knew that was the way to do business."[89] In 2010 General Stanley McChrystal inelegantly mocked Vice President Joseph Biden who preferred a different strategy in Afghanistan with the words "Are you asking about Vice President Biden? Who's that?"[90]

Third, the conduct of contemporary war is difficult to grasp. The practices of war fighting are increasingly complex, specialized, and compartmentalized, as is knowledge about the conduct of war. Complexity is nowhere more evident than in nuclear weapons and nuclear war fighting. Although the decision was taken early in the nuclear era that civilian political leaders should control nuclear materials and the authority to use nuclear weapons, civilian knowledge of nuclear weapons and the plans for their use is limited. Journalist Thomas Powers wrote about the revision of the plans for nuclear war, the Single Integrated Operational Plan (SIOP), in 1985 in *The Washington Post*, "With the arguable exception of Jimmy Carter, no American President has ever acquired more than passing knowledge of how we planned to use nuclear weapons in War." But the ignorance, according to Powers was more widespread: "Representatives and Senators I have talked to seem vaguely sure *somebody* must be briefed on these matters." Powers found in 1985 that:

[87] Quoted in Cooper, "The Politics of Air Strikes," p. 72.

[88] General Michael C. Short, Commander, Allied Air Forces, Southern Europe, Air Force Association, Air Warfare Symposium 2000, 25 February 2000, http://www.afa.org/aef/pub/short200. asp. Short's criticism ignores the fact that he and General Wesley Clark had different views of the target set that would yield victory. Clark was focused on destroying the Serbian Army while Short favored the "strategic targets" in Cooper, "The Politics of Air Strikes," pp. 80–81.

[89] Short, Air Warfare Symposium 2000, February 25, 2000.

[90] Quoted in Ann Kornblut, "McChrystal Article Renews Attention to Split with Biden over Afghanistan," *Washington Post*, 23 June 2010, http://www.washingtonpost.com/wp-dyn/content/article/2010/06/23/AR2010062301109.html.

This confidence that somebody has these matters well in hand is not limited to Congress. The whole National Security establishment, from the President on down, seems to share it. But when you get particular and look around for the people in charge, you find that nobody, no agency or committee, no appointed or even self-appointed group in the White House, the Pentagon, or the Congress has been asked to question the SIOP and its implications for the planet in rigorous detail on a regular and continuing basis.[91]

Fourth, militaries are always loathe to discuss war plans, weapons, and conduct during war for fear of exposing secret plans, tactics, or technologies to enemies. As weapons technology has become more sophisticated, the urge to keep it secret has grown and, in this regard, nuclear weapons are the extreme case. The initial decision to build nuclear weapons was secret, the exact numbers of nuclear weapons held by the United States was secret in the early nuclear era, and the debate over whether to produce the more powerful hydrogen "super" bomb was also held among a very small circle of military, scientific, and political advisors. When US Senators asked for a briefing on the plan for nuclear war in 2000, they were frustrated by a lack of information. Senator Bob Kerrey noted:

> In fact, when asked for detailed targeting information we were given three different answers. First, we were told that they did not bring that kind of information. Then, we were told there were people in the room who were not cleared to receive that kind of information. Finally, we were told that kind of information is only provided to the Senate leadership and members of the Armed Services Committee. Because members of the leadership and the Senate Armed Services Committee indicated they had never received such information, I can only surmise there must be a fourth answer.
>
> We find ourselves in an uncomfortable and counter-productive Catch-22. Until we as civilians provide better guidance to our military leaders, we are unlikely to affect the kind of changes needed to update our nuclear policies to reflect the realities of the post-cold-war world. Yet, providing improved guidance is difficult when we are unable to learn the basic components of the SIOP....
>
> While I still believe this briefing is needed, we need not wait for a briefing on the details of the SIOP to answer the question of how many nuclear weapons are needed to deter potential aggressors. In truth, it is important for citizens, armed only with common sense and open-source information, to reach sound conclusions about our nuclear posture and force levels.[92]

[91] Thomas Powers, "What's Worse than the MX?" *Washington Post*, 31 March 1985.
[92] *Congressional Record*, 30 June 2000, Senate S6292.

Fifth, there is a concern to avoid discussions at a level that might engender questioning or dissent at home, or worse, "encourage" the enemies of the United States. When in January 1991, President George H. W. Bush asked Congress for a resolution of support of his actions and the United Nations resolutions, he warned of "encouraging Iraqi intransigence." Bush said, congressional action "would help dispel any belief that may exist in the minds of Iraq's leaders that the United States lacks the necessary unity to act decisively in response to Iraq's continued aggression against Kuwait....Anything less would only encourage Iraqi intransigence."[93] These factors tend to reinforce each other so that it is difficult for nonmilitary experts to question the conduct of war.

Too Much Civilian Oversight during Vietnam?

The conventional wisdom among many civilians and members of the military in the United States is that civilian oversight over military conduct was too intrusive during the Vietnam War. As Colonel Harry Summers, Jr. wrote in a widely read analysis of the Vietnam War, "our civilian leadership in the Pentagon, the White House, and in the Congress evidently believed the military professionals had no worthwhile advice to give."[94] The US former commander in Iraq, Lt. General Ricardo Sanchez repeated the charge in his 2008 memoir: "Civilian leaders in the White House micromanaged many aspects of the Vietnam War. They did not allow the US armed forces to utilize the full extent of its resources to achieve victory. Instead, the military was forced to fight incremental battles that led to a never-ending conflict."[95] The belief that unhindered, the US military could have won the war was widespread.[96] And Vietnam is understood as a peak of civilian intrusiveness. Is that so?

The US military involvement in the Vietnam War began with a small number of military advisors in the early 1960s and by 1964 had reached about 18,000 troops. The US began covert air and naval attacks on North Vietnamese targets in retaliation for North Vietnam's sponsorship of a rebellion in South Vietnam in the mid-1960s. A clash on 2 August 1964 between North Vietnamese patrol boats and a US Navy destroyer in the Gulf of Tonkin and another incident two days later where the Navy again fired were portrayed as a major assault and a threat to not only regional but

---

[93] George H. W. Bush, quoted in in Crabb and Holt, *Invitation to Struggle*, p. 157.

[94] Harry G. Summers, Jr., *On Strategy: The Vietnam War in Context* (Carlisle Barracks, PA: U.S. Army War College, 1981), p. 42–3.

[95] Ricardo Sanchez and Donald T. Phillips, *Wiser in Battle: A Soldier's Story* (New York: Harper, 2008), p. 29.

[96] Robert Pape, *Bombing to Win: Airpower and Coercion in War* (Ithaca, NY: Cornell University Press, 1996), pp. 186–188.

global peace. The second attack never occurred, although nearly everyone in the United States thought that there had been an attack.[97] On 5 August, Johnson spoke to the American people of the North Vietnamese aggression—"deliberate attacks against U.S. naval vessels operating in international waters"—and of the responses he had already taken. On 6 August, congressional debate began, and on 7 August, the Gulf of Tonkin Resolution was passed, 88 to 2 in the Senate and 416 to 0 in the House of Representatives. The resolution gave congressional approval and support for the president "to take all necessary measures to repel any armed attack against the forces of the United States and to prevent further aggression."[98]

The tension between the US military and US civilian leadership over Vietnam strategy was simple and irreconcilable: the US military wanted the authority to destroy the military of North Vietnam, while most US civilian leaders were convinced that gradual escalation and the threat of more force would induce the North Vietnamese to negotiate.[99] The tensions were played out in every aspect of the war, but perhaps nowhere more clearly than in the several bombing campaigns. For example, President Johnson's advisors objective for the Rolling Thunder bombing campaign of 1965 to 1968 was to pressure North Vietnam to make concessions at the bargaining table by steadily ratcheting up the pain to civilians. "From late 1966 on, they intended to make the North's civilian populace wince from the destruction of military objectives."[100] The military objective of Rolling Thunder was to interdict the flow of material supplies and troops from North Vietnam to the South by targeting both the source of the supplies in North Vietnam and the supply routes themselves. The targets associated with interdiction dominated the first part of the bombing campaign.

US air strikes were subject to limitations with the aim of avoiding civilian casualties. Specifically, there were two zones around Hanoi. In the inner "prohibited" zone of 10 miles, strikes required White House authorization and there was no restrike authority. Outside that was a 30-mile "restricted" area, where specific White House approval was required for striking targets and restrike authority also required White House authorization. The prohibited and restricted zones around Haiphong were 10 and 4 miles, respectively. White House authorization was required for striking bridges and dikes, levees, dams and hydroelectric plants were not authorized targets. In addition, when the North Vietnamese acquired Surface to Air Missiles (SAMs) to augment their other Anti-Aircraft guns, the White House restricted attacks on

[97] Louis Fisher, *Presidential War Powers*, 2d ed., revised (Lawrence: University Press of Kansas, 2004), pp. 132–133.

[98] Joint Resolution of Congress, H.J. RES 1145, 7 August 1964.

[99] Russell F. Weigley, *The American Way of War: A History of United States Military Strategy and Policy* (New York: Macmillan, 1973), p. 464; Pape, *Bombing to Win*, pp. 177–181.

[100] Mark Clodfelter, *The Limits of Air Power: The American Bombing of North Vietnam* (New York: The Free Press, 1989), p. 127.

those sites as well. SAMs could only be targeted if they were preparing to fire on US aircraft or if they were not located in populated areas. The United States could only attack SAMs in populated areas if they were actually firing at US aircraft. The North Vietnamese capitalized on these limits by putting their anti-aircraft and SAM sites in these restricted locations, including dikes, while at the same time beginning an evacuation of Hanoi and Haiphong in 1965 which, according to US intelligence esti-mates, by 1967 had reduced the population of the capital by half and the population of Haiphong to one-fourth of its pre-evacuation size.[101] The military services, the Office of the Secretary of Defense, and the State Department selected targets and the White House approved them. White House control over the approval of targets for bombing was tight. Each Tuesday, after lunch, the president, Secretary of Defense McNamara, and other military advisors met to discuss the details of the campaign. Potential bomb-ing targets were categorized along four criteria: military advantage, risk to US aircraft and pilots, estimated civilian casualties, and danger to third country nationals.[102]

Thus, during the escalation of the bombing campaign, civilians in the Johnson administration were vetting the targets according to political criteria, with the presi-dent himself engaged in the process on a regular basis. This mirrored a long-standing devolution of power toward civilians during the early Cold War. Civilian analysts grad-ually came to dominate analytical practices in World War II and in the Cold War, as they applied "systems analysis" to policy planning for nuclear weapons procurement and nuclear war planning. McNamara accelerated the use of systems analysis and other mathematical modeling and increasingly used the civilian planners for conventional strategy as well. As military historian Colonel H. R. McMaster wrote, "The president and McNamara shifted responsibility for real planning away from the JCS to ad hoc committees composed principally of civilian analysts and attorneys, whose main goal was to obtain a consensus consistent with the president's pursuit of the middle ground between disengagement and war."[103] In McMaster's view, the civilian analysts did not understand war and hence their strategy of "graduated pressure was fundamentally flawed. "Human sacrifices in war evoke strong emotions, creating a dynamic that defies systems analysis quantification." McNamara, he argued, "viewed the war as another business management problem" and "refused to consider the consequences of his rec-ommendations and forged ahead oblivious of the human and psychological complexi-ties of war."[104]

---

[101] W. Hays Parks, "Rolling Thunder and the Law of War," *Air University Review*, vol. 33, no. 2 (January/February 1982): 2–21, 9–12, Ward Thomas, *Ethics of Destruction: Norms and Force in International Relations* (Ithaca, NY: Cornell University Press, 2001), pp. 152–153 and 190; William W. Momyer, *Air Power in Three Wars* (Washington, DC: Air Force, 1979), pp. 134–135.

[102] Parks, "Rolling Thunder and the Law of War," pp. 13–14 and Earl H. Tilford, Jr., *Crosswinds: The Air Force's Setup in Vietnam* (College Station: Texas A & M University Press, 1993).

[103] H. R. McMaster, *Dereliction of Duty: Lyndon Johnson, Robert McNamara, the Joint Chiefs of Staff and the Lies that Led to Vietnam* (New York: Harper Perrenial, 1997), p. 329.

[104] McMaster, *Dereliction of Duty*, p. 327.

The restrictions on bombing were gradually eased and the bombing escalated in the summer of 1967.[105] Civilians in Southeast Asia faced a pounding from the air that the US military hoped would drive North Vietnam to submission when Rolling Thunder was followed by Linebacker I and II and the strategic bombing of Cambodia and Laos.[106] In addition to bombing, the US escalated the ground war. Although some in the military may have wanted even fewer controls, civilian leaders did not, for the most part, attend to tactics such as the use of defoliants, bombing by F-4 Phantoms, or the dropping of napalm and white phosphorous by helicopter.[107] The "lesson" the US military took from Vietnam was that civilian oversight was too intense. Some blamed the significant losses of US aircraft to North Vietnamese air defenses on the political restrictions on targeting air defenses and on the pauses in US bombing that were meant to give the North Vietnamese time to think about whether they should negotiate.

The complaint that the Vietnam War had been characterized by too much interference of civilians in the details is a caricature, perhaps mostly of President Johnson and his weekly lunch/targeting sessions, but also of Robert McNamara and the "whiz kids" of the Pentagon. Senator Barry Goldwater made this argument in a statement on the Senate floor in 1985:

> U.S. military forces did not lose the Vietnam War, civilian policymakers did.
>
> The rules of engagement caused a piecemealing of air operations which allowed North Vietnam to adjust to the U.S. air bombing campaign by importing war materials through routes immune from attack and then to disburse and store the materials in guaranteed sanctuaries. From these safe areas North Vietnam infiltrated the material to South Vietnam and Laos. The rules allowed the enemy to protect its forces and material, provided it with military training and staging areas free from attack and permitted it to erect massed air defense weapons. One of the most tragic consequences of the rules was the impact on American aircraft and pilot losses by giving North Vietnam time to build up its sophisticated air defense system.
>
> The lesson of Vietnam is that once civilian policymakers decide on war, the result of placing military operations under day-to-day management of unskilled amateurs and rejecting the advice of the best military professionals may be loss of the original objective for going to war. Such rules must never again be applied to our armed forces.[108]

---

[105] Pape, *Bombing to Win*, p. 188.

[106] See Pape, *Bombing to Win*.

[107] See Allen R. Millett, Peter Maslowski and William B. Feis, *For the Common Defense: A Military History of the United States* (New York: Free Press, 2012) pp. 507–566; Robert Neer, *Napalm: An American Biography* (Cambridge: Harvard University Press, 2013) pp. 109–125.

[108] Goldwater, 131 *Congressional Record*, S5431, 6 May 1985.

It is true that during the Vietnam War, political leaders set limits on conduct that often conflicted with the military's sense of what would be effective. It is also true that one Air Force General was fired for ordering air strikes that violated those restrictions. Further, those limits did not lead to success in Vietnam in the ways that civilians had hoped. But even after the "gloves were taken off," and they were, the bombing strategy did not succeed. Henry Kissinger, who took over as National Security Advisor in 1969 recalled, "For years, the military had been complaining about being held by a leash by the civilian leadership. But when Nixon pressed them for new strategies, all they could think of was resuming the bombing of the North."[109] Yet, the specter of too much civilian interference in the details of the Vietnam War remains to this day.

The Moral Responsibility of Political Actors and "States"

Civilian oversight is not only for the utilitarian purpose of military necessity, so that military means are appropriately calibrated to political objectives, but also so that moral considerations and responsibility can be engaged. The state necessarily tells the military when to go to war and it is obliged to monitor the conduct of its instrument.

After World War II, the focus of international law turned to individual responsibility for war crimes. Before Nuremberg and the turn to individual responsibility for war crimes, the focus of accountability was states.[110] While the focus of legal considerations of responsibility is still on individuals, the legal responsibility of states for violating the norm of noncombatant immunity is currently being debated by international lawyers. The International Law Commission Draft Articles on "Responsibility of States for Internationally Wrongful Acts" of 2001, makes explicit recognition of the state as a legally responsible actor and implicitly assumes that states can be held morally responsible for wrongful acts.[111] According to the draft articles, states committing wrongs are first obliged to cease the act, then obliged not to repeat it. Further, the state is obliged to make "full reparation for the injury caused."[112] Importantly, the draft articles retain legally relevant distinctions among different levels of legal responsibility, rather than collapsing all responsibility to the state level: individuals, even when "acting on behalf" of the state, and international

---

[109] Kissinger, quoted in Summers, *On Strategy*, p. 104.

[110] Nina H. B. Jørgensen, *The Responsibility of States for International Crimes* (Oxford: Oxford University Press, 2000).

[111] United Nations International Law Commission (ILC) Draft Articles on "Responsibility of States for Internationally Wrongful Acts." The text can be accessed at http://www.un.org/law/ilc/, *Official Records of the General Assembly*, Fifty-sixth Session, Supplement No. 10 (A/56/10). The ILC report to the United Nations also contains commentaries on the draft articles.

[112] Article 31 of the Draft Articles on "Responsibility of States for Internationally Wrongful Acts."

organizations, may still be held responsible for wrongs.[113] Further, although the word is not used in the draft articles, the notion seems to be that to be wrongful, the act must be intentional.

The draft articles treat states as though they were unitary actors and overlooks organizations within the state to focus on the individual level of responsibility. "The conduct of a person or group of persons shall be considered an act of a State under international law if the person or group of persons is in fact acting on the instructions of, or under the direction or control of, that State in carrying out the conduct."[114] This treatment of the state as a unitary actor might be appropriate understanding of state responsibility from an external view, but states are clearly not unitary actors. Viewed from inside, specific responsibility for systemic collateral damage is associated with the formal roles of the state institution. In this sense, elements of states—legislatures, executives, judiciaries, and military organizations—are responsible before the fact (prospectively) and after the fact (retrospectively) for putting the military in situations where systemic collateral damage is more or less likely to occur and for the broad outlines of their conduct in war.[115]

Political Responsibility to Soldiers

During the same period that the US military began to understand and institutionalize the value of protecting civilians, it began to emphasize force protection, what has been called "casualty aversion" or a "bodybag syndrome." For example, Harvey Sapolsky and Jeremy Shapiro argued in the US Army journal *Parameters* in 1996 that "in particular, we have grown ever more sensitive about casualties—our own military casualties, opponent and neutral civilian casualties, and even enemy military casualties—and we seek to avoid them. This limits our ability to exercise the tremendous power we possess and makes us susceptible to pressures others can ignore."[116]

---

[113] Article 57 of the Draft Articles on "Responsibility of States for Internationally Wrongful Acts" refers to the responsibility of international organizations and Article 58 refers to individual responsibility.

[114] Article 8 of the Draft Articles on "Responsibility of States for Internationally Wrongful Acts."

[115] From the perspective of the draft articles, systemic collateral damage results from "composite" acts, defined as "1. The breach of an international obligation by a State through a series of actions or omissions defined in aggregate as wrongful occurs when the action or omission occurs which, taken with the other actions or omissions, is sufficient to constitute the wrongful act. 2. In such a case, the breach extends over the entire period starting with the first of the actions or omissions of the series and lasts for as long as these actions or omissions are repeated and remain not in conformity with the international obligation." Article 15 of the Draft Articles on "Responsibility of States for Internationally Wrongful Acts."

[116] Harvey Sapolsky and Jeremy Shapiro, "Casualty, Technology and America's Future Wars," *Parameters*, vol. 26, no. 2 (Summer 1996): 119–127. http://www.carlisle.army.mil/usawc/Parameters/96summer/sapolsky.htm.

Many have argued that it was after Vietnam, and the shift to an all-volunteer armed force, that the United States became casualty averse. The lives of volunteer soldiers perhaps seemed dearer to commanders, and there was a concern that high casualty wars would lead to a decline in public support. "As the trauma of the Vietnam War began to fade, we came to realize that even defeat did not matter in these distant conflicts....What mattered was the domestic interpretations of the fighting, the cost to families and to public life of the casualties we suffered and inflicted. The potential political effects of these reactions began to constrain US leaders more than did assessments of opposing forces. Although we do not fully appreciate the consequences even today, we were by the 1970s quite constrained."[117] Yet, as I argued above, the norm of force protection can conflict with the norm of protecting civilians and we see these norms in tension quite dramatically during the later part of the twentieth century, and the early years of US war in Afghanistan and Iraq.

Who is morally responsible for this state of affairs? The military has begun to see suicide prevention as their moral responsibility. However, as Larry May argues, moral responsibility for soldiers extends more broadly. "If a person's vulnerability is increased by the society, then it is the society that has the responsibility either to remove the vulnerability or to help minimize its harmful effects.... Even those who voluntarily join the military, but who are then coerced into the most dangerous of positions, can have their increased vulnerability imputed to the society, or the State."[118] May continues: "The society, or state, owes a minimally safe environment to those whom the society sends of to do its bidding. In wartime, it might seem that nothing is safe and all such restraining considerations are off the table. But there are, indeed, safer and less safe ways for war to waged."[119] So suicide prevention during and after deployments is an organizational responsibility. The choice of whether and how to fight is a political responsibility. Further, more often than not, it leaves a traumatic trace on the physical bodies, brains, and souls of soldiers, and the anguished violence when soldiers snap may not be restricted to a military front and the heat of battle. Soldiers may kill each other in brawls, beat their children, rape or kill their wives, or harm themselves with alcohol and drug abuse. The violence of war creates a new collateral damage at home.

Thus, the first responsibility of civilian leaders is to limit those occasions where the lives of soldiers are put at risk to only those that are truly necessary. Second, because, if they fight long enough, war breaks warriors and they "lose it" on the battlefield war, the mental health of active duty soldiers and veterans must be protected and treated. The care for the physical and mental health of soldiers' families must also be considered as part of the obligation of the state which makes war.

[117] Ibid.
[118] Larry May, *War Crimes and Just War* (Cambridge: Cambridge University Press, 2007), p. 38.
[119] Ibid., p. 39.

Third, it is also the case that states should treat veterans who "lose it" with some measure of mercy. When soldiers are told to fight a counterinsurgency, they are authorized to fight a particular kind of war with foreseeable likely consequences. Psychiatrist Robert Jay Lifton argues that "those crimes [in Haditha, Guantanamo, and Abu Gharaib] are a direct expression of the kind of war we are waging in Iraq."[120] Robert Lifton's argument is not simply that responsibility for war crimes goes to the top of the military political chain of command. Counterinsurgency and wars of occupation mean that soldiers will likely be confronted with civilians who are themselves faced with difficult choices. For example, the practice of night raids often yields civilian casualties. It is the practice of night raids that needs to be examined as much or more than the conduct of individual soldiers. It should not be the case that if the military regularly puts soldiers in situations where they are likely to kill large numbers of civilians, because civilian leaders have declared this kind of war, that we should hold soldiers fully responsible when they do.

Conclusion: Exercising Political Responsibility

The civilian leadership of the United States has a long habit of deference to military leadership regarding the conduct of war. Civilian governmental responsibility for the conduct of the military in the United States is more or less today exercised in an ad hoc fashion. Different bureaus within the Executive branch itself vary in their oversight of military actions—with the civilians in the Pentagon exercising the most direct oversight and policymakers within other parts of the executive more concerned with strategy and goals than conduct. Within the Legislative and Judicial branches, there is even less oversight. There may be the occasional congressional hearing or lawsuit about the treatment of prisoners of war, or a criminal case against an individual perpetrator where organizational practices are discussed, but these are not the kind of routine and institutionalized inquiries that constitute consistent oversight. [121]

For many this habit of deference is seen to be a virtue. By contrast, I argue that the habit of deference vitiates the important prudential, practical and moral reasons for civilian oversight. The US civilian leadership has missed opportunities to exercise their moral agency and responsibility in the post-9/11 US wars in Afghanistan, Iraq, and Pakistan, and in the drone strikes in Yemen.

While the cycle of moral agency for civilians begins with members of the Executive, Legislature, and Judiciary performing their constitutional roles,

---

[120] Robert Jay Lifton, "Haditha: In an 'Atrocity-Producing Situation'—Who is to Blame?" *Editor & Publisher*, 4 June 2006.

[121] Howell and Pevehouse argue that the Congress does have the capacity to shape the broader public debate through national and local media and that this translates to an influence on public opinion. Howell and Pevehouse, *While Dangers Gather*, p. xxiii.

those roles are underspecified and the structure of information to civilian leaders is titrated so closely that it is difficult for civilians to understand, evaluate, and advise military operations. The danger of leaving operations under the sole purview of military professionals is that they are too close to the values and beliefs of the military to have a fresh perspective. The Legislature, Executive, and Judiciary should provide oversight of and assure the accountability of the military organization.

How could political institutions exercise oversight of the conduct of war with regard to ensuring respect for civilians on the other side? One of the chief barriers to oversight is a dearth of information given to Congress. I suggest three specific steps that would increase the ability of Congress to acquire information: civilian government audits and reports of civilian and military casualties; regular reviews and hearings on the conduct of wars; and greater direction by civilian authorities on the conduct of war and the choice of weapons.

Civilian auditing and reporting of civilian and military casualties is essential. Although the Fourth Geneva Convention (1949) requires that occupying powers provide information about the deaths of protected persons, the United States provides no such information with any consistency for either Iraq or Afghanistan. Indeed, no one knows for sure how many Iraqis or Afghanis, whether civilian or military, have died as a direct result of US action. But how is one to know, for instance, if precision-guided weapons do a more or less better job at reducing the level of civilian casualties if no records are kept?

Independent government auditors should monitor and regularly report (perhaps monthly and bi-annually) on the effects of military tactics and strategies on both combatants and noncombatants.[122] Current reports by the US Congressional Research Service about casualties are minimal. Specifically, they make regular reports compiling the numbers of civilians, military, and police killed in Iraq and Afghanistan. The Congressional Research Service data for both conflicts uses information provided by the US military and reports on studies by nongovernmental organizations and the governments of Iraq and Afghanistan, respectively. The authors of the 2010 Congressional Research Service reports acknowledge the weaknesses of the data—"because the estimates of…casualties contained in this report are based on varying time periods and have been created using differing methodologies, readers should exercise caution when using them and should look to them as guideposts rather than as statements of fact."[123]

---

[122] ACBAR in Afghanistan has recommended that international bodies keep and publish these statistics, but it should also be the responsibility of the states that are prosecuting a war to do so. ACBAR, "Protecting Afghan Civilians," p. 3.

[123] See, for example, Susan G. Chesser, "Afghanistan Casualties: Military Forces and Civilians," Congressional Research Service, 14 September 2010, R41084; Hannah Fischer, "Iraq Casualties: U.S. Military Forces and Iraqi Civilians, Police and Security Forces," Congressional Research Service, 7 October 2010, R40824.

These reports, while a first step, however, are not detailed and analytical. They are simply numbers. For example, the CRS reports do not connect the effects of weapons used or of tactics and rules of engagement on the numbers of casualties. This is the duty to look at the big picture, to add up individual incidents to see if there is a pattern. More comprehensive audits and analysis should function as early warning. For example, in the United States such an auditing function could be based in the Congressional Research Service or the Government Accountability Office and be tasked with making unclassified reports to the National Security Council, the Office of the Secretary of Defense, and appropriate congressional committees. But while the Government Accountability Office and Congressional Research Service could potentially fill some of the knowledge gap, these offices are often overworked and sometimes hamstrung by their desire to maintain collegial relations with the Department of Defense, and the GAO, in particular, does not at times ask hard questions or push for answers. In the conclusion I suggest how congressionally directed monitoring and reporting could be coupled with the work of nongovernmental organizations.

Second, regular Executive branch reviews and congressional hearings on the conduct of war should be held. Presidents Bush and Obama gave regular reports on "progress" in the wars in Iraq and Afghanistan, but these progress reports were geared toward assessing how well the United States has done in achieving certain benchmarks. This is certainly appropriate. But in every war, the conduct and consequences of military operations must be assessed on a regular basis. When potentially troubling patterns of either combatant or noncombatant killing are identified in the regular audits and reports, the venues for deliberation within the state could then be engaged. Within the Executive this means that the civilian leadership of the military and National Security Council should engage an independent analysis of the meaning of the findings of the auditors. Within the Legislature, appropriate committees should hold regular hearings.

Third, when either elements of the Executive or Legislature found that policies, practices, or weapons were causing systemic collateral damage or were increasing the risk to US soldiers, the Congress should be able to trigger changes in the practices of the military by requiring the Executive to so do. Such action is indeed implied by the language of the US Constitution—"To make Rules for the Government and Regulation of the land and naval Forces; ... To provide for organizing, arming, and disciplining, the Militia, and for governing" the armed forces. This may mean, in some cases, requiring the military to change its training or its rules of engagement. Congressional hearings, congressional resolutions, and the power of individual members to catalyze the media and the public sphere through public statements can start a process of more intensive deliberation. On occasion, the Legislature may have to act to ban weapons, such as cluster bombs, that the military has not removed from the arsenal.[124] If the military resists

---

[124] For example, the US House of Representatives, H.R. 996 Cluster Munitions Civilian Protection Act of 2011 and Senate S 558 introduced respectively on 10 March 2011 and referred to the relevant committees on the same day.

providing information or changes in operations that members regard as essential, the Legislative branch may have to take up specific challenges through the judicial system.

In sum, if the debate about the role of civilians in war is continually resolved in favor of civilian deference to the military and president as commander in chief, then prudence and the practical virtue of a tighter link between political goals and military means will likely be diminished. But more important, it is the moral responsibility of civilian institutions, as the moral agents who have ordered that war be fought, to monitor and direct the military instrument.

8

Public Conscience and Responsibility
for War

An action is ours the execution of which we have laid upon another.
—Samuel Pufendorf,
De Jure Naturae et Gentium (On the Law and Nature of Nations)[1]

One is not normally responsible for a war in a way that leads to moral
blame. Rather, what one is responsible for is the way one reacts to
that war.
—Larry May, *Sharing Responsibility*[2]

Our duties to be and become effective moral agents may turn out to be
ones that are genuinely demanding.
—Barbara Herman, *Moral Literacy*[3]

Soldiers, commanders, the military, and civilian institutions should care about collateral damage because it is their role responsibility. But why should members of the US public, most of whom care about civilian casualties, believe that it is their responsibility to act and that their actions can somehow make a difference? Most members of the public do not have direct causal responsibility for killing either the soldiers or the noncombatants of the other side. Indeed, the norm of civilian immunity in war is rooted in the fact that the general public poses no direct threat to the other side. If no member of the civilian public approved the killing of innocent people, and if the civilian public could not have stopped a specific incident, how could the public be morally responsible for killing the civilians of the other side?

[1] Samuel Pufendorf, *De Jure Naturae et Gentium (On the Law and Nature of Nations)*, 1688, translated by C. H. Oldfather and W. A. Oldfather (Oxford: Clarendon Press, 1934), p. 66, quoted in Larry May, *War Crimes and Just War* (Cambridge: Cambridge University Press, 2007), p. 36.

[2] Larry May, *Sharing Responsibility* (Chicago: University of Chicago Press, 1992), p. 22.

[3] Barbara Herman, *Moral Literacy* (Cambridge, MA: Harvard University Press, 2007), p. 275.

And if others are more directly responsible for collateral damage, what could a caring public possibly do that would have any effect?

In the introduction, I suggested four reasons that collateral damage should concern citizens, civilian government, and the military. The first reason to care about "enemy" civilian casualties is moral: killing civilians is not only wrong when it is deliberate but also sometimes wrong and blameworthy when it is unintended and foreseeable. Specifically, I argued, the idea that collateral damage incidents are always unforeseen and unpreventable accidents is misleading. Further, individual incidents are sometimes the result of foreseeable, foreseen, and calculated trade-offs between civilian life and the values of military necessity and force protection. Noncombatants rightly have special protection—they have done nothing to deserve ill-treatment, even if it was unintentional. My second reason was pragmatic. The wrongness of killing noncombatants is associated with strong moral disapprobation, pain, grief, and anger among survivors that does not increase their love for those who cause it. On the contrary, resentment and resistance grow. Clearly, winning hearts and minds means we must stop killing civilians. The third reason was the moral high ground that Americans often assert. Claims of moral high ground are more credible if Americans ensure that their military takes great care to avoid harming noncombatants. The fourth reason concerned the balance of risk on the battlefield: if we ask soldiers, for pragmatic reasons (because we want their hearts and minds "population centric" strategy to succeed), or for moral reasons, to protect noncombatants at potentially greater risk to themselves, then citizens and soldiers must be fully aware of any additional burden of risk to soldiers, and acknowledge their potential and actual sacrifice.

But there is at least one more reason why the public ought to not simply be concerned, but active with regard to questions of the resort to and conduct of war. It is our moral responsibility as citizens in a democracy to monitor and hold to account the actions of governmental leaders and institutions when the state makes war. War is undertaken on behalf of the public, by political organizations for political purposes as it is said, in the public's name, in contrast to murder—the unjustified taking of another's life—which is usually a private act. Or, as John Finnis says, war is "paradigmatically a social and public act." As Finnis argues, war is a "public policy which members of the society are invited or required to participate in carrying out."[4] The public is invited and required to participate in war because of both the moral and legal requirement that war be justified and the material requirement of the enormous resources and mobilization required to project power for political ends. The view that causal responsibility for war is out of the public's hands and resides only in the hands of a small group of political leaders, is a conception of the

---

[4] John Finnis, "The Ethics of War and Peace in the Catholic Natural Law Tradition," in Terry Nardin, ed., *The Ethics of War and Peace: Religious and Secular Perspectives* (Princeton: Princeton University Press, 1996), pp. 15–39, 19.

role of the public in making public policy that refers to a time before democratic institutions allowed for wider citizen participation, when kings and queens were sole sovereigns.[5] Continuing to think of war as the business of the sovereign state in a time when the public does have political power fosters an attitude of public passivity with respect to war.

Because war is a public act, with a political justification, it ought to be that the public is accountable for it. As Lieber suggested in General Orders 100, "Men who take up arms against one another in public war do not cease on this account to be moral beings, responsible to one another and to God."[6] Lieber's focus was clearly on the responsibility of the soldier and commanders, but he was also concerned with standards of civilization and the larger moral climate that shapes conduct in war. The Lieber Code notes that "public war is a state of armed hostility between sovereign nations or governments. It is a law and requisite of civilized existence that men live in political, continuous societies, forming organized units, called states or nations, whose constituents bear, enjoy, suffer, advance and retrograde together, in peace and in war."[7] While I would not necessarily state the case this emphatically, I agree with the gist of the argument that "persons are morally responsible for what they *bring about*, what they *intend* to bring about, and what they help to bring about; they are also responsible for what they *endorse* and for that which they chose to *identify themselves*."[8] Yet, the public's responsibility for the state is not as simple as that. Public moral agency and responsibility is indirect and secondary to the primary and direct moral agency of soldiers, commanders, and the military organization itself.

An argument that the public's role in matters of war ought to be active engagement, rather than deference to authority, is not uncontroversial. In the next sections, I summarize and respond to the arguments against public moral responsibility for conduct in war. I then discuss how citizens should exercise moral responsibility, and I offer suggestions for how to increase the deliberative capacities of the public with

---

[5] See Michael Green, "War, Innocence and Theories of Sovereignty," *Social Theory and Practice*, vol. 18 (1992): 39–62 and Igor Primoratz, "Michael Walzer's Just War Theory: Some Issues of Responsibility," *Ethical Theory and Moral Practice*, vol. 5, no. 2 (June 2002): 221–243.

[6] United States, *Laws of War: General Orders 100* (1863), Article 15.

[7] Ibid., Article 20. Lieber and others have advanced the argument to say that because the public does contribute to war through various means, the public can be a target of military force. I do not go that far because it is impossible to discriminate between the innocent and the guilty and because even if economic and infrastructure is attacked, the consequences to infrastructure are indiscriminate, the idea of public responsibility does not give a license to target civilians and civilian infrastructure. An interesting discussion of these questions is contained in Primoratz, "Michael Walzer's Just War Theory."

[8] G. Brennan and L. Lomansky, *Democracy and Decision: The Pure Theory of Electoral Performance* (Cambridge: Cambridge University Press, 1993), emphasis in the original. This is an old idea, found for example in Hobbes *Leviathan* although Hobbes did not appear to believe that the public was always obligated by or bound by the actions of the state if those actions were unauthorized.

respect to questions of war and the use of force, and how to enhance the capacity of the public to act as moral agents.[9]

Five Arguments against Public Engagement

Five factors could potentially disqualify the public, or large portions of it, from deliberating about authorizing resort to war, and after wars have begun, conduct in war.[10] Each of these objections questions whether the public can be understood to have moral agency and moral responsibility in matters of the cause and conduct of war—that is whether the public has the capacity to deliberate and act in ways that make it responsible.

The first potential objection to public responsibility concerns the public's causal agency and moral responsibility. One might argue that because the public does not directly control the levers of war and foreign policy, the public is not directly causally responsible when a state undertakes war or for how the state prosecutes wars once begun; military organizations and commanders bear more or less direct causal responsibility for what happens in war. By contrast the role of the public in war is indirect: unless they have volunteered or been conscripted, civilians are not soldiers, who have a duty to follow lawful orders; nor do civilians procure the weapons, train the troops, or write the rules of engagement that tell soldiers when and how they may kill in any specific situation.[11] In this, the traditional view, the sovereign and the agents of the state are morally responsible because they are caus-ally responsible. Civilians, in this view, have no significant causal role and, using the "it's not my job" argument, civilians have no significant moral responsibility for war.

Yet, as I argue above, lack of direct causal responsibility does not vitiate moral responsibility. Indeed, even if one agrees that the public does not have a direct causal responsibility, one might believe that the public moral responsibility for killing civil-ians is greater, in a moral sense, than the responsibility of soldiers or commanders because the war is prosecuted in democracies for the ends that the public approved and consented to. At a minimum, as the argument for secondary responsibility goes,

---

[9] My arguments are focused on war. Many others have taken up the general question of citizen's responsibility. For a recent statement, see Laura Valentini, *Justice in a Globalized World: A Normative Framework* (Oxford: Oxford University Press, 2011).

[10] The public must also consider instances when the state is not using military force and it would be appropriate and urgent to do so, most obviously in situations where a regime is organizing or waging mass killing or a genocide of its own or others' civilians. In other words, some uses of military are justi-fied and indeed would seem to be a moral imperative. The citizen in this case may urge humanitarian intervention. Unfortunately, I do not have space to discuss humanitarian intervention here.

[11] Some members of the public make weapons or work as private military contractors. Those civil-ians may have a direct role in armed conflict.

the citizen as the principal in this relationship of authority must see that its agents exercise their roles appropriately.

Further, the public has an indirect causal role in war; public participation, in fact, is essential, the sine qua non for modern war. Rapid and widespread consent can speed military mobilization and sustain a war through thousands of casualties. Even in non-democracies, the public is needed for the formation of armed forces, the production of weapons, and the provision of taxes. Conversely, the political public has the power to withhold all those things, and in a democracy the public may give or withhold their approval. Even in the most minimal democracy citizens have the nominal power to vote out advocates of a particular war or to censure the advocates of certain practices in war and to vote in others. And in this they are not simply acting as individuals but more likely to be organizing to change the climate of belief among the political public.

The assertion of indirect causal responsibility and public moral responsibility for war and conduct in war raises two valid concerns. On the one hand, one must be careful to not slip from arguments about of public moral responsibility to assertions of collective guilt. The assertion of collective guilt has several problems, not least of which is the potential to conclude that if a society is collectively guilty, their members may deserve collective punishment. It is right to avoid assertions of collective guilt and the urge to collective punishment because a collective punishment would not discriminate among those who are actually culpable for wrong-doing, and those who had nothing to do with either endorsing or implementing the actions that produced harm. On the other hand, there is the problem of intention. Most members of the public do not intend their militaries to either deliberately kill or unintentionally kill civilians on the other side. The public may be "guilty" of inattention, but this is not guilt in a legal sense, nor should that guilt necessarily lead to legal sanction. Nevertheless, while avoiding collective guilt and its corollary, collective punishment, it is still important to consider the ways that publics can be and are morally responsible in a prospective sense for war. The distinction between combatants and noncombatants must still be preserved. As international law provides, only direct participation in hostilities makes one a combatant and a lawful target.

The next four objections concern whether the public is capable of acting as a moral agent—able to understand and make decisions about the complex and specialized issue area of war and its conduct. Specifically, the second argument against public responsibility for war suggests that the public is simply not competent to participate in deliberations about war. One might argue that war is so particular an exercise, and that the conditions that might lead to war so complex, it would be impossible to educate the public on all the relevant factors, especially if time is of the essence. To understand war we must master many areas—from technical details, to politics, to matters of ethics and human emotion. In short, the argument goes, the public is not qualified to deliberate on these questions; only experts should weigh in on matters where technical or specialized knowledge is required to make an informed judgment. Taken further, this view tends toward what might be called the Goldwater argument: the meddling of "unskilled amateurs" will do more harm than good. If the general public is not well suited to deliberate about war, then how could the public hold the military or civilian leaders to account in those instances when a war is undertaken unjustly or when its conduct is immoral, illegal, or reckless?

The third objection to public participation in debates about the resort to war and its conduct is the claim that it is a contradiction in terms for democratic peoples to authorize the use of force and then attend to the details of its use. Democracy is about the renunciation of force within the state so that problems may be resolved through deliberation and accountability for wrong decided by the rule of law. As Randall Forsberg argues, "democratic institutions have prompted, or paralleled, a growing rejection of violence as a means of achieving political or economic ends within and between nations." For Forsberg, it is not an exaggeration to say that democracy and a commitment to nonviolence are synonymous—"commitment to non-violence lies at the core of democratic institutions."[12] Democratic publics should be experts in the practice of deliberation, not coercion. A call for civilians to attend to how force is used in their name is asking them to become educated in the ways of non-democratic politics. This tension is, at least for the foreseeable future, unavoidable.

A fourth concern, related to the previous argument, is that the public is simply too squeamish about its own or other's casualties, and if one pays too much attention to public opinion, the options of leaders will be hamstrung. Christopher Gelpi, Peter Feaver, and Jason Reifler describe this as the conventional wisdom. "The general public, so the argument goes, is highly sensitive to the human toll, and this sets severe constraints on how American military power can be wielded....Americans stop supporting wars that produce casualties, and voters punish political leaders who deliver such policies."[13] Yet, using public opinion research, Gelpi, Feaver, and Reifler show that the US public is not so casualty averse as some have argued.

Yet, there is another fear about American squeamishness, expressed by the journalist Robert Kaplan below: if the public knows too much about the conduct of war, it will withdraw its support of the military. Kaplan uses the phrase "Indian Country" to describe the war in Iraq.

---

[12] Forsberg also argued, "Though little recognized, the renunciation of violence as a means to any ends except defense is as much a cornerstone of democratic institutions as its widely recognized counterpart, freedom of expression and other civil liberties. Commitment to nonviolence protects and preserves freedom of expression and other civil liberties by precluding intimidation or coercion by violence or the threat of violence. Within democracies, wherever nonviolence is not the rule...other democratic rights and freedoms are lost or severely compromised." Randall Caroline Watson Forsberg, "Toward a Theory of Peace: The Role of Moral Beliefs" (Ph.D. dissertation, Political Science, MIT, 1997), pp. 34 and 35.

[13] Christopher Gelpi, Peter D. Feaver, and Jason Reifler, *Paying the Human Costs of War* (Princeton: Princeton University Press, 2009), pp. 1–2.

In Indian Country, it is not only the outbreak of a full-scale insurgency that must be avoided, but the arrival in significant numbers of the global media. It would be difficult to fight more cleanly than the Marines did in Fallujah. Yet that still wasn't a high enough standard for independent foreign television voices such as al-Jazeera, whose very existence owes itself to the creeping liberalization in the Arab world for which the U.S. is largely responsible. For the more we succeed in democratizing the world, not only the more security vacuums that will be created, but the more constrained by newly independent local medias our military will be in responding to those vacuums. From a field officer's point of view, an age of democracy means an age of restrictive rules of engagement.

The American military now has the most thankless task of any military in the history of warfare: to provide the security armature for an emerging global civilization that, the more it matures—with its own mass media and governing structures—the less credit and sympathy it will grant to the very troops who have risked and, indeed, given their lives for it. And as the thunderous roar of a global cosmopolitan press corps gets louder—demanding the application of abstract principles of universal justice that, sadly, are often neither practical nor necessarily synonymous with American national interest—the smaller and more low-key our deployments will become. In the future, military glory will come down to shadowy, page-three skirmishes around the globe, which the armed services will quietly celebrate among their own subculture.[14]

Kaplan's statement that "an age of democracy means an age of restrictive rules of engagement" and his argument that democracy means "demanding the application of abstract principles of universal justice that, sadly, are often neither practical nor necessarily synonymous with American national interest" suggests that if people know too much about war, it will get in the way of the expedient prosecution of it by "field officers."

The final objection to civilian participation in debates about the resort to war and the conduct of war is that regardless of the outcome of public engagement—whether or not it is squeamish—public deliberation about war is simply too slow to be of practical utility. The sixteenth-century Spanish theologian Francisco de Vitoria argued that "a prince is not able and ought not always to render reasons for the war to his subjects, and if the subjects cannot serve in the war except they are first satisfied of its justice, the state would fall into grave peril."[15] Vitoria's logic

---

[14] Robert. D. Kaplan, "Indian Country: America's Military Faces the Most Thankless Task in the History of Warfare," *Wall Street Journal*, 25 September 2004, http://www.opinionjournal.com/extra/?id=110005673.

[15] Quoted in Michael Walzer, *Just and Unjust Wars: A Moral Argument with Historical Illustrations*, 3d ed. (New York: Basic Books, 2000), p. 39.

appears to rest on the need for expediency in times of peril, and on this same logic it would appear that the conduct of war should also be left to the prince.

Arguing for Public Responsibility

While agreeing that the requirement for public consent could slow a march to war, the eighteenth-century philosopher Immanuel Kant argued that such caution was to be desired. The power of the prince needs to be checked because the prince might otherwise be too cavalier with other's lives and treasure: "in a constitution which is not republican, and under which the subjects are not citizens, a declaration of war is the easiest thing in the world to decide upon, because war does not require of the ruler, who is the proprietor and not a member of the state, the least sacrifice of the pleasures of his table, the chase, his country houses, his court functions, and the like. He may, therefore, resolve on war as on a pleasure party for the most trivial reasons." The public knows the costs of war all too well. "If the consent of the citizens is required in order to decide that war should be declared (and in this constitution it cannot but be the case), nothing is more natural than that they would be very cautious in commencing such a poor game, decreeing for themselves all the calamities of war."[16]

> Among the latter would be: having to fight, having to pay the costs of war from their own resources, having painfully to repair the devastation war leaves behind, and, to fill up the measure of evils, load themselves with a heavy national debt that would embitter peace itself and that can never be liquidated on account of constant wars in the future.[17]

When Kant says that because the people bear the costs of war more directly than the sovereign, they may be better judges of whether the war is worthwhile, he is arguing that they are more directly interested in war than the sovereign—they have more at stake. When Kant argues that "philosophers" should be consulted about issues of war and peace, he is suggesting that their views are to be valued because they are more dispassionate. "But it appears humiliating to the legislative authority of a state, to whom we must naturally attribute the utmost wisdom, to seek instruction from subjects (the philosophers) on principles of conduct toward other states. It is very advisable to do so." Kant believed it wise for the state to encourage philosophers to "publicly and freely talk about the general maxims of warfare and of the establishment of peace (for they will do that of themselves, provided they are

---

[16] Immanuel Kant, *To Perpetual Peace: A Philosophical Sketch,* translated by Ted Humphrey in *Perpetual Peace and Other Essays* (Indianapolis: Hackett Publishing Co.: 1984), pp. 107–143, 113.

[17] Kant, *Perpetual Peace,* p. 113.

not forbidden to do so)."[18] Kant emphasizes the role of reason when he suggests that philosophers be participants in deliberations about war because they would exercise reason that was unaffected by an interest in power. "That kings should philosophize or philosophers become kings is not to be expected. Nor is it to be wished, since the possession of power inevitably corrupts the untrammeled judgment of reason. But kings or kinglike peoples which rule themselves under laws of equality should not suffer the class of philosophers to disappear or to be silent, but should let them speak openly. This is indispensable to the enlightenment of the business of government, and, since the class of philosophers is by nature incapable of plotting and lobbying, it is above suspicion of being made up of propagandists."[19] Thus, while Vitoria argues that the political leadership should not be unduly constrained by public deliberation, Kant argues that the restraint of "universal human reason" is good.

As Vitoria implied and Kant argued, an engaged public whose sons, daughters, and siblings are fighting may better see the costs of war in blood and treasure. Further, the public's emotional distance from and more general/less immediately involved perspective on questions of war can be an asset for evaluating the justice and conduct of war.[20] This is perhaps what Georges Clemenceau, French Prime Minister during the latter years of World War I, meant when he said war is too important to be left to the soldiers.

Soldiers, commanders, and the political officials who are tasked with waging the war may feel conflicted about their moral duties. We expect them to perform their jobs and work to achieve victory and at the same time, to act as citizens in the sense of questioning the ends and the means of war.[21] The military and civilian political leadership want to win particular battles and the war; they are often concerned not to risk their soldiers in an effort to protect enemy noncombatants. The military and political leadership are likely to see more "military necessity" than the public. Though certainly interested in the outcome of the war, the public can perhaps better make judgments about proportionality and military necessity. If the

---

[18] Kant, *Perpetual Peace*, second supplement.

[19] Kant, *Perpetual Peace*, p. 126.

[20] This is not to say that the public is dispassionate about war. Indeed, the opposite is generally the case. I am arguing that the public often sees itself as having less at stake in war than politicians whose careers may depend on the initiation and successful prosecution of a war.

[21] Marion Smiley frames this tension quite nicely. "The tension between our role as citizens and our more particular role becomes especially troublesome when our particular role is closely tied to citizenship itself. Here the case of a foot soldier confronted with the problem of stopping his sergeant at the My Lai massacre is illustrative. On the one hand, the foot soldier may have construed his role as United States citizen in terms of obedience to his military superiors in times of war. On the other hand, the role of United States citizen clearly does not include standing by while others rape and pillage. Hence, he is forced to choose between two roles." Marion Smiley, *Moral Responsibility and the Boundaries of Community: Power and Accountability from a Pragmatic Point of View* (Chicago: University of Chicago Press, 1992), p. 200.

barriers to public political deliberation and agency can be overcome (and this is an open question) in the ways I suggest below, the public may be better able to judge the conduct of war in some respects than soldiers and their military and civilian commanders.

On the question of moral blame for unjust wars, there is also a division of opinion. John Locke believed that the public's responsibility was limited by their causal role in abetting wrong acts.

> For the People having given to their government no Power to do an unjust thing, such as is to make an unjust War, (for they never had such a power in themselves;) they ought not to be charged, as guilty of the Violence and Unjustice that is committed in an unjust war, any farther, than they actually abet it; no more, than they are to be thought guilty of any Violence or Oppression their Governors should use upon the People themselves, or any part of their Fellow Subjects, they having impowered them no more to the one, than to the other.[22]

Karl Jaspers, a German professor of philosophy who suffered under the Nazi regime, argued for a wider sense of responsibility—including criminal guilt for those who violate laws, political guilt for statesmen and citizens, moral guilt for failures of individual conscience, and metaphysical guilt, or the inner feeling of guilt. Jaspers's idea of political responsibility is like Locke's causal notion of abetting harm. "Political liability is graduated according to the degree of participation in the régime."[23] Jaspers argues that moral and metaphysical guilt extend beyond the active participation in wrong. "But each one of us is guilty insofar as he remained inactive. The guilt of passivity is different.... Its anxious omission weighs upon the individual as moral guilt. Blindness for the misfortune of others, lack of imagination of the heart, inner indifference toward the witnessed evil—that is moral guilt."[24]

During US congressional hearings about the Vietnam War in 1971, Congressman John Seiberling echoed Karl Jaspers's views on public moral responsibility when he questioned the lack of American attention to Vietnam. He said, "One of the most shocking and depressing aspects of the disclosures of German atrocities after World War II was the fact that so few citizens in that great nation raised their voices in protest or even took pains to learn the truth. This is understandable in a people living under the iron grip of a totalitarian regime; it is unthinkable in human and

---

[22] John Locke, *Two Treatises of Government* (Cambridge: Cambridge University Press, 2002), p. 388. Quoted in Uwe Steinhoff, "Civilians and Soldiers," in Igor Primoratz, ed., *Civilian Immunity in War* (Oxford: Oxford University Press, 2007), pp. 42–61, 48.

[23] Karl Jaspers, *The Question of German Guilt* (New York: Fordham University Press, 2000), p. 37.

[24] Ibid., pp. 63–64.

civilized democracy. We must know the truth before we can deal effectively with our nation's problems."[25] Seiberling's anguished statement articulates the concern that even more is at stake than public attention to the conduct of a war and events on a specific battlefield; the health of a democracy is tested by how the public attends to its moral and political responsibilities for war. John Finnis also suggests that deliberations about war should go beyond philosophers: "Individual citizens can, in principle, assess the public policy, the announced reasons for going to war, the announced war aims, and the adopted strategy (so far as they know it) and assess the justice of the war."[26]

Michael Walzer suggests that both the public and the soldiers who fight the wars have limited responsibility for deciding the justice of war and in evaluating its conduct. Walzer seems to place most of the burden of moral responsibility and blame on political leaders. When Walzer quotes Vitoria's argument that it is impractical to give the responsibility for undertaking war to the average citizen, he implies that it is the political leadership that ought to make decisions about the justice of war.[27] Walzer, like Locke, wants to limit responsibility for conduct in war to those who actually do something. Specifically, the fact that an individual belongs to a common political community and shares in its fate "says nothing about their individual responsibility."[28] Specifically, he argues that "it might be better to say of loyal citizens who watch their government or army (or their comrades in battle) doing terrible things that they feel or should feel ashamed rather than responsible—unless they actually are responsible by virtue of their particular participation or acquiescence."[29] Thus, for Walzer, moral responsibility is closely tied to direct causal responsibility.

But Walzer also argues that citizens in a democracy are more responsible than those in authoritarian settings. Walzer approvingly quotes the arguments of J. Glenn Gray:

> This is Gray's principle, which I mean to adopt and expound: *"The greater the possibility of free action in the communal sphere, the greater the degree of guilt for evil deeds done in the name of anyone."* The principle invites us to focus our attention on democratic rather than authoritarian regimes. Not that free action is impossible even in the worst of authoritarian regimes: at the very least, people can resign, withdraw, flee. But in democracies there

---

[25] Congressman John Seiberling, Citizen's Commission of Inquiry, ed., *The Dellums Committee Hearings on War Crimes in Vietnam: An Inquiry into Command Responsibility in Southeast Asia* (New York: Vintage, 1972), p. 8.

[26] Finnis, "The Ethics of War and Peace in the Catholic Natural Law Tradition," p. 19.

[27] Walzer, *Just and Unjust Wars*, p. 39.

[28] Ibid., p. 297.

[29] Ibid.

are opportunities for positive response, and we need to ask to what extent these opportunities fix our obligations, when evil deeds are committed in our name.[30]

Walzer goes on to argue that in a perfect democracy citizens would be obliged to do all they could to prevent an unjust war. Yet, Walzer recognizes that we do not live in perfect democracies, and so he focuses his attention on the active and relatively well-informed citizen to oppose unjust wars as best they can. Walzer's description of the public's role in the Vietnam War highlights, in equal measure, the public's responsibility for the decision to go to war and the war's conduct: "the American war in Vietnam was, first of all, an unjustified intervention, and secondly, carried on in so brutal a manner that even had it initially been defensible, it would have to be condemned, not in this or that aspect, but generally."[31] Thus citizens ought to do more than assess the worthiness of going to war: the conduct of war is also public business.

The military's own investigation of the My Lai massacre, the Peers Report, noted organizational failures and lapses among those who were higher up in the chain of command. The philosopher Kurt Baier argues that responsibility for My Lai includes those who created the cultural and political context within which the atrocity occurred. Baier is concerned that the United States had a culture characterized by an easy acceptance of killing others as the price of victory. "Let us assume that there is a certain attitude toward the lives of others, particularly those of other cultures, which is not uncommon among soldiers anywhere, and that under the sort of pressure to which Calley was exposed, this attitude leads almost inevitably toward war crimes." In Baier's view, the "sovereign people" may share responsibility for creating a permissive atmosphere.

> Those who put victory above everything else, who at most pay lip service to international law, who would cover up war crimes, who can see no difference between unavoidable killings of non-combatants and deliberately executing them to avoid inconvenience, who advocate methods of indiscriminate mass killing and destruction—these are on the way to adopting the attitude I mean. Those who see the connection between this attitude and the proneness to war crimes under conditions of strain, yet themselves adopt that attitude and encourage it in others, fail in their internal responsibility and I believe can be said to bear a share—collectively a not inconsiderable share—of the responsibility for My Lai.[32]

---

[30] Ibid., p. 298.

[31] Ibid., p. 299.

[32] Kurt Baier, "Guilt and Responsibility," in Larry May and Stacey Hoffman, eds., *Collective Responsibility: Five Decades of Debate in Theoretical and Applied Ethics* (New York: Routledge, 1998), pp. 197–218, 216–217.

Baier's argument that military institutions and the wider culture that supports war may be responsible for creating the climate that results in deliberate killing has never gained much traction. If Baier is right, the dominant American culture that led to and condoned the US war in Vietnam was so militarized, that it could condone such violence. Yet, it is difficult to convince ourselves that we, who are not on the battlefield, share responsibility for deliberate killing.

Baier's idea that the public can share in responsibility is rooted in the relationship between roles and role responsibilities. Those whose job it was to prevent such killing were, as Baier argues, in "task" responsible roles. Others have what Baier calls "internal" responsibility: "if we are as a group (answerable-) responsible for our government and for the Army it uses to carry out its policies, then all of us are— as a group, not individually—(answerable-) responsible for failures in the Army's (task-) responsibility." Baier argues that those who protested the Vietnam War have "surely done much toward discharging that internal responsibility."[33] This division is similar to the familiar principal-agent description of authorizing and implementing roles, and Robert Goodin's notion of primary and secondary responsibility, where those with secondary responsibility have the role of ensuring that those with primary responsibility do their job.

There are contemporary versions of this debate. Legal scholar Mary Dudziak articulates the Kantian perspective with regard to the US war in Pakistan when she argues that "drones are a technological step that further isolates the American people from military action, undermining checks on...endless war."[34] Similarly, in describing the adoption and expansion of the Predator drone program of air strikes into Pakistan the journalist Jane Mayer argued that "it's easy to understand the appeal of a 'push-button' approach to fighting Al Qaeda, but the embrace of the Predator program has occurred with remarkably little public discussion, given that it represents a radically new and geographically unbounded use of state-sanctioned lethal force." Further, because the CIA Predator program has been so secret, Mayer argues that "there is no visible system of accountability in place, despite the fact that the agency has killed many civilians inside a politically fragile, nuclear-armed country with which the U.S. is not at war."[35] In this view, the public's lack of engagement with the use of drone aircraft is symptomatic: not only is there little discussion of the use of drones, there is little public understanding of, oversight, and accountability for the consequences of US strategy and conduct.

In sum, the public has moral responsibility for the resort to war and for its conduct because democratic publics authorize war, potentially benefit from a successful war, and contribute to war by the providing resources (blood and treasure) that make war possible. Even if citizens do not explicitly or even implicitly authorize the

---

[33] Baier, "Guilt and Responsibility," p. 216.
[34] Mary Dudziak, quoted in Jane Mayer, "The Predator War," *The New Yorker*, 26 October 2009, p. 40.
[35] Ibid., p. 38.

parts of war that constitute illegal actions or unintended harm, they could be seen to be morally responsible. As Iris Young argues, "individuals bear responsibility for structural injustice because they contribute by their actions to the processes that produce unjust outcomes."[36] Further, whether or not the state is democratic, the public has an interest in war; the public bears the burdens and reaps the benefits of war because of and to the extent that war shapes the purposes, resources, and behavior of the state at home and abroad. The public and the private are thus thoroughly intertwined at a practical and moral level.[37] Finally, although we are all members of a particular state, one could add the humanitarian argument that we are also all human beings who would agree that the innocent should be protected from harm.

Humanitarian Law: Public Conscience and Moral Deliberation

The international humanitarian laws of war are premised on our shared humanity, and they offer important and clear protection of civilians against deliberate killing. What could the attention of the public to civilian casualties add to humanitarian law and the direct actions of the military? The lawyers who drafted the international rules that protect civilians believed that the law alone was not enough to ensure that military necessity would not trump humanitarian concerns. Rather, their language suggests that they believed that public attention adds moral urgency and a wider moral vision, an attention to our humanness.

The law is not enough because international humanitarian law holds military necessity and civilian protection in tension, while the practices of military organizations privilege military necessity. The doctrine of double effect can enable concern for civilian harm to be trumped by presumed military necessity when the harm is unintended; and the idea of necessity is elastic and depends not on the eye of the beholder but on those who make war. The Lieber Code, the Hague Regulations, the Geneva Conventions, and the Additional Protocols to the Geneva Conventions allow that military necessity may trump civilian protection. Although the 1977 Additional Protocols of the Geneva Conventions defines civilians and civilian protection and prohibits indiscriminate attacks, the Protocols implicitly allow action that could be anticipated to harm civilians if it is not "excessive in relation to the concrete and direct military advantage anticipated."[38] In sum, expansive notions of

---

[36] Iris Marion Young, *Global Challenges: War, Self-Determination and Responsibility for Justice* (Polity: Malden, 2007), p. 175.

[37] As Barbara Herman argues, "We live in and through social institutions that shape our moral lives, sometimes in ways that empower us and sometimes in ways that challenge our will to act well." Barbara Herman, *Moral Literacy* (Cambridge, MA: Harvard University Press, 2007), p. vii.

[38] Geneva Convention Additional Protocol I, Part IV, Chapter 2, article 51, paragraph 5b. In general see Articles 48 to 51.

military necessity and a permissive understanding of proportionality permeate even the conceptions of civilian immunity. The law as written for specific circumstances (*lex specialis*) is not perhaps the law as it ought to be, or may be in the future (*lex ferenda*).

I argue that the call to go beyond the law is explicit in many treaties, although perhaps some lawyers see those words as rhetorical flourish. Specifically, the law of war frequently refers to the significance of the "laws of humanity, and the requirements of the public conscience." For example, in the 1899 Martens Clause of the Hague Convention (and later, the 1907 Hague Convention) called the "dictates of the public conscience." Martens, the Russian delegate to the 1899 Hague Peace Conference, was highlighting the fact that not everything that ought to be regulated in the future was included in the Hague regulations.

> Until a more complete code of the laws of war is issued, the High Contracting Parties think it right to declare that in cases not included in the Regulations adopted by them, populations and belligerents remain under the protection and empire of the principles of international law, as they result from the usages established between civilized nations, from the laws of humanity and the requirements of the public conscience.[39]

This clause is generally understood as affirming the role of existing state practice, or customary law. But the Martens clause in its original and later formulations also looks to the future and to public moral discourse that is wider and deeper than international treaty law and which precedes codification into treaties. Public conscience is the place where norms are formed and where the excesses of political leaders and institutions are checked. But there is a debate about the public capacity to participate in deliberation about the problems of war, about the public's duties before, during and after war, and the public responsibility for crimes of war. The role of public conscience defining and enlarging international law is suggested in the 1980 "Convention on Prohibitions or Restrictions on the Use of Certain Conventional Weapons Which May be Deemed to be Excessively Injurious or to Have Indiscriminate Effects."

> *Confirming their determination* that in cases not covered by this Convention and its annexed Protocols or by other international agreements, the civilian population and the combatants shall at all times remain under the protection and authority of the principles of international law derived from established custom, from the principles of humanity and from the dictates of public conscience.
>
> ...

---

[39] "Marten's Clause," Convention with Respect to the Laws of War on Land (Hague II), 29 July 1899.

Reaffirming the need to continue the codification and progressive development of the rules of international law applicable in armed conflict.[40]

More recently, international treaties have referenced public actors in the development of weapons prohibitions that are intended to protect noncombatants.
Specifically, the 1997 Anti-Personnel Land Mine Treaty stresses "the role of public
conscience in furthering the principles of humanity as evidenced by the call for a
total ban of anti-personnel mines and recognizing the efforts to that end undertaken
by the International Red Cross and Red Crescent Movement, the International
Campaign to Ban Landmines and numerous other non-governmental organizations
around the world."[41] And the 2008 treaty banning cluster bombs, mentions public
conscience in two sections of its preamble. "*Reaffirming* that in cases not covered
by this Convention or by other international agreements, civilians and combatants
remain under the protection and authority of the principles of international law,
derived from established custom, from the principles of humanity and from the dictates of public conscience." And, in language that parallels the Land Mine Treaty, the
cluster bomb treaty stresses "the role of public conscience in furthering the principles
of humanity as evidenced by the global call for an end to civilian suffering caused by
cluster munitions and recognising the efforts to that end undertaken by the United
Nations, the International Committee of the Red Cross, the Cluster Munition
Coalition and numerous other non-governmental organisations around the world."[42]

Public Moral Agency and Phases of Public Responsibility

So far, I have argued that the public has a role to play in questions of war and peace,
and that this role includes moral responsibility. My argument about moral responsibility for collateral damage is now almost complete: moral responsibility is shared
among actors according to their role in directly acting to create collateral damage
and indirectly creating the conditions that lead to collateral damage or fail to halt or
prevent it.[43] As Larry May suggests, "we are only morally required to pay attention

[40] "Convention on Prohibitions or Restrictions on the Use of Certain Conventional Weapons
Which May be Deemed to be Excessively Injurious or to Have Indiscriminate Effects."

[41] "Convention on the Prohibition of the Use, Stockpiling, Production and Transfer of
Anti-Personnel Mines and on Their Destruction," 18 September 1997, http://www.un.org/Depts/
mine/UNDocs/ban_trty.htm.

[42] "Convention on Cluster Munitions," 30 May 2008, http://www.icrc.org/ihl.nsf/FULL/620?Open
Document.

[43] One could take arguments about moral responsibility of particular agents farther to other publics, international institutions, and nongovernmental organizations. For example, Iris Young argues
that there is a global public sphere that took up its responsibilities to protest the initiation of war in Iraq
in 2003. Young, *Global Challenges*.

to those actions of others that risk harm and that, given our roles, it is reasonable to think that we should try to prevent."[44]

The role responsibility of actors is clear with regard to deliberate killing, but less clear in cases of inadvertent collateral damage killing. Yet collateral damage killing and injury, in fact, often constitute the greater burden of harm on noncombatants. If collateral damage is foreseeable and often foreseen, we cannot imagine that our moral responsibility is negligible simply because no one intended to harm or kill civilians. I argued above that in cases of systemic and proportionality/double effect collateral damage, the harm was foreseeable, and sometimes foreseen and authorized. The US public is indirectly responsible for the conditions that lead to systemic and proportionality/double effect collateral damage when it authorizes or consents to wars that are likely to cause large numbers of civilian deaths. The public is also responsible when it fails to monitor the conduct of wars, or to push actors with primary responsibility for the conduct of war to monitor and control operations.

I argued above that for individuals to have moral agency and exercise moral responsibility, they must be able to acquire information, deliberate without undue pressure, and act. No one is completely free to act in war, and neither are individuals in a political public. Karl Jaspers says that "impotence excuses."[45] But no adult of sound mind in a democracy is completely impotent. A group or a political public is potentially able to exercise a powerful, albeit limited form of moral agency. When the public does become engaged, research shows it can and does constrain the initiation and conduct of war.[46] To affect the resort to war, and the conduct of war, the group has to create and protect the conditions that allow for the exercise of moral agency and public responsibility.

In this section, I describe the key areas where the political public must assert its moral agency with respect to the decision to go to war, conduct in war, and how the state should behave after wars end. This section is filled with should and ought statements and the descriptions of public moral responsibility are aspirations, not how the public generally approaches the problem of war. Having the abstract moral responsibility for the resort to war and conduct in war does not necessarily mean that one has the real life and real time capacity required to act on one's responsibilities. The next section is more concerned with how to realize these goals for public deliberation about war and I suggest how public moral agency can be enhanced.

The political public has a duty to constrain the state from entering into unjust wars because they have indirect causal responsibility for war and can exercise moral agency with regard to war. The political public also has a duty to refrain from enlisting in the military and working in arms factories when their efforts to prevent the

---

[44] May, *Sharing Responsibility*, p. 95.
[45] Jaspers, *The Question of German Guilt*, p. 63.
[46] For example, see Howell and Pevehouse, *While Dangers Gather*, p. 31.

state from undertaking an unjust war have not worked.[47] Further, when the conduct of the war leads to large number of civilian casualties that the state (individual commanders, the military organization, and political institutions) does not sufficiently move to prevent, the moral failure of the state's executive and deliberative bodies establishes a moral responsibility for the public to act to draw attention to the problem of systemic collateral damage. Specifically, if the state fails to act to halt systemic collateral damage, the political public is obligated to organize responses that will push the state to act. At a minimum, individual members of the public must withhold their consent in the most basic way they can, through the ballot box, while using the public sphere to articulate alternative policies.

The time before war, when war might be avoided altogether, is as Clemenceau suggests "too important" to be left to the generals and the politicians. So well before war, the public should be debating the meaning of security and whether and which specific threats to security can be effectively met by military force and which are most effectively met by other means. The political public ought also, in this phase, to think carefully about the weapons that are being procured, and how the military is being trained. Deliberation before war should also include a discussion about how to avoid the use of military force altogether, for example, through the use of law enforcement mechanisms, economic sanctions, or negotiation.

Second, public deliberation before and during war must include a discussion of the costs associated with military action in both the short and the long term. There is a tendency to take a short-term view of the costs of war—focusing on estimates of military operations and procurement. But the public must keep in mind that the economic costs of war usually do not end after the fighting stops—veterans' benefits must be paid, survivors must be compensated, and in the case of wars financed by borrowing, interest payments on war debt must be estimated.

The public also has a duty to remain critical of the conduct of war and to take care that the mission does not expand so that the war might be concluded as quickly as possible. The public should not assume that the commanders or the rest of the political leadership is adequately performing the monitoring of the conduct of war and its intended and unintended consequences. Indeed, bureaucracies are notoriously places of conformity and so the monitoring and questioning that can uncover and correct negligence or abuse cannot be left to members of the bureaucracy alone. The public must monitor the conduct of war and act as the last check on military

---

[47] The question of whether citizens should refrain from paying taxes when the state is engaged in an unjust war deserves much more attention than I give it here. The financing of war can be a complex matter of accounting—taxes and the selling of war or treasury bonds may fund the war; alternatively, some wars are financed by borrowing. Further, wars are paid for over many decades—well after the fighting stops—as weapons and equipment are replaced and as veterans draw on their medical, disability, housing, and education benefits. Legislatures have much more direct power over the financing of wars.

and political institutions. When military organizations and the political leadership fail to monitor the military's conduct in war or to correct abuses, the public ought to mobilize, through nongovernmental organizations, a critique of the policy and a political response. When members of the public have good reason to believe that the conduct of the war is leading to too many "accidents" against the other side's noncombatant population, the public must act as the last check on the military organization and on the commanders and political leadership. In other words, the public must call the political and military leadership to do its job to protect not only its own soldiers but also to protect the noncombatants on the other side.

When the state goes to war, the public must understand how wars are being fought and in particular how the conduct of war affects both human life (combatants and noncombatants) and political objectives. This requires that the public have a basic understanding of the weapons in the arsenal, the terms of war, and the conduct of war. The public can weigh in on strategy to the extent that it understands a particular strategy or set of tactics and their alternatives. But civilians often don't have the foggiest idea of what goes on in a battlefield, or even in the decision to procure weapons such as cluster bombs, made well before a war. With regard to understanding the potential for systemic collateral damage this means that the public must have much the same information as political leaders about the conduct of war and its consequences. In other words, it is not only the military and civilian leadership that needs the potential to see whether the war is producing systemic collateral damage as opposed to the occasional accident or a deliberate atrocity.

Third, public deliberation ought to occur at the conclusion of a war. The political public must assess the costs of war and debate how to make amends where necessary. Evaluations are just that: to evaluate does not necessarily mean to question an individual soldier's heroism or sacrifice. It *does* mean that the political purpose and military strategy are being reviewed.

In sum, I have thus far argued that most discussions of public moral responsibility for war place the responsibility for *jus ad bellum* decisions in the political realm and the responsibility for *jus in bello* decisions—whether they affect one's own soldiers or the welfare of noncombatants on the other side—in the realm of military decision-making by commanders. There is relatively little discussion of how the public ought to address the military's conduct in a particular war. Again, it is generally assumed that this is the province of the military commanders. We might, as Walzer does, argue that if a war is unjust, the public has a duty to do its best to prevent and halt such a war.

> The real burden of the American war fell on that subset of men and women whose knowledge and sense of possibility was made manifest by their oppositional activity.... The expression of... self-righteousness, however, is not a useful way to get one's fellow citizens to think seriously about the war or to join the opposition.... It is not easy to know what sort of action

might serve these purposes. Politics is difficult at such a time. But there is intellectual work to do that is less difficult: one must describe as graphically as one can the moral reality of war, talk about what it means to force people to fight, analyze the nature of democratic responsibilities. These, at least, are encompassable tasks, and they are morally required of the men and women who are trained to perform them.[48]

What is the guilt or liability of a people that does not exercise its moral responsibility for the conduct of its military in war? Hannah Arendt warns us that assigning blanket collective responsibility can degenerate into collective guilt and to a sort of meaninglessness. "When all are guilty, nobody is.... Guilt... is strictly personal."[49] Still, if Arendt is right, we cannot simply throw up our hands and say that the collective cannot be judged.

What is the responsibility of a public that asks its soldiers to take on more risk so that the noncombatants on the other side can be less at risk? When we, for example, urge commanders to order their pilots to fly lower so that they can discriminate between combatants and a wedding party, we are also asking commanders to heighten the risks to those pilots and their crews. Surely the lives of a nation's soldiers are just as valuable as the noncombatants of the other side. Do we not violate the categorical imperative in such a case by treating the pilots as a means to our admittedly praiseworthy ends? What does the public owe its soldiers? Specifically, if the public demands that their soldiers take greater risks so that the noncombatants of the adversary can be protected, is the public then morally responsible for those greater risks and the injury and death to one's own soldiers that may occur so that we might feel better about taking care to protect the other side's civilians?

What is the moral responsibility of the public on the other side? Walzer argues that the potential noncombatant victims of war bear some responsibility for their fate. "Even indiscriminate fire is permitted within the actual combat zone. Civilians ought to be forewarned by the proximity of the fighting."[50] Does this public not have the duty to get out of the way? Yes they do, and they often try to flee. In some cases, they are prevented from leaving. In others, they do not have the means to exit a war zone, or they take the gamble that the risk of staying at home to protect their property is less than the risk of travel or of seeking shelter in a refugee camp. I think we must assume that those who are in a war zone are doing the best that they can to avoid harm. We should not blame them if they are harmed.

I have not answered all the relevant questions. But as citizens of democratic states, or at least of states aspiring to be more fully democratic, we ought to pay more attention to our moral responsibilities for conduct in war. This includes making amends

---

[48] Walzer, *Just and Unjust Wars*, p. 303.

[49] Hannah Arendt, *Responsibility and Judgment* (New York: Schocken Books, 2003), p. 147.

[50] Walzer, *Just and Unjust Wars*, p. 318.

to those at home who bore the burden of war—principally, soldiers and their families—as well as amends to those whose abroad whose rights were infringed or lives were harmed during the war.

Enhancing Public Agency and the Public Sphere

It [Thoreau's essay, *On Civil Disobedience*] just blew me away. Just the idea that we as a people have responsibility not only to be aware but to be involved and to know. That we have to demand a better government. So many times we just roll over. Because our lifestyle now is so convenient and it's so leisurely that it's hard for people to care about issues. And so me being directly affected because I'm in the military kind of force me to be concerned and care about stuff.[51]

What would public moral agency look like? What does it mean to have moral agency in a democracy? How can we move from the assertion of an abstract moral responsibility for war to a situation where people can actually productively assume those responsibilities? Deliberation includes the capacities to acquire relevant information, engage in moral reasoning about war, and to form considered opinions. There are three levels at which public moral agency must be enhanced. The first is what Barbara Herman calls the "moral literacy" of the individual citizen. She argues against theories of moral agency that take individual deliberative capacity as a given and suggests that our moral agency can be consciously developed and educated.[52] Of course, there are many cognitive errors that we all make, and those get in the way of deliberation, but awareness of those errors can help us overcome them.[53] The second level where public moral agency should be enhanced is in our habit of engagement and linking to others, what political theorists call the resources and habits of association in civil society or the public sphere. The "public" has the potential and acts as a collective moral agent when it exercises the ability to deliberate in the public sphere and act through associations and in aggregation. In other words, an unfocused and unorganized public can organize to become a deliberative polis or political public sphere.

---

[51] Ricky Clousing, quoted in Matthew Guttman and Catherine Lutz, *Breaking Ranks: Iraq Veterans Speak Out against the War* (Berkeley: University of California Press, 2010), p. 122.

[52] Herman, *Moral Literacy*. Increasing our capacities for moral deliberation and overall moral agency would be useful for many subjects, not simply questions of war and its conduct. See Neta C. Crawford, "No Borders, No Bystanders: Developing Individual and Institutional Capacities for Global Moral Responsibility," in Charles R. Beitz and Robert E. Goodin, eds., *Global Basic Rights* (Oxford: Oxford University Press, 2009), pp. 131–155.

[53] For a review, see Daniel Kahneman, *Thinking Fast and Slow* (New York: Farrar, Strauss and Giroux, 2011). Also see Eric Beerbohm, *In Our Name: The Ethics of Democracy* (Princeton: Princeton University Press, 2012).

And third, there is the level of the structural environment in which the individual citizen and political associations must attempt to exercise their agency. But the use of the term "level" implies that the capacities of individuals are distinct from the civil society and from structural factors such as the mechanisms for voting or access to secret information; rather, the levels are intertwined and mutually influencing. Barriers can block deliberation and public agency at more than one level.

In the previous section, I set out the ideal role of the political public. But there are barriers to enhancing public deliberation related to deeply ingrained habits of thinking about war. Specifically, two sets of beliefs, which parallel the beliefs held by international lawyers, have shaped the American public's response to noncombatant killing in war. The first is a focus on the intentions of those who hurt civilians: if the harm was unintended it is forgivable. The idea that someone intended to hurt civilians or is "just following orders" is unacceptable. The second set of beliefs shaping public views of collateral damage is a focus on the agency and responsibility of individual perpetrators. Organizational responsibility is not generally considered. A larger sense of responsibility is not required if the locus of responsibility is assumed to be the intentional actions and calculations of individual perpetrators.

Historian Sahr Conway-Lanz also stresses the role of beliefs about intention in the public understanding of responsibility for civilian killing. Conway-Lanz argues that Americans have traditionally believed in noncombatant immunity and did not abandon this belief even after the use of nuclear weapons against Japan. Rather, Conway-Lanz says that Americans "tenaciously clung to the optimistic assumption that violence in war could still be used in a discriminating manner despite the increased destructiveness of weapons."[54] Conway-Lanz suggests that "in effect, they [Americans] continued to deny a contradiction between the American way of war and noncombatant immunity, placing their faith in the ability to control and direct precisely the violence of modern war."[55] Conway-Lanz argues that the reconciling the dilemma of indiscriminate weapons and noncombatant immunity was accomplished in the post-World War II era.

> The Korean War and the hydrogen bomb made it difficult to ignore completely that American military action had inflicted or would inflict massive harm on civilians. Therefore in the early 1950s, a new American interpretation of noncombatant immunity emerged which incorporated elastic definitions of a 'military target' in war, but more significantly made intent the dividing line between justifiable and unjustifiable action. It became common for Americans to claim that any harm the United States inflicted on noncombatants was unintentional, a tragedy the responsibility for which

---

[54] Sahr Conway-Lanz, *Collateral Damage: Americans, Noncombatant Immunity, and Atrocity after World War II* (New York: Routledge, 2006), p. 19.

[55] Ibid.

was diffuse. The notion of atrocity for Americans had shrunk. Only the calculated killing of people uninvolved in the fighting of wars remained generally condemned as inhumane and indefensible.[56]

Public opinion research—funded by the US Air Force and conducted by the RAND Corporation—supports Conway-Lanz's observation that Americans do care about civilian casualties but are most concerned if they believe the killing is either intentional or a result of gross negligence. When Americans are persuaded that everything possible was done to avoid civilian casualties, they are much more likely to maintain support for US operations when those casualties do occur. Specifically, according to the research, "the principal support for U.S. military operations and civilian casualties is the belief that the United States is making serious efforts to avoid civilian casualties: Those who hold this belief are more likely to support U.S. military operations than those who do not, and this result holds both in the American public and foreign publics."[57] The RAND research included advice for Pentagon public affairs personnel to prepare the American public for the "eventuality" of collateral damage and to emphasize that as much as possible was being done to prevent civilian killing. Moreover, the report's authors stressed in their recommendations that it was important to improve communication with the media and the public about these incidents. "Such improvements also would have the salutary benefits of reducing the likelihood of constantly changing (or even contradictory) explanations that can erode credibility."[58] The RAND report stressed the importance of shaping a positive message of US care in incidents that lead to civilian death.

> Finally, over the longer term, by emphasizing the efforts that are being made to reduce civilian casualties (e.g. increased precision, smaller blast effects, improved target verification, and so on), the Air Force and DoD can help ensure that the U.S. Congress and public have continued reason to trust that the U.S. military is seeking new ways to reduce the prospects of civilian deaths in future military operations. A demonstrated commitment to a philosophy of continuous improvement may be what is needed to ensure this trust in the future, and in the case of foreign audiences, to build trust in the first place.[59]

Official attention to shaping public impressions of US treatment of civilians is not new. For example, the US military was concerned in the Vietnam War to

---

[56] Ibid., pp. 19–20.

[57] Eric V. Larson and Bogdan Savych, *Misfortunes of War: Press and Public Reactions to Civilian Deaths in Wartime* (Santa Monica, CA: RAND Corporation, 2007), p. 209.

[58] Ibid., p. 216.

[59] Ibid.

not just take care with civilians but to avoid the public impression that it was not. One memo, from US headquarters in Vietnam "Mistreatment of Detainees and PW [prisoners]" from February 1968 urged subordinates to avoid adverse media reports. "Extensive press coverage of recent combat operations in Vietnam has afforded fertile ground for sensational photographs and war stories. Reports and photographs show flagrant disregard for human life, inhumane treatment, and brutality in handling of detainees and PW. These stories have served to focus unfavorable world attention."[60]

The belief that the military institution is doing all it can to reduce the risk of harm to civilians reinforces the tendency to focus on the conduct of individual soldiers in cases of noncombatant killing, or to see incidents of noncombatant killing as, isolated, unforeseen accidents. The focus on the individuals who commit deliberate atrocities, that are considered to be exceptions, has deep roots in American military history. I have in this book tried to denormalize these taken for granted beliefs by arguing first, that collateral damage is not natural and inevitable and the military can and has increased its efforts to prevent collateral damage, and second, that the framework of individual moral responsibility for deliberate killing is incomplete. We ought to attend to the unintended and foreseeable consequences of war-making.

Yet, these are not the only barriers to deliberating about war and collateral damage. Even in democracies, public participation in decisions about when to go to war is often low and participation in decisions about how to fight is generally even lower. The barriers are high for the political public to act independently from and with even more difficulty against civilian and military leaders. Specifically, there are four general challenges to public deliberation about war, the habit of deference, a dearth of knowledge of the causes of war and how it is fought, the passions that emerge or which can be stoked in war, and a general weakness of the institutions and the traditions of deliberation.

The first barrier is the habit of public deference to military experts. The American public tends to give great deference to the military and civilian leadership, especially in times of war. Further, the public also defers to military leaders and tends to see military sources as more credible. The "National Credibility Index" ratings for "sources of information on using military force" showed that most respondents put military experts and military leaders well above others in perceptions of credibility in the United States (see table 8.1).

Trust in the military has been stable. More recent public opinion surveys, cited by the US military, underscore the confidence the US public places in the military. For example, in late 2010, the US Department of Defense reported that polls

---

[60] Message, Headquarters U.S. Military Assistance Command, Vietnam, MACJ15, quoted in Mark Martins, "Rules of Engagement for Land Forces: A Matter of Training, Not Lawyering," *Military Law Review*, vol. 143, no. 1 (Winter 1994), pp. 1–160, 49n.

Table 8.1 **The National Credibility Index**

Rank	Information Source	Mean Rating
1	Military Affairs Expert	81.2
2	Secretary of Defense	80.4
3	Chairman, Joint Chiefs of Staff	80.4
4	Foreign Policy Expert	79.0
5	High Military Officer	77.7
6	National Security Advisor	75.5
7	Secretary of State	74.4
8	US United Nations Ambassador	74.4
9	Member of the Armed Forces	72.5
10	Representative of National Veterans Group	71.4
11	US President	69.6
12	US Vice President	69.3
13	US Senator	67.1
14	US Congressman	66.3
15	Representative of a Human Rights Organization	57.0
16	National Religious Leader	55.5
17	Major Newspaper/Magazine Reporter	53.2
18	National Civil Rights Leader	52.6
19	National Syndicated Columnist	52.2
20	Local Religious Leader	51.9
21	Ordinary Citizen	51.4
22	TV Network Anchor	51.0
23	Student Activist	36.9
24	TV/Radio Talk Show Host	35.6
25	Famous Entertainer	27.6

Source: Public Relations Society of America Foundation, *The National Credibility Index* survey Credibility Ratings for Sources of Information on Using Military Force in Foreign Affairs. Sample size 1,501; survey September 1998.

showed high public confidence in the US military as an institution. "Americans have more confidence in the military than they have in banks, the media, public schools and organized religion, according to a recent national poll." In fact, "respondents had more confidence in the U.S. military than in Congress; state, federal and local governments; the Supreme Court; and print, broadcast and online news."[61] Because the military and military leaders have such high credibility among the general public, a democratic society needs to have at its disposal nongovernmental organizations and experts who can critically evaluate government statements.

We are often told that it is our obligation to support the troops and some imply that questioning a war is unpatriotic or hurts the troops. For example, during the 1991 Gulf War a 70 percent majority of the public believed that although it was possible to speak out against that war and still be patriotic, a similar percentage believed antiwar protests, "hurt the troops."[62] The 1991 Iraq war was popular. But even though the 2003 Iraq War was viewed as a mistake by the majority of Americans by 2005, protests against the war declined.[63] Critics will become silent if they fear their patriotism will be questioned and thus, those who question war must have their speech protected. An accounting of the likely and actual costs in blood and treasure should also be part of the deliberation before war.

Second, war, in particular, tends to be associated with the kind of fear, hostility, and feelings of revenge that blinds the public and even perhaps tends to make member of the public indifferent to the suffering of enemy others—whether combatants or noncombatants. Once wars begin, fear and hatred grow and the citizen will often be less able to see beyond the haze of those emotions. Those who do retain their critical capacities, and who have doubts about either the justice of the war or its prosecution have reason to feel timid. As J. Glenn Gray writes: "A state at war reveals itself to the penetrating eye in its clearest light and the spectacle is not beautiful. Nietzsche's likeness of a cold snake is, from one perspective, not greatly exaggerated. The awakened conscience will recognize a part of this spirit of the nation in the hate-filled speeches of the politician-patriots, in the antipathy toward dissenting opinions about the utter virtue of its cause, in the ruthlessness with which the individual is sacrificed for real or alleged national advantage."[64] As a profession, the military is dedicated to preparing for "worst case" scenario threats and has cultivated a healthy regard for the dangerousness of the "other." Once the passions are engaged, it is difficult to distinguish what one ought to be legitimately afraid of and what is not a mortal danger.

Further, the argument that particular military operations or rules of engagement are "necessary" to accomplish military ends, will be given the benefit of the doubt in a climate of fear and hate. A culture that is deeply militarized—that assumes

---

[61] Cheryl Pellerin, "Poll Shows High Public Confidence in Military," American Forces Press Service, 22 October 2010, http://www.defense.gov/news/newsarticle.aspx?id=61388.

[62] Los Angeles Times poll taken 16-17 February 1991, cited in John Mueller, Policy and Opinion in the Gulf War (Chicago: University of Chicago Press, 1994), pp. 314 and 315.

[63] Pew Research Center for the People and the Press, "Public Attitudes toward the War in Iraq," 19 March 2008, http://pewresearch.org/pubs/770/iraq-war-five-year-anniversary.

[64] J. Glenn Gray, The Warriors: Reflections on Men in Battle (New York: Harper Collins, 1959), pp. 196–197.

military force is usually effective and efficient—will tend to give greater credence to military means and to soldiers than a less militarized society. The philosopher Larry May argues, "When the world is a blue of emotions and violence, the best thing is to get people to stop and think, to shake them out of their normal ways of reacting to each other as evil enemies and instead see each other as just fellow humans."[65] This deference to the military in war time is bolstered by the fact of a general trust and confidence in military leadership, especially in times when other public and private institutions are perceived to be less than competent.[66]

Third, a public that might be disposed to be critical of the experts still often lacks the information necessary to make an assessment. Secrecy and complexity are high hurdles. When they are informed that a threat is looming, the public has to acquire independent information about potential threats and deliberate about the risk they may pose. Yet, although the reports, assessments, estimates, and projections of enemy capacity can be very wrong, as they have been numerous times in US history—from the Bomber Gap, to the Missile Gap, to the Gulf of Tonkin, to the Window of Vulnerability, and the fear of nonexistent Iraqi weapons of mass destruction—the public may have little basis to say which threat assessments are wrong or right. The mass of the public, after all, does not have the detailed military plans, estimates, and the quality of intelligence briefings available to the political leadership.

Fourth, the public sphere, where citizens deliberate, argue, and organize, is not robust.[67] A public sphere can coalesce in coffee houses, public libraries, on the steps of a courthouse, on the pages of a newspaper, in blogs and social networking sites, university forums, and as Alexis de Tocqueville argued, in political associations. Public spheres may function more or less well to foster deliberation. Specifically, the press, the citizens in their associations, and the intellectual class associated with universities may be unable to act or fail to engage in discourse, debate, and political mobilization. The inability or failure of publics to deliberate, organize, and act may be caused by ignorance, fear, apathy, or a general decline in the habits and infrastructure for deliberation within the public sphere. Unless the society is brutally authoritarian, the potential for public deliberation and action, and therefore public agency, is always there. How does public moral responsibility differ in instances where the democracy is robust as opposed to when it is less than well functioning?

As the philosopher Larry May suggests, "being morally or politically responsible is something that takes a lot of work; it is not merely a matter of conforming to a

---

[65] Larry May, *War Crimes and Just War* (Cambridge: Cambridge University Press, 2007), p. 11.

[66] Cheryl Pellerin, American Forces Press Service, 22 October 2010, http://www.defense.gov/news/newsarticle.aspx?id=61388.

[67] See Jürgen Habermas, *The Structural Transformation of the Public Sphere* (Cambridge, MA: MIT Press, 1989) and Craig Calhoun, ed., *Habermas and the Public Sphere* (Cambridge, MA: MIT Press, 1992).

list of minimal rules."[68] Nevertheless, I suggest ways that the public sphere—where deliberation and arguments about the resort to and conduct of war occur—can be made more robust so that those challenges and barriers can be reduced and overcome. These are ways to enhance public deliberation and participation. Further, I focus on the problem of urgency and the argument that there is simply not time for deliberation. I argue in particular against the notion of urgency that underpins the resort to preventive war and short-circuits the public's role in deliberation about war.

These barriers to responsible public deliberation must be lowered before democratic publics can effectively enact their responsibilities to assess legitimacy of a particular war, evaluate the conduct of war including the causes of civilian death on the other side, and whether their military and political leaders are taking due care.

The first barrier to robust public deliberation about the causes and conduct of war is the level of individual citizen's preparedness and capacity for deliberation. Most states do not inculcate or encourage deliberative capacities in their citizens. Rather, many in a "democracy" believe that their democracy is "robust" if they are allowed regular opportunities to select a slate of political leaders in "free and fair" elections. This thin, polyarchic, view of democracy has become the norm so that many are unclear about the characteristics of robust political deliberation about war or indeed many public policies.

Yet even if all or at least more members of the public had the disposition to discuss the most politically charged issues, not all members of the public are equally able to deliberate and act collectively within a public sphere. Inequalities of education, financial resources, and deliberative capacity limit the effective members of the public to the political public—those who are potentially able to influence public policy. Further, those who are very old, very young, or ill sometimes cannot participate at all, or with any effectiveness. Those who fail to organize or affiliate with groups will also have limited capacities within the political public. Further, to the extent that there is a dominant discourse that reflects the dominant cultural and political beliefs of the day, those whose ideas are radically different will have limited ability to participate in the public sphere since their ideas may not be welcome or even comprehended. The presence of those different ideas in public forums is essential to counterbalance the tendencies of countries at war to slip into less critical patriotism.

The steps to lowering the formidable barriers of individual disposition and capacity to deliberate about war are fortunately the same actions needed to increase the robustness of individual political capacity for all citizens. Citizens must see themselves as entitled to deliberate and must become capable of political deliberation. One of the most important elements of preparation for democratic deliberation is learning to make arguments and to listen to each other. As Karl Jaspers wrote: "We

---

[68] Larry May, *Sharing Responsibility* (Chicago: University of Chicago Press, 1992), p. 3.

want to learn to talk with each other. That is to say, we do not just want to reiterate our opinions but to hear what the other thinks. We do not just want to assert but to reflect connectedly, listen to reasons, remain prepared for new insight. We want to accept the other, to try to see things from the other's point of view; in fact we virtually want to seek out opposing views. To get at the truth, an opponent is more important than one who agrees with us."[69] These skills—the dispositions and habits of deliberation, and the capacity to make and evaluate arguments—must be nurtured in primary and secondary education and practiced in public meetings and civic associations.

How can we lower the second barrier to considered deliberation, more specific to the occasion of war, the passions that are associated with the threat and waging of war so that it is possible to think more clearly about war? I actually don't think the fear and hatred associated with war can be so easily erased. But to that fear one can heighten other emotions such as empathy and respect for the combatants of the other side. Empathy and respect can be enhanced by increasing the cultural knowledge we have about others.

The third barrier to public deliberation about war, at both the civil society and institutional level is epistemic—concerns what it is possible to know with reasonable certainty. Specifically, in times of war, as it is often said, the first casualty is the truth. Without the "truth"—or at least some sense of what is happening where, when, and why—and in a context where most members of the political public have little understanding of the details of strategy and tactics, it will be difficult for civilians to judge whether civilian deaths on the other side were preventable. How can this barrier be overcome? This is largely the responsibility of the "experts" and the institutions of the public sphere making it possible for two processes to occur. First, those with the knowledge must be able to openly debate and question each other in public forums. Second, the media, universities, and cultural institutions must make the space for such discourse and exchange.

The fourth barrier to considered deliberation about the causes and conduct of war is the health of institutional "democracy" in a state at war. In other words, close behind the casualty of truth is often the diminution of democratic rights of free speech and assembly. In this way, the "public" itself is harmed as the institutions of the public sphere are first diminished and sometimes destroyed in a "garrison state" atmosphere. As the political scientist Harold Lasswell warned in 1951, though militarization would not necessarily lead to diminished civil liberties, he argued, it might well do so gradually, through "tiny declivities."

> To militarize is to governmentalize. It is also to centralize. To centralize is to enhance the effective control of the executive over decisions, and thereby to reduce the control exercised by courts and legislatures. To centralize

---

[69] Jaspers, *The Question of German Guilt*, pp. 5–6.

is to enhance the role of military in the allocation of national resources. Continuing fear of external attack sustains an atmosphere of distrust that finds expression in spy hunts directed at fellow officials and fellow citizens. Outspoken criticism of official measures launched for national defense is more and more resented as unpatriotic and subversive of the common good. The community at large, therefore, acquiesces in denials of freedom that to go beyond the technical requirements of military security.[70]

These four barriers to considered public deliberation, judgment, and action about war are linked. A public that is ill-prepared to deliberate—because citizens lack the disposition to do so or the knowledge that would enable deliberation, will find it difficult to grow in their deliberative capacities in a political system that has limited venues for deliberation or that limits argument and fears dissent is unhealthy. Those who have a different analysis of war, potentially have valuable perspectives and arguments but their voices are too often stilled by fear and the sense that their interventions will not be welcomed. The level of fear must be lowered by a clear-eyed assessment of threats. So also must the fear and hatred of the other, our potential and actual adversaries, be lowered through the development of knowledge of and empathy toward the "other." But this is very difficult in peacetime, much less than in wartime. The institutions of the public sphere and the deliberative capacities of individuals must be made more robust before a public can effectively constitute itself as a collective agent and can act in the public sphere to monitor its government and make a difference.

Again, all of this is difficult for individuals to do, especially in a time of war. Thus, a democracy must develop these capacities and preserve them in peacetime. And both the habits of deliberation and the venues where this deliberation can occur must also be developed during peacetime. Indeed, nongovernmental organizations (NGOs) are a resource for the citizen who does not necessarily have all the time required to gather and digest information about war.[71] NGOs can mobilize the public for collective action, and their techniques for doing so—investigation, reports, and exhortation—can be effective only to the extent that there is a receptive audience in the public and among elite decision-makers.

The News Media and the Public Sphere

Independent media, including reporters who are not embedded with the armed forces, are a necessary part of a healthy public sphere in times of war. The media

---

[70] Harold Lasswell, "Does the Garrison State Threaten Civil Rights?" *Annals of the American Academy of Political and Social Science*, vol. 275 (May 1951): 111–116, 111.

[71] As Eric Beerbohm notes, we cannot all be "superdeliberators." "We need a division of democratic labor sensitive to our decision-making powers." Beerbohm, *In Our Name*, p. 166.

must strive to gain access while still remaining critical and independent. As a study by the University of Maryland of US media coverage of weapons of mass destruction found, reporters were not critical of official government claims. "Many stories stenographically reported the incumbent administration's perspective on WMD, giving too little critical examination of the way officials framed the events, issues, threats, and policy options."[72] If the media or public intellectuals fear questioning received wisdom in a climate of war, the tendency to rally around the flag will be unchecked. If the dominant model of political deliberation is shouting down opponents, then there is little hope for reasoned discourse to be heard and assessed. The press must be allowed access to and free reign in reporting what happens in the battlefield. Embedded reporters (whose lives depend on the soldiers with whom they travel) and pools cannot take the place of independent reporters.

Although the arguments of skeptics should be given more prominent play in the media at times of war, the arguments of critics and skeptics are very hard to find in the mainstream media. One recent case underscores this point. More than a year after the Iraq war began, the *New York Times* apologized for its lack of critical reporting of claims of Iraqi weapons of mass destruction. The bulk of the paper's self-criticism was about its less than skeptical reporting of claims made by Iraqi defectors; much too late, the paper realized that the men it was quoting were biased and simply not credible. But the *New York Times*'s lack of skepticism extended to official sources, a problem that was compounded by the paper's tendency to give page-one prominence to official views and to bury or not to publish internal dissent or external expert assessments of Bush administration claims.

> On Sept. 8, 2002, the lead article of the paper was headlined "U.S. Says Hussein Intensified Quest for A-Bomb Parts." That report concerned the aluminum tubes that the administration advertised insistently as components for the manufacture of nuclear weapons fuel. The claim came not from defectors but from the best American intelligence sources available at the time. Still, it should have been presented more cautiously. There were hints that the usefulness of the tubes in making nuclear fuel was not a sure thing, but the hints were buried deep, 1,700 words into a 3,600-word article. Administration officials were allowed to hold forth at length on why this evidence of Iraq's nuclear intentions demanded that Saddam Hussein be dislodged from power: "The first sign of a 'smoking gun,' they argue, may be a mushroom cloud."

[72] Susan D. Moeller, "Media Coverage of Weapons of Mass Destruction: May 5-26 1998, October 11-31, 2002, May 1-21, 2003," Center for International Security Studies at Maryland, University of Maryland, 9 March 2004, p. 3.

Five days later, The Times reporters learned that the tubes were in fact a subject of debate among intelligence agencies. The misgivings appeared deep in an article on Page A13, under a headline that gave no inkling that we were revising our earlier view ("White House Lists Iraq Steps to Build Banned Weapons"). The Times gave voice to skeptics of the tubes on Jan. 9, when the key piece of evidence was challenged by the International Atomic Energy Agency. That challenge was reported on Page A10; it might well have belonged on Page A1. [73]

Of course, the New York Times was not alone among news media in neglecting to challenge official claims or in failing to publish the analysis of those who were skeptical of government arguments and evidence. Nor is such a failure unique to the Iraq war. The news media ought to report alternative arguments and question public officials before conflicts are undertaken, when deliberation is most essential. There are many reasons the media may not be inclined to be skeptical at these times, including the desire to have access to government officials. Indeed, a bit too much skepticism may lead to the denial of access that reporters fear.

But two additional reasons for credulity and a lack of critical reporting are worth noting. First, the news media may not challenge officials because it believes the public does not want it to ask hard questions of the military and national security experts. Second, reporters and editors may believe that the issues of war and peace are too complex to be explained with any confidence to a general public that may lack the background knowledge to make sense of reports. In that case, it may be easier to let glib claims by public officials go unchallenged.

Once war begins the news media must be there to report it. Of course, the news media often lack the resources to get to war zones or once there, media access may be restricted by the military. Independent reporters may be at greater physical risk because they travel unprotected. In fact, many reporters have been killed in the wars in Iraq and Afghanistan. Too often, the media turns to retired colonels and generals who are less than independent analysts. Well into the Iraq war, it was, for example, disclosed that many of the retired military were in fact paid spokespersons for the United States. And finally, when the media does publish something that might be understood to be less than supportive of the military, reporters can be excoriated by public officials for "endangering" the troops. For example, in 2007, the former commander of US forces in Iraq General Ricardo Sanchez accused the media of bias in their reporting of the Iraq war. Sanchez accused the media of "straying" from its own "ethical standards" and of "unscrupulous reporting, solely focused on supporting an agenda and preconceived notions of the U.S. military."[74]

---

[73] Editors, "The Times and Iraq," New York Times, 26 May 2004.

[74] Sanchez, quoted in Fox News, "Sanchez: Media's Reporting of Iraq War Endangered Soldiers Lives," Fox News, 15 October 2007, http://www.foxnews.com/story/0,2933,301676,00.html.

In late 2012, the *New York Times* published an editorial calling for the administration to develop rules on targeted killing and make those rules public.[75] Indeed, the *Times* broke the story that the administration was developing those rules in late 2012. This kind of editorial was more illustrative of the exceptional and occasional coverage and questioning by the mainstream news media even after eleven years of war, than it was the rule. Such calls for accountability should be the norm.

Acting Responsibly

The focus thus far has been on how the public deliberates about going to war. But what else can and should the public do besides talk and form opinions about the justice of war and the conduct of war? First, one should never underestimate the power of democratic deliberation in the formation of consent and legitimacy. Deliberation is a form of action when conclusions lead to the giving or withholding of consent and resources to political authorities. Deliberation includes questioning authorities about the reasons they give for actions. Second, as suggested earlier, even in democracies where the main avenue of participation is voting, where venues and occasions for deliberation are limited, there is still voting to be done at regular intervals. And third, individuals may join or support organizations that take action to prevent wars or to constrain actions in war.

The political theorist Igor Primoratz asks about those civilians who "neither support their country's unjust war nor oppose it in any way: who choose to get on with their lives as if nothing very untoward was taking place, who refrain from voting in elections and referenda, perhaps even from voicing any opinion on the subject in public?" When asked, these citizens may have one or more reasons for not taking a stand: they may feel they don't know enough or that they are too busy to get involved and must by necessity leave everything to the experts. Primoratz suggests that such a stance is irresponsible.

> Since something very untoward *is* happening, since *their* state is waging an unjust war, *their* government is in charge and *their* armed forces are doing the killing, maiming and destruction, it seems to me that they don't really have the option of sitting on the fence; their refusal to be involved is tantamount to passive support of the government and the military. They live in a democracy and are both entitled and supposed to take part in the political process. To be sure, one also has a right not to take interest in politics. But this is a right in normal times.... When one's country goes to war, the times are no longer normal.[76]

[75] Opinion, "Rules for Targeted Killing," *New York Times*, 30 November 2012, p. A26.

[76] Primoratz, "Michael Walzer's Just War Theory," p. 237. Again, as noted above, the question can go both ways—preventing an unjust war or urging the waging of a just war. For example, it may be that it is urgent to push the state to intervene for humanitarian purposes, perhaps to avert or halt a genocide. See Samantha Power, *'A Problem from Hell': America and the Age of Genocide* (New York: Basic Books, 2002).

It seems then that the one thing that adults who have the capacity to deliberate and act ought not to do is to be disinterested and uninvolved on questions of war and peace. Karl Jaspers believes that those who are passive feel, or ought to feel, "moral guilt" because they let evil occur.[77] In some cases it is unclear whether a war is right or wrong. Indeed, whether a war or its conduct is "evil" is precisely the first question the public should debate. It is perhaps less useful before and during war to think of the guilt of passive civilians than to emphasize the duty and potential for moral action from this point in history, going forward.

Does my argument about public responsibility mean that I am placing civilians in the chain of command and therefore blurring the distinction between combatant and noncombatant and that responsible civilians could therefore be the object of legitimate attack? Indeed that is, roughly, the argument that some terrorists make when they say that civilians are responsible for their government's policies and have lost their immunity from attack. To be absolutely clear, I am not making that argument. Civilians do not pose an immediate armed threat to others and therefore they have done nothing to lose their immunity from attack. Someone may not like them or their governments' policies, but they cannot be killed. Whether or not a democratic public acts responsibly, it is never right to think that if they support an unjust war, members of the public are legitimate targets—that they have lost their immunity, as civilians, from attack. Nor would it be right to punish civilians, indiscriminately, after a war, for their government's actions in launching or prosecuting a war. My argument for civilian responsibility recognizes that most civilian members of the public do not exercise authority over their government. They do not call the shots. Moreover, even if the majority of civilians did agree with the launching and prosecution of an unjust war, there would be no way to distinguish in an attack between those who agreed with an unjust war and those who did not or who had no power to change the course of events.[78] That is the trouble, as I suggested above, with collective guilt—it does not make sufficient distinctions and it is associated with criminal liability and punishment. The citizens do not have primary responsibility for the war. Those with primary responsibility are those who should be held to account. Those with secondary responsibility should use it to hold those with primary responsibility accountable before and during a war.[79]

[77] Jaspers, *The Question of German Guilt*, pp. 57–58 and pp. 63–64.

[78] Igor Primoratz, "Civilian Immunity in War: Its Grounds, Scope and Weight," in Igor Primoratz, ed., *Civilian Immunity in War* (Oxford: Oxford University Press, 2007), pp. 21–41, 34–35.

[79] On post-conflict justice, see Bronwyn Leebaw, *Judging State-Sponsored Violence, Imagining Political Change* (Cambridge: Cambridge University Press, 2011).

9

Collateral Damage and Frameworks of Moral Responsibility

As Robert Goodin says, "Vulnerabilities, and the responsibilities growing out of them, are not only relational but also relative." Goodin continues, "Dilemmas arise because discharging our responsibilities with respect to some of those who are vulnerable to us entails defaulting on our responsibilities with respect to some others who are also vulnerable. Whom we should favor depends...upon the relative vulnerability of each party."[1] Civilians are to be protected from targeting in war when and because they are noncombatants, because they are vulnerable and pose no threat to those who are making the war. Indeed, noncombatant civilians generally and simply want to get out of the way of the violence. Soldiers, of course, do not relish the risks they take, but it is the relative vulnerability of civilians that makes them the subject of protection.

The idea that civilians should be protected is also an aspect of the aspirational identity of American civilian and military leaders. As Secretary of Defense Donald Rumsfeld said in July 2002, "We can also take pride in the fact that coalition forces have gone to extraordinary lengths not only to avoid civilian deaths but to save civilian lives."[2] And, more recently, the imperative to protect civilians has become a key element in declared US policy and in the strategy of the counterterror and counterinsurgency wars that it has been fighting: win hearts and minds, and win the war; kill or hurt the people, make more enemies, and lose the war.

Part I discussed the concept of collateral damage and described its incidence in recent US wars, in service of three main arguments. While the principle of civilian immunity applies to deliberate targeting of civilians and civilian objects, civilians may still, legally, be harmed if the harm is unintentional and incidental to the military's objectives. In sum, the first argument was that collateral damage is legal and often taken for granted as a necessary and ordinary consequence of war.

Second, I reject the fatalism about collateral damage of the sort also articulated by Donald Rumsfeld in July 2002; Rumsfeld said that, "it's an unfortunate fact of

---

[1] Robert E. Goodin, *Protecting the Vulnerable: A Reanalysis of Our Social Responsibilities* (Chicago: University of Chicago Press, 1985), pp. 118–119.

[2] Quoted in Thom Shanker, "Rumsfeld Calls Civilian Deaths Relatively Low," *New York Times*, 23 July 2002.

war that, inevitably, innocent civilians are killed. This has been true, true throughout the history of warfare, and it remains true even in this age of advanced technology and precision-guided munitions."[3] By describing the incidents of collateral
damage in recent wars, I showed that there are really three different kinds of collateral damage: genuine accidents; systemic collateral damage, the foreseeable if
unintended consequence of rules of engagement, weapons choices, and tactics; and
double effect/proportionality killing, accepted as military necessity. Systemic collateral damage has been in a moral blind spot, where systemic collateral damage has
often been seen as an accident, and its occurrence and general incidence as natural
and unaffected by policy choices. Proportionality/double effect collateral damage
also occurs in a moral blind spot—because it is legal and the result of the conscious
choice to prioritize a military goal "military necessity," over the lives of civilians,
a proportionality calculation that excuses the deaths as an unintended, "double
effect" of the operation.

Third, I argued that both systemic collateral damage and proportionality/double
effect collateral damage are produced in part by expansive and permissive conceptions of military necessity. The other causes of systemic collateral damage are found
in the organization of war making—the institutionalized rules, procedures, training,
and stresses of war. Depending on choices that are made at the organizational and
command level, the likelihood of causing civilian casualties may rise or fall. When
those factors (including beliefs about military necessity) change, the incidence of
collateral damage also changes.

In sum, it is a mistake to believe that all the unintended killing of civilians is
always or even usually an unforeseen or unforeseeable accident. Indeed, a focus on
intention and individual actors leaves room for a great deal of systemically produced
harm. Collateral damage is a foreseeable and, as we have seen, often preventable
consequence of choices made in both the war zone and far from the battlefield and
sometimes well before a war was begun.

Arguing that collateral damage is not natural and inevitable situates it in the
realm of a moral problem, subject to human agency, and in Part II, I turned to the
questions of moral responsibility. We all know the wrongness of deliberately killing
civilians and there is nothing controversial about condemning the deliberate killing
of noncombatants. Individuals who deliberately kill civilians are often demonized.
The bad apples, malevolent leaders, and policies that deliberately target civilians
should be blamed. Yet to blame individual soldiers for "snapping" is to be, in a sense,
blind to how the moral agency of soldiers is shaped and compromised by the institutions of war making and realities of combat and not all pernicious consequences
are produced by malevolent actors with a deliberate intention to cause harm.

Because collateral damage is defined in such a way that it is legal, the problem
of unintended yet foreseeable harm to noncombatants is, for practical purposes,

---

[3] Quoted in ibid.

outside international criminal law, with its focus on individual moral and legal responsibility or intentional acts. There is the potential to prosecute an individual's negligence, but with the focus on deliberate intention, the bar is set very high. It is, in fact, not only the "reality of war" but also the structure of the law with regard to noncombatant immunity and military necessity that creates the potential for large-scale, regular, systemic collateral damage in war as the "ordinary" consequences of military operations. And so, to accept collateral damage as an inevitable if tragic aspect of war is to ignore its systemic roots in rules of engagement, standard operating procedures, and international humanitarian law. The instrumental reasoning that allows military necessity to trump civilian immunity is the same reasoning that transfers the risks from civilians to soldiers when it is decided that winning requires a "population centric" strategy of protecting civilians.

Part II addressed the moral responsibility of the primary actors, both individual and organizational—soldiers, commanders, and the military. In focusing on how military organizations both enable and constrain individual moral agency and are themselves moral agents, I have pushed the usual boundaries of conceptions of moral responsibility. My argument is that the extension of agency and responsibility to organizations is necessary because the reality of war includes its collective and social organization. There would be no war without organization and organizations. Organizations create the framework and conditions that lead to systemic collateral damage. The key innovation of the discussion of organizational responsibility above was my argument that organizations, specifically in this case, the US military can and have demonstrated moral agency. Organizations always already are the institutionalization of normative beliefs and they are always engaged in a cycle of moral agency. My work has been to show how the military has done both the active work of institutionalizing respect for civilian immunity and also how it has created the conditions for systemic and double effect/proportionality collateral damage.

I also pushed the boundaries of theorizing about moral responsibility in war in Part III by attending to political and public moral agency and responsibility in terms of roles and procedures for deliberation. War is a social and political act, and thus both frameworks for understanding and assigning individual and collective responsibility are required. In these discussions of organizational, political, and public moral responsibility, I have necessarily become more prescriptive and descriptive of the ways that moral responsibility can and should be exercised. Moral responsibility at the level of military and political organizations and the public requires a mix of individual role responsibility and procedures which encourage better analysis and deliberation. Moreover, each level of moral responsibility ought to be attentive to the other level. So if an individual fails in their role, the organization should call on that individual to act responsibly. Conversely, if an organization fails to act responsibly, individuals must, courageously call the organization to account.

Carl von Clausewitz's call for commanders to have the "courage to accept responsibility, either before the tribunal of some outside power or before the court of one's own conscience"[4] is just as important today as it was when he was a soldier in the Prussian Army. This moral courage and moral responsibility is everyone's call. It is the moral integrity, which, Larry May argues, "involves the notion that our actions and omissions need to conform to our principles, for we are responsible for what we do and who we are."[5]

Concrete Lessons and an Action Plan

Although several of the chapters contain specific recommendations, much of what I have said is at a level of abstraction that may suit the general public and students and scholars of war and international law who are searching for a way to understand the larger issues of civilian killing. I have made suggestions about a long-term agenda for increasing moral responsibility for collateral damage. For example, I argued in the chapter on norms in tension that civilian vulnerability ought to be weighted more than military necessity. In the chapter on public responsibility, I underscored the importance of enriching public understanding of the way that war is fought as a route to increasing the public's capacity to understand and if necessary intervene on questions about the conduct of war.

But an equally important set of readers includes specialists (congressional staff, the staff of think tanks and the National Security Council, judge advocates, and soldiers) who are searching for a way to reform and reorganize their organizations and operations to reduce the occurrence of systemic collateral damage. They may also be searching for ways to rethink proportionality/double effect killing. For those readers, I summarize five concrete suggestions that could be immediate and medium-term action items. I do not know that all civilian deaths in war can be avoided. Certainly, those deaths will occur as long as humans continue to use war as a political tool. There are changes at the organizational and political level that could reduce the likelihood of killing and maiming civilians. Halting or changing practices that are likely to cause harm to civilians is the first step. Some fixes are relatively easy. We should make sure that they are implemented as a down payment on the assumption of our moral responsibility. These are examples of how a deeper respect for noncombatant immunity can be institutionalized in US and other nations' operations. While international law does not require these steps, they are implied by the ethical analysis contained in this book.

1. *Systematically record and analyze the deaths of noncombatants.* Some collection and concatenation of data, and some analysis, about civilian killing for these

---

[4] Carl Von Clausewitz, *On War*, edited and translated by Michael Howard and Peter Paret (Princeton: Princeton University Press, 1976), p. 101.

[5] Larry May, *Sharing Responsibility* (Chicago: University of Chicago Press, 1992), p. 101.

wars has already been conducted by various actors (e.g., NATO/ISAF, the Rand Corporation, and US military organizations). A more systematic analysis is by nongovernmental and governmental organizations would serve the functions of acknowledging civilian killing and providing the raw data and analysis that is necessary to formulate to reduce foreseeable civilian harm. The data and results (stripped of personal identifying information) should be publicly available.[6]

2. *Review weapons procurement, deployment, and use so that weapons and practices that are difficult to use in a discriminate way and are likely to cause foreseeable harm are retired from the arsenal.* These weapons include those that immediately cause collateral damage and those with delayed effects. The international community has already restricted antipersonnel landmines (1997) and cluster munitions (2008) because of their immediate threat to noncombatants and long-term threat they pose. The United States has not signed the land mine and cluster munitions treaties. I have already suggested that the United States should accelerate its retirement of cluster munitions. Other weapons and practices to review include the use of large bombs (500-2,000 lbs.) in villages and urban settings where they cannot be used discriminately. Such a review and recommendations to change the arsenal are an organizational and political responsibility—data must be gathered and analyzed, and recommendations must be drawn.

3. *Review operational instructions and targeting criteria, specifically rules of engagement.* As noted in the discussion of the steps the Army took in Iraq to reduce civilian killing at checkpoints, the review of rules of engagement and their modification can and does save lives—not only of civilians but also of combatants. But while rules of engagement are constantly reviewed in the field, the review must be systematically connected to the analysis of effects.

Targeting of infrastructure and "dual use" facilities such as power plants should also be reviewed. Current doctrine sees little problem with such targeting if the intention is not to kill civilians but perhaps only to deny the enemy resources and civilian support. But targeting infrastructure foreseeably causes long-term harm to civilians—malnutrition, disease, and death. Again, while strictly legal, this harm may be immoral. As C.A.J. Coady argues, the fact that immediate death does not result from an attack on infrastructure does not eliminate responsibility for the long-term consequences of such attacks.

> When attacks on infrastructure are aimed at destroying civilian morale, they stand condemned under the principle of discrimination, but even when viewed from a dual-purpose perspective, there must be doubts about many such attacks. The dual-purpose strategy tends to see the

[6] Standardization of best practices in casualty recording is underway in the Oxford Research Group "Every Casualty" programme. See http://www.everycasualty.org/practice/methods-research.

infrastructural features of an enemy population as connected with short-term military gains and short-term civilian discomforts, but the moral gaze needs to be broader than that because, especially in modern societies, the infrastructures are increasingly crucial to well-being, survival, and even sometimes to life itself. Something like this point can be extended to the problems raised by direct or incidental damage to the natural and human environment of the enemy's country.[7]

4. *Make the criteria used in targeted killings such as drone strikes and the data about the effects and effectiveness of those killings available to the public.* The United States under both the Bush and Obama administrations repeatedly asserted that its targeted killings by drone strike are legal and effective. But in the absence of disclosure of the criteria and the data these assertions remain just that.[8] If this information is made public, it will almost certainly be challenged. A government confident in its reasoning should not fear such a challenge. Further, the argument about drone strikes and other means of targeted killing rests on assumptions that need to be questioned, namely that the possible future actions of individuals deprives them of their rights and makes them a legitimate target. But it is on just such a logic that preventive war is not allowed in most understandings of the law and justice of war. Targeted killings that entail risks to noncombatants indeed blur the distinctions between combatant and noncombatant while they may also elevate the idea of military necessity to the point that the lives of many noncombatants can be risked.

5. *Establish an institutional home within the military, in combination with an academic research institute or the US Institute for Peace, for ongoing review and analysis of the problems of civilian killing in war.*[9] Military lawyers currently conduct much of the more systematic research.[10] Nongovernmental organizations such as CIVIC also acquire data. In

---

[7] C. A. J. Coady, "Bombing and the Morality of War," in Yuki Tanaka and Marilyn B. Young, eds., *Bombing Civilians: A Twentieth Century History* (New York: The New Press, 2009), pp. 191–214, 213.

[8] Scott Shane, "Election Spurred a Move to Codify U.S. Drone Policy," *New York Times*, 25 November 2012, p. 1. Opinion, "Rules for Targeted Killing," *New York Times*, 30 November 2012, p. A26.

[9] CIVIC, urges the creation of a "high-level" position in the Pentagon to oversee and coordinate policies, strategies, and tactics that focus on civilian harm. "United States Military Compensation to Civilians in Armed Conflict," May 2010, Washington, DC, CIVIC. "A new high-level position would: unify, refine, and strengthen efforts to prevent harm and address casualties when they occur; study lessons learned; encourage procurement and deployment of new weapons and tactics designed to diminish harm; ensure proper civilian damage estimates and combat damage assessments; ensure proper investigative and statistical data on casualties; ensure culturally appropriate condolence measures are in place and effectively implemented." I agree that these are necessary. My argument, however, is that while the military needs greater institutionalization, other institutions inside and outside the government should be engaged as well. "United States Military Compensation to Civilians in Armed Conflict" (Washington, DC: CIVIC, May 2010), p. 13.

addition, ad hoc reviews and investigations of specific incidents have resulted in changes in rules of engagement and other recommendations. But a larger organization that includes civilians and those without a stake in a military career, tasked with review, analysis, and recommendations will have the capacity to look back and forward and potentially conduct more comprehensive and critical analysis. Part of the charge of such an organization would be the public dissemination of its findings so that Congress and the public could engage in these issues.

Mercy and Taking Responsibility

This book is about when, how, and why American soldiers too often kill innocent people, either deliberately, or more often in recent years as an inadvertent, albeit "ordinary" consequence of their operations and about the command, organizational, political, and public moral responsibility for those deaths. I make a moral argument that begins with identifying collateral damage as something that is not "normal" or inevitable, although international law and the Just War tradition have made it seem that way. I show that even though it is legal, foreseeable collateral damage is a moral problem not just when large numbers of civilians are killed, but because it is a regular and often adjustable feature of war planning. I argue—against the dominant framework of individual moral responsibility—that the moral responsibility for collateral damage is not simply individual, but a consequence of the organization of war. The causes and remedies for collateral damage are thus about organizational changes.

In this way, the book is also, in some sense, about those at the point of the spear, the soldiers. And as each month passes in the post-9/11 wars, the deaths and serious injuries of American soldiers mount. At the time of this writing, more than two million veterans, many who spent more than one combat tour in these wars, have come home, many thousands missing limbs or suffering traumatic brain injury, and tens of thousands experiencing the symptoms of trauma. Some speak with pride of their accomplishments: they saved lives, they built schools, and they found and killed insurgents and terrorists. Many are silent. Some have committed suicide—in some years that number surpassing those killed in combat.

And a small but growing number of veterans express remorse for their part in killing civilians or torturing prisoners. These men and women have echoed the cry of Vietnam veterans: we need to stop and think about what we are doing to them "over there" and ourselves here. An effort to understand moral responsibility for war and the killing of civilians—men, women, and children who often wanted no part in

---

[10] See, for instance, the work of the Center for Law and Military Operations. An example is their report, *Forged in Fire: Lessons Learned during Military Operations (1994-2008)*, (Charlottesville, VA: United States Army, 2008).

the war—is the least that I can do for those civilians and US soldiers. But a call for understanding our responsibility also entails the assumption of the duties implied by taking responsibility. And we must all do that.

Prospective moral responsibilities are expectations about how people and institutions should act in particular situations and the institutions that we put in place to ensure responsible action. Retrospective responsibility is the act of looking back at what we have done and assigning praise or blame according to how well prospective responsibilities were met. Taking responsibility retrospectively entails both acting responsibly in the present and looking backward. If in looking backward we find wrong, we should expect individuals and collectives to change those practices that brought harm, if they have not already done so, and to make repair.

Two authors have articulated the sense of shared moral responsibility that I am trying to extend. The nineteenth-century legal theorist and one of the first authors of American rules of war, Francis Lieber and his coauthors wrote in the 1863 US laws of war that were intended to govern the northern army: "Men who take up arms against one another in public war do not cease on this account to be moral beings, responsible to one another and to God."[11] Writing more than 100 years later, Larry May wrote:

> It is true that we are all partially responsible for many of the defects of our selves or the harms of the world. But because our lives are interdependent with the lives of others it is misleading to speak of people as being radically free. We are not free to change the world overnight, although in combination with others we often are able to change the world over the long run. Because of our dependence on the help of others to change the world, it makes more sense to speak of shared rather than personal responsibility in a great many cases over which we could exert some control.…
>
> One is not normally responsible for war in a way that leads to moral blame. Rather, what one is responsible for is the way one reacts to that war, and here again we are back to personal responsibility for self.[12]

And though we are not able to change the world overnight and all by ourselves, we are capable of seeing how it is that choices made far from the battlefield, long before any war, and choices made during wars, can lead to not only the deliberate killing of enemy soldiers but also the deliberate and unintentional killing of noncombatant civilians. To be morally responsible in contemporary war—as a warrior, commander, politician, and citizen—requires that we understand how the division of labor and the now prevalent understanding of responsibility, which stresses individual agency and intention, can mask the unintended yet foreseeable consequences

[11] United States, *Laws of War: General Orders 100*, 1863, Article 15.

[12] May, *Sharing Responsibility*, pp. 21–22.

of our ostensibly reasonable, and legal, choices. We may not soon change the organization of labor that produces war and simultaneously masks the responsibility for its unintended consequences. But we can see more clearly how our actions have unintended yet foreseeable consequences and act so as to assume responsibility for those consequences.

As long as the US military and civilian leadership conceive of protecting noncombatants as another tool employed in the service of winning a war, then ironically, civilian protection may be more difficult to achieve, and perversely, the United States will continue to undermine its war aims. If the United States were to explicitly value human life as an end in itself, and not primarily as a means to victory, and stop practices that the civilians in these war zones consider brutal and cynical—calculations of "military necessity" versus acceptable levels of "collateral damage" that too often lead to civilian death—then the United States would arguably be much more successful at "winning hearts and minds." But, even if protecting civilians did not ease the path to victory, it is a value and set of practices worth promoting, in and of itself.

Finally, the public has moral responsibility for the resort to war and for its conduct in its public role, because democratic publics authorize war and contribute to its prosecution by providing resources. As Iris Young argues, "individuals bear responsibility for structural injustice because they contribute by their actions to the processes that produce unjust outcomes."[13] Further, whether or not the state is democratic, the public has an interest in war; the public bears the burdens and reaps the benefits of war. Finally, although we are all members of a particular state, we are also all human beings who would agree that the innocent should be protected from harm. The tasks involved in the assumption of moral agency are not easy at either the individual or institutional level. Yet, if we attend to the problems of agency and responsibility, the benefits are well worth the effort.

Kenneth Waltz once responded to his critics that "not everything need go into one book and not everything can go into one theory."[14] Indeed, much about the development of the norm of noncombatant immunity, moral responsibility, and the cycle of moral agency remains to be explored. I have focused on war and the problem of collateral damage. But the arguments about unintentional systemic harm that is produced by standard operating procedures, and the role of individuals and organizations in creating or ameliorating such harm, can be applied to other organizations and areas of collective action. We might use this framework, for example, to understand the moral responsibility for the predictable industrial accidents or such large-scale problems such as global warming, famine, and deforestation. As human interactions become more dense and are increasingly mediated by large

---

[13] Iris Marion Young, *Global Challenges: War, Self-Determination and Responsibility for Justice* (Polity: Malden, 2007), p. 175.

[14] Kenneth N. Waltz, *Realism and International Politics* (New York: Routledge, 2008), p. 51.

organizations, we need a way to think about both individual and collective moral responsibility because it is not only military technology that has the capacity to produce unintentional and indiscriminate effects.

What I am suggesting requires new ways of thinking about individual moral responsibility and new ways of designing institutions and the law so that the exercise of responsibility within a cycle of moral agency is easier. On the other hand, once these new ways of thinking—attending in particular to how organizations and political institutions can create the conditions for more or less unintended harm— and new procedures to promote moral agency and accountability are institutionalized, there are potential benefits in many areas of social, political, and economic life.

ACKNOWLEDGEMENTS

In a book that took about ten years to complete, it should be no surprise that I have many to thank. First among them, for her patience with this longer than anticipated project, I am more than grateful to my daughter, Rose Jordan Crawford. For as long as Rose can remember, the United States has been at war. Rose also cannot remember a time when I wasn't working on this project. Rose kept urging me on and showed great forbearance—when she wasn't teasing me about how *long* I was taking. She has also told me on more than one occasion to not work so hard—that it was time to read a book with her, kick a soccer ball, bake bread (or perhaps cookies), or to build something out of maple, oak, or mahogany. I will never forget giving a presentation about the book in St. Andrews, Scotland, and my pleasure that Rose, at 9 years old, both listened with attention and seemed to find it interesting. More amusing was her reaction when I said that the book was accepted for publication. She smiled and jumped, singing, into my arms, with what I am sure was a combination of simple relief over a long journey nearly ended, and happiness. Her frequent questions—"are you done yet?" or "when will you be done?" and, "but I thought you said you would be done already?" reminded me that this was really a mutual journey.

My brother Robert, a fine artist and carpenter, renovated the attic in my house; he gave it insulation, a floor, and windows, and made it a beautiful space. That room was supposed to be my workspace. But I was too impatient to work, so I set the books and papers in a porch that overlooks the Mystic River. With a view of swans, Great Blue Heron, dog walking neighbors, and the occasional jumping fish, that porch is the first room one sees when entering the house and Rose put up with the piles of library books and government documents with good humor. I tried to keep a path clear for my great neighbors, houseguests, and friends, including Sabina Berretta, Jill Breitbarth, Orit Ditman, Kelly Feller, Doug Kincade, Karen Kurlander, Barbara Macy, Catherine Manegold, Mary Raczko, Katie Pakos Rimer, Seth Itzkan, Lisbeth Gronlund, and David Wright. Some friends were very funny—including Alexa

Arlos, Laurie Richardson, and Jeremie Jean-Baptiste. Rachel Manley, Christina Shea, and Tracy Isaacs, three fine writers, raised the bar and inspired. Friends, you have no idea how I would (sometimes) move stacks of books and pull down the cover to my roll top desk before you came over, or struggled to find my keys among the papers so we could meet elsewhere for coffee or canoeing or soccer. You have all commented supportively, if also with that same wonder as my parents, Robert and Jeanne Crawford, at how long I could keep at it. Only in the last year of writing did I finally move to the attic. Rose, Chris Low, and Juliette Low Fleury metaphorically leapt with joy when the big move occurred and everyone audibly sighed when the piles of books and papers just seemed to get bigger and then migrate back downstairs.

I thank my colleagues in the United States, Canada, United Kingdom, and France and the universities that invited me to present the chapters and papers that eventually became this book. Your comments at the presentations or afterwards were invaluable. Joshua Cohen, Jeremy Weinstein, and Lynn Eden at Stanford; Henry Shue at Oxford; Tom Weiss at CUNY; Cathy Lutz and Keith Brown at Brown; Toni Erskine at Aberystwyth; Janice Stein and Emanuel Adler at University of Toronto; Karyna Korostelina and Daniel Rothbart at George Mason; Samy Cohen at Sciences Po, Paris; Amy Gurowitz at University of California Berkeley; and Robert Lifton at Harvard. Near the end of writing this book, I was able to present the entire argument at Harvard, the University of Minnesota, St. Andrews in Scotland, Princeton, and Cornell. Steve Walt, Bud Duvall, Kathryn Sikkink, Joan Tronto, Tony Lang, Peter Katzenstein, Nick Rengger, Karin Fierke, Andy Muravchic, and Ian Hurd were excellent interlocutors. Others commented on early versions of this work at the annual meetings of the American Political Science Association, the British International Studies Association, and the International Studies Association or at other conferences including a meeting on Just War theory at the United States Institute of Peace. I am grateful to Martin Cook, Cian O'Driscoll, Richard Price, Hugo Slim, Colin Kahl, Sebastian Kaempf, Robert Goodin, Marianne Hanson, Howard Adelman, Albert Pierce, Lt. Col. David Barnes, Peter Liberman, Karin Fierke, and Carol Cohn. I thank Robert Goodin and anonymous reviewers at *The Journal of Political Philosophy* where I first published some of the ideas presented here.

I have enjoyed correspondence, exchanged citations, and had stimulating conversations with Nasrina Bargzie, Sara Cobb, Janina Dill, Lynn Eden, Matt Evangelista, Marc Garlasco, John Sloboda, Ira Houck, Sarah Holewinski, Joy Gordon, David Luban, Jonathan Manes, Meg McLagan, Alex Downes, Sahr Conway-Lanz, Rachel Reid, Jessica Stern, John Tirman, and Iris Marion Young. My friends and colleagues at Boston University, and in the greater Boston area, who dared to ask what I was working on were also supportive and I thank Andrew Bacevich, David Mayers, Cathie Jo Martin, and Gina Sapiro, for conversations and suggestions. More than that, some of you suggested that I read particular books, which expanded my historical knowledge and understanding of international law. Many times, I wish I had just read those books first—so much time would have perhaps been saved. And while those scholars—Claudia Card, Tony Coady, Larry May, and Marilyn Young—have not directly commented on this work, their scholarship, cited throughout, has helped me to expand and refine my analysis. Judith Herman, Catherine Lutz, Robert Lifton, and Howard Zinn were my coauthors on a short piece about civilian casualties in what has turned out to be the middle of these wars. Cathy Lutz and I have worked intensely together over the years. It is always a pleasure to work with someone with such integrity.

Sahr Conway-Lanz, Ellen Caulo, Matthew Evangelista, Allen Forbes, Joy Gordon, Tony Lang, and Henry Shue took time to read large unpolished chunks of the manuscript and to make critical comments on several chapters. You were and are ideal readers. Late in the project, Mark Osiel gave the entire manuscript a perceptive reading and many helpful suggestions for which I am also extremely grateful.

Three graduate students helped at various stages. Grant Marlier performed able research on numbers for me very early on. Near the end, James Gillcrist read the manuscript and was supposed to help me cut it. Instead, he used his experience as a US Army infantry Captain in Iraq to make helpful suggestions. I don't think the book is shorter for his input, but it is richer. Brian Smith diligently checked the final proofs. Laura D'Amore, Pat Sills, and Wes Soper, successive administrators in the Political Science Department at Boston University, also helped.

I was fortunate to have a short residency at the Blue Mountain Center in mid 2010 where I was able to spend hours in uninterrupted work on what were the most difficult parts of the project. And when I could read and write no longer I was able to talk with the scholars, artists, and staff at the BMC, or take a walk along the water, or climb a small mountain. What an important gift! I thank Rose for letting her mother take the time away from her to work there, Ellen and Grace Caulo for helping Rose and Herschel get along while I was away, and the BMC for using a beautiful space to bring stimulating people together. In particular, I thank Anne McClintock for passing articles and citations to me, the artists Camille Gage and Susanne Slavick for their images, the writers Dahr Jamail and Ann Jones, and all the others there for stimulating conversation. Tamar Diesendruck, thank you for suggesting that I apply.

Everything I write has the imaginary audience of now absent friends and family. Jane Low effortlessly lived empathy and compassion and showed me both; Jane would have appreciated the careful copy editing Oxford University Press gave this book. Jonathan Tucker, one of my dearest friends for more than twenty-five years was a model of integrity and principled engagement with the tough issues of public policy from outside government and inside it. I also wrote with Hayward Alker's ears in mind, in the desire that it might interest him; a curious mind, a generous warm heart, and a playful, challenging teacher, so honest and unafraid. And with Randy Forsberg's penchant for precision keeping me on my toes, her heart and dedication to persuasive argument, my inspiration. I remember Randy's blue blue eyes and how they saw farther and better than most. For Randy, information was the power to open and change minds. She believed in evidence, the force of the better argument, in the use of reason in the search for truth, practicing a form of argumentation that engaged the other respectfully. Like Jonathan and Hayward, Randy used her brilliance honestly, without deception, meeting the arguments of the other with better arguments and acknowledging when others had a better case. And I always write with the desire that my grandmother Odell would have found the prose readable and the purpose good. Grandma could make a world long past appear with her musical words. In Jane, Jonathan, Hayward, Randy, and Odell, I could have no better exemplars of intellectual honesty, passionate engagement, and a commitment to others.

I may have forgotten some of those who gave this project respectful attention. Please forgive me; nearly ten years is a long time to keep track. But I will never forget my insightful, encouraging, and long-suffering editor, the historian Dave McBride.

Finally, the last two years of writing were interrupted by illness and two other demanding projects. Chris W. Low nursed and nourished me (mostly) patiently and playfully through these challenges, while posing new ones.

INDEX